"Helen-ophiles, rejoice! *Helen of Troy* gives you everything you ever wanted to know about 'The Face That Launched a Thousand Ships.'. . . Hughes has brilliantly and exhaustively covered . . . her subject from more angles— romantic, historical, archaeological, mythological, psychological—than even Paris could dream of on his best night." —Steven Pressfield, author of
Gates of Fire and *The Virtues of War*

"The nuggets garnered from archaeology in particular are often revelatory. . . . The details coalesce to conjure up an aspect of this age in its satisfying entirety, a place the reader can enter and explore."
—*The New York Times*

"Hughes splendidly reclaims Helen from centuries of helpless victim-hood. . . . This book puts Helen of Troy at the centre of a world in which, as Bettany Hughes convincingly explains, the primordial power was female." —*The Observer* (London)

"Vivid and evocative. . . . Underpinned by a sure-footed sense of narrative flow. It will be a resource for students and scholars as well, I think, as a great pleasure for the wider public. I enjoyed it thoroughly and recommend it most highly." —Lesley Fitton, Chief Bronze Age Curator in the department
of Greek and Roman Antiquities, British Museum

"Hughes's portrait is as close to a real, living Helen as we are likely to get. In an increasingly sexualized culture, the questions Helen raises are more alive than ever." —*Financial Times*

"The most exciting thing about this book is its hot fascination with the past, its almost ecstatic pursuit of a sensuous history. . . . A passionately sensed and recorded homage to Helen. . . . Hughes reminds us now, at the end of a long history of Puritanism and misogyny, of a time when women's dominion over the produce of the earth, and their own sexual powers, made some of them potent subjects and radiant objects of worship, adoration and desire." —Page DuBois, professor of Greek History and
Cultural Studies, University of California, San Diego,
in *The San Diego Union-Tribune*

"Fantastic. . . . I have never, EVER, read anybody write so well about travels in Greece and going to explore archaeology." —Edith Hall, professor of Greek history at Durham University

"A real tour de force. It combines astonishing erudition and knowledge of the early classical world with a wonderful, easy fluency of writing. It has taught me a lot, and I have enjoyed every page." —John Julius Norwich

"An investigative achievement." —*The Guardian* (London)

"An extraordinarily comprehensive account of one of the most enigmatic women of all time; a brilliant and fascinating history." —Professor Lord Robert Winston

"A wonderful read. It's what great history is all about—excitement, a fast-moving story, packed full of information, accessible and brainy, a dazzling combination. Bettany Hughes puts women slap-bang right back at the heart of things." —Kate Mosse, author of *Labyrinth*

"Evoking in sensuous and gorgeous prose the citadels, the palaces and the luxuries of that long-vanished world, history and mythography have been dazzlingly elided. In this passionate book, Hughes adds to Helen's mystery . . . powerfully." —*The Sunday Times* (London)

"Never before has the world of Homer's epic, the thirteenth century BC, been brought so vividly to life. Hughes brilliantly evokes the sights and sounds of the Bronze Age, the heady smells of women's perfumes and oils, the rustle of linen over their thighs and breasts, the whisper of their prayers and liturgies. . . . A fascinating, compelling argument. . . . A gripping read." —Dr. Jenny Wallace, Director of Studies in English, Peterhouse College, Cambridge University, in *Times Higher Education Supplement*

"Hughes skilfully brings this period back to life. A fascinating window on to the power politics of an age. A genuinely exciting historical narrative." —*The Sunday Telegraph* (London)

BETTANY HUGHES

HELEN OF TROY

Bettany Hughes is a cultural and social historian, writer, and television presenter. She received degrees in ancient and medieval history at Oxford University and has carried out research in the Balkans, Greece, and Asia Minor. She has presented numerous documentaries and historical series for the BBC, PBS, and the Discovery Channel, and also writes pieces on popular history for several newspapers and magazines.

BETTANY HUGHES

HELEN OF TROY

THE STORY BEHIND THE MOST
BEAUTIFUL WOMAN IN THE WORLD

VINTAGE BOOKS
A DIVISION OF RANDOM HOUSE, INC.
NEW YORK

For my mother and father
who taught me everything

And for Adrian, Sorrel and May, from whom I'm still learning

FIRST VINTAGE BOOKS EDITION, JANUARY 2007

Vintage ISBN: 978-1-4000-7600-0

www.vintagebooks.com

Printed in the United States of America
10   9   8   7   6   5   4   3   2

CONTENTS

@@@@@@@@@@@@@@

Illustrations   xi
Text Acknowledgements   xv
Maps   xvii
Timeline   xxiii
Dramatis Personæ   xxxi
Family Trees   xxxii
Foreword and Acknowledgements   xxxv

INTRODUCTION

Cherchez la Femme   1
An Evil Destiny   4
Helen-Hunting   8
Goddess, Princess, Whore   10

PART ONE

HELEN'S BIRTH IN PRE-HISTORY

1   A Dangerous Landscape   17
2   A Rape, a Birth   22
3   The Lost Citadel   29
4   The Mycenaeans   34
5   The Pre-historic Princess   41

PART TWO

THE LAND OF BEAUTIFUL WOMEN

6   The Rape of 'Fair Hellen'   49
7   Sparte Kalligynaika   55
8   Tender-eyed Girls   62

PART THREE

THE WORLD'S DESIRE

9   A Trophy for Heroes   71
10 The Kingmaker   77
11 A Royal Wedding   81

PART FOUR

KOUROTROPHOS

12 Hermione   91
13 A Welcome Burden   96
14 Helen, High Priestess   100
15 La Belle Hélène   106

PART FIVE

A LOVER'S GAME

16 The Golden Apple   115
17 Bearing Gifts   120
18 Alexander Helenam Rapuit   131
19 The Female of the Species Is More Deadly
      Than the Male   136

PART SIX

EROS AND ERIS

20 Helen the Whore   143
21 The Pain of Aphrodite   148
22 The Sea's Foaming Lanes   153

PART SEVEN

TROY BECKONS

23	East Is East and West Is West	165
24	The Fair Troad	172
25	The Topless Towers of Ilium	177
26	The Golden Houses of the East	186
27	A Fleet Sets Sail	191

PART EIGHT

TROY BESIEGED

28	Helen – Destroyer of Cities	203
29	Death's Dark Cloud	210
30	A Beautiful Death – Kalos Thanatos	214
31	The Fall of Troy	219

PART NINE

IMMORTAL HELEN

32	Home to Sparta	229
33	The Death of a Queen	235
34	The Age of Heroes Ends	240
35	'Fragrant Treasuries'	244
36	The Daughter of the Ocean	250

PART TEN

THE FACE THAT LAUNCHED A THOUSAND SHIPS

37	Helen in Athens	259
38	Helen Lost and Helen Found	267
39	Helen, Homer and the Chances of Survival	271
40	Veyn Fables	277
41	Helen of Troy and the Bad Samaritan	281
42	'Perpulchra' – More Than Beautiful	289

43   Dancing with the Devil   298
44   Helen's Nemesis   308

                    APPENDICES

1   The Minotaur's Island   315
2   La Parisienne   321
3   Women of Stone and Clay and Bronze   328
4   Elemental Helen – She-Gods and
     She-Devils   332
5   Royal Purple – The Colour of Congealed
     Blood   339
     Epilogue – Myth, History and Historia   342

     Abbreviations   345
     Notes   347
     Bibliography   413
     Index   445

ILLUSTRATIONS

@@@@@@@@@@@@@

Maps

All maps drawn by Henry Buglass, Institute of Archaeology and Antiquity, University of Birmingham.

1 The Mycenaean World; 2 Laconia, the Argolid and Central Greece: Major Mycenaean settlements and traces of roads; 3 The Hittite World (Map 1, 'The World of the Hittite' taken from *Life and Society in the Hittite World* by Trevor Bryce, 2002, by permission of Oxford University Press); 4 The Troad in the Late Bronze Age; 5 Bronze Age trade routes in the Mediterranean; 6 Helen's itinerary through the Eastern Mediterranean and the location of her cult sites.

Part-Title Images

Page 1 Helen's seduction and return. Red figure *skyphos*, 490–480 BC. From Campania or Sessola (© 2005 Museum of Fine Arts, Boston); **Page 15** Signet ring (*The Demon Ring*) with ritual scene. Gold, *c.* 1500 BC. From the 'Tiryns Treasure' (National Archaeological Museum, Athens); **Page 47** Statuette of a girl runner. Bronze, *c.* 550 BC. Found in the sanctuary of Zeus at Dodona (National Archaeological Museum, Athens); **Page 69** Mycenaean diadem. Gold, *c.* 1550 BC. From Shaft Grave III on the Acropolis at Mycenae (National Archaeological Museum, Athens); **Page 89** Ivory Triad, *c.* 1300 BC. From the 'Sanctuary Deposit' north of the palace on the Acropolis at Mycenae (National Archaeological Museum, Athens); **Page 96** Linear B inscription, *Tablet Ab 553* (© Diana Wardle); **Page 113** Linear B symbols of 'Man' and 'Woman' (© Diana Wardle); **Page 141** Human skull from Mycenae (Mycenae Museum); **Page 163** 'The Jewels of Helen'. Gold earring, *c.* 2500 BC, discovered by Heinrich Schliemann (*bpk*/Museum of Antiquities, Berlin; photography by Klaus Goeken); **Page 201** Arrow and spearheads found outside the walls of Troy. Bronze (Troia Project, Tübingen University); **Page 227** Helen. Marble relief carving from altar at Lacus Juturnae, 1st century AD (© German Archaeological Institute, Rome); **Page 257** Female figurine. Marble, *c.* 2500 BC (Archaeological Museum, Naxos); **Page 313** Snake goddess votary. Faïence, *c.* 1600 BC. Excavated by Sir Arthur Evans, 1903 (Archaeological Museum, Heraklion).

1 The Birth of Helen. Campanian red-figure bell *krater* vase, *c.* 340 BC. The Caivano Painter (Naples National Museum); 2 The ruins of Troy. Manuscript, 15th century AD. From *Liber insularum archipelagi* by Cristoforo Buondelmonti (© Biblioteca Apostolica Vaticano, Rome); 3 Wall painting from the cult centre at Mycenae *c.* 1250 BC. Pen and ink with partial reconstruction (© Diana Wardle); 4 Terracotta mounted female figure, votive offering. Pen and ink reconstruction, late 4th/early 3rd century BC (Artwork © Melanie Stéiner; original figurine, Sparta Museum,); 5 Perfume jar inscribed with dedication to Helen. Bronze *aryballos, c.* 675 BC. Found at the *Menelaion,* 1975 (Sparta Museum, photograph courtesy of H.W. Catling); 6 Mirror with handle in form of a nude woman. Bronze, *c.*540 BC. (National Antiquities Collection, Museum of Munich); 7 and 8 Theseus' Abduction of Helen. Proto-Corinthian *aryballos,* perfume vase, *c.* 680 BC (Louvre Museum, © Photo RMN/© Hervé Lewandowski); 9 Goddess from Mycenae. Terracotta figure, made *c.* 1300 BC, deposited at the cult centre at Mycenae *c.* 1230 BC (Mycenae Archive, Birmingham University); 10 Mycenaean female figure riding a horse. Terracotta, (?) 13th century BC. Said to have been found in a tomb at Mesogeia, Attica (Stathatos Collection, National Archaeological Museum, Athens); 11 Crouching Lion. Ivory, deposited 1230 BC, from the cult centre at Mycenae (© Mycenae Archive, Birmingham University); 12 *Kourotrophos* figurine with child and parasol. Clay, *c.* 1300 BC. From Chamber Tomb 80 at Mycenae (National Archaeological Museum, Athens); 13 'Priam's Treasure'. Photograph, 1874. Artefacts *c.* 2500 BC, from Heinrich Schliemann's excavation of Troy. (Reproduced in *Trojanische Altertümer* [1874], Leipzig); 14 King Priam meets Helen of Troy. Manuscript, 1470 AD. From *Chronique Universelle* by Jean de Courcy (© Photo SCALA, Florence/Pierpont Morgan Library, New York); 15 The Marriage of Paris and Helen. Manuscript, mid-14th century AD. From *Historia destructionis Troiae* by Guido delle Colonne, 1287 AD (Fondation Martin Bodmer, Geneva); 16 Mycenaean Charioteer. Watercolour reconstruction of 13th century BC decoration from the *megaron* at Pylos. Piet de Jong, 1955 (Courtesy of the University of Cincinnati); 17 Lion-hunt dagger. Bronze inlaid with gold, niello and electrum, *c.* 1550 BC, found in Shaft Grave IV, Grave Circle A at Mycenae (National Archaeological Museum, Athens); 18 Linear B, *Tablet Un1314.* Clay, *c.* 1200 BC. From the Palace of Nestor at Pylos (National Archaeological Museum, Athens); 19 *Helen of Troy.* Oil on canvas, 1898. Evelyn De Morgan (De Morgan Centre, London/Bridgeman Art Library, London); 20 The confrontation of Helen and Paris. Fragment of Attic white-ground *calyx-crater, c.* 450 BC (Cincinnati Museum of Art); 21 *Helen of Troy.* Oil on panel, 1867. Frederick Sandys (National Museums Liverpool/Walker Art Gallery); 22 *Helen.* Oil on canvas, 1881. Sir Edward John Poynter. (Art Gallery of New South Wales/Photo by Brenton McGeachie for AGNSW); 23 Cover image of *The Private Life of Helen of Troy* by John Erskine. Illustration by Earle Bergey, 1952

(Popular Library, 147 [1947, Reprinted 1952]); **24** The Rape of Leda. Marble relief, date unknown (British Museum); **25** *Zeuxis Choosing his Models for the Image of Helen from among the Girls of Croton*. Oil on canvas, 1789. Andre-François Vincent (Louvre Museum, © Photo RMN © René Gabrielle Ojéda); **26** Zeuxis painting a statue of Helen. Manuscript, 1282 AD. From Cicero's *Rhetoric*, The French School (Bridgeman Art Library/Musée Condé, France); **27** 'The Royal Citadel of Mycenae' and **28** 'The Lion Gate at Mycenae'. Artwork by Donato Spedaliere from *Mycenaean Citadels c. 1350–1200 BC (Fortress 22)* by N. Fields and D. Spedaliere (Osprey Publishing [2004], © Osprey Publishing); **29** Troy, 13th century BC. Computer generated reconstruction, Hans Jansen (© Hans Jansen, Tübingen University, Troia Project); **30** Reconstruction of the South Gate of Troy, *c.* 1250 BC. Watercolour, acrylic and gouache. Christophe Haussner, 2004 (© Christophe Haussner); **31** The ruins of a royal palace at Büyükkale, *c.* 1260 BC. Aerial photograph by Ayse Seeher (Courtesy of Hattusa Excavations); **32** The *megaron* at Pylos. Watercolour reconstruction by Piet de Jong, 1955 (Courtesy of the University of Cincinnati); **33** Signet ring. Gold, 15th–13th century BC. Mycenae Acropolis Hoard (National Archaeological Museum, Athens); **34** Pin with rock-crystal head. Bronze, late 17th century BC. Excavated from Grave Circle B at Mycenae (National Archaeological Museum, Athens); **35** 'Clytemnestra' figure. Terracotta, made *c.* 1300 BC, deposited *c.* 1230 BC. Found at the cult centre in Mycenae (© E.B. French); **36** Funeral shroud. Sheet gold, second half of 1600 BC. From Shaft Grave III, Grave Circle A at Mycenae (National Archaeological Museum, Athens); **37** Woman carrying a *pyxis* (cosmetic box). Graphic depiction of a fresco fragment found within the palace at Tiryns, *c.* 1300 BC. Artwork by Gilliéron (National Archaeological Museum, Athens); **38** Female saffron-gatherer: girl wearing Minoan dress. Fresco, *c.* 1600 BC, from 'Xeste 3' at Akrotiri, Thera (Greek Archaeological Society); **39** Female saffron-gatherer. Fresco, *c.* 1600 BC, from 'Xeste 3' at Akrotiri, Thera (Greek Archaeological Society); **40** Mature woman. Fresco, *c.* 1600 BC, from the 'House of the Ladies' at Akrotiri, Thera (Greek Archaeological Society); **41** Boxing Children. Fresco, c.1600 BC, from the 'West House' at Akrotiri, Thera (National Archaeological Museum, Athens); **42** Head of young man. Ivory, deposited *c.* 1300 BC, the cult centre at Mycenae (Mycenae Museum, © Mycenae Archive); **43** Spartan dancing girl. Bronze, *c.* 550–520 BC. Found at Prizren, Serbia; possibly made in or near Sparta (British Museum); **44** *Young Spartans Exercising*. Oil on canvas, 1860. Edgar Degas (© 2005 National Gallery); **45** Eris, the Goddess of Discord. Attic black-figure cup interior, *c.* 560 BC (© *bpk*/Antiquity Collection, National Museums of Berlin/photograph by Ingrid Geske); **46** *The Abduction of Helen*. Egg tempera on wood, attributed to Zanobi Strozzi, *c.* 1450 (© 2005, National Gallery); **47** Sappho: *No. 47, Fragment 16*, c. 600 BC. Papyrus copy, late 1st–early 2nd century AD (Bodleian Library, University of Oxford); **48** Detail of *The Rape of Helen*. Oil on copper, mid-18th century. Johann Georg Platzer (Wallace Collection); **49** *L'enlèvement d'Helene*. Oil on poplar, *c.* 1470. Liberale da Verona (Louvre Museum, © Photo RMN, © René-Gabriel Ojéda); **50** *The Abduction of Helen*. Egg tempera on wood, *c.* 1450. Master of the Judgement of Paris (© 2005, National Gallery); **51** Mycenaean woman/goddess. Lime-plaster, *c.* 1300 BC. Found near the cult centre at Mycenae (National Archaeological Museum, Athens); **52** *The Toilet of Helen*. Oil on canvas, 1914. Bryson Burroughs (Walters Art Museum, Baltimore); **53** The sacrifice of Iphigeneia. Manuscript, 15th century AD. From *Recueil* by Raoul Lefevre (National Library, Paris); **54** Neoptolemus batters Priam. Black-figure amphora vase, 540 BC, made in Athens (British Museum); **55** The rape of Cassandra. Attic red-figure vase, *c.* 430 BC (Louvre Museum, © Photo RMN/© Hervé Lewandowski); **56** The murder of Cassandra. Hammered bronze sheet from a coated wooden box or piece of furniture, 675–650 BC (National Archaeological Museum, Athens); **57** Menelaus and Helen. Red-figure *amphora* vase, 470–450 BC, made in Athens (British Museum); **58** Nemesis and companion. Attic red *amphora* vase, 530 BC (© *bpk*/Antiquity Collection, National Museums of Berlin); **59** *The Building of the Trojan Horse*. Oil on canvas, *c.* 1760. Giovanni Domenico Tiepolo (© 2005 National Gallery); **60** *Helen at the Scaean Gates*. Oil on canvas, *c.* 1880. Gustave Moreau (photograph © RMN, Gustave Moreau Museum, Paris; caption: *Euripides*, Helen by George Seferis, translation by E. Keeley and P. Sherrard from *George Seferis: Complete Poems*, (1995), Princeton University Press; **61** *Helen Recognising Telemachus, Son of Odysseus*. Oil on panel, 1795. Jean-Jacques Lagrenée (State Hermitage Museum, St Petersburg); **62** The Ludovisi Throne: The Birth of Aphrodite. Stone relief carving, 460–450 BC. Found in 1887 on the grounds of a now demolished villa in Rome (© Photo SCALA, Florence, National Museum of Rome); **63** Black figure *mastos* (breast-shaped cup). Clay, made in Athens 520–500 BC, excavated in Etruria (British Museum); **64** *Kore* Statue. Marble, *c.* 2nd century AD. Excavated at the Roman Stadium, Samaria in 1932 (photograph © 2005 Palestine Exploration Fund, London; Rockefeller Archaeological Museum); **65** Dioscuri helmets. Limestone, relief carving, date unknown. Excavated at Roman Kore Temple by Eliezer Sukenik in 1931 (© 2005 Palestine Exploration Fund, London); **66** Representation of a theatrical mask. Stone, 1st–2nd century AD (British Museum); **67** *Elizabeth I and the Three Goddesses*. Oil on panel, 1569. Hans Eworth (Royal Collection © 2005, Her Majesty Queen Elizabeth II); **68** *The Circle of the Lustful*. Pen and ink and watercolour over pencil on paper, 1824–1827. William Blake (© Birmingham Museums and Art Gallery); **69** A lyre player. Watercolour reconstruction of 13th century BC fresco from the *megaron* at Pylos. Piet de Jong, 1955 (Courtesy of the University of Cincinnati).

TEXT ACKNOWLEDGEMENTS

〇〇〇〇〇〇〇〇〇〇〇〇〇

Grateful acknowledgement is made for permission to reproduce material from the following translations: J. Balmer, from *Sappho: Poems & Fragments* (1992) Bloodaxe Books; C. E. Boer, from *Homeric Hymn to the Earth* (1980), Spring Publications; D. A. Campbell, Reprinted by permission of the publishers and the Trustees of the Loeb Classical Library from *Greek Lyric: Volume I*, Loeb Classical Library® Volume 142, translated by David A. Campbell, p. 73, Cambridge, Mass.: Harvard University Press, copyright © 1982 by the President and Fellows of Harvard College. The Loeb Classical Library® is a registered trademark of the President and Fellows of Harvard College; M. Davies, from *The Epic Cycle* (1989), Bristol Classical Press by kind permission of Gerald Duckworth & Co. Ltd; R. Fagles, scattered excerpts from the *Iliad* by Homer, translated by Robert Fagles, © 1990 by Robert Fagles. Used by permission of Viking Penguin, a division of Penguin Group (USA) Inc.; scattered excerpts from the *Odyssey* by Homer, translated by Robert Fagles, copyright © 1996 by Robert Fagles. Used by permission of Viking Penguin, a division of Penguin Group (USA) Inc., and by Gerald Duckworth & Co. Ltd.; A. E. Galyon, from *The Art of Versification* (1980), Iowa State University Press/Blackwell Publishing; H.J. Magoulias, reprinted from Harry J. Magoulias (trans.) *O City of Byzantium: Annals of Niketas Choniates*, p. 360 © 1984 The Wayne State University Press, with the permission of the Wayne State University Press; A. M. Miller, from *Greek Lyric: an anthology in translation* (1996), reprinted by kind permission of Hackett Publishing Company, Inc. all rights reserved; W.H. Parker, from *Priapea: Poems for a Phallic God* (1988), Routledge; P.H. Young from *The Printed Homer: A 3000 Year Publishing and Translation History of the* Iliad *and the* Odyssey © 2003 Philip H. Young, reprinted by permission of McFarland & Company, Inc., Box 611, Jefferson NC 28640, www.mcfarlandpub.com; P. Vellacott, from *Euripides' Orestes and other plays* (1972), Penguin; N. Wright from Joseph of Exeter, *Trojan War*, reproduced by kind permission of the translator.

Grateful acknowledgement is also made for permission to reproduce material from the following publications: HD (Hilda Doolittle), 'Helen' from *Collected Poems 1912–1944* and from *Helen in Egypt*, copyright © 1961 by Norman

Holmes Pierson, both reprinted by kind permission of New Directions Publishing Corp., and for UK and Commonwealth rights by kind permission of Carcanet Press Ltd; Carol Ann Duffy, 'Beautiful' from *Feminine Gospels* by Carol Ann Duffy, by kind permission of the author and Macmillan Publishers Limited; Lord Dunsany, 'An Interview' from *Mirage Water* (1938), reproduced with permission of Curtis Brown Ltd, London on behalf of The Dunsany Will Trust, copyright The Dunsany Will Trust; Lawrence Durrell, 'Troy', Faber & Faber Ltd; D. Parker, 'Partial Comfort' from *The Portable Dorothy Parker* by Dorothy Parker, edited by Brendan Gill © 1928, renewed © 1956 by Dorothy Parker. Used by kind permission of Viking Penguin, a division of Penguin Group (USA) Inc.; S. B. Pomeroy from *Spartan Women* copyright © 2002 by Sarah Pomeroy. Used by kind permission of Oxford University Press, Inc.; W.B. Yeats, 'Leda and the Swan' and 'Lullaby' by kind permission of A.P. Watt Ltd on behalf of Michael B. Yeats, reprinted with the permission of Scribner, an imprint of Simon & Schuster Adult Publishing Group, from *The Collected Works of W. B. Yeats, Volume I: The Poems, Revised*, edited by Richard J. Finneran. Copyright © 1928 by the Macmillan Company; copyright renewed © 1956 by Georgie Yeats.

Every effort has been made to trace and contact copyright holders. The publishers will be pleased to correct any mistakes or omissions in future editions.

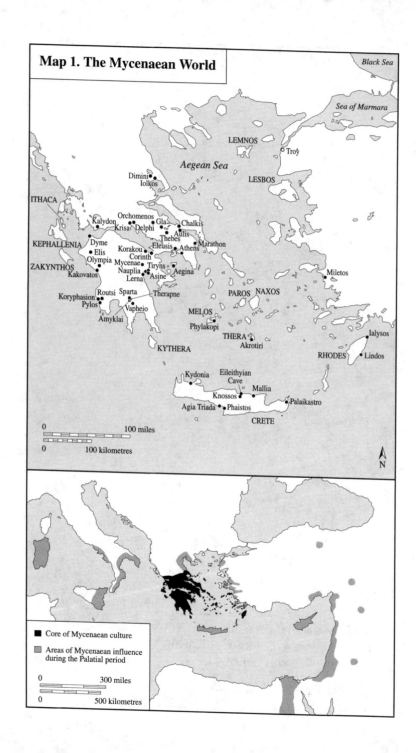

Map 1. The Mycenaean World

Black Sea

Sea of Marmara

LEMNOS

Troy

Aegean Sea

LESBOS

Dimini
Iolkos

ITHACA

Orchomenos
Kalydon
Krisa Delphi Gla Chalkis
Aulis
Thebes
KEPHALLENIA Dyme Korakou Eleusis Athens Marathon
Corinth
Elis Mycenae Tiryns
Olympia Nauplia Aegina
ZAKYNTHOS Kakovatos Lerna Asine Miletos

Koryphasion Routsi Sparta
Pylos Therapne PAROS NAXOS
Vapheio
Amyklai MELOS
Phylakopi

KYTHERA THERA
Akrotiri Ialysos
RHODES Lindos

Kydonia Eileithyian
Cave
Mallia
Knossos Palaikastro
Agia Triada Phaistos
CRETE

0 _____ 100 miles

0 _____ 100 kilometres

N

■ Core of Mycenaean culture

▦ Areas of Mycenaean influence
during the Palatial period

0 _____ 300 miles

0 _____ 500 kilometres

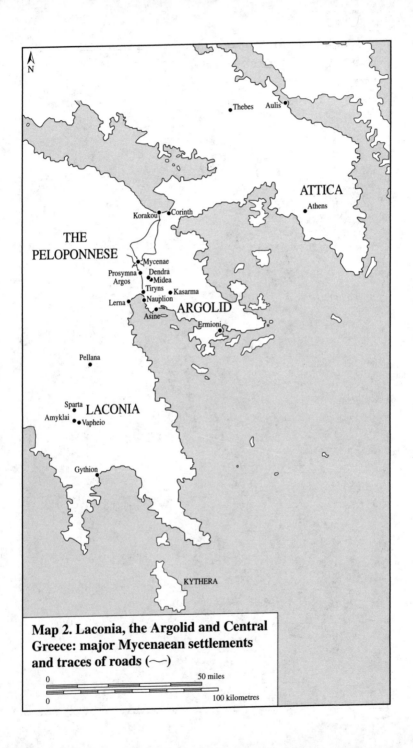

Map 2. Laconia, the Argolid and Central Greece: major Mycenaean settlements and traces of roads (⌣)

| 0 | | 50 miles |
| 0 | | 100 kilometres |

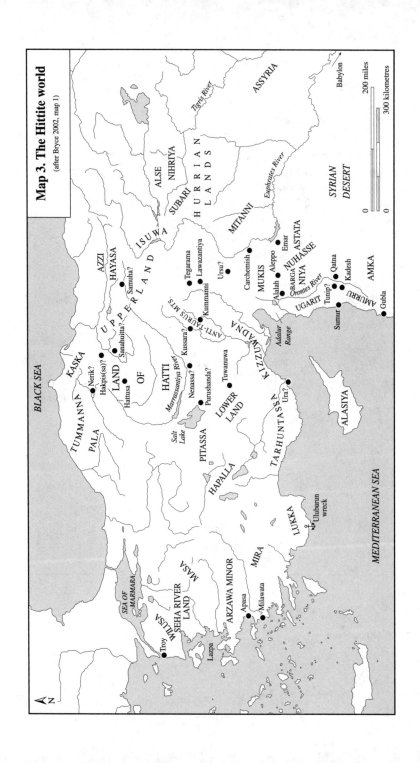

Map 3. The Hittite world

(after Bryce 2002, map 1)

N

BLACK SEA

KASKA

TUMMANNA

Nerik?

PALA

Hakpis(sa)?

Hattusa

Sanahuitta?

Samuha?

AZZI

HAYASA

UPPER LAND

ISUWA

OF HATTI

Marrassantiya River

Salt Lake

Kussara?

Nenassa?

Purushanda?

PITASSA

HAPALLA

LOWER LAND

Tuwanuwa

Kummanni

ANTI-TAURUS MTS.

Tegarama

Lawazantiya

Ursu?

KIZZUWADNA

Addur Range

TARHUNTASSA

Ura?

ALASIYA

ALSE

NIHRIYA

SUBARI

HURRIAN LANDS

MITANNI

Tigris River

Euphrates River

ASSYRIA

Babylon

SYRIAN DESERT

Carchemish

MUKIS

Alalah

Aleppo

Emar

ASTATA

NUHASSE

NIYA

BARGA

UGARIT

Orontes River

Tunip?

Sumur

AMURRU

Gubla

Qatna

Kadesh

AMKA

WILUSA

Troy

SEA OF MARMARA

MASA

SEHA RIVER LAND

Lazpa

ARZAWA MINOR

MIRA

Apasa

Milawata

LUKKA

Uluburun wreck

MEDITERRANEAN SEA

200 miles

300 kilometres

0

0

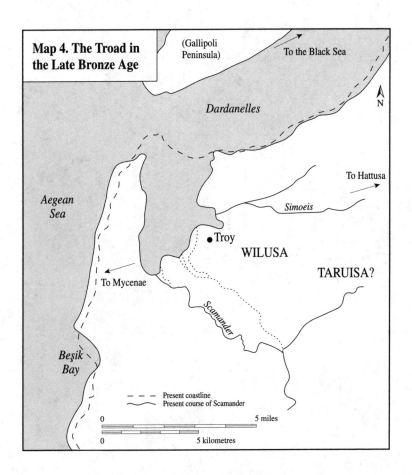

Map 4. The Troad in the Late Bronze Age

(Gallipoli Peninsula)

To the Black Sea

Dardanelles

N

To Hattusa

Aegean Sea

Simoeis

●Troy

WILUSA

TARUISA?

To Mycenae

Scamander

Beşik Bay

- - - Present coastline
── Present course of Scamander

0   5 miles

0   5 kilometres

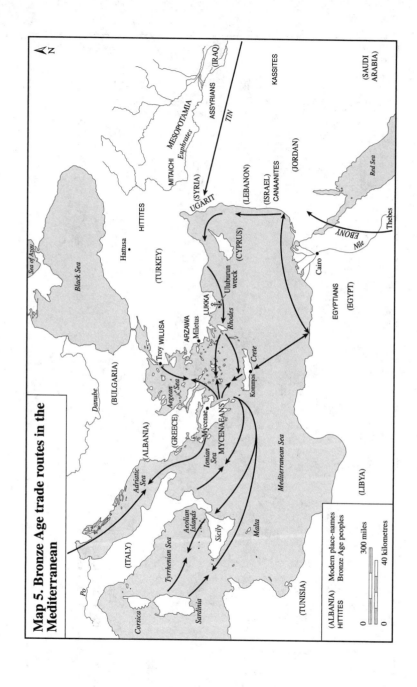

Map 5. Bronze Age trade routes in the Mediterranean

(SAUDI ARABIA)

KASSITES

(IRAQ)

ASSYRIANS

MESOPOTAMIA

MITAICHI

Euphrates

TIN

(JORDAN)

Red Sea

(LEBANON)

(SYRIA)

UGARIT

(ISRAEL)
CANAANITES

HITTITES

Hattusa

(TURKEY)

Black Sea

Sea of Azov

Thebes

EBONY

Nile

Cairo

(CYPRUS)

EGYPTIANS

(EGYPT)

Uluburun
wreck

LUKKA

Rhodes

ARZAWA
Miletus

Troy WILUSA

(BULGARIA)

Danube

Crete

Kommos

Mediterranean Sea

Aegean
Sea

(GREECE)

(ALBANIA)

Mycenae
MYCENAEANS

Ionian
Sea

(LIBYA)

Malta

Sicily

Aeolian
Islands

Tyrrhenian Sea

Sardinia

Corsica

(ITALY)

Po

Adriatic
Sea

(TUNISIA)

| (ALBANIA) | Modern place-names |
| HITTITES | Bronze Age peoples |

0   300 miles

0   40 kilometres

N

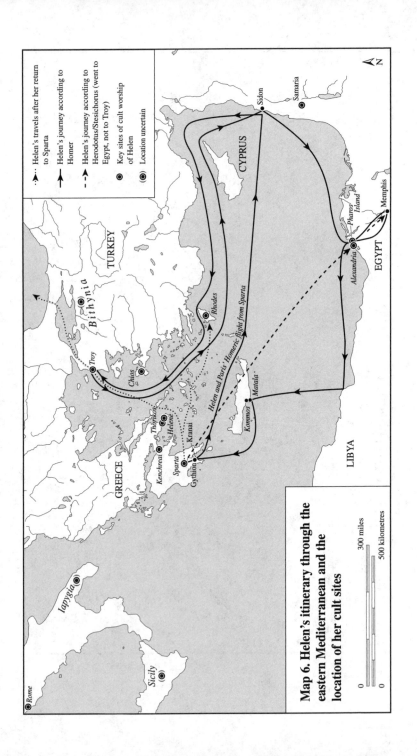

Map 6. Helen's itinerary through the eastern Mediterranean and the location of her cult sites

····▶ Helen's travels after her return to Sparta

——▶ Helen's journey according to Homer

– –▶ Helen's journey according to Herodotus/Stesichorus (went to Egypt, not to Troy)

◉ Key sites of cult worship of Helen

◉ Location uncertain

N

Rome

Iapygia

Sicily

GREECE

Troy

TURKEY

Bithynia

Chios

Thorikos

Helené

Kenchreai

Sparta

Kranai

Gythion

Rhodes

Helen and Paris' Homeric flight from Sparta

Matala

Kommos

CYPRUS

Sidon

Samaria

Pharos Island

Alexandria

Memphis

EGYPT

LIBYA

0   300 miles

0   500 kilometres

TIMELINE

@@@@@@@@@@@@@@

All dates before 500 BC are approximate unless otherwise stated.

BRONZE AGE CRETE

2000 BC	MIDDLE MINOAN (MM) period starts MM I–II Old Palaces at Knossos and elsewhere are built Destroyed *c.* 1700 BC by earthquakes
1700 BC	MM III New Palaces are built
1600 BC	LATE MINOAN (LM) period starts
1425–1370 BC	LM II–IIIAI Linear B in use at Knossos. Mycenaeans begin to dominate the Aegean and influence Minoan culture
1370 BC	Destruction of palace at Knossos

BRONZE AGE GREECE

1600 BC	LATE HELLADIC (LH) period starts
	Grave Circles A and B at Mycenae
? 1550 BC	Eruption of Thera/Santorini
1525–1450 BC	(LH IIA)
	Early *tholos* and chamber tombs constructed at Mycenae
1450–1410 BC	(LH IIB)
	Warrior panoply found near Midea, the 'Dendra armour'

1410–1370 BC	(LH IIIA1)
	Treasury of Atreus constructed at Mycenae
1370–1300 BC	(LH IIIA2)
	Uluburun shipwreck
	Tomb of Clytemnestra built at Mycenae
1300–1200 BC	(LH IIIB1)
	? Trojan Wars? *c.* 1275 BC–1180 BC
	'Mycenaean Lady' fresco from the House of the High Priest Cult Centre at Mycenae
	Extant Linear B tablets found at mainland Greek sites date from *c.* 1200 BC
	Evidence of destruction in Mycenaean palace settlements

THE HITTITE WORLD

1400 BC	First mention of Wilusa (Troy) and Ahhiyawa (Greece) in Hittite texts. Hittite Empire at its height
1360 BC	Horse-training manual written by Kikkuli
1300 BC	Alakšandu rules over Wilusa, correspondence: the 'Alakšandu treaty'
1275 BC	Battle of Kadesh between Egyptian pharaoh Rameses II and Great King of Hatti
1275–1250 BC	Destruction of Troy VIh
1275–1180 BC	The Trojan War?

1250 BC	'Tawagalawa letter' sent to King of Ahhiyawa
(c. 1265–1240 BC)	Hattusili III reigns at Hattusas, with Puduhepa as his queen
1230 BC	Crisis between Hittite states of Ugarit and Amurru over marriage alliance
1223 BC	Last mention of Ahhiyawa in Hittite text
1200 BC	Last mention of Wilusa in Hittite texts
1175 BC	Collapse of the Hittite Empire

'DARK AGES' OF GREECE

1100–800 BC	Mycenaean citadels abandoned, literacy appears to be lost
1000 BC	Dorians settle Sparta and Lakonia

ARCHAIC GREECE

800 BC	Sparta expands to include settlement at Amyklai
700 BC	Homer's epics, the *Iliad* and the *Odyssey*, written down
650 BC	Poems of the Epic Cycle composed, including the *Cypria*
650 BC	Works of Hesiod composed – *Works and Days*, *Theogony*, *Catalogues of Women and Eoiae*
	'Helen's Temple' or the Menelaion: shrine to Helen and Menelaus dedicated at Therapne, Sparta
650–550 BC	Lyric poems of Sappho, Stesichorus, Alcaeus and Alcman featuring Helen composed
	Earliest extant votive offerings left for Helen at the Menelaion

650 BC	The Mykonos vase is created, one of the earliest surviving images of Helen and the Trojan War
	Reform of Spartan society attributed to Lycurgus

CLASSICAL GREECE

- -

506 BC	Sparta and Peloponnesian League allies invade Attica
500–450 BC	Persian Wars between Greeks and Persians
480 BC	Battle of Thermopylae
	Persian king Xerxes visits Troy
500–400 BC	Radical development of Athenian democracy and cultural 'golden age' of Athens
447 BC	Building of the Parthenon begins
	Tragic plays by Aeschylus, Sophocles and Euripides composed and performed at Athens, including those that deal specifically with Helen or the Troy story:

472 BC – Aeschylus' *Persians*
458 BC – Aeschylus' *Agamemnon*
415 BC – Euripides' *Trojan Women*
412 BC – Euripides' *Helen*
411 BC – Aristophanes' *Lysistrata*
408 BC – Euripides' *Orestes*
c. 405 BC – Euripides' *Iphigeneia at Aulis* (posthumous)

431–404 BC	Peloponnesian War between Athens and Sparta. Ends with Spartan hegemony of much of Greece
430 BC	Herodotus' *Histories*
	Thucydides' *History of the Peloponnesian War*

400 BC	Gorgias' *Encomium of Helen*
390–350 BC	Plato's philosophical works, include reference to Helen
370 BC	Isocrates' *Encomium of Helen*
335–322 BC	Aristotle's philosophical works
336–323 BC	Alexander the Great of Macedon conquers territories from Greece to India
334 BC	Alexander visits Troy
280 BC	Foundation of the Library of Alexandria
270 BC	Theocritus' *Epithalamium for Helen* written at Alexandria

IMPERIAL ROME

- -

31 BC–AD 14	Octavian defeats Mark Antony and Cleopatra at Actium Reign of Octavian, henceforth known as Augustus. Birth of imperial Rome
19 BC	Death of Virgil, and publication of the *Aeneid* – telling of the travels of Aeneas after the fall of Troy
c. 25 BC– AD 17	Works of Ovid, including *Art of Love, Heroides* and *Metamorphoses* – many of which make Helen their subject
AD 14–68	Julio-Claudian dynasty. Includes reigns of Tiberius (AD 14–37); Claudius (AD 41–54); Nero (AD 54–68)
	AD 64 Fire of Rome (Nero reported to have sung of the fall of Troy)
	AD 66 Alleged 'discovery' of Dictys' account of the Trojan War
AD 69–96	Flavian Dynasty

AD 79	Eruption of Mount Vesuvius, destroying towns of Pompeii and Herculaneum. Death of Pliny the Elder, author of the *Natural History*
AD 96–192	Age of the Antonines. Includes reigns of Trajan (AD 98–117); Hadrian (AD 117–138); Marcus Aurelius (AD 161–180)
c. AD 160	Pausanias' *Guidebook to Greece*
	Works of Lucian, including *Dialogues of the Dead*
c. AD 200	Works of Christian writers such as Irenaeus, Hippolytus, Clement of Alexandria and Justin Martyr, with testimony on Simon Magus' life in the first century AD
	Statue of *kore*/Helen from Samaria-Sebaste
	Cult of Simon Magus and Helen at Rome
	Dictys' account of the Trojan War written
AD 306–337	Reign of Constantine I Official recognition of Christianity
(*c.* AD 300–600)	Dares' account of the Trojan War?
	Statue of *kore*/Helen destroyed

MEDIEVAL TO TWENTY-FIRST CENTURY

c. AD 500	Collapse of Roman Empire in the West
c. AD 700	Isidore of Seville inscribes Helen's name into account of 132 seminal events in the history of the world
AD 1122–1204	Life of Eleanor of Aquitaine

c. AD 1170	Benoît de Sainte-Maure writes the *Roman de Troie* for Eleanor
c. AD 1175	Matthew of Vendôme's *Art of Versification*
c. AD 1180	Joseph of Exeter completes his *Trojan War* tale
AD 1204	Sack of Constantinople, destruction of Helen's statue in the Hippodrome
AD 1475	William Caxton produces the first printed book in English, the *Recuyell of the Historyes of Troye*
AD 1594	The first recorded performance of Christopher Marlowe's *The Tragical History of Dr Faustus*
AD 1864	Premiere of Offenbach's operetta, *La Belle Hélène*
AD 1870	Heinrich Schliemann begins excavations at the site of Troy
AD 1876	Heinrich Schliemann excavates at Mycenae – Grave Circle A
AD 1880s	Gustave Moreau paints a number of Helen canvases including *Helen at the Ramparts of Troy*
AD 1952–3	Michael Ventris and John Chadwick decipher and publish Linear B
AD 1961	Publication of Hilda Doolittle's (H.D.) *Helen in Egypt*
AD 2004	Wolfgang Peterson's *Troy*

DRAMATIS PERSONÆ

@@@@@@@@@@@@@

ZEUS king of the gods and father of Helen
LEDA wife of Tyndareus and mother of Helen, raped by Zeus disguised as a swan
TYNDAREUS Helen's adoptive father and king of Sparta
HELEN wife of Menelaus of Sparta, abducted by Paris of Troy
CASTOR & POLLUX Helen's twin brothers, also known as the Dioscuri
CLYTEMNESTRA sister of Helen and the Dioscuri, wife of Agamemnon
THESEUS hero-king of Athens, attempts to abduct Helen
MENELAUS king of Sparta and husband of Helen
AGAMEMNON king of Mycenae and brother of Menelaus
IPHIGENEIA daughter of Clytemnestra and Agamemnon, in some traditions
   the daughter of Helen and Theseus
EILEITHYIA pre-Greek goddess of childbirth and fecundity
HERA goddess-wife of Zeus, favours the Greeks in the Trojan War
POSEIDON god of the sea, younger brother of Zeus

@@@@@

PARIS Trojan prince who abducts Helen from Sparta
PRIAM king of Troy and father of Paris and Hector
HECTOR Trojan prince, brother of Paris, and finest Trojan warrior
HECUBA queen of Troy, mother of Hector, Paris and Deiphobus
DEIPHOBUS Trojan prince who marries Helen once Paris is dead
CASSANDRA sister of Paris and Hector, a prophetess whose curse is never to
   be believed
APOLLO divine protector of Troy, son of Zeus and Leto
APHRODITE goddess of sexual love, mother of Aeneas, champion of Troy and
   in particular of Paris
ARES god of war, another protector of Troy, son of Zeus and Hera

GREEK GODS

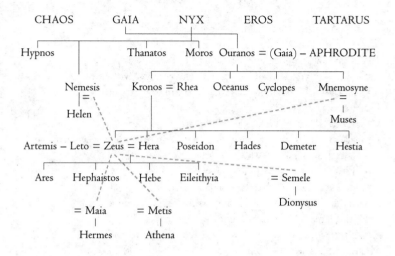

CHAOS　　　GAIA　　　NYX　　　EROS　　　TARTARUS

Hypnos　　　　　Thanatos　　Moros　Ouranos = (Gaia) – APHRODITE

Nemesis　　　Kronos = Rhea　　Oceanus　Cyclopes　　Mnemosyne
　=　　　　　　　　　　　　　　　　　　　　　　　　　　=
Helen　　　　　　　　　　　　　　　　　　　　　　　　Muses

Artemis – Leto = Zeus = Hera　Poseidon　Hades　Demeter　Hestia

Ares　Hephaistos　Hebe　Eileithyia　　　= Semele

　　　　　　　　　　　　　　　　　　　　　Dionysus

　= Maia　　= Metis

Hermes　　Athena

HOUSE OF TROY

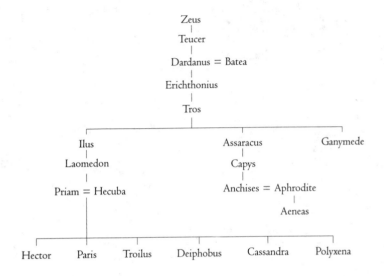

HOUSE OF ATREUS AND THE TYNDAREIDS

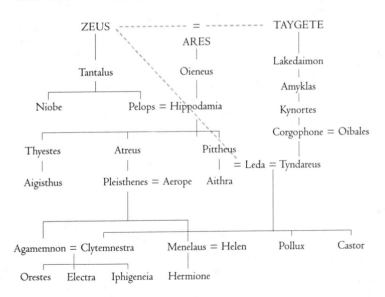

FOREWORD
AND ACKNOWLEDGEMENTS

THE STUDY OF HELEN as a real character from history has been consistently neglected. Historians and romantics alike have enthusiastically sought out the heroes of Greece and by-passed its heroines. It has been too tempting perhaps to remember Helen as 'the most beautiful woman in the world', too appealing to keep her vapid and perfect – too disappointing to discover the world's desire¹ and to find her flawed. Yet there is now a sufficient weight of scholarship to root Homer's account of Helen, the *Iliad*, in an epoch known as the Late Bronze Age (1600 to 1050 BC). Tracking the life of a Late Bronze Age aristocrat from birth to death, I hope to put flesh on Helen's beautiful bones. To put into context a name that is familiar, but strangely insubstantial.

Because Helen is not just one story, but many, told over and over across Europe and the Eastern Mediterranean, I have also travelled through the landscape to bring together a promiscuous range of 'Helens'. There is no single arterial route to the truth of Helen of Troy, but a number of paths that wind across time: Helen grazes the historical record and when written sources are absent I have allowed artefacts, art and the landscape to become articulate. This fusion of ideas and things, people and places, the past and the present, is very Greek; for the early societies around the Mediterranean, boundaries were blurred between the physical and spiritual worlds, between aesthetics and politics. My hope is that this book is an '*historia*' in the sense used by the ancients: an account which encompasses observation and narrative, inquiry, analysis and myth;² a physical quest in search of a woman who was renowned, above all, for the physical impact she had on those around her.

There are a number of things this book does not attempt to do. I do not seek to prove the historicity of the Trojan War or indeed of Helen but to examine the character and historical context of both. Erudite works have been written demonstrating that Helen was a vegetation goddess – this is not one of them. A definitive survey of the reception of Helen would run to many volumes; in this book I have focused on those examples that seem to me to demonstrate, particularly vividly, what she has meant to women and men for over twenty-eight centuries.

I use the phrase 'the Greeks' to describe those who lived on the Greek mainland and in Greek territories, and 'Anatolians' for the inhabitants of what is now predominantly Asiatic Turkey;[3] to avoid confusion, Greece, Crete and Turkey describe geographical areas rather than political entities. Where appropriate I use the Roman name for Anatolia – Asia Minor. In the Bronze Age the Greeks appear to have been variously called the Achaioí, Danaoí, and Argeioí almost certainly explaining why Homer refers to them as the Achaeans, the Danaans and the Argives.[4] This group of peoples I describe collectively as the Mycenaeans – a nomination they were first given in the 19th century AD. When I talk of a Bronze Age Helen I am describing evidence of the real queens who did indeed live in the Eastern Mediterranean and who were, I believe, a prototype for Homer's Helen. Even if Helen was just an archetype, she was an archetype with distinct historical features. 'The ancients' is a loose term, here applying to those who lived between the 8th century BC and the 3rd century AD, a period known as 'antiquity'.

I have transliterated all Greek, including the Bronze Age version of ancient Greek, 'Linear B'; hence PA – MA – KO has become *pharmakon* ('useful little things' – the 3,500 year old root of our word pharmacy). In general I have Latinised figures and place-names from ancient literature. Words from Modern Greek have been given their rough phonetic equivalent.

I have referenced the works, both ancient and modern, on which I have relied heavily or which might be of further interest to the reader. I am indebted to many scholars and adventurers who have gone before me and in particular to those who have been kind enough to help me with this project. They include: Peter Ackroyd, Robert Arnott, Dr Bruce Barker-Benfield, Professor Jonathan Bate, Professor Mary Beard, Dr Lisa Bendall, Rebecca Bennett, Professor Julia Boffey, Dr Julian Bowsher, Professor Nicholas Boyle, Dr Jerry Brotton, Professor Trevor Bryce, Dr Lucilla Burn, Gill Cannell, Professor Paul Cartledge, Richard Catling, Dr Hector Catling, Nick Chlebnikowski, Dr Paul Cohen, Professor Robin Cormack, Mary Cranitch, Dr James Davidson, Professor Jack Davis, Professor Wolfgang-Dietrich Niemeier, Dr Aude Doody, Nicole Doueck, Professor Christos Doumas, Dr Mark Edwards, Matti and Nicholas Egon, Henry Fajemirokun, Dr Lesley Fitton, Dr Katie Fleming, Professor John France, Dr Elizabeth French, Professor Simon Goldhill, Dr Nikolaos Gonis, Dr Barbara Graziosi, Dr Myrto Hatzaki, Professor David Hawkins, Professor John Henderson, Carol Hershenson, Professor Simon Hornblower, Professor Richard Hunter, Dr Hans Jansen and the Tübingen team working at Troy, Dr Richard Jones, Hari Kakoulakis, Dr Michael Keefer, Professor John Killen, Dr Julia Kindt, Professor Dr Manfred Korfmann, Dr Silvin Kosak, Dr Olga Krzyszkowska, Professor Jennifer Larson,

Dr Michael Lane, Dr Miriam Leonard, Dr Maria Liakata, Dr Alistair Logan, Professor Deborah Lyons, Dr Laurie Maguire, Professor Sturt Manning, Professor Rosamund McKitterick, Professor Christopher Mee, Dr Daniel Orrells, Professor Elisabeth Oy-Marra, Professor Thomas G. Palaima, Professor Spyros Pavlides, Paul Pollak, Professor John Prag, Dr Laura Preston, Dr Cemal Pulak, Professor Dr Gilles Quispel, Professor George 'Rip' Rapp, Professor Colin Renfrew, Dr Roman Roth, Dr Deborah Ruscillo, Professor Lynne Schepartz, Professor Cynthia Shelmerdine, Professor Alan Shepherd and Dr Kim Yates, Professor James Simpson, Dr Nigel Spivey, Professor Jane Taylor, Dr Theodore Spyropoulos, Dr Natalie Tchernetska, Professor Bella Vivante, Dr Sofia Voutsaki, Dr Diana Wardle, Dr Kenneth Wardle, Professor Peter Warren, Rev. Peter Watkins, Dr Michael Wedde, Dr Martin West, Dr Todd Whitelaw, Dr Gotthelf Wiedermann, Michael Wood, Dr Jenny Wormald, Dr Neil Wright, Dr Sofka Zinovieff.

The staff at the Ashmolean Museum, British Museum, Louvre Museum, Cambridge University Library, Matthew Parker Library (Corpus Christi College), Trinity Hall Library, the National Gallery of Scotland and Wilton House have been enormously helpful.

I must reiterate heartfelt and special thanks to Paul Cartledge for his exceptional support and numerous readings; to Ken and Diana Wardle, Trevor Bryce and Lisa Bendall for detailed assistance well beyond the call of duty and to Colin Renfrew, Peter Millett, Richard Bradley, Justin Pollard, Lesley Fitton, Sofia Voutsaki, Cynthia Shelmerdine, Jane Taylor, Alistair Logan, Mark Edwards, John France, Julian Bowsher, Laurie Maguire, Bruce Barker-Benfield and Stephen Haggard for reading chapters or the full manuscript in draft form and responding with invaluable suggestions. Diana Wardle produced the Linear B images on pages 96 and 113 with just a few hours' notice. Ellah Allfrey elegantly honed the manuscript and Dr Annelise Freisenbruch, who has been my constant ally throughout the research and writing periods, has been nothing other than splendid.

Thank you too to Kristan Dowsing for coffee and above all to Jane who put this book before something far, far more important.

INTRODUCTION

Cherchez la Femme

◎◎◎◎◎◎◎◎◎◎◎◎◎

Il y a une femme dans toutes les affaires; aussitôt qu'on me fait un rapport,
je dis: 'Cherchez la femme'

There is a woman in every case; as soon as they bring me a report, I say,
'Look for the woman'

ALEXANDRE DUMAS, *Les Mohicans de Paris*, 2, 3

IN THE HEART OF THE PELOPONNESE, in the centre of Sparta, there
is a small square, filled with palm trees and roses. Across dappled paving
stones and behind an erratic fountain is the Sparta Museum. Built with
Greek-American money in the 19th century, the museum has seen better
days – the paintwork must have been yellow ochre once; now it is patched
and peeling, the colour of creamed butter. Classical sculptures, headless,
many with limbs missing, flank the entrance. All is quiet and faded. Inside,
there is a small number of artefacts from pre-historic, archaic and classical
Greece: each is special and precious in its own way, but the labelling is
minimal and rather listless: '*Possibly of the 6th century BC*'; or '*From Therapne,
thought to be an offering to a Goddess*'.[1] Every time I visit, the guards are squashed
into a back room watching a Greek shopping channel and I have the place
to myself.

My first stop is to pay my respects to a limestone block half a metre
high. Two thousand five hundred years old and edged with carved snakes,
it dominates one of the rooms. The stone has, front and back, a tanta-
lisingly eroded scene. On one side, a warrior tenderly holds a young girl.
On the other, the same warrior is lunging forward, his sword to the woman's
throat, ready to kill. But because the woman has turned towards the man,

I

the impact of her face has transformed his attack into an embrace.[2] The man is Menelaus, King of Sparta, the woman, his queen, Helen of Troy.

Helen, *whose beauty summoned Greece to arms, / And drew a thousand ships to Tenedos*,[3] has been known for millennia as a symbol of beauty, and also as a reminder of the terrible power that beauty can wield. Following her double marriage – first to the Greek king Menelaus and then to the Trojan prince Paris – Helen came to be held responsible for an enduring enmity between East and West. She was, according to the oldest surviving ancient Greek written sources, put on the earth by Zeus to rid the world of its super-fluous population:[4] *'[there was] a god-like race of hero men . . . grim war and dread battle destroyed a part of them . . . [war] brought them in ships over the great sea gulf to Troy for rich-haired Helen's sake.'*[5] For nearly three thousand years, she has been upheld as an exquisite agent of extermination.

As soon as men in the West began to write, they made Helen their subject. Hesiod, born around 700 BC and one of the earliest named authors in history, was the first to chronicle her 'wide renown stretching over all the earth'; the poet Sappho described 'her beauty surpassing all mankind'.[6] The epithets endured; it is how Helen is remembered today. When the *New Scientist* magazine debated how to quantify beauty, it was suggested that the measure should be the *millihelen*.[7] In El Paso, Texas, a multi-million-dollar business, Helen of Troy Ltd, distributes beauty products worldwide from its modernist, metal-clad headquarters. The company's website beckons with the catch-phrase: *'Look – and feel – fantastic with Helen of Troy.'* She is still a household name, still commemorated as the gold standard of physical perfection.

෴

A stone's throw from the candyfloss and the Punch and Judy delights of Bournemouth Pier on the south coast of England, just up the breezy cliff path, is an extravagant Victorian mansion that houses the Russell-Cotes collection of art and curiosities. Inside there is an oil canvas, painted by Edwin Long in 1885 and entitled *The Chosen Five*. The setting of the painting is a workshop in southern Italy. Pressing in on a middle-aged man are five gorgeous creatures. One is blonde. One, naked apart from a necklace, has a mane of red hair caught up in a gold circlet. A brunette has her back turned, her chiton half-off, draped around her hips. A handsome Romanesque girl leans over a table playing draughts. The fifth, darker than the rest, has a lyre balanced in her naked lap and a leopard-skin rug licking around her thighs. All are statuesque but impassive. The male artist stares hungrily at the women but none meets his gaze.

This scene tells the story of a master-painter from the 5th century BC: Zeuxis, a man much in demand, particularly in Magna Graecia.⁸ Commissioned to produce a picture of Helen of Troy for the temple of Hera at Agrigentum in Sicily, Zeuxis decided he could realise his task only if the city supplied him with the five most beautiful maidens in the region as models – the sum of their beauty might at least approach Helen's. The selection process started in the town's gymnasium. Inspecting young men as they exercised, Zeuxis asked to see the siblings of the most handsome. Word went out and the pretty sisters of the pretty boys began to line up. Edwin Long created another painting, *The Search for Beauty*, which illustrates what happened next. It is a voluptuous scene. Here Zeuxis is 'auditioning' his models. Scores of women crowd around him; many begin to remove their clothes. One woman is drawing out a pin to let fall her blue-black hair. These girls had to be palpably perfect, perfect in every last detail if they were to become second Helens.⁹ Zeuxis surveys them eagerly, relishing the task in hand.

Across the English Channel and on the second floor of the Louvre in Paris there is another Zeuxis, attempting to paint another Helen.¹⁰ The scale of this 18th-century canvas is worthy of its surroundings: it is a mammoth thing, 4 m across and 3.3 m tall. Here there are five eager girls – again, each is a wonderful specimen. One blonde, with a blue ribbon in her hair and pearls around her neck, is undressed, her modesty precariously preserved by a flimsy drape of cloth – an old woman pokes at her, staring covetously at the plump young flesh which is about to be immortalised. Yet what dominates this painting is not the cluster of beauties – it is the bleak, virtually empty canvas in the centre of the composition. This is where Helen should be: a void that Zeuxis is desperately, abortively, trying to fill.

Because, of course, the wonderful irony about the most beautiful woman in the world is that she is faceless. There are no contemporary representations of a Spartan queen from the 13th century BC, the putative date of the Trojan War. The extant images of high-born Greek women from this period – the Late Bronze Age – are all standards, all recycled replicas within a genre. At this time there was no characterisation in Greek art. Excavators have turned up striking Bronze Age death masks – but only of men. There are precious signet rings belonging to the aristocrats of the time, but the female faces they bear are of abstracted, quasi-divine creatures; these are no portraits.

By the 7th century BC the ancient world does start to paint Helen's picture, or inscribe her form on stone, clay and bronze.¹¹ Yet these too are stylised, copybook approximations – the vase painters, sculptors and fresco artists of Greece and Rome worked to a recognised formula; we have no lifelike representation of Helen from antiquity. Museum storerooms around the world have shelves crammed with vases showing Helen at various points in her life-story and in her evolution as an idol — Helen as a girl, Helen as queen, Helen as a demi-goddess, Helen as a whore — but these images, without exception, are all made up; they reveal not who Helen was, but who men have wanted her to be.

An Evil Destiny

◎◎◎◎◎◎◎◎◎◎◎◎

On us the gods have set an evil destiny,
That we should be a singer's theme
For generations to come.

Helen, from Homer, *Iliad*[12]

ALTHOUGH HELEN HAS COME TO BE MEMORIALISED for the patina of her beauty, she is far more than just a pretty face. She also represented something so potent, complex and charismatic that the finest author of the ancient world composed an epic masterpiece in which she is pivotal. Just a few generations after the ancient Greek alphabet was invented[13] at the beginning of the 8th century BC, the *Iliad*, an epic poem running to 15,693 lines, was written down.[14] Thirty or so years later came the *Odyssey*. In over 200,000 words of ancient Greek, Homer told the world what women like Helen could make men do. He gave the West its earliest and most influential work of literature. He promoted Helen as a captivating and troubling icon.

Homer's poetry roars and whispers. He talks of passion and revenge and duty and disloyalty, of loss and love, deploying characters who wear wolf-pelts and leopard-skins: they think like us and they dress like cavemen. At the most basic of readings the *Iliad* — which describes the Achaean Greeks and the Trojans battling it out for possession of Helen — is a tale of boy meets girl meets boy — leading to the mother of all bust-ups. At its most complex, it is an exploration of the relationship between gods and mortals, women and men, sex and violence, duty and desire, delight and death. It asks why humanity chooses paths it knows to be destructive; why we desire what we do not have.

With the *Iliad* and the *Odyssey*, for the first time in the West, we find notions of personal morality being tested. Helen is a vital part of this interrogation because she is a paradox. A bedazzling, unfaithful queen, a duplicitous home-wrecker who causes decades of misery, she none the less survives unscathed: an inscrutable mix of self-will and suggestibility, intellect and instinct, frailty and power. Created at a time before good and evil were regarded as distinct entities, Helen embraces both. She is physically perfect and yet her perfection spawns disaster. She is clearly dangerous and still men cannot stop loving her. She enters the record as a woman who demands engagement.

When Homer was composing the *Iliad* in the 8th century BC, there were no preconceived ideas of how societies should constitute or conduct themselves. Everything was an experiment. The Eastern Mediterranean was a vast social and political laboratory. During Homer's lifetime and for the three hundred years after his death, the Greeks tried all manner of ventures: tyrannies, democracies, totalitarian boot camps, proto-communist utopias. Anything went, but there was one important constant. All these experiments measured their own success against the achievements of a distant past described by the epic poets, and, in particular, by Homer. This glittering epoch became known as 'the Age of Heroes'.[15] And the single most important female figure from this heroic age was the Spartan queen, *orea Eleni*, 'beautiful Helen'. Helen's story therefore became a benchmark by which the classical world judged itself.

The long-dead heroes (and heroines) from the Bronze Age were envisaged as giants in mind, body and spirit. Dinosaur bones were touted around classical Greece and Rome as relics of the über-men and women who were believed to have inhabited the pre-historic past.[16] Enormous stone building blocks, the remains of Bronze Age fortifications, were described as 'Cyclopean' because it was presumed only giants – such as the one-eyed Cyclopes – could have moved them into place.[17] At Olympia, a monstrous shoulder-blade – thought to belong to Heracles' great-grandson Pelops – was displayed with deep reverence in a specially built shrine.[18] All this was considered proof-positive that the Greeks' ancestral heroes were men and women to revere. In their outsize lives could be found the ultimate expression of what it meant to be human.[19]

Homer's words[20] were as close as the pagan, polytheistic Greeks got to an over-arching orthodoxy, and so his ideas became theirs. For the ancients, the bard's work was canonical – in many quarters the *Iliad* had the authority of a sacred text. Sappho, Plato, Aeschylus, Euripides and Aristotle picked up Helen's theme. The conflict at Troy came to represent the war not to end, but to start, all wars. Homer's Helen became a paradigm for the female sex and for the hazards of the entangling female embrace.

Yet Helen is not contained by the works of Homer. The *Iliad* and the *Odyssey* deal with only a fraction of her narrative. These two epic poems cover only a short period (the *Iliad* only fifty-one days) in a rich and eventful life. When Helen is first mentioned by Homer in Book 2 of the *Iliad* she is given no introduction. The author presumed his audience was familiar with her colourful back-story. Although Helen's presence is felt throughout the poem – hovering in the wings, a hated *casus belli* – there is a great deal that Homer does not tell us about her. We know from vase paintings and fragments of stories that turn up in plays, poems, or philosophical debates that the men and women of antiquity were well versed in other intimate details of Helen's extraordinary tale.

Alternative epics were to carry on where Homer left off. Most of these are long lost – or displaced; some we can assemble piecemeal, others survive in name only: works such as the *Little Iliad*, the *Sack of Ilium*, the *Homecomings* and the *Cypria*.[21] Helen was writ particularly large in the *Cypria*, a group of poems composed soon after Homer's death.[22] Originally part of an Epic Cycle that dealt with the origins of the world and reached to the end of the Age of Heroes, this collection seems to have focused on Helen's early years. Now in desultory fragments, this would have been one of our best sources for Helen's epic life.

❦❦❦❦❦

In this book I will follow Helen's fortunes as recounted by Homer. I will also explore the evidence offered by these other less familiar literary sources and by archaeology – piecing together Helen's life-story from her conception to her grave. I will trace her evolution as a human character from the Late Bronze Age, as a spiritual power and as an icon of peerless beauty and erotic love; and follow in her footsteps across the Eastern Mediterranean.

Mine will be a physical journey and a journey across time. Helen's lament in the *Iliad*, that on her the gods had laid an evil curse, making her '*A singer's theme for generations to come*', was prophetic. How Helen has been sung. Where women have in general been written out of history, Helen has been written in. She is one of the few, evergreen female personalities to survive from antiquity.[23]

The Romans claimed their city was founded by descendants of a Trojan War veteran, Aeneas, and therefore stories of Troy were at the heart of

Roman inheritance. When the megalomaniac emperor Nero redecorated his opulent *Domus Aurea* – his Golden House – the elaborate fresco cycles he commissioned told the story of the Trojan War; and when he fiddled while Rome burned, it was said that he sang of Troy.[24] Even after the fall of Rome, as the ruling dynasties throughout Europe competed to prove themselves the true inheritors of Roman power, royal households traced their ancestry back, directly, to the heroes of Troy – men who were made heroic in battling for Helen.

In the 7th century AD, Helen's rape by the Trojan prince Paris was credited by Isidore of Seville in his *Etymologies* – a work immensely influential in medieval thought – as one of 132 moments that shocked and shaped the world. When William the Conqueror invaded England, his military performance against King Harold was compared (favourably) by one of his biographers, Guillaume de Poitiers, to that of Agamemnon seeking to rescue the Spartan queen: 'where Agamemnon took ten years to break down Troy, William took one day'.[25]

Scribes in the ancient and medieval worlds carefully copied Helen's story on to papyrus, parchment and vellum, and once Caxton had brought the printing press to Westminster in 1476, her tale was mass-produced – the basis of *The Recuyell of the Historyes of Troye*,[26] the first book ever to be printed in the English language. The initial production of *The Recuyell* was laborious: it took Caxton between five and six months to print the 700-odd leaves of the book, but from this moment on, Helen would inhabit not just the popular imagination, but the mass media.

Dante, Fra Angelico, Chaucer, Leonardo, Marlowe, Shakespeare, Spenser, Dryden, Goethe, Jacques-Louis David, Rossetti, Gladstone, Yeats, Berlioz, Strauss, Rupert Brooke, Camus, Tippett and Ezra Pound: all have kept the idea of Helen alive. Cultures have created their own Helens, consistent with their own ideals of beauty. She is irresistible because she is recondite. No model, no substitute, is ever quite good enough. Zeuxis' answer was to manufacture a composite, but even that amalgam fails to satisfy. Because Helen is elusive, her appeal endures. She is prodigious, part of the cultural, and the political, make-up of the West.

Helen-Hunting

◎◎◎◎◎◎◎◎◎◎◎◎

They called me Helen. Let me tell you all the
truth of what has happened to me.

EURIPIDES, *Helen*[27]

ANCIENT AUTHORS TELL US that Helen travelled extensively through
the Bronze Age world, zigzagging across Greece, besieged in Anatolia
and journeying to Egypt. They believed that after her death her spirit lived
on in the landscape.

In Helen's case, locations are particularly germane because we will never
hear her voice, first hand, through textual evidence. Although the character
of Helen derived from an epoch that used writing (an early form of Greek
now called Linear B), the Linear B tablets that have survived – accidentally
preserved when they were baked hard by the very fires that destroyed many
Bronze Age palaces – deal with relatively mundane details of Bronze Age
life. These are administrative lists, tallies of wine, pots, grain, oils and livestock – the material culture that warrior-overlords controlled.

The Linear B script is utilised primarily for bureaucracy. In the tablets
dug up to date there is little that is immediately recognisable as the inner
voice of a civilisation, no self-conscious historical record.[28] This is not a
culture that employed written symbols as a form of emotional expression.
For that, we have to wait until the reintroduction of writing around the
time of Homer just after 800 BC. Greece in the 13th century BC, Helen's
age, still stands in pre-history.

But Helen's is a story of two civilisations – of Greeks and of Trojans.
There are fuller written sources from the 'other' side. Paris, Helen's Trojan
lover, occupied territory in the Troad, the coastal buffer-zone, now in
modern-day Turkey, which in pre-history sat at the edge of the Anatolian
landmass dominated by the great Hittite Empire. At the turn of the 20th
century, excavators in central Turkey uncovered a cache of Hittite texts:
diplomatic treaties, ritual tablets, royal biographies, accounts of trade and
conflict. Tens of thousands of inscriptions have since been discovered. Some
are carved into rocks and along remote mountain passes, others are still
being dug out of the earth. Many tablet fragments have lain, undeciphered,
in museum storerooms since they were first excavated a hundred years ago.
About seven thousand fragments have yet to be published: there are simply

not enough Hittite scholars, or research funds, to do the work.[29] These Hittite texts give an eastern perspective to the Troy story that has not been fully explored. If Helen is to be explored as a real woman as well as an icon, and in a Bronze Age context, then they are vital testimonies.

అంఅంఅం

Since recorded time, men have believed in Helen. They have believed in her both as an actual historical character and as an archetype of beauty, of womanhood, of sex, of danger. In my own pursuit of Helen, I will look not just at what she has come to mean, but what she meant to the populations of the past. I will explore the praxis of Helen, trying to imagine how she was experienced in antiquity and beyond, as men and women walked past her shrines, as they watched the priestesses of her cult inspect bloody entrails to determine her will, as they scratched lewd graffiti about her onto the walls of Rome, as they listened to politicians and philosophers enveloping her in their rhetoric, as they decorated their palaces and their temples with her image.

Helen's admirers (and her detractors) have been many and various. Medieval nuns pored over an imagined exchange of love-letters between Helen and Paris from the *Heroides*, written by Ovid – honing their own skills in literary flirtation as versions of the poems were smuggled out to men, or even passed between the girls in the convent.[30] In Renaissance England the rebellious named their daughters 'Helen' despite its categorisation by pamphleteers as an appellation that would bring disgrace.[31] In 17th-century Europe artists were commissioned to decorate buildings with giant scenes of Helen's abduction. One example, by Giovanni Francesco Romanelli, still survives in the old Bibliothèque Nationale in Paris. A horribly compelling composition, it soars on the ceiling of the Galerie Mazarine. In the neo-classical boom of the late 18th and early 19th centuries men such as the philosopher, historian and dramatist Friedrich Schiller used the name 'Helen' as a term of abuse, to mean a flirt, a tart, an immoral woman.[32] Strolling through the Montmartre district of Paris in the 1860s you would have rubbed shoulders with a bohemian throng and an occasional royal, the Prince of Wales or the Tsar of Russia – all heading to the Théâtre de Variétés to watch Offenbach's operetta sensation, *La Belle Hélène*.[33]

Dreamy 19th-century paintings portrayed Helen – anachronistically – as a plump, blonde, classical Greek beauty, dressed in diaphanous clothes. Scores of prostitutes found themselves plucked off the streets to be immortalised in oils, as 'Sweet Helena'. The Spartan queen has spawned some of the most beautiful poetry of the 20th century, and some of its ugliest. There are sites on the internet that today invoke her as a powerful white witch, others that hail her as the first recorded female role-model. Helen encourages speculation in its truest sense – holding a speculum, a mirror, up to her ever-changing face to see what worlds can be glimpsed in the reflection behind.

Goddess, Princess, Whore

@@@@@@@@@@@@@@

There is no art in turning a goddess into a witch,
a virgin into a whore, but the opposite operation, to give dignity
to what has been scorned, to make the degraded desirable,
that calls either for art or for character.

J.-W. GOETHE (from posthumous papers)[34]

HISTORY IS AT ONCE BAFFLED AND ENRAPTURED BY HELEN; we can trace nearly three millennia of ambiguous attitudes towards her. She is difficult to categorise for good reason; a pursuit of Helen across the ages throws up three distinct, yet intertwined, guises. When we talk about her, we are in fact describing a trinity.

The most familiar Helen is the brilliant regal beauty from the epics, particularly Homer's Helen: the Spartan princess with divine paternity fought over by the heroes in Greece and then won by Menelaus' wealth. The queen who – led on by the goddess of love, Aphrodite – welcomed a Trojan prince into her bed while her husband was overseas. The head-strong, capricious aristocrat who deserted the Greeks, sailed across the Aegean and then languished in Troy, hated by all around her. The exile who watched heroes suffer agonies in her name – fleet-footed Achilles, red-haired Menelaus, sharp-witted Odysseus, Agamemnon, the king of men; and of course the lads from the eastern camp – Hector, breaker of horses, Priam, lord of a glorious citadel, and Paris with his glistening love-locks.

This is the invidious Helen who walked around the Trojan Horse, imitating the voices of the Greek wives, attempting to dislodge her erstwhile countrymen from their equine siege-breaker. The adulteress who, after ten sad, punishing, faithless years in Troy, was still so entrancing that her cuckold husband, Menelaus, could not bear to kill her. The enigmatic figure who sailed back to Sparta while Paris' body smouldered on the Trojan plain, back to a daughter whom she had left motherless, back to a bed she had left cold. The creature – flawed and yet strangely dignified – who demonstrated that female beauty was something to fear as well as to crave.

But Helen was not just a finely drawn character from the Greek epics, not just a 'sex-goddess' in literary terms. She was also a demi-god, a heroine, worshipped and honoured at shrines across the Eastern Mediterranean. She was perceived as an integral part of the spiritual landscape. Men and women made propitiation to her earthy power. In Sparta she was invoked by young virgins; in Egypt she had uxorial duties, caring for newlyweds and old wives; and in Etruscan society her half-dressed form was carved on the funerary urns of high-born women – a valued companion for the journey into the afterlife.[35] Some scholars believe that a mortal Helen never existed, but that she is, instead, simply the human face of an ancient nature-goddess, a full-blown divinity, a pan-Hellenic spirit of vegetation and fertility. A visceral force that brings with it both life and death.

Then there is the *'shameless whore'*,[36] the *'traitorous bitch'*[37]; the *'Aegeyan bitch, her of the three husbands, who bare only female children'*;[38] the *'strumpet'*;[39] the beautiful, libidinous creature irresistible to men; the pin-up, golden-haired, phantom Helen, lambasted in theological texts and draped across the art galleries of Europe, an erotic *eidolon* – a Greek word meaning a ghost, an image or idea – an idol of female beauty and sexuality, both lusted after and despised.[40]

⌒⌒⌒⌒⌒

I believe that all three incarnations – princess, goddess and whore – find their root in a Bronze Age Helen, that the template for Helen of Troy was provided by one of the rich Spartan queens who lived and died on the Greek mainland in the 13th century BC; a woman who slept at night and woke at dawn, a flesh-and-blood icon, an aristocrat responsible for *orgia* – secretive, mysterious fertility rites – a woman so blessed, so honoured, so powerful, she appeared to walk with the gods. A mortal who, down the centuries, has become larger than life.

Because Helen is such an alluring figure of fantasy, because she dazzles as she goes, she can make it hard to see the women of substance who walked through the Bronze Age palaces of the Eastern Mediterranean. But ongoing archaeological and historical projects demonstrate that these women were prominent and significant: broken writing tablets tell us that female aristocrats were used as diplomatic trading chips, highly valued commodities passed from one state to another, the Bronze Age equivalent of the Black Tulip. Within the context of her world, Helen is a historical possibility.

Greece and Anatolia had a complicated, fractious and intense relationship at the end of the Bronze Age. Magnates from both sides married each other's women, fought over each other's territories and joined together in trade. In Turkish waters divers have found Bronze Age ocean-worthy vessels laden with precious goods, which sank as they made the journey between the Greek mainland and Asia Minor. Official letters sent across the Aegean from one great leader to another can flatter or they can simmer with scarcely contained fury. Stockpiles of sling-shot have been discovered at the walls of Troy. And the civilisations that Helen and Paris represent – the Mycenaeans (based on the Greek mainland) and the Hittites (in command of much of Turkey and the Middle East), along with their allies such as Troy – imploded in a dramatic rush of flame and confusion at the end of the 13th century BC. At the height of their power, something or someone brought these giants to their knees.

Slowly pieces of the jigsaw puzzle are fitting together. As more Bronze Age texts are translated, as more material culture is recovered in archaeological excavations, Homer's epic, describing the conflict between the Greeks[41] and the Trojans, edges closer to fact and Helen's story rings ever more true. Digs at Troy have not yet produced Prince Hector's mangled body, nor the remains of a god-like hero called Achilles, an arrow piercing his heel, nor, miraculously preserved in anaerobic conditions, the fetlock of a giant wooden horse. And they are never likely to do so. But what they have yielded is a city destroyed by fire and a culture rocked to its core. The Hittites and the Mycenaeans were mighty – less than a hundred years after the putative date of the Trojan War, they disappear.[42] What Helen has come to mean is universal; but her story is proving increasingly appropriate to the circumstances of the Late Bronze Age.

A caveat: to date, no human remains of a 13th-century BC Spartan queen have been identified. Until we discover a Late Bronze Age burial in Sparta itself, containing a skeleton with sufficient uncontaminated DNA to test positively as female, lying next to a Greek king, both corpses wearing Trojan gold, the site surrounded by dedications marked '*eleni*' written in a Bronze Age script; then, and only then, can we say, categorically, we have found our human Helen. And the wait for such an eventuality will almost certainly be interminable.

Pre-history is a temporal land of ifs, buts and maybes, a land that up until a hundred and fifty years ago still lay buried and mute. But it conceived the idea of a woman who became the cause célèbre of the most influential work of epic literature in the West. We have the story, and now it is up to us to find its roots.

If Helen is a confection, an artistic construct, she was originally the construct of the pre-historic mind; if she is a nature divinity, her worship began in pre-history; if she is real, she lived and loved as a pre-historic princess. To understand all three Helens, we have to start our journey in her pre-historic world. A world which is other, rich and strange.

PART ONE

HELEN'S
BIRTH IN
PRE-HISTORY

1

A DANGEROUS
LANDSCAPE

Suddenly down from the mountain's rocky crags
Poseidon stormed with giant, lightning strides
and the looming peaks and tall timber quaked
beneath his immortal feet as the sea lord surged on.
HOMER, *Iliad*[1]

To UNDERSTAND THE DISQUIET LANDSCAPE that nurtured Helen, we must begin our story 175 miles south-east from Sparta, Helen's traditional birthplace, across the Aegean Sea on the Cycladic island of Thera.[2] Here, over three and a half thousand years ago, a single, cataclysmic event directed the course of western civilisation.

☙☙☙☙☙

Between 1859 and 1869, labour-gangs were employed on the island of Thera to quarry raw materials for cement. Huge amounts were needed: this was preparatory work for the construction of the new canal at Suez. The workers were after pozzolan, a powdered pumice-stone which, combined with lime, produces a cement so fine that it is like plaster; they were digging in the right place. Here were layers of pumice a full 10 m thick: the tell-tale sign of massive geo-physical activity. The volcanic island of Thera had erupted a number of times, and as the navvies dug deeper and deeper it became clear that the most spectacular explosion pre-dated the Romans, the classical Greeks and Homer himself. When the pick-axes finally hit the bedrock, the workers had made their way through extruded volcanic material 3,500 years old to the archaeological level of the Aegean Bronze Age. What was being quarried was the fall-out of a gargantuan natural disaster.

The landscape of present-day Thera still signals the force of an earth that is uneasy. Take a little boat out to the collapsed centre of the volcano and you crunch your way through its hills and hummocks built up of dusty, aerated lava. Pumice stones skitter and slide underfoot at the approach to the volcano's centre. The ground still breathes out attenuated plumes and wisps of smoke. Footpaths wind past giant rocky outcrops: once molten ooze, these subterranean minerals have now hardened into titanic chunks of shiny, black, broken treacle. For centuries, the Theran landscape would have been a stark aide-memoire, telling the ancients that men were mere matchwood when it came to the anger of the earth, the sea and the sky.

Thera is a shocking and savage enough place today – just imagine it as the volcano erupted around 1550 BC.[3] Earthquakes a month or so before would have been the first signal that the gods were uneasy. Then the massive mountain in the sea would have started to exhale clouds of ash, a dark stain in the sky, an ugly blur visible for a hundred miles. With a scream of released pressure, steam would have escaped in voluminous billows and tight jet-blasts. And then the *coup de théâtre*: between 30 and 40 km of pumice, rock-shards and ash hurtling into the atmosphere in the giant eruption column. Magma spewing up from the volcano's mouth; pyroclastic flows leaving deposits 20 to 50 m thick in some places; electrical storms ripping open the sky.[4]

Although it may have taken only three or four days for the volcano to erupt, the effects were far-reaching. The global temperature would have gone down as volcanic aerosols were released, blocking solar radiation to the earth's surface. As far away as Lake Golcuk in the Bozdag mountain range in Turkey, 320 miles north-east of Thera, a 12 cm-thick layer of Theran tephra has been found.[5] Sediment cores from the Black Sea also contain Theran material. Ash would have drifted over an area of 500,000 square km, smothering crops, stifling livestock.

Following the volcanic eruption there were other horrors to come. As sea water was displaced by the shift of the earth and rushed into the collapsed magma chamber – the newly gaping Theran caldera sinking over 480 m below sea level – a giant wave, a tsunami, began to gather and hurtle towards shores in the region. It is estimated that the largest tsunami created by the eruption of Thera – just one in a train of waves – would have been up to 12 m high, travelling at well over 160 km per hour.[6] Just 111 km away, the north coast of Crete was particularly badly hit. Near the Bronze Age palace of Malia on the island, tiny fossilised sea-shells have been found in mud deposits, shells that under normal conditions exist only in deep ocean. Small boats would have been plucked from the shallows and hurled onto the hills. And as the decomposing bodies of the volcano's victims were washed back ashore, diarrhoeal diseases – cholera and typhoid – would have spread. The destruction and death toll would have been immense. The Bronze Age world was brutalised.

But for one group of people who lived in scattered settlements on the Greek mainland, the explosion of Thera offered an unexpected opportunity.

⊙⊙⊙⊙⊙

From the 19th to the 15th centuries BC, the islanders of Crete – the Minoans (thus named in 1895 by the archaeologist Arthur Evans after the legendary ruler of Crete, King Minos) – had dominated the sea-ways of the Aegean.[7] Floating between Europe, the Middle East and Africa, the Minoans successfully exploited their pole position. For five hundred years communities around the Eastern Mediterranean not only traded with 'the people of Keftiu', as the Minoans were probably known in the Bronze Age, but also followed their political and religious lead.[8] Secure on their island home, the Minoans were wealthy, vigorous and influential. They have been described as a '*thalassocracy*' – a sea-power, rulers of the waves.

The eruption of Thera changed Minoan fortunes. This was a sophisticated culture, a culture that relied on contacts with the outside world to keep its workshops fed with tin and copper, with semi-precious stones and with oils and unguents. But all boats moored along the busy north and east coasts of the island – a fleet essential for Minoan well-being – would have been destroyed by the tsunami that followed the Thera eruption. Patterns of trade and communication across the Aegean were disrupted. Vital farmland was flooded. As refugees fled Thera itself they could have brought with them unfamiliar pathogens which would have radiated quickly from the crowded shanty towns that mushroomed on Cretan coastlines.[9]

The psychological impact of the disaster must have been far-reaching. For a fundamentally superstitious pre-historic culture like the Minoans, a perversion of nature such as this could be explained only in spiritual terms. The column of water which appeared from nowhere and hit the island at a horrifying, incomprehensible speed, the eerie afterglow of the volcanic explosion hanging on the horizon, must have been interpreted as momentous signs from enraged gods. The confidence of the Minoans – who had, for centuries, seemed blessed – would have been shaken to its core.

Helen's Mycenaean ancestors were equipped to step into the breach.[10]

The Mycenaean civilisation first comes into focus around 1700 BC. Centred on mainland Greece – particularly its southern landmass, the Peloponnese – the Mycenaeans founded citadels, carved up agricultural districts and established a network of roads and trade-routes. This was a well-organised, ambitious and materialistic culture; each generation of the warrior-elite expanded Mycenaean territories and the treasure stores of Mycenaean palaces. As the Mycenaeans looked to the south, Minoan palaces and ports must have tempted them – control of Cretan territories would have offered a clear trade-route through to Egypt and across to Asia Minor. It is little surprise that after years as a fledgling culture, when the Mycenaeans decided to spread their wings, they had Crete in their sights. Thera's explosion triggered a political as well as a geological shift in power.

Throughout the 16th century BC the Minoans appear slowly to lose their grip on the Aegean; then, around 1450 BC we find Mycenaean pottery simply replacing Minoan artefacts. At the great palace complex of Knossos in the north of the island, a Mycenaean administration takes the reins. Across the island, fires destroy all other palatial centres. All Minoan administrative records come to be written in the Greek language. Independent Minoan culture is eclipsed. For the next three hundred years it would be the Mycenaean Greeks, not the Minoans, who dominated the region. Following the eruption of Thera, the leaders of the mainland Greeks slowly join the ranks of the most powerful men on earth – by the 13th century BC Helen's ancestors are, like the rulers[11] of Egypt, Babylonia, Assyria and Anatolia, described as 'Great Kings'.[12]

⌒⌒⌒⌒⌒

And so, although many artists have imagined Helen and her peers as soft, sun-kissed creatures, wafting indolently in front of classically fluted columns in diaphanous chitons, if we are to hold in our mind a picture of the real women of the Late Bronze Age and the environment they inhabited, we must add harsher colours to the palette.

The eruption of Thera was the most showy disaster in the Late Bronze Age, but there were others. This was a fragile, edgy epoch in which communities were frequently destabilised by both political and environmental forces. The Eastern Mediterranean stretches over a tectonic-plate boundary – a zone where two plates in the earth's crust push and pull like testy lovers; Helen's story is set in one of the most seismic – as well as one of the most volcanic – regions of the world. In addition to the extreme eruption of Thera, for the Late Bronze Age populations of the Aegean natural disasters were regular and unwelcome visitors. There were 'storms' of earth-quakes, as well as unusually frequent cosmic activity.[13] From the 14th to the 12th centuries, on average, the Peloponnese would have suffered an earth tremor, an earthquake, or a cosmic strike every decade.

Across the Bronze Age Aegean there is evidence of these disasters in the form of 'destruction layers' – jumbled masses of disjointed architecture, artefacts, plant and animal remains. Everyday objects in the archaeological strata are in unlikely places or positions. In the most extreme examples, debris has been pulverised or burnt, human bones are crushed in rubble; the disorder bears witness to moments of great crisis. At Thebes – the main Mycenaean settlement in Boiotia, central Greece, which Homer tells us contributed fifty ships to the Trojan War effort – a destruction layer from a Mycenaean building on the hill of Kadmeia is a full metre thick. Trapped in one horribly compressed upper room is a skeleton, probably that of a woman aged between twenty and twenty-five, who seems to have been killed by a violent blow to the head as the building was ripped apart.[14]

Destruction layers witness trauma. They are public signifiers of private tragedies – but there were also devastating events that leave little archaeological trace. Landslides and dust-clouds, water springs blocked at the source, flash floods, rivers diverted: life abrupted.[15] From 1800 to 1100 BC many of the settlements in the Eastern Mediterranean appear to have been hit not once, but repeatedly.[16] Helen's inheritance was vexed. She was born as a woman or as an idea when heaven and earth were in pugnacious mood. The mortar binding the foundation myths in a court such as hers would have been streaked with blood. The Mycenaeans clawed their way to prominence in the Eastern Mediterranean over rubble and detritus and broken lives; theirs was an ascent back-lit by flames. As they reach supremacy in the 13th century BC, the smell of death – whether brought by man or by nature – still hangs in the air.

Little surprise that Helen's story is brooding and uncomfortable.

2

A RAPE, A BIRTH

◎◎◎◎◎◎◎◎◎◎◎◎

A shudder in the loins engenders there
The broken wall, the burning roof and tower
And Agamemnon dead.
W.B. YEATS, 'Leda and the Swan' (1928)

ELEN'S TRADITIONAL breeding-place, the Peloponnese in the southern Greek mainland, is, even when not rocked by natural disasters, a place of extremes. In her home town, Sparta, summer temperatures can reach up to 104 degrees Fahrenheit (40 degrees Celsius), while in the winter choking mists clog up the valleys and the almond trees are laced with hoar-frost. High in the mountains that ring the town, there are icicles the size of a grown man. Widows at the roadside will tell how the weak and very poor still die from the cold. This can be a savage land and it has given birth to correspondingly savage stories.

Helen's conception is a prime example. According to Greek myths, Helen came from good stock, but her genesis was violent. Her father, Zeus, was chief among the pantheon on Mount Olympus. Helen was Zeus' cherished and only mortal daughter. Her mother, Leda,¹ the wife of Tyndareus, King of Sparta, was famed for her beauty. One day, as Leda bathed on the banks of the Eurotas, the lush river that irrigates the Spartan plain, Zeus saw the young queen and was enraptured. Determined to have Leda, he turned himself into a giant swan and raped her.

In classical Athens, remembering these distant stories, the chorus in Euripides' play *Helen* bemoans the moment: '*so sorrowful was that destiny, lady mine, that befell you, a life better unlived given to you, yes given, when Zeus blazed in the bright air, in the snowflash of the swan's wing to beget you upon your mother. What grief is there you have not known? What in life have you not lived through?*'²

It was a beginning recalled as being at once brutal and erotic. In a mosaic from a sanctuary of Aphrodite at Paphos on Cyprus a gloriously plump-bottomed Leda, with her back to us, runs the edge of her gossamer shawl over the swan's beak.[3] Early Greek representations of the story are relatively tame, the bird small, with Leda simply petting him. But as time goes on, the bird grows bigger, the atmosphere more violent. In Argos, a tombstone commissioned by a rich Greek merchant immortalises in marble the moment when the swan enters the young woman.[4] The sculpture stands at the entrance of the small Argos Museum. Leda is doubled over – in pain or in ecstasy – her hand making its way towards her vulva. It is impossible to tell whether she is trying to drag Zeus out or help him in. In a wall-painting from Herculaneum, the town buried along with Pompeii by the eruption of Vesuvius in AD 79, the fowl-god bites Leda's neck. Michelangelo's 16th-century Leda[5] seems to be abandoned to sensual pleasure; after its donation in 1838, a copy of the painting was hung in the office of the director of London's National Gallery rather than put on display as it was considered inappropriate for the public gaze.[6]

Leonardo da Vinci's famous drawing of the subject was rumoured to have been destroyed by the Vatican,[7] but copies were made just before the work was consigned to the flames. Rubens painted his explicit oil (here the swan is pressed tight into Leda as she sucks his beak) from one of the hastily done sketches.[8] In the 18th century, gentlemen would carry pocket watches that concealed the scene of Leda's brush with bestiality and rape under a golden, finely worked lid. In one of D.H. Lawrence's paintings, Leda is lying on her back, while the swan's neck snakes its way up between her breasts. When Lawrence's painting was shown in 1929 in the Warren Gallery in London, after 12,000 people had seen it, and the *Daily Telegraph* had dubbed the exhibition 'gross and obscene', the Leda (along with twelve other paintings) was seized as pornographic material by the police and impounded. Like her daughter Helen, Leda pays for the blessing of beauty. The perfection of these women cannot simply be enjoyed; it has to be tampered with, its abuse dwelt upon.

Although time can give representations of this story the veneer of respectability, we have to imagine many in their ruddy, primal form. Recently I visited the Palazzo Nuovo in Rome, now a part of the Capitoline Museums, at sunset.[9] It was one of those halcyon days of late January. The low sun on the brick of the courtyard, refracting through the thick old glass of the windows, gave everything a soft, pale tinge – the light was the colour of apricots and cream. The galleries are lined with one marble sculpture after another, and turning right at the top of two flights of broad, generous steps, I stumbled upon a Leda from the 1st century BC.

With her pallid companions this young woman looked serene and demure – the two figures, the swan and the queen, carved from the same block of stone, have a companionable unity. But imagine the sculpture coloured as it would originally have been. Painted, the thick column of the swan's neck, resting on Leda's stomach and between her legs, would take on the appearance of a phallus – the swan's beak its glans tip. Leda pulls up her cloak to hide her face, revealing one perfect carmine breast. Sand-blasted and neutralised, the statue blends into the crowd, and becomes inoffensive fodder for the tourists who file past. But when created this was a lurid and shocking scene, a titillating work of art which bore witness to an unnatural, forceful impregnation.

ᘓᘓᘓᘓᘓ

Although we give no credence to the stories of Helen's bestial conception, the ancients would have been very comfortable with the idea that Helen's divine genes came to her in the form of a bird. Birds (eagles, swans, larks, doves, swallows) were believed to be wherry-men for divine spirits.[10] With the beat of the Swan-Zeus' wings on Leda's thigh came immortal power. The beautiful monster conceived on the banks of the Eurotas was an intoxicating mix – enough of a woman to be enjoyed, enough of a deity to be sublime.

The storytellers recounted that, following Leda's rape on the banks of the Eurotas, the young queen produced a curious clutch of eggs.[11] Some said Leda was pregnant at the time, and so Helen shared Leda's womb with Tyndareus' brood.[12] They were a singular group of siblings. Helen's half-sister Clytemnestra would go on to murder her husband Agamemnon in cold blood, and then be murdered in turn by her son Orestes. Helen's twin brothers Castor and Pollux, the Dioscuri,[13] boys famous for riding white stallions and for their own successful rape of two sisters – Hilareia and Phoebe (known as the Leucippides)[14] – would spend their short lives trying, with varying degrees of success, to protect their much sought-after sister.

Harbouring her testy chicks, Leda's eggs were left to hatch in the protective foothills of Mount Taygetus, the king mountain in the range that flanks the west side of Sparta – then, as now, fragrant with rosemary, myrtle, wild pear and juniper.[15] The eggs were found by a shepherd, gathered up, and taken back to the Spartan palace. It was from here that Helen would assert her position as a matrilineal heiress to a great temporal power.

Artists have been intrigued by the idea of Helen's unconventional birth. In a number of canvases she is shown emerging from her egg, a white, fat, grub-like little thing. One such example, painted on wood between 1506 and 1510 by Cesare da Sesto in Leonardo's Milan studio, now hangs in Wilton House, a stately home on the Dorset/Wiltshire borders in the south of England. Dimly lit in a corner, this is a masterpiece well worth seeking out. Strawberries, a symbol of fertility and abundance, cluster in the bottom left-hand corner around Helen's egg. The skin of the newborn princess has a pallid, waxy quality. Helen's avian gestation was given as one reason for her fine, albuminous beauty: *'She is white, as is natural in the daughter of a swan, and delicate, since she was nurtured in an egg-shell'.*[16]

Bizarrely enough, the last time I went to study the painting, a new version of Jane Austen's *Pride and Prejudice* was being filmed in the gardens of the house. The star was an English beauty, famous for her pale skin. I asked one of the staff why they thought this porcelain creature was a good choice – 'She looks like a doll,' he said, 'men like that.'

Helen's pallor was deemed an important part of her desirability. Having white skin was certainly a mark of supreme beauty when Homer composed his epics, and most likely in the Late Bronze Age too. Goddesses were frequently described as 'white-armed' and 'pale-faced'.[17] Mycenaean fresco fragments of high-born women always show them with chalky limbs and faces. Some of the most exquisite and highly valued anthropomorphic arte-facts from the Mycenaean world, male and female, are carved out of ivory. Traces of white-lead in a number of Athenian tombs housing female skele-tons show that a thousand years on, in the 3rd century BC, women blanched their skin in pursuit of physical perfection.[18]

In the West, whiteness came to have its own currency – little surprise that the most beautiful woman in the world was always imagined to be perfectly pale. In one representation of Helen's story by Johann Georg Platzer[19] (now hung at the Wallace Collection in London) a death-white, half-naked Helen is being bundled onto a boat by Paris and his troops. The sea and sky glower. The men pressing around the Spartan queen are hoary and dark. Her pallid body stands out, a pearl being wrenched from its shell.[20]

Helen's snow-whiteness, perfection waiting to be spoiled, was an inspir-ational theme for writers too, allowing poets and prosaists to relate Helen's brutal origins in delicate terms. A search through the 14th-century manu-scripts at Corpus Christi, Cambridge, yields this description of Helen by a medieval theologian, Joseph of Exeter:

> Leda's daughter partakes more deeply of Juppiter's starry
> character, and there breathes through all her limbs the spirit of

the milk-white swan which deceived her mother. Her forehead flaunts its natural ivory, her head produces the gold of her hair in even tresses, her white cheek is like linen, her hands like snow, her teeth like lilies, and her neck like white privet.[21]

∽◯∽◯∽◯∽

The Greek author Pausanias,[22] writing around AD 160, tells us that, once Helen had hatched, her birth-egg was lovingly preserved and that in the middle of the 2nd century AD, the remains of her egg-shell, tied up in ribbons, were still suspended from the roof of a temple on the Spartan acropolis.[23] Pausanias travelled to Sparta to visit the sanctuary, dedicated to Hilareia and Phoebe (those sisters who, according to myth, were stolen during a cattle raid by Helen's twin brothers Castor and Pollux), in order to see this curious relic for himself.

Originally from Asia Minor, Pausanias worked his way across the Aegean, producing a tour guide as he went. He noted what he saw, gathering intelligence from locals and other travellers. We are greatly indebted to him when it comes to tracing the physical remains of figures from Greek myth and history through the Aegean landscape – remains which have been described as 'the archaeology of nostalgia'.[24] Although not all of Pausanias' extensive work is reliable, much does show meticulous research in the field. When finished, his opus, *Periegesis Hellados*, 'A Guide to Greece', ran to ten volumes.[25]

If you visit the Spartan acropolis today you will no longer find Helen's egg. With the exception of the Roman theatre, here there are little more than a series of knee-high ruins. The position of the acropolis is splendid, even though its monuments are few and far between – scraps that come to some as a terrible disappointment after the glories of Athens. Visitors are rare. The half-excavated theatre is most favoured by the town's teenagers – kids who practise bicycle stunts on its slopes. But the northern side of the acropolis is peaceful, sheltered by avenues of eucalyptus trees whose dagger-shaped leaves shudder and shiver in the breeze. Ancient Greece has been described as 'a spiritual landscape rustling with invisible presences',[26] and sitting up there early in the morning it becomes easier to appreciate why this was believed to be so.

Surveying one of the most fertile valleys in Greece, one can imagine the populations of ancient Greece marvelling at Helen's relic and honouring the spirit of Helen as they did so. For the Greeks, an egg was a recognised symbol of fertility and sexual potency.[27] Immense eggs have not lost their totemic status; ostrich eggs can still be found, gaudily decorated, hanging from Greek Orthodox churches in the region. Throughout antiquity, a trickle of pilgrims would have visited Helen's egg in the temple, and, standing under the remains of her egg-shell, would have prayed that they too would be blessed with the power of the Tyndareid women, Leda and Helen, of sexual attraction and fecundity.[28]

What Pausanias saw may well have been a relic from the Late Bronze Age, strung up in the roof of the classical temple of Hilareia and Phoebe – the Mycenaeans did import ostrich eggs from Africa and surviving artefacts from pre-history were often thought by the ancients to have hidden powers.[29] We shall never know. But, whatever its provenance, in the 2nd century AD, an egg – decorated with ribbons and surrounded with stories – was there. Helen, Leda's hybrid love-child, was commemorated at Sparta under the cracked remains of her curious ovum.

ᔆᕽᕽᕽᕽᕽ

Pausanias' egg is a cogent reminder that Helen was a much revered presence in the city of Sparta. From at least the 7th century BC onwards, she was venerated at Spartan shrines as a heroine – a patron and protector. Men and women left precious dedications to her. They carried out animal sacrifices in her honour – devotions usually reserved for gods and goddesses. Young Spartan girls would incant her name on the eve of their nuptials.[30] Up until the Roman period dynasties of priests and priestesses avidly maintained her cult. Spartans, then and now, fiercely defend their conviction that Helen was a local girl, even though the attitude towards her in the modern-day city is somewhat ambiguous. Waiters in hotel lobbies will still attempt to get the attention of young women by comparing them to *their* Helen of Troy. The old men who meet every day in the *kafeneio* to smoke, drink coffee and watch the world go by get surprisingly heated when debating her merits; a number still damn her as a 'bad woman'[31] and yet the city's first DVD guide has been narrated by the 'voice of Helen'.

Sparta lies in a valley, surrounded by what Homer describes as *'Lacedaemon's lovely hills'*. When I was last there, in early spring, from my hotel room I could see the snow-capped peaks of Mount Taygetus in the distance, the eagles wheeling round it, the foothills fringed with fields of wild iris.[32] Camomile and thyme grow rampantly in the tiny archaeological sites that are scattered throughout the city, and the evening air is tinged with their scent. This, the ancients told each other, was the rich domain that a newborn Spartan princess would inherit. And it is in this vigorous, redolent landscape that we have to look for traces of our Bronze Age Helen.

3

THE LOST CITADEL

@@@@@@@@@@@@@

Look, Pisistratus — joy of my heart, my friend —
the sheen of bronze, the blaze of gold and amber,
silver, ivory too, through all this echoing mansion!
Surely Zeus's court on Olympus must be just like this,
the boundless glory of all this wealth inside!
My eyes dazzle . . . I am struck with wonder.

Odysseus' son Telemachus describes Helen's and Menelaus'
palace to the son of King Nestor. HOMER, *Odyssey*[1]

A MYSTERY SURROUNDS HELEN'S PALACE. The Sparta of the Age of Heroes features prominently in the canon of Greek myth — and yet no obvious palatial remains have been uncovered, no monumental Bronze Age structure that one can imagine being a spur to the Homeric tales of court intrigue and warrior honour — or the awestruck hyperbole of Telemachus' report as he wonders at the opulence of Helen's Spartan home. Recent archaeological discoveries in Greece[2] suggest that modern-day Lakonia was indeed a distinct territory in the Late Bronze Age;[3] the poets tell us it was a rich kingdom. So where is the royal seat of Lakedaimonia, the headquarters of the Mycenaean clan that held sway here three and half thousand years ago? Where is the home of a Spartan Queen, our Bronze Age Helen?

Archaeologists have looked for a Mycenaean palatial complex buried beneath present-day Sparta but have drawn a blank. Preliminary investigations suggest that the earliest remains of occupation and permanent settlement under the modern town date from the 10th or 9th century BC. There is a slim chance that Late Bronze Age walls, chambers and grand halls could be hidden there, but until such a footprint has been located we have to look elsewhere to try to identify where the Bronze Age Spartan clan would have been raised.

The prime candidate is just outside Sparta itself on a hill called

Therapne. The road to Therapne lies to the south-east of the city. It follows the River Eurotas upstream for a mile or so and then branches – one metal sign for an archaeological site signals a turning right into a low ridge of hills. The situation is impressive, but the archaeology scant. The German archaeologist and adventurer Heinrich Schliemann, who famously 'discovered' the site of Troy, came here at the end of the 19th century and was disappointed – he declared this was no home for Homeric heroes. But local farmers had more faith. As they worked their fields primitive artefacts made of bronze and terracotta – votive offerings – were turned up by the plough. Some came forward with their finds; in 1909 archaeologists from the British School at Athens began to dig.[4]

The earth leading up to the summit of Therapne is a rich burnt red; even in spring the grass that covers the hill has already been bleached to a sandy gold. On the high ground, the warm winds start to move quickly. Here you can see a 50-mile span north to south of a domain rich in natural resources. Stretching out beneath the shadow of the hill is the flat, fertile Tayegetan plain, now a market garden for Athens and beyond – Spartan oranges end up as pulped juice around the world. The *horta* – wild greens – that gave the ancients a mineral-rich diet, and kept the modern Greeks going through German occupation, still grows on the hillside. Faunal remains attest to the presence, in the Late Bronze Age, of the quarry of hunts enthusiastically portrayed in Mycenaean art: venison, hares, duck, geese, wild boar and partridge.[5] The Eurotas meanders through the valley all year round, crystal clear in the spring, rusty after the November rains when it tears its banks.

Up here on this river bluff there are two distinct areas of archaeological significance. The oldest is a truncated Late Bronze Age building surrounded by tantalising clues of human activity: painted pottery sherds, female figurines[6] and beads made of semi-precious stones, spindle whorls, loom weights and pots for food preparation. The second archaeological feature, crowning a misshapen natural rock core, is a crumbling rectangle of archaic stone blocks – the remains of a religious structure – a structure that has just been shown to have late Bronze Age foundations. For the last two millennia, this particular remnant of the early days of Greece has been known as the *Menelaion*.[7] But before that, the building that stood here, dating from the late 8th century BC and rebuilt in the 5th century BC, was called, simply, *TES HELENES HIERON* – 'HELEN'S SHRINE'.[8]

From at least the 7th century BC onwards, 'Helen's Shrine' was believed to be the spot where Helen was buried alongside her husband Menelaus. Here great honours were paid her.[9] The Spartans could have chosen to worship anyone at this prominent location: Athena, Heracles, Poseidon, or the king of the gods, Zeus himself. But for at least a thousand years this breath-taking, confident, awe-inspiring site was reserved for Helen and for Helen's family[10] and as late as AD 300 Helen was still described by a poet called Tryphiodorus, who wrote another epic version of her rape, as 'the bride [*nymphe*] of Therapne'.[11]

Archaeological discoveries back up the connection made with Helen in the literary record. The hilltop was first excavated in a rather piecemeal way in 1909 and 1910 – and then left fallow for over sixty years. But when archaeologists started to work more systematically in 1974 they immediately turned up evidence of cultic activity; pits at the corner of 'Helen's Shrine' to accommodate offerings of holy food; in front of her shrine a deep cistern providing water for the purification of celebrants and for the communal feasts that played a key part in cult worship.[12] The words 'For Helen' have been incised into a 6th-century *harpax*,[13] a meat-hook dedicated as an offering. This vicious-looking eight-clawed instrument (now in the Sparta Museum), used for hanging meat, suggests that Helen was worshipped with animal sacrifices and feasting: 'sacrifices worthy of gods not just heroes', says Isocrates in the middle of the 4th century BC.[14] A fine bronze perfume jar, an *aryballos*, was also found here. Dating from the 7th century BC, it too is inscribed, roughly, with Helen's name.[15] Difficult to make out, the inscription reads: 'Deini[s] dedicated these things [in gratitude] to Helen (wife) of Menelaos.'[16]

Three hundred or so terracotta figurines, a number of them women, riding horses, have been excavated at Therapne. These could be images of Helen herself[17] or, perhaps more likely, of her worshippers. *Fibulae* – sturdy bronze and iron dress pins – have also been found on the hill; dedicated perhaps by girls who communed with the spirit of Helen and then left their girlhood and their girlish clothes behind them, descending the hill as a rite of passage when dressed as mature women.[18] A steady flow would have tramped up that hill between *c.* 700 and 200 BC clutching their gifts for Helen, thinking fervently of her as they came.[19]

So if this was the location of Helen's shrine, could the Late Bronze Age building, a hundred yards off, be Helen's palace? For years excavators and romantics have debated whether the compact Late Bronze Age remains – described by the most generous as a 'mansion' – might have held the royal household, might have been where Helen grew up, the palace to which she was brought by Menelaus after her dangerous liaison with a prince of Troy, where – in a scene that was vividly imagined by Homer – she entertained Odysseus' son Telemachus and heard stories told of how the Western world had risen in arms to bring her home from a foreign city.[20] However, there is a problem. Other palatial complexes, built and ruined at about the same time are significantly larger. 'Nestor's Palace' at Pylos, a hundred kilo-metres west, appears to be five times the size of the Spartan offering. The other grand citadels in the Peloponnese dwarf the Therapne remains. In the Argolid plain the palace complex of Mycenae covers an area of *c.* 110,000 square feet (10,220 square m) with a surrounding community spread over *c.* 32 hectares; the Tiryns and Pylos complexes are *c.* 55,000 square feet (5,110 square m).[21] Helen, always billed as a wealthy woman, would surely have inhabited something approaching this scale.

Here then is a bewildering state of affairs; at Therapne evidence of a vigorous cult of Helen – and a fortifiable hill standing above a fertile plain just as the Mycenaeans liked it (almost without exception they favour elevated defensive positions). Here is a Late Bronze Age building of the 13th century BC, the most likely date of a Trojan War, scattered with Mycenaean pottery. We have a Linear B reference to a district called Lakedaimon; and yet visible signs of a palace are absent. There is no hint of the grand citadel-complexes found at the other seedbeds of Mycenaean culture. No showy home for a rich Spartan queen.

The latest research does, however, shed some light.[22] The eastern slopes of the hill of Therapne are very exposed – the summit is particularly prone to erosion and the clay sub-soil easily subsides. The remains of that little 'mansion' have now been identified simply as substantial basement storage areas. Late Bronze Age sealings for clay stoppers have been found here; this is where food and wine supplies would have been stored. These modest remains do not look like a palace, because they were not one. Any Mycen-aean palace would have towered high above, away and to the left as you stand facing the setting sun. There are faint traces of this building on the highest point of the hill and a rough staircase leading from the 'basements' to where the upper rooms would once have been. The basements are a frac-tion of a larger complex and have survived only because of their more protected position on the hillside.

But the area of ground where that palace would have stood has been eaten by the elements. The hill of Therapne is itself now much smaller than it would have been three thousand years ago – as a result of natural erosion vast quantities of earth have, over time, slowly but surely slipped down the hillside. And as the ground disappeared so too the Spartan palace walls would have cracked and tumbled. Mycenaean treasures, broken and exposed, would have been eagerly picked off by human scavengers. We cannot find the palatial complex of the Late Bronze Age king and queen of Sparta, because in its entirety it is no longer there to find. Even if Helen has not escaped from history, her home has almost certainly escaped the archaeological record.

But one enigmatic woman from the Late Bronze Age has been left up on Therapne hill. While excavating close to the basements, archaeologists found three skeletons.[23] The first was a human female – aged about thirty; the two others were children. The woman has her legs drawn up to her chin, suggesting she has been trussed up with her hands behind her back.[24] She was unworthy of even a shallow grave, her body left on a rubbish tip. Hers was no natural death. She was, almost certainly, either the victim of an attack or has been left as a human offering – a sacrifice. At the time that she died the basements had been scorched by a fire of such intensity that large areas of the palace above must have been weakened or destroyed. Here, towards the end of the 13th century BC, the community living at Therapne witnessed a dreadful calamity. The destruction of the palatial buildings at Sparta is symptomatic of the closure of the 'Age of Heroes', when across the Greek mainland once powerful Mycenaean centres crumble and fall. Archaeological evidence describes the features of this demise but not its cause. At Sparta we have only one adult witness left – and she is long silent.

It seems as though the Spartan palace, immortalised by Homer as blazing with gold, amber, bronze, silver and ivory,[25] will never be teased back out of the earth. So, to envisage more fruitfully how a Late Bronze Age princess such as Helen would have spent her early years, we have to look elsewhere: we have to travel 120 kilometres north-east of Sparta to the plain of Argos and the place that gave Mycenaean civilisation its name – the grand citadel of Mycenae.

4

THE MYCENAEANS

◎◎◎◎◎◎◎◎◎◎◎◎◎

Mycenae rich in gold

HOMER, *Odyssey*[1]

IN 1871, HEINRICH SCHLIEMANN, a man who had started life as a
sickly grocer's assistant but accumulated a fortune – in the indigo trade
in St Petersburg, during the gold rush in California, and finally dealing
in saltpetre and brimstone at the inception of the Crimean War – went to
the Eastern Mediterranean in pursuit of Helen of Troy and the old gold
of the Age of Heroes. Schliemann was ravenous for knowledge and archaeological experience. He had taught himself eighteen languages, including
Greek, Latin and Hebrew, and, as an adorer of the works of Homer, he
determined to find physical proof of the *Iliad* and the *Odyssey*. At the age
of forty-eight he travelled to Turkey in search of Troy and started to dig
– in the right place.

Schliemann's luck matched his millions. Throwing his money at the
excavation of a hill called Hisarlik he swiftly uncovered a wealth of pre-
historic artefacts. Within a year the German amateur declared he had
discovered King Priam's splendid citadel and the jewels of Homer's heroes.
But then came a problem. Failing to share his treasure-trove with the
Ottoman authorities as agreed, Schliemann was banned from excavating on
Turkish soil. Frustrated, fired up, irrepressible, he fixed his sights on Greece.
In 1874 he moved to the Peloponnese and began a series of unofficial
excavations at the Bronze Age site of Mycenae.

Mycenae was the legendary home of the greatest of all the Greek tribal
leaders: Agamemnon, 'the king of men'; the warrior who returned home
victorious, a purple cloth laid beneath his feet as he stepped back through
the gates of his citadel;[2] a short-lived welcome as it transpired, for lying in
his bath the returning hero was stabbed to death by his unfaithful wife –
Helen's half-sister, Clytemnestra – and his bones thrown to the dogs. The
gruesome tale appealed to the dark imagination of the ancient Greeks. In

the Hellenistic period tourists visited Mycenae to see the drama played out in front of them during alfresco performances of Greek tragedies (such as the *Oresteia*) above the very scenes of these legendary crimes.[3]

For Schliemann, Mycenae would prove as rich a vault as Troy. On discovering a gold death mask from one of the royal shaft graves within the citadel at Mycenae, Schliemann made his — famously exaggerated — claim that he had located another home of a warrior hero and had 'gazed upon the face of Agamemnon'.[4] Following the showman-archaeologist's romantic pronouncement, a motley crew of scholars, writers, poets, artists and empire builders converged on Mycenae, to gaze and wonder. We know about the influx of these archaeo-tourists in unusual detail because many stayed in Schliemann's old lodgings just down the road from the Bronze Age citadel, a little house called *La Belle Hélène*.

La Belle Hélène still welcomes visitors. Sitting under the neon light of the new extension the current owner regales guests with tales of his own ancestors, his grandfather and his Uncle Orestes, men who pulled Mycenaean gold out of the earth with their bare hands. And then, after the obligatory trip to Herr Schliemann's old room, the patron will proudly list just some of the enthusiasts for Mycenaean culture who, over the years, have slept under his roof. Sartre was here, Virginia Woolf and the Frys, and Agatha Christie. Nazis stayed too, Goebbels, Himmler and Herman Goering — drawing lessons from the warrior-cultures of the past. The composers Debussy and Benjamin Britten, the Beat poet Allen Ginsberg — they all came, and as they passed through they left their own paper-trail behind them, signing the fat visitors' book before returning home.[5]

Although '*Mycenae rich in gold*' is shattered walls and bare stone now, the massive site — which spans a full hectare — still signals its original impact. Of all the Late Bronze Age palace-fortresses excavated on the Greek mainland, Mycenae appears to have been the grandest, the most audacious.[6] It is cradled by the Arachneion mountain range,[7] and if you approach from the modern village of Mikines, the citadel is a diminutive, humble echo of the mountains' great limestone splendour — a toy-town version of the rock masses, themselves giant fortresses. But then, walk through the famous Lion Gate and survey the Argolid plain from the citadel itself and the impression is entirely different. Now Mycenae laughs at the landscape below. Seemingly impregnable, crammed with the finest art and fiercest armaments in the known world, this was the home of history's winners — here it becomes apparent why the Mycenaeans are a legendary civilisation.[8]

A traveller in the 13th century BC would have passed through swathes of dramatic virgin countryside, much of it uninhabited, some unfarmed, and then, breaking the brow of a hill or turning the corner into a valley, there would have stood one of the Mycenaean warlords' great citadels, typically elevated on a hill or rocky outcrop with the grand *megaron* — the great hall or royal throne room — at its heart. To reach the *wanax* (the Mycenaean king) and his queen, a physical ascent had to be made — privileged access granted only to a few. There would not be disappointment on arrival — the royal apartments were richly furnished. One Linear B tablet describes a throne from Pylos made predominantly of rock crystal, decorated with blue-glass paste, 'mock' emeralds and precious metal; on its back, the figures of men and palm trees picked out in gold.[9]

Religious sanctuaries were also contained within the citadel — these palace-fortresses were the homes of gods as well as men, places where power, both real and perceived, resided.[10] Little wonder that Homer should speak of Mycenae rich in gold, of the high-roofed chambers and dazzling halls of the Spartan palace, of men and women adorned as gods, little wonder that wandering heroes should marvel at the 'polished walls' of the clan leaders' homes which were themselves 'troves of treasure'.[11] Around 800 BC Homer recalls the impact these places must have had on contemporaries — an impact that survived in the popular imagination for at least five hundred years, transmitted from one generation to the other by storytellers and by gossip in modest homes around low fires late at night.

Schliemann, and others after him, discovered at Mycenae a mass of wealth to match Homer's eulogies. In one of Schliemann's excavation reports, details of the rich finds from a single tomb spread across nearly fifty pages. Here was a finely carved ivory lion, small enough to rest in the palm of a hand. The lion is crouched waiting to pounce — its muscles flex in readiness: the genius of the craftsmanship is immediately apparent. There are solid gold drinking cups,[12] rock crystal carvings and sandstone grave-markers bearing rich abstracted pictures. The inlays on daggers, swords and jewellery beaten from gold, silver and niello (a compound of sulphur and silver) are as fine as spun sugar. A delicate head of a boy, carved out of ivory,[13] gazes out at the world with a subtle, melancholic expression.

Many of these treasures were preserved because they were buried along with the Mycenaean dead in *tholos* tombs (cavernous round structures) and in shaft graves (burial chambers cut into the bedrock). The contents of shaft graves show that Mycenaeans had a passion for gold.[14] Gold leaf, seemingly fine enough to be used as a confectioner's decoration, would be worked into jewellery or made into death masks for kings. In two apparently isolated instances from Mycenae, the gold has been pressed out paper-thin and then wrapped around the bodies of dead babies. Craftsmen created life-size gold flowers resembling the *ianthos* that grows profusely in Greece today; gold discs were punched with images of women, and then sewn onto clothes. Many of these treasures would be buried with their owners, but some would be kept by the living, used as gifts for the gods or passed down as totemic heirlooms from father to son, from mother to daughter. A princess such as Helen would have been cocooned in her Peloponnesian citadel by the bullion of her ancestors.

Painted figures once strode out across the frescoed walls of the Mycenaean citadels – part of the grand decorative schemes which covered the richest rooms. All are fragments now but are still dynamic. One woman holds out a necklace – an offering to a deity perhaps. Her tight, scooped-out bodice is dyed saffron yellow, and a translucent yellow gauze thinly veils her breasts. Her left hand, painted it seems with the finest sable brush, stretches out elegantly.[15] These were the women who, so the bards sang, waited in the Peloponnesian palaces and prayed as the siege at Troy dragged out another long year. The women who, we are told, first cursed Helen's name.

The riches of the citadels excavated by Schliemann and his successors make it clear that although Homer was composing in the 8th century BC this was indeed the world commemorated in his poetry.[16] A land of opulent palace-complexes inhabited by a warrior elite. A feasting, booty-grabbing, gold-loving society that enjoyed a clannish co-operation. An ambitious culture with a finely developed technological sense.

Of course there are moments of brilliance in the years that separated Homer from the Late Bronze Age, a period from 1100 to 800 BC that has come to be called the 'Greek Dark Ages' – but there is nothing to touch the marvels of Mycenae and the expansive civilisation it represents. Little surprise that Homer and Hesiod should think of Helen's era as an 'Age of Heroes',[17] a time that had to be remembered, a time populated by men and women with an extraordinary capacity to achieve.

৩৩৩৩৩৩

The Mycenaean citadels were glorious – but kept so only by a population of unsung heroes. These shadowy masses are the labourers of the Bronze Age, men and women all but forgotten by the poets and the history books, who in the Greek landscape have left unusually vivid clues.

The observant traveller in the Peloponnese will notice the odd, roughly thatched shack made of mud-brick: each the colour of burnt sienna, these *kalyvia* are shelters for herdsmen and itinerant labourers. They function remarkably well; mud-brick is warm in the winter, cool in the summer. A stone's throw from the Mycenaean palatial site at Tiryns, half-hidden in an avenue of pomegranate trees, are the dilapidated walls of one of these mud-cottages – abandoned now. Before long, the rest of this modest house will collapse and the rains will wash the mud back into the earth.

Up on the citadel of Tiryns itself there is a proud note from the German team who have been excavating the site since 1967.[18] Just outside the settlement walls the archaeologists have found evidence of cheap, rough homes nudging up against one another – the shacks of Mycenaean workers – each one made of mud-brick, with proportions that match those of the 21st century. It is ironic to think that, whereas the most powerful from the Late Bronze Age would walk through their smashed, burnt, empty palaces today and weep, the slaves, bondsmen and child labourers might find a more familiar landscape, their humble mud-brick homes, apparently, still standing.

A civilisation as aspirational as the Mycenaeans' needed to mobilise a mass of muscle – a human resource to do its dirty work. And into these mud-huts would have squashed the men and women who executed the elite's back-breaking jobs: grinding corn, beating flax to produce linen, sweating away lives, lifting those giant Cyclopean blocks into place to build the glittering citadels. Just east of Tiryns, thousands of tonnes of earth were moved in the Late Bronze Age, damming and diverting the natural flow of a watercourse – the handiwork still visible today. A handful of channels and dykes that were built in the Bronze Age still work perfectly, irrigating farmlands in the Peloponnese. Until recently, women in the Argolid used the weirs around Mycenae to wash their laundry.[19] Such construction would have involved a workforce of many hundreds. It is little surprise to find that the Linear B tablets have, etched into their soft surfaces, a category of men and women called *do-e-ro* and *do-e-ra*, male and female servants or slaves.[20]

Slaves were almost certainly bought and sold – at Pylos, for instance, is a group of women described as *Aswiai*, 'Asians',[21] who could well have been bartered or even kidnapped in exchange for wine or gold. Some of Homer's greatest lines speak of the fate of women during military conflict: rape and enslavement following the slaughter of their husbands, brothers and sons.[22] There are certainly more women listed in a subservient context on the Linear B tablets than there are men. It is easy to imagine the scenario: a domineering power like the Mycenaeans, expanding their territories and happily putting female captives to good use once they have executed their menfolk and acquired new lands. A time described by Homer, where territorial expansion (and the Trojan War is a prime example) is undertaken for glory and for material gain – the greatest commodity of all, humans.

In their prime the Mycenaeans were certainly not contained by the Peloponnese. Their influence can also be traced in North Africa, Cyprus, Palestine (Israel) and Phoenicia (the Lebanon) – as far north as Croatia, as far west as Italy. Mycenaean rapiers have been found in the Danube Valley, broken bowls in rubbish dumps on the east bank of the Nile at Tel el Amarna, 587 km south of Cairo. On the plinth of a statue from the funerary temple of the Egyptian pharaoh Amenophis III[23] we hear of a powerful city that lay to the north, a city called Mukana.[24] Mycenaean pots have been excavated in eastern Spain, tiny Mycenaean beads have been found in graves in Syracuse on Sicily; and still the artefacts come out of the earth – construction workers building Amman Airport in Jordan[25] unexpectedly uncovered a collection of finely made Mycenaean vases.[26]

Miletus on the east coast of Turkey was a Mycenaean settlement, as was the area of Chalkidiki in the north of the Greek mainland. The importance of the Mycenaean control of coastal territories and contacts across the water is reflected in their calendar. The first month of the Greek year in the Late Bronze Age was called *Plowistos* – the month of sailing. There would have been talk around Mycenaean traders' fires of the wild and wonderful lands that lay beyond the reach of even the most adventurous sailor, but there was more than enough to occupy these bully-boy buccaneers in the Eastern Mediterranean. Once they had taken over Minoan Crete,[27] it has been argued, they turned their eyes east, to the coast of Anatolia and the rich city of Troy. Another culture to loot. Another people to enslave. Another city to fell. This is too early in time for there to have been a sense of nationhood within Greece but the Mycenaeans were clearly capable of consolidated action – both in peacetime and in war.[28]

The contents of Mycenaean graves speak of a belligerent society. Schliemann calculated that in Shaft Grave V at Mycenae, three men from the 16th century BC had been buried with ninety swords between them. Almost all extant skeletal remains have suffered trauma. A man, in his late twenties,[29] has an oblong depression 2.3 cm long in his skull – a healed wound originally inflicted by a sharpened weapon. At the coastal site of Asine a warrior in his mid-thirties has a deeply bruised left shinbone – a result of the continual impact of a shield during warfare or battle-practice. Abrasions this low on the leg may well have been made by a 'tower-shield' – the model owned in the *Iliad* by Ajax and widely represented in Mycenaean art. The skeleton of a twenty-five-year-old male from Armenoi in Mycenaean-occupied Crete shows ten vicious cut marks, probably from an axe – at some points his bones have been sliced right through.[30]

Women too are shown invested with swords, armour and the distinctive Mycenaean 'figure-of-eight' shields. Come the 13th century BC (the peak of Mycenaean power) even religious figures (priests and priestesses, gods and goddesses) bear arms.[31] Some argue that the Warrior Goddess – a woman who rides in a chariot brandishing a spear and wearing a helmet made of boar tusks – was a Mycenaean invention.[32] It was from such an environment as this that Helen's story was drawn – and in which a Spartan aristocrat would have been raised. These would have been the robust lessons of childhood for a Mycenaean princess.[33]

5

THE PRE-HISTORIC PRINCESS

@@@@@@@@@@@@@

By maunding and imposture Helen came,
Eater of the white fig, the sugar-bread;
Some beauty, yes, but not more than her tribe
Lathe-made for stock embraces on a bed.

LAWRENCE DURRELL, 'Troy' (1966)

LIFE FOR OUR BRONZE AGE HELEN would have been sensuous and
short. The average age of death for Mycenaean females was twenty-
eight. Women were mothers at twelve, grandmothers at twenty-four,
dead before they were thirty.[1] The majority of the population was carried
off in its prime by disease. Homer talks about the 'scurf of age', but in
real terms pre-historic Greece was a land populated by the very young –
and it had a cultural energy to match.

Archaeological finds attest to trade in gold, silver, amber, carnelian,
andesite, obsidian, red jasper, lapis lazuli and ivory from both elephants and
hippopotamuses. In *pithoi*, giant storage jars, there are traces of olive oil,
frankincense, myrrh and wine; coriander and sesame were used to flavour
food, rose-petals, sage and anise to sweeten perfumes.[2] The clothes of the
richest Mycenaeans, made of wool and linen and even fine wild-silk, were
coloured with saffron and a purple dye extracted from a species of sea-snail.[3]

The Mycenaeans' was a magpie culture. Great sea journeys would be
undertaken to bring the finest raw materials and manufactured goods back
to the Greek mainland. The more successful a clan-leader was, the more his
palace would have glittered – storerooms and tombs would have been stacked
with relucent treasure. Cult images were dressed in cloth that had been
impregnated with olive oil to give the material a distinctive sheen; privileged mortals too would have worn clothes treated in this way.[4] Those of
the highest rank are – for the first time – literally, illustrious. Perhaps this
is what the bards meant when they recalled that Helen was 'radiant', 'fair',
'shimmering', 'golden'.[5]

And so we can imagine the young Helen, starting her day, being decked in the treasures and baubles that marked her out as a princess. Sitting perhaps, with her feet resting on one of the fine footstools inlaid using the 'aiamenos' technique, with ivory men, horses, lions or octopuses – a decorative effect recorded both in Homer[6] and in the Linear B tablets.[7] Her jewels would have been taken out of an ivory trinket box.[8] Some extant examples are decorated with human heads, animals and shields, others are in the shape of ducks – a bird that symbolised female sexuality.[9]

The necklaces worn by a young noblewoman, a number of which have survived and can be found in the National Archaeological Museum of Greece, are still startling to look at: handsome, colourful things made of agate, steatite, red carnelian and amethysts. Some have matching bangles. Beads range from the size of gobstoppers to split lentils. Gold jewellery also survives: diadems, belts, a chain of showy rosettes separated by delicate triangular cut-outs. Large, gold hoop earrings, portrayed on frescoes and rescued from Late Bronze Age graves, would have dangled and swung in the ears of the highest-born women.

Those of high rank flashed gold and silver signet rings – or, if they were really exalted, rings decorated with iron, since iron at this stage was a rare and precious metal. A female skeleton discovered in 1965 in Tholos Tomb A at Archanes had, lying on her chest, a giant signet ring, depicting a scene from a tree-cult.[10] The position of the ring on the woman's breastbone suggests that it (and other rings like it) may have been worn as a pendant. These impressive, mysterious jewels were etched with images of religious festivals, bull-leapers, hunters, battles and voluptuous female figures. Red jaspers the size and texture of boiled sweets look disarmingly simple, until you run your finger across the surface and feel the shapes of bees, bulls and leopards, priests and high-priestesses – carved out to mark distinctive seal-stones. These intaglios were important status symbols for both male and female potentates. In one area at Mycenae, tentatively labelled by archaeologists a 'cult complex', an enigmatic fresco was excavated in 1968. Women dominate. Of the three shown, certainly two, possibly all three, have seal-stones strapped to their wrists.[11] In graves of the 14th and 13th centuries BC, male and female skeletons have been found with the seal-stones still close to their wrist-bones.

The rooms where a girl like Helen spent most of her time would have been emblazoned with colour. The walls, covered with lime plaster, were decorated with vivid patterns in blue, yellow ochre and deep salmon pink – still visible on the fresco-fragments that have survived. Pattern and form were created using both the *buon fresco* and *fresco secco* techniques – the paint being applied in different sections when the plaster was wet and again when it was dry. Even some of the floors were technicolor – decorated with paint or vivid cut stones; at Pylos there are geometric patterns, and an octopus glides close to the central hearth of the palace. Columns as high as three men, also coated in a rich pink wash, would have supported the roof and provided a colonnade through which a young princess could wander – perhaps on her way to the *megaron,* one of the most richly appointed areas of the building.[12]

We know from Linear B tablets that flax-products – oil and fibre, used to make clothes, sail-cloth, thread, strings and nets[13] – were an important export for the Peloponnese, particularly from the region around Pylos. The flax crop would have lit up the land with a brilliant blue when each plant bloomed from dawn until its petals fell at noon. Many of the grandest women wore moulded glass-paste beads, some the colour of speedwells, some indigo, some deep turquoise. As they passed through their territories, carried in litters by slaves, their jewellery would have been a guileless, bijou echo of the landscape around.

The finds from the Mycenaean citadels and graves illustrate the centrality of visual signals in pre-history. Before writing was employed as a tool of propaganda, appearance and experience are *all*-important. Images have to speak louder than words. The ruling classes of the Mycenaeans had access to precious raw materials from across the Eastern Mediterranean – of a calibre and variety never before imagined. And so in marked contrast to the rest of the population, the high-born made sure they gleamed, perpetually, with an artificial lustre. A girl like Helen, sparkling and glinting as she would have done, would have had it reinforced day in and day out, from a very early age, how important, valuable and desirable she was.

This was an infant society and yet we find on the Greek mainland for the first time a systematic, ubiquitous and extreme division between rich and poor, between town and countryside. Bone evidence speaks of the effects of social segregation – the aristocrats, well-nourished during life and buried within or next to the citadels are on average a full 5 cm taller than the Mycenaean workers, who, in contrast, both in shanty towns and in villages, show the effects of regular starvation.[14] The citadels were exalted and exclusive. Fairytale palaces when the resident clan-leaders served your needs or protected your family; sinister castles when they turned their might and their systems against you.[15]

ᘏᘎᘏᘎᘏ

Today, the massive building blocks of the grand Mycenaean citadels have been softened. At Mycenae, each year, a million or so tourists trail around the citadel and the stones and footways are gently burnished by centuries of wear and tear. At different points in the year where one stone meets another there are splashes of bright pink and yellow, the flower-heads of tiny wild cyclamen and autumn crocuses clinging to the crevices.

The sun-baked ruins with their airy, open spaces might present a pretty picture today. But imagine walking through each room closed in with many thousands of tons of solid stone, with exterior walls up to 7.5 m thick. Large areas of the palace complexes would have been dark and musty – the smell of burnt vegetable and mutton fat from natural oil lamps lingering in the corridors. And from the workshops in the citadel the acid tang of metal being forged – because towards the end of the Mycenaean age a mass of armaments was produced.[16]

For the bulk of the Bronze Age population, life was strained and precarious. Most Mycenaeans did not have Cyclopean walls to protect them. Tomorrow could bring a new earthquake or a new leader, and then those wild flowers would be dancing not in the breeze, but in the back-draught of enemy fires. Rival clans might choose to extend their boundaries to notch up new territories with a body count to match. There was, too, always the chance that devastation could come from across the oceans. Think of the heart-stopping anxiety of looking out to sea, spotting a small speck on the horizon, not knowing whether it was a trader or a messenger, or the advance guard of a hostile force; malcontents making their way slowly and steadily towards you, with the explicit purpose of burning your crops, razing your property to the ground, maiming your husband, enslaving your children or raping your wife.

In the *Iliad*, Homer weaves his story around a network of allies – men variously described as the Achaeans, the Danaans or Argives.[17] Their clan-leaders – Agamemnon, Odysseus, Menelaus, Achilles and the rest – had a sense of collective identity, but on the battlefield, back at camp and in bed, they were torn apart by personal rivalries and dog-fights – within the Greek confederacy there is a great deal of posturing. These tribal micro-conflicts – in many ways the meat and drink of the *Iliad* – bear out a likely scenario in the Late Bronze Age in which each territory was run by a warlord, his wife and their loyal coterie of aristocratic elite. Tribes in competition with those across the valley.

On one vase, ranks of elite foot-soldiers march doggedly across the surface. This 'Warrior Vase' is a solid, roomy thing – 40 cm high, made late, around 1150 BC and now in the National Archaeological Museum in

Athens. At first glance one can be deceived into thinking that all the figures are male. The automaton warriors are striding into battle, but behind them is a lone figure, waving. It is a woman. Is she a mother saying goodbye? Is she a Mycenaean Greek waving for help? Is she an alien (a Trojan even) about to be attacked? Is she a queen sending her soldiers off to die? We do not know the story of the vase, but we can read its message. At the tail-end of Mycenaean civilisation – in precarious, blood-thirsty times – this is what men are brought up to do: to stand together and fight while women stand and watch.

PART TWO

◎◎◎◎◎◎◎◎◎◎◎

THE LAND
OF BEAUTIFUL
WOMEN

6

THE RAPE OF 'FAIR HELLEN'

@@@@@@@@@@@@@

I sat beauty on my lap
I found her bitter
And I insulted her.

RIMBAUD,
Season in Hell (1873)

HEN THEY RECOUNTED HELEN'S LIFE as a young woman growing up in Sparta, the authors of antiquity did not imagine it to have been easy. As well as her most famous abduction, by Paris the prince of Troy, they recalled that Helen – still only a child – had been violated on the banks of the River Eurotas by the aged King of Athens, Theseus.[1] Theseus was fifty; some sources say Helen was twelve,[2] some ten,[3] some as young as seven[4] – already 'excelling all women in beauty'. The princess had been exercising and dancing naked with other young virgins when Theseus, recently widowed, caught sight of her. With eyes for no other, consumed by lust, he seized the Spartan princess.

Isocrates, writing in the 4th century BC,[5] describes how, despite the king's might and standing, Helen became the summation of all earthly desires: '*[Theseus] was so captivated by her loveliness that he, accustomed as he was to subdue others, and although the possessor of a fatherland most great, and a kingdom most secure, thought life was not worth living amid the blessings he already had unless he could enjoy intimacy with her.*'[6]

@@@@@@

Tracing the site of those dancing grounds in Sparta early one summer, along the river-banks of the Eurotas, I lost my way.[7] The bulrushes here are 3 m high – the perfect hiding place for a Theseus, prowling around the young girls. Twisting and turning I ended up in one of the orange groves, hundreds of which now edge the river and carpet the Eurotan plain. In the next-door field, women were lopping olive trees, to allow the top growth all the strength it needed. As they burned the branches, smoke mixed with the smell of the jasmine which wound around the mature boughs. I was investigating the scene of a crime, but the sensuous charge of the place was sweet and overwhelming. The 5th-century BC poet Pindar wrote this about the Greeks' subterranean equivalent of heaven, Elysium, and he could have been describing Sparta on that balmy afternoon:

> *For them the sun shines at full strength.*
> *The plains around their city are red with roses*
> *And shaded by incense trees, heavy with golden fruit.*
> *And some enjoy horses and wrestling, or table games and the lyre*
> *And near them blossoms a flower of perfect joy.*
> *Perfumes always hover above the land*
> *From the frankincense strewn in deep-shining fire of the god's altars.*[8]

A poignant place for a rape.[9]

Some said that Helen was dancing in a religious sanctuary devoted to the goddess Artemis Orthia when Theseus attacked her. Artemis Orthia was a hybrid deity – a potent conflation of Artemis, the virgin huntress and protector of mothers and children, and Orthia, a Dorian goddess[10] associated with youth, fertility rites and the dawn. From at least 700 BC[11] this was a site much frequented by women: a huge number of votive offerings, including over 100,000 small lead figurines, many of girls dancing or riding, have been excavated here; some are thought to represent Helen, left by those who adored her.[12]

Today the sanctuary is neglected and ugly. Old plastic bags eddy around the remains of the archaic altar or stick in the chicken-wire fence that hems the site in. The religious complex is close to the River Eurotas and built on swampy ground: gnats whine to and fro across the broken stones. A bumpy, dusty track leads to the archaeological remains. Each time I have visited, there has been unexpected company: the gypsy camp down the road spills over with curious, grubby children, eager to see who it is that is visiting their local ruin.

But the musty atmosphere of the holy site is strangely appropriate. One of the reasons young girls of Classical Sparta – first Greek and then Roman – would visit the place was to celebrate the onset of puberty. Boys too would come, to undergo a brutal rite of passage. Faced with a challenge to reach the goddess's altar and steal cheeses from it, they had to brave a gauntlet of whips wielded by older adolescents. Meeting the lashes face on, the boys had two options: reach their goal, or die, flayed alive in the name of education and social development. The sanctuary of Artemis Orthia is a sordid site, a site steeped in blood.[13]

And Theseus, true to form, precipitated the catalogue of blood-letting when he came here to take Helen by force. This was a hero who lived with the smell of another's fear in his nostrils. The ancients told each other stories of how, as well as raping young virgins, Theseus famously slew the Minotaur on Crete, attempted to abduct Persephone from the underworld, and made love to the Queen of the Amazons.[14] Even after his death, his ghost turned up in the 5th century BC, a giant apparition running in front of the Athenian troops at the Battle of Marathon to spur them on to victory. Theseus was the kind of champion Athens approved of – the mascot of a city-state as famous for its aggressive, ruthless expansionism as for its art, philosophy and politics.

The story goes that following the rape, Theseus locked Helen in the hill-fortress of Aphidna near Dekeleia.[15] While her assailant was off in pursuit of yet another woman (this time Persephone),[16] Helen's brothers, Castor and Pollux, stormed the prison. The abduction of the Spartan princess by the Athenian king had thrown down the gauntlet to the Lakedai-monian clan. The liberation of Helen was used by her noble brothers as a pretext for invading Attica: '[they] laid waste all the country round about'[17] and then enslaving Theseus' mother Aethra.[18] Theseus' defilement of Helen was legendary but the outrage burned in the minds of the Spartans – becoming an excuse for further aggression. Each year between 431 and 425, during the Peloponnesian War, Sparta raided Attica.[19] The only region they left untouched was Dekeleia – in gratitude to the Dekeleian men of old who, it was said, had led Castor and Pollux to Theseus' Aphidna hideout.[20]

The rape of women from another social group was an act of defiance which required retaliation.[21] Helen's rape was triply offensive: an incursion onto another's territory, the disruption of a ritual of paramount impor-tance (the dance-display of young virgins in a sacred site) and, of course, an attack on an under-age royal.[22] Her abductions became scores that needed settling. In the minds of the Greeks, at a tender age Helen had begun her career as a creator of conflict.

☙☙☙☙☙

Helen's rapes – both by Theseus and by Paris – were of timeless political relevance to the city of Sparta. The Spartans who dominated the classical landscape were in fact interlopers – Dorians who had invaded the region in *c.*1050 BC. Whereas Sparta's rivals the Athenians claimed to be autochthonous (sprung from the soil, self-earthed), a tribe born and bred to rule Athenian territory, the Spartans were viewed as Johnnies-come-lately: a historical fact to which they were extremely sensitive. They promoted their antique heritage vigorously – and one of their claims to rightful ownership of Spartan lands was that they were direct descendants of beautiful Helen.

In the Spartans, Helen found an idiosyncratic fan-base. The epithets Spartan (austere, hardy, rigorous) and Laconic[23] (brief, using few words) have made their way into the English language. They are appropriate mementoes of a society which was indeed extreme, hard-line and taciturn. The Spartans believed, above all, in duty and self-sacrifice. Deriving inspiration from a shady – possibly mythical – figure called Lycurgus 'the Law-Giver' they outlawed money, banned prostitutes and perfume and shunned the sartorial embellishments much loved by other Greek city-states; the true Spartan lived bare-footed and wore a thin ragged cloak summer and winter. Spartans discouraged outsiders: in a codified policy known as *xenelasia* (literally 'the avoidance of strangers') they forbade overseas trade. All social and political structure was designed to preserve the 'purity' and strength of the Spartan city-state.

Although Sparta was totalitarian and secretive, the Spartans' rigid political and social systems were attractive to a number of Greeks – appearing to guarantee *eunomia*, good order. 'Lakonophiles' – lovers of Lakonia – included the philosopher Socrates and the historian Xenophon. *Eunomia* was largely maintained thanks to rigid social engineering. Boy-children were taken away from their mothers at the age of seven and reared in the *agoge* – an all-male training camp: the overriding purpose of their instruction, to manufacture loyal and invincible soldiers. Spartan men did not have to trouble themselves with the more variegated demands of life – the Spartan state was supported by helots, a slave population, and the *perioikoi*, craftsmen who lived 'round about'. Spartan citizens lived to be professional soldiers; a male Spartiate was commemorated with a named headstone only if he fell in battle and a female Spartiate only if she died in childbirth. There was no interaction between the ranks. Spartan women (in theory) bred exclusively with full-blown Spartan citizens.[24] Because all Spartan men between the ages of seven and thirty spent their days in army camp, and their nights together in the *syssition* (the mess), the running of the household and, on occasion, of day-to-day affairs of state fell to Spartan women.[25]

Unlike the Athenians, the Spartans despised the pursuit of visible wealth and the pomp of grandiose monuments. The Spartans did not trouble themselves with large-scale artistic patronage – they never built a Parthenon.

The lucid, terse 5th-century historian Thucydides pointed out that, had Sparta been deserted (and only the foundations of its sacred and secular buildings left standing), no one would have had any idea from its meagre architecture how important a city it was.[26] The remains of the ancient *polis* are indeed sparse, and because it promised little, Sparta was one of the last sites to be excavated in the nineteenth-century race between European states to lay claim to ancient monuments. The first spades breached the soil of the Spartan acropolis only in 1906.

The British led the Spartan digs. Conditions were challenging, progress slow; the mid-19th-century neo-classical town of Sparti had been built directly on top of the ancient city.[27] Then, intriguing artefacts started to come out of the earth. There were the anticipated figurines of hoplite soldiers,[28] inscriptions commemorating glorious achievements in brutal close-combat competitions and sculptures of the warrior-perfect Spartan Ideal. But there were also more sensual objects: fine ivory combs, perfume bottles, kohl eye-liners, intricate mirrors and terracotta and bronze figurines: girl musicians, girl dancers, female equestrians – some riding side-saddle – many dedicated at Helen's cult sites. Yet the female figurines were put aside in cardboard boxes and tucked away in the bottom of archives – many undisturbed to this day. This disrespect towards the detritus of female cults, including the cult of Helen, the ancient Spartans would have found unconscionable.

Every man, woman and child of ancient Sparta lived with vivid, tangible mementoes of their celebrated ancestor. In the form of carvings, inscriptions and figurines, Helen was present across the city until the end of Roman rule. As well as her cult sites at the Menelaion and Platanistas, she had a shrine in the centre of the city near the tombs of the poet Alcman and Heracles.[29] Stone steles featuring Helen – created to be displayed in public – were carved by one generation after another. One dating from the 6th century BC, shows Helen with her birth-egg.[30] On another, from the 2nd century BC, Helen is flanked by her brothers, the Dioscuri; she is striking, her head crowned with long rays of light – a representation of the celestial sphere.[31] Curious fillets dangle down from her hands – to the untrained modern eye these look like strings of onions, but to the Ancient Greeks, who knew that these knotted bands of cloth or rope had a sacral nature, they would have signified Helen's ritual power.[32]

From the Hellenistic period onwards,[33] exclusive societies – whose members' names were inscribed on slabs of stone – organised feasts and sacrifices for Helen and her twin brothers.[34] Only those who were 'in' could worship Leda's children in this way. There were strict codes of behaviour.

One of the club officials was a '*gynaikonomos*': an individual who made sure that women in the religious society dressed and behaved appropriately. In the Roman period, hereditary priesthoods – priests and priestesses – claimed Helen and the Dioscuri as their ancestors; Helen's seers inspected the entrails of sacrificed animals for divine messages.[35] Spartan girls prepared themselves each year for the lush, orgiastic festivals of the spring, anniversaries of Helen's youthful dances at Artemis Orthia's sanctum and on the banks of the River Eurotas. Helen's name was sung, her memory lauded at formal civic occasions. Whether or not 'the world's desire' enjoyed a mortal life, there is no question that she lived, vividly, prominently, in the minds of the ancient Spartans. We call her Helen of Troy – for the Greeks she was, indisputably, Helen of Sparta.[36]

7

SPARTE KALLIGYNAIKA

๏๏๏๏๏๏๏๏๏๏๏๏๏

No Spartan girl could grow up modest, even if she wanted to.
You never find them staying at home; no, they go out with bare
thighs and loose clothes, to wrestle and run races along with
the young men. I call it intolerable.

EURIPIDES, *Andromache*[1] (428–424 BC)

ELEN'S LOT AS A SPARTAN WOMAN — so the authors of antiquity
would have us believe — was to progress from rape-victim to child-
bride, to cheating lover, to trophy mistress and back to dutiful wife.
The stations of her life were given marked sexual divisions. Almost no
attention was paid to those years that did not involve some kind of intoxicating, erotic encounter. It is no coincidence that once Helen is no longer
being chased by men, she fades from Homer's epic poetry. The last we see
of her in the *Odyssey* is retiring to bed with Menelaus in the Spartan palace
on the royal couple's return from Troy.[2] Homer does not care about her
quiet old age. Through the twists and turns of her time on earth this story-
book Helen encounters many men and learns how to deal, only too well,
with the manifestations — and consequences — of the sexual urge.[3]

The Spartan city-state recognised that its prominent ancestor — whose
remembered life comprised a series of rites of passage — was an expert in
sex. Beautiful Helen was not shamed because of this. Instead she was considered well placed to foster the development of young Spartan girls. And
so she stood at the heart of state-sponsored rituals — rituals that aimed to
socialise the city's adolescents, to turn ingénues into good wife material, to
lead them from the state of *parthenos*, virgin, to *nymphe*, newlywed.

An islet in the River Eurotas was, almost certainly, the site of Helen's
cult worship by Spartan virgins. Located near the sanctuary of Artemis
Orthia, this marshy area, a liminal place — half-water, half-land — was called
the Platanistas, after the plane trees that once shaded it. Here the river-
banks are wide and flat, the mud firm. It is a natural athletics ground.

Ritual dancing in honour of Helen was practised at the Platanistas by Spartan girls from the 7th century BC onwards. The displays aimed to replicate those performed by Helen herself when she was a youngster growing up in the city. In the Sparta museum there are racks of grimacing terracotta masks[4] reminiscent of gargoyles carved in medieval churches — some believe that these grotesques were used to hide the faces of the adorants as they danced and sang to each other.[5] To honour Helen the virgins were left alone together throughout the night. Their rituals would have been heady, pulsating affairs, throbbing with adolescent energy. They danced in the hours of darkness, paused, and were back again just before sunrise for more. There was torchlight, drinking and almost certainly sumptuous feasts.[6] The celebrants whirled their way from childhood to maturity, starting the night as innocent virgins who by dawn had been transformed into 'beautiful' young women ready for marriage.[7] The dances, it seems, were intended to drum out of the earth and the air some of Helen's sublime appeal: '*kharis*' is the Greek word.

Kharis is the root of 'charisma' and 'charismatic' and can simply mean grace or charm. But the original Greek also has a more sexualised connotation — a grace which ignites desire. *Kharis* was a gift of Aphrodite, the goddess of sexual love. It is that quality of raw seductive power that Helen possessed above all others. The girls who danced at the Platanistas — led on by the example of their presiding spirit, Helen — were experiencing a rite of passage that made them beautiful in that they were becoming charismatic, sexually mature and sexually available. For them, Helen was not the most 'beautiful' woman in the world, she was the most erotic.

These all-female orgiastic rites inspired by Helen's story[8] have been immortalised by the Spartan poet Alcman.[9] In the 7th century BC, Alcman wrote *Partheneia*, choral odes that were practised by groups of girls in secret and then sung as part of choral and gymnastic contests. These *Partheneia* were a central part of the Spartan girls' education, and were learnt and performed by one generation after another. The poems exalt female beauty — particularly the beauty of blondes. They laud the physical achievements of the Spartan woman.

Alcman's poetry is ardent and evocative. In the following segments each *parthenos* — girl or maiden — praises another's beauty. The lines that have survived are only fragmentary and therefore the rhythm of the verse is much denuded — but it is still possible to appreciate the timbre of the songs.

Alcman, *Partheneion 3*

Olympian Goddesses . . . about my heart . . . song and I . . . to hear the
voice of . . . (5) of girls singing a beautiful song . . . will scatter sweet
sleep . . . from my eyelids and lead me to go to the contest where I
will surely toss my blond hair
(10) delicate feet . . .
(61) with limb-loosening desire, and more meltingly than sleep and
death she gazes toward . . . nor is she sweet in vain.

The precious papyri on which these poems are written are preserved in
the Sackler Library in Oxford and the Louvre in Paris.[10] Originally de luxe
productions (witness the fine hand and the generous margins on the document), they are now sadly derelict. Some scraps are the size of a fingernail
– the Greek lettering pricked into the surface impossible to decipher. The
work in the Louvre, discovered in Saqqara, Egypt, in 1855, is desperately
damaged (the document was used to mummify a crocodile, so little surprise)
and is kept safely away from the light by the museum's curators.

In one poem the beauty of the girls is compared to the scorching heat
of Sirius the Dog Star – a cosmic body associated with sinister powers and
wantonness. The girls are singing directly to one another of each other's
passion and fine form; the words caress; the flirtation – with a hint of the
tribadic about it – is striking.

Alcman, *Partheneion 1*

(45) For she herself is conspicuous, as if one set among the herds
a strong horse with thundering hooves, a champion from dreams in caves.
(50) Don't you see? The mount is a Venetic: but the hair of my cousin
Hagesichora blooms like pure gold;
(55) and her silvery face – why need I tell you clearly? There is
Hagesichora herself; while the nearest rival in beauty to Agido will
run as a Colaxian horse behind an Ibenian.
(60) For the Pleiades rise up like the Dog Star to challenge us as we bear
the cloak to Orthria through the ambrosial night.
(65) There is no abundance of purple sufficient to protect us, nor our
speckled serpent bracelet of solid gold, nor our Lydian cap,
adornment for tender-eyed girls, nor Nanno's hair (70) nor Areta
who looks like a goddess, nor Thylacis and Cleesithera.
. . .

— *no, it is Hagesichora who exhausts me with love.*
For Hagesichora with the pretty ankles is not here beside us.
. . .
And she with her thick blond hair . . .[11]

The Spartans might have left little in the way of written history, but rare, literary sources such as the Alcman *Partheneia* hint that the Spartan girls' reputation in the classical world as proponents of homosexuality and homoeroticism was justified.[12] It is men who have famously fallen in love with Helen, or with the idea of her, but by singing rapturous lines, such as those of Alcman, women too had a chance to adore her.

For these young Spartan girls, practising their peculiar paeans together alone at night, Helen was real. It might take a little help to feel her breath on a cheek or hear her voice in the air, but the torchlight, all-night dancing and drinking probably altered the youngsters' senses sufficiently for them to believe that Helen walked in their midst. To suggestible minds she was not just a metaphysical, but a physical, presence.[13] It can be hard to imagine how vivid and present long-dead Helen would have felt to the archaic and classical Spartans, but consider this: for the Ancient Greeks, gods and goddesses, *daimons* and spirits did not hover in the ether – or in the hearts of men – but occupied real, temporal homes.[14] And so we find Zeus residing at Olympia, Athena on the Athenian acropolis and, from at least the 7th century BC, Helen living on as a nurturing spirit in the city of Sparta.

৩৩৩৩৩

Homer first describes Sparta as *Sparte kalligynaika*,[15] 'the land of beautiful women', an epithet almost certainly inspired by Helen's example. The hugely respected and influential Delphic Oracle endorsed Spartan girls as *kallistai* – 'the *most* beautiful', 'the finest', or, simply, 'the best'.[16] Helen's sublime beauty was a resource for Spartan women – a gift to the city-state released when carefully constructed rites such as the dances on the Platanistas were performed. 'Being beautiful' was an overt goal for the Spartans who, rejecting material fripperies, fetishised the natural beauty of the unadorned human body. It was said that physical beauty was admired in Sparta above all other attributes.[17]

In pursuit of physical perfection, Spartan women had the advantage over their Athenian counterparts. Unlike Athenians, Spartan girls were given the same food rations as boys and were allowed to drink unwatered wine.[18] Adolescent girls were subjected to a strict training regime that made them

every bit as fit as their brothers and boy-cousins. Women could be econom-
ically independent. They could ride. They were trained in music and poetry
recital.[19] In the sanctuary of Artemis Orthia a unique collection of metal
figurines has been found – girls playing cymbals, flutes and the lyre.[20] We
hear tell of a female poet (rare in Greece) called Megalostrata who, like
Helen, was 'golden-haired'.[21] One, probably apocryphal, tale describes the
self-confident Spartan womenfolk manhandling Spartan bachelors around
an altar.[22] All in all, they possessed an intimidating reputation: the polar
opposite of the ideal woman from Athens who would 'see, hear and speak
as little as possible'.[23]

Spartan girls exercised naked or semi-naked and their manoeuvres were
so vigorous (one involved beating their buttocks with their heels as many
times as possible – a move called the *bibasis*[24]) that they earned the nick-
name 'thigh-flashers'. Classical sources list as part of a girl's education racing,
wrestling, throwing the discus and javelin, and trials of strength.[25] These
youngsters are represented on the handles of fine bronze mirrors – they
are toned, nude (it is unusual to find the naked female form this early in
Greek art), some with flowers behind their ears, their long hair tucked away
ready for exercise.

These were the virginal beauties who in archaic and classical Sparta,
worshipped Helen. Her cult attendants were called *poloi*, 'foals' – juveniles
not yet subdued by the yoke of marriage.[26] When the playwright Aristophanes pictured Helen's acolytes as fillies in his *Lysistrata*, he was tapping
into a common ancient Greek notion that perceived in women the allure
of the unbroken mare[27] – all the more exciting because she hovered on the
edge of domestication.[28]

It could be that the reputation of these young Spartan girls as concu-
piscent, physically fit viragos was simply invented as part of the Spartan
'mirage', part of the mystery and secrecy and exoticism that lay like the mist
of the Eurotas around this exceptional city-state. The Spartans chose not to
write about themselves, not to promote their own histories and mores. And
so other Greeks only heard of strange Spartan goings-on second-hand.[29]
Their reports might, possibly, have been exaggerated. But come the Hellenistic
and Roman periods there is no doubting as to the athletic, body-conscious
credentials of Spartan girls. Now the Spartans' excessive characteristics were
actively promoted. Boys were whipped and girls raced naked in an odd kind
of sado-tourism which attracted visitors from across the Roman Empire.
Augustus Caesar himself came to watch such displays in the newly rebuilt
Roman theatre on the Spartan Acropolis[30] and one Spartan girl was imported
to Rome to grapple in public with a Roman senator.[31]

Excitable authors imagined Helen in similar lurid scenarios. Ovid, for example, waxes particularly lyrical about the young Spartan princess wrestling naked in the palaestra.[32] Other authors enjoyed recounting the story that an unclothed child-Helen, her skin gleaming with olive oil, exercised, raced and danced with her peers. The Roman poet Propertius[33] – recalling Helen's youth in one of his erotic elegies – lets his imagination run away with him as he describes the Spartan girls' 'admirable regime':

> *There a young woman properly exercises her body in physical sports, wrestling naked with the young men, throwing a ball too fast for them to catch, spinning a nifty hoop; or at length stands panting, smeared with the mud of the wrestling-floor, bruised in the rough pancration; or binds the leather straps to her brave fists, or swings and tosses the weighty discus, or races her horse around the ring, the scabbard bouncing against her snow-white thigh, a bronze helmet protecting her virgin head; or swims as the bare-breasted Amazon regiment swam in the waters of Thermodon; or maybe hunts with a pack of native hounds across the long mountain ridges of Taygetus.*[34]

Although outsiders focused on the prurient pleasure the Spartan women's exercises and dances gave to others,[35] there is every reason to believe that this active life empowered its participants. One bronze statuette[36] made in Sparta in around 520 BC (but found in Prizren in Serbia, taken home perhaps as a tourist's memento) represents a girl with honed biceps and strong calf muscles. The figure is in the middle of a dance – leaping forwards while looking back. Such a girl would have pounded the Spartan training grounds. I have held this figure in my hand and although she is only small she speaks clearly of the vigour and zest of the women of Sparta. Women who worshipped Helen.

The very thing about Helen that made the majority of ancient authors recoil – her liberty, physicality and initiative – may have helped to give Spartan girls a sense of themselves. Helen of Sparta was not a femme fatale but a role-model, thought to occupy the most sacred precincts of the rich Spartan lands.

⌒⌒⌒⌒⌒

Herodotus, the 5th-century BC 'father of history', recounts a magical little tale about the purview of Helen's sublime beauty. A baby girl, born in Sparta, was terribly disfigured (the Greek is *dysmorphia*, 'misshapenness' or 'ugliness'). She was well born, and her nurse had the bright idea of taking this ugly child up on the hilltop of Therapne to Helen's shrine to seek a cure. As with all Classical sanctuaries, framed by a small stone structure,[37] here there would have been an *agalma*, an image of the residing spirit. Helen's statue, perhaps made out of carved wood, stood, year in, year out, as it was approached by devotants such as Herodotus' suppliant. One day as the nurse sat on the warm stones, next to the idol of Helen, a beautiful woman appeared from nowhere and laid her hand on the child's head. As the years went by, following the blessing of the mysterious apparition (Helen, naturally) the disfigured girl grew up to be the most comely in the kingdom.[38]

Writing eight hundred years after Herodotus, Pausanias, who visited Sparta around AD 160, went to the Menelaion to try to ascertain why the shrine to Helen and her husband was so revered.[39] He adds a detail relevant to our story.[40] When retelling the anecdote about the clever nurse and the transformation of the unfortunate baby, Pausanias makes a subtle linguistic point. Helen's intervention turns the ugliest *girl* into the most beautiful *woman* – *gunaikon to eidos kallisten* is the phrase used: the most beautiful wife-woman. The story ends with this newly attractive *gunē* not only being married by a friend of Sparta's King Ariston, but then involved in a messy and difficult love triangle, desired by the king himself.

On the hilltop of Therapne; by the banks of the River Eurotas; in the streets of Sparta: Helen's beauty took on a spiritual aspect. Powerful, sometimes pernicious, her *kharis* was believed to be undimmed by the centuries, her homeland hectic with her energy.[41] This is how Helen was adored in Sparta in the historical period – as a carnal *alma mater*, a spirit of nature, a proponent of female fecundity. And a thousand years earlier, in the Late Bronze Age, archaeological evidence, still under excavation, suggests that a historic princess, a living Helen, would have been glorified in a remarkably similar way.

8

TENDER-EYED GIRLS

⊚⊚⊚⊚⊚⊚⊚⊚⊚⊚⊚⊚

> We have exiled beauty; the Greeks took up arms for her . . .
> Once more, the philosophy of darkness will break and fade
> away over the dazzling sea . . . Once more the dreadful walls
> of the modern city will fall to deliver up – 'soul serene
> as the ocean's calm' – Helen's beauty.[1]
>
> ALBERT CAMUS, 'Helen's Exile' (1948)

IN 1987, ON THE NORTHERN COAST OF CRETE at Chania, during routine site clearance at a private address, 4 Odos Palama, builders uncovered something rather unexpected – a series of Late Bronze Age tombs. Inside were twenty-nine skeletons dating to the 14th century BC.[2] The remains were carefully analysed and dental examination pointed to stress problems in the teeth of the females between the ages of eleven and twelve – a textbook indicator of the advent of puberty. If at twelve years old girls in the Bronze Age were ready to become sexual partners, it is almost certain that at twelve a Mycenaean aristocrat, a Bronze Age Helen, would have been put on the marriage market.

The adolescent, marriageable girl was recognised by early Mediterranean societies as a vital and precious commodity – a nubile creature whose burgeoning fecundity would ensure the continuation of the community. It is no chance that Helen frequently was given a twelve-year-old age tag at the time of her abduction by Theseus – a point was being driven home: this was the defilement of a child at the very moment she became most valuable.[3] We have no written testimony from the Late Bronze Age for the quantifiable desirability of twelve-year-old girls; however, we do have cogent clues – pictures that suggest how pubescents in Helen's Bronze Age world looked, the rites of passage they underwent and the high value they commanded.

Young women are represented on frescoes of the 13th century BC at Mycenae, Tiryns and Pylos and on tiny gold discs, gold rings[4] and carved ivories,[5] but to find the most striking examples we have to travel back three hundred years in time and, geographically, across the Aegean to the Cycladic island of Thera.[6] When that angry volcano exploded, destroying the lives of its native population and reshaping the development of the Western world, it showed us a few cultural kindnesses. Preserved in the volcanic residue at Akrotiri was a splendid surprise.

Excavations in 1967[7] revealed something extraordinary – an entire and unexplored Bronze Age settlement in the pumice. Here there were streets and courtyards, sanctuaries and houses – many exceptionally well preserved. As more finds emerged it became clear that pre-historic Akrotiri had been a busy, wealthy town. A clever and complicated drainage system underpinned the settlement, many buildings were two or three storeys high and most were richly appointed. But the greatest discovery was yet to come. As archaeologists delicately brushed away the pumice from a number of the internal walls, they uncovered staggeringly beautiful frescoes; naked boys carrying strings of freshly caught fish, boats decked out for a celebration, exotic rivers populated by fantastical creatures. And, particularly salient to a search for Helen, a number of scenes featuring high-born women at various stages of sexual development.

The original frescoes are now stored in Athens, but it is worth the journey to Thera to reflect on their provenance. Arriving by boat is best – a chance to appreciate this rocky island as Bronze Age traders would have done. The dark rock mass rears out of the Aegean. Modern-day Thera perches – like frosting on a devil's-food cake – on the caldera left behind when the central section of the volcano caved into the sea some time between 1650 and 1525 BC. A horrifying pyrotechnic spectacle for the Bronze Age world.

Now the island has become a playground for world travellers and the rich and famous. Walking through the chic little streets selling Barbie bikinis and killer cocktails, through lanes and passageways that twist from the edges of the cliff to the museum where the replica frescoes are housed, at first it is hard to imagine pre-historic Thera – a brooding giant, fertile and strategically placed, attracting and supporting a hardy merchant population. Thera enjoyed the profits of Bronze Age trade – until the earth started to behave abnormally, sending out warning signs, earthquakes, precursory falls of pumice from the uneasy magma chamber, erratic and inexplicable steam blasts shooting out of the ground. The digs revealed Bronze Age workshops hastily abandoned with pots of paint and plaster left half-empty as Thera's population took to the seas, fleeing to nearby Crete with the few possessions they could cram into their boats.

Inside the Museum of Pre-historic Thera, away from the modern-day tourist attractions, there is a display of replica Bronze Age fresco fragments which sweeps the visitor back to that earlier, evacuated world. In one series of rooms (the Xeste 3 complex) women dominate. Here there are 'classic' symbols of divinity: a griffin on a red leash, lotus flowers. A blue monkey reaches up to a central, elevated female figure[8] who rests on rich bundles of cloth and is bedecked in jewels. Around her neck is a string of beads, red, yellow and blue, carved in the shapes of ducks and dragonflies. This goddess-girl, whose breasts are just budding,[9] is accompanied by four female acolytes. The goddess-figure seems to care for the youngsters; on her wrists are bangles decorated with moon-shapes[10] – lunar imagery is often associated with the menarche – a sign that this is a chaperone-spirit who nurtured the girls' physical development.

The walls are studded with pastoral scenes.[11] Swallows dive through the sky, courting or feeding their young above a variety of natural landscapes. There are craggy rocks – reminiscent of Thera's own morphology. Young deer confront each other; lilies, the papyrus plant and rock-roses wave in the breeze. This is a celebration of the cycle of the seasons, of the glory of nature and of the place of women and emergent sexuality within both.

One flower is particularly conspicuous on the walls of Akrotiri: saffron, a frail, delicate plant, the stamens of which were worth more than their weight in gold – a herb used as a yellow dye for fine clothes and as a culinary flavouring. Huge amounts of saffron had to be gathered to be employed effectively – 4,000 stamens to produce just one ounce (28 g) of the distinctive golden colourant.[12] Early societies recognised that this diminutive plant also had qualities beyond the cosmetic. Skilfully employed, saffron is an efficacious pain-reliever – this was a highly prized crop. Clumps of saffron crocuses (their formation here probably suggests they were farmed rather than collected wild) cover the back walls of the fresco, the goddess's bodice is edged with flowers, stamens cover her clothes and mark – possibly tattoo – her cheek.[13] Elsewhere at Akrotiri a merchant-boat is decorated with saffron, an indication perhaps that this magical crop was exported in bulk. Certainly, come the historical period, Thera had a reputation for producing the finest saffron flowers in the Eastern Mediterranean.[14]

The women and girls who harvest the saffron crop are clearly the highest-born and are distinguished, in minute detail, by their clothes and hairstyles: these frescoes present detailed impressions of a Bronze Age princess.[15] This is how Helen would (almost certainly) have looked had she walked through a Mycenaean citadel – first as a juvenile and then with the new hairstyle of a bride-to-be. The youngest girls of Thera have their heads close-shaved with just a lock of hair above the forehead and a tiny ponytail at the back. Blue paint has been used to designate shaving and so the young-sters look as though they are wearing blue skull caps with tufts of hair escaping at jaunty angles. The four attending the goddess have had a rectan-gular area of hair removed just above their ears. One carries a shell-shaped incense burner – her lips and ears have been picked out in deep-red make-up. Another girl approaches a doorway which drips with blood.[16] The appearance is extreme and exotic – these tonsured young aristocrats could not be further from the saccharine-sweet, rose-coloured princess Helens conjured up by the artist's brush down the centuries.

In adolescence it appears that girls were allowed to grow their hair slightly longer and curlier (although still with a bushy forelock and pony-tail), and then, once they reached full maturity, the razor was put away. Mature women have luxuriant locks, sometimes elaborately bound with ribbons and beads – and buxom, exposed breasts. While adult women wear full-length robes, the girls have calf-length dresses with short sleeves. The youngsters chat as they collect their valuable saffron harvest. One young woman has hurt herself and sits on the floor cradling her foot, peering at her bleeding sole, her hand clasping her head in pain.[17] A girl walks forward holding out a necklace, an offering perhaps for the deity; another, smiling, wends her way through a field. A number of the women wear large hoop earrings and chunky ankle-bracelets – jewellery which is matched precisely by finds in the archaeological record.

During preservation work, it became clear that at least one of the girls, standing directly behind the girl-goddess, has tawny-red hair and blue eyes.[18] This was unforeseen – an intriguing revelation, and again one relevant to Helen's story. The Homeric heroes and heroines are frequently referred to as being *xanthos*, red- or golden-haired – think of red-haired Odysseus, red-haired Menelaus, golden Helen. For years it was presumed that *xanthos* was simply a trope, a literary device used to indicate 'goldenness' – heroic or divine status. But the Thera frescoes suggest something else. The gene for tawny or blonde or red hair must have been present or at the very least recognised in Bronze Age aristocratic circles. All other women represented across the Aegean Bronze Age have dark hair. In a population that would have been predominantly brunette, perhaps women and men born blond were thought to be blessed in some way, worthy of special status.[19] The red-head at Thera is positioned close to the deity and is the only 'mortal' allowed to wear a necklace, made, apparently, of cornelians, stones much prized because of their rich red colour.

The beatified young women in paintings like these – particularly those who are *xanthai* – might not be divine but, rather, thought to be touched by divinity. The religious imagery implies some kind of ritual activity. Is this red-head the prototype for Helen? A golden-haired girl who was thought to be 'special' and was therefore entrusted with particular religious authority? A woman who appeared to carry with her a divine gift? A woman who, centuries later, in the epics of Homer, came to be remembered as a child of the gods? Speculation – and yet at the same time, a historical possibility: the golden girl at Thera was honoured with immortalisation on the walls of a rich mansion; 'golden' Helen was honoured with immortalisation by the bards of the Peloponnese.

What we see at Thera when we look at those busy young girls is a subset of society so cherished, so consequential, that as they approach sexual maturity they are entrusted with the care of one of the most estimable crops in the ancient world.[20] Perhaps picking saffron itself was a rite of passage, an apprenticeship in stewarding nature – a neat combination of both commercial and spiritual activity. Without a written history, interpretations of the rich frescoes in the Xeste 3 complex on Thera have to remain just that – interpretations. But however we read the wall-paintings one thing is glaringly obvious: men barely get a look in.[21] It is instead well-dressed young women, the female elite of society, who are responsible for the precious saffron flower. If we are to carry an image in our minds of a Bronze Age princess such as Helen on the cusp of marriage, a rich prize, a woman believed to hold both temporal and religious sway, then the adolescents on the frescoes at Thera should be our first point of reference.

The active, bucolic, abandoned representations from pre-historic Thera stand in marked contrast to the prevailing, repressive view of young Greek women, particularly Athenian women, which had developed a thousand or so years later, by the 5th century BC. This is the century that generated some of the most enduring takes on the Helen story. The century that took Helen and turned her into a 'lustful bitch', a 'destroyer of cities'. The comparison is made beautifully explicit by a little *pyxis* – a cosmetics box – dating from 470 BC featuring Helen, now in the British Museum.[22] Here Helen sits as a demure young girl with her sister Clytemnestra. Helen is positioned by a basket of wool, ready to sew: the perfect pursuit for a docile Athenian girl – only a mirror, hovering between the siblings, suggests the presence of a worrying beauty.

There are other memorable heroines here too – but all are trapped indoors, grooming themselves or fruitfully employed in domestic labour. Iphigeneia ties a band around her head; Cassandra, the sister of Paris, is handed a work-basket; Clytemnestra holds out a perfume bottle. All images appropriate for the owner of the *pyxis*, a well-to-do wife who sat at home and took out jewels or ointments to beautify herself.

Unlike their pre-historic Greek ancestors – the Bronze Age pre-pubescents from Thera – these restricted vase-girls are not living full lives, the sun on their faces, stones underfoot, a lucrative crop to secure. Nor are they dancing around a tree, their breasts bare, high on opiates – as you will find Mycenaean women on a number of rings and seal-stones.[23] *Alia tempora, alii mores*. Athenians suppressed, feared and demoted the female sex. The Classical Greeks never went to war over a woman. Although the Helen most familiar to us has been filtered through the Classical Greek world, the essence of a primordial Helen should not be sought in the vase-painting work-shops of Athens and Corinth, but on the colourful, crumbling walls of the Late Bronze Age.[24]

PART THREE

@@@@@@@@@@@

THE
WORLD'S
DESIRE

9

A TROPHY FOR HEROES

@@@@@@@@@@@@@

Wise men in Greece in the meanwhile to swagger so about a whore

THOMAS NASHE, *Of Lenten Stuff* (1599)

HE FRESCOES AT THERA suggest that a pubescent, pre-historic princess was quite some prize. And now, the architects of Helen's story tell us, in Sparta, in the Age of Heroes, this was a prize that had to be played for. Helen's brush with sexuality on the banks of the Eurotas had been premature. In one sense she was a spoiled woman. But her assailant Theseus was, at least, a king. Helen had not been defiled by a nobody. This was a princess with land and standing – she still had worth. Whoever married her might not get a virgin, but they would get the rich Spartan kingdom. They would – we are told – also get a fair woman, shining, golden, a young girl blessed with incomparable beauty. Messengers were sent across Greece and beyond: Tyndareus' peerless daughter was to be fought for. Down to the 3rd century BC, Greek families boasted that their ancestors had gone to Sparta to vie for Helen's hand. Losing was no shame – competing with such a prize at stake was honour enough in itself.[1]

Because Helen was worthy of only the finest, her father, Tyndareus, organised a marriage contest in which all the warriors of the land had to compete in shows of strength and offers of wealth.[2] There is no consensus as to where the contest took place, other than at Tyndareus' home. Some ancient writers say Sparta itself,[3] others just leave a blank. But in Euripides we find Tyndareus' domain coupled with a reference to the name Amyklai.[4] Amyklai was originally a pre-historic settlement 7 km due south of Sparta. It is surrounded by plenty of flat land which could have accommodated the contests of heroes – chariot-driving, foot-racing, wrestling – not to mention the bulkier bribes the suitors brought with them: the poet Hesiod tells us that in a bid to win Helen, the hopeful heroes imported vast herds of oxen and sheep as well as gleaming pots, pans and cauldrons.[5] So let us imagine the marriage contest for Helen taking place here.

Amyklai is an atmospheric place – face east and at your back is the Tayegetan mountain range that keeps its snow long into the summer. Look out across the little promontory of the site and you are greeted by a soft green patchwork of farmland – hummocky and ramshackle, where elfin fields are peppered with copses of olives. Sapling trees and oleanders grow over half-excavated blocks of stone. The peace is broken only by the sound of tractors chugging up and down the lane below, delivering the agricultural produce which has always been particularly plentiful in this sheltered spot.

Close by at Vapheio, up a neat avenue of olive trees, there is a deep beehive tomb dating from the 15th century BC – the final resting place of a Mycenaean warrior. The tomb had been plundered down the centuries, but robbers overlooked a sunken burial pit, which was then excavated in 1889 by the Greek archaeologist Christos Tsountas. Here alongside the accoutrements of the dead – perfume vases, a mirror, daggers, knives, hunting spears, axes, beads and an ear-pick – were found two lavish gold cups, both moulded with rippling scenes of bull-taming.[6]

At Amyklai itself there are only a few remnants from pre-history. The site seems to have been occupied after many of the larger palatial complexes such as Mycenae had been destroyed around 1200 BC. The Mycenaean objects uncovered here included unique finds – human clay figures of almost life-size who would have overseen some kind of ritual activity. Here too there was a plethora of rough female figurines. This was a place of cultic significance. Amyklai, serene now, once witnessed idiosyncratic and fervent rites, long since lost to time.

Throughout the archaic and classical periods this was the home to alfresco festivals such as the *Hyakinthia* which was held in honour of Apollo and Hyakinthus.[7] The textual references are matted, but there is a strong possibility that Helen was worshipped here too in a festival called the *Heleneia*.[8] Families would take tents, picnics and plenty of wine to the sanctuary and eat, drink and dance long into the night. Girls would drive here in *kannathra* from the town of Sparta: some of these gaudily decorated carts were in the shape of fantastical creatures – griffins or goat-stags.[9] The whoops and cries of the drivers and the jingle of tack would be heard for miles about as the young Spartans raced each other in Helen's honour. The course ran through the outskirts of Sparta to Amyklai, or to '*eis to Helenes*' – to Helen's sanctuary.[10] The races were popular, the competition fierce. It is all a far cry from Athens, where women were allowed to ride in chariots only to weddings and funerals.

൭൭൭൭

The notion of a Bronze Age precinct here at Amyklai, or at Sparta itself, packed with suitors, the tense and sweaty pick of male Mycenaean society, is vivid – and was inspirational to the earliest known authors in the West. Hesiod lists the heroes who came to fight for the Spartan princess on that first occasion – because, of course, they are to meet again, competing for Helen on the battlefields of Troy. He mentions one suitor, Philoctetes, and then quickly, and elegantly, moves on to describe the heroes' prize. Throughout this catalogue of the great and the good Hesiod drops in little reminders of Helen's beauty. She is *'neat-ankled'*, *'rich-haired'*, *'the girl whose renown spread all over the holy earth'*.[11]

We have only fragments of Hesiod's poem and so cannot trace a complete list of heroes, although tradition has it that anywhere between twenty-nine and ninety-nine men turned up. Helen's husband-to-be, Menelaus, one of the princes of Mycenae, did not attend, although his older, richer brother Agamemnon was there.[12] Achilles, being too young to come, was conspicuous by his absence. Hesiod points out, in a barbed aside, how lucky Menelaus was to get Helen: *'Menelaus could not have won Helen nor would any other mortal suitor, if swift Achilles returning home from Pelion had encountered her.'*[13]

Each hero, each clan-leader in the stories, had his own coterie of likely lads, or *'etai'*. This was a social rank that has its counterpart in the Late Bronze Age *hequetai*, who seem to have been a chariot-driving warrior caste. Contests such as these are not figments of the classical imagination. The Bronze Age elite would certainly have met together in fierce combat-sports to sort out the men from the boys: to determine among them which of the aristocrats really was the best (*aristos* in ancient Greek) and who therefore deserved control (*kratos*). On a variety of visual sources from the Bronze Age we find men slugging it out – not in battle, but in complicated 'friendly' combats, engagements that were designed to perfect close-quarter combat skills. Submission fighting, submission wrestling, mock battles with pikes and shields and boxing are all represented. These contests were important preparation for war, but also served to identify the real 'heroes' within the citadels. Their ancient Greek name, *agones*, is the root of 'agony'; the etymology goes some way to convey the intensity of such contention.

Dressed to impress, to strut in front of each other, and perhaps Helen, the Mycenaean hopefuls would have worn short kilt skirts or tailored tunics made of linen, or goat or sheep wool. Frescoes from Pylos show men with black leather skirts, cut into points, the leather offering a second-skin protection. It appears that only the elite were allowed to wear pleated tunics – those of lower status have a simpler garment, on occasion decorated with braids. Workers wear loin-cloths.[14]

Homer was eloquent when recounting the impact the elite would have made, massed on the battlefield: '*Argives armed in bronze*'.[15] Then in 1960, in the Argolid at Dendra near the Mycenaean citadel of Midea, came a staggering discovery: a Late Bronze Age tomb harbouring a warrior's fine armour dating from *c.* 1400 BC. The village that peters out just before the site has a scruffy old-world charm; small-holdings abutting the site are ramshackle; scrawny hens pick their way around rusting cars. Nothing prepares you for the stern glory of the panoply that was dug up a few yards away. The bronze plates are 1 mm thick; skilfully wrought, they would have been lined and laced with leather, and stitched together, a high collar covering mouth and chin. The overall impression is bold, inhuman – designed to intimidate.

This fine panoply, three and a half thousand years old, now stands quietly on the first floor of the Nafplion Museum – a half-hour drive from its point of discovery. The Nafplion Museum looks directly out over the town's central square, a place bright with activity, serving ice-cream and pungent coffee late into the night. Most of the diversions on offer are fresh and brassy. There are children's boutiques, pool bars and an unfeasible number of shops selling rainbow-coloured *komboloi* – worry beads. In the museum, the armour, although one of the oldest inhabitants of the area, seems almost out of place: discoloured and dull from its many centuries in the earth, alien, sterile, awkwardly weighty. But imagine that bronze new and polished as Homer did and suddenly the armour sparks with life:

> As ravening fire rips through big stands of timber
> high on a mountain ridge and the blaze flares miles away,
> so from the marching troops the blaze of bronze armour,
> splendid and superhuman, flared across the earth,
> flashing into the air to hit the skies.[16]

Also found at Dendra were the bronze cheek-pieces (*chalkoparios* in Homer meaning 'of brazen cheeks') that would have been attached to a boar's-tusk helmet. Extant archaeological examples that pre-date Homer by five hundred years match his account perfectly.[17] Here forty or so split tusks are wrapped around in concentric circles – up to ten adult animals would have been killed for each helmet. Hard boar's tusks would have made a good barrier, cradling the warrior's skull – but they were also symbolic. Of all the animals potentially fatal to Bronze Age populations, it was the grouchy, belligerent wild boar that would have been encountered most frequently. An animal behaviourist told me while we were analysing pre-historic hunting techniques that he would far rather be left in a cage of wolves than in the wild boar enclosure.[18] A boar's-tusk helmet signalled both a successful hunter and a warrior who carried the fighting spirit of a fearsome animal with him.

A marriage contest in the Bronze Age for a woman such as Helen – a Spartan heiress – would have sponsored an excess of preening and posturing, since otiose display was at its heart. Showy panoplies such as that found at Dendra and boar's tusk helmets would have been dusted down and paraded in front of the assembled company. In a society whose good relations were based firmly on gift exchange, a unique prize such as Helen would have attracted only those able to promise substantial material reciprocation.[19] A sexually mature princess, a living, precious asset, was joining herself to the member of another clan and to merit such an honour, he and his family would have to deck themselves in their finest attire and dig deep into their pockets. Opening his doors to the glory of Greece, Tyndareus must have smiled as he thought 'And may the richest man win.'

ᚖᚖᚖᚖᚖ

In Mycenaean Greece money was yet to be coined. So a Bronze Age hero would hope to impress in other ways. Recent discoveries suggest that in addition to gift-giving one form of social display – a way of broadcasting superiority – may well have been an equitation. In the 13th century BC horsemanship was already well advanced east of the Bosphorus, but appears to have been in its infancy on the Greek mainland.[20] There are a number of representations of Mycenaean chariots and charioteers on frescoes, sealstones and grave-markers – but up until the middle of the 20th century, none had been found of a mounted rider. Then in 1953, a miniature figurine, a man dressed in armour and riding a horse, was found at Mycenae.[21] Forty years later there was an extraordinary discovery: five clay figurines excavated in the destruction layer of a cultic shrine at Agios Konstantinos near Methana, each showing a man on horseback. The riders sit high up, their arms flung around the horses' withers, their hands wound into the animals' manes. One figure in particular looks as though he is half-standing, leaning against the horse's neck in a streamlined position, the stance of a jockey winning a race.[22]

The movement and poise of these figures is not tentative, it is confident. Riding might have been a novelty, a skill in its infancy, but these are men in charge of their mounts. With the Methana discovery it was evident that on the Greek mainland in the Late Bronze Age, a select band of men could ride – and could ride well. Mastering this new mode of transport-cum-fighting-machine would have been both the privilege of the elite and its distinguishing mark. Homer's depiction of Agamemnon's father, the King of Mycenae, as *'that skilled breaker of horses'*,[23] of the *'stallion land of Argos,'*[24] now seems appropriate. We can indeed imagine the Mycenaean heroes on horseback, signalling their superiority as they rode through Peloponnesian territories.[25]

When the eager suitors thundered through the Taygetan plain to Sparta, their horses spittle-flecked and colourful, a caravan of gifts behind in preparation for the marriage contest ahead, they would have cut quite a figure.[26] All yearning to win glory and a peerless princess. To take possession of a thing of beauty. This moment of anticipation was brilliantly evoked in the 7th century BC by Hesiod as he coupled male sexual imagery (a spear) with a description of Helen's god-given charisma:

> . . . Philoctetes sought her, a leader of spearmen
> . . . most famous of all men
> at shooting from afar and with the sharp spear.
> And he came to Tyndareus' bright city
> for the sake of the Argive maid [Helen] who had the beauty of
>   golden Aphrodite,
> and the sparkling eyes of the Graces.[27]

But as they rode into the Spartan domain, the old King of Sparta, Tyndareus, made them promise one thing before they fought, raced, sang and bid for the princess. Since there could be only one winner and many losers, they had to swear eternal allegiance to he who was successful. Even if they were not lucky enough to claim Helen, they must remain loyal to each other, must help each other whenever asked, must not allow jealousy to divide them.[28] As a sign of the enormous importance of the pact, Tyndareus sacrificed a horse.[29] The heroes of Greece would keep their word.

10

THE KINGMAKER

@@@@@@@@@@@@@

[Tyndareus] told his daughter To let sweet Aphrodite's wind blow where it would, And from the suitors name the husband of her own choice. She chose — I curse the day he won his wish — Menelaus. So then this Paris, the man — you know the tale — who judged The three goddesses, left Troy for Sparta. His gown gleamed With flowers; gold sparkled in barbaric luxury. He loved Helen, and she him.

EURIPIDES, *Iphigeneia in Aulis*[1] 5th century BC

SHOW-FIGHTING WAS A FIXTURE at grand social gatherings in the Bronze Age.[2] Trying to identify more precisely what this would have entailed, a group of body-building experimental archaeologists helped me in my research by mounting a display of wrestling techniques.[3] In a quiet gymnasium in the suburbs of Athens they demonstrated holds and moves which they had painstakingly derived from Bronze Age visual sources.[4] Knowing that these were mock displays, I expected something rather camp and theatrical. But the men hurled each other around with terrifying force. Their backs crashed onto the ground each time they were thrown; their skin wrinkled, bulged and flushed purple as they were squeezed and pinned down in a variety of holds. The bones of men from the Late Bronze Age typically show severe trauma; bony nodules in the cervical, lower thoracic and lumbar vertebrae point to over-exertion in training exercises such as these[5] — some of their wounds would not have been sustained in battle but during similar 'play-fights'.

This is how the ancients believed that Helen was won — with loot and brawn. The heroic tournament for her hand became so iconic that a thousand years later in classical Greece, it was carefully re-enacted. A figure of speech bandied around the streets of 5th-century BC Greece was: 'Hippokleides cares nought for that' — an expression approximating to our notion of 'not giving a toss'. The historian Herodotus gives us the origin of the phrase – a marriage-contest that took place in the early 6th century BC at Sicyon in the north-east Peloponnese organised by the tyrant of Sicyon, Cleisthenes, and closely resembling Tyndareus' competition for Helen.[6] Those of 'manly worth' from all over Greece were invited by the tyrant to compete in wrestling and running and shows of strength. In the evening, around the dinner table, their social and musical skills were scrutinised.

Despite the rigour of the selection procedure, after a full year of wrestling, boxing and stick-fighting, there were a number of contestants still standing. It was time for Cleisthenes to choose the lucky bridegroom. The tyrant took the role of judge and following minute analysis of all the competitors, a contestant from Athens – none other than Hippokleides – emerged as the favourite. Cleisthenes slaughtered a hundred oxen, stoked up the fires to start the wedding feast and was on the verge of honouring his new son-in-law with a toast, when things started to come apart at the seams. Hippokleides – celebrating with an amphora of wine too many, one imagines – started larking around, dancing on the tables, striking ludicrous poses and then finally resting his head on the bench, wiggling his bottom and legs in the air. Cleisthenes was horrified, rejected Hippokleides and chose for his daughter another, more sober and decorous man. The buffoon was said to have retorted, 'Hippokleides cares nought for that.' One wonders whether, the following morning, with a sore head, a lonely bed, and empty pockets, this young wag would have been so phlegmatic.

While there is plenty of lively, literary testimony describing marriage contests in both the classical and the pre-historic periods, marriage remains one of those 'invisible' Late Bronze Age activities where the lack of contemporary documents from the Mycenaean world is frustrating. Detailed accounts of aristocratic unions – politically expedient, sexual, even romantic – from Hittite and Egyptian courts exist, but nothing for the Mycenaeans. With the lack of contemporary written evidence, we have to turn to the one source available – to the Greek epic tradition – for guidance.[7]

Time and again in literature and myth-stories we hear that women are the kingmakers, that the right to monarchy does not pass from husband to son, but from mother to daughter. Men have to win a crown by winning a wife. Helen's half-sister Clytemnestra makes her lover, Aigisthos, king while her husband Agamemnon is overseas, fighting the Trojan War; Pelops (who gave his name to the Peloponnese) becomes King of Elis through his marriage to Hippodamia; Oedipus is crowned the King of Thebes when he marries Queen Jocasta. Even faithful Penelope, left at home by Odysseus, seems to have the prerogative to choose who will be her next king. And, of course, Menelaus becomes King of Sparta when he marries Helen.

Tradition tells us that along with his daughters Helen and Clytemnestra, Tyndareus had two sons – Castor and Pollux. And yet there is no suggestion that either of them will inherit their father's title when he dies. It is Helen who will become queen and it is only marriage to Helen that will bring regal status and sovereignty over the Spartan territory. We hear from Pausanias,[8] amplifying Homer,[9] that it is not one of Menelaus' sons, not even his 'favourite son', who becomes king of Sparta.[10] Instead it is the children of Helen's *daughter* Hermione who succeed to the throne. And it is only once Orestes marries Hermione that he, in turn, becomes the new ruler of Spartan territories.

To judge from the literary evidence, it seems that young men were mobile across the Greek diaspora and – although rooted into locales by marriage to a high-born heiress – they kept their familial connections up and running through agnatic ties. A king might have ruled at Mycenae or Sparta or Argos thanks to his wife's position as local landowner – but his kudos and heritage also came from belonging to a particular dynasty. Ties of loyalty were not linear, but politically and geographically lateral, spread across the Aegean like a fine net.

Homer describes Late Bronze Age politics as familial and dominated by the 'House' system. Menelaus from the House of Atreus at Sparta has a brother, Agamemnon, at Mycenae. Adrastus from the House of Sicyon keeps contact with his son-in-law Diomedes at Argos. If it was assumed that women were kingmakers, and that inheritance was matrilineal, by marrying princes off to wealthy aristocrats in citadels across the Greek mainland a web of power would be created. And given that men had no right of succession, then the acrid squabbles of sons over inheritance would be avoided.

Travelling through the Peloponnese from the archaeological remains of one Mycenaean powerhouse to another, it becomes clear that there must have been some kind of system of loyalty to keep these communities from in-fighting over territories and resources. Each citadel was largely self-sufficient, but the cultivatable land between kingdoms was at a premium. A journey along the old National Road from Argos to Mycenae brings home what a vast and difficult terrain is contained within the region. The mountain ranges here are coherent barriers. For Late Bronze Age populations – without the viscous glue of blood-ties – those geological boundaries could have afforded a magnificent opportunity for retrenchment and political division.

And yet the Mycenaeans clearly co-operated with one another. They had, by 1450 BC, taken over, lock, stock and barrel, in Crete. In the centuries that followed they entertained the same expansionist ideas when they looked east to Anatolia.[11] The Anatolian towns of Miletus and Muskebi were certainly under Mycenaean control. In the Late Bronze Age, some kind of understanding allowed for the combined action of disparate communities from across the Greek mainland. Perhaps the weft and warp of loyalty through marriage ties and agnatic bonds explains how there could have been a unified act of aggression against a land as rich as Crete and even against a foreign city as tempting as Troy.

☙☙☙☙☙

If this is an accurate picture of dynastic politics in Mycenaean Greece, then in such a scenario women like Helen were more than just golden, sitting ducks, waiting to be hunted down. Helen is mentioned seventeen times in the *Iliad* – on eight occasions her name is coupled with the word *ktema*, 'treasure' or 'possession'.[12] This wealth – which Paris rustles away to Troy when he steals the Spartan queen – is ascribed not to Menelaus, but to Helen. We hear in Troy that Paris begins to 'fight Menelaus for Helen's treasure'. If wealth was the honey-pot which attracted suitors like Menelaus, women like Helen appear to have owned and enjoyed the honey.[13]

On the Linear B tablets[14] there is a surprising number of women who have responsibility for temporalities. In one series from Pylos that deals with landholding,[15] two women, one called Kapatija (the 'Keybearer') and the other Erita ('the Priestess'), have large lots of land. Half of those listed in the series who possess *onata*, 'benefits' of land allotments, have feminine names.[16] The suggestion is that women could be landholders and had a right to exploit their estates.

One might imagine that a woman in possession of such riches would have had some say in whom she married. In one version of the wedding story,[17] Helen *chooses* her suitor by garlanding him with a crown of flowers.[18] Euripides picks up the theme: in his play *Iphigeneia in Aulis*,[19] with the lines that open this chapter, Helen, he says, *chose* the younger son of the House of Atreus, the prince of Mycenae. Whoever did the choosing, hero or heroine, Helen ends up with the richest man in town. We hear that Agamemnon's coffers – the booty from Mycenae – outweighed those of all his rivals, and so, on behalf of his younger brother, 'war-like' Menelaus,[20] he provoked the release of the greatest counter-gift of all.[21] The wealth of the monumental House of Atreus had won the world's desire, beautiful Helen. The wedding preparations could begin in earnest.

11

A ROYAL WEDDING

@@@@@@@@@@@@

Now, in Sparta once, in the palace of golden-haired Menelaus,
There were girls who wound fresh hyacinths into their hair, and
Stepped into the dance outside his freshly-painted bridal room –
Twelve girls, from the city's foremost families, the great glory of
Sparta's youthful womanhood . . .

THEOCRITUS, *Epithalamium for Helen*[1] (THIRD CENTURY BC)

I N THE 3RD CENTURY BC the Greek-Macedonian Ptolemies, who
controlled the ebullient court at Alexandria on the Mediterranean coast
of Egypt, patronised numerous poets. One, Theocritus, a man from
Syracuse in Sicily, wrote tenderly of the Spartan queen. In his *Epithalamium
for Helen*[2] he describes – in luxurious language – Spartan girls, on the cusp
of sexual maturity, re-enacting the moment when the young Helen became
a bride. These bridal songs were, in turn, then sung by Spartan girls on the
eve of their own weddings.

The protagonists of Theocritus' poem are twelve young virgins and
the verses are rapturous. Theocritus was obviously inspired by the
7th-century BC poet Alcman,[3] delighting as the Archaic poet had done in
the wistful potential of his setting and his characters.[4] There are idolising,
pastoral descriptions of Helen: her beauty is like the dawn, it is like a
cypress tree in a garden, it is the arrival of spring after winter. The girls'
thoughts of Helen are as tender as a lamb's longing for the teats of
its mother.[5]

As the poem develops, the twelve virgins smother the ground around
a sacred plane tree with olive oil and carve Helen's name into its bark.
Whereas we might expect a romantic graffito like this to read 'Helen loves
Menelaus', it is the tree – a symbol of fertility in both Bronze Age and
classical Greece and perhaps thought to harbour Helen's spirit – that is
being adored. Here is a love triangle – the threesome not Helen, Menelaus
and Paris, but Helen, young Spartan virgins and nature herself.

For you first [Helen], we will weave a wreath of the lotus growing
   close to the ground,
And place it on a shady plane tree.
And first we will pour liquid oil from a silver flask
And let it drip beneath the shady plane tree.
And on its bark shall be inscribed in Dorian so that a passerby may
   read
'Revere me. I am Helen's tree.'[6]

Lotus flowers, olive oil – this precursor of the marriage of Spartan girls seems sensual and sylvan: by all accounts precisely what a Spartan wedding ceremony in the classical period was not. The Greek author Plutarch tells us that the Spartans endorsed 'marriage by capture'. In this – to us – curious rite, a girl was taken from her home to her chosen husband's at the age of eighteen[7] and dressed as a boy.[8] The room was sealed from the light. Her hair was shaved off and she was left alone in the dark lying on a straw pallet. The prospective husband would come from the all-male military camp where he lived; in some versions he was expected to 'seize' his betrothed from a number of girls. He would then copulate with his androgynous bride. Having had sex with her (some sources suggest this was anal, some between the thighs rather than vaginal penetration) he would then leave.[9] The pair were now married but saw each other infrequently. The new bridegroom returned to his peers in the *syssition* – the all male-training camp in which Spartan boys lived between the ages of seven and thirty. The newlyweds saw each other every few months or so to have sex – it was thought such abstinence would promote more vigorous offspring.

Marriage by capture may sound humiliating but there are two possible interpretations of this elaborate piece of sexual theatre. The first is that a teenage girl masquerading as a boy might have been less disconcerting to the young Spartiates who knew only close physical and emotional relationships with father figures, having lost all contact with women at the age of seven. The second explanation is that by shaving her hair and dressing as a man, the Spartan girl was being recognised as an important part of the citizen body. Spartan women kept their heads shaved after they were married. This was *not* humiliation, but 'promotion' to masculine status for sexual engagement.[10]

On the night before the wedding the bride danced and sang with her girlfriends. Given Helen's highly coloured personal history – particularly her abandonment of the king of Sparta for an eastern prince – it might seem strange that Theocritus' *Epithalamium for Helen* should be recited on this occasion, and perhaps a little odd that Spartan men were happy for their women to invoke her as an example during their pre-nuptials. A wayward wife is an unexpected choice as chaperone for a girl on the last night before a wedding. But we have to remember to look at Helen through Spartan eyes. This is not yet the faithless harlot who, down the centuries, has become cloaked in choler – but a more noble Helen, a full-blooded woman, a fount of erotic power, an irresistible force of nature.

Elsewhere in the *Epithalamium for Helen*, there is a playful suggestion that a rather staid, tipsy Menelaus should go to bed early while Helen stays out late, cavorting with her close circle of girlfriends. Menelaus is a gooseberry, insignificant; Helen is the centre of attention, and very much in charge. The poem describes a gifted and blessed woman. The young friends remember the races they have run together, their skin massaged, gleaming with oil. The Spartan princess is at her happiest, sharing a last, glorious night with her adolescent, female friends before she embarks on the life of a wife.

But the long night must become morning: Menelaus will rouse himself from his stupor: Helen has to leave the girls; she has to marry.[11] Menelaus welcomes his 'Adored Helen'[12] into his chamber and locks the door. The virgins weave garlands of hyacinth flowers; Helen has a crown of lotus; the royal wedding has begun.

⊙◎⊙◎⊙◎

To honour a union such as this, in the Bronze Age, the ruling family of Sparta would have prepared what Homer describes as a *gamos* or *gamelia* – a word that can mean either a marriage or a marriage feast. As work on Linear B progresses, it becomes clear that banquets in the Mycenaean citadels were vast operations, sometimes accommodating thousands of people. For the biggest feasts additional support staff would be seconded from within the palatial economy. We even have reference to a number of bedsteads being shipped in – almost certainly these were pallets for workers;[13] something a little more fancy would be provided for honoured guests.

From the analysis of residues on the interiors of pottery sherds we know of a selection of the dishes that would have been passed around to the assembled company: lentil broths flavoured with cumin, celery and coriander; chick-pea pancakes; grilled meat, fruit stews; roast boar, hare, duck and venison.[14] The vast spreads were not necessarily laid on by the tribal leaders – these were often bring-your-own parties,[15] guests vying to provide ever more lavish supplies in the hope of social advancement.[16] A ruler could demonstrate his standing merely by the quantity of food he managed to garner from his population. Individuals might give, for example, a single goat.[17] Those who had more to prove and had the resources to meet their ambition could rise to the heights of generosity displayed on one tablet: 1 cow, 2 bulls, 13 pigs (1 fattened), 1 ewe, 15 rams, 13 male goats, and 8 yearlings, not to mention around 375 litres of wine and over 1,000 litres of olives.[18] The names of individual donors have, in some cases, been carefully recorded – this was a good list to be on. Linear B experts debate whether or not these tablets represent obligatory taxes or prestigious gifts. But whether the food was brought in voluntarily or under obligation, it was undoubtedly there in enormous quantities.[19] A single tablet from Pylos lists animals ready for sacrifice (bulls, sheep, goats and a fatted pig) whose carcasses would have produced over 1,600 kg of meat.[20] Each and every animal was chosen because it was a plum specimen.[21]

The doorways in the palace-fortresses are noticeably wide – were they thus designed in part to accommodate these rushes of livestock? Pouring into the citadels or into the designated killing-yards the animals must have panicked as they smelt the death ahead of them, slipping and sliding on the stone surfaces which would have run with muck and blood. Animals were ritually slaughtered before they were eaten, using sets of sacrificial instruments: stunning axes from Crete, knives and gold-leaf-covered restraining chains.[22] Carbonised faunal remains from Pylos tell us – almost certainly – that burnt offerings, including the tongues of oxen, were offered up to the gods.[23] A sarcophagus from Crete shows a woman at an altar, responsible for the kill; if we are to envisage Helen officiating at the grand feasts of the Late Bronze Age, perhaps at her own wedding celebrations, we should picture her with a sacrificial knife in her hand.[24]

Homer talks a great deal about the consumption of animal flesh by his hero-protagonists. For years this was considered epic exaggeration, and that, in fact, the Greek elite survived on a diet that consisted predominantly of vegetables and a kind of fruit porridge. Together with the evidence from Linear B, bone analysis now shows that Helen and her peers would have been pretty resolute carnivores and serious drinkers to boot.[25] Special storage spaces had to be created at Nestor's palace in Pylos for 2,856 *kylikes* (long-stemmed drinking vessels). When the palace was first excavated in 1939, the *kylikes* were found stacked neatly in storerooms, some waiting for their baptismal use. One tablet appears to record over 1,700 litres of wine ready to be drunk.[26] Analysis of the organic residue in a number of vessels reveals that as well as neat wine the Mycenaeans drank a lethal cocktail of honey mead and retsina,[27] a recipe reminiscent of the 'honeyed, mellow wine' quaffed by the heroes in the *Iliad*.[28] In the palace at

Knossos, aristocrats on one of the fragmentary frescoes sit on drinking stools and sup from their deep cups.[29]

The higher up one was in the pecking order at a grand feast, the closer one was, physically, to the centre of things. Some of the population would be served outside in the palace courtyard, these have-nots gratefully eating out of the pots and cups made of rough clay that have been found in nearby rooms and were possibly used to serve the people.[30] From here the lower orders could still appreciate the beneficence of their ruler, and perhaps glimpse the king and queen themselves in the magnificent central *megaron* — or at least watch as their food, served in fine, gleaming metalware,[31] was brought to and from their table.[32] The archaeology supports Homer's picture of careful social apartheid on the rich occasion of a marriage feast.[33]

> *What a fine thing it is to listen to such a bard*
> *as we have here — the man sings like a god.*
> *The crown of life, I'd say. There's nothing better*
> *than when deep joy holds sway throughout the realm*
> *and banqueters up and down the palace sit in ranks,*
> *enthralled to hear the bard, and before them all, the tables*
> *heaped with bread and meats, and drawing wine from a mixing-bowl*
> *the steward makes his rounds and keeps the wine-cups flowing.*
> *This, to my mind, is the best thing that life can offer.*[34]

Homer tells us that accompanying the food, at a marriage such as that of Helen and Menelaus, there would have been music and song. '*The gods made music and banquets to go together*'[35] says Odysseus. He describes the *hymenaios*, the wedding song accompanied by the music of lyres and flutes, theatricalised with torchlight and whirling dancers.[36] Archaeological finds demonstrate that the courtly life of a woman such as Helen would indeed have had a varied and sophisticated soundtrack; metal and clay rattles, finger cymbals, a whistle made from the tooth of a hippopotamus, and tortoiseshells to be used as the resonating box of a lyre, have all survived.[37] There is one tantalising Minoan seal-stone that seems to show a girl leading a procession, blowing a triton shell.[38] Tritons — or other conches — were used both as libation vessels and cups; the girl might be drinking from the shell, or using it to form a rare sound. In the Museum at Agios Nikolaos in Crete there is an exquisite man-made version of the conch that suggests the engraved seal-stone does indeed denote a young girl at the head of a musical procession.[39] Sitting proudly in a case by itself the stone conch has been skilfully carved out of serpentine.[40] It is solid, a good couple of kilos in weight, its surface crusted with demons and sea-creatures. Identified as a libation vessel, it has an aperture at one side that makes a perfect mouthpiece. Certainly one museum official managed to get a good — and eerie — note out of it.

The instrument most in evidence in the Late Bronze Age was the lyre. Helen's epic story is itself lyrical — composed by bards to be sung to the lyre. Homer imagined his gods and heroes 'plucking strong and clear on the fine lyre': Achilles plays to 'delight his heart'[41] and Paris plays the lyre to delight Helen — an image that has proved perennially inspirational. It was said that when Alexander the Great landed at Troy in 334 BC, the leaders of the city came out to honour him, offering up as a gift the lyre with which the prince of Troy had serenaded the 'world's desire'.[42] Alexander, with his much discussed predilection for men, allegedly retorted that he would have preferred the instrument Achilles used to woo his own warrior-love, Patroclus.

Paris was said to have learnt his seductive, mellifluous art while a young man out tending flocks of goats in the countryside around Troy. The image of the Trojan prince, rustic, unaware of Helen's existence, happily strumming, was a popular one in antiquity — much replicated on vases from the 6th century BC onwards. In a number of the depictions we learn of the next chapter in Helen's story: that as he sat alone on that rock, Paris was visited by three goddesses who had hastily left another wedding party, this time on Mount Pelion, to lay a dreadful challenge in front of the young cub — a challenge that would draw him to Helen's bed. On one vase, now in the Louvre, the Trojan prince, overwhelmed by the task ahead of him, has sensibly grabbed his lyre and is beating a hasty retreat out of the picture.[43]

Over two thousand years later, in 1788, the French painter, Jacques-Louis David painted a canvas featuring Paris and his lyre.[44] Oozing sentimentality and sexual imagery, it shows the young lovers, Helen and Paris, tenderly entwined. Paris' modesty is preserved by a finger of cloth, but a priapic lyre rests, heavily, on his thigh. At first glance the image is sweeter and more intimate than the other grand Davids in Salle 75 of the Louvre where the painting now hangs. The lovers are pressing against each other but they seem contented and still; the palette the artist has used is warm and velvety. Yet the painting's title, *Les Amours de Paris et d'Hélène*, is fitting. Paris' colour is high, Helen's see-through dress has already slipped off one shoulder, jets of water spurt into a sunken bath in front of the amorous couple.

Whereas Paris is staring directly at Helen, one thing on his mind, Helen looks demurely down, lost in thought. This is one of the most perceptive portraits of Helen that exists. There is something resigned about her. This Helen is both victorious and vanquished. The momentary act of abduction is subsumed by a greater problem: the problem of being the most beautiful woman in the world.

◦◦◦◦◦

We know that Iron Age bards such as Homer strummed their lyres and sang about Helen 'the beautiful problem'. But what of the Bronze Age: was the lyricist really a feature of Helen's world?[45] Could Paris have wooed Helen with its sweet sound? Was Helen part of a story sung by Bronze Age bards? Lyres certainly existed in the Late Bronze Age; fragments of them have been found at Mycenaean sites, they appear in art, and miniature versions of the instrument – probably votive offerings to the gods – are scattered around shrines.[46]

Perhaps lyre-players and singers recorded the deeds of the Mycenaeans as eye-witnesses. Even if the words of the *Iliad* were first written down in the 8th or 7th century BC, could they have started off life in the Mycenaean palaces themselves? In 1953 a fragmented fresco of a bard with his lyre – in the same scheme as two aristocrats who appear to be drinking and a giant bull trussed and waiting for sacrifice – was uncovered at Pylos, generating much excitement in the academic world. Suddenly a 13th-century BC bard-singer, whose job was to celebrate his palatial patrons, entertaining with an exposition of events past and present, was found right at the heart of one of the Mycenaean palatial complexes. Here was a man, commemorated on the walls of the palace throne room itself,[47] who could have recounted, verbatim, the tales of his king and queen. Just such a man might have transmitted the original Bronze Age version of Helen's story.

So, as the aristocrats of the Late Bronze Age ate, we can hold a picture in our mind's eye of the court musicians adding music to the *gamelia*, feasts and marriage celebrations, and a singer of songs recalling the deeds of mighty ancestors, celebrating the achievement and the ambitions of those around him. Imagine that lyrical music, that bright, rich sound stealing through the palace – notes coming in an *ioe*, a 'rush' or a 'sweep' as Homer says,[48] filling the central hall and then drifting down the corridors beyond.

Helen, 'the pearl of women', had been won. Menelaus must have felt his brother's generosity rewarded many times over. On their wedding night, in the imagination of the Hellenistic poet Theocritus, Menelaus lies 'breast pillowed upon breast, breath mingling love and desire'.[49] The younger son

87

of the House of Atreus has kudos: he has won the girl, and has a stock-pile of gifts left by his rivals, the scores of unhappy, thwarted suitors. But the audience of the ancient poets knows what he does not; within a few years, after an affront of international proportions, the 'happy groom', as Theocritus calls him,[50] will be travelling five-hundred-odd miles east to try to win wife, treasure and reputation back again.

PART FOUR

KOUROTROPHOS

1 Helen emerges from an egg. In some versions of the story, Helen's mother was not Leda but Nemesis – the spirit of Fate or Revenge – who took the form of a goose and mated with Zeus.

2 From the Classical period onwards, men have searched for the site of Troy. This illustration from a 15th century AD manuscript gives an artist's impression of the settlement. Troy was a totemic site for both the East and the West – after taking Constantinople in 1453, the Ottoman ruler Mehmet the Conqueror visited, declaring his desire to avenge the age-old Trojan dead.

3 Women appear to dominate the religious rituals of the Mycenaean age. This fresco was discovered in the cult complex at Mycenae in 1968. The imagery is obscure. One woman holds a giant sword, another a staff, a third ears of wheat. Two tiny male figures tumble down in front of the armed ladies.

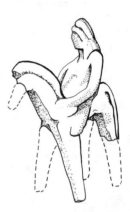

4 Helen was worshipped in the town of Sparta itself and on the nearby hill of Therapne. These are two of the votive offerings left to her: a mounted terracotta female figure and a perfume jar inscribed with Helen's name (5).

6 Spartan girl-athletes dedicated mirrors, such as this 6th century BC example, at religious sanctuaries. These were expensive, finely wrought items.

7 Theseus' abduction of Helen could relate to a broader mythological story: the seizure of a young woman who represents fertility (spring and summer) and whose absence brings winter to the earth. In this early image (*c.* 680 BC) Helen has monstrous proportions, suggesting she is being represented as a quasi-divine figure (8). Theseus and Peirithous seize her, but she is about to be saved by her two brothers, Castor and Pollux, mounted on horses.

9 This female figure from Mycenae clasps her breasts – a defining gesture of a goddess. Dots represent bracelets and a necklace.

10 The mounted goddess figurine could suggest that highborn women were permitted to ride in the Late Bronze Age.

11 Mycenaean delight in visible beauty is demonstrated by this finely carved ivory lion.

12 In the Late Bronze Age, female figurines were produced in great numbers. This example, found at Mycenae, carries one child in her arms while another is strapped to her back underneath a parasol. She is a *kourotrophos* – a nurturer of shoots/youngsters.

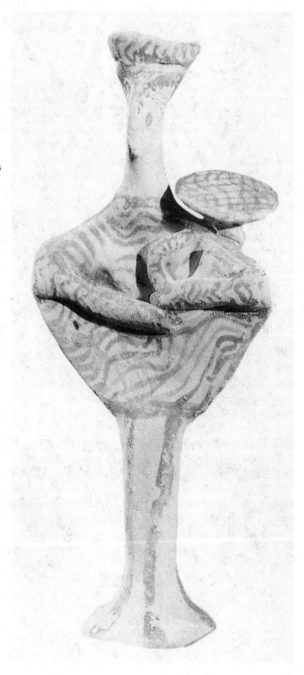

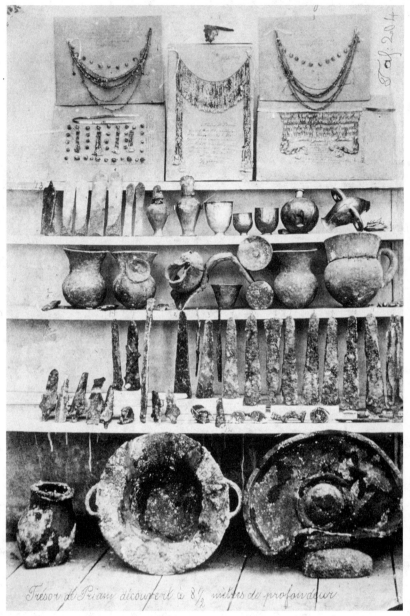

Trésor de Priam découvert à 8½ mètres de profondeur

13 Schliemann proudly presented 'Priam's Treasure' (a misnomer) to the public in this archive photograph taken in 1874. To access finds such as these, during his first excavation season at Troy, Schliemann moved 78,000 cubic metres of earth.

14 A number of European dynasties traced their lineage back to the Romans (as the Romans did back to the Trojan hero Aeneas). In both these medieval scenes, Helen is welcomed into Troy as an honoured and respected aristocrat. But in fig. 15 Cassandra, the prophetess, hints at the doom to come as she tears out her hair.

quas deuotio affectibz ꝫ leta fronte susapir   vbis p̄apitatum ruinas...

16 Mycenaean chariots have wheels with only four spokes (the Hittite chariot has six) and are lighter than their Hittite counterparts.

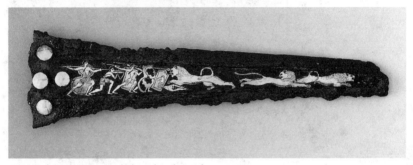

17 Much Mycenaean art deals with military themes or the joy of the hunt. The decoration on this dagger shows Mycenaean warriors killing a lion. Note the large rectangular 'tower-shield' and the shields covered in hide. In the *Iliad*, Ajax is described as bearing a shield '*like a wall*' covered in ox-hide.

18 Linear B tablets were incised blocks of clay. This tablet lists the herbs and spices (such as *e-pi-ka* – hibiscus) used for culinary and medicinal purposes. The word *pa-ma-ko* (the root of pharmacy) has also been inscribed.

12

HERMIONE

> Let the premature guzzle wine that is hardly fermented,
> I'll take wine from a jar mellowed in vintage with time.
> Only the full-grown tree resists the heat of the sunlight,
> Meadows too recently sown offer the barefoot no joy.
> Who wants Hermione, if Helen is his for the taking?
>
> OVID, *The Art of Love*[1] 1st century BC/AD

BEFORE DISASTER STRIKES, the poets allow Helen and Menelaus a little happiness. In the Spartan palace they have a child, a beautiful daughter, Hermione.[2] Hesiod tells us this was a difficult confinement: 'she bore fair-ankled Hermione in his halls — though the birth had been despaired of'.[3] Difficult and singular. In the *Iliad*, while slipping in the information that Menelaus had sired a son (Megapenthes — 'great grief') by a slave girl, Homer relates:[4]

> *To Helen the gods had granted*
> *no more offspring once she had borne her first child,*
> *the breathtaking Hermione,*
> *a luminous beauty gold as Aphrodite.*

To try to solve their fertility problems, both the Helen of the epic poems and our Bronze Age queen would have made propitiation to the goddess of procreation and childbirth, Eileithyia. The name means 'she who appears' or 'she who arrives'. A divinity first attested on Crete, where she appears on Linear B tablets as *Eleuthia*.[5] Eileithyia was a popular goddess who came to be worshipped at cultic sites across the Aegean.

In the 6th century BC a stone effigy of Eileithyia was hacked out of a lumpy piece of rock: it now stands alone against a side-wall of the museum at Sparta. I noted during one visit to the museum that curators had hedged their bets and the figure was described on its faded cardboard label as

'Eileithyia/Helen/Hera'.[6] The form is beautiful and undeniably earthy. The figure's sex organs are marked by a deep gash at the vulva, and the woman is clearly in labour: either side of her there are daimons or spirits, clutching her belly, helping her get through the terrible pains of childbirth.[7]

Travel south from Sparta for a day and a night by boat, and you find Eileithyia again. About half an hour inland from Crete's cramped Heraklion airport, in the summer packed with tourists, mainly British, there is an underground cavern known as the Eileithyia cave. No longer an official tourist attraction, the cave can be reached by scrambling off the roadside and forcing a way through a small overgrown copse of olive trees. Inside the air is dank and bitter. As eyes grow accustomed to the dark, phallic and vulvic rock-forms loom out of the shadows. The walls are moist with a pale green fluid that drips down the rock-face.

Votive offerings left here reveal virtually continuous use as a sacral site from 3000 BC. There are potsherds spanning time from the Bronze Age to the medieval period – including the remains of Christian lamps from the late Roman Empire. A Linear B tablet from Knossos indicates that in the Late Bronze Age honey was brought to the cave as an offering to Eleuthia.[8] The cavern is described in the *Odyssey* as the haunt of the goddess of childbirth and labour.[9] Just inside the entrance there is a stomach-shaped flat rock, worn smooth over 5 millennia by the gyrations of countless, nameless believers: pilgrims hoping to enhance their own fertility through contact with the divine spirits of the place.[10]

It was as a pregnant, twelve-year-old woman, following her abduction by Theseus, that Helen was said to have founded her own shrine to Eileithyia in Argos. The sanctuary was noted by Pausanias as he migrated around Greece:[11] commemorating the rape of a young girl and a bastard birth, the shrine was still the locus of devotions well into the Roman period.[12]

❧❧❧❧❧

And it would have been as a twelve-year-old that a Bronze Age Helen would be charged with the responsibility of producing heirs for the Spartan citadel. Skeletal evidence from the Late Bronze Age indicates that women had lower life-expectancy than men – largely because of the trauma associated with continuous pregnancies and childbirth. A seminal osteo-archaeological survey of Late Bronze Age female bone-material across the Eastern Mediterranean has drawn the conclusion (from traumatised pubic bones) that women would typically have sustained five pregnancies by the time of their death.[13] Other studies of the period show that women might have produced at least one child a year.[14] A Late Bronze Age aristocrat – typically dead by the time she was twenty-seven or twenty-eight[15] – would never have become menopausal; she would have seemed eternally fecund.[16]

Yet we know that the high-born of the Late Bronze Age tried to avoid pregnancy: there are descriptions from contemporary societies of recipes and gadgets used by women to afford themselves some contraceptive protection.[17] The Egyptian records are particularly explicit. Because of their regular contacts with Egypt through trade,[18] it is absolutely possible that the Mycenaeans would have had access to the Egyptian contraceptive recipes which had been in circulation since around 1850 BC.[19] Documents from Egypt show that the Egyptians exchanged remedies with the Minoans during the period of Mycenaean occupation.[20] In the vicinity of the cult centre at Mycenae, Egyptian blue-green faience doorposts, inscribed with the throne-name and birth-name of Amenophis III, flanked a room that some argue was set aside as an Egyptian 'consulate', a place specifically dedicated to the mediation of Egyptian interests and information, including medical knowledge.[21]

The Egyptians favoured contraceptive suppositories (both oral and vaginal) and creams. Some, such as those made of elephant or crocodile dung, must have formed a rather dubious barrier. But old wives on occasion knew what they were doing; one preparation incorporates the tips of acacia (containing gum arabic), which produces lactic acid during fermentation – and lactic acid is a constituent of many modern contraceptives. Many of these unguents and embrocations were bound together with honey and held in place by natural sponges – precursors of honey-caps, today's contraceptive of choice for the eco-friendly.

There is no extant evidence of contraceptive use in the Mycenaean world – we have to wait until the classical period before *Greek* prescriptions and potions are written down. One thing that is clear once documentary evidence is available is that many women relied on polypharmacy for both contraception and abortion; that is, throwing in as many ingredients as possible and keeping their fingers crossed. Cedar resin was applied to the mouth of the womb; sponges were soaked in vinegar and oil; *Vitex agnus castus*[22] was eaten. According to many ancient sources, the latter brought on contractions in labour, promoted the flow of breast-milk, could act as an early abortifacient or suppress sexual desire (the Latin *agnus* comes from *agnos*, which in Greek means 'chaste'). Modern research shows that over a period of time, derivatives from the shrub act as a hormone balancer and can indeed be used to treat a number of gynaecological problems.

It was vital to keep all these tricks and treatments used by women under surveillance, because without healthily reproductive females ancient communities could not survive. So, some time at the end of the 5th century BC, the *Peri Partheniōn* is written – part of the Hippocratic Corpus. It deals with subjects such as menstruation, the hysteria of adolescents, appropriate treatment of the hymen, and far-fetched theories including the peregrinations of the womb around the female body during the menstrual cycle. In the ancient world girls and their periods were a serious, if baffling, business.

Those women in classical Greece who were expected to produce heirs for the family and the community were subjected to regular and intimate physical examinations. The progression from maiden (*parthenos*) to wife (*gyne*) was marked by three kinds of bleeding: menstruation, loss of virginity and childbirth.[23] All these stages would be tabulated by other members of the household. And a woman was thought to be a true *gyne*, or wife, only if she had passed *lochia* (normal discharge) after the birth of her first child. There was intense pressure on a Greek woman's body to behave in an 'orthodox' biological fashion.

∞∞∞∞

Still, the Helen remembered in the stories of the ancient Greeks had passed this test – she had proved herself fertile and, in an apparently matrilineal society, had succeeded in producing an heir for the Spartan citadel. Hermione was the obvious person to pick up the mantle of Helen's perfect, enticing beauty and authors of antiquity fantasised about the daughter as they did about the mother; witness the Roman writer Plutarch quoting a fragment of Sophocles:

> . . . *that young maid, whose tunic, still unsewn,*
> *Lays bare her gleaming thigh*
> *Between its folds, Hermione.*[24]

There are towns named after Hermione, songs written about her, small tokens of honour. Sappho[25] lists her among the great beauties, in a fragment that bears only the words, '. . . *[for when] I look at you face to face, [not even] Hermione [seems to be] like you, and to compare you to golden-haired Helen [is not unseemly]* . . .'[26] But the girl who would be abandoned by the Spartan queen never managed to reach her mother's iconic status. She was attractive, but lacked her mother's ability to floor men – an also-ran if ever there was one. First, she was branded by Helen's misbehaviour.[27] In Euripides' *Helen*, Hermione sits alone in Sparta, unmarried because she has a harlot for a mother.[28] In another Euripidean play, *Andromache*, we hear that once she has become a mature woman, her husband finds her unattractive because she is barren and 'unfit'.[29] But most importantly, because thousands of men willingly fought and died for Helen, it is the mother who is exalted. Helen's beauty is magnified by the blood shed in her name. Whereas Helen still blazes a trail after the Trojan War, many imagined Hermione's life to be cauterised by her mother's crimes. Hermione is a blameless beauty – and she is less exciting because of it.

Down the centuries, however, Hermione proved useful as a foil for Helen's disgrace. By emphasising that Hermione was an innocent, a reject, a victim, authors could really stick their knives into the Spartan queen. The Roman poet Ovid, in his clever, manipulative style, manages to evoke Hermione's grief in his *Heroides*[30] (a collection of fictitious letters from one ancient celebrity to another):

> Oh my mother, you did not hear your daughter's
> childish words, you neither felt her arms
> around your neck nor felt her weight on your lap;
> it was not your hand that cared for me;
> when I was married no one prepared the bed.
> When you returned, I went to meet you –
> I tell the truth – but I did not know your face.
> You were the most beautiful woman
> I had ever seen, you had to be Helen,
> but you asked which one was your daughter.[31]

Maternal neglect is another notch on the tally of Helen's transgressions. As ever, following her footsteps one encounters not only history and myth, but the preoccupations and prejudices of those who have made her their subject.

13

A WELCOME BURDEN

37 bath attendants
13 girls
15 boys
c. 10661 of wheat
c. 10661 of figs
Children, half rations

Linear B Tablet, Ab553 : Rations of Wheat and Figs
for Women and Children. *c.* 1200 BC

CHILDREN ARE DIFFICULT TO TRACE in the distant past – they leave little clutter behind them. In most cases, their bodies have been scavenged centuries before any archaeologist can get to them and their bones are often too fragile to survive in the archaeological record. Sometimes, however, an unexpected ghost of their presence appears. Linear B tablets from Knossos show the delicate palm-prints of small children who had been patting out the clay tablets in preparation for use by adult scribes. In one grave in Chania, Crete, a humble, nineteen-year-old woman has been buried with a late-term embryo, presumably hers. Here, mixed in among the finger-bones of the woman, is a single leg-bone of the baby. Someone clearly thought it important that the two – mother and child – travel to the afterlife together.[1]

It is the Mycenaean homes for the dead that tell us most about Mycenaean lives. But, frustratingly, child burials are scant in number, and thanks to the common pre-historic practice of communal burials and the timeless practice of grave-robbing, it is impossible to trace infant burial patterns with any real confidence. Some burials are plain and simple whereas others burst with gifts. A few are in tombs, others in pits (small holes in soft rock) and cists (oblong graves usually lined with stones) or even under floors, behind walls or in staircases.[2]

One aristocratic girl who died in Mycenae in the 17th century BC, aged about five or six, was buried, hemmed in with vases.[3] Her body was draped with jewellery – a necklace of rock crystal with a blue pendant, a ring of coiled gold wire on the little finger of her left hand and a diadem decorated with gold rosettes on her head. Semi-precious stones – carnelian, amethyst and rock crystal – were looped across her temples.[4] Undecorated gold foil was pressed around the tiny corpses of two other children buried in Shaft Grave III, Circle A. The bodies themselves are long gone – and a finer foil drifts over the place where each infant's face would once have been.

Some dead children appear to have been left with toys[5] – perhaps thought to harbour friendly spirits.[6] Mycenaean 'feeding bottles' have also been excavated from a number of children's graves. These are well-designed receptacles – perfect for the weaning toddler. A number contain residues of honey and dairy products but recent analysis of organic deposits caught and preserved in the rough clay interior suggests that these spouted jugs were used to carry a whole range of substances – including drugged wine. One pretty, striped example from Midea[7] contained a concoction of wine, barley beer and mead. A potent mix. The use of a feeding bottle to administer alcohol does not preclude its being given to infants. A dead baby has usually been a sick one. It is more than likely that drugs and alcohol were used to dull the child's senses as it struggled with a fatal illness or infection.

This being a world before advanced medicine, many children, particularly the poor, would have succumbed to disease. The results of bone tests from the cemetery at Armenoi in Mycenaean Crete tell a sorry tale.[8] All the individuals studied lived between 1390 and 1190 BC. The infectious diseases osteomyelitis (infection of the bone marrow), brucellosis (which produces flu-like symptoms or even degradation of the central-nervous system when the Brucella bacterium is ingested in milk) and tuberculosis were present. There were nutritional hazards, osteoporosis, scurvy, rickets, iron-deficiency and anaemia, as well as cancer. Forty per cent of the children in the sample from this particular cemetery died before they were two, 50 per cent before they were five.[9]

Although a child's life was in constant jeopardy even in aristocratic circles, it does not seem to have been cheap. There is one artefact from Mycenae which hints not at insouciance, but tenderness – perhaps even at mother love within palace-culture. It is a small ivory group – originally rainbow-coloured and inlaid – found on the Mycenaean citadel in 1939.[10] Carved in the round, two women – who share a woollen shawl between them – hug a young child, proudly and protectively, in their laps. The girl or boy (the jury is still out, although the figure does wear clothes usually worn by young girls) sports a full-length dress, tied in at the waist, and has earrings and a necklace similar to that of the older women. She or he is draped across the knees of one woman and leans on the thigh of another; doing that childish thing of taking up as much adult attention as is physically possible. One of the women has her arm curved across the child's back. Her hands are slender but this is a strong embrace.

Whether the tableau personifies divine or mortal characters, it is clearly a representation of the human form and an acute observation of the bond between adult and child.[11] Now the trio rests in the cool confines of the refurbished National Archaeological Museum in Athens. But even there, protected from human touch by glass and security alarms, the group radiates intimacy.

When I first saw the carving[12] I was researching dress-styles in the Mycenaean period but words of Helen's, from the *Iliad*, immediately came to mind. In Troy, Helen confides in King Priam, confessing the things she misses from home:

> *And Helen the radiance of women answered Priam,*
> *'I revere you so, dear father, dread you too —*
> *if only death had pleased me then, grim death,*
> *that day I followed your son to Troy, forsaking*
> *my marriage bed, my kinsmen and my child,*
> *my favourite, now full grown,*
> *and the lovely comradeship of women my own age.'*[13]

The comradeship of women — not, I think, simply poetic imagination. Mycenaean signet rings and wall-paintings imply that women conducted religious rituals in same-sex groups.[14] Frescoes from the palaces show finely dressed women processing along side by side. Linear B tablets tell us that working women spent their days together with their children in labour-gangs.[15] We are even given the names of some of those who laboured side by side: Wordieia ('Rosie' or 'garden of roses'),[16] Theodora, Alexandra and Mano.[17] In tribal Mycenaean culture women, both the rich and the poor, spent a great deal of time in one another's company. It is no surprise that Homer's Helen admits to missing not just her kith and kin, but her female attendants and her companions in the decorated halls.

ↄ◌ↄ◌ↄ◌

In the Argos Museum, almost lost among a medley of artefacts in a glass case, there is another sculpture of a woman from the Late Bronze Age —

a simple, terracotta figurine. She is what archaeologists call a Phi-type terra-cotta. These rudimentary human figures, usually 10–20 cm tall, and often a lone woman with raised arms, could have represented a number of things: the caring powers of women, female fecundity, a votary or a goddess, no one yet knows. But what is certain is that they would have formed part of the day-to-day experience of a Bronze Age noblewoman such as Helen. The figurines are always women with breasts high and far apart – each mammary the shape and size of a squashed pea. They are called Phi-figurines because they resemble the Greek letter Φ: there are also Psi (Ψ) and Tau (T) types.[18]

The little woman in Argos is in fact a *Phi-kourotrophos* – a nursing mother. Someone has rolled a wormy shape out of the mud and given the woman a baby, wrapped in a shawl, to cradle. So far, around seventy of these *kourotrophos* figures from the Mycenaean world have been discovered. Most nurse single babies – usually cradled to the left breast (as you would expect, to keep the child's head close to a beating heart and leave the carer's right hand free). In a handful of versions there are two babies. An example from Tomb 41 at Mycenae shows the woman figure nursing one baby carefully on her chest with a parasol balanced over a second precious bundle on her back.[19]

Archaeologists usually find such figurines in graves, but during the life of their owner they could well have sat on the floor or a shelf, whether in a Mycenaean palace or a shack: gifts of thanks for a newborn child, good-luck charms to keep the gods on side throughout the difficult business of conceiving and then bringing up a young family – the original talis(wo)men. A full 9,000 fragments of the Phi, Psi and Tau female figurines have been found at Mycenae alone, where around 200 new fragments a year are discov-ered.[20] In the settlements of the 13th century BC they would have been virtually omnipresent. And the figurines or figures of men?[21] They are simply not there. The *kourotrophoi* terracottas raise one question about the bond between woman and infant in the Late Bronze Age, and as a collective pres-ence the female figurines posit an even greater one about the spiritual landscape of the Late Bronze Age – and the role of women within it.

14

HELEN, HIGH PRIESTESS

@@@@@@@@@@@@@

At Pylos: 14+ female slaves on account of the sacred gold[1]

Linear B record of 'temple offerings' perhaps to a priestess *c.* 1200 BC

THE *ILIAD* DEALS WITH A NUMBER OF TESTY RELATIONSHIPS: between Helen and Paris, Paris and Menelaus, Agamemnon and Achilles. But the most dysfunctional of all is that between Zeus and mankind. Zeus reigns but he is a flawed and fickle god, who treats humankind like a box of tin soldiers, and just as with a spoilt child, you can never quite be sure when he will tire of his game and start kicking his phalanxes all over the floor.

> . . . *but all night long the Master Strategist Zeus*
> *plotted fresh disaster for both opposing armies —*
> *his thunder striking terror —*
> *and blanching panic swept across the ranks.*[2]

From the Iron Age onwards, audiences who listened to the *rhapsodes* — the singers of epic poetry — would have identified with the struggles of those blanching warriors. These men and women knew that their lives too were governed by the immortal egos on Mount Olympus. They also knew that the gods and goddesses themselves were subject to the whims, foibles and tantrums of the king-god Zeus. Zeus 'the cloud-gatherer' is central to the *Iliad*, because by the time the epic was written down in the 7th century BC, he had become the undisputed ruler of the Olympian pantheon and therefore of the known Greek world. He was, to quote Hesiod, 'the father of gods and men . . . the most excellent among the gods and supreme in power'.[3]

But it had not always been thus. A Bronze Age Helen would have lived in a world in which Zeus was a mere upstart — an ingénu yet to prove himself on the celestial scene. Zeus does get a mention on Linear B tablets, but there is no evidence whatsoever that he was supreme.[4] To date, four, possibly five, figures of a 'smiting god' (a male anthropomorphic deity with his arm raised aggressively, almost certainly Zeus or Poseidon) dating from the 13th and 12th centuries BC have turned up in the Aegean,[5] but so far these are isolated finds. When it comes to the number of totemic female images that have been uncovered, these smiting gods are mere dust on the foothills of mountains.

For the men and women of Helen's pre-historic world, female spirits and their earthly representatives had a pedigree stretching back tens of thousands of years. Gathering up all the figurines and artefacts and fresco paintings created in the twenty thousand-odd years before the Trojan Wars would generate an assemblage of predominantly female forms. A mere 5 per cent would be of men.[6]

Come the Bronze Age, representations of women are still abundant – often shown as creatures who sit somewhere between the temporal and spiritual worlds. They are found in particularly notable form on *pithoi* – the clay jars used for the storage of precious grain, oil and wine. These vessels, vital for the continuation of a settled, farming community, were habitually made in the shape of giant wombs. On some *pithoi* women's facial features, bodies and sex organs have been carved or painted. In the Heraklion Museum, one vase dating from *c.* 2000 BC has been lightly moulded into the shape of a girl – two spouts jutting out in the place of her nipples. Lactating women weren't hidden away, they were glorified, magnified into ingenious terracotta creations that could spurt choice liquid from their breasts.

Just as these vessel-women were the source of life-giving nutrients, they could also nurture death. In some cases *pithoi* are found storing not food but bodies. Corpses have been bent into a foetal position, crammed back into these giant jars and then covered with honey. Honey would have embalmed the flesh with some success for around eight weeks[7] – mirroring the amniotic fluid that had originally cosseted life.[8] Still-births and miscarriages would have been very hard to explain: women appeared to bring forth the dead as well as the living. The womb was also a tomb. Whether she was real or imaginary, Helen was the perfect paradigm for this duality: she was the woman who made love and war, a force charged with both the positive and the negative.

Even in the dog-days of the Late Bronze Age, a time of religious, political and social flux, women are conspicuous by their presence. They march across the palace walls, they are carved onto seal-stones and conjured out of clay. Some link arms and process together, others ride in chariots. On one fresco in the cult complex at Mycenae a woman carries a giant sword, another a staff, a third two sheaves of wheat. A pair of men are there too but they are Lilliputian figures tumbling down, naked, helpless in front of the armed females. These painted ladies give the impression of a gender still holding its own (even if they were doing so by the skin of their teeth).

Priestesses are landholders, they have their own servants (including male attendants), and one Linear B tablet seems to show them dealing in 'sacred gold'.[9] Priestly women have controlled access to supplies of stored food and are called the *klawiphoroi*, the 'key-bearers'.[10] *Potnia* is a term that can refer both to a goddess and the 'mistress' of the citadel.[11] In chronologically parallel societies (the Hittites, the Egyptians, the Babylonians) the highest-born women have central religious roles – they are the chief representatives of the gods. There is every reason to believe that a Mycenaean queen – a Bronze Age Helen – would also have been a high priestess, a religious as well as a temporal potentate. Although Homer's Helen is half-mortal, half-divine, it is as a woman, as a Spartan queen, that she speaks confidently to the gods and goddesses in the epic; she addresses her altera ego Aphrodite as an equal.

Homer's tale of the Trojan Wars, of the final flourish of the Bronze Age, describes the end of an era. For Homer's audience, this story about Helen had to do two things. It had to explain the influence of a woman to an audience who, living in a man's world, knew that this power had been eclipsed. And – even subconsciously – it needed to describe a moment in historical time of displacement and flux: a time when it was still not entirely clear whether the boy (god) Zeus would be king, or what kind of earthly kingdom he would have power over. For Homer (and for almost all sub-sequent authors), Helen was a contradictory creature: a female Janus, with one face turned to the future and the other looking back, a Bronze Age Everywoman who represented a world in temporal and spiritual transit. A paradox. A troubling reminder of the way things once were.

⊛⊛⊛⊛⊛

Sexual politics, particularly pre-historic sexual politics, constitute a puzzle whose complexity rivals King Minos' famous labyrinth. But by following the story of Helen's Bronze Age peers, we can perhaps find some kind of path through the maze.

Let us imagine we are walking through the citadel of Mycenae some-time around the middle of the 13th century BC. We enter through the famous Lion Gate. It is our first point of reference – frequently cited as an appropriately male gateway for the macho rulers of Mycenae. But comparison with engravings on seal-stones of the period shows that this domineering portal is flanked by two worn, carved animals – not a pair of lions, but lionesses,[12] for the animals at Mycenae have smooth necks whereas lions of this period are typically shown with luxuriant manes.

The shrines and sanctuaries of the Mycenaean palace-fortresses have none of the blustering grandeur of Egyptian or Classical Greek temples – none of the 'look-at-me' architecture that typically accommodates the deities of a male-dominated pantheon. The cult centre at Mycenae, dating from the mid-13th century BC, enjoys such conspicuous modesty that it was discovered only in 1968.

I made my initial visit to the cult centre while it was still being investigated – hoping to get a clearer sense of religious practice in Helen's Late Bronze Age world.[13] The inner sanctum, the holy of holies, at first seemed little more than a glorified garden shed. A creaky wooden door swung open to reveal beetles scuttling across the floor and festoons of cobwebs. Eroded earthen steps led to an empty platform. But the investigation was fruitful: this was a secret chamber where grotesque figures, nearly all women, had been stored. Each of the stolid, hook-nosed terracotta idols, now safe in the Museum at Mycenae, stands about 50 cm high and is punctured with small holes: on the torso; above an eyebrow; on a cheek; burrowed through an upper arm – niches on which amulets and sacred offerings could be hung.

Most of the idols have their arms raised, bent at the elbow and facing flat out in front of them. This gesture usually denotes a worshipper, so it is thought that these figures perhaps represent the female populations of the citadel – given their grotesque appearance, maybe even the spirits or demons (the word comes from the Greek *daimon*) within them. One particularly unsettling figure was found with her face turned into a corner. The grotesque, with her worrying evil eye, was left staring for over three thousand years at a wall which would once have been brightly painted and decorated; it is degenerate earth now.

A 'goddess' figure, also recovered *in situ* in the cult centre, is only 29 cm tall.[14] Perfect round dots which circle the divine doll's neck and hang down her chest represent a bead necklace, and her cheeks are decorated with the same spotted lozenges that appear on the faces of women on the frescoes and the 'Sphinx' head from Mycenae.[15] Unlike the disingenuous, pierced, terracotta women, the face of this female figure is kindly and open. She is holding her breasts up high, an attribute typical of representations of a goddess.[16]

Finely moulded rings and carved seal-stones hint at the ecstatic rites that the women of the palaces performed to keep such deities on side. Central to Bronze Age religious practice, both on Crete and on the mainland, is the idea of epiphany, literally the 'showing' of a divine spirit. And in Mycenaean Greece, the divine spirits frequently chose to 'show' themselves to high-class women. Long before Homer writes about Aphrodite on the battlefield, or we hear of Athena's spinning contest with the cocky, competent peasant-girl Arachne, men and women thought that gods and goddesses walked among them and that, given the right propitiatory rituals, at any moment, a spirit might appear.

As Mycenaean women dance or shake trees or collapse over altars, divinities materialise in the heavens, in the form of doves and shooting stars. They peep from behind figure-of-eight shields. One signet ring originally found at Mycenae and now on display in the National Archaeological Museum in Athens, only an inch and a half across (34 mm) has a whole world on its moulded surface – a world where only women are present.[17] One sits down as others dance attendance on her; all are bare-breasted. The largest seated figure is offered lilies and poppies by two adorants; she shakes a plump bunch of poppies which she holds in her left hand. There is a fourth small female figure (a child perhaps?) reaching up to a tree. Just visible, drifting out of the sky concealed by a figure-of-eight shield, is a goddess. The ring is edged with lions' or lionesses' heads; the moon and the sun are in the sky.

The scene is enigmatic. But the proliferation of trees and vegetation suggests that a fertility rite is in progress.[18] And the poppies make one thing clear – these women are employing narcotics to approach their gods. Many other Mycenaean rings and seal-stones bear similar scenes.[19] One golden ring found at Thisbe, near the Gulf of Corinth, shows a female figure offering poppy capsules to a divinity, and a seal-stone from the same site is inscribed with the picture of a woman who seems to be rising up out of the earth, helped by a young man.[20] On another golden ring from Isopata near Knossos a number of women are dancing through lilies, while a figure hovers above them: the ecstatic hallucination of a transported priestess perhaps – or a vision of a godhead conceived by a worshipper who had enjoyed the mind-altering gift of the goddess?

On occasion invisible spirits inhabit a human body, broadcasting their power through a mortal. The women (and occasionally men) who are the honoured subjects of an epiphanic visitation sit on high pedestals or soar above the heads of the crowd. A divine spirit radiates through them. These were women and men with feet of clay, but they were blessed, touched by the force of the gods. Perhaps this belief in epiphany could help further to explain Helen's divine credentials. A high priestess who, during prominent religious ceremonies was thought to be possessed – who enjoyed unusually clear channels of communication with the spirit world. A human with a divine tinge.

∽∽∽∽∽

In the past, the pre-eminence of women in the religious sphere in the Late Bronze Age has been discussed in patronising, faintly pitying tones, as if while men got on with the business of fighting, women simply tended the shrines. But if worship is at the heart of all temporal affairs, it is, by definition, less marginal. And given that women in the Late Bronze Age appear to have had particular responsibility for the successful production and storage of vital agricultural produce, they immediately become fundamental rather than incidental. Women were not occupied with arranging church flowers, as it were, while their officer husbands manipulated international affairs; they were protecting and marshalling the staff of life.

The women that we find represented at Mycenae, Pylos, Tiryns, Knossos and Thebes appear significant, prominent, gorgeous. A striking Spartan queen, in charge of her lands and responsible for the spiritual health of her people, could well have been the prototype for Helen – rich, influential, hallowed. But down the centuries this vaunted position could not be maintained. Helen was a woman who could not be allowed simply to be wonderful. As Homer's reluctant home-breaker, as Hesiod's promiscuous princess – the girl with neat ankles and the sparkling eyes, as Euripides' 'bitch-whore', as Ovid's flirtatious, artful queen, Helen is best remembered for being a flawed human. As she travels through time her brilliance becomes luciferous; the storybook Helen is a fallen angel, forever damned for committing that familiar crime of falling in love with the wrong person.

15

LA BELLE HÉLÈNE

@@@@@@@@@@@@

Heavenborn Helen, Sparta's queen,
(O Troy Town!)
Had two breasts of heavenly sheen,
The sun and moon of the heart's desire:
All Love's lordship lay between
(O Troy's down, Tall Troy's on fire!)

DANTE GABRIEL ROSSETTI, '*Troy Town*' (1869)

ALTHOUGH THE STORYTELLERS FALL SILENT and the vase painters put down their brushes when it comes to the nine years that Helen was supposed to have spent, happily, ruling Sparta together with Menelaus before the arrival of Paris, Bronze Age sources are rich in their representations of the lives of those in power. And the material evidence from the citadels and royal graves frequently tallies with Homer's evocations of Helen as queen.

In the *Iliad* and the *Odyssey*, Helen is typically referred to in luminous terms: she gleams and glistens. At one point, during her sojourn in Troy, Homer envisages Helen wrapping herself in shining linen:

> And with those words
> the goddess filled her heart with yearning warm and deep
> for her husband long ago, her city and her parents.
> Quickly cloaking herself in shimmering linen,
> Out of her rooms she rushed.[1]

This might not just be a literary conceit. As we have seen, a high-class woman from the Late Bronze Age could have contrived a certain lustre: the rich used olive oil not just as a food but to give their skin and clothes a silky sheen. In the *Odyssey* Homer describes women working oil through fabric: '*some weave at the loom, or sit and twist yarn, their hands fluttering like the leaves of a tall poplar, while soft olive-oil drips from the close-woven fabrics they have finished';*[2] he talks of boys who *'wore fine-spun tunics rubbed with a gloss of oil'*.[3] Scholars have puzzled over the meaning of these passages. Is a cleaning process being described? Are the words just metaphorical? Are these clothes really oily, or are they stitched with gold?

A cache of Linear B tablets from Pylos offers an explanation. At the Mycenaean palace of Nestor 100 km west of Sparta there was a flourishing trade in olive oil. On a number of these tablets have been scratched the words and symbols for 'perfumed unguents' – that are to be used on cloth.[4] It seems these unguents do more than just soften. Olive oil, rubbed into linen cloth and then washed out again, leaves a distinct afterglow. Using the unguents is a time-consuming, expensive business; wearing 'shining linen' would have been an honour reserved only for the finest in the palace. An honour reserved for a queen such as Helen.

A lucrative sideline to the olive oil industry was the manufacture of perfume.[5] Fragrances included sweet sage, hyssop, cyperus (an aromatic marsh plant) and rose. Some oils were coloured an earthy red with henna. Women and men (who both wore their hair long) would have massaged the oils into their chests, faces and scalps. The fresco evidence from Mycenaean palaces suggests that women typically twisted and coiled their hair – Helen's famous golden curls[6] may have been decorated with the products of the 'makers of hair braids' who lived and worked near Pylos.[7]

My most recent visit to Pylos[8] was with a cameraman, and (as he put it) we looked and felt like something out of a cheesy drinks advertisement. I was driving a white, open-topped jeep, while he filmed in the back seat. Ancient Pylos is perched right on the top of a steep hill, Epano Englianōs, and so the road that leads directly up to it from the coast describes a series of neat, hairpin bends. As we screeched around the corners, in his viewfinder you would get the odd wisp of my hair, a very blue sky (when I unwittingly made an emergency stop) and ranks upon ranks of the bright pink oleander that grows wild here and lines the roadsides.

It seemed a fitting environment for a Bronze Age perfume business.[9] Given the procedures involved, three and a half thousand years ago you would not have smelt just oleander as you came up that hill. The air would have been saturated with scents – anise and rose and that rich tang from the burning, broken olive stones that were used by artisans and craftsmen as a smokeless fuel.

The organic signals left on the interiors of clay pots now enable us to put together a fuller picture of aromatic workshops across the Eastern Mediterranean. Workers would be chopping and pulverising coriander, cardamom, or the resin from terebinth trees – all substances that have the ability to break down organic material.[10] Obsidian blades have been found, used to slice raw ingredients; these are stone razors whose cutting edge can end up a fraction of a millimetre thick – a blade worthy of any medical instrument. One enthusiastic archaeologist in England asked for his own obsidian blades to be used during a surgical operation.

Soaked in wine or water, the plant pulp made an astringent paste which was then boiled up with oil. Aromatics such as sage and rose petals would be crushed and heated. Oil of iris (extracted from the iris root) was an important ingredient: four thousand years on, oil of iris is still being used in the manufacture of perfume, and today sells at around £3,000 per kilo. The Bronze Age vegetable cornucopia would then be left to steep for a few days before it was stored in elegant stirrup jars. Archaeologists working at Mycenae report that when they removed the clay stopper from one of these, a sweet fragrance hung on the air for a moment and then evaporated.[11]

Pylos clearly produced more perfume than was needed for a local economy. Perfumed oils – liquid gold – were exported by the Mycenaeans in exchange for luxury goods, as well as that raw material that kept the Bronze Age world turning, copper (which combined with tin makes bronze) from Cyprus. Mycenaean stirrup jars – the standard carriers for liquid goods – have been found as far south as Nubia and as far east as the upper Euphrates.

For a Bronze Age Helen, the beauty regime did not stop at a massage with aromatic olive oil. Representations of women reveal dark, smoky eyes – kohl perhaps on their upper and lower lids. Recipes and organic analysis confirm that at this time in Egypt kohl was made from a confection of charred almond shells, soot and frankincense.[12] Galena (a dark grey ore of lead) was also used.[13] The kohl must have ended up as a sticky gunge – essential because this was beautification with a triple purpose: make-up that protected women's eyelids from sunburn as well as acting as an insect-repellent.

All the women on Mycenaean frescoes have gleaming white skin. The range of implements and mixing bowls found in women's graves indicates that substantial quantities of make-up were produced – enough to cover parts of the body as well as the face. White lead oxide was available in the Late Bronze Age, and the iconography of the frescoes suggests that, for particular religious and state occasions, women's heads, breasts, hands and arms would have been painted white and then decorated with colourful symbols.

A striking painted sculpture of a female head dating from the 13th century BC, found at Mycenae and now sitting in a case at the National

Archaeological Museum, stares, glazed, through narrowed kohl-rimmed eyes.[14] Her lips are a cherry red, on her cheeks and chin are red circles, surrounded by dots – they have the appearance of scarlet suns. These symbols also appear on the cheeks of terracotta female figures (such as the 'goddess' from the cult centre) and of a number of women on Mycenaean frescoes. On other frescoes from Pylos, Malia and Thera, women seem to have had their ears rimmed with scarlet. The overall effect is mesmerising.[15] Women made up in this way have great impact: they become walking effigies. Their faces take on the appearance of a mask – their painted bodies move from the natural to the supernatural.[16]

⌒⌒⌒⌒⌒

The sartorial culture of the world in which a Late Bronze Age queen grew up would have been the same for generations. Dresses represented in the art of the Mycenaean citadels are almost identical to those originating, three hundred years earlier, on Minoan Crete, and indeed on the Cycladic island of Thera. The clothes a Helen could have worn would have mimicked those of her great-great-great-great-grandmother. Made from wool or linen, her dresses, skirts, cloaks and under-skirts would have been dyed with saffron, indigo, purple, madder red, onion skins or cochineal from the eggs of the coccus. All the colours were made fast with vinegar, salt or urine.

Linen – the Linear B word for flax is *linon* – stretched to the point where it becomes a flimsy, frivolous material, more reminiscent of organza, would have wrapped around her legs. Richly decorated, heavier fabrics, layered in strips one on top of the other, like roof tiles, were pleated over the top.[17] And still emerging from the earth are punched gold discs – also from the wardrobe of a Mycenaean aristocrat. For decades archaeologists assumed these were a form of coinage; but in fact they are decorations – giant Mycenaean 'sparkles' liberally sewn onto the clothes of their most honoured.

Ivory carvings, frescoes and inlaid gold rings show that aristocratic women, at least on special occasions such as a state celebration or a religious ritual, wore their breasts bare or covered only with a gossamer cloth of silk and linen, and there is no reason to think that a Spartan queen would have dressed differently.[18] The classical Greeks certainly presumed that at times Helen had an extreme décolletée. In Euripides' *Trojan Women*, Paris' mother Hecuba warns Menelaus not to meet Helen again after the fall of Troy, in case the sight of the reprobate in all her half-dressed glory overwhelms him. He does and it does. Helen's shawl has slipped to her waist, she kneels and clutches his knees,[19] the position of a suppliant, but also, with breasts exposed, an act of erotic stimulation.

Whether or not it was sexualised, the female breast was certainly idolised in the Late Bronze Age. Women appear with bare breasts during rituals involving trees and plants clearly associating the mature female figure with a celebration of fertility and procreation. A female breast, cupped in the hand, was the arresting design of a string of delicate beads made of gold, cornelian and lapis lazuli.[20] On one particularly striking fresco from the Mycenaean palace at Thebes, a procession of bare-breasted women – all of generous proportions – stride purposefully together.

Down the centuries Helen's beautiful breasts have been fetishised. The Roman elegiac poet Propertius talks amorously about Helen and her family: '*Thus on the sands of Eurotas Pollux was to excel in riding and Castor in wrestling, and Helen is said to have armed for exercise just like them, breasts uncovered, and her divine brothers did not blush.*'[21] And the poet Ovid goes further: in his imagined love-letter from Paris to Helen – the author lingers just that moment too long when he remarks:

> *Once, I remember, your robes fell open and your breasts were revealed to my eyes – breasts so much whiter than snow or milk or whiter than Jove as he embraced your mother.*[22]

The Roman author, Pliny the Elder, in his popular work *Natural History*,[23] tells the story of a ritual goblet in the Temple of Athena at Lindus on Rhodes, made of electrum and reputed to be cast in the dimensions of one of Helen's breasts. Breast-shaped cups were on occasion used by the ancient Greeks to hold holy liquid – one survives and is on display in the British Museum.[24] Fifteen centuries later, Madame de Pompadour was said to drink out of champagne goblets inspired by Helen's chest. Maurice des Ombiaux in his essay '*Le Sein d'Hélène*' gives the 'mythological' background to the story:

> Helen appeared with her attendants, looking as radiant as a
> Phoebe among the stars . . . the veil which covered her bosom
> was lifted and one of the two globes was revealed, pink as the
> dawn, white as the snows of Mount Rhodope, smooth as
> the goat's milk of Arcadia . . . with wax provided by the golden
> daughter of Hymettus, the shepherd Paris . . . took the cast of
> the breast, which looked like a luscious fruit on the point of
> falling into a gardener's hand. When Paris had removed the wax

cast, the attendants hastened to replace the veil over Helen's gorgeous breast, but not before her admirers had glimpsed a teat whose freshness was as tempting as a strawberry.[25]

Helen's chest in the Late Bronze Age might have been covered with the sheer 'wild' silk spun from the cocoon of the native silk-moth, or with finely stretched linen, but whether bare or translucently veiled, her breasts would have been framed by a tight corset. This bodice, which looks from the art of the time to be intentionally figure-hugging, was edged with braid, crossed over the torso and fastened tightly below the diaphragm. On some frescoes (from Akrotiri on Thera) women wear tassels which swing to and fro at elbow level.

As Helen, or a woman like her, emerged from her sleeping quarters, dressed in all her finery, she must have seemed a vision. Plump from the choicest meats, nourished by the produce of one of the most fertile regions in Greece, her skin rubbed down with perfumed oil, she would have appeared extraordinary. 'Sashed and lovely', as Homer says, 'in all her radiance, her long robes';[26] her own countrymen, as well as visiting diplomats and traders, would have caught glimpses of her moving from one area of the palace to another, or officiating at a ceremony: all that gold draped around her, catching the light and reflecting up onto her face and arms[27] – turning her flesh the colour of freshly collected honey.

Just think of the chink and clatter those generous decorations would have made as the women moved around their palaces. Passing through the corridors, Helen would have been heard before she was seen. There is something fabulously proud about a noisy entrance. No need to slip in or out of sight: when you have high status, the world must take you on your own terms. And in the Mycenaean citadels there would have been a swish and rustle of skirts, outsize sequins clanking, jewellery jangling, hand-held beads click-clacking, leather shoes tapping, as the feet of a Bronze Age queen paced across her decorated floors.

ੰࠕ࠘ࠕ࠘ࠕ

We cannot say what actual value beauty had in the Late Bronze Age: how a beautiful woman was assessed or what she was thought to be worth. But the importance of outward show and of material culture is self-evident. The rulers of the Bronze Age loved and invested in bright, beautiful things. Beauty was traded in the form of gifts. When the richest died, they made their spiritual journeys accompanied by the things that had sparkled around them in life. To associate oneself with beauty was a mark of success and power. Come the 8th or 7th century BC when Homer composed his epics, possession of a living, breathing beauty was thought to enhance both *kleos* (heroic fame) and *kudos* (standing in the eyes of humanity). Late Bronze Age texts from the Near East show that princesses were avidly traded between one ruler and another – their beauty vaunted in the diplomatic letters that set up the deal. In both Bronze Age and Iron Age culture, *kharis* and *kallos*, beauty, and *kleos* and *kudos*, reputation, were powerful currencies. Currencies in which Helen was rich.

A
LOVER'S
GAME

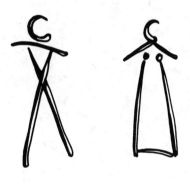

16

THE GOLDEN APPLE

@@@@@@@@@@@@@

*. . . for beauty she [Helen] possessed in the highest degree,
and beauty is of all things the most venerated, the most precious
and the most divine. And it is easy to determine its power; for
while many things which do not have any attributes of courage,
wisdom, or justice will be seen to be more highly valued
than any one of these attributes, yet of those things which lack
beauty we shall find not one that is beloved.*

ISOCRATES, *Encomium of Helen*[1] (*c.* 380 BC)

BRONZE AGE HELEN would certainly have been aware of her own
beauty. One female skeleton from the 13th century BC discovered
in Archanes on Crete was buried holding a mirror, its cold surface
pressed right up close to her face. Early mirrors such as this are made of
metal — some curved, many about the same proportions as our own hand-
mirrors. Like our mirrors too, the frames and handles of those from
pre-history were often finely decorated. They are familiar, instantly recognisable objects. One can readily imagine men and women picking them up
and searching for their image in the disc in front — trying to understand
who they were from the outside, in.[2]

In the classical world, an image of Helen often appears at the base of
a mirror. It is almost as if the owners can fool themselves that the representation of Helen in front of them is, in fact, their own reflection, or that
by holding an image of Helen, some of her superlative, iconic beauty might
rub off on to them.[3] There is a particularly fine example of Helen on the
back of a mirror in the Victorian grandeur and gloaming of the Fitzwilliam
Museum, Cambridge. The Fitzwilliam is neo-classical, charmingly romantic;
Corinthian pillars on the outside, plum and taupe marble within. The Helen
mirror here was made sometime between the 3rd and 2nd centuries BC out
of bronze. Now the metal is a dull green but in its day it would have been
buffed to a high, reflective gloss.[4] Helen sits with Zeus, in his rapist guise

as a swan, and a wantonly naked Aphrodite – she is in powerful company.

A popular vase design of the 4th century BC, much replicated, showed Helen leaning forward, staring into a mirror, lost in her own image while Paris stands behind brandishing his spear.[5] In *Trojan Women* by Euripides – where Helen is a sinister figure – much play is made of the fact that Helen owns '*the golden mirrors in which maidens delight*',[6] and in *Orestes*, the anti-hero scoffs at Helen's Trojan slaves, '*chaps who polish her mirrors and set out her scents*'.[7]

Despite the corpus of created Helens we have surprisingly few clues from antiquity as to what men and women *imagined* Helen saw as she looked into her mirrors of gold. When she is described, stock epithets are used; she is '*white-armed*',[8] her hair is '*lustrous*'[9] and '*golden*'.[10] The ancients were in no doubt that she existed yet there is no attempt to define, physically and severally, what made her so beautiful. Quintus of Smyrna retelling *The Fall of Troy* in the 4th century AD writes that '*shame sat on her dark-blue eyes and cast its flush over her lovely cheeks*'.[11] This is about as specific as we get; the further back in history one travels, the more *the face* that launched a thousand ships is an irrelevance. Helen's physiognomy is less important than how she made people *feel* – what her extraordinary charisma made them *do*. She is not just invisible, she is ineffable.

For classical, pagan antiquity her beauty is too important, too powerful simply to set down, to shackle with portraits or words. Helen's beauty cannot be defined by a face alone. It is literally unspeakable. To witness Helen's beauty, coming as it does from the gods, verges on a religious experience. When the old men of Troy see her walking along the ramparts, they know that this is a war worth fighting, but they describe her beauty as 'terrible' – like that of a goddess.

'Terrible beauty' would have meant more to the ancients than it does to us today – they knew of the dreadful things that could happen if one looked on the transcendental face of a goddess or a monster-woman. The Gorgon's stare turns her victims to stone; when Actaeon, a young man hunting in the woods, catches sight of the goddess Diana bathing naked in a pool, she turns him into a stag who is then chased down and torn to pieces by his own faithful hounds as unwitting friends urge the dogs on.[12] This is why Helen becomes Byron's Greek Eve.[13] If we understand the Spartan Queen in the way the ancients did, her beauty cannot simply be viewed, it is coercive: she forces men and women alike into a state of longing, she forces them to act. Those who look at her cannot walk away unscathed. She catalyses desire. She is an *eidolon* that burns with projected emotion.

☙☙☙☙☙☙

Discourses on the power and meaning of beauty have been mulled over since the advent of the written record.[14] Sappho, Plato and St Augustine all put their minds to the thorny question of where beauty came from, what it meant and what it was *for*. Considered a gift of the gods, beauty clamoured for attention. In Greek thought everything had an intrinsic meaning, nothing was pointless – beauty had a purpose, it was an active, independent reality, not a passive and nebulous quality that came into being only once it was discerned. Men such as Plato and Aristotle, Herodotus and Euripides would have had some trouble with Hume's oft-repeated sentiment of the 18th century AD – beauty is in the mind of the beholder. For them, nonsense. A discrete entity, beauty could be measured and quantified. It was a psycho-physical parcel that had as much to do with inner character as with chest-size.[15] Far from being insubstantial it was thought to wield distinct and determinate power.[16]

The value of beauty – and specifically of Helen's beauty – was analysed, publicly, by some of the greatest thinkers and rhetoricians in classical Greece.[17] One man, a Sicilian called Gorgias, developed such a popular discourse on the meaning of Helen that he played to crowds of thousands in the Athenian agora – all paying for the pleasure.[18] Called the *Encomium of Helen*, Gorgias' was a blistering piece of work – a tongue-in-cheek defence which set up Helen as a paragon; his purpose primarily to prove his own wit and alacrity – to demonstrate that he was capable of defending the indefensible. But in doing so he promoted the 'irresistible force' of physical beauty. Identifying Helen's nature and her blood-line as contributors to a beauty that 'equalled that of the gods' Gorgias argued that seeing her annihilated resistance or logic. Her beauty was spellbinding – an assertion that, in a superstitious age, carried worrying weight.[19]

As an animate attribute, pulchritude needed to be quantified, evaluated and monitored, and as a result *kallisteia*, 'beauty contests', were an important fixture in classical Greece.

☙☙☙☙☙☙

In the 4th century BC,[20] callaesthetic competitions are described in the city of Elis, where the event was called the *krisis kallous*, 'the battle' or 'the judgement' of 'beauty'. There were competitions[21] in Tenedos and on Lesbos, where the format sounds remarkably similar to modern-day Miss World events – women being judged as they walked to and fro.[22] Men too could enter –

although the sexes were always judged separately. The interior of a 5th-century BC drinking cup shows one male competitor transformed into a living maypole – ribbons were tied around particularly winning features of the contestants such as a bicep or a calf-muscle and this well-endowed victor is festooned with strips of cloth.[23]

In Sparta we are told there were competitive ritual races in honour of Helen herself, 240 pubescent girls, naked and oiled, charging along the banks of the Eurotas, all hoping to achieve Helen's level of physical perfection.[24] By measuring up against Helen, though, these girls raised the odds too high, winning was an empty victory – no one could ever be as beautiful as the most famous Spartan woman of all time, the very incarnation of physical perfection.[25] In the poem that commemorates the race, the competitors castigate themselves for falling so short of Helen's mark.[26] Helen is both winner and prize – *the* barometer by which all other beauty was judged. In the 4th century BC, the epitaph inscribed for the daughter of a friend of Socrates, who had run a philosophy school at Cyrene, said that she was '*the splendour of Greece, and possessed the beauty of Helen, the virtue of Thirma, the pen of Aristippus, the soul of Socrates and the tongue of Homer*'.[27]

The *kallisteion* also features prominently in myth. One of my favourite stories is of the foundation of a temple of Aphrodite Kallipugos ('Aphrodite of the Beautiful Buttocks') in Sicily. The story goes that a decision had to be taken as to where a sanctuary to Aphrodite should be located. A living exemplar of the power of human beauty would make the choice. Two amply proportioned farmer's daughters battled it out, the best endowed given the honour of choosing the site of the shrine.[28] Winning a beauty contest could indeed be a matter of religious importance. Since it was presumed that beauty was both a gift of the gods and a pleasure to them, in some contests, such as at Elis, the winners became prime celebrants in a public religious ritual. Carrying sacred vessels to the goddess Hera, 'the beautiful people' led the sacrificial ox to the slaughter stone and then offered up the beast's innards to the gods on the sacrificial fire.[29]

☙❧❦❧❦❧❦☙

Of course, Helen's narrative itself begins with a beauty contest, 'the Judgement of Paris'.[30] It could even be said to begin with that universal of human history, the challenge of an overlong guest list for a wedding. Picture the scene – the nectar is flowing, Apollo is tuning up his lyre decorated with silver and ivory, everyone who is anyone is there on Mount Pelion, because Thetis and Peleus are getting married. Thetis was a nymph, and very popular with the Olympian pantheon. Peleus had sailed with Jason as an Argonaut, a hero and a king. All the gods and goddesses turn up to bear witness to the union, but one – Eris, the goddess of discord and strife, has been left out. Limiting numbers at a wedding is always tricky, but this omission was a big mistake.

As befits the very best of the bad fairies (Eris is rarely portrayed in classical art, but when she is, she is often ugly, sometimes with black wings and pointy, black boots), the goddess of strife is enraged by this social slight, and turns up regardless. Arriving at the wedding feast, Eris hurls down a golden apple (probably a quince) with the words 'For the fairest', written on it. It is a subtle and clever little act of de-stabilisation.

The three most powerful goddesses from Mount Olympus, Hera (Zeus' wife), Athena (Zeus' daughter) and Aphrodite (the goddess of sexual love), each assumes the apple is meant for her. Zeus does not want to get drawn into a cat-fight, so he sends the trio with his messenger Hermes, to Mount Ida near Troy, to nominate Paris as judge. At this point in his career, Paris is simply a young (lyre-playing) herdsman, exiled by his father the mighty King Priam because of a prophecy that the prince will bring destruction to the great walls of Troy. The goddesses assume it will be easy to sway such an ingénu with worldly gifts and so each proffers a bribe.

Hera offers Paris sovereignty over a vast empire, Athena tempts with invincible prowess in war and Aphrodite, fluttering her eyelashes and stroking her thighs, simply promises him the most beautiful woman in the world. Paris is a young man – he is swayed by Aphrodite's bribe, he chooses Helen.

So Aphrodite wins the golden apple. And with that judgement, Paris – having made himself a couple of divine enemies (heaven and hell hath no fury like a goddess scorned) – is granted by Aphrodite *machlosyne*, 'the aura of sexual attraction radiating onto others'.[31] The handsome young prince of Troy is on course to get the Queen of Sparta. He musters an elite force of men – his cousin Aeneas among them – and points the prows of his black-beaked, cypress-wood ships towards the Peloponnese. Homer was right to commemorate Paris' boats as '*trim freighters of death*'. Paris' lust spelt trouble: hidden amongst his cargo of glittering gifts and olive branches, there were swords.

17

BEARING GIFTS

@@@@@@@@@@@

Beauty is a greater recommendation than any letter of introduction.

Quotation attributed to Aristotle by Diogenes Laertius[1] *c.* 4th century BC

EXHIBIT NO. 13396 in the National Archaeological Museum in Athens is a slightly larger-than-life-size statue of Paris, frozen at the moment the Trojan prince stretches out to offer the golden apple to Aphrodite.[2] Even in the bustle of Athens' busiest museum the Trojan prince commands attention. He challenges one to stop; a proud expression, perfect features. When I have been in the musem before opening hours, cleaners, fags dangling, who have swept past Paris at 5.00 a.m. for years, still pay him their respects with a nod and a sigh.

The sculpture, made in around 340 BC and rescued from the sea off the coast of the island of Antikythera, has been cast in bronze, its eyes picked out in rock crystal. Each muscle and sinew is lovingly modelled, the lips are full and slightly parted. Famous himself for being wonderfully beautiful, in many of his classical representations Paris glares balefully out at the world. A passionate specimen, although one destined to be the cipher of a more memorable lover.

According to Homer, the second-born prince of Troy was a bit of a peacock, a man enamoured of his own good looks and eager to further contrive his god-given loveliness.[3] In the anxious minds of many classical Greeks,[4] aware in the 6th and 5th centuries BC of the very real threat of invasion by their forceful neighbours across the Bosphorus, the Persians, Paris came from 'the East', from the 'other side'. Depending on the political machinations of the moment, Helen was either landing a rich and exotic catch or she was sleeping with the enemy.

Western Turkey was Paris' playground, in particular, the Troad, the rich crescent of land that borders the Bosphorus and the Aegean Sea. The myth-stories divulged that early on in life Paris had learnt to cope the hard way.[5] While the first-born prince, Hector, stayed on in the palace, as an infant

Paris was exposed on Mount Ida, left to die because his father, King Priam, had been warned in a vision that his handsome newborn son would bring great destruction to the mighty city of Troy. But he survived and returned as an angry young man to take his place in the palace and, eventually, to fulfil his father's prophecy.

Paris' beauty is much talked about in the *Iliad*. He has the grace of a dancer and a face framed by glistening love-locks. If Sparta was the land of beautiful women, then the Troad was thought to be the land of beautiful men – the mythical home of Ganymede, the son of an early king of Troy, who felled Zeus himself with his unwarranted physical perfection. It was geographically appropriate that a prince of Troy should be stunning. Fitting that he should enter the *Iliad* – and therefore the written record – with the flourish of a matinée idol:

> . . . *Paris sprang from the Trojan forward ranks,*
> *a challenger, lithe, magnificent as a god,*
> *the skin of a leopard slung across his shoulders.*[6]

Down the centuries, Paris has been described as having a youthful, fine, peachy beauty that would make any girl jealous. Euripides details his *'gown gleaming with flowers'*. In a 6th-century AD version of the Trojan War story, his hair is *'soft and blond'*.[7] Later accounts, written from an 'eastern', Byzantine perspective, picture Paris as a luscious thirteen-year-old: '. . . *a blossom of spring and a fresh rose, admired by all those who look upon him. He outshines Aphrodite herself . . .'*[8]

Paris may have had his admirers, but the consensus of both the ancient and the modern worlds is that his dewy good looks made him weak and effeminate – that he was a sap. The Roman poet Horace revels in a description of Paris fleeing Menelaus 'as the deer flees the wolf'. Over one and a half millennia later, translating Horace's *Odes* in 1684, Thomas Creech sneers:[9]

> *In vain shalt thou thy Safety place*
> *In Venus' Aid, and paint thy Face;*
> *In vain adorn thy Hair;*
> *In vain thy feeble Harp shall move,*
> *And sing soft Tales of easie Love,*
> *To please the wanton and the fair.*[10]

Although designed to censure, overblown descriptions such as this unwittingly give a better impression of how a Bronze Age Paris would have looked than does that classical statue in the National Archaeological Museum. The rulers of the Near East commemorated themselves on rock carvings and tombs, they detailed their personal possessions in carefully kept state archives, and so we have an extremely good idea of 13th-century BC court fashions. An Anatolian prince would indeed have 'adorned his hair'. He would also have been crusted with the jewels and dazzlers that were the mark of the Anatolian aristocracy – earrings, necklaces and finger-rings. The statue in Athens is heroically naked, with cropped locks, but a Bronze Age Paris would have been clean-shaven with his hair hanging to his shoulders or below.[11] If he followed Hittite fashions he would have sported shoes with extravagantly turned-up points and round his neck glittering pendants – little groups of charms and amulets, lunate or in the shape of animals and fancy footwear.[12] These Anatolian boys were the original medallion men.

And just as Homer describes Paris with a leopard-skin flung across his shoulders, so too a prince of the Late Bronze Age would have been draped in furs on the battlefield. Late Bronze Age representations from both the Greek mainland and Anatolia show men dressed in animal hides. On the walls of the palace of Pylos, Mycenaean Greeks fight shaggy, skin-clad warriors. Homer talks of the heroes of the Trojan War wrapped in lion-skins, the pelts of grey wolves, caps of weasel-skin and leopard hides.[13] During the excavation season of 1995 at the Bronze Age site of Troy, a lion's jaw – dumped in the refuse along with horses' bones – was dug up in a ditch in the lower town.[14] The warrior-princes of Troy would have identified with hunters from the animal world, borrowing the coats of the kings of beasts, lionising themselves in order to swagger and intimidate on the battlefield.

So, the story goes that Paris, a rich young man with the body of a god and a weakness for women, sailed from Turkey to the Greek mainland.[15] This was a troublesome prince. Strong and lithe, he focused his energies on making love. *'Paris, appalling Paris!'* his elder brother Hector wails. *'Our prince of beauty – mad for women, you lure them all to ruin!'*[16] The poets of Greece imagined him racing across the white-flecked waters of the Aegean, accompanied by Aeneas[17] – drawn to the court of the king and queen of Sparta, tracking Helen down.

We hear from fragments of the *Cypria*, the epic that dealt with those early years of Helen's life, that Paris was entertained in Sparta as a *'xenos'*.[18] *Xenos* is an important, though equivocal, Greek word that translates as a stranger, guest or friend. The concept of *xenos* was fundamentally important to Greek society. Its derivative, *xenia*, denoted an understanding that bound together neighbours and travellers, guest and host. *Xenia* was a code of conduct, an unwritten convention that crossed state boundaries and stitched together the communities of the Eastern Mediterranean. It was demonstrated by a recognised etiquette, involving gift-giving and feasting, and originated in the Late Bronze Age – *xenwia* (which becomes *xenia* in ancient Greek) appears on Linear B tablets where it translates as 'for guest-gifts'.[19] *Xenwia* would indeed have ordered the ingress and egress of foreign visitors to the palaces of the Peloponnese in the 13th century BC.

To mark his arrival at the Spartan palace, Paris was honoured as a *xenos* with a great feast and in return he brought rich gifts from his homeland for Helen and her king. Later authors, knowing of the outrage that was to follow, recognised the irony of the situation: they tell us that at the outset of his stay, Paris, the adulterer, was 'welcomed' into Menelaus' palace.[20] But at this point in the story the Spartan queen and the Trojan prince are dealing with each other in an entirely appropriate way – both in moral and in historical terms. Paris fills Helen's palace with treasures,[21] she fills his plate with the best food Lakonia can offer.

◌◦◦◦◦◌◦◌

Thanks to contemporary Near Eastern records, we know in minute detail of the luxurious and exotic gifts that aristocrats and ambassadors would have brought to their hosts on a diplomatic or trading trip such as this in the Bronze Age. These were not mere knick-knacks – the token gifts and delicate bribes of modern-day diplomacy: chest-loads, boat-loads of treasure exchanged hands. Each item was designed to impress and to solidify relations between rulers. A tacit way for the aristocracy to engage in trade without seeming to lower themselves to the ranks of merchantmen.

In the Late Bronze Age the Hittites controlled the area we now know as Turkey. An Indo-European people whose ancestors had crept over eastern Anatolia during the third millennium BC, they established a central power-base by incremental expansion of their territories. At the height of their command in the 14th and 13th centuries BC the Hittites ruled over a vast landmass, an area that covered much of modern-day Turkey and extended through to northern Syria, the Black Sea and the western fringes of Mesopotamia, abutting the frontiers of the Egyptian kingdom in southern Syria. The Hittites were active participants in the politics of the region; fortunately for us, they were also excellent record-keepers.

The city of Troy was part of an entity known as Wilusa on the fringes of this influential empire. Wilusa was almost certainly a wealthy vassal – a principality, loyal and subordinate to the giant powerhouse that ruled from the east. Documentary evidence attests to (sometimes) friendly relations between Trojan and Hittite authorities stretching back 150 years from the mid-13th century, a relationship maintained by envoys travelling between the two. Troy was a very useful, and very rich, buffer.[22]

෧෧෧෧෧෧

Throughout the 19th century AD, western travellers had sent back reports of curious stone carvings and abandoned cities in central Anatolia. Their context remained an enigma: it was only in 1876, in a lecture given to the Society of Biblical Archaeology by the Rev. Archibald Sayce, a professor of Assyriology at Oxford, that the Hittites were 'officially' re-discovered. Having recognised similarities between rock carvings at Boğazköy, Karabel and Carchemish, Sayce proposed that a great empire had once straddled Asia Minor. Could these, he asked, be the enigmatic Hittites or sons of Heth who are given passing references in the Bible but who had been presumed to be a Canaanite tribe living in Palestine?[23]

Considering the Battle of Kadesh in 1275 BC between the Egyptian pharaoh Rameses II and the Great King of Hatti (a battle which halted the northward expansion of the Egyptians), Sayce realised that he had identified, in the King of Hatti, a leader for the sons of Heth. An archive of clay tablets found in El Amarna (1887) included two letters from the 'Kings of Hatti'. Slowly Bronze Age Anatolia was coming into focus, showing itself to be the homeland of one of the great 'lost' civilisations of the world.

෧෧෧෧෧෧

Today the journey from Istanbul to Hattusa, the Bronze Age capital of the Hittite Empire, takes a good twelve hours, but on my first visit, twenty years ago, hitch-hiking my way east, it lasted two days. These are the high heartlands of Anatolia, reached by travelling for many hundreds of miles across sparsely inhabited plains, via modern industrial centres and through deep, wooded valleys. I was drawn by excavations in the area where new fragments of inscribed stone and clay tablets had been discovered. The voices, ideas and wealth of information flowing from the finds were extraordinary. Having already seen some of the texts in translation in London, I now wanted to investigate their provenance.

Nothing had prepared me for the visual and physical impact Hattusa would make. I had known intellectually about the power of the Hittite civilisation, and had looked at the treaties and the letters that witnessed international relations stretching across the Eastern Mediterranean and beyond. But it was only by walking around this vast complex, wrapped up against the sub-zero temperatures that complement a typical winter season, through the hills and rock escarpments and vales contained within the 160-hectare settlement (1.6km²), that I began to understand what a fearsome force the Hittites had been at the end of the Bronze Age.

And it was only once I looked out across the line of the perimeter walls over and beyond the miasmic plains, at one time the home of lions, panthers, bears and wild boar, and then imagined the reach of these rulers continuing further than the eye could see, up to the coast of the Black Sea, to Babylon in the south and across to Troy in the west, only then did I begin to comprehend what it would have meant in the Late Bronze Age to take on the might of the kings and queens of Hattusa and their allies.[24] Although classical Greek sources came to talk about the Anatolians who lived east of the Bosphorus as 'barbarians', this was a pre-historic civilisation more powerful, more cosmopolitan and more advanced than that of the Mycenaean Greeks.

The central ramparts of Hattusa are 100 feet (30 m) long and 600 feet (180 m) across, bisected with a carefully engineered tunnel known as *Yerkapi*, 'the gateway into the earth'. A section of the walls that protected the site was reconstructed by a team of German and Turkish archaeologists in 2004. These were towering fortifications, made of brick covered with mud-plaster and cow dung. Probably painted white, the walls were topped with distinctive triangular crenellations. As the archaeologists worked, local schoolchildren dressed in royal-blue smocks and chewing on sweets would drift up from the nearby village to watch the walls rise. A number of the diminutive houses from their village down below were made using the same method and materials, but the children of the 21st century were slack-jawed – this was architecture on a scale never before experienced.

In 1905, a team commissioned by the German Oriental Society and Kaiser Wilhelm II had made an unprecedented discovery at Hattusa. While excavating the storage rooms of the Great Temple (the temple alone covers an area of 65 by 42 m, almost the size of a football pitch; the whole temple complex is 14,500 square m), in the central rib of the site they uncovered over ten thousand fragments of tablets in the ruins. As the years went by more and more fragments were discovered, until eventually over thirty thousand had been prised out of the earth.[25]

Each tablet had originally been stored in the serried ranks of wooden shelves that lined the temple and palace scriptoria. Here were the central archives of the Great Kings of Hatti; treaties, diplomatic letters and administrative files as well as scores and scores of religious texts (another indicator that many of the activities we would think of as secular, in the Late Bronze Age fell within religious parameters). Hittite laws were laid down in minute detail – who could and could not marry, the punishment for adultery, the punishment for bestiality, the definition of abduction, and so on.

With the translation of these tablets, the Hittites, at a stroke, had not just a name, but a history. Literate Hittites revealed themselves to be articulate and garrulous – the language used is often fresh and expressive. One scholar has pointed out that the glyphs – the graphic symbols or characters used by the Hittites along with cuneiform – can be scattered energetically across the writing surface.[26] The art of writing was relatively newfangled, yet the Hittites seemed to understand how to exploit it to its full potential.[27] While the Mycenaeans lingered in pre-history, the Hittites were learning what it meant to express themselves through the written word.

Some of the discoveries at Hattusa are particularly relevant to the story of Paris and Helen. The tablets were written in a variety of languages, but one, Akkadian (a Semitic language originally from Mesopotamia), seems to have become the 'international language' of travellers, tradesmen and diplomats in the 2nd millennium BC. In among the haul of fragments found at Hattusa and at other Hittite sites were diplomatic letters that were the equivalent of a pro forma: scribes filled in the gaps where appropriate. Counterparts to these Hittite letters can be found in Babylonian and Egyptian administrations. There is no doubt that in the 13th century BC there was an internationally recognised language of diplomacy and behaviour that was adhered to (all things being equal) by powers across the Eastern Mediterranean.

It is from these diplomatic letters that we learn in detail about the kind of tributes and guest-gifts a royal envoy such as Paris would have been carrying on a trip to an alien court. The tablets that survive deal with relations between the Hittites, the Babylonians, the Hurrians (who controlled much of the northern half of modern-day Iraq), the Egyptians and the Mycenaeans. They are evidence of *xenia* in action and record in minute detail the material sweeteners that passed between rulers. Each treasure would be carefully itemised in an accompanying letter and then packed away ready for the long, dangerous journey ahead. From Egypt, we hear of gift-lists citing golden razors, gold-plated chariots, beds inlaid with ivory, silver sieves, mirrors and washing bowls. Once a silver monkey with a baby in its lap did its diplomatic duty, proffered as proof of friendship, unity and prosperity.[28]

These gifts were paraded or unpacked in front of the assembled court with great ceremony. On some occasions this must have been quite a performance; the Hurrians from Mesopotamia sent out fine horses, complete with tack and chariots. Every power trafficked human cargo, sometimes as many as 300 people at a time. If the offerings fell below expectation the consignment was likely to cause offence. Kings and queens were thought to be *personally* responsible for the calibre and safe arrival of their tributes. Around 1350 BC, the Babylonian king Burna-Buriyash received one suspiciously grey-looking delivery of gold from the pharaoh Akhenaten. (When gold is mixed with a baser metal, it loses some of its sheen and clarity.) Burna-Buriyash had the consignment melted down and was furious at the results: 'Forty minas of gold had been brought to me, but I swear that when I put it all into the kiln, not even 10 minas came out!' He carries on with the finger-wagging: 'My brother must *not* delegate the handling of the gold which he is going to send to me to somebody else; my brother must check it *personally*, seal it and then send it to me.'[29]

Despite all the security measures, heists were a real problem. There were many hostile territories to venture through, many petty kings to be tempted as the diplomatic caravan passed, many soldiers open to bribes. That gold might have left Egypt as yellow as butter, but the journey to Babylon had clearly been long and fraught.

Although gift-exchange was a cryptic way for the great leaders to trade with each other, the political and diplomatic function of all this show was as important. The men and women who exchanged these gifts were *the* players of the day. The bigger and richer the consignment, the higher up the pecking order you were seen to be and, by definition, therefore, you were. In what was becoming an increasingly inter-regional and international (rather than local) economy, guest friendship kept the markedly material Late Bronze Age world turning.

☙☙☙☙☙

But back at the palace of Sparta, the carefully constructed edifice of *xenia* was about to be breached. We are told that Menelaus, almost as soon as Helen had met her fine, gift-bearing guest, hurriedly and unexpectedly set sail for Crete.[30] As one might imagine, given her standing and influence, the queen of Sparta was left in charge of things — with explicit instructions from her husband to entertain their wealthy, honoured and handsome stranger. Who could have supposed that the ambassador she entertained would turn aggressor? Hesiod tells us that 'Helen disgraced the bed of fair-haired Menelaus';[31] had Paris taken her in battle or seized her on the road, things would not have been so bad, but he was a *guest* — ancient authors reeled at his arrogance. It was as though a visitor had not only left the bath grimy, but had nicked the towels and the gold taps to boot. By stealing Helen, Paris defiled the fundamental principles of hospitality, principles that underpinned society and international relations. This was not just a seduction, it was an act of war.

There is another provocative possibility – an often neglected Egyptian rendition of the story picked up by Herodotus[32] and then again in the 1st century AD by the Greek sophist Dio Chrysostom. In this version of events – relayed according to both authors by Egyptian priests – Paris claims to be Helen's legitimate spouse, having been invited to compete for Helen's hand along with 'many suitors [who] came from outside Greece also because of Helen's beauty and the power of her brothers and father'.[33] Dio's rationale for Paris' being at Sparta is carefully laid out; Troy was close to the Greek mainland, there was 'much intercourse between the Trojans and the Greeks', and the Trojan prince had with him, courtesy of his father King Priam – one of the wealthiest men in Asia – coffers packed with Asian gold.

By travelling back to Troy with Helen, in Herodotus' account, the Trojan prince protests he was simply claiming what was his by rights. Swept off-course and onto the coast of Egypt, he swore blind in front of the Egyptian king that he too had been invited to compete for Helen, and that he (and his boatful of Trojan treasures) had, in fact, won the day. The King of Egypt, Proteus, unconvinced, is appalled by Paris' story. He rages – not at the rape, theft and abduction of a wife, but at the flagrant flouting of the unspoken international law of *xenia*. This was simply not the way to behave. Proteus confiscates Helen and the Spartan treasure and gives Paris three days to leave town. It was only local custom that stopped the Egyptian king slaughtering Paris on the spot.[34] Even if Paris was, by rights, the warrior who should have claimed Helen from her father Tyndareus, by stealing Helen he abused something far more important than a woman.

Herodotus is keen to emphasise that his research is cutting-edge and Dio Chrysostom overtly sells an anti-Homer line, endeavouring to prove that the great bard had got it all wrong. But still, could a Bronze Age Paris have been one of Helen's suitors? An Anatolian hero who joined the Greek warriors to compete for a young heiress' hand in King Tyndareus' domain? Was a Spartan princess perhaps betrothed as a child – as Hittite sources tell us many aristocrats were – to a foreign potentate? Were the gifts that Paris brought exchange for a promised Greek princess? Contemporary sources are full of references to fine objects and talents of gold being sent across the seas in return for a bride; we know the Mycenaeans and the Trojans had a close relationship.[35] Did the Greeks steal back a royal woman who was by rights Trojan property? Once again, in the absence of a written history this is *all* speculation, but perfectly possible.

The setting for Helen and Paris' infidelity – embellished and adapted down the centuries – has all the ingredients of a pot-boiler, but it also encompasses central characteristics of the Late Bronze Age. The courts of the 13th century BC would certainly have hosted foreign envoys. Princes, kings and queens would have showered each other with gifts, they would have slept in each other's beds and married each other's women. There is too written evidence that there were acrid disputes between clan-leaders both over the inanimate and the living treasures that exchanged hands.

෧෧෧෧෧

One, particularly pertinent, diplomatic crisis demonstrates that the bad behaviour of a Late Bronze Age female aristocrat could send ructions throughout the region.

Around 1230 BC, Hittite negotiators had been brought in to negotiate peace between two states on the brink of war.[36] The King of Ugarit, Ammistamru II, had married the daughter of the King of Amurru, a man called Benteshina. As was usual with such bridal arrangements, the marriage was a diplomatic one, intended to strengthen the alliance between these two vassal states of the great Hittite Empire. But things did not go according to plan. Shockingly, the girl was sent back to Amurru in disgrace. From the language used in the correspondence it was clear that while in the Ugarit court, the young woman had transgressed some deep-seated code of behaviour: '*she has only sought to do him harm*', the text of the divorce says. It is hard to imagine what she could possibly have done – other than have refused to sleep with the king or, even worse, have slept with someone else instead.[37]

And the story does not end there. Although the princess had been repatriated, the King of Ugarit was clearly still seething. Not satisfied with exiling the princess from his kingdom, he then demanded that she be returned to the Ugarit court for further punishment – almost certainly execution. Eventually, after protracted negotiations, the affair seems to have been resolved. The two states never actually came to blows[38] but the case demonstrates that the scandalous behaviour of aristocratic women in the Late Bronze Age could have significant political implications.

There have always been those sceptical of the notion that the Greeks and Trojans would have gone to war over a woman. But this sort of thing could and did happen in the Late Bronze Age. Even if Helen and her sweet-talking lover Paris are fictitious, a scandal such as theirs would, in the

13th century BC, have been a perfect excuse for Mycenaean aggression on the western coast of Turkey. And although, down the centuries, authors have been quick to label Paris a rapist, a Bronze Age Helen, a Peloponnesian queen, could well have played more than just a passive role – as is suggested by the following fragments of one of the earliest poems written about the Helen affair:

> . . . and fluttered the heart of Argive Helen
> in her breast. Maddened with passion for the man
> from Troy, the traitor-guest, she followed him
> over the sea in his ship,
>
> leaving her child at home . . .
> and her husband's richly covered bed . . .
> . . . her heart persuaded by desire . . .
> [line missing]
>
> [line missing]
> . . . many of his brothers the black
> earth holds fast, laid low on the Trojan plain
> for that woman's sake,
>
> and many chariots in the dust . . .
> . . . and many flashing-eyed . . .
> . . . trampled, and slaughter . . .

ALCAEUS, FRAGMENT 283 (6th century BC)[39]

18

ALEXANDER HELENAM RAPUIT

@@@@@@@@@@@@@

She won the heart
of every man she saw.
They stood in line, sighed,
knelt, beseeched *Be Mine*.
She married one,
but every mother's son
swore to be true to her
till death, enchanted
by the perfume of her breath
her skin's celebrity.

So when she took a lover, fled,
was nowhere to be seen,
her side of the bed unslept in, cold,
the small coin of her wedding ring
left on the bedside table like a tip,
the wardrobe empty of the drama of her clothes it
was War . . .
. . .
Meanwhile, lovely she lay high up
in a foreign castle's walls, clasped
in a hero's brawn, loved and loved
and loved again, her cries
like the bird of calamity's,
drifting down to the boys at the gates
who marched now to the syllables of her name.

CAROL ANN DUFFY, extracts from *'Beautiful'*"

131

Paris' seduction of Helen in the palace at Sparta has been inspirational for three millennia.[2] Most ancient Greek accounts of the seduction – or at least the extant fragments of those accounts – are fairly elliptical. The *Cypria* simply states that after giving Helen gifts, '*Aphrodite brings the Spartan queen together with the Prince of Troy*'.[3] Apollodorus, writing in the 2nd century BC, records that after nine days of enjoying Menelaus' hospitality, Paris 'persuaded Helen to go off with him'.[4] But for later writers, such as Ovid, this episode is a spur to the imagination. In his *Heroides* 16, the poet describes how Paris '*swells up with envy*' at the sight of Helen and Menelaus together. Paris moans: '*When he presses your body to his I drop my eyes, and food I have not tasted sticks in my mouth because I cannot swallow.*' Helen in her turn, trembles: '*I have seen, traced on the table's flat top, my name spelled in spilled wine, and there beneath it, the two words, "I love".*'[5]

This moment in the story of Helen has particular pathos: the Spartan queen is seduced because her husband Menelaus has been called away to tend to his grandfather's funerary rites in Crete.[6] Soaking up Lakonian hospitality, Paris seems, at first, to keep himself in check. He might have watched the Spartan queen too closely as they dined together, she might have left her hand in his just a moment too long as they said goodnight. But so far, so good. Things are as they should be. The regal host has her fine gifts, the Trojan prince his audience with the representative of a foreign super-power.

All would have been well had not Menelaus, the dutiful grandson, dallied one night too many with a Cretan concubine after burying his grandfather Catreus. But dally he did, and in the heat of that Mediterranean night it was not Menelaus' but Paris' shadow that fell across Helen's threshold. The bards' audience must have enjoyed sucking in their cheeks with disapproval as the story unfolded: 'Isn't it terrible, do tell me more.' For visual artists down the centuries the fascination with Helen's abduction or rape – her *enlèvement* – has also proved resolute.

The Louvre Palace and Museum in Paris holds several representations of *l'enlèvement d'Hélène*. With its marble floors, Greek columns and rooms full of treasure, the Louvre is a labyrinthine place. A Mycenaean princess might have felt at home here; she could even have admired the Cyclopean architecture of the new extension – an appropriate place to go Helen-hunting. But just as the Louvre has cherry-picked its architectural inspiration from the ancient world, similarly, the depictions of Helen in the museum show that throughout history this Peloponnesian girl has been represented in a subjective and pernicious way.

One crisp December day I visited the Louvre, in my search for Helen, armed with a list of archive references and the numbers of scores of display cases; I was expecting a visual journey through Helen's life.[7] Instead, what I saw was a catalogue of sexual violence. Throughout the ages, whether in the illuminations of a medieval manuscript, on a grand canvas or a ceramic plate destined for the Pope's table, artists and their patrons have wanted to remember one thing above all else: the fact that Helen was taken by force. I spent an afternoon looking at thirty ways to rape a woman.

On one platter, almost 18 inches (45 cm) in diameter, painted by Avelli in 1540, a muscly Helen has become the subject of a tug of war.[8] Watched over by a kindergarten golden sunset whose neat rays are reflected in the seething, swirling sea, Spartan guards drag Helen back by her cloak, while the Trojans, with their arms around her waist, manhandle her onto their waiting boat. Helen grabs one of the Trojans by the hair; she is desperate. On another plate made in the same year, Helen is strangely childlike.[9] Innocent and sexual at the same time, half-naked, she clings to her captor with her legs wrapped around him. She looks as though she is being given a piggy-back, but her eyes, wide with shock and terror, tell a darker story.

A medallion, just 10 cm across, primarily monochrome with a hint of blue, shows an anguished Helen surrounded by a rough, primitive looking crowd – wild men from the East who apparently cannot wait to sully this pure Greek beauty.[10] A bronze statuette from the 18th century has a more positive passion. Only a couple of feet high, the two figures dominate the room. Originally this piece could be seen in the Palais des Tuileries during the reign of Louis XV. Helen and Paris are caught up in a whirlwind of their own creation. The artwork is vital. Helen surges above Paris, he stares up at her, and their clothes billow around them. She seems weightless, his face lifted by hers rather than she by his arms.[11]

It was that moment of passion enjoyed by Paris and Helen – a moment not of violence but 'ate'[12] (abandonment or delusion) – that brought about the deaths of thousands of men, women and children, and tied up the Greek heroes in a pointless and protracted war. One sexual slip that took on epic proportions. A peccadillo that grew in popular imagination until men like Herodotus could write of it in his *Histories*: '. . . great crimes are matched with great punishments by the gods.'[13] The Judaeo-Christian tradition is often blamed for making sex a woman's problem. But Helen is easily Eve's equal. As one scholar has put it, 'clustered about her [Helen] are all the problems which men perceive about female sexuality, i.e. how their desire for women turns into a problem to be blamed on women'.[14] Helen's culpability is quickly magnified. By telling Helen's story, men manage to make sex the root of evil, and to identify women as the source of both.

A piece of curved, painted wood from the 16th century AD, also on display in the Louvre, encapsulates the situation perfectly. Paris and Helen are placed dead centre. The focus of attention, Helen has one hand to her head in a gesture of despair. Her hair waves but otherwise she and Paris seem frozen – the still centre of a seething storm, for around them, piled one on another in a monstrous, heaving, sweaty crush, are the Greek and Trojan armies. Everywhere is hate, fear, distress and cruelty. Helen and her selfish infidelity are central and primordial.

Sex is powerful. This the ancients knew. In the *Iliad*, Homer writes a steamy passage about the goddess Hera preparing to seduce her husband Zeus. The goddess needs to distract Zeus' attention from the battle down below to give her favourites of the moment, the Argives, a better chance of victory. Helen is never mentioned, but the message is clear – this is what women do to manipulate men, this is how they use love as a weapon. And as one reads, aware that the larger narrative here is the love affair between Paris and the Queen of Sparta, one immediately pictures not Hera, but Helen, preparing herself in her quarters for her guest Paris – as he scents her perfume and paces outside, up and down, up and down, in his chambers at the Spartan palace.

> *The ambrosia first. Hera cleansed her enticing body*
> *of any blemish, then she applied a deep olive rub,*
> *the breath-taking, redolent oil she kept beside her . . .*
> *one stir of the scent in the bronze-floored halls of Zeus*
> *and a perfumed cloud would drift from heaven down to earth.*
> *Kneading her skin with this to a soft glow and combing her hair,*
> *she twisted her braids with expert hands, and sleek, luxurious,*
> *shining down from her deathless head they fell, cascading.*
>
> *. . . and into her earlobes,*
> *neatly pierced, she quickly looped her earrings,*
> *ripe mulberry-clusters dangling in triple drops*
> *and the silver glints they cast could catch the heart.*[15]

❧❧❧❧❧

That night, when Paris and Helen were left alone in the Spartan citadel and the nightjars called, as the palace slept, who, in fact, hovered at whose doorway? Who made the first move? In the *Iliad* and the *Odyssey* Helen is the subject of both blame and praise, so who stole whom?

A host of ancient authors are very clear and articulate on the matter – and given that inventory of violent seductions imagined by latter-day artists, their opinion is perhaps a little surprising. Paris certainly did not have the upper hand. According to Homer, once Helen has teamed up with the Trojan prince, she is never described as his whore or sex-slave, not even as his enthralled bride – but only as his legitimate, equal partner. She is first Menelaus' *'parakoitis'*[16] and then Paris' *'akoitis'*[17] – words which translate as bedmate, spouse or wife. Both the Spartan king and the Trojan prince are described as her *'posis'*, her consort.[18] Helen is never given the title *'damar'* – subservient wife.[19]

The fact that Helen is to be seen across the art galleries of Europe portrayed as a victim is a later manifestation of a rape fantasy. As far as the ancient Greeks were concerned, Helen, instructed by the goddess of sexual love, Aphrodite, made herself irresistible to Paris. The title of this chapter should in fact read *Helena Alexandrum rapuit.*[20]

19

THE FEMALE OF THE
SPECIES IS MORE DEADLY
THAN THE MALE

@@@@@@@@@@@@@

Some an army of horsemen, some an army on foot
And some say a fleet of ships is the loveliest sight
On this dark earth; but I say it is what-
ever you desire:

and it is perfectly possible to make this clear
to all; for Helen, the woman who by far surpassed
all others in her beauty, left her husband —
the best of men —

behind and sailed far away to Troy; she did not spare
a single thought for her child nor for her dear parents
but [the goddess of love] led her astray
[to desire]

SAPPHO, *Fragment 16* (7th century BC)[1]

.

OMPOSING WITHIN A HUNDRED YEARS OF HOMER, the female
poet Sappho was certain that the Spartan queen seduced Paris, or
was, at the very least, willing to go with him, certain that inspired
as Helen was by the passion of Aphrodite, she was not stolen but left of
her own free will.

Sappho's treatment of Helen is important for two reasons. The first —
and most obvious — is that if you believe Sappho lived, she is a rare,
surviving, female voice from the ancient world.[2] She does not write with a
man's idea of what Helen should be. The second reason is that Sappho was
held in high esteem across centuries of antiquity. The Athenian lawgiver

Solon was said to have memorised a Sappho song at a drinking party, 'So that I can learn it and then die.'[3] Plato talks of Sappho as one of the 'wise men and women of old'.[4] In the Hellenistic period she was compared to Homer and was even honoured with the epithet 'the 10th Muse'.[5] Her ideas mattered and so, partly because Sappho and her work were much talked and gossiped about, for centuries no one could quite shake off the idea that Paris might be Helen's plaything, not vice versa.

Along with Helen, Sappho is one of the few female figures from the ancient world who is still a household name. Yet virtually no historical evidence exists for her life. With the exception of one complete poem, nothing remains of her poetry but tattered fragments. When one looks down at these scraps, Fragment 16 is sandwiched between two glass sheets in the Bodleian Library in Oxford – a pathetically incomplete jigsaw – the poetry shows itself to be more absent than present. But when first examining the tiny pieces I realised that in the frieze of intellectual illuminati that had been painted around the walls of the library between AD 1615 and 1620, Sappho was the only woman depicted: testimony to the acumen of the scant words that have survived.

We are fortunate to have Sappho's thoughts on Helen at all; at the end of the 19th century a number of Greek fragments came to light in Egypt on ceramic potsherds or on tiny pieces of papyrus that had been recycled to wrap up mummies or to use as compost. Luckily a sharp labourer spread the news that he was turning up these precious scraps as he farmed his fields, and eager collectors from Europe came to gather up the slithers before they were ploughed back into the earth.

Fragment 16, the poem to Helen, was discovered in the centre of a giant rubbish tip at a place called Oxyrhynchus ('Town of the Sharp-Nosed Fish'), once Egypt's third city and now the little village of Bahnasa 160 km south-west of Cairo. The morsel, which implies that Helen actively decided to leave Menelaus and elope with a lovely eastern prince, was 2.5 m below the surface in a pile of decomposing manuscripts thrown away in the 5th century AD.[6]

We know that Sappho was probably a lyric poet – she composed verses to be sung with the accompaniment of a lyre. The consensus is that she was a woman born some time around 630 BC, of good family, and that she came from Mytilene on the island of Lesbos. It seems that she was a mother: '*I have a lovely child, whose form is like gold flowers.*' Although her poems were committed to papyrus by the end of the 5th century BC, we have no way of knowing whether or not she was herself literate.

Sappho is compelling. Even in the little we have, she speaks to us directly, and through her voice we get a tantalising glimpse of the culture of archaic Greece. Her poetry embraces big themes – death, love and the gods – but her most famous lines seem to serve some kind of educational purpose, guiding and socialising other (younger) women. And Sappho employs Helen to illustrate how, when it comes to love affairs, the female of the species can pull her weight. If her reputation is anything to go by, she was quite a mentor. The ancient world credited Sappho with being the first both to speak directly about love and to describe *eros* as a 'bitter-sweet' experience (in fact she describes it as *glukupikros*, sweet-bitter), as well as inventing the plectrum and creating a new musical mode later used by tragic poets.

Helen was an ideal subject for Sappho, a poet genuinely interested in analysing the disconcerting power of beauty and physical attraction. Anyone who has enjoyed or suffered an intense passion can identify with any number of Sappho's lines: '*My tongue is frozen silent, stiff, a pale flame seeps under my skin, I can no longer see, my ears whirl and hum.*'

In Sappho's version of Helen's story this is the queen of Sparta's call. She already has a husband, but Paris, a younger, fitter, better option, comes along, and she chooses him instead. This was a view subject to soft-censorship. When fragment 16 was first being jigsaw-puzzled together in 1906, the male editors, Grenfell and Hunt, originally had Helen merely cooing over Paris' masculine heroism rather than acting on instinct and actually jumping ship.[7]

It is hard to ignore in Sappho's portrayal of Helen a distant echo of the renowned Spartan practice of polyandry. Polyandry ('husband-sharing' or having a number of male partners) may be part of the Spartan mirage. It may be an outsider's fanciful notion of the lengths that Spartan girls would go to exploit their reputation as viragos. But then again, it may just be true. We first hear explicitly about polyandry from Polybius, a well-born Greek author who was writing in the 2nd century BC, describing practices that he termed 'traditional' – that is, stretching back to at least the 8th century BC, possibly beyond.[8]

By *choosing* the prime specimen (Paris), perhaps Sappho's Helen was living out a custom that the poet was familiar with from travellers' tales of contemporary Sparta. We are told by Plutarch, the author of the *Life of Lycurgus*, that for over five hundred years, in Spartan tradition, women had been allowed by their husbands to pair up with nubile lovers if they thought the young bloods would father more vigorous and successful offspring.[9] If this was fact rather than a later fabrication, perhaps Sappho had heard of this practice. Perhaps she thought it perfectly natural that Helen, a Spartan princess should – back in the mists of time – have indulged in a spot of polyandry.

We may also be witnessing the impact of the memory of Helen on the mores of classical Sparta – where Spartan women were inspired by the tales of their feisty, adulterous ancestor. Plutarch says they are polyandrous, like Helen. This is not to suggest that Spartan girls took attractive youths home as the *continuation* of a tradition that originated with a real Helen's true-life relationship with Paris in the Late Bronze Age. But rather that, given Sparta's intimate involvement with the Helen story, her track record would have been a useful cultural alibi for such a practice. If Helen was plangently polyandrous, then, naturally, other Spartan wives would be vindicated in following the example of their city's role model.

Although it was Helen the rape victim or the scheming, grabbing seductress who came to find most favour with writers and artists down the centuries, there were also those who followed Sappho's line and saw in Helen a woman who, helpless against the powers of Aphrodite, abetted Paris as he stole her away. During the Napoleonic Wars, soldiers brought back from North Italy an 11th-century manuscript copy of a new epic poem. This poem was unknown by scholars: dating to the 5th/6th centuries AD, it had been composed by an Egyptian called Colluthus of Lycopolis.[10] The poem turned out to be another interpretation of the love triangle, another 'Rape of Helen'. In this version Helen, a *'fair-ankled' 'Argive nymph'*, is a willing participant in her elopement.

Colluthus tells us that Helen is stunned by Paris' beauty. She dilly-dallies, she is 'perplexed', but in the end physical attraction wins out over good sense and she resolves to take the plunge. *'Come now, carry me from Sparta unto Troy . . .'* she says. She has welcomed into her house her destruction, just as Troy will welcome in not one but two Trojan Horses, the first – Helen herself. This familiar frailty is emphasised by the repetition of the Greek word *aneisa*, meaning to unbar, let loose, give in to fate or pleasure. Just as Helen has *'unbarred the bolts of her hospitable bower'* to greet Paris, so at the end of the poem, Troy *'unbarred the bolts of her high-built gates and received on his return her citizen that was the source of her woe'*.[11]

In yet another (this time anonymous) retelling of the story from the 6th century AD, the *Excidium Troie*, Helen actually asks Paris to abduct her. The *Excidium Troie* was a standard school text. It was written in Latin, but sparked all sorts of vernacular versions across the West, among others the 13th-century Norwegian *Trjumanna Saga*, the German *Trojanerkrieg*, the Spanish *Sumas de Historia Trojana* and the 14th-century Bulgarian *Trojanska Prica*.[12] Following the same tradition in a French illuminated manuscript of 1406 now housed by Trinity Hall in Cambridge, Helen climbs down a ladder to meet Paris.[13] Helen stares directly at Paris, a slick of rouge on her cheeks, her leg cocked over the parapet as she grips Paris' shoulders. Not the climax of the abduction story we have come to expect. Hardly the behaviour of a reluctant sexual partner.

⊗⊗⊗⊗⊗

In the course of researching and writing this book I made a point of asking friends and colleagues for their own thoughts of Helen. The majority described her as 'the most beautiful woman in the world' but a bit of a nonentity, a push-over. When I spoke to one legendary actress, fresh from her cameo in the Hollywood film *Troy*, she described Helen as 'just a pawn'. And indeed, the Helen in this 21st-century blockbuster bears a worrying resemblance to the other vacuous, submissive Helens that dominate the corpus of western art.[14] We have become used to thinking of Helen as a passive prize, but it is only in relatively recent history that she has earned this reputation. For two and half millennia an alternative tradition recognised a feistier heroine. Not just a woman of straw, but a dynamic protagonist, a rich queen. A political player who – with the help of Aphrodite – controlled the men around her.

PART SIX

@@@@@@@@@@@@

EROS
AND ERIS

20

HELEN THE WHORE

@@@@@@@@@@@@@

O adulterous beauty! Barbarian finery and effeminate luxury
overthrew Greece; Lacedaemonian chastity was corrupted by
clothes, and luxury, and graceful beauty; barbaric display proved
Zeus' daughter a whore.

CLEMENT OF ALEXANDRIA, *The Instructor*
(2nd century AD)[1]

GIVING HELEN INITIATIVE AND A SEXUAL APPETITE does not
automatically grant her standing. Far from it. When Helen is the
active rather than the passive partner, men across time and space
rush to label her a whore. And after the 2nd century AD, in an increasingly
Christianised world, the notion of 'Helen the wanton' takes firm hold. She
becomes typecast not simply as a wilful woman but as a tart. The fact that
Paris brought gifts to the Spartan court was, to the Christian writers, further
proof that Helen's elopement was prostitution by any other name.

The search for Helen the whore leads to the paradoxically serene
surroundings of Corpus Christi College in Cambridge. In the 16th century
AD, a theologian called Matthew Parker bequeathed to the college an assemblage of rare manuscripts. The original collection is still housed in the
Parker Library, where sound is muffled by oak panels and sage-green blinds;
the place speaks of stillness and order.

Here there is a compact little codex. One of the entries is a poem by
the theologian Joseph of Exeter, entitled *Ylias* or *Bellum Troianum* or *Trojan
War*.[2] Joseph seems to have spent most of his life in the French court –
with a brief foray into crusading. His own Troy epic ran to six books which
were completed some time around 1184. Carefully written out in the 13th
century AD on vellum, the lines of chocolate-brown ink are minute and
controlled, each letter less than a couple of millimetres high. In the regular
lines the only hint of the colourful contents of the poem is that a capital
letter every few inches or so is picked out boldly in vermilion-red.

Joseph's diatribe, written in medieval Latin, is both funny and sad. He clearly derives great pleasure from describing Helen's attributes, even making a reference to her *crurumque decora* – the grace of her legs.[3] But Helen has become just another nail in the coffin of womankind. Christianity carried on where the classical Greeks – particularly the Athenians – had left off, demonising women and their sexual power. Female physical beauty was coming to be thought of as a mark of evil rather than of inner strength and spiritual merit.[4] The medieval literature might make for a diverting read, but the outraged language has a bedrock of bigotry. Men such as Joseph clearly derived great satisfaction from immortalising Helen's sin.[5]

Joseph's *Ylias* makes it clear that Helen, as an active partner in her own abduction, is not Helen the empowered woman but Helen the dangerous slut. Having conceded that it is Paris' access to the exotic treasures of the Orient that brings about '*an easy seduction*', Joseph then expands in a passage that is strikingly salacious:

> *Lying on him with her whole body, she [Helen] opens her legs, presses him with her mouth and robs him of his semen. And as his ardour abates the purple bedlinen that was privy to their sin bears witness to his unseen dew. What evil! O wicked woman, were you able to put a check on such passionate desire? Was your lust waiting for a purchaser? What marvellous power in the gentle sex! Woman holds back her precipitate lust to obtain wealth and does not deign to give joy unless her smile has been paid for!*[6]

When Joseph was writing in the 12th century, it was considered a sin for women to be on top during intercourse. Anything other than the 'missionary position' was unnatural because it made the woman physically superior; it was the mark of a whore and was thought to pervert the course of semen.

So, branded by theologians not only as adulterers but as sexual deviants, Helen and Paris feature prominently in influential Christian texts such as *The Plaint of Nature*, written between 1160 and 1175 by the poet and theologian Alan de Lille,[7] and conceived as a heartfelt cry from Mother Nature herself at the abuse of her natural laws; de Lille even manages to blame Helen for encouraging Paris to turn to other men to satisfy his excess of lust.

> Why did I deify with a godlike beauty the face of Tyndareus' daughter who forced the use of her beauty to decline to the abuse of harlotry, when, sullying the covenant of her marriage-bed, she formed a disgraceful alliance with Paris.

No longer does the Phrygian adulterer chase the daughter of
Tyndareus but Paris with Paris performs unmentionable and
monstrous deeds.[8]

For committing similar sexual sins, the medieval laity would expect to have
to perform a series of penitentials. For 'unnatural' sexual positions penances
could last forty days or even more. Denial, fasting, fines, constant prayers,
standing outside the church wearing a white hat or carrying a white wand
were all typical penances for the period. For adultery the 7th-century *Canons
of Theodore* prescribe for a three-year period of two days of abstinence from
sex every week, plus three blocks of forty abstinent days. Women who
committed adultery had to do penance for seven years.[9] In the 11th century,
St Peter Damian preaches a required period of twenty-five years fasting and
penance for married couples over the age of twenty who have indulged in
'deviant' sexual positions. These 'bestial acts' and 'whorish embraces' were
thought to lead to all kinds of human misery; one late medieval theologian went so far as to say that God had sent the biblical Flood because
he'd espied a couple having sex with the woman on top.[10]

And, of course, despite all these warnings, despite the carmine caveat
that Helen became, despite the bile that dripped from the pens of these
theologians, ordinary men and women carried on abusing Mother Nature
and incurring the wrath of the Church, regardless. For every woman that
was branded a Helen and wore a white penitential cap in the corner of a
church, there was a novice in the convent library who pored over translations of Ovid's love letters. For every poet that wanted to see Helen and
Paris burn in hell, there have been ten who held the curtains aside to let
the Trojan step into the Spartan queen's bed.

Homer's Helen was created in a time before good and evil were thought
to be two vast, magnetic forces – each at a different pole, each sucking
humankind towards it. For the Greeks, things were less clear-cut; the gods
themselves were in part good, in part bad. Helen is the perfect example of
a Greek archetype, a woman who is ambiguous, who is at once *chiaroscuro*.
But for the Christianised West this was a difficult concept to deal with.
Although the Christian writers do not dispute Helen's breeding or deny her
her cultic crown, it is hard to describe Helen as very, very good, and therefore she has to be very, very bad – in fact, a diabolical whore.

When Chaucer painted a rather gallant picture of Helen as the 'faire
queene eleyne', he was quite possibly playing on a homophonic connection
with the word for a harlot, 'a quene'.[11] In Dante's *Inferno* Helen inhabits
Circle Two – the sphere of the carnal and the lustful. And come the

Elizabethan period she is frequently found in the ranks of those damned for whoring. In 1578, the author of *The Reward of Whoredome by the Fall of Helen*, Thomas Proctor, paints her as a courtly prize and then comes in for the kill by describing her as encapsulating prostitution's 'vilde filthy fact'.[12] In Richard Robinson's *The Reward of Wickedness* (1574), she suffers indescribable torments alongside 'Popes, harlots, proude princes, tyrants and Romish bishops'.

Five hundred years after *The Plaint of Nature* was written, the notion of Helen as whore was still in vogue. Take the influential words of Alexander Ross, a reforming Scottish minister, who, in 1648, brought out a populist and popular guide to the classics, a kind of alphabetical myth-dictionary:

> . . . for she had a deform'd soul, playing the strumpet, not only in her younger years with Theseus . . . but also being married to Menelaus, forsook him, and became a whore to Paris; and not content with him, committed incest with Gorythus, the son of Paris and Oenone; afterward betrayed the city of Troy to the Grecians, and treacherously caused her husband Deiphobus to be murdered in his bed by Menelaus . . . thus we see, that outward beauty of the body, without the inward graces of the mind, is but a gold ring in a swine's snout.[13]

If their implications were not so tragic, diatribes like this might amuse. Helen is the woman men love to love and love to hate.

❧❧❧❧❧❧

When following Helen's progression through time it is important to remember one thing: medieval society came to see Helen's affair with Paris as an act *against* God.[14] But for the Greeks and Romans it was most commonly believed to be the act *of* a god, or, rather, of a goddess – Aphrodite. Not simply a woman of unbridled lusts, Helen is also a prism through which Aphrodite's power shines. Erotic impetus comes from Aphrodite – thus, for example, in the *Iliad* and the *Odyssey*, Helen preserves an air of wronged innocence. This is all the goddess's doing, not hers. Helen is simply playing by love's rules, as the Roman poet Ovid in his *Art of Love* – admittedly with his tongue planted firmly in his cheek – expounds:

> While Menelaus was away, Helen, that she should not lie alone, was welcomed at night by the warm bosom of her guest. What

folly was this, Menelaus? You went away alone; your wife and her guest were beneath the selfsame roof. Madman, do you trust timid doves to a hawk? Do you trust a full sheepfold to a mountain wolf? In naught does Helen sin; in naught is that adulterer to blame: he does what you, what anyone would have done . . . Helen I absolve from blame: she used the opportunity a courteous lover gave.[5]

21

THE PAIN OF APHRODITE

In her bed, peace of mind is a rare prize.
Blessed is anyone who finds calm there,
Where most are driven mad.
Eros the hovering golden-haired boy with the bow
Has but two arrows in his quiver.
The one brings bliss.
The other casts a net of confusion
And chaotic pain

The chorus of maidens from Euripides,
Iphigeneia at Aulis[1]

W HEN HE AGREED TO ADJUDICATE the beauty contest between the three goddesses at Mount Ida, Paris probably had not banked on being a judge who would never be able to shake off one of the contestants. Because where Helen goes, Aphrodite goes too. She is there on Greek vases at the Spartan palace as Paris arrives: indomitable, blocking Helen's escape into another picture or another story. She is there at Troy, plucking Paris from the battlefield, as the pathetic prince crumples in a man-to-man fight against Menelaus. Coddling her playboy, the goddess both saves and shames the handsome second-born son of Troy.

In many retellings of the story, Aphrodite acts as Helen's fluffer. Take, for example, the following description of Aphrodite (one of the first ever written down). The goddess is on her way to meet Paris on Mount Ida. Aphrodite's mission, to persuade the boy that of the three premier goddesses she is the fairest – she wants that golden apple. Embedded in the lush, dewy, fecund setting of the natural world, it is immediately obvious the young lad does not stand a chance:

She set on her skin the garments which the Graces and the Seasons had made
and dyed in the flowers of spring-time, garments such as the Seasons wear,

dyed in crocus and hyacinth and in the blooming violet and in the fair flower of the rose, sweet and fragrant, and in ambrosial flowers of the narcissus and the lily.[2]

Over a thousand years later, the author Colluthus (the man who describes Helen unbarring her door to Paris) imagines how, during the Judgement of Paris, the goddess *'lifted up her deep-bosomed robe and bared her breast to the air and had no shame. And lifting with her hands the honeyed girdle of the Loves she bared all her bosom and heeded not her breasts.'*[3]

Aphrodite does not go so far as to make love to Paris, but she clearly gets more than a little vicarious pleasure out of leading Helen and Paris to each other's beds. Homer, for example, describes how in the dog-days of the Trojan war, Aphrodite stands at the door of the prince's bedchamber, ordering Helen in, rousing and commanding her two royal work-horses to worship her in the act of sex. Helen whips round on the goddess (her confidence an indication of her own quasi-divine pedigree) and asks: *'Where will you drive me next? Off and away to other grand, luxurious cities, out to Phrygia . . . Have you a favourite mortal man there too? . . . Well, go to him yourself – you hover beside him! Abandon the gods' high road and be a mortal!'*[4]

Aphrodite is only ever moments away, because she is both Helen's muse and her altera ego. And Helen is Aphrodite's mortal surrogate. In some traditions the pair are mother and daughter. If Aphrodite is the goddess of sex, Helen is sex incarnate. The two are a potent combination and they are inextricable. Paris has got himself caught up in an intense love triangle; he is outnumbered and he is to be pitied, not envied: Aphrodite's bed is a place you are 'driven mad' as Euripides instructed his 5th-century BC audience.[5]

So why is the goddess of love so terrible? Why is she such a pernicious partner for Helen? Why is Helen's allure so destructive? Why do the Greek playwrights and poets sing of her beauty and then describe her as a bitch, a whore, a demon? Why should it seem inevitable that Helen's and Paris' excessive love would lead to an excess of killing on the battlefields of Troy? Why credit Helen with the crime of loving and being loved to excess, of willing Eros' second arrow out of his quiver?

To answer those questions, we have to look way back in Greek mythology, back to the origins of being, back before the beginning of time. Back to Aphrodite's birth. Hesiod, in the 7th century BC, wrote a revisionist theology – the *Theogony* – that told of the origins of the gods and of the earth. As with Homer, Hesiod's works became canonical. Some of his most striking passages deal with the world's emergence from disorder and Aphrodite was one of the first inhabitants of this primordial world, the only divinity who was thought to have survived from the origins of the cosmos through to the establishment of the Olympian pantheon. Euripides described her as 'greater even than the gods'. An archaic hymn articulates the power she has over gods and men alike:

> *The sacred Heaven feels the desire to penetrate the Earth (Gaia), the Earth is consumed by the desire to enjoy coitus: the rain comes down from the Heaven husband like a kiss toward the Earth, and it gives birth to herds that graze for mortals and the fruit of life of Demeter, as the spring foliage comes to an end under the dew of the hymen, and I am the one who is cause of all this,*[6]

The world began with Chaos – a hideous mêlée of nothingness and everything. Out of Chaos, Earth (Gaia) and her dark underbelly Tartarus emerged. Earth then gave birth to Ouranos, the 'starry heaven', and proceeded to sleep with her heavenly child. Among the offspring of this grand pairing were the Titans and monsters. Ouranos feared these monsters so he continually copulated with Gaia in order to trap their hideous children inside Mother Earth's womb.

But Gaia wanted her brood released and persuaded her firstborn Titan son to collude in a dastardly scheme. Together they cut off Ouranos' erect penis and testicles while he was engaged in his eternal love-making. The bloody castrates were hurled into the ocean and Aphrodite emerged from the foaming spume, dragging herself out onto the shores of Cyprus (hence her alternative name Cypris).[7] It was a suitably gory genesis for a female who brought with her as much pain as she did pleasure. Aphrodite was a being to fear as well as to solicit. The ancients talked of love as 'Aphrodite's disease', a sickness that invaded and controlled the mind and body, causing both to melt or wither away. Pausanias reported that some Greeks would bathe in a river in Achaia called the Selemnos because they thought it would bring a cure for the dreadful affliction of love itself.[8]

Detailing the generation of the divine powers, Hesiod tells us of Aphrodite's birth and that immediately after her come Night's children. The three firstborn are all given the names of morbidity: *Moros* (destiny), *Ker* (death) and *Thanatos* (everlasting sleep). Swiftly following on their heels is *Eris*, strife. The little deaths, the *petites morts*, follow Aphrodite as she sweeps through others' lives. They clutch at her fine *chiton* (when she is wearing one) but as she passes, the scent she leaves on the air can carry the cloying sweetness of decay.

Also hanging on to Aphrodite's skirts is her wounding son Eros. When

Aphrodite cannot be there herself with Helen and Paris she sends this spiky spawn in her place. With his beating wings fanning the flames of passion, Eros commits Paris to a febrile death:

> *'Thou wilt bring conflagration back with thee! How great the flames thou seekest over these waters, thou dost not know!' A truthful prophetess was she; I have found the fires of which she spoke, and flames of fierce love rage in my helpless breast!*[9]

Authors continually played on Helen's fervid nature. Her beauty sears. It lights a touch-paper, it sparks the infernal abandon of sex. Ovid's poem *Heroides* 16 is profligate in its use of inflammatory language. Paris declares he is '*on fire with love*'. Misunderstanding Hecuba's prophecy at his own birth he muses: '*One of the seers sang that Ilion would burn with the fires of Paris — that was the torch of my heart, as now has come to pass!*' He tells Helen: '*Like a great queen you will make your progress through the Dardanian towns, and the common crowd will think a new goddess come to earth; wherever you advance your steps, flames will consume the cinnamon, and the slain victim will strike the bloody earth.*'[10]

There was duplicity in all this fiery talk. Fire gave light and warmth and comfort, but it was also perilous — one of the greatest hazards of the ancient world. The archaeological record shows that domestic, military and natural infernos were by far the most common agents of destruction. '*Paris himself is said to have burned at the sight of Helen naked, when she rose from the bed of Menelaus.*'[11] The ancients chose their words carefully — consumption in a sexual conflagration was thrilling and equivocal. Beautiful Helen, allied with Aphrodite and Eros, delights and she destroys.

☙❧☙❧☙

It would take four hundred centuries or so for Greek Eros to become Roman Cupid — a cheeky, impish little *putto*, destined to pierce hearts with his arrows of love on mawkish Valentine cards. For the Greeks, particularly the early Greeks, Eros, born out of chaos, is something far more pernicious — forget the cute, plump little baby and think instead of a malevolent, rangy boy. For the Ancient Greeks Aphrodite and Eros catalyse a crazed, keening frenzy for lust and lust for frenzy.

Eros was well taught by his mother. In ancient Greek literature he consumes flesh and spirit; he can invade like a virus, he can corrode like a poisonous chemical.[12] Socrates (if we believe he was faithfully represented by his interpreters) was equally imaginative in his description of the effects of love. For him, love's kisses resembled the bite of a venomous spider – worse in fact, since Eros[13] did not need physical contact between two organisms to start his poisonous work.[14] Not only does Eros destroy, he also emasculates. Hesiod's articulation of Eros' power has close parallels with the impotence of the moment of death. Eros is *'lusimeles'*: he who unbinds, who loosens, who breaks the limbs.[15]

The Greeks delighted in the subtleties of language, in the power of words. Alcman, the poet who gave those young Spartan girls such sensuous lines to sing, such rhythms to dance to, sees women as an even more powerful agent of dissolution than death itself. 'By the desire that loosens the limbs [*lusimeles*], she [a woman] has a gaze that is more liquefying [*takeros*] than Hypnos (sleep) or Thanatos (death).'[16] Odysseus' swineherd Eumaios says of Helen *'she loosed the knees of many men'*.

Aphrodite was a primal creature, and when men loved women like Helen, they were embracing a murky, primordial power. Aphrodite was wild in all senses of the word[17] and since Helen was a city girl, as she served Aphrodite, she brought that wilderness to the beds of princes and kings, to the citadel of Sparta and to *'the topless towers of Ilium'*.[18] Coaxing unpredictable, fickle, fathomless nature back into the new culture of the city meant destruction was inevitable. For the Greeks, the weeds that have now seeded themselves in the broken walls of Troy, and the grasses that grow over neglected flagstones, would have been reminders of Helen.

In very many she created very strong amorous desires; with a single body she brought together many bodies of men.[19]

22

THE SEA'S FOAMING LANES

@@@@@@@@@@@@@@

> . . . [Paris] braved the seas in his racing deep-sea ships,
> trafficked with outlanders, carried off a woman
> far from her distant shores, a great beauty
> wed to a land of rugged spearmen.

HOMER, *Iliad*[1]

T HE DIE IS CAST. Stealing together out of the royal apartments, Helen and Paris race from the Spartan citadel towards the coast. This is a nocturnal adventure. They have just a few hours before the alarm bells are sounded. Colluthus in his epic poem *The Rape of Helen*, tells us that it was only the following morning that Helen's absence was noted. He imagines an abandoned, nine-year-old Hermione dashing through the Spartan palace. The young girl is innocent and unsuspecting, weeping inconsolably. Her mother has vanished, so too has the handsome prince who visited the court from Troy. Hermione presumes that Helen must have been taken by wild beasts, or have been drowned in a stream. Of course, she could never, never have done anything as despicable and shameful as running off with another man:

> *And Hermione cast to the winds her veil and,*
> *as morning rose, wailed with many tears. And often taking her handmaidens*
> *outside her chamber, with shrillest cries she uttered her voice and said:*
> *'Girls, whither hath my mother gone and left me in grievous sorrow, she*
> *that yester-even with me took the keys of the chamber and entered one bed*
> *with me and fell asleep?' So spake she weeping and the girls wailed with*
> *her. And the women gathered by the vestibule on either side and sought to*
> *stay Hermione in her lamentation.*[2]

But the weeping would be in vain: it was too late. From Homer we learn that the fugitives spend their first night of passion together on the tiny island of Kranai. Ten years later, in the *Iliad*, as bodies tumble around the walls of Troy, Paris relives the moment. His words are heavy with yearning, spiced with the sorrow of illicit sex. Helen and Paris have just had a row and pricked by Paris' poor show against Menelaus, Helen lashes out at her feeble lover. But her sharp tongue excites rather than chastens:

> But come [says Paris]
> let's go to bed, let's lose ourselves in love!
> Never has longing for you overwhelmed me so,
> no, not even then, I tell you, that first time
> when I swept you up from the lovely hills of Lacedaemon,
> sailed you off and away in the racing deep-sea ships
> and we went and locked in love on Rocky Island . . .
> That was nothing to how I hunger for you now —
> irresistible longing lays me low![3]

Poor Paris, for the last two thousand years, his making passionate love in the afternoon like this, even to his 'wife', has been, for a number of commentators, the final nail in the young man's coffin, proof positive that he was dissipated and amoral.

※※※※※

To get to Kranai from Sparta you leave the protective embrace of the Taygetan mountain range and travel southwards to the little port of Gythion.[4] Today, with its bobbing fishing boats and pastel-painted guest houses, Gythion is the perfect place for a romantic tryst. Approaching the town there are small hills to climb through and the way can be rough. A traveller from the Hellenistic period onwards would have passed a little shrine on the roadside harbouring 'Helen's sandal' – a holy relic left in the mad dash to get from the Spartan citadel to Paris' waiting boats.[5]

Kranai is easily visible from the harbour-side at Gythion. It is a tiny island, little more than a rock and so close to the mainland that the two are now joined by a causeway. Homer was right to describe it as '*kranae*' – 'craggy' or 'rocky'; the island is still ringed with a curious dove-grey volcanic outflow. These rocks are unevenly eroded; if you try to cross them to get to the shoreline, your hands will be lacerated and your shoes punctured by their edges as sharp as spears. Kranai is a hard place to lose yourself – but at least Helen and Paris would have been alone here. If indeed Helen had been seized by force she could have been raped in the flimsy boat built of cypress wood, held up against the interior skin of stretched, oiled linen, and violated while Aeneas and his men took a break from cataloguing their loot, to watch. Perhaps Kranai was thought to be an opportunity for private passion, a sex act more appropriate to a queen.

The stories tell us that this was a brief stop-over, just enough time for the Trojan contingent to load supplies from the traders at Gythion, Sparta's port in antiquity and a natural harbour in the 13th century BC.[6] Although Homer's description of that first night of passion may just be a fable, this is certainly an appropriate setting; there was indeed a Bronze Age settlement here.[7]

~~~~~~

What were all the world's alarms
To mighty Paris when he found
Sleep upon a golden bed
That first dawn in Helen's arms?

YEATS, 'Lullaby' (1929)

Whether Paris was a rapist or a complicit liberator, at this moment his cup was running over. The prince had Helen and he had a boatload of treasure – plunder from the Spartan citadel. The idea of the booty and the beauty leaving Sparta together has offered artists down the ages a lewd and luscious subject. Nicolo dell' Abate drew a version in 1512 which was then touched up a century later by Rubens, who added details that make the scene bristle with violence.[8] In his version Helen's hair is being dragged back, though in the original she seems resigned to her fate. Rubens forces her to stare back at the Spartans in desperation. Paris is redrawn: his left leg now kicks one of the Greeks in the groin, while a Trojan sailor sinks his hands into the robes of Paris' living, lovely prize.

Scholars have made a good argument for the pronounced emphasis on the theft of treasure as well as of Helen herself, simply being a way of 're-masculating' the Greeks. From the classical period onwards, a number of writers have found the idea that Greece should rise to arms over a woman ludicrous and belittling. And so references to the stolen treasure crop up again and again. When Agamemnon led his men to Troy, he was not just drawn by a woman, which would be the act of a feeble fool, but went to steal back Greek riches.

If an aristocrat had made a sea journey from one palatial centre to another in the Late Bronze Age, it is highly likely that the elegant galley would indeed have been heavy with swag. Paris and his men would have loaded their boats with Mycenaean goods and precious raw materials, as well as with the beautiful Helen. In a sense Bronze Age society was ultimately materialistic – the Eastern Mediterranean was becoming one baggy, local economy and each royal court derived great standing from the exotic effects it could acquire. This was, after all, an age without coined money. The world would have to wait for coinage until the Lydians, in the second half of the 7th century BC, punched out roughly shaped discs of electrum, a natural alloy of gold and silver. Instead, wealth comprised material goods. So axes, daggers, rings, seal-stones and hides, rich tapestries and bronze armour, hippopotamus ivory and rare stones were used for trade and gift-exchange.[9]

The mechanisms that kept the flow of Bronze Age raw materials, artefacts and spoil in circulation were the oceans, rivers and tributaries that linked one great trading port with another – seas that were 'wine-dark', sings Homer; 'the Great Green', say the Egyptians. It is worth stating the obvious – that the Mediterranean region is the only landmass identified by its adjacent sea. We think of waterways as barriers but the Aegean, the Bosphorus and the Mediterranean and Libyan Seas were the highways and byways of pre-history. Homer even calls them 'the sea's foaming lanes'. A single boat of the period had almost 200 times the haulage capacity of a donkey;[10] although land trade-routes were well developed, the oceans were heavily patronised by merchants, aristocrats, journeymen, pirates and buccaneers.

We might characterise Helen as an inanimate object, who famously sat out a ten-year siege at Troy, yet in fact her story is a kinetic one and the rivers and oceans of the Eastern Mediterranean are central to her tale. She is conceived when her mother is raped on the banks of the Eurotas by a giant waterfowl. Eight, nine, ten, eleven, twelve years later she too will be violated on the banks of the river. Paris comes to her by boat, and she leaves with him to cross back over the waters. A naval expedition is launched by the Greeks to retrieve her. Once Helen leaves Troy she spends seven years sailing with Menelaus; she visits Cyprus, the Phoenician city of Sidon, Crete and Egyptian Thebes where she is given gifts including a fine golden spindle.[11] Even after her death Helen flits between the Isles of the Blest and earthly cult sites (many on islands, a number next to natural springs) from Bithynia to Egypt. Or she watches over the Oceans as a star alongside her brothers, the twins Castor and Pollux.[12]

Interestingly, it is in the late medieval paintings of Helen's story that the maritime setting really comes to the fore. The 13th century AD marked a rejuvenation of international trade. The Italian Renaissance was partly funded by the money that came in through Italian ports.[13] Perhaps artists and their sponsors felt an affinity with a tale that told of the transfer of precious treasures, back and forth across vast, dangerous seas. During this period Helen is often depicted at the water's edge; a rowing boat or a fine Trojan galleon in the bay ready for her.

One version of the story of Troy, written in the 6th century AD, has Paris stealing Helen's heart as she worships Aphrodite at a seaside temple on the island of Kythera.[14] (There are archaeological records of a shrine to Aphrodite on Kythera from the 6th century BC, and of her eastern predecessor Astarte from the 8th century BC.) This coastal version of Helen's rape was a popular choice for Italian marriage chests or birth trays, '*desco da parto*'. It may seem a little odd that young brides or first-time mothers would be honoured with a scene of such abuse and uxorial duplicity, but Helen's story is a series of rites of passage – and so as women (flattered perhaps by their conflation with Helen) made their own journeys, becoming wives, mothers and widows, Helen came with them.[15]

One such birth tray, in the establishment, neo-classical glory of the National Gallery in London, painted in egg tempera on wood around 1440–50 and attributed to an anonymous artist known as 'the Master of the Judgement of Paris', has a nightmarish quality about it.[16] It is dark; a sliver of moon lights a black sea sprinkled with islands. Helen's elegant courtiers stand and watch and talk, inert as Helen is seized. The two figures that immediately beg attention, leaping out of the frame, are Helen and Paris. In a setting where everything is still, they are turbulent. Paris' yellow-lined cloak whips out in the wind, and his hand grasps Helen's dress in a thick clump under her buttocks. Helen's feet are flaying, her delicate red pointy shoes kicking up her white dentate petticoat as she struggles and thrashes about. Paris stares up at Helen's face hungrily, and still the courtiers do nothing – Helen strains back out to reach them, but still they stand and watch and talk. They are frozen and impotent. Helen's destiny is the waiting boat, the inky stretch of the sea.

In one of the ground-floor cases of the Heraklion Museum on Crete there is a scattering of bronze shapes – reminiscent of a selection of beaten-up horse brasses. In fact these are the broken remains of a tripod base, made in the 8th century BC, left as a votive offering and found on the floor of the Idaean Cave in Crete. A boat has been drawn out of the metal. In the prow there are two figures: archaeologists debate whether they should be identified as Theseus and Ariadne or Paris and Helen. Whoever they are, they cling together, tiny black silhouettes looking across the changing, unimaginable volume of the sea.

∽∽∽∽∽

One soft autumn day in late October – while looking for traces of Helen's cults, many of which are by rivers or coastlines – I found myself stuck at the small town of Hermione (Ermioni) on the Greek mainland, clearly just about to muff my 8.00 p.m. rendezvous on the island of Hydra.[17] I had with me only my powder compact, 40 euros and a mobile phone. I had missed the last hydrofoil and turned down the offer of a lift from some drunk teenagers in charge of a worryingly large yacht. It all seemed rather hopeless until I remembered noticing a ragged, handwritten scrap of paper pinned to a bench near the harbour advertising sea-taxis. I rang the number, and within eight minutes a little boat buzzed up, the driver tanned the colour of tar. The only other passenger was an old goat. I trusted that my new friend was the equivalent of a London cabbie, and with bouzouki music on the ship's radio for company, headed off towards the horizon.

It was an entirely 21st-century experience. Yet because it was novel (and somewhat random), I felt, for a moment, the frisson of travelling to the unknown by sea and a fleeting sense of what it was to be a part of a seafaring nation. This short adventure was a taste of how ancient water-ways once operated. A number of Bronze Age bays would have had their taxi-boatmen, navigating little fishing boats, coast-hugging vessels, with whom one could strike a bargain and hitch a ride. As a Bronze Age Helen and Paris sailed along from west to east they would have passed seasonal beach markets and ports pockmarked with colour, pungent with the smells of livestock and spices, their traders standing by ready to tout their wares. Out on the open sea there would be pirates waiting to relieve the ocean-traveller of vital supplies and priceless consignments of hippopotamus ivories and the like.

Archaeological finds and Bronze Age written sources have given us a surprisingly detailed picture of the luxury goods that would once have criss-crossed the waters. From the Amarna tablets in Egypt, for example, written in the 14th century BC (and packed with political and social detail for the period), we get tantalising lists of the kinds of artefacts trafficked between royalty and aristocrats across the East Mediterranean. Some of the tablets, first discovered in 1887 by a peasant woman tilling the soil, are now stored in the British Museum.[18] The lists are minutely detailed and fascinating, but they deal only with the final flourish of a culture, the end-point of creation – here we have evidence of achievement rather than process.

Then, in 1983 at Uluburun (near the modern-day town of Kaş), thanks to the sharp eyes of a Turkish man diving to collect living sponges, an extraordinary find illuminated the Bronze Age trading scene.[19] The diver reported 'biscuits with ears', metal ingots weighing between 17 and 26 kg each. Archaeologists investigated and found, tucked into the silt, a Bronze Age shipwreck. Suddenly, precise, untouched examples of Bronze Age cargo could be examined.

Here there were the copper and tin ingots necessary to manufacture bronze; the lumps of cobalt-blue glass that would be melted down and re-cast as striking figure-of-eight beads, worn around the necks and wrists of women like Helen. There was amber from the Baltic, hippopotamus ivory and a beautiful drinking cup made of faience in the shape of a ram's head. Ivory trumpets and tortoiseshell sound-boxes lay muted by the sea. On board were ebony logs: dendro-chronological dating from some sections of the wood has been used to indicate that the boat sank sometime between 1318 and 1295 BC.[20] The presence of the scarab of Nefertiti shows the boat certainly sailed some time after 1345.

Along with the sophisticated artefacts – the female figurine with her feet and lower arms dipped in gold, the scarab marked with Queen Nefer-titi's name, the cosmetic boxes made in the shape of ducks (with movable wings for lids), the fine oil lamps – here too was a 'ghost cargo': the base ingredients of seven civilisations, the raw materials that are rarely preserved for posterity.

Boats like these, if they began their journey in the south, could have cut a direct course from Egypt through to Crete and then on to Turkey, but most would have meandered from the Nile along the Libyan coasts, up to Crete and Italy, perhaps, or stopping off at the island of Kythera and then on to mainland Greece, past the Cyclades, Rhodes, Anatolia and then down to Cyprus, Syria-Palestine and, finally, back to Egypt.[21]

In one of the earliest written sources for the Helen story, the *Cypria* (we hear this particular detail via Herodotus), it was explained that in just three days the two lovers bolted straight across the sea to Troy.[22] I have made the trip, and – at a headlong dash, in a boat comparable to the most sophisticated Late Bronze Age vessels of 15–17 metres, with oars and a sail – it is possible, with the benefits of modern sailing technology to make the trip in just under two and a half days. Homer, however, tells us the fugitive lovers followed the route of those Aegean traders, brigands and buccaneers. We hear, in the *Iliad*, that en route Paris picked up rich cloths and Sidonian (Phoenician) women.[23] These slaves from the literary record join the real lists of human cargo that we find incised into Bronze Age clay tablets.[24] Once again, the Helen and Paris story intersects very neatly with Late Bronze Age reality.

☙◦◦◦◦◦❧

There is an unfamiliar version of the Trojan War story by the poet Stesichorus, writing in Sicily in the 6th century BC.[25] In his interpretation of Helen's 'history', the Spartan queen never goes to Troy, but sends an *eidolon* (a body double or phantom) across the hazy-bright waters while the flesh-and-blood Helen actually lies low in Egypt for ten years. Plato recounts that Stesichorus wrote his version after he had been blinded for slandering Helen.

Once Stesichorus had come to his senses and realised what a powerful (angry) creature he was dealing with, he made propitiation to Helen by producing a poem defending the 'real' Helen in which she sits out the Trojan War blamelessly, in Egypt. As a result of his judicious volte-face his eyesight was restored.[26] There is a possibility that Stesichorus visited Sparta[27] (there were close political connections between Sicily and Sparta in his lifetime). Perhaps what we hear in his verse is a more patriotic rendition of the Helen story, a version promoted by the Spartan population, determined to maintain the dignity of their iconic royal ancestor. Although never the most tenacious or popular reading of the tale, this exegesis interested a number of ancient authors.

The historian Herodotus adds weight to this Egyptian version of events by piling in with his own evidence – saying that while on Helen's trail he personally travelled to Egypt and interviewed the Egyptian priests at Memphis.[28] The priests checked their records, he says, and confirmed that Helen had indeed spent ten years in Egypt around the time of the Trojan War. Herodotus also claims to have found a sanctuary in which there was a statue of a beautiful woman. The inscription, he reports, read: 'The Foreign Aphrodite'; Herodotus assumes this alluring icon was Helen. So suddenly we have not just an earlier extended visit to Egypt, but a sojourn there for centuries as a divine spirit.[29]

The evidence from Egypt is significant. Herodotus, the 'Father of History', may have been wrong when he identified the statue of the 'Foreign Aphrodite' as Helen, but tellingly he thought it perfectly possible that a queen of Sparta should have travelled to Africa, and believed that she could have made such an impact on locals that they were still talking about her eight hundred years later. Just as he didn't underestimate Helen's reach, neither should we.[30]

Herodotus, in his *Histories*, very carefully lays out the case for Helen never actually making it to Troy. As with most writers, the 'Father of History' has a personal and emotional take on Helen's story:

> . . . had Helen really been in Troy, she would have been handed over to the Greeks with or without Paris' consent; for I cannot believe that either Priam or any other kinsman of his was mad enough to be willing to risk his own and his children's lives and the safety of the city, simply to let Paris continue to live with Helen. The fact is they [the Trojans] did not give Helen up, because they had not got her; what they told the Greeks was the truth.[31]

Clearly for Herodotus, love does not conquer all.

The Egyptian journey is as interesting historically as it is symbolically. Pre-historic Crete and the Peloponnese seem to have maintained vigorous contact with Africa.[32] For the Greeks, Egypt was the nearest point of the African continent. The sailors of the Bronze Age and antiquity – for obvious reasons – preferred to plan their routes along shorelines rather than forging out into open seas. The Greek route to Africa followed the southern coast of Asia Minor, around Cyprus and past Syria. Helen's Egyptian sojourn was remembered for a reason – because it told the descendants of the Bronze Age that contact with Africa was an important part of the Mycenaean Bronze Age experience. And it should remind us that the Eastern Mediterranean was not yet divided into the Occident and the Orient, but was instead a charged interface of commerce and territorialism.

Whether this was history, or just a story, Helen's route to Troy, and Homer's roll-call of the countries she visited on her way back, reinforced a shared, mental map of an international age.[33] It is a perception that Helen's story enunciates. Her route reminded Homer's audience who the players were among their Mediterranean ancestors, who, out of nations and rulers and commercial centres – the jostling nexus that was the Eastern Mediterranean – really counted. And of course the climax of her tale reminded them that this doughty region was irreversibly destabilised sometime in the 13th century BC.

෧෨෧෨෧෨

So far Helen and Paris have been the protagonists in a love story. There may have been some physical and emotional casualties as they left Menelaus' palace, but up until now there has been no massacre. All that will change. In the minds of the ancients this Heroic Age was to be brought down – by the over-love of a Spartan queen. For Helen, all chance of anonymity was forfeit when she left her homeland to travel with the prince of Troy. She would be forever remembered as an enemy of both eastern and western interests. The ripples that Helen and Paris' boat made as they crossed the sea spread wide – the cargo making its way towards Troy was a dangerous one.

PART SEVEN

TROY
BECKONS

23

EAST IS EAST AND
WEST IS WEST

@@@@@@@@@@@@

For then it was, because of the rape of Helen, that Troy began
to summon against herself the chieftains of the Argives, Troy —
O horror! — the common grave of Europe and Asia, Troy the
untimely tomb of all heroes and heroic deeds.

CATULLUS (1st century BC)[1]

THE RELIGIOUS SITE OF DELPHI in the north of Greece is —
despite the coachloads of tourists — still an awe-inspiring place. High
in the hills, hugging the southern slopes of Mount Parnassus, the
air is light and sweet. Delphi was considered by the Greeks to be the *omphalos*
— the navel of the earth, the centre of the world.[2] Throughout antiquity,
men would come here from as far away as Syria and Sicily to make their
religious devotions, to trade, to hone political deals and to try to comprehend the cryptic pronouncements of the Delphic oracle.[3]

The oracle handed out advice in all degrees. Some came with domestic
problems: should they marry? How could they get a son? Statesmen arrived
with grander questions: what sort of law codes should they introduce?
Should they invade their neighbours' territory? Treasuries and embassies
crowded along the Sacred Way. Here the leaders of the day met to talk and
admire the self-aggrandising portraits commissioned for the busy highway.
Every four years (when it was first instituted, every eight) gymnasts, boxers
and charioteers — a polyglot crowd — would limber up for one of Greece's
busiest religious festivals, the Pythian Games. Delphi was a place that
mattered, and the pronouncements of its oracle were taken very seriously
indeed.

One section of the ancient site is not open to the public. Although
reaching the spot is quite a hike and would probably pick off the less determined sightseers, here the landscape is peaceful and strange. Close to the

fine, classical stadium there is a peculiar, bulbous stone – once a pint-size temple hacked out of volcanic rock. The rock was the home of the Pythia, an old woman symbolically dressed in a young virgin's clothes, who, high on the fumes of roasted henbane seeds or crushed laurel, would babble out the Delphic oracle. These mumblings would then be analysed by a male priest who turned them into hexameter verse. Generally the oracle's prophecies were translated into such obtuse riddles that they could be interpreted in a number of ways. But the pronouncements pertaining to Helen were unambiguous. Recorded on stone, the stark words told the ancient world that:

Helen would be brought up in Sparta to be the ruin of Asia and Europe and for her sake the Greeks would capture Troy.[4]

ᗪᗪᗪᗪᗪ

Any modern-day traveller through Turkey is sure to remember the moment sailing over the Bosphorus, or crossing the Atatürk Bridge by coach, passing over the swordfish and dolphins and anchovies swimming down below, and being told through the proud nasal tones of a tannoy that one is leaving Europe to enter Asia. Our world-view – partly informed by the reception of tales of the Trojan War – is that the globe is indeed split in two: that the Orient and the Occident exist as distinct (often antagonistic) entities.

Was there a moment when two Bronze Age lovers crossed some kind of imaginary fault-line – the moment when West became East? This was certainly an idea that caught hold of the popular imagination in the 5th century BC – at a time when tensions between Europe and Asia were to the fore. Since the 6th century BC, the Persians had made it clear to the Greeks that their ambitions lay in the west. The Persian Empire was indeed mighty – at its peak between 522 and 486 BC during the reign of Darius I, it reached from the coast of modern-day Turkey to Afghanistan and Pakistan and included parts of Egypt, Armenia, Iran and Iraq. Greece was outranked and, with their backs against the wall, the Greeks were quick to vilify their towering rivals across the waters.[5]

The immoral, degenerate Persians were much talked about in plays and literature, often contrasted with the tough, wily Greek underdogs.[6] In either 479 or 478 BC the popular orator Simonides delivered an elegy, equating the Persian and Trojan Wars.[7] The earliest extant Greek tragedy, Aeschylus' *Persians*, produced on stage in 472 BC, dealt with the hostility between Persia and Greece – Aeschylus himself was a veteran of the Persian conflict. The sack of Troy, an exponential Greek victory, gave great hope to the beleagured Athenian Empire. The Trojan War story swiftly became a part of political and cultural polemic. Aeschylus equated the Bronze Age Trojans with the modern-day Persians – or, as he calls both peoples, the 'Phrygians'.[8]

The historian Herodotus, writing in the 5th century BC, is very clear that the oracle at Delphi was sound, that it was Helen's crime that had marked a totemic division between east and west, the start of an enmity between Europe and Asia. Twice he quotes Persian sources as proof: 'in their opinion, it was the taking of Troy which began their feud with the Greeks'; and again, 'the Greeks, all for the sake of a Lakedaemonian woman, mustered a great host, came to Asia, and destroyed the power of Priam. Ever since then we have regarded the Greeks as our enemies.'[9]

Herodotus was born into the instability and bloodshed of the Persian Wars, when the Greeks and 'men from the east' were once again enemies. The conflict witnessed epic-worthy contention, the battles of Marathon, Thermopylae, Salamis, Plataea. In 449, the Peace of Kallias achieved an uneasy truce: it did nothing to allay the suspicion and mistrust that the Greeks and Persians felt towards one another. As Herodotus gathered his material and wrote his histories it was important for him to find the inception of this ethnic fault-line.

During the Persian wars, both sides had committed dreadful atrocities. Temples had been torched and populations massacred or enslaved. Herodotus claimed that, as they entered enemy territory, the Persian forces turned the most beautiful boys into eunuchs and sent the most beautiful girls as slaves to their king. Advancing towards the Battle of Marathon, the Persian armies spread across the landscape, a malign 'net' of men, wiping out whatever was in their path.[10] The stories of their ferocious brutality came thick and fast. These were the horrors whispered fearfully at night, passed from one village to another as the smoke of enemy fires was spotted snaking up on the horizon.

Herodotus came from Halicarnassus (modern-day Bodrum in Turkey) on the edge of Asia Minor, and therefore spent his earliest years within the Persian satrapy, or province, of Lydia.[11] Today Bodrum is a high-octane tourist town that welcomes international travellers – here you can find the best (and most expensive) carpets and massages in Turkey. It is as cosmopolitan now as it was then. Halicarnassus tolerated a diverse population which embraced Ionian, Dorian and Carian influences. As a young man Herodotus and his family had been exiled to the island of Samos following their political struggles against the Persian-backed local tyrant Lygdamis. Ten years later Herodotus was in Athens (possibly again an exile) and by the end of his life he had been granted citizenship of Thurii in southern Italy.[12] He was a man who had lived and suffered, who had seen the world and understood men – Greeks and non-Greeks alike.

Although Herodotus was famously dubbed 'the Father of History' his historiographical technique would sit more happily on the desk of a roving (and brilliant) journalist in Fleet Street today than in the ivory towers of our great educational establishments.[13] Herodotus was peripatetic: as he gathered information for his histories (his '*historia*' or enquiries), he claimed to have covered massive distances – from Babylon to the Black Sea, from Tyre to Thessaly. He met officials, gathered local knowledge and kept his ear to the ground. The scale of some of his expeditions must have been exaggerated, but, importantly, Herodotus had the chance to assimilate attitudes and opinions as well as hard data. And what he found around him was hostility between east and west.[14]

A useful place to test the temperature of popular thought has always been the theatre, and in 5th-century Greece it is on the stage that we find an 'anti-barbarian' polemic oft repeated. Xenophobia is a lazy crowd-pleaser, and so in a number of dramas 'the Athenian' becomes typified as democratic and egalitarian and manly, 'the Barbarian' as tyrannical, hierarchical and effeminate. Helen is a pivotal character in this theatricalised discussion of East vs. West. Hecuba, Paris' mother, condemns Helen and broadcasts the perceived intemperance of the east in Euripides' *Trojan Women:* 'In Argos you were used to a small retinue; having got rid of the Spartan city, you looked forward to a deluge of extravagance in Phrygia with its rivers of gold. The halls of Menelaus weren't large enough for your luxury to wanton in.'[15] And in his play *Helen*, written three years later, the Spartan queen bewails: 'There is no man living but Helen is his hate, notorious through all Hellas as having betrayed my husband, to live in the golden houses of the East.'[16]

The stereotypes on stage could also be found in the workshops of Athenian artists. Dark easterners (like Paris) covet white-armed Greek women (like Helen). On vase paintings and murals from the 5th century BC, Trojans are increasingly painted in Persian garb. Gradually the two ethnographically and historically distinct groups morph into one another: Persia = Troy = Bad News.[17]

On occasion, Helen is praised for uniting the disparate communities on the Greek mainland against the East. But the eulogy is deeply ironic. The xenophobic proto-nationalism that was becoming the norm in classical Athens is evident here. Take, for instance, Isocrates' praise-song for Helen, his *Encomium:*

Apart from the arts and philosophic studies and all the other benefits which one might attribute to her and to the Trojan War, we should be justified in considering that it is owing to Helen that we are not the slaves of the barbarians. For we shall find that it was because of her that the Greeks became united in harmonious accord and organised a common expedition against the barbarians, and that it was then for the first time that Europe set up a trophy of victory over Asia . . .[18]

In the classical corpus, Helen is more typically cited as ruinous – the cause of an agonising death for Greeks and Trojans alike:

> *You plague, holocaust, blight*
> *Of both nations – see this graveyard of heroes*
> *And the naked bones lying all over*
> *The plain unburied. Your nuptials strewed them.*
> *For you spurted Asia's blood, spurted Europe's,*
> *As you viewed duelling husbands – indifferent,*
> *Unsure of your wish.*[19]

⊙⊙⊙⊙⊙

It was Homer who introduced the concept of barbarism – *barbarophōnoi*, 'bar-bar-speakers', – alluding to men whose language was so indistinct and incomprehensible to the Greek ear that it simply sounded like 'bar-bar-bar-bar-bar'.[20] And yet Homer treats Greek and Trojan with equity – he sees the hero and the degenerate in both. The *Iliad* is not a document of oriental/occidental division although it has been promoted as such down the centuries: Homer has been hijacked.[21]

There is no contemporary indication that Bronze Age populations thought in terms of east and west. The Eastern Mediterranean was quite simply a fractious theatre of power. What we do have is hard evidence that in the Late Bronze Age the traffic of people between east and west was two-way. A tablet known as the Tawagalawa letter was sent by a king of the Hittites to a Mycenaean ruler in around 1260 BC.[22] In the letter the Hittite king Hattusili III bemoans the fact that no fewer than 7,000 of his Western Anatolian subjects from the Lukka Lands in Ahhiyawan territory have been resettled in Greece. Recent analysis has proved that what we call 'Mycenaean' territory was, in the Late Bronze Age, 'the land of Ahhiyawa'.[23] Those Anatolian immigrants could have been used by their Greek overlords to flesh out the workforce that went on to build the giant Mycenaean citadels. Over a thousand years later, Strabo says it was the Cyclopes (giants from Lycia – corresponding to the Bronze Age Lukka Lands) who built Tiryns.[24] The outsize blocks of stone that make up the walls of the Mycenaean citadels and engineering projects are often of an unfeasible bulk and size. Did folk memory in Strabo's time recall Lycian natives heaving monstrous masonry into place? An act that could have been carried out only by giants?

Another clay tablet, very fragmentary, appears to document a dispute between the Greek mainlanders – the king of Ahhiyawa – and the king of the Hittites over the ownership of lands 'off Assuwa' (most probably Lemnos, Imbros and Samothrace), which may have been given in exchange for a princess, the daughter of a man called 'kadmu' (possibly the ruler of Thebes).[25] Natives of Greece and Turkey today would recognise the tension. It is pertinent to the Helen story that a princess was thought a worthy exchange for such strategic territories.[26]

So in the Late Bronze Age there were both close connections and uncomfortable tensions across the waters. The Mycenaeans and the Trojans were powerful neighbours, although separated by stretches of sea. These were communities that bought and sold each other's goods, worked each other's land, slaved for each other's rulers and were able to communicate with each other. They were also embroiled in each other's politics. For any trader or migrant travelling up the Dardanelles in the Late Bronze Age, the idea that the men from the West were in some way more advanced than and superior to the men from the East, would have seemed risible. The Greeks were not sailing to Troy to confront a bunch of culturally inferior barbarians. Think in reverse. In the Bronze Age it was the Greek mainland that was on the edge of things. Greece was itself the western tip of a far older civilisation, a civilisation originating predominantly in Mesopotamia and interfacing directly with the Greek mainland via the Hittites and their allies.

ᘒᘒᘒᘒᘒ

Helen's beauty and infidelity (not, you notice, Paris' hubris and lust) were seen as the trigger for disintegration and conflict on an international scale and for enmity between Europe and Asia. There are usually many contributory causes to international conflict, to the end of civilisations; the ancient Greeks needed only one: the promiscuity of a beautiful woman.[27]

Helen is a piece of creation so perfectly beautiful that like the butterfly, called by the Greeks *psyche* – a soul or life-breath – she was thought to hover somewhere between the real and the fantastical.[28] But Helen is also a perfect exemplar of the butterfly effect. In the grand scheme of things, she is of little significance – she is a regent in Lakonia and Paris a princeling of Troy. This is not the story of the greatest power-brokers of the age, a scandal involving the Queen of Mycenae or Thebes, the King of Troy himself or his heroic, *firstborn* son Hector. Helen and Paris start out as bit-players, but their sexual peccadillo changes the world: a private, local act that ends up dragging human history along behind it.

So as the Troy-bound lovers listen to the sounds of the night, and stroke each other's arms, as the waves lap the boat's side and Helen pushes her 'loose and lustrous hair' back out of her eyes, the picture of mortal bliss, there is a dreadful inevitability about what is going to happen next.[29] A butterfly has flapped its wings. Chaos is on its way.

24

THE FAIR TROAD

@@@@@@@@@@@@

Oh Violet it's too wonderful for belief. I had not imagined
Fate could be so benign . . . I've been looking at the maps.
Do you think perhaps the fort on the Asiatic corner will want
quelling, and we'll land and come at it from behind and they'll
make a sortie and meet us on the plains of Troy? . . . Will the
sea be polyphloisbic and wine dark and unvintageable . . . ?

RUPERT BROOKE (February 1915)[1]

I T IS ONLY ON HEADING EAST from Sparta's port of Gythion by boat
that it becomes clear just how close Troy is to the Greek mainland.
Hugging the coastline, the safest route passes through the Aegean Sea
and then wends its way around the Cycladic islands and thereon up into
the straits of the Dardanelles and the Bosphorus. With a fair wind, this is
a simple journey. On foot, following the Mycenaean roads and trackways
that still appear as ghosts in the Peloponnesian landscape, the trek from
Mycenae to Sparta would have taken over three days. By sea the Mycenaean Greeks could have reached a whole new continent in the same time.
For the warrior-lords of Greece, the Anatolian coast must have felt very
close; and very tempting.

I first arrived at Troy by boat.[2] In the owl-light, the sea heaved with an
ugly, oily swell. It was a disturbed night. Homer describes moments like
this perfectly: 'wave on blacker wave, cresting, heaving a tangled mass of
seaweed out along the surf'. For hours I watched the breakers on the coastline, but then, as dawn lit up the land, the bleakness of the Turkish coast
came as a shock. The sea, now an innocent, speedwell blue stretch, was
broken by squat hills and long listless beaches. Troy inhabits a raw landscape – an appropriate setting for the raw passion and attenuated, desperate
fighting that Homer tells us it once sustained.

On the opposite side of the Dardanelles, there were other pilgrims
visiting another battlefield. One day I walked behind them along a narrow

stony path. The dust in front and behind was kicked up by these serious young men and women, heads down, making their own pilgrimage to the site of Gallipoli where in 1915 during the First World War so many died, thirty-odd centuries after the Trojan War. The dead at Gallipoli are commemorated in row upon row of simple marble tombs. On their headstones they are promised a uniform comfort: 'THEIR NAME LIVETH FOR EVERMORE.'

The small museum near to the battleground houses a smattering of artefacts that belonged to these young martyrs. When I first visited the site in the mid-1980s, in one glass case were the remains of a tin of chocolate and a pair of hand-knitted woollen mittens, sent by a British woman to keep her teenage grandson warm. My back was wet with the sweat from the long walk in baking heat, and inside the museum my eyes took some time to adjust after the glare of the sun: no gift could have felt more inappropriate. Nor indeed could the bright-eyed verve of the soldiers who sailed up the Dardanelles – boys who left home with Homer's words spinning in their heads – an irony not lost on those they left behind:

> Bees hummed and rooks called hoarsely outside the quiet room
> Where by an open window Gervais, the restless boy,
> Fretting the while for cricket, read of Patroclus' doom
> And flower of youth a-dying by far-off windy Troy.
>
> Do the old tales, half-remembered, come back to haunt him now
> Who leaving his glad school-days and putting boyhood by
> Joined England's bitter Iliad? Greek beauty on the brow
> That frowns with dying wonder up to Hissarlik's sky![3]

There are many ghosts along the coast of the Troad. This is a place where innocents died in both the 20th century AD and, perhaps, in the 13th century BC, far from home, men fighting for political and military juggernauts whose cause was obfuscated or long forgotten.

ᖆᖇᖆᖇᖆ

In pre-history, pulling into the Bay of Beşik, five miles or so south-west of Troy, would have been a welcome respite from the challenging sailing conditions of the Dardanelles. Between May and October, watermen would have to deal with the double trouble of strong currents powering from the Sea of Marmara to the Aegean and a north-easterly wind blowing head on as they tried to enter the straits.[4] Three and a half thousand years ago an arm of the sea would also have stretched inland from the coastline here – some think right to the town of Troy itself. Little surprise that the ports of Troy and their associated citadel, positioned as they were to serve the three seas, the Aegean, the Black Sea and the Sea of Marmara, should become so iconic, so hallowed.[5] It must have been with some relief that sailors arrived within sight of Beşik Bay. Here, at last, was some security and an opportunity to trade.

Every new boatload that turned up to anchor at Troy's ports would have merited a turn of the head, a greedy glance from the merchants and slaves who worked there. This would have been both a crossroads and a checkpoint. Here there would certainly have been a great bar-bar-ing, but it would be the sound of men from all over the Eastern Mediterranean talking to each other. Doing deals, learning each other's songs, worshipping each other's gods. The variegated Anatolian states in the Hittite commonwealth were not sea-powers, but they relied on foreign boats to bring in the raw materials that motivated the civilisations of the Eastern Mediterranean – tin and copper, to make the bronze that was so coveted by the rulers of the age.

The range of pottery and other artefacts retrieved from the site of Troy and its environs bears out the city's literary reputation as a cosmopolitan hub; there are ivory beads here from Greece, amber from the Baltic, pottery from Crete and foodstuffs from Babylon, Cyprus and the Lebanon.[6] The foundations of exceptionally spacious buildings within Troy itself have been diagnosed as massive storage centres for grain, oil and wine. The Uluburun shipwreck heading west from the Turkish coast, contained traces of pomegranates, almonds, pine nuts, ostrich eggs and a full ton of the pungent terebinth resin. These are the kinds of goods that would have been lowered, along with human cargo, at the anchorage points close to Troy.

Any Mycenaean Greek arriving at Beşik Bay would have been greeted by a babble of different voices. No one knows for sure what the lingua franca would have been. Eight written languages are recorded at the Hittite capital Hattusa,[7] and in order to operate here, linguistic competence would have been essential.[8] Scholars in the past have used the fact that Trojans and Greeks appear to communicate effortlessly on the battlefield to dispute the *Iliad*'s historicity. But even were this intended only as a dramatic device, it would also have been a historical possibility.[9] Given their close trading links, Bronze Age Trojans and Mycenaean Greeks would indeed have been used to understanding one another.[10]

Beşik Bay is a strange, forgotten place now. Sandy enough to pass for a pleasure beach, on occasion it hosts visitors – mainly locals – for walks and dips in the sea. Approaching the site of the Late Bronze Age anchorage points, there is a scrubby area that serves as a car park, boasting an occasional broken bin, from which the litter escaped long ago; plastic bags perch and flutter in the nearby trees like flocks of ragged, brightly-plumed birds. Onto the shoreline itself, grey seaweed has been tossed in giant clumps. Herds of goats pick their way through the dunes, defecating as they go.

On first impression, there is nothing here that speaks of heroes or of the cosmopolitan interchange that the bay would have witnessed three and half thousand years ago. But excavations in 1984 and 1985 produced irrefutable evidence of Mycenaean presence. Just three hundred yards inland a cemetery was discovered. Here there are well over a hundred burials of men, women and children.[11] Identification of the goods found within the graves shows them to be from the 13th century BC and not all Anatolian, but predominantly Greek or Greek imitation. In one elaborate 'grave-house' melted metal suggests that men were cremated along with their swords and daggers. Some of the dead have been buried in giant *pithoi*. Elsewhere cenotaphs have been found, marking empty graves.

The human remains at Beşik Bay may represent a subsidiary Mycenaean group providing supplies to a hostile force of Greeks, or even just a mongrel trading community, men and women who dealt peaceably with the Trojans. From the evidence we have, this is clearly not the graveyard of an epic battlefield. If the remains speak of violence, they are more likely to tell of a series of small skirmishes in the area around Troy. But whatever the circumstances of the deaths in that little Grecophile community, whether the Mycenaeans came to the shores near Troy in peace or in war, there is no doubt that they were here.

There is another clue in the landscape to the significance of Beşik Bay: a peculiar hummock, a further 455 m inshore, now named Beşik Tepe but for centuries known as the 'Mound of Achilles'. This grand extrusion has been the focus of much political posturing and was visited by the great generals of antiquity;[12] Xerxes, the leader of the Persians came here in 480 BC, having already honoured the dead Trojan heroes with libations and the sacrifice of a thousand cattle to Athena of Troy.[13] Alexander the Great, visiting in 334 BC, styled himself a second Achilles, with his beloved companion Hephaestion ably filling the role of Patroclus: *'Fortunate youth, to have found in Homer an herald of thy valour!'*[14] we are told he shouted out during his visit, jealous of Achilles' immortality.[15]

As it stands, this cone of earth, the 'Mound of Achilles', is an accretion of the centuries. Excavations have shown the bulk of the construction to be Hellenistic – so Alexander and others were honouring a phantom grave. When I last visited Beşik Tepe, the excavation had been back-filled, the mound restored. Braving the vipers and brambles I scrambled to the top. Standing on the stony summit with my back to the sea, I could just pick out, five miles inland, perched on a small hill called Hisarlik, the extant remains of Troy. It was almost certainly this settlement that Homer had in mind when he wrote his tale of *Ilios* and this is where countless authors and adventurers from both the ancient and the modern worlds have wanted to believe that King Priam's glorious palace once stood.

A huge gateway has been identified on the western edge of Hisarlik Hill. It is 3.5 to 4 m across, and looks out to sea, facing west. Recent excavations show that from this gate a paved roadway would have led out across the Scamander Plain towards Beşik Bay.[16] Naturally a town such as Troy that looked to the travelling salesmen of the sea for its income would save one of its most imposing approaches for the ocean. Another major gateway in the southern section of the citadel walls stands next to the remains of what would have been an imposing watchtower – the Trojans knew they attracted enemies as well as acolytes. The ingress and egress of vessels and cargo in Beşik Bay and up to Troy's harbour would have been carefully monitored. Boats could bring disease and enemies as well as trade. They could bring a Helen.

25

THE TOPLESS TOWERS
OF ILIUM

೦೦೦೦೦೦೦೦೦೦೦೦೦

a suspect stranger from Greece,
is she a slave or a queen?

H.D., *Helen in Egypt* (1961)[1]

ISARLIK HAS ATTRACTED VISITORS AND INTEREST for
millennia. The Late Bronze Age buildings here would have been
abandoned at the latest in 950 BC but there was an unbroken local
tradition – almost certainly transmitted by Homer – that this ruined site
was indeed the *Ilios* of the Age of Heroes.[2] Overlooking the rich, arable
plain of the River Scamander the citadel was rebuilt and reoccupied in the
Archaic, Hellenistic and Roman periods.[3] In AD 324 the Emperor Constantine began to found his 'new Rome' close by at Yenishehir before he moved
the operation 200 miles north to Byzantium, or, as he rechristened the city,
Constantinople. Amateur classicists were thrilled to think they had found
in the region tangible evidence of Troy and the Trojan War. In 1631 an
endearingly callow sailor-boy left his mark on a piece of masonry he believed
to be Hector's tomb:

> *I do suppose that here stood* Troy
> *My Name it is* William *a jolly boy,*
> *My other Name it is* Hudson, *and so,*
> *God Bless the Sailors, where ever they do go.*
> *I was here in the Year of our Lord 1631,*
> *and was bound to Old England,*
> *God Bless her.*[4]

Another English traveller, Edward Clarke, was the first formally to
identify Hisarlik as the site of Troy but half a century would pass before

any exploratory soundings were made of the large grassy knoll.[5] In the 19th century AD, the land to the east of the hill was owned by the Calvert family – a dynasty involved in the region for some time as landowners, diplomats and businessmen. One son, Frank was convinced he had the 'topless towers of Ilium' on his doorstep. In 1865 he started to dig, tentatively: Calvert's investigations were careful and perceptive, but there was insufficient cash to mount a serious excavation. Troy looked set to keep its secrets until an angel of mercy (or despair, depending on your view of his methods of excavation) came in the form of the German businessman Heinrich Schliemann.

Schliemann claimed he had had an obsessive determination to find Homer's Troy from the tender age of eight. Forty years later, conversations with Calvert convinced him that it was on Hisarlik that he should focus his search. In 1868 he declared to Calvert in a letter: 'I am now quite decided to dig away the whole artificial mount of Hisarlik.'[6] He was true to his word. In 1870, with dogged enthusiasm he and his workmen, a force that could number 160 at any one time, cut a vast trench from north to south through Hisarlik Hill, 14 m deep and 79 m wide, gouging out the central and potentially most fecund area of the archaeological site. Hisarlik had been a trading centre since *c.* 3000 BC. There are forty-one habitation layers on the site at Troy, and in his haste to find Helen, Achilles, Hector and the rest, Schliemann tore through most of them, destroying irreplaceable evidence of the past.[7]

The self-taught showman-archaeologist was, at first, disappointed. Schliemann was looking for the grand palace of Priam, the man with fifty sons and untold wealth – and yet, he admitted in private to a colleague, the entire settlement seemed to be 'hardly larger than Trafalgar Square'.[8] Still, his core enthusiasm was not dampened. Schliemann's driving motive, rather than to understand the Late Bronze Age, was to try to find proof of Homer's stories and – behaving like a puppy with its first toy – when he came across a sloping road (dating in fact from 2500 BC, over a thousand years before the most likely date of the Trojan War) he triumphantly concluded that this was none other than the broad pathway up which the Trojans had pulled the malevolent Wooden Horse.[9]

Convinced he had rediscovered Helen's love-nest, Schliemann tried to bring Helen back to life. His methods, if not cavalier, were certainly wilful. When his workers dug up a terracotta statuette at Troy, he immediately identified it as a 'bust of Helen'.[10] And in May 1873,[11] as he came across an extraordinary hoard – copper lances, silver knife-blades, gold cups, a large silver vase – Schliemann fell on the finds, dubbing these 'Priam's

Treasure"[12], and the diadems, necklaces, bracelets and finger rings – packed tight in the vase – 'The Jewels of Helen'. Schliemann's fantasies about the Spartan queen continued beyond the grave. At his funeral, while copies of the *Iliad* and the *Odyssey* were lodged next to his corpse, Helen's funeral speech for the dead hero Hector was recited – by his own Greek wife – over his grave.[13]

For Schliemann had already gone so far as to ship in a Greek beauty to glide through the ruins of Troy. Before he divorced his first, Russian wife (with whom he had three children), Schliemann had instructed a Greek archbishop, Theokletos Vimpos, to find for him someone . . . 'of the Greek type, with black hair and, if possible, beautiful . . .'[14] A sixteen-year-old Greek girl called Sophia Engastromenos was sourced and an interview was arranged at her family home. Schliemann – whose stipulations also included poverty and education – asked the girl to recite Homer and to answer a question about Roman history. Sophia delivered, and shortly after the interview the two were married. According to Schliemann it was a happy match: 'She loves me as a Greek, with passion, and I love her no less. I speak only Greek with her, for this is the most beautiful language in the world. It is the language of the gods.'[15]

Schliemann dressed his newly acquired Hellenic spouse in 'the Jewels of Helen' and photographed her, creating for the chattering classes who followed his digs a dazzling image of a legendary queen. The tiny finger rings (8,750 gold ornaments in all were found) are too delicate for this matron's fingers. Her jet-black hair might set off one of the jewelled head-dresses rather well, but she is no Helen. The diadem, made up of fine gold-wire and of 16,353 worked gold pieces,[16] would have complemented Helen's famous golden curls, the tresses that men found so hard to resist. But it is all chimerical. Expert examination of the treasures shows them to be 1,200 years too old to have been worn by a 13th-century Bronze Age queen – these could have belonged only to a woman who would have been dust in the earth at the time a real Helen arrived at Troy.[17]

Just as Schliemann dressed Sophia up in 'Helen's Jewels', so he built for her a Trojan palace in the heart of Athens: *Iliou Melathron*, he called it, the great hall of Troy.[18] Here he kept his wife, their two children and a complement of servants. The children's bedrooms are decorated with hand-painted picture-postcard scenes of Greek landscapes and half-excavated ruins. During one visit to the *Iliou Melathron* I found archaeologists and art students in the process of renovating the frescoes – neglected for decades. Refreshed, the images gleamed with an ebullient clarity. Schliemann clearly hoped his own offspring – little Agamemnon and Andromache – would fall asleep dreaming of the heroic adventures to come in their technicolor Mediterranean playground.[19]

It is easy to mock Schliemann's romanticism and to criticise his gung-ho methods of excavation. But subsequent investigation has proved that his instinctive approach paid dividends. Not all was lost when the massive trench was dug through the mound. Digs in the 1930s[20] and 1980s turned up a wealth of clues to the life and influence not of a literary, but a historical, reality – a powerful Bronze Age settlement called, in contemporary texts, 'Wilusa'.[21] This was a city that was home to a rich king, a city that dealt with Mycenaean Greeks and suffered attack and privations in the 13th century BC. It is almost certainly Homer's Ilios or Troy.[22]

The campaign of excavations begun in 1988 under Professor Manfred Korfmann, which stretch across the plateau to the south of the mound, right down to the location of Troy's inland port, offer a satisfying picture of how this Bronze Age community would have operated. Although the scale of the 'palace' originally disappointed Schliemann, Troy is indeed turning out to be a massive settlement, one of the largest fortified urban developments of the region. It is now clear that the site is a full fifteen times larger than had been previously imagined. And so if we are to think of a Bronze Age Helen arriving at Bronze Age Troy, we can hold in our mind's eye her destination: Hisarlik Hill.

৩৩৩৩৩

The Boston Musem of Fine Arts is home to a vase, painted between 490 and 480 BC, which bears a particularly elegant depiction of Helen and Paris.[23] The couple have left Sparta behind them. Helen seems tense – her chest is pulled in as if she holds her breath, her neck stoops. Aphrodite fusses maternally with the Spartan queen's headdress while Eros touches Helen's brow – ensuring it is love and love alone that she sees before her. Behind the pair hovers Peitho, the goddess of persuasion. Whatever doubts the fugitive lovers may have, Peitho will ensure that this *mania* (a Greek word originally meaning an erotic madness) seems the right, the only possible, course of action. Meanwhile Paris holds Helen by the wrist – a courteous gesture which would have sent out a clear message to contemporaries that this is neither rape nor kidnap. This symbolic physical contact was the clear signifier of a legitimate marriage ceremony.

There is a twist to this fine, uxorious piece of pottery. On the reverse, time has advanced ten years. Now Helen is not walking, but on the run, fleeing from her husband Menelaus who has come to Troy to bring her home, Paris is nowhere to be seen. The King of Sparta charges his wife, head down, his rage mimicked by the charging bull inscribed on his shield. The vase was discovered in 1879 during excavations of the cemetery of Suessula, a town just south-east of Capua in Italy; when uncovered it still contained the fatty ashes of a burnt sacrifice; the lower portion of the painting is in fact remarkably well preserved thanks to the emollience of the animal fat. Not simply a record of the legitimacy of Helen and Paris' union, this valued item was left as a gift to the gods. For the dead, a morbid reminder of the intimate, inevitable relationship between *eros* and *eris*.

But we should allow that vase to remind us of something else. The Helen in the Boston Museum, even though she is aided and abetted by the powers of persuasion, lust and love, walks in step with Paris. This match is a gallant one, the passion mutual. Here is the Helen the Greeks knew – a woman complicit in her own abduction.

Although less popular than the raped Helen, this eloping dignitary frequents western art – particularly in secular medieval illustration. The patrons within the European ruling dynasties were fully aware that Helen was a queen – some even went so far as to trace their lineage back to the nobility of the Age of Heroes. The Trojan tale speaks of the life of the high-born and when commissioning fine works of art from their illuminators and scribes, aristocratic patrons were asking for a portrayal of 'us' not 'them'.

In one such manuscript, originally produced in northern Italy and now housed in Madrid, Helen steps lightly down a gangplank, and trumpeters clarion her arrival.[24] Her wimple preserves her modesty: this is a seemly queen. On another manuscript, a Flemish one made in 1470, Helen enters a city of gothic arches on a white palfrey replete with henin hat and floating veil.[25] In the late 15th century, her 'marriage' to Paris was stitched into a Franco-Flemish tapestry.[26] Paris' left hand cradles Helen's, his right holds, with a theatrical flourish, the ring. Around the pair is a swirl of silks and brocades – the fine stuff of Helen's handmaids who, we hear in all literary sources from Homer onwards, came to Troy with the Spartan queen.[27]

The notion that Helen travelled to Troy with a number of her female attendants nourished all manner of lurid stories down the centuries.[28] Authors have eagerly dwelt on the image of Helen entering Troy as a willing captive surrounded by the rustle of skirts and the flutter of Greek eyelashes, a gorgeous woman with equally beguiling ladies-in-waiting. While 17th-century travellers have been blamed for sparking the fashion for 'orientalising' – that is, fantasising about groups of women living closely together in the women's quarters and royal harems of the east[29] – this is a tradition which in fact begins much, much earlier.

The *Souda* was an ambitious and unparalleled encyclopaedia of the Byzantine world, amassed in the 10th century AD. The compilers were anonymous but assiduous – the *Souda* comprises 30,000 entries. One such concerns Astyanassa, a maidservant to Helen, or, more specifically, a *therapaina*, 'a body servant who cared for [*therapeuo*] her mistress's personal health and appearance'. Inspired by her unfeasibly lovely employer, the *Souda* claimed that Astyanassa was the first person ever to compose a sex manual. More precisely, she was '*the first to discover the ways of lying in bed* [katakliseis] *for intercourse, and* [*she*] *wrote "on the Postures* [skhēmatō] *for Intercourse"*'. The manual was very popular, used so the *Souda* tells us by no less than Philaenis and Elephantine,[30] the notorious harlots much berated by the Christian Fathers.[31] Manuals like this were presumed to be based on personal experience.[32]

As you might expect, Helen's advent within the Trojan citadel was imagined to be noxious as well as exciting – many authors played on the horror that the Spartan queen brought with her. The playwright Aeschylus spikes his picture of Helen tripping 'lightly into Priam's Troy' by pointing out that she imports 'death and destruction as her dowry'.[33] On another Italian vase, made around 350 BC, Helen marries Paris once again, but instead of hiding a divinely beautiful face, her veil conceals a grotesque mask.[34] In an illustrated 14th-century AD manuscript of Guido delle Colonne's 13th-century AD account of the Trojan legend, Helen arrives at Troy, comfortably seated on a horse, and then marries Paris in the presence of priests. Standing to the left of the frame is Paris' sister Cassandra, the prophetess who had been cursed by Apollo: although possessing the gift of true prophecy, she was never to be believed. Cassandra's hair streams down her back, she rakes at her cheeks in despair, a harbinger of the terrors that are to come. And in a Neapolitan 14th-century manuscript now held by the British Library, Helen greets Paris, but extends her hand around his back towards one of the other Trojan princes clustered behind.[35] *Semper mutabile femina.* This promiscuous queen has only just arrived at Troy and already she is keeping her options open.

❧❧❧❧❧

Had Helen really walked into the citadel of Troy in the 13th century BC she would have been greeted by a wash of mongrel scents, drifting up from the magazines of the city. We know that at this time in the Eastern Mediterranean, frankincense, oil of iris, cumin, coriander and the sulphurous-smelling yellow mineral orpiment were unloaded in the ports and beach harbours of Bronze Age Turkey.

Aromatics were important commodities here — as they were in Mycenaean Greece. Those who came up smelling of roses had proved they could rise above the ordinary stinking world: Homer uses scent to denote standing: *'Andromache pressed the child to her scented breast, Smiling through her tears.'*[36] Helen's apartments in both Troy and Sparta earn the epithet *'richly scented'*, as do her robes. There is more than just poetic imagination at work here: only the rich of the Late Bronze Age could afford to smell good. The greatest rulers on the Greek mainland and in Anatolia alike scent-marked their territories.

Another odour carried on the air around the city of Troy would have been that of horses. Homer describes Troy as 'famed for its horses' and the hero Hector as a 'breaker of horses'. When the Hittites appear in the Bible they are the proponents of horse-power: 'The Lord had caused the Arameans to hear the sound of chariots and horses and a great army, so that they said to one another, "Look, the king of Israel has hired the Hittite and Egyptian kings to attack us!"'[37]

During recent excavations at Troy, a complete horse skeleton has been found along with substantial numbers of dislocated horse-bones.[38] Could this indeed have been an equestrian training and trading centre? In Anatolia, horse-handling was more advanced than it was on the Greek mainland, a feature of aristocratic life from at least 1600 BC. The Horse Book of Kikkuli, a Hittite text dating from 1360 BC, gives a detailed account of how to rear, break and train horses.[39] Eastern-style equine tack has been found in a grave at Mycenae.[40] East of the Bosphorus the horse's potential as a tool of war was being exploited.

In an effort to approximate sights and sounds that would have surrounded our Bronze Age Helen and Paris, a team of experimental archaeologists and I embarked on an empirical investigation in 2004 in the shadow of Hisarlik. Chariots are well represented in Mycenaean and Hittite art.[41] Drawing from visual and textual sources,[42] and using the raw materials that would have been available to both Greeks and Trojans in the 13th century BC, the team created replica Anatolian and Mycenaean chariots, trained up pairs of horses from the local gypsy encampment and then put both together on the plains of Troy.[43]

In Greece the Late Bronze Age chariots appear relatively lightweight. The wheels have only four spokes and the frames — particularly of those bearing arms — remain uncovered by hides. Anatolian chariots are represented on an intricate stone relief recording the Battle of Kadesh of 1275 BC. These carriages are chunkier, and the wheels have six spokes. Standing proud in the middle of the Kadesh relief is Rameses, the ruler of Egypt, bow and arrow in hand, picking off lesser warriors as his swift chariot circles the battlefield. It is a sight that would also have been seen outside Late Bronze Age Troy.

We know that by the 8th century BC, chariot warfare had all but disappeared. Chariots were still being exploited in battle by the Syrians, for example, but not by the Greeks or Anatolians. This is one instance when Homer is writing about his own Iron Age world, rather than that of the Bronze Age. In Homer we find chariots seldom used in actual combat but rather as taxis or chauffeur-driven cars, dropping off and picking up the great and the good between camp and battlefield.

Until recently Homer's understanding of chariot-use was orthodox: it was thought that the Greeks did not employ chariots as weapons of war. But we now have textual evidence of an intimidating number of Mycenaean chariots on Anatolian soil. In around 1400 BC a Greek tribal leader called Attarssiya is recorded as operating on the western edges of Hittite territory with an army of infantry and one hundred chariots.[44] To have had any kind of effective engagement with the Trojans, the Mycenaeans must have brought their chariots with them for tough service in battle: even though the Mycenaean vehicles were lighter than those from Anatolia our experiment showed them to be highly effective on the flat Scamander plain.

The 13th-century Hittite chariot had a crew of three: a driver, a fighter (archer or spearman) and a shield-bearer whose mission was to protect his colleagues.[45] All the charioteers had to be firm-footed horse-whisperers. These were men who devoted no little time to the perfection of their art. With no collars or traces, with the horses' hind-quarters swinging around wildly, staying upright in these lightweight carriages requires a high degree of concentration and aptitude. Managing to keep one's balance as well as one's hands free to use the pikes, arrows and sling-shots that allowed a fighter to kill and maim as he sped by is, as we discovered, quite a feat.

But a master charioteer would have been able to wreak much damage. As well as picking off rival heroes he could also have smashed through a huddle of infantry; the carnage would have been sickening. As the reconstructed chariot reeled around corners the leather would have groaned and creaked. The war-horses wore bells on their harnesses to provide an aural 'baffle' — essential in the maelstrom and cacophony of battle. Some of Homer's most harrowing lines describe the howls of the heroes as they fought on Scamander Plain for Helen:

> *Screams of men and cries of triumph breaking in one breath,*
> *fighters killing, fighters killed, and the ground streamed blood.*[46]

The charioteers in 13th-century combat would not have been massed: this was engagement by the few to destroy and impress the many. Frescoes show the chariots with brightly decorated sides and covered in striking black-and-white rawhide. Those riding in them are immediately lifted above the ordinary on the battlefield: they are distinctive, memorable – fight well in one of these and an opportunity for immortal fame would swiftly present itself. We know from Hittite texts that those in Anatolia who manned chariots were typically not just drivers, but high-ranking agents of the state. Men of privilege, representatives of a vastly outnumbered ruling class who needed to make an immediate and lasting visual impact on those around them – both friend and foe.

At the end of our experiment with the replica chariots we were applauded only by the tomato and cotton-pickers as they too rattled to and fro in their own horse-drawn carts through the fields. Of course, ours were not deeds that would echo down the centuries, but we had edged a little closer to understanding the reality of military engagement outside the walls of the city. The Mycenaean chariot fared well as a mobile missile platform. Neat enough to allow for excellent manoeuvrability, it could still accommodate a driver and two soldiers who, supplied with bows and arrows or pikes, had great fire-power. The chariot-technology of the Greek mainland was clearly sufficiently advanced to meet whatever it was that a prince of Troy might choose to throw at the Mycenaean Greeks.[47]

And so, hearing the horses in their stalls, sniffing the air as she travelled into the fortress of Troy itself, what would our Bronze Age Helen have thought of her new home? As she stood on top of the citadel, whipped by winds then as now, her view of the lower town, of the packed little shanty homes, and the sandy bay stretching out to the Dardanelles, must have appeared very different from the Lakonian heartlands she had left behind. Here the swampy lagoon encourages disease – malarial mosquitoes and ague.[48] Today, in the fields around Hisarlik, blazing sunflowers hang their heads towards the dusty earth. It is all quite different from the mossy, moist Eurotan plain and the twists and turns of Taygetan foothills.

In the stories, Helen has turned her back on Greece. To try to understand the life such a woman would have enjoyed in the Trojan citadel in the Late Bronze Age, we too have to turn away from the West and from the Mycenaeans and instead set our sights on the evidence of the East.

26

THE GOLDEN HOUSES OF
THE EAST

@@@@@@@@@@@@

Armies of allies crowd the mighty city of Priam,
true, but they speak a thousand different tongues,
fighters gathered here from all ends of the realm.

HOMER, *Iliad*[1]

THE STORY OF HELEN AND PARIS, Achilles and Hector,
Agamemnon and Priam draws in visitors to the site of Troy from
across the globe. While the impoverished archaeology there gives no
quickfix impression of the hubbub of the Bronze Age city, the influx of
tourists is curiously appropriate. Here there are many nationalities of men
and women of all ages from all walks of life – just as it would have been
three and half thousand years ago. Materials from Assyria, Babylon, Mycenaean Greece and Cyprus have been excavated at Troy – brought by traders
whose quarters would have been in the town. Diplomatic texts show us
correspondence between heads of state regularly passed in and out of Trojan
gates: here there were chancelleries and scribes, diplomats and envoys. In
the 13th century BC, this centrifugal power-base would have been a colourful,
jangling place.

Because we have no extant written records from within Troy itself –
Schliemann's wilful destruction of the central belly of the site may well
have put paid to any chances of discovering a Trojan archive – we have to
derive a detailed picture of Bronze Age life from other, contemporary
sources. Troy was a vassal state of the Hittites. Socially, politically and
culturally there are striking similarities between a kingdom such as Troy and
the other great settlements within the Hittite empire.[2] To try to understand
the impact upon a foreign visitor, or captive, such as our Bronze Age Helen,
of the culture of the Near East we must turn to the eloquent evidence
excavated from the Hittite capital, Hattusa.

Because the Hittites kept meticulous written records of their affairs on tablets which are still emerging from the earth – more than three thousand fragments were excavated at Sapinuwa, north-east of Hattusa in 1990 – we have a strong taste of the characters any visiting aristocrat from the Greek mainland would have encountered.[3] Here there were priests, priestesses and temple assistants, medical advisers, barbers, doormen, grooms, bureaucrats, scribes, sword swallowers, acrobats (there are wonderful rock carvings of 'ladder-men' who compete to see who can balance on a free-standing ladder for the greatest length of time),[4] bagpipe, castanet and cymbal players, dancers and a phalanx of general domestic staff. In the 13th century BC – when the Hittite civilisation was at its most ebullient – the citadels would have heaved with people.

Once again, as within Mycenaean society, women are conspicuous by their presence. Criss-crossing the broad streets paved with their wide, heavy flagstones, there would have been large numbers of concubines – the *naptartu* – women imported to join a harem of official bed-partners. The Hittites also have a name for a 'secondary wife', the E-ŠER-TU (or *esertu*). These were consorts often imported to strengthen links with other countries and brought to the royal bed to create a dynasty of little princes and princesses.[5] Anatolian royal families needed official offspring to use as diplomats, or marriage fodder and as clan representatives within the kingdom or in the wider world. Priam was famous for having fifty sons, and texts from the Late Bronze Age show that Anatolian potentates did indeed seed huge families. Controlling the movement and marriages of women in the palace was the Tawananna (sovereign queen).[6] This is the dynastic and social environment within which our Bronze Age Helen would have been enveloped, whether as a captive, a 'secondary wife' or a premier consort.

One fragmentary Hittite tablet known as the Alakšandu Treaty, tells us that the sons of concubines could succeed to the throne.[7] A liberal interpretation of the text may even draw the conclusion that the Trojan prince referred to in the tablet, a man called Alaksandu, has a Greek concubine as a mother.[8] As we have seen, Homer has an alternative name for Paris in the *Iliad* – Alexander – almost certainly a Greek form of Alaksandu. There is simply not enough evidence to draw a line connecting Alexander the prince of Homer's Troy – a man with a taste for Greek women – and Alaksandu the Late Bronze Age prince of Wilusa, who possibly was of Greek blood, but the reference bears witness to the international nature of dynastic relations within the great royal courts of pre-history.[9]

Anatolian royal families, packed together in relatively isolated quarters, seem to have enjoyed familial relations worthy of any soap-opera, and oracles and texts refer to quarrels and catfights. One can just imagine the rivalry – not to mention the insurrections. One of the few texts that speaks of Trojan history describes the deposition of a king there called Walmu.[10] As early as 1500 BC, the Edict of Telipinu (following the murder of the epony-mous king's wife and daughter) had tried to put an end to the wranglings and bloody power struggles of the Anatolian courts.

> Who will become king after me in future, let his brothers, his sons, his in-laws, his further family members and his troops be united! Thereupon you will hold the country subdued with your might. And don't speak as follows: 'I will eradicate it', for you won't eradicate anything. On the contrary, you will only implicate yourself! Do not kill anybody of your family, it is not right.[11]

One woman whose intrigues and power-broking make for apposite – and diverting – reading is Puduhepa: a Hittite queen who was particularly active between 1280 and 1230 BC – the putative era of the Trojan War. We meet Puduhepa face to face in a weathered rock carving in Cappadocia, southern Turkey: the Firaktin relief. Dressed in a priestess' robes, she pours a libation to one of the premier deities in the Hittite pantheon – the sun goddess Hepat of Arinna. This, our only surviving representation of the queen, is a fitting one. Puduhepa had started off life as a priestess, a 'hand-maiden of Ishtar'. She had a reputation as a great beauty and the king, Hattusili III, declared that he had been compelled to marry her following a vision in a dream. Years later he writes that the goddess Ishtar has blessed them with 'the love of husband and wife'.[12] Ishtar looked after affairs of the heart in Anatolia as Aphrodite would come to in Archaic Greece and beyond.[13]

> *A man and his wife who love each other and carry their love to fulfilment:*
> *That has been decreed by you, Ishtar.*
> *He who seduces a woman and carries the seduction to fulfilment:*
> *That has been decreed by you, Ishtar.*
>
> Hurrian Hymn to Ishtar *c.* 14th century BC[14]

Deeply pious, Puduhepa energetically re-organised a number of the reli-gious festivals in the Hittite calendar. We know of the extent of her influence because she left behind her an excellent trail – not of paper, but of stone and clay.

As with a number of female consorts of the time, Puduhepa shared a seal with her king. In October 2004, fortified with the Turkish coffee that stands as thick as soup in its cup, following a tour around the vast site of Hattusa, I went to investigate one of the few surviving imprints of this vital tool of royal bureaucracy, now sitting in the quaint Museum of Bogazkale in the modern village that abuts the archaeological site.

The seal imprint has a number of cracks and it crumbles a little at some of the edges, but it is a good size, about an inch across and fairly easy to read. In the palm of my hand, the artefact hardly registered any weight — extraordinary that this discrete, diminutive piece of mud, stamped out over three thousand years ago, has survived at all. On the clay surface it is possible to make out Puduhepa's name in Luwian hieroglyphs and, next to her name, that of her husband. It was fairly common for Hittite queens to share a seal, and to enjoy some degree of independence from their consorts. But Puduhepa took things one stage further, she had her *own* seal cast.[15] In complex judicial arrangements (for example, a difficult case brought before the royal court regarding ownership of sunken treasure once a ship had been attacked) it is not King Hattusili, but Queen Puduhepa who is, repeatedly, the voice of authority.[16]

When Puduhepa comes to be involved in the negotiations surrounding her daughter's marriage to the King of Egypt, Rameses II, we get a real taste of her *kudos*. Not only does she receive from Rameses exact duplicates of the letters he sends to her husband, but then, not at all happy with the way things are proceeding, she takes the Pharaoh himself to task.

In *c.* 1270 BC there had been a fire in Puduhepa's treasure house at Hattusa.[17] The queen contacts Rameses to tell him that as a result, diplomatic affairs are delayed, in the immediate future she will not be able to send over one of her daughters as a bride to the Egyptian court. Rameses seems to be pushing her to advance the matter — presumably because he wants to get hold of the girl's dowry as well as the girl. Puduhepa's response is acerbic.

> Does my brother possess nothing at all? Only if the son of the Sun-God, the son of the Storm-God, and the sea have nothing do you have nothing! Yet, my brother, you seek to enrich yourself at my expense. That is worthy of neither your reputation, nor your status.[18]

Puduhepa was confident enough to chastise one of the most powerful men on earth. Her history reminds us that in the 13th century BC, given sufficient force of character, aristocratic women could make a lasting mark on the world around them. When you turn the spotlight onto a queen such as her, it becomes apparent that this was not just an Age of Heroes but an Age of Heroines too.

ᕙᕗᕙᕗᕙᕗ

As well as giving us a sense of courtly life, the texts from Hattusa are invaluable when trying to understand the central premise of Helen and Paris' story. A vast selection deal with legal affairs and a number of these texts show that rape, abduction and adultery were live issues. Within the collection of Hittite state laws, out of 200 clauses, fourteen deal with sexual misdemeanours.[19]

There is an assumption in the Hittite texts that, in order to be protected by law, marriages are monogamous and that such unions brought with them material gain and material responsibilities. If a man ran off with another man's betrothed then he (not the girl's family) would be personally responsible for recompensing the rejected suitor with the equivalent value of the girl's dowry.[20] Generally, marriages were arranged and it was accepted that on occasion they would not work out; if there was an amicable divorce then any property would be divided equally between both husband and wife. In the case of rape though there was less equity. Although women did have redress in law, if a woman was raped in her own home then there was an assumption that she was complicit and therefore guilty.

> If a man seizes a woman in the mountains (and rapes her), the
> man is guilty and shall die, but if he seizes her in her house, the
> woman is guilty and shall die. If the woman's husband catches
> them (in the act) and kills them, he has committed no offence.[21]

Suspected rape or adultery might bring the death penalty.[22] The Hittites recognised that passion could interrupt a well-planned marriage – there is ample legislation that deals with elopement. The concept of a lover is given a name, the 'pupu'. But if you made love to another man's wife you diced with death. Under Anatolian law, Helen's liaison with Paris was, potentially, a capital offence. A Bronze Age Paris and his illegitimate amour would not have been surprised to hear that a vengeful husband was in pursuit, the cuckold confident that he would be justified in meting out the harshest possible punishment.

27

A FLEET SETS SAIL

@@@@@@@@@@@@@

Because of his longing for something gone across the sea
a phantom seems to rule the rooms,
and the grace of statues shaped in beauty
comes to be an object of hate for the man.
In the absence of eyes
all Aphrodite is vacant, gone.

AESCHYLUS, Agamemnon[1] (c. 458 BC)

I N TROY, AS THE HELEN OF THE EPIC CYCLE looked out west, across the sea, she would have seen two small dark shapes on the horizon.[2] Two boats – preliminary envoys from Greece.[3] We hear from a variety of literary sources that when he learns of his wife's absence, Menelaus' first reaction is not to spill blood, not to effect a lightning strike, but instead to attempt to sort out the whole sorry business with diplomacy.[4] The Greek army has already been raised and is waiting in Tenedos, but the hapless Spartan king sails with Odysseus to negotiate for Helen's release.

Cut off from the rest of the army, Menelaus and Odysseus are exposed and outnumbered. As they take their request to the Trojans, Paris attempts to engineer an assassination, bribing another Trojan, Antimachos, to persuade the assembly to butcher the Greek heroes.[5] But the libidinous prince could have saved his gold. The assassination attempt is bungled and the stalwart Greeks endeavour to persuade Priam and the assembled court to hand Helen back – adding, with more than a glimmer of a threat, that by doing so they will save themselves much adversity. The Trojans choose the path of greatest resistance and vote not to give up their prize. Greek audiences would have watched this moment played out in a drama by Sophocles, now lost, called *Helenes Apaitesis*, 'The Request for Helen'. It is an eternally popular theme – the empty privilege of hindsight – an impotent vision of bloodshed avoided, of the better, happier place the world could have been.

But there is more than just pathos in play here. This version of events reflects international relations in the Late Bronze Age, when pacts and treaties and diplomatic negotiation stitched populations together; war was an expensive and unpredictable business. Great store was set by negotiation. The King of the Hurrians negotiates with the King of Babylon, the King of the Hittites writes to rulers on the Greek mainland and, in one of the most celebrated treaties from the ancient world, the Hittites and the Egyptians enter into a peace treaty, the 'Eternal Treaty' (now popularly known as the Treaty of Kadesh) to try to prevent widespread, unsustainable, mass conflict. A copy of the clay tablet on which the treaty was inscribed in 1259 BC is posted outside the United Nations Security Council. It was an agreement sealed thirteen years later by a royal marriage – that of a Hittite princess to the King of Egypt, Rameses the Great:

> [The treaty which] Ramses [Beloved] of Amon, Great King, King [of Egypt, Hero, concluded] on [a tablet of silver] with Hattusili [Great King], King of Hatti, his brother, in order to establish [great] peace and great [brotherhood] between them forever . . . I have now established good brotherhood and good peace between us forever, in order likewise to establish good peace and good brotherhood in [the relations] of Egypt with Hatti forever.[6]

The clay and bronze tablets that carried messages and information from one head of state to another were written by men and women who clearly had a common understanding although the icy respect and honey-tongued, thinly veiled threats of some of these diplomatic texts are only too familiar. The language of diplomacy seems to have changed very little down the millennia. Take, for example, the King of the Hittites, writing to Kadashman-Enlil II, the King of Babylon, some time between 1263 and 1255 BC:

> When your father and I established diplomatic relations and when we became like loving brothers, we did not become brothers for one day only; did we not establish permanent brotherly relations based on equal understanding?
> . . . after the death of your father, I dried my tears and dispatched a messenger to the Land of Babylon, and sent the following message to the high officials of Babylon; 'If you do not keep the son of my brother as ruler, I shall become your enemy, I will go and invade Babylon; but (if you do, then) send

me word if an enemy rises against you or if any difficulty threatens you, and I will come to your aid!'[7]

The tablets reveal something of central importance to the Late Bronze Age. In many ways, it was appropriate that this distant era should be nominated as heroic. Not simply because this was a time of storybook wealth, vigorous ambition and massive achievement before an age of retrenchment that we have labelled 'the Dark Ages', but also because those in charge of the palace-citadels of the Eastern Mediterranean were, in a sense, giants of men. Read the treaties written by the Hittites and the other great leaders of the day and the language used clearly demonstrates that these are agreements not between states, but between individuals: between singular men (and sometimes women) – heroes and heroines whose actions could indeed direct the course of entire civilisations.

The Hittite king, for example, frequently styles himself 'Great King, Hero'.[8] Given that single aristocrats could mobilise vast forces in the Late Bronze Age – 47,500 allied Hittite forces at the Battle of Kadesh,[9] we are told by ancient accounts – it is little surprise that these all-powerful rulers became larger-than-life characters in the popular imagination and that their decisions and actions became legendary.

Still, even if this was an age of diplomacy, of negotiation between heroes, in the narrative of the Trojan War, diplomacy failed. Paris would not release his exotic new queen, and the Greeks were sent back to their ships empty-handed. Whether Helen had walked lightly into Priam's great city, or had been dragged through the gates, bruised and traumatised by her rape, the Trojans were not going to give her up. Licking their wounds, the Greek leaders Menelaus, Odysseus and Agamemnon began to draw up their battle plan.

They recalled the vows of loyalty that they and all the other heroes of Greece had made to each other over the sacrificed corpse of a horse when contesting for Helen's hand. They agreed that when an infiltrator, a foreigner, came and made a mockery of their honour and their self-sacrifice, came and took Helen while a guest of the Spartan palace, they had sustained a collective affront. Agamemnon, the most powerful king in Greece and the elder brother of the cuckolded Menelaus, had the perfect excuse to mobilise the army. Doubly, triply insulted, next time the Greek tribal-leaders were not going to take no for an answer.

❧❧❧❧❧

As Helen lay in Paris' bed, weeping or laughing at the news that Menelaus had been sent back from his diplomatic sortie empty-handed, his tail between his legs,[10] the Greek fleet, following an earlier, abortive attempt to land on the Troad, was gathering at Aulis on the eastern coast of Greece near Thebes.[11] The Greeks were not to be cheated of their prize-woman. Supplies were loaded, and the drummers drummed as soldier after soldier marched up and down the beaches preparing for battle. The glory of Greece was there – the warrior-heroes who between them ruled over Crete and the Greek mainland. Women had been left in charge in palace-fortresses back in Greece and the clans had put aside their differences to form a unified war machine. Their blood was up. The shores of Troy promised revenge and plunder and women a-plenty. Later in the narrative of the conflict, Thersites provides an inventory of the spoils of war: bronze, gold and *'Best of the lot, the beauties'*.[12] Spurring one of his men on, Agamemnon offers *'a tripod, or purebred team with their own car or a fine woman to mount and share your bed'*.[13]

Everything was set and yet the wind was against the Greeks; the boats, lined up at Aulis, could not set sail. An enervating lingering dragged out, day after day. Only an extreme act would bring catharsis. Helen's was an act of love that famously precipitated an act of war, but the killing starts long before the Greeks land on the Anatolian coast. Her affair set in train a whole catalogue of murders. The first victim was a young child – Agamemnon's daughter Iphigeneia.[14]

The reason the Greek ships had found themselves trapped at Aulis was because a Greek soldier – some whispered Agamemnon himself – had killed a deer in the sanctuary of the goddess of the hunt, Artemis. To make matters worse, the arrogant hunter then boasted that this was a feat that bettered any kill of the gods. The goddess was enraged. Artemis would only be appeased with a blood gift of the most perfect kind. And so Agamemnon sends wily-tongued Odysseus to tempt his young daughter Iphigeneia to her death. 'Tell her that Achilles is waiting,' says the desperate king, 'tell her she shall be married to the greatest of all heroes.'[15] Iphigeneia travels from Mycenae with her mother Clytemnestra. But when she arrives, she is not taken to put on her wedding clothes, but instead to an altar slab by her father. Here she is to be sacrificed; ostensibly to appease the goddess – but in reality for Greek honour, to ensure that men can fight for an emblem of beauty. It is a desperate moment. Iphigeneia cries out to her father, but is still lifted *'like a goat, face downward, above the altar'*. She is *'gagged, the bit yanked roughly, stifling a cry that would have brought a curse down on the house'*. She knows all her assailants, but she can do nothing but *'with pitiful arrows from her eyes'* shoot the sacrificers, '*vivid as in a picture, wanting to speak, to call each one by name.*' And all this, as the watchman acidly points out, is Helen's fault. Iphigeneia is sacrificed to '*safeguard, / A war of vengeance over a woman*'.[16]

The hideous brutality of Iphigeneia's death drives Agamemnon's wife, Helen's half-sister, Clytemnestra, to kill Agamemnon on his return from Troy. Horror at his father's murder, in turn, spurs Orestes to kill his mother Clytemnestra and her lover Aegisthus. Orestes is persecuted, driven mad by the Furies for his unfilial hatred. Helen is the catalyst of one of the most famous tragic cycles in the world.

ⓖⓥⓖⓥⓖⓥ

The story of Iphigeneia deals with fundamental issues – the conflicts of love and duty, of ambition and humility, of superstition and belief. And because of this the slaughter of a virgin-princess from Mycenae is still enacted on stages across the world. Recently I saw a small poster advertising a production of Goethe's version of the tragedy in a little theatre above the Prince Albert pub in Notting Hill, West London. Interested to see how a regular theatre crowd would react to the tale of the sacrifice of a pre-pubescent, I bought a ticket on impulse and waited half an hour for the show to start. The theatre audience was sitting in the bar downstairs, talking about film-stars and shopping alongside the fashionable of Notting Hill. Conversations were shouted to compete with the TV and thudding piped music while the electric ceiling fans above whirled busily, necessary in this crowded smoky venue even on a chill November evening. Single men smoked, read the *Evening Standard* and talked on their mobile phones – a lot of day-to-day business to get through before moving upstairs to be pounded by a drama first staged 2,500 years ago.

And of course all those thoughts about passion and principle, free will and fate, hooked to the story of a woman butchered so that the Greeks could get on with the business of retrieving Helen from Troy. In Euripides' version of the tale, Iphigeneia's mother Clytemnestra begs her husband to reconsider his decision, which, even to an ancient Greek mind, seems nefarious.

> *Tell me: if someone asks why you are killing her,*
> *What will you say? Or must I speak your words for you?*
> *'So that Menelaus may get back Helen.' A splendid act,*
> *To pay a child's life as the ransom for a slut!*
> *To buy what we most hate with what we most dearly love!*[17]

Just before he kills her, Agamemnon tries to justify, to his own daughter, her imminent death. He articulates the close connection between *eros* and *eris*, blaming a form of the love goddess for rousing his men to a passion to leave Greece and fight. 'Some kind of Aphrodite has frenzied the army, made them mad to set sail as soon as possible.'[18] Small comfort to the young girl.[19]

Iphigeneia is stretched across the altar and the high priest brings his knife to her throat. In some versions of the story there is a crash of thunder and a flash of lightning and the girl is whisked off by Artemis herself to Tauris (present-day Crimea on the Black Sea). In others, the blade hits home. But the fate of the daughter of Agamemnon is now an irrelevance because suddenly, miraculously, the leaves around the sanctuary begin to stir. The wind is back and the soldiers and generals let out a great sigh – they are on their way to Troy: 1,186 ships, bearing between them 100,000 men, sail from the port of Aulis to reclaim Sparta's wandering queen.[20]

Today the coastline of Aulis is a sad place, dominated by a vast cement factory – the intrusion of industrialisation on the landscape is uncompromising. There are classical and indeed Mycenaean ruins here, and a sanctuary of Artemis, but all is covered in a fine layer of cement dust. The air is bitter. Occasionally little posies are left on marble slabs in memory of the young Iphigeneia. An innocent who has come to represent the inexorable brutality of war and of blind ambition.

⊚⊚⊚⊚⊚

Homer does not deal with the Iphigeneia story but his famous roll-call of Greek maritime might, 'the Catalogue of Ships', sheds an interesting light on the origins of the *Iliad*. We are told that twenty-nine naval contingents are launched from Aulis in Boiotia, in northern Greece. This catalogue is surprisingly similar to the lists of foodstuffs and taxes and personnel, the property distribution and the hierarchies, which are scratched into the clay of the Linear B tablets. It is bald, bland and repetitive, a blatant and meticulously detailed assertion of power. First listed are the regions and towns that have contributed to the war effort; then we learn the names of the commanders and finally the number of ships and crew members.

It is impossible that this comprehensive list was researched and formulated by one man, concocted as a giant memory test to flesh out an already long poem. Of all 178 names recorded by Homer not one is fabricated and almost every one of the places catalogued is given an appropriate geographical position.[21] Indeed, prominent parts of Homer's 8th-century BC Greece are conspicuous by their absence; the bard is not simply detailing the centres of power in his own Iron Age world. These omissions indicate the historicity of this element of the epic – the excluded towns and regions were indeed not part of 'Greece' in the Bronze Age. Described by some as an 'order of march' the list is a plausible compilation of the forces available to a Late Bronze Age general.

In 1993, the discovery of a single Linear B tablet in Thebes[22] threw an entirely new light on the Catalogue question. The tablet was uncovered by accident, when a water pipe was being laid in Pelopidas Street in central Thebes. The waterworks were suspended and an archaeological investigation begun. The dig has been productive and, to date, over 250 tablets have surfaced. These tablets show that Thebes was in fact the centre of a massive territory, a territory larger than Pylos or Sparta or Mycenae itself.[23] If the Theban district was a vitally powerful region in the Late Bronze Age, it suddenly makes sense that a consolidated movement of Greeks should set sail from Thebes' port – the port of Aulis.

The new Theban tablets list a town, Eleon, which had always given archaeologists and historians some trouble – it is mentioned in the Catalogue of Ships, part of the naval contingent from Boiotia. Yet Eleon seemed to have vanished off the face of the earth. As a northern Greek settlement it is not mentioned in any other source from antiquity. And so, scholars argued, this town must have been simply a figment of Homer's imagination.

The Thebes tablets dating from the 13th century BC tell a different story. Eleon appears on tablet TH Ft 140.[24] Homer's lines, in this case (as in many others), are transmitting information direct from the Bronze Age past.

And by comparing Homer's verse with the hard evidence of the Late Bronze Age, another snag in the Trojan story can be unravelled. It has often been asked why Homer uses two names for Troy. Why does he call the town both *Troia* and *Ilios*? Why do we have a book called the '*Iliad*' that tells the story of the '*Trojan*' war? The answer has now revealed itself thanks to a collaboration between linguists and historians of the Hittite world.

Homer was probably an Ionian Greek; he could have lived in Smyrna or in Chios. By the time his words were written down in the 7th century BC, in the Ionian region the 'w' that often preceded the letter 'i' would have been lost (the Aeolian dialects kept their 'w' for longer; Sappho, for example, would have used it). The Hittite texts tell us that in the Troad there were two territories in the region of Troy – one was called Wilusa, the other Taruwisa.[25] If these names are remembered down the centuries, and then sung by a bard who drops his 'W's, Wilusa becomes (W)Ilusa, then (W)Ilios and eventually Ilios, and Taru(w)isa, becomes Taruisa and eventually Troia. Hence we get the story of Ilios, the *Iliad*, and the wars of Troia, Troy.

The rhythm of the *Iliad* too can guide us towards the certain knowledge that a number of Homer's lines were composed in the Mycenaean period. The entire poem is written in hexameter. Many of the verses read perfectly, and yet the meter of some lines is simply unsatisfying, there are jolts and jars where normally the poetry flows. But write those lines using elements of Linear B, Bronze Age rather than Classical Greek – in the language that the Mycenaeans would have used – and the lines scan perfectly.[26]

☙❧☙❧☙❧

Despite the historical roots of the Catalogue of Ships the quest to reclaim a wayward queen could never have launched a *thousand* ships. If the Mycenaean elite had left for Troy in such a number, with each fifty-oared boat carrying thirty warriors, each of those warriors with at least one high-born valet, the Mycenaean economy would simply have disintegrated. In the 13th century BC, the sighting of just seven ships off the coast of the Levant spread panic through the region.[27] And in legend, Heracles was said to have sacked an older city of Troy with a mere six ships. We have to wait close on a thousand years before a fleet remotely approaching the size of Homer's Catalogue is ever recorded and even then (when the Persians sail to Greece in the hope of a takeover) the number reaches only five hundred or so.[28]

Back in the Cyclades where those stunning Bronze Age frescoes were preserved by the violent eruption of the Thera volcano, one diminutive example shows a nautical procession setting sail. Here the boats are finely decked out, fluttering with garlands of flowers, the skins of sacrificed animals, flags, and coloured cloths – they are clearly ready for some kind of grand state occasion. In the background men and women scurry around a vast citadel; soldiers are in evidence, and it is difficult to tell whether the boats are being welcomed or repulsed. There were no dedicated war-fleets in the Late Bronze Age. Those boats in the paintings would have been multi-purpose vessels that delivered sometimes goods, sometimes traders and diplomats, sometimes soldiers to far-flung shores. Camphor and incense could be burnt in the prows – there would have been lights to deal with the endless blackness of the ocean.[29]

It would have been boats like these that carried the contingents of Mycenaean Greeks to Beşik Bay. And, if there is any truth in the stories, it would have been boats such as these that brought Ajax, Achilles, Odysseus and the glory of Greece hurtling eastwards across the surf, the greatest warriors of the known world, leaving their homes and families, leaving their citadels unprotected, their crops rotting in the fields, to honour a promise made on a plain close to Sparta ten years earlier.[30] And keenest of all, the cuckhold King of Sparta, Menelaus, with the sails on his boat bellying, crossing the high seas, to bring back his queen.

⊚⊚⊚⊚⊚⊚⊚⊚⊚⊚

PART EIGHT

TROY
BESIEGED

28

HELEN – DESTROYER
OF CITIES

@@@@@@@@@@@@

So now let no man hurry to sail for home, not yet . . .
not till he beds down with a faithful Trojan wife,
payment in full for the groans and shocks of war
we have borne for Helen.

Nestor, in Homer, *Iliad*[1]

THE GREEK VERB φρίσσω (phrisso) is an interesting one, the root
of our word frisson. A useful word, it is flexible and while it can
be interpreted in a number of ways it is always evocative. It is a
word used by Homer in connection with Helen. In Troy we learn from her
that πάντες δέ με πεφρίκασιν, 'all around me cringe or bristle with fear'.
Elsewhere she is ῥιγεδανὴ Ἑλένη, 'Helen who makes you shudder' or 'makes
you tremble'. She is sweet poison – both dreadful and delicious.[2] And now
that she has come to Troy, because Helen trails disaster in her wake, the
plains of Troy too will bristle with arms. As Cassandra has predicted, as
Zeus has planned, the Greeks want Helen back.

Homer paints a vivid picture of the boats, clustered up on the shore
of the Bosphorus, row upon row, blackening the sand with their hulls until
the beach below is submerged. The armies are like swarms of flies, seething
over freshly collected milk.[3] Elsewhere in the *Iliad* he speaks of the fires
around the new Greek camp glowing in the dark, and the men in their
bivouacs, tense and expectant. And he imagines these soldiers rank with
aggression. Listen to the first lines of the *Iliad*.

Rage – Goddess, sing the rage of Peleus' son Achilles,
murderous, doomed, that cost the Achaeans countless losses.[4]

Homer makes it clear from the outset of the epic that the *Iliad* is a story of hate as well as of love, of human lives adulterated by the maw of conflict. Furious passages in Book 1 describe two men jarring over a woman – not Menelaus and Paris over Helen, but 'brilliant' Achilles and Agamemnon 'lord of men' over Briseis 'the girl with the sparkling eyes'. Agamemnon has already been filibustering about another girl, Chryseis. We do not hear much about Chryseis directly, but we are told that her father, the priest Chryses, loves her and is outraged that she is being used as Agamemnon's whore. She has been dragged from the temple of Apollo and seems destined to become a spoil of war, as Agamemnon barks at Chryses:

> The girl – I won't give up the girl. Long before that,
> old age will overtake her in my house, in Argos,
> far from her fatherland, slaving back and forth
> at the loom, forced to share my bed![5]

There are echoes of Helen's fate, if we believe that she too is a woman forced to share the bed of a foreigner a long way from home. The lines also pre-echo the fate of the women of Troy, a fate described with sometimes unbearable brilliance by the tragedians Euripides and Aeschylus. Homer makes it clear to us that men will always use the possession of women to score points over one another. Agamemnon brags to Achilles that he will have another woman, Achilles' Briseis: 'So you can learn just how much greater I am than you.' The Greeks are on Trojan soil and they are ready to punish all women, who, like Helen, weaken men by love. Ready to force open the gates of Troy and to force open the women protected by the city's sloping walls.

As Homer fleshes out the narrative of the Trojan War, we come across a use of language that does not presume a dividing line between the lust for love and the lust for blood. Swords and rapiers stab at yielding bodies. The heroes seek satisfaction in slicing open their enemies' flesh. Hector teases and intimidates Ajax: 'My long spear will devour your white flesh.'[6] Or, as Fagles puts it in his translation of the same line: 'If you have the daring to stand against my heavy spear, its point will rip your soft warm skin to shreds!'[7] Suddenly, in the heat of battle, towering Ajax has become female: in Greek artistic and literary iconography it is usually women who boast soft, lily-white flesh.

Aphrodite's lovers were Ares the god of War, and Hermes the guide of the dead.[8] And so unfortunately for Paris and for Helen, where love travels, eris (discord or strife or deadly conflict) will follow. Helen's is a gutsy love in pursuit of which much blood will be spilled. She is as deadly as she is delectable. When we talk about desire and death, sex and violence, we couple them because they are distinct, contra. But for the ancients these were close cousins, the malign progeny of unbridled nature, building blocks of the cosmos, creatures close to Chaos. Helen's love was lethal. She is famous for inspiring men to fuck and to fight. Consequently we remember her, not as Helen of Sparta, but as Helen of Troy.[9]

The conflation of sex and violence in the Greek mind can be traced through the language. Both lovers and warriors can mingle together: *meignymi*. *Damazo* could mean to slaughter or rape or to seduce or subdue. *Kredemna* denotes either a city's battlements or the veils of a woman. When Troy falls, both will be ripped and blasted – the thing they had hidden will be defiled and destroyed. Writers such as Thucydides and Euripides used the word *eros* in metaphors to describe the fever that roused men to fight. The Spartans sacrificed to the spirit of Eros before they went into battle.

It is little surprise that 'much-desired' Helen enters extant written record as spoil. We first hear about her in Book 2 of the *Iliad* where she is described both as 'a trophy' and as an instrument of destruction. The gods are gossiping. Hera is warning Athena that the Argives have lost hope and are sailing home:

> . . . *Inconceivable!/ . . . All the Argives flying home to their fatherland,/ sailing over the sea's broad back? Leaving Priam/ and all the men of Troy a trophy to glory over,/ Helen of Argos, Helen for whom so many Argives/ lost their lives in Troy, far from native land.*[10]

Helen's casual introduction here into the plot of the *Iliad* demonstrates that Homer does not need to explain her origins, confident as he was that his audience was already familiar with a fuller Helen narrative. The poems of the Epic Cycle, written a hundred years or so after Homer, which tell of Helen's earlier life, must have been echoes of older songs, lost now, that dealt in more detail with the tale of the Queen of Sparta.

When we meet Helen face to face in the *Iliad*, in Book 3, she is brought in to survey the men fighting for her on the plains of Troy. Priam, the great king who is about to see the pride of Greece crawling over his lands, slaughtering his men and enslaving his women, calls her over to watch: '*Come over here, dear child. Sit in front of me . . . I don't blame you*'.[11] So there is Helen, famous, beautiful and desired. A prize for Trojans and Greeks alike. She is watching men slug it out for her, just as they did twenty years before in the marriage contest arranged by her father. But now the bar has been raised as Anatolian heroes too have entered the fray. The need to possess the ultimate beauty will spur Greeks and Trojans alike to a ruthless odium.

∞∞∞∞∞

Today it is still possible to stand on the citadel walls of Troy to look over the Scamander plain which does indeed stretch out beyond the 'Scaean Gate'. Tourist guides promote a rag-bag of Trojan tales in an impressive array of languages as they shepherd their charges along the walls. Walking the ramparts, looking down over the 'lower town', now scrubland, with a copy of the *Iliad* in hand, the romantic can fancy, following Homer's lead, the hungry, worn Trojans gathering to watch as Helen, a willing captive, was shown off to the assembled crowd. The displays were intended as morale-boosters, reminding the tired, benighted inhabitants why they had to endure such suffering and why, with such a prize at stake, it was still worth fighting this long and bloody war.

These showy personal appearances were designed to galvanise spirits, and they worked, even after years of privation and personal loss; the elders at Troy, according to Homer, declare that Helen's radiance is indeed worth the disintegration of their lives. As she passes, the old men start to chatter; their voices rising and falling like cicadas.[12] She has a face like a goddess they say. In a world where divine power could be malign or benign, that might be a terrible as well as a wonderful thing:

> And catching sight of Helen moving along the ramparts,
> they murmured one to another, gentle, winged words:
> 'Who on earth could blame them? Ah, no wonder
> the men of Troy and Argives under arms have suffered
> years of agony all for her, for such a woman,
> Beauty, terrible beauty!'[13]

∞∞∞∞∞

As she passed along the ramparts of Troy, this is what a Bronze Age Helen would have seen. In the 13th century BC, there were five gateways, three of them massive, on the citadel at Hisarlik Hill, each providing access through the citadel walls – which were, in parts, 9 m high. At some point these gates have been burnt to the ground. Watchtowers[14] were built into the walls – remembered three thousand years later by Marlowe as 'the topless towers of Ilium'.[15] As at Mycenae, the aristocratic zone is terraced, and two-storeyed mansions surround a central 'palace'. The streets of Troy, as Homer says, are walled and 'well-laid' – although three thousand years on, the broad, cracked flags buckle and bulge.

The excavations begun by Professor Korfmann in 1988 and subsequent magnetometer surveys of the site have delivered a more complete picture of the 13th-century BC city than was ever before available. The south-western 'Scaean Gate', operational until just after 1300 BC, was subsequently blocked up — the infill is still clearly visible. Just beyond the gated ramparts there is a marked concentration of small-scale finds (evidence of a busy shanty town at Troy's walls) and then, further out still, south of the citadel, Troy's lower town. The lower town (which Schliemann never found — dying before he could begin his planned excavations in 1891) has been shown to be protected by two ditches: one is 400 m from the citadel, the other 500 m. Both ditches are U-shaped, cut straight out of the limestone bedrock and around 11½ feet (3.5 m) wide, 6½ feet (1.95 m) deep — almost certainly dug to protect against chariots — that ferocious weapon of the Late Bronze Age. The area, enclosed perhaps by palisades, is at least 270,000 square m (75 acres).[16]

With this discovery, the city of Troy has now been shown to have been large enough to accommodate anything between seven and ten thousand people. Here there are storage pits, pavements and cobbled streets, traces of figs and vines, and (interestingly) a fair amount of Mycenaean pottery — both imported and imitation; the Trojans clearly had a taste for Greek style.

Typical of other Anatolian fortress-towns of the time, Troy was indeed — as described by Homer — both a trading town and the seat of a royal family.[17] And protecting those aristocrats and merchants, circling the citadel were great sloping walls, Homer's *euteikheion*, 'well-walled' city. In the *Iliad*, Homer constructs a vivid scene where Achilles' lover, the Greek hero Patroclus, tries four times to scale the 'jutting walls' of Troy. With gargantuan effort, the eager hero nearly succeeds.[18] But this is a war between the gods as well as between men and eventually Patroclus is blasted back by the wrath of Apollo, the god worshipped with great piety at Troy, protecting the city that was dear to him.

Homer talks a good deal about Apollo's love for Troy, and recently archaeologists have turned up a tantalising piece of evidence from the 13th century BC.[19] Across Turkey you will find giant carved 'god-stones' at doorways and gateposts. The Bronze Age Anatolians believed that these megalithic blocks protected the spirits of their deities and spirits. God-stones have been excavated at Troy too — at the time of writing, seventeen have been found. An inscription on the Alaksandu treaty tells us that one of the 'swear-gods' particularly revered at Wilusa was a male god, *Ap(p)aliunas*. Homer makes it clear in the *Iliad* that the god Apollo was the pre-eminent deity in the city – is this another instance where he was right? Was *Ap(p)aliunas*, Apollo?

With its god-stones and sanctuaries, its stocks of weapons and mansions, its stores of fine perfumed cloth and its gold, its cosmopolitan population, in both the minds of the ancients, and in Bronze Age reality, Helen or no, Troy would certainly have been a city worth sacking.

⚭⚭⚭⚭⚭

The siege of Troy famously lasted for ten years. While looking for reminders of Helen from the classical world, I once travelled to Manchester in the north of England where a number of remarkable pieces are held by the University of Manchester Museum.[20] Here there is a finely painted black figure-*skyphos* (a deep wine-cup) from Attica, which speaks of the yawning stretch of years and the duller, drearier days of such a lengthy campaign. The heroes Achilles and Ajax are bent over a gaming board.[21] The men are lost in the counters in front of them, enjoying their absorption in something other than death and destruction. A mitigation from the tense tedium of a protracted – and perhaps pointless – campaign. In the quiet of the museum it is a tacit reminder of the gentler moments of any grand military campaign.

In reality it would have been impossible for the Trojans (or for any Late Bronze Age city) to endure a ten-year siege. The Mycenaeans too would have been entirely debilitated after camping out in the Troad for ten winters.[22] But arrowheads and stores of sling-shot and burnt walls do show that Troy suffered sustained periods of attack in the Late Bronze Age. Throughout the second millennium BC the fortifications of the site are built with increasing vigour, and new archaeology reveals that the population of Troy would have had the wherewithal to withstand and survive shorter onslaughts. Homer talks about underground springs and rivers at Troy. Not only have references to 'subterranean water channels' been traced in the Hittite texts which describe Wilusa,[23] but recent excavations[24] have revealed Troy's hidden strength, a concealed underground water channel – a 'water-mine' possibly built as early as 3000 BC. Up to 306 gallons (1,400 litres) of water still run through it every day.[25]

When I last visited, the place was easy to find. Reeds grow around it and one of the dogs that make the site their home will lead you there to have a quick drink from the oozing puddle outside the mouth of the channel, now barred by a metal grille. Behind the grille stretch four channels – one large, three small; the deepest is 100 metres long. Deep in the cave is a reservoir, the overflow caught in storage tanks. Although aesthetically unin-spiring, this is a strangely moving spot. Perhaps these man-made water cisterns complemented the 'washing pools' that Homer describes close to the banks of the Scamander River (itself still 'broad and sandy') at Troy.[26] Hearing the gentle splash of water one is reminded that whether or not this natural resource kept Helen alive, it would, over years of Trojan history, have saved the lives of many.

So what inspired those stories of a ten-year siege? A muscular Mycen-aean presence on Trojan territory? An aggressive neighbour staking out a patch in a cosmopolitan little kingdom? Or maybe the story of the Trojan War is a conflation of any number of micro-conflicts suffered by those on the glittering crescent of coastal land around the Troad? Skirmishes over land and taxes and trading routes and slave labour, ugly little squabbles that become inflated into an epic event in the popular imagination? All inter-pretations are possible.[27]

What is certain is that in the 13th century BC and again *c.* 1180 BC, the Trojans experienced great perdition.[28] Cracks in the citadel's fortifications and massive rock-falls have been diagnosed as earthquake damage — fires followed.[29] Could a natural disaster have sounded the death knell for a city already weakened by human agency? There are a few human skeletons from this period at Troy; all have been mutilated. By 1180 BC the *'topless towers of Ilium'* were destroyed. Archaeology cannot yet give us the definitive cause of its destruction — but for over two and a half thousand years men have been swift to blame not fire, or earthquakes, or military ambition, but Helen.

29

DEATH'S DARK CLOUD

@@@@@@@@@@@@@

Idomeneus skewered Erymas straight through the mouth,
the merciless brazen spear point raking through,
up under the brain to split his glistening skull –
teeth shattered out, both eyes brimmed to the lids
with a gush of blood and both nostrils spurting,
mouth gaping, blowing convulsive sprays of blood,
and death's dark cloud closed down around his corpse.

HOMER, *Iliad*[1]

TROY MAY HAVE SMELLED SWEET ONCE but it would soon be running with filth. Fighting for possession of Helen, the Greeks and the Trojans lock in a tortuous struggle, as first one, and then the other, gains the upper hand.

Paris and Menelaus challenge each other to a duel. Too many lives are being squandered. This is a matter of honour and so they will sort out the whole deranged business the hero's way, man to man, close-quarter fighting. Dressed in their finest, glinting armour they march to the dust-bowl that was once arable and mark out the ground. The duel begins symbolically, with showy moves: each throws a spear; Menelaus runs at Paris with a silver-studded sword. But then it becomes messier, more personal; the Greek king and the Trojan prince hurl themselves at each other, grappling together on no man's land. Menelaus is the stronger, and the more experienced warrior, it is clear he is going to win. He grabs Paris by the strap of his helmet and begins to drag him towards the points of Greek swords.

Aphrodite cannot bear to see her beautiful prince pulverised. She conceals herself within a cloud of mist and swoops down to scoop Paris off the battlefield – laying him out languidly on his 'large carved bed'. Disguised as an old woman, the goddess seeks out Helen and orders her back to service her second husband. Helen is furious – both with Aphrodite 'who supplied the lust that led to disaster' and with the feeble failure of

19 The romantic Helen – a blonde, Classical pin-up. Evelyn De Morgan painted Helen as many have imagined her to be – rose-tinted. The artist has given Helen a golden mirror; she appears transfixed by her own beauty, but does not, cannot, look directly at her reflection.

20 Helen's image was frequently used to decorate the richest of vases. The white background and colour paint on this sherd shows this was an expensive piece. Helen lowers her chin, but glances up at Paris from underneath long eyelashes.

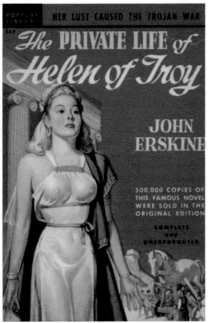

21-23 The images painted of 'the world's desire' tell us as much about men's ideas of women as they do about Helen herself. Frederick Sandys' Helen sulks (**21**, *above*).

Sir Edward John Poynter's Helen realises, too late, what she has done (**22**, *right*).

Earle Bergey's cover (**23**, *left*) for John Erskine's titillating novel, originally written in 1925 and then reprinted 1952, is literally pornographic (a demonstration of *porneia* – unchastity).

24 Zeus, disguised as a swan, rapes Leda, Queen of Sparta, and Helen is conceived – a popular theme much reproduced throughout the Greek and Roman periods. This *stele* is a Roman-period copy of a Greek tombstone.

25 The story told of the 5th century BC artist Zeuxis' attempts to recreate Helen became an allegory for the artist's struggle successfully to depict nature's perfection.

In this manuscript from 1282 (**26**), Helen is not a painting but an idol. The action is arrested at the moment Zeuxis reaches out to give 'the most beautiful woman in the world' a face (an impossible task). Behind the artist, young men practice their spear-throwing technique.

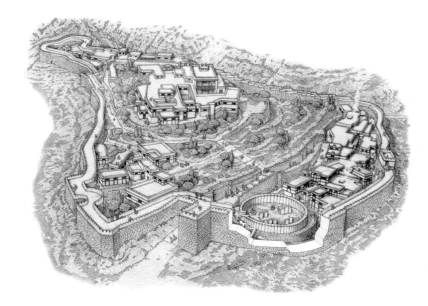

27 The royal citadel of Mycenae was strengthened in the 13th century BC; a period when the Greek inhabitants were clearly uneasy.

28 The 'Lion Gate' at Mycenae. The entrances of both the Greek citadel of Mycenae and the Hittite citadel of Hattusa were protected by immense, carved beasts – now known to be lionesses.

29 Troy in the 13th century BC. Current surveys indicate that Troy had an extensive lower town. The centre of the Bronze Age site of Troy was virtually eradicated by Schliemann, but Greek and Roman settlers had already destroyed much of the palatial area with their own building schemes.

30 Note Troy's sloping walls. An unusual number of horse-bones have been found at Troy, suggesting this could have been a Bronze Age equine trading centre.

31 The royal citadel at the site of Hattusa – the capital of the Hittite world. In the 13th century BC the Hittites commanded much of modern-day Turkey and large parts of the Middle East. Troy was a kingdom loyal to the Hittites and influenced by them. The *Iliad* concerns the clash of peoples from both sides of the Dardanelles Straits, both Greeks and Trojans; the epic should be studied from an Eastern as well as a Western perspective.

32 A reconstruction of the *megaron* – the throne room at Pylos. Some details are conjectural but the overall impression is very good. Mycenaean royalty favoured vivid decorative schemes – visual stories are told in frescoes around the walls.

33 The scenes on a number of large gold signet rings represent ritual activity, often the cult of trees; here, a bare-breasted woman dances, a man shakes a branch vigorously and another young woman collapses onto an altar.

34 The poppy-head frequently makes an appearance in Mycenaean art and artefacts – and is handled by women, suggesting that narcotics were an important part of religious ritual. This pin made of bronze and rock crystal was found in an elite grave at Mycenae.

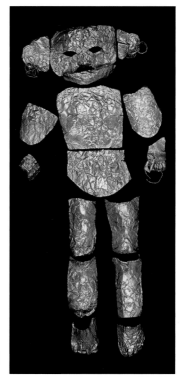

35 The terracotta figures found at Mycenae give a sense of the horror as well as the ecstasy that seems to have formed a part of religious practice. This ghoulish lady, dubbed 'Clytemnestra' by her excavators, was found in the cult-centre at Mycenae where she had been left c. 1230 BC.

36 The corpses of the Mycenaean dead were often draped in gold and other ornamentations. Two babies found at Mycenae had been covered with the gold sheeting.

The young Helen would almost certainly have worn make-up – this woman from Tiryns in the Peloponnese carries a large cosmetics box (**37**, *left*).

A 'princess' Helen would have had her head shaved as a young girl (**38**, *right*).

Adolescents grow their hair a little longer – this is as close as we can get to the impression of a Mycenaean aristocrat on the eve of her wedding (**39**, *below left*).

The mark of a mature woman is long hair. Older women are portrayed with pendulous breasts and with dabs of red paint in the corners of their eyes (**40**, *below*).

41 Physical beauty and prowess were valued in men as well as women in the Bronze Age. This image from a fresco found at Thera shows two boys boxing.

42 This soulful head of a young Mycenaean man has been carved out of elephant ivory. He wears a band around his head and his ears are pierced.

43 A Spartan girl caught in the middle of a dance, turning forward and looking back. Originally a decoration on the rim of a large metal vessel. Although artists of all periods have fantasised about young Spartan virgins exercising naked or semi-clothed, the archaeological record suggests they did indeed perform dances and athletics with very little on. At a separate women-only festival in honour of Hera at Olympia, Spartan women would race competitively.

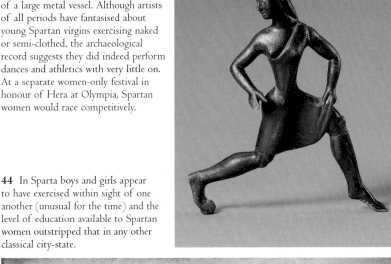

44 In Sparta boys and girls appear to have exercised within sight of one another (unusual for the time) and the level of education available to Spartan women outstripped that in any other classical city-state.

45 The story of Helen and Paris' love affair begins at a wedding on Mt Pelion where proceedings are disrupted by Eris, the goddess of strife. Few representations of the goddess were made, or survive.

46 Helen is raped throughout European art in a number of ways. Although archaic and classical Greek artefacts typically show Helen's liaison with Paris as an elopement, and Sappho, in *Fragment 16* (**47**), describes Helen leaving Menelaus of her own accord, down the centuries the encounter with the Prince of Troy becomes more violent.

48 By the 15th century when figs. 49 (*right*) and 50 (*below*), were commissioned, Helen's journey to Troy is almost always a forced abduction.

51 The female face of the 13th century BC. This woman-goddess from Mycenae is heavily made up, with red 'suns' on her cheeks, chin and forehead.

52 This image, painted in 1914, is what Helen has become; not a part of the Eastern Mediterranean but distinct from it, a white woman attended to by an oriental slave. A vain and shallow creature, lost in her own image while behind her Troy burns.

her cocksure amour. She tries to resist both the goddess and the goddess' plaything, but Aphrodite, chilling, threatens to dash Helen's beauty, her one security. Helen slinks back to Paris' chamber where the beautiful boy is in infuriatingly ebullient mood. He has danced away from death and although Helen scorns him he begs her to lose herself in love: '*He led the way to the bed. His wife went with him. / And now, while the two made love in the large carved bed, / Menelaus stalked like a wild beast, up and down the lines — / where could he catch a glimpse of magnificent Paris?*'[2]

Deprived of his prey, the King of Sparta succumbs to redoubled hate. And as Paris and Helen worship Aphrodite under the 'high-vaulted roof' of the prince's 'sumptuous halls', outside in the dust the battle and the atrocities continue. At one point Menelaus suggests making a Trojan soldier a prisoner-of-war rather than executing him. His elder brother Agamemnon, saturated with blood-lust, roars at the disgraced King of Sparta:

> *No baby boy still in his mother's belly,*
> *not even he escape — all Ilium blotted out,*
> *no tears for their lives, no markers for their graves!*[3]

The *Iliad* is an orgy of killing. Homer's poetry pairs heart-piercing verse with a delight in the minutiae of death and suffering. To read it can be distressing.[4] In one extended narrative scene that would have filled a number of parchment or papyrus sheets, the Greek Diomedes drives his way through the Trojan ranks:

> *One he stabbed with a bronze lance above the nipple,*
> *the other his heavy sword hacked at the collarbone,*
> *right on the shoulder, cleaving the whole shoulder*
> *clear of neck and back.*

Over a hundred lines on, the butchery continues . . .

> *With that he hurled and Athena drove the shaft*
> *and it split the archer's nose between the eyes —*
> *it cracked his glistening teeth, the tough bronze*
> *cut his tongue at the roots, smashed his jaw*
> *and the point came ripping out beneath his chin.*[5]

The bone evidence from the Late Bronze Age bears out Homer's assertion that there were many ways to die in armed combat. Forensic studies reveal the dreadful injuries sustained by both Bronze Age Anatolians and Greeks. Within the city of Troy itself a girl aged between sixteen and seventeen has been hastily buried, her feet burned by fire.[6] At the balmy site of Asine on the Greek mainland – a place mentioned in Homer's Catalogue of Ships,[7] where a picture-perfect sea abuts the Mycenaean remains and prickly oak grows among the stones – was the body of a man who had been subject to therapeutic trepanations. The scalp has been cut back in flaps, to remove cranial bone fragments that had been driven into the brain during armed conflict. There is skeletal re-growth, suggesting that the warrior survived both the initial head injury and the subsequent operation.[8]

Near the Athenian agora, a middle-aged, Late Bronze Age man has had an incision carved into his right shoulder-blade – almost certainly gouged by a spear or a rear arrow attack. Warriors have sustained severe trauma as the result of 'parry thrusts' to their right forearms. And to counter the injuries made by the weapons they had invented – the rapiers, the slashing swords, the daggers – the Bronze Age populations developed an impressive array of medical equipment. At the Palamidi-Pronoia cemetery near the seaside town of Nafplion a hoard of what seem to be surgical instruments was found during excavations in 1971 – a long saw, forceps, a curved razor, a scoop, two long probes and three chisels.[9]

A gruesome and primitive array – and yet much Bronze Age surgery seems to have worked. The body of a woman from Grave Circle B in Mycenae (clearly an aristocrat) has a perfectly healed, fractured humerus – someone has given her excellent medical attention. On Linear B tablets we find the words *pharmakon* (as remarked in the Foreword, origin of our 'pharmacy'), and on tablet Eq 146 from Pylos is *iater*, which means 'doctor'. *E-ri-ka* (possibly hibiscus) and *Althea officinalis* (marshmallow) crop up on Linear B tablets; today marshmallow root is one of the key ingredients of de-toxifying teas as it mollifies gastro-intestinal problems. The terebinth resin (*kirtanos* in the Linear B tablets, the sap from the 'turpentine tree') – used in the perfume industry – also had medicinal qualities. Its efficacy as an antiseptic was clearly exploited: a staggering quantity of it, a whole ton's weight, carefully packed into a hundred jars, was found in the Uluburun shipwreck. When the resin was taken out of its pots and rolled between the fingers of the excavators, the tangy, terebinth smell came stealing out.

Little surprise that antiseptic was needed in such quantities in the period. If a warrior was not killed in hand-to-hand combat (or subsequently by the surgeon's knife) there was still the risk of Apollo's 'black bolts of plague' which, Homer tells us, sought out many soldiers on the plains of Troy.[10]

For nine days, in the *Iliad*, following the outbreak of plague 'the corpse-fires burned on, night and day, no end in sight'.[11] Once again, the skeletal evidence attests to relentless epidemics in the region. And even for those who managed to avoid fighting or disease, each day's pillaging could bring a premature death. There are descriptions in Homer of the rank and file dividing up loot – no cash economy here, so anyone in the path of the invading army would have been mercilessly plundered.

While bearing in mind their real and extraordinary achievements, and their sometime sophistication, when we try to imagine the life of a pre-historic princess and her peers we should never forget to what degree superstition, prejudice and ignorance would have been a part of their lives. One particular ritual act bears relevance to Helen's story. At the beginning of the 13th century BC, the Hittite king's wife, Gassulawiya, was mortally ill. In desperation she sent a substitute, a human representative, to the temple of the great goddess Lelwani. This was a woman chosen specifically for her beauty. The sick queen begs: 'this woman shall be my substitute. I am presenting her to you in fine attire. Compared to me she is excellent, she is pure, she is brilliant, she is white, she is decked out with everything. Now, O God, My Lord, look well on her. Let this woman stand before the god, My Lord.'[12]

Perhaps this 'brilliant', 'white' woman was to be sacrificed. The text is so damaged we shall never know. But it is certain that her beauty made her worthy of sacrifice, of becoming sacred. A dying queen – one of the most powerful women in the Near East – believed that of all the things on the known earth, of all the things the massive wealth of the Hittite empire could buy, a beautiful woman would be most pleasing to the goddess. A beautiful woman was her single hope. If there had been a preternaturally beautiful woman born in the Eastern Mediterranean in the 13th century BC we should not be surprised to find her totemic. We should not be surprised to hear that men went to war over "a Helen". But just as Menelaus and Paris found that Helen's beauty did not bring the perfect world it promised, so for Gassulawiya the sorcery of beauty proved sour. The queen died.

30

A BEAUTIFUL DEATH – KALOS THANATOS

@@@@@@@@@@@@

Tales of great war and strong hearts wrung,
Of clash of arms, of council's brawl,
Of beauty that must early fall,
Of battle hate and battle joy
By the old windy walls of Troy

And now the fight begins again
The old war-joy, the old war-pain.
Sons of one school across the sea
We have no fear to fight –

CHARLES HAMILTON SORLEY,
'I Have Not Brought My Odyssey'[1]

LTHOUGH THE MOST BEAUTIFUL WOMAN IN THE WORLD was – in Greek eyes – a credible trigger for the war to end all wars, the heroes of Troy were fighting not just for a woman, but for honour and for all the glories that death could bring. *Kalos thanatos*, 'a beautiful death', *euklees thanatos*, 'a glorious death' and *kleos aphthiton*, 'deathless fame' were fundamental reasons to live (and die). The *Iliad* articulated a code for male, aristocratic Greek society – a belief-system embodied in the ultimate warrior, Achilles. The true hero was a man who loved both a glorious life and a glorious death.[2]

Yet where was the glory in the agony and putrescence of the battle-field? How could the call of fame be heard when the screams of death and pain were all around? When swords and spears ripped open linen armour, when careering chariots splintered bones and stretched skin from muscle, when poisoned arrows turned blood black, made the hero shit and vomit uncontrollably, when fathers, brothers, sons died hundreds of miles from home, and the crows pecked out their eyes: how could that be a thing of honour? How could it be the mark of a real man, to be cut off in what the Greeks called his *akme*, his prime?

In the archaic and classical mind, violent death on the battlefield could in fact be the very best, the most illustrious way to die.

Given the right, fairly prescriptive, set of circumstances, death might actively be sought out by the would-be hero.[3] By accepting that a premature demise was his life's ambition, a hero such as Achilles diced daily with mortality. For him, even a life that was nasty, brutish and short was more attractive than a long and happy one. Better to die young than to live contentedly, with the creeping humiliations of old age. Better to be remembered as a hero than to be forgotten by peers and by history.[4]

Of course this kind of immortality, this celebrity, was impossible without becoming *aoidimos*, 'worthy of being sung'. A warrior only garnered *kleos*, 'glory', by being heard of (the root of *kleos* is *kluo*, 'to hear'). Archaic art was not just an imitation of life; it could give life (and death) its very meaning. The epic poetry cycles were the mechanism through which heroic honour was recognised. In city-states such as Athens and Sparta, a recital of Homer's poetry was taken to be a defining moment for polite society — Helen's story was a constituent of the genetic make-up of western civilisation.

Those in armed conflict emulated the Homeric model — but the bar was high. Even when a warrior lay dead on the battlefield after an awe-inspiring display of heroism, his immortality was not guaranteed. If his body was abused as Hector's was, when it was tied to the back of Achilles' chariot by the heels and dragged in the dust around the walls of Troy, or if his corpse became carrion, then the ugly, tattered, physical ignominy would wipe out all the glory gathered by dying well. Dead, decaying and defiled, the hero loses the chance to be perfect, and to achieve a perfect immortality.

I have held the bones of men and women from pre-history whose corpses have been left out in the open to rot.[5] Many are punctured and gnawed by canine teeth. It is impossible to tell whether these would have been domesticated dogs, or the wild dogs and wolves that hovered at the edges of human settlements. But whatever the breed of beast, the frenzy would have been the same as the body was ripped: the sick-sweet smell of decomposing flesh, the growls as human meat was fought over.

And so to avoid this disgrace, the dead heroes in the *Iliad* are swiftly collected from the battlefield and are sent off on their journey to the after-life as perfect as they can physically be. They are washed and oiled, their wounds are soothed over with ointments, their hair and clothes and skin are sprinkled with perfumed olive oil. Scrubbed, stroked and massaged, their bodies are laid on funeral pyres. And at this point in the epic tradition, as the kindling is lit and the fires take hold, the shining flesh leaps into flame. The hero's body spits, crackles and glows its way to immortality:

> *There is no fitter end than this.*
> *No need is now to yearn or sigh.*
> *We know the glory that is his,*
> *A glory that can never die.*
> *Surely we knew it long before,*
> *Knew all along that he was made*
> *For a swift radiant morning, for*
> *A sacrificing swift night-shade.*

> CHARLES HAMILTON SORLEY,
> 'In Memoriam'[6]

This was a fantasy and a reality lived again by the young men who fought in the First and Second World Wars. During the 1914–18 conflict particularly, many soldiers carried into combat copies of Homer, Hesiod, Herodotus and Euripides. Some drew on their classical education for inspiration and comfort.[7] Others recognised the desperate fact that ill-advised, ill-planned, ill-omened conflicts are a constant of human history. They read and re-read those passages of the *Iliad* that are a damning and thunderous survey of the inconsistencies and messiness of war, where Homer recognises that the enmities and allegiances, motives and strategies of Greeks and Trojans are as fragile as a glass made of sugar crystal. And over three thousand years after the fall of Troy, some recalled Helen's name as they questioned the purpose of conflict and suffering. One soldier, Patrick Shaw-Stewart, fighting at Gallipoli, seems to have borrowed from the work of the classical playwright Aeschylus in the lines:

> *I saw a man this morning*
> *Who did not wish to die:*
> *I ask, and cannot answer,*
> *If otherwise wish I . . .*

> *O hell of ships and cities,*
> *Hell of men like me,*

Fatal second Helen,
Why must I follow thee?[8]

〇〇〇〇〇〇

Although death — the virile *Thanatos* — could be viewed as welcome and honourable by the Greeks and those inspired by heroic ideals, it also had a more terrifying, female aspect: *Ker*. This death is blood-thirsty, bleak and vengeful:

*And Strife and Havoc plunged in the fight, and violent Death [*ker*]*
now seizing a man alive with fresh wounds, now one unhurt,
now hauling a dead man through the slaughter by the heels,
the cloak on her back stained red with human blood.[9]

Helen's complicity with *Ker* survives to the present day. She is still blamed for the multiple bereavements of the Trojan war — memorialised as the progenitor of the horror, rather than the glory of death.

〇〇〇〇〇〇

In the 19th century AD, when the French romantic painter Gustave Moreau made Helen his subject, the Spartan queen has turned her back on *Thanatos*.[10] Moreau's Helen is indeed *Ker*'s friend. In Moreau's picture, *Helen at the Ramparts of Troy*, the sky is gunmetal-grey, and corpses are slumped in piles at Helen's feet as she stares balefully out from Troy's walls at the desecration. This Helen is a moulder of hearses, not heroes. She is not shocked by what she sees. She is sullen and complicit.

I went to visit Moreau's house, 14 rue de la Rochefoucauld, in the Trinité district of Paris, to try to get a sense of the origins of this and the many other Helens the artist imagined stalking the Trojan citadel.[11] Moreau's paintings are prolific, crammed onto every square inch of every wall of the house, now a museum. Visitors are forced to crane their necks and peer up into dark corners to make out the host of quasi-mythical characters — the majority of them are women — that crowd into the space. Here is Salome, here Cleopatra, here Leda. And here, a striking number of times, is Helen.[12]

Making my way up to the second floor of the house-cum-museum, twisting around the spiral staircases and creaking across the original wooden floorboards, I found what has to be one of the most haunting images ever created of the Spartan queen. In many of his depictions, Moreau has given

Helen a solid body but a blank where her face should be.[13] And the epitome of this ghoulish, faceless Helen can be found on a canvas painted in 1880: *Helen at the Scaean Gate*. Here Helen's body is as ghostly as her face. She is white and insubstantial, an *eidolon*, more akin to the wisps of smoke rising from Troy than to a real woman. Crawling over this vision there are gobbets of gore; swirls and strands of paint – crimson, black, blue and brown. It is a sickening, livid, dribbling representation of the death and suffering that Helen has brought to Troy. This mess, that surrounds and clings to Helen, also seems to burn.

Here is the horror that the Spartan Queen has become. In those pernicious little blobs of paint, the incriminating flicks and stabs of the artist's brush, we are reminded that for centuries, Helen has been blamed for all this carnage; she has come to represent man's ability to use love as an excuse for hate. And while the heroes who killed and died in her name are still thought of as glorious, Helen is remembered as sordid.

et oceiroient le roy priant ses
enffans et tous ceulx du
parc et destruisoient la cite
De ces nouuelles furent les
grecois forment resiouys

et en firent feste sollennelle
Et receuprent calcas en
leur compaignie par soy
et serment Et lui prom
mirent de faire du bien

Temple de Dyane

laste Dandille

Agamenon

effigenie

Le temple de la deesse drane
Comment les grecois
a moult grant nature
se mirent en nage pour
aller vers troye Et de ce quil
leur aduit sur mer Et pour
faire cesser le tempeste agamenō
sacfya sa fille effigenie

Dez ceste feste
que les grecois
auoient me
nee pour les
bonnes respō
ces dappollin
Calcas sen alla lendemain
en sa compaignie de achilles

53 Either as a pawn of the gods or as a manipulator of men,
Helen was associated with the hideous violence of the Trojan War.
Helen's niece Iphigeneia (some versions say Iphigeneia was Helen's
daughter, the pregnancy following her rape by Theseus) was the
first to be sacrificed to its cause.

54 Here Priam is beaten to death by a club created from the body of his own grandson (Astyanax) and Paris' sister Cassandra is raped in Troy by Ajax while clinging to a statue of Athena (55, *below*).

56 There were mixed homecomings for the heroes of Troy. This Bronze relief from the Argive Heraeum, made in the 7th century BC, shows Clytemnestra (Helen's half-sister) killing Paris' sister Cassandra. Agamemnon was said to have brought Cassandra home from Troy as his concubine.

57 Menelaus drops his sword as he discovers his wayward wife in Troy – Greek dramatists made much of the fact that it was the sight of Helen's wonderful breasts that overwhelmed the king of Sparta.

58 As Aphrodite counsels Helen to make love to Paris, Nemesis points an accusing finger at the Spartan queen. Disaster is inevitable.

59 The construction of the Trojan Horse came to represent the triumph of Greek (Western) wile over Trojan brawn.

60 The artist Moreau painted Helen a number of times (*top right*). Here Troy disintegrates. All for nothing – for a blank, an empty face. As the poet George Seferis wrote in his poem 'Euripides' Helen': '*And the rivers swelling, blood in their silt, / all for a linen undulation, a filmy cloud, / a butterfly's flicker, a whisp of swan's down / an empty tunic – all for a Helen.*'

61 Unlike many of her counterparts, Helen's return home was relatively painless. Once back in the palace at Sparta she displays her sagacity by recognising Odysseus' son Telemachus (*bottom right*). In contrast to later Greek authors, Homer continually emphasises Helen's mental acuity. In fact, in the *Iliad* Bronze Age intelligence seems to be a distinguishing mark of a number of female characters: Agamemnon lists among the virtues of a good woman: '*build...breeding...mind...works of hand*' (*Iliad*, 1. 135).

62 Helen's cultic sites are often found by oceans or springs. Sexual power – in the form of the goddess of love, Aphrodite – was thought to have originated in the sea. This Greek relief shows the birth of Aphrodite from water. Images of spirits and deities associated with sexual power were bathed in water in the hope that their fecundity would be refreshed.

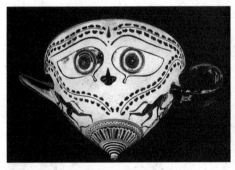

63 Helen's breasts were said to have provided the dimensions for a sacred cup, still used on the island of Rhodes in the 2nd century AD. Breast-shaped cups did carry holy liquid in classical Greece – this particular example was made in Athens in 520-500 BC.

64 The broken statue of the *kore* – almost certainly Helen – found at a pagan sanctuary in Samaria.

65 The distinctive caps of Castor and Pollux from the same sanctuary in Samaria, each crowned with a star.

67 Queen Elizabeth, tutored by Roger Ascham, was well versed in tales of Helen. Here she 'confounds Juno, Minerva and Venus' in a parody of the Judgement of Paris. Elizabeth carries her golden orb as Paris did his golden apple. Note that, in various details, all three goddesses resemble Elizabeth.

66 Helen features prominently in Athenian tragedy – her character would have been played by a man wearing a rigid mask – horsehair was possibly used to replicate Helen's 'golden curls'.

68 Because of her pronounced sexuality, Helen comes to be damned in a number of medieval and renaissance theological tracts. In Dante's *Inferno* she is consigned to the rank of the whore – howling through the circle of the lustful – as illustrated by William Blake.

69 Was Homer a historian? A fresco image of a lyre player found in the Late Bronze Age palace of Pylos tells us that there were, almost certainly, bardic singers whose job it was to recite the deeds of the Bronze Age kings and queens of the Near East. The *Iliad* is looking less and less like a fairy tale.

31

THE FALL OF TROY

@@@@@@@@@@@@@@

> Did my mother bear me as a monstrosity in men's eyes?
> My life and fortunes are a monstrosity, partly because of Hera,
> partly because of my beauty. I wish I had been wiped clean like
> a painting and made plain instead of beautiful . . .
>
> EURIPIDES, *Helen*[1]

THE PICTURE HOMER PAINTS OF HELEN IN TROY is a poignant and lonely one; he hints that these were ten long years of self-recrimination. Helen calls herself a vicious, scheming bitch and wishes she had been swept away by a storm before causing so much unhappiness.[2] In her funeral speech for Hector — the last great oration of the *Iliad* — she talks about her 'doom-struck, harrowed heart', and wishes a premature death had pre-empted her meeting with Paris 'as magnificent as a god'. Four times in Homer she refers to herself as a *kuōn*, 'a bitch'.[3] The Greek word was chosen carefully: those who listened to the *rhapsodes* would have remembered the scavenger-beasts that gnawed at human flesh. And like the dogs that prowled (and still prowl) around the walls of Troy, Helen too was half a part of the city, half an exile.

Starving, cut off from their millennia-long links with the sea by the line of Greek ships on Beşik Bay, even despite her beauty, by the end of the war the Trojans have come to hate Helen. They shudder as she passes — whispering and turning away. We cannot tell how quickly her own doubts set in, when she realises what she has started. The moment the flirtation was consummated on Kranai? Or when Paris loses his gloss and the first flush of the affair is over? What Homer seems to suggest is that pretty soon the scales fall from Helen's eyes and she realises what a peacock Paris is. He has become '*blind, mad Paris*'. Talking to Paris' brother, Hector, flirting masterfully, she opines: '*I wish I had been the wife of a better man, someone alive to outrage, the withering scorn of men.*'[4] And once the eldest-born prince of Troy has been killed by Achilles, leading the songs of sorrow Helen keens:[5]

And so in the same breath I mourn for you and me,
my doom-struck, harrowed heart! Now there is no one left
in the wide realm of Troy, no friend to treat me kindly —
all the countrymen cringe from me in loathing![16]

Helen's relationship with men in the *Iliad* sets her up to be a fickle woman,[7] but it is with the advent of the Trojan Horse that she is unambiguously established as an archetype of duplicity.[8] The Trojan Horse is mentioned only once in the *Odyssey* and does not feature at all in the *Iliad*; the fullest account of it is given by Virgil in the *Aeneid*. The earlier poem terminates with the death of Hector before Troy is sacked; however, with the help of Greek vase paintings, plays, and the snatches of lost epics that resurface in later works of antiquity, we can see the drama to its conclusion.

We hear how the Greeks, demoralised and weak after ten years of campaigning, ten years of camping out, both summer and winter, have put all their faith in a lunatic, brilliant gambit from the master-mind of Odysseus. The Greeks hide close by at Tenedos and burn their camp – at last, it seems, they have relinquished Helen. The one thing that still stands outside the walls of Troy is a giant wooden horse. The Trojans are divided: should they throw this brute creation over a cliff, or would that be sacrilegious – is the horse a gift for their beloved goddess Athena? Tired, gullible, quixotic and superstitious, they decide to welcome the horse in. The people of Troy celebrate with flowers and sacrifices. Helen, Virgil adds, runs like a bacchante around the town, dancing with intemperance – delighting now that Troy will soon be destroyed.[9]

But whose side is she on? Helen is also bait, endeavouring to tempt her onetime countrymen out to certain death. Circling the horse three times, stroking its flanks as she walks, she imitates the voices of the women the Greeks have left behind at home – murmuring sweet nothings, torturing the men inside with the memory of their loved ones.[10] One hero, Anticlus, is so desperate to leave, so tempted by her siren song, that Odysseus has to kill him before he betrays the crack squad inside. For once, though, Helen's charms are not strong enough. The Greek soldiers hidden inside – any number from thirteen to three thousand, so the storytellers said – sit tight.[11] As the moon rises, one Greek, Sinon, slips out of the horse and lights a beacon to tell Agamemnon's forces waiting patiently at Tenedos that the ruse has succeeded. The Sack of Troy can begin.

As the Greeks break into the citadel there are manifold atrocities. Paris' sister Cassandra is raped by Ajax. Hector's young son Astyanax is either thrown over the walls or used as a human club with which to beat old King Priam to death.[12] On one of the earliest visual representations of the story, a vase dating to 700 BC, now standing alone in the British Museum, children lie bleeding, stabbed by warriors with thick swords.[13] The women of Troy are left to watch the homicide, and to wait for their own degradation and agonies.

Extant legislation from the 13th century BC makes it clear that enslavement, often following a military campaign, brought with it deplorable adversity:

> A slave who provokes the anger of his master will either be
> killed or have his nose, eyes or ears mutilated; or his master will
> call him to account along with his wife, his children, his brother,
> his sister, his in-laws, his family, whether it be a male or female
> slave . . . If ever he is to die, he will not die alone; his family
> will be included with him.[14]

The moment of subjugation is hauntingly, shockingly described by Euripides in his play *The Trojan Women*. Troy has been torched. The sad, certain violation of shrines and homes and lives is described by the chorus. The cycle of violence will be unbroken. The soldiers will make their captives suffer because they too have suffered. The women, maimed and petrified, press together. Written during the time of the Peloponnesian War, the twenty-seven-year-long struggle between Athens and its rival Sparta,[15] *The Trojan Women* also had political overtones. The play tells the story of Helen and of Troy, but it was too an exploration of the privations and furies of military conflict. Euripides' audience was being asked to confront the lot not of conflict's victors, but of its victims.

The sometimes cocky Athenian audience must have shuddered as they watched. A hallmark of the ongoing Peloponnesian War had been the hideous brutality meted out by both sides: both had razed cities to the ground (the worst instances were at Plataea by the Spartans in 427[16] and on Melos in 416[17] by the Athenians) and massacred their men, selling the women and children into slavery. The actors spoke their lines with the very real spectre of military, moral and psychological collapse hovering in the wings.

The playwright Aeschylus also knew how dreadfully perfect this cycle of violence could be. 'They raped our queen, we raped their city, and we were right . . .'[18] The ingredients of his play – sexual politics, civic identity, abstract universals and military strategy – were already seething; to add Helen was to throw fat on the fire. Because she was, of course, not just Helen, she was Helen of Sparta. In the eyes of Athens, at war with Sparta, this libertine queen was both their political and moral enemy.

Bronze Age texts tell us that enormous numbers of men and women ended up as the spoils of war in the 13th century BC. In Hittite texts, these are known as 'booty-people'. On Linear B tablets from Pylos and Thebes which described human commodities are etched the names *Tros* and *Troia* – Trojan and Trojan women.[19] In a world where all depended on manpower, wars were started to appropriate not just territories but peoples. One Hittite king, Mursili II, boasts that following a particularly successful campaign he herded 15,000 newly conquered captives back to his city.[20] It is no surprise that these atrocities were burned into the consciousness, into the popular mythology of the Eastern Mediterranean – and telling that a woman's lust should be remembered as their aboriginal spark.

⌒⌒⌒⌒⌒

And what of Paris? Neither the *Iliad* nor the *Odyssey* graces his death with a single line. We hear from the *Little Iliad* that he is killed by an arrow – by the archaic period a weapon considered to be effeminate and unheroic.[21] It is a sufficiently ignominious end for a man without honour,[22] a pretty, eviscerated prince who, unlike Helen, amounted to little more than moonshine. And once he has gone, Helen, with unseemly haste, takes on another prince of Troy, Deiphobus.[23] Learning that the Greeks are inside the city, Helen steals her new husband's sword and leaves him to the mercy of Menelaus and Odysseus.[24] It is a final act of treachery dwelt on with perverse delight by Virgil in Book 6 of the *Aeneid*. The hero Aeneas is travelling through the underworld, where the Spartan queen's perfidy is revealed to him:

> Here too he [Aeneas] saw Deiphobus, son of Priam, his whole body mutilated and his face cruelly torn. The face and both hands were in shreds. The ears had been ripped from the head. He was noseless and hideous. Aeneas, barely recognising him . . . went up to him and spoke . . . 'Deiphobus, mighty warrior, descended from the noble blood of Teucer, who could have wished to inflict such a punishment upon you? . . .' To this the son of Priam answered . . . 'It is my own destiny and the crimes of the murdered from Sparta that brought me to this. These are reminders of Helen.'[25]

As the fires of Troy-town blaze, Helen is tearing through the streets, desperate to find sanctuary. She is surrounded by hatred: Stesichorus tells us that the Greeks and Trojans gather to stone her to death.[26] When Menelaus finally roots her out, cowering in a temple (ancient authors dispute whether the temple was consecrated to Athena, Apollo or Aphrodite) his sword is aloft, ready to kill.

But, so the ancients recounted, the fires of lust proved stronger than the fires of revenge. Menelaus drops his sword.[27] Electra wails: '*O misery me! Have their swords lost their edge in the face of that beauty?*'[28] The scene is vividly recreated on vases across the classical world. Although Menelaus has the perfect opportunity to slice Helen open, the perfect excuse to run her through, he does not do it. He loves her instead, and because of this she is both exciting and terrible. She tricks men into 'sheathing their swords' with the promise of perfect sex.[29] Even presented with his specious, disgraced queen, trapped in a corner in front of him, Menelaus cannot dominate. She is a woman to remember, a woman who is sexual but not subservient, and because of this she is a warning to history.

One of the earliest surviving images of Helen is on a giant *pithos* discovered by chance by a smallholder on the island of Mykonos.[30] This fabulous 7th-century BC piece is now displayed in the Archaeological Museum on the island. The surface is a press of images. Menelaus threatens Helen with a gargantuan blade – the metal shaft must be a good 4 feet long. All around her there are terrible scenes: soldiers dying, women and children being killed. But Helen does not flinch. She simply pulls her veil around her head, an action that is continually repeated in the representations of her discovery. It is hard to tell whether the Spartan queen is loosening her veil or wrapping it tighter around her. The gesture is common in Greek art and can be interpreted in three ways. Sometimes it is a fearful reaction: the woman hides her face when she is afraid. Sometimes it signifies marriage: maybe Helen is welcoming back her lawful husband. And some suggest it is an erotic ploy, a way of letting slip her clothes to hint at pleasures to come, teasing Menelaus with a peep of her famous breasts.[31]

'*When Menelaos caught a glimpse of Helen's breasts – naked in whatever way – he threw away his sword,*'[32] recites one character in Aristophanes' *Lysistrata*; and in Euripides' *Andromache*, Menelaus is berated: '*casting sheep's eyes on her bosom, you unbuckled your sword and puckered up for kisses, petting that traitorous bitch.*'[33]

On a number of the artefacts that depict Helen's recapture by the King of Sparta, she has wild, distrait hair; on one mirror, delicately etched by the Etruscans using the tang technique, Menelaus' fingers are meshed through Helen's curls, dragging her away from the image of Athena to which she clings.[34] Elsewhere, though, a tender Menelaus respectfully leads her by the hand to his waiting ship. A bronze shield-band from Sparta itself (almost certainly) shows Menelaus with sword aloft looking back at a Helen who carries a wreath – there is no threat here.[35] But even though he takes her home, the majority of depictions make it clear that Helen's actions will be neither forgiven nor forgotten.

In Aeschylus' play *Agamemnon*, beacon fires are lit to bring the news of the defeat of the Trojans to the Greeks. The archaeologist Dr Elizabeth French (who has spent many years working in the Aegean landscape) estimates that the Mycenaean citadels were so well placed that Greeks on either side of the Bosphorus could indeed have watched as the beacons were torched first from Mount Ida in Turkey, then on Lemnos, Mount Athos, Cithairon and finally at Mycenae's own watchtower, Agios Elias in the Arachneion range that cradles the great citadel above the Argive plain.[36] The fires signalled the fall of Troy, they told of a Greek triumph, and they announced that the Spartan queen would be coming back home.

I

Hot through Troy's ruin Menelaus broke
To Priam's palace, sword in hand, to sate
On that adulterous whore a ten years' hate
And a king's honour. Through red death, and smoke,
And cries, and then by quieter ways he strode,
Till the still innermost chamber fronted him.
He swung his sword, and crashed into the dim
Luxurious bower, flaming like a god.

High sat white Helen, lonely and serene.
He had not remembered that she was so fair,
And that her neck curved down in such a way;
And he felt tired. He hung the sword away,
And kissed her feet, and knelt before her there,
The perfect Knight before the perfect Queen.

II

So far the poet. How should he behold
That journey home, the long connubial years?
He does not tell you how white Helen bears

Child on legitimate child, becomes a scold,
Haggard with virtue. Menelaus bold
Waxed garrulous, and sacked a hundred Troys
'Twixt noon and supper. And her golden voice
Got shrill as he grew deafer. And both were old.

Often he wonders why on earth he went
Troyward, or why poor Paris ever came.
Oft she weeps, gummy-eyed and impotent;
Her dry shanks twitch at Paris' mumbled name.
So Menelaus nagged; and Helen cried;
And Paris slept on by Scamander side.

RUPERT BROOKE, 'Menelaus and Helen'[37]

PART NINE

○○○○○○○○○○○○

IMMORTAL
HELEN

32

HOME TO SPARTA

◎◎◎◎◎◎◎◎◎◎◎◎

When the war ends, Helen resumes her place as a matter
of course in the house of Menelaus. She bears it with
unconstrained and perfect dignity; and her relations to her
husband carry no mark of the woeful interval, except that
its traces indelibly remain in her own penitential shame.

RIGHT HON. W.E. GLADSTONE, DCL, MP
for the University of Oxford[1]

WAS IT THE CURVE OF HELEN'S NECK that stopped Menelaus'
steely blade? The gift of beauty, of *kharis*, the queen's only shield?
Was Menelaus simply overpowered by his old love for her? I
suspect not. Whether he was the real bridegroom of a Mycenaean land-
holder, or the mythical consort of a half-divine woman, the beautiful creature
in front of him had superb connections. By aligning himself with Helen
– and thanks only to that association – Menelaus is told on the journey
home to Sparta that he has an opportunity for immortality:

> But about your own destiny, Menelaus,/ dear to Zeus, it's not for you to
> die/ and meet your fate in the stallion-land of Argos,/ no, the deathless ones
> will sweep you off to the world's end, the Elysian Fields . . . /where life glides
> on in immortal ease for mortal man;/ . . . /All this because you are Helen's
> husband now – the gods count you the son-in-law of Zeus.[2]

How could Menelaus have cut Helen's throat as she cowered in a corner
of Troy? He would have been slicing through his one connection to rich
Lakonian lands, killing the only mortal daughter of Zeus, and denying
himself the chance of an eternal life in the Elysian Fields. Where Helen
leads, Menelaus follows.

The ancients imagined Helen's return on the Spartan king's boat to be,
in some ways, as heady and as charged as her outward dash over a decade

before with the Trojan prince; the royal couple had all those lost years to pick over. So much resentment, so many questions. Had she left her heart in Troy? Had the east changed her? Was she defiant, was she humbled? Was she raging, was she broken? Was she snaggle-toothed[3] or stooped? Was she – as the tragedian Euripides asked in a rare comic aside – fat?

> MENELAUS: *She'll be shipped aboard, Be cargoed home.*
> HECUBA: *Not on your ship!*
> MENELAUS: *Why not? She's put on weight?* [4]

Fat or thin, termagant, defiant or burning with shame, at this point in the story, one would imagine that Helen – a dishonoured woman, 'her hair scabbed with dead men's blood'[5] – is humiliated and dragged back to her homeland. Not so. Menelaus has dropped his sword. There are surprisingly few recriminations. It seems the adulteress is going to get off scot-free.

The reunited royals have time aplenty to kiss and make up because homeward bound, along with other Greek heroes, they are caught in a storm at Cape Malea and their boat is blown a long way off-course. So begins the difficult journey home for the heroes of Troy – recorded in detail in another fragmentary epic, the *Nostoi* ('The Homecomings'). Homer, famously, charts Odysseus' ten years of peregrinations on the high seas in his *Odyssey*. His wife Penelope has spent the duration of the Trojan War loyal to her husband, but her palace at Ithaca is overrun by voracious, opportunist suitors. Agamemnon is delayed by a storm and at the end of a grand feast to celebrate his homecoming, along with his Trojan concubine Cassandra, is murdered in his bath by his wife Clytemnestra and her lover Aigisthus.[6] Diomedes' wife too is faithless, his kingdom no longer his when he returns. Nestor makes his way back to Pylos safely to 'grow rich and sleek in his old age at home' but many – Ajax, Achilles and Patroclus – are now dust on the plains of Troy.[7]

Helen and Menelaus too have troubles ahead. Hostile winds take them to Gortyn on Crete and to Cyprus, Phoenicia, Ethiopia and Libya. Once again, within Homer's poetry, Bronze Age trading routes are being tabulated. And for all authors – Homer, Stesichorus, Herodotus, Euripides, the anonymous composers of the Epic Cycle – the great, rich lands of Egypt 'where the houses overflow with the greatest troves of treasure'[8] are an important part of the royal couple's journey home.[9]

When Herodotus chronicles the fact that the flesh-and-blood Helen stays in Egypt while the warriors fight for a phantom in Troy,[10] he also reports that even here blood is shed – because her presence leads to a human sacrifice.[11] Having left Troy and travelled up the river Nile to Memphis, Menelaus has discovered Helen in Egypt, and, impatient to get his (now blameless) wife back home, he tries to set sail. But the winds are against him. Furious, he sacrifices two native children, earning, as he does so, the enmity of Egypt and of its king, Proteus. The Spartan king and queen have to flee for their lives, getting as far as Libya where, for the outraged Egyptians, the trail then goes cold.[12]

Herodotus' story is, of course, not the first time Helen has been associated with ritual murder. The most notorious sacrifice is of Iphigeneia, her niece (or her daughter, depending on the source), and the Delphic oracle too connects Helen to ritual death, making reference to a tenacious plague in Sparta: the solution, the annual sacrifice of high-born Spartan virgins. One year, it is Helen who is led to the altar stone. Just before the knife enters the flesh, an eagle swoops down and rips the weapon out of the priest's hands, dropping it, point down, onto a heifer. From that moment on it is young cows rather than young girls that are lined up for the priests' cold blade.[13]

Without hard evidence it has always been immensely difficult to judge whether human sacrifice was in fact a part of the Bronze Age experience.[14] But on Crete, a staggering excavation appears to have exposed incontrovertible remnants of ritual murder. Just below Anemospilia (the 'Cave of the Winds'), a half-hour drive inland from the capital Heraklion, there is a redolent site. When I first visited, retracing the literary Helen's steps on the way back from Troy, I had to brush past tall grasses thick with herbs to reach the sanctuary.[15] The Aegean stretches out beneath, the peak of Mount Juktas towers above.[16] Here in the 1970s, four bodies were found – three men and one woman – all dating from around 1600 BC. Analysis of the human remains showed them all to be well built, well fed and well dressed: the elite of society. One man had been carrying a large bowl, a second had collapsed on the floor. Jugs filled with a viscous fluid stood nearby. The third man, aged about eighteen, was lying on an altar, with a bronze dagger laid across his chest. His feet had been bound and his body bled dry. Further forensic tests show that on the left-hand side his neck had been sliced through. The scene is so shocking that some scholars – quite rightly – have been careful to propose less sensational interpretations. But it is very hard to read this as anything other than the sacrifice of the young man.[17]

It is too simplistic to bring our 21st-century sensitivities to the idea of human sacrifice. A sacrifice means 'to make something sacred'. For ordinary humans to become part of the divine stratosphere may have been perceived and experienced as a great honour, though an honour bestowed only *in extremis*. Helen's story is an extreme one (her impact on the world around her both affirmed life and denied it) and I suspect this is why we find her name linked with a number of human sacrifice stories. In the minds of the Ancient Greeks, it was no surprise that Helen catalysed the ritual murder of her fellow men. After all, this was a woman who traded in blood as well as in beauty.

〰〰〰〰〰

And yet, in Homer there is no scandal attached to Helen's stay in Egypt, there are no untimely deaths. Instead the royal couple gather up stories and treasures to bring back with them to Sparta. Among the gifts lavished on Helen during her Egyptian sojourn is a golden spindle – a romantic, story-book prop if ever there was one. But real golden spindles have now been discovered in the graves of Anatolian women; one particularly fine example comes from Alaca Höyük in central Turkey. Whether or not '*precious gifts: a golden spindle, a basket that ran on casters, solid silver polished off with rims of gold*'[18] were given to a Mycenaean queen, again we find that Homer is not fantasising, but itemising specific details of the Bronze Age past.[19]

So Helen is on her way home. And, according to Homer, once she lands back on Greek soil, she does so with impunity. Her Trojan husband is dead, his body burned on a Trojan funeral pyre; she is free to become a good Greek wife once again.[20] In the *Odyssey* we find her back at Sparta, in the palace of her birth, relaxed and in control. She runs the household; she chats to guests; when Trojan War veterans arrive she pulls up a chair to listen to their tales and to add her own (note that it is Helen rather than Menelaus who initiates the storytelling session – a sign in Homeric society of the respect due to her); she impresses the assembled company by interpreting, correctly, an omen in the sky.[21] She is reunited with her estranged daughter – as her niece Electra bitterly points out in Euripides' play *Orestes*: '*In her [Hermione] she takes her joy and forgets her troubles.*'[22] She seems fulfilled and content. It is, almost, as if nothing untoward had ever happened.

But beneath the surface there are hints of trouble. What Homer does, very skilfully, is to paint a picture of a woman who is both relaxed and wary, both resourceful and tricky. The royal couple are hosting a wedding party – Hermione is to marry the son of Achilles, and among their guests is Telemachus, the son of Odysseus. The palace is full. In jubilant mood, a bard plays on his lyre, '*a pair of tumblers dashed and sprang, whirling in leaping handsprings, leading on the dance*'.[23] Helen enters this scene from her '*scented, lofty chamber*' with a train of women. But when the feasting is over and the lights are low, the mood changes and thoughts turn to the pain and suffering of the last ten years. Tales told of dead heroes make the entire room weep inconsolably. Helen has the answer.[24]

> *Into the bowl in which their wine was mixed, she slipped a drug that had the power of robbing grief and anger of their sting and banishing all painful memories. No one who had swallowed this dissolved in wine could shed a single tear that day, even for the death of his mother and father, or if they put his brother or his own son to the sword and he were there to see it done.*[25]

The drug was most likely opium – which, when mixed with alcohol becomes pure laudanum.[26] There is no doubt that opium would have been used within palatial culture in the Late Bronze Age – and it was much loved by the Mycenaeans. As well as rock-crystal pins made in the shape of poppy seed-heads, Mycenaean women wore beads carved out of red carnelian representing poppy flowers[27] and gold rings depicting orgiastic rites to which opium poppies were central.[28] One of the goddesses found in Crete, dating from the Mycenaean occupation of the island, has a diadem made of woven poppy seedheads. This stiff, somnolent figure with her arms bent and palms facing out, flat on, has a glassy stare. The seedheads crowning her brow have been split open – the optimum moment for opium latex to be extracted. Homer tells us that *nepenthes* drugs were imported from Egypt – for the ancients, 'made in Egypt' implied top-grade medicinal goods.[29] But forensic analysis shows that opium poppies, *Papaver somniferum L.*, were home-grown in the Peloponnese in the Late Bronze Age. At Tiryns and at Kastanas opium poppy seeds have been recovered from excavation levels relating to the late 13th century BC.[30] As well as acting as an effective pain-killer *Papaver somniferum L.* has acute psychotropic effects.[31]

There is no doubt that a Mycenaean queen, with the privilege of rank, perhaps a high priestess, would have known how to use these powerful narcotics, just as the Homeric Helen does. Opium is a useful tool to heal wounds, both physical and psychological; it opens a path to dreams. Mixing her drugs, interpreting omens, captivating the assembled company, the Homeric Helen is both a sorceress and a salve, intoxicating to the last. Having stupefied her household, she puts away her golden spindle and her purple-tinted wool, to bed down with Menelaus: '*Menelaus retired to chambers deep in his lofty house with Helen the pearl of women loosely gowned beside him.*' This is the last time we see Helen in the works of Homer.

While at Troy Homer tells us Helen embarked on an intricate tapestry – a never-ending creation that tolds the tales of heroes and of war. Now, it seems, the final stitch is completed, the running thread snipped. But this is a story destined to be reworked again and again; Helen's prophecy in the *Iliad*, '*On us the gods have sent an evil destiny, that we should be a singer's theme for generations to come*', will be fulfilled. Helen might have completed her own epic work of fabrication back in Troy, but now there would be a whir and a clatter as others settled themselves at the loom to begin their own versions of the life of the Spartan Queen.

Our Homeric Helen may have sailed home to a warm welcome. The Helens that followed her centuries later described a bleaker route through history.

33

THE DEATH OF A QUEEN

@@@@@@@@@@@@

Orestes: Our watchword for today: 'Kill Helen' — there it is.

Pylades: You have it/ . . . There'll be cheering in the streets,
Bonfires will blaze to all the gods, and prayers rise up/ For
blessings on us both, because we justly shed/ The blood of a bad
woman. Kill her, and your name/ Of 'matricide' will be forgotten,
giving place/ To a more glorious title: you'll be called 'the man
Who killed the killer of thousands, Helen'.
. . .

Electra: Kill, stab, destroy her, both of you!/ Aim your swords —
in! — in!/ Two hungry blades flashing in your hands!/ Kill her!
She deserted her father, she deserted her Husband;/ Countless
Hellenes died in battle by the riverside — And she killed them!
Tears flooded upon tears,/ There, where iron spears flew/ Beside
the seething Scamander.

EURIPIDES, *Orestes*[1]

I N HIS TRAGIC DRAMA *ORESTES*, Euripides is one of the few to write
of the death of the Spartan queen. The play is set in the royal palace at
Argos visited by Menelaus and Helen on their way back to Sparta from
Troy, just six days after Orestes has murdered his mother Clytemnestra. As
the royal couple arrive, Orestes is surrounded by armed guards, with a death
warrant from the Argive court hanging over his head. Menelaus refuses to
endorse his actions, or the complicity of his sister, Electra — a reluctance which
enrages the eponymous anti-hero who (with his accomplice Pylades) hatches
a plot to kill Helen and thus drive Menelaus raving mad. Pylades articulates
this as an act of sweet revenge — the killing of Helen, he argues, will mean
that all Greece will forget Orestes' infamous matricide and instead call him
'the man who killed the killer of thousands, Helen'. Orestes is persuaded —
within moments we hear Helen's wretched screams from inside the palace.

It is Helen's Trojan slave who describes the murder. The slave stands beside the Queen of Sparta, fanning her with feathers, while she spins a gossamer thread – intended to decorate the purple robe she will lay at the tomb of Clytemnestra. Orestes entices Helen to an altar, while Pylades locks up Helen's other slaves. Helen is surrounded. As the assassins pull their swords from under their purple cloaks, she runs away with her golden sandals clattering, but Orestes catches her by the hair, bends back her neck and prepares to slit her throat.

After a brief interlude, Hermione bursts in only to be greeted by the sight of her mother's corpse, twisted in its death-throes, laced with blood. Orestes and Pylades charge at the girl, and once they have caught her, turn back to their original prey. But Helen has mysteriously disappeared. Was this a miracle? An act of magic? Did the gods steal her away?

The news of the outrage is leaked to Menelaus and the war-weary king musters his strength and hurtles off in pursuit, but finds Orestes with a sword, this time, to Hermione's neck. Swearing vengeance, the Spartan king calls upon the citizens of Argos to take up arms and do away with Orestes, but just as he bellows out his last plea, Apollo appears and explains that he snatched Helen up to safety:

> For Helen's beauty was to the gods their instrument
> For setting Greeks and Trojans face to face in war
> And multiplying deaths, to purge the bloated earth
> Of its superfluous welter of mortality.
> So much for Helen . . .[2]

> Now, soaring aloft to the star-bright sphere,/ Helen I will conduct to the mansion of Zeus;/ There men shall adore her, a goddess enthroned/ Beside Hera and Hebe and great Heracles./ There she, with her brothers, Tyndareos' sons,/ Shall be worshipped for ever with wine outpoured/ As the seamen's Queen of the Ocean.[3]

This is a textbook *deus ex machina*. There is no corpse because Helen, saved by the gods, has become a star. And this was how many Greeks imagined her, always perfect, always present – but just out of reach.

෧෧෧෧෧

Because the premier extant chronicler of Helen's life, Homer, leaves her end unresolved there is no one favoured account of her death, but instead myriad theories. For some she lives out her life contentedly as Queen of Sparta. The Roman poet Ovid imagines her caught at last by time, weeping as she sees her 'aged wrinkles in the looking glass, and tearfully asks herself why she should twice have been a lover's prey'.[4] Other authors describe her as exiled and lonely, suffering a horrible and violent death.[5] Three ideas surface again and again. The first is that this adulteress, trailing a past that drips with gore, ends up not tormented in the underworld but as one of the blessed, in Elysium. The second is that Helen gets some kind of retribution for all the suffering she has caused, before her final journey to meet her makers. And the third finds her attaining sparkling immortality – no one wants to lose Helen, no one wants her to die.

⁙⁙⁙

Because Mycenaean tombs offer the richest of all archaeological finds, we can extrapolate a detailed reconstruction of the funerary rites that would have been staged in honour of our Bronze Age Helen.[6] There are caveats – structures such as the 'Treasury of Atreus' (built c. 1370 BC) or the 'Tomb of Clytemnestra' (c. 1300 BC) at Mycenae are showy pieces of archaeology begging to be raided.[7] When archaeologists arrive at the heart of a grave the contents are often strewn and sparse, bones jumbled together and the most precious objects long gone.[8] Sometimes grave-robbers are the culprits, sometimes tomb-raiders masquerading as officials and sometimes it is the Bronze Age populations themselves, moving aside one corpse and its gifts so that another from the clan could be laid to rest.[9] Still, piecing together reliable evidence from across the Late Bronze Age Mycenaean world we can form a composite picture of the burial of a high-born, female aristocrat, and in that picture it does appear that women had as extravagant a send-off as men.

In order to prepare a woman such as Helen for this moment, her body, carefully washed, smoothed with perfumed oil and dressed in a bespoke funerary dress, would be laid out gently on a bier. A finely carved seal-stone would be placed on her wrist,[10] on her finger a silver ring, on her head perhaps a gold diadem.[11] Golden spirals might be twisted into her hair,[12] a shawl laced with beads wrapped over her head and shoulders, and necklaces of faience and amber fastened around her death-white neck.

Once this fine, gem-studded corpse was fully dressed, it would be covered from head to toe in a shroud.[13] The funeral cortège would then make its way towards the entrance of the tomb – in the 14th century BC perhaps down a *dromos* (a walled corridor) towards a *tholos*, a distinctive beehive-shaped grave. At the Tomb of Clytemnestra, the sobering corridor entrance is 36 m long. In the Treasury of Atreus, the inner lintel block itself weighs over 100 tonnes. The audacious architecture of these mausoleums still astounds.

In front of the freshly dead body, hugging close to the head, there would almost certainly have been children, and behind them women, some raising their hands to their heads, others with torn clothes and scratched faces.[14] Paintings on Bronze Age *larnakes* (chestlike coffins) from Tanagra in Boiotia depict children and female mourners clustered around the corpse. On a broken-up *krater* (a large vase) from Agia Triada Palaioboukounia in Elis, a funeral scene shows a child standing right next to the head of the corpse.[15] Homer demonstrates that women were important players in funerary rites – a reminder that the females of this distant world were thought to bring life and death in equal measure.

Once inside the chill, cavernous space of the tomb, the aristocrat's precious goods would be laid all around her or on a carefully constructed little bench. The Tomb of Clytemnestra, at Mycenae, on being re-opened in 1876 and 1891, contained a crumpled cornucopia of delights – evidence of the capital chosen for the dead.[16]

Among the treasures found in the tomb itself and in a grave-pit in the *dromos* was an exquisite bronze mirror with a carved ivory handle, lapis lazuli decorations and the images of two plump women with tight curls, sitting on palm leaves.[17] There were embossed gold strips pierced so that they could be sewn onto the corpse's clothes, heart- and lily-shaped gold beads, polished amethysts and broken terracotta figurines of women and animals. In one tomb on Crete,[18] dating from around the 14th century BC, the female skeleton was found holding a bronze mirror in her left hand, pressed right up close to her face.[19] Would a Bronze Age Helen have been left alone with a metal mirror in the cold earth, to stare for eternity at her own lovely face?

I recently visited the site of one rich discovery at the Late Bronze Age necropolis of Dendra, in the gentle farmland that rolls out south-east from Mycenae, taking with me an account of the original excavation of 1926.[20] Above the tombs, I read the report – the excitement of the revelation was transparent. The leader of the dig, a Swede called Axel Persson, described how in the sweltering July heat, working with knives and small picks, workers exposed a skeleton lying in a layer of blue clay shot through with charcoal particles, and then . . .

gold began to appear; round the neck and on the breast was a great Mycenaean necklace of gold rosette beads, 18 large ones and 18 small. It measured almost 80 cm in length after we had re-threaded it. The large rosettes were found on the breast, the small ones at the back of the neck . . . below the chest there lay the gold binding of a girdle and 35 spiral pendants of thin gold leaf which no doubt had also adorned the girdle . . . It was a *little princess* we had found.[21]

On 30 July the excavators went on to discover a woman who had apparently been left with a small steatite lamp to light her way into the afterlife. She cradled a gold cup in her right arm. Decorated with gold bulls'-heads, silver and niello, once cleaned with a soft brush and water the cup was found to be still serviceable. Persson and his team filled the liberated offering with Nemean wine, and, along with a gathering of local villagers, toasted their success, the glories of Greece, and then passed the cup round for everyone to share.

Although this theatrical treatment of artefacts would be considered sacrilege by today's archaeologists, it was in fact a sympathetic gesture. In a *tholos* tomb at Kokla, near Argos,[22] two drinking cups[23] had been drained and then smashed. Did these hold final toasts for the dead? In the Minoan cemetery at Armenoi in western Crete, analysing the organic traces found in drinking and cooking vessels dating from *c.* 1390–1190 BC, scientists have found evidence of resinated wine (wine mixed with pine resin, partly to preserve and partly to mask the sour taste as the alcohol turns rancid) and wine mixed with barley. These are potent alcoholic drinks. The Mycenaean dead had a good send-off.

As the invocations and prayers died out, as the flautists and lyre-players fell silent,[24] with an aromatic mist still hanging in the air from the incense burners and the small fires that had fumigated the burial chamber before the corpse's arrival, the tomb would be closed and the entrance sealed. In some burials the *dromos*, the corridor, has been back-filled. And as the last lick of flame in the lamp next to the body guttered, the aristocrat and her glittering prizes were left in the dark.

In a tomb such as this, Helen's body would have been laid to rest.[25]

34

THE AGE OF HEROES ENDS

๏๏๏๏๏๏๏๏๏๏๏๏๏

[Helen's beauty] exhausted the divine genius of Homer . . . [and] tired out many great and famous painters and carvers.

BOCCACCIO, *Concerning Famous Women* (AD 1364–70)[1]

THOSE BRONZE AGE CORPSES were left alone, but not undisturbed. Just as, in the minds of the ancients, Helen's actions caused the Age of Heroes to implode, so the Mycenaean civilisation really did disintegrate at the end of the Bronze Age. Glittering palaces would fall, trade would evaporate, heroes would melt into the shadows – and all in the span of a lifetime.

The dating of 'the Trojan War' is a vexed and thorny issue. The traditional systems of the ancient world set it anywhere from 1334 to 1135 BC.[2] The most popular date, however, was *c.* 1184 BC; archaeology tells that around this time, the cultures of Crete and the Greek mainland and Anatolia did indeed evaporate and current research suggests that there were a series of devastations at Troy: battles and court intrigue in the first half of the 13th century BC, fire in 1200 BC, fire and perhaps earthquakes around 1180 BC, cauterisation of the city as an economic entity for the next 100 years, total abandonment by 950 BC. Popular memory had one thing right: Helen's death heralded the death of a whole way of life.

Around the end of the Bronze Age, much of what is now Greece and Turkey experienced intense seismic activity: 'storms' of earthquakes. The storms would impact an area of up to 2,000 sq km over a period of around fifty years. So, for instance, in an intensely active period in recent recorded history, say between AD 1900 and 2000, in the eastern Peloponnese an earthquake with a magnitude of over 6.5 on the Richter Scale occurred every thirty or forty years.[3] With sophisticated architecture damage is minimal – with the building techniques of the Late Bronze Age[4] devastation would have been extreme and it looks as though many of the Bronze Age centres were hit not once, but repeatedly.[5] Crude oil lamps have been found by their thousands in Late Bronze

Age sites. As buildings collapsed, as sanctuaries juddered and palaces fell down, these lamps would have been sent flying – starting devastating fires. Those not killed by the quakes and flames would have watched as frescoes and painted floors, golden cups and stores of handspun cloth, the trappings of Bronze Age civilisation and the marks of the heroic age, were consumed in front of them. Excavations of Late Bronze Age magazines at Thebes have uncovered carbonised fruit. At the tranquil site of Midea six miles inland from Argos, there are the charred remains of chick-peas, lentils, bitter vetch, grass peas, fava and broad beans; hoarded for men but consumed by fire.

In the expansive storerooms of the Mycenaean palatial complexes one of the most precious and prolific commodities was olive oil kept in giant stoppered *pithoi* each holding around 40 gallons (182 l) of highly flammable liquid. Inexplicably, at the point that Mycenaean palaces were destroyed, the necks of a number of these *pithoi* have been sawn off – as if the jars were being used as incendiary devices. In one palace on Crete, at Agia Triada, in the intense heat of the inferno, the Bronze Age equivalent of a fire in an oil refinery,[6] the stone floor of the oil storeroom has not only buckled and serrated; it has vitrified – turned to glass.

Helen's world was not wiped out by these calamities, but the impact would certainly have been enough to destabilise Mycenaean society. The chaos would have galvanised local opportunists: men and women empowered to question the authority of leaders (both religious and secular) who had clearly inspired the gods to great ire. The meticulous administrative systems of the Mycenaeans would have been interrupted. Deities were demoted: the strange female figures in the cult centre at Mycenae are laid to rest, the frescoes of beautiful women on the walls are carefully whitewashed. A fine film of soil is sprinkled over the cult items and dedications and large stone slabs are laid along the side of the room to cover the significant, potent objects whose home this had once been.[7]

The spirits of the earth and sky had expressed their displeasure. Were the goddesses and fine female figures on the wall in disgrace? Were they being tactfully demoted? Did these earthquakes and the subsequent fires, which may well have contributed to the collapse of Mycenaean civilisation, herald a new era? An era in which that arriviste god Zeus – who almost certainly originated in the east – became dominant?[8] An era which would see the end of female supremacy in the religious sphere, an era which would be remembered and distorted by bards through the 'Dark Ages' of Greece? An era celebrated with longing and fear by epic poets like Homer as an Age of Heroes? An era whose warriors had risked all for a woman and cursed her as they did so?

That end, that petering out of a once powerful people, is palpable in the flat lands north of Mycenae. A lone, battered, blue road-sign points to the archaeological site of Archaiai Kleonai. The settlement lies beyond the main road, across a railway track, past row upon row of drying tobacco leaves and low-level vines. Homer describes Kleonai in the *Iliad* as 'sturdy, strong Kleonai'.[9] Now the settlement is virtually non-existent. In fact, all that is left is a much denuded, much later, Hellenistic Temple of Heracles – there is no sign of Bronze Age glory. Travellers who passed through the area at the beginning of the 20th century reported that a few Mycenaean remains were still standing. But this is prime farmland – when I last visited the site, the rhythmic swish of itinerant labourers' skirts as they passed to collect the grape harvest was a reminder that agriculture is now the priority here. Those Bronze Age stones and artefacts, which must have been just an irksome impediment to the business of farming, are long gone, chopped up by the plough or cannibalised by locals. Palatial masonry has become the foundations for barns and cow-sheds; sacrifice stones have turned into hearths.

If we estimate that the events described by Homer relate in large part to the late 13th century BC, then a hundred years or so after Helen's mortal storyline ends, this would have been the fate of many of the great citadels. Some continued in reduced form – at Elateia in Phokis and Lefkandi on Euboia. There would still have been populations on the Mycenaean settlements at Athens, Amyklai and Mycenae itself. But most are abandoned by the ruling elite. From around 1150 BC, instead, squatters live in the ruins of the rooms of kings, pigs root in the sanctuaries of the old gods. As the great Mycenaean civilisation drags to its end, the Greek Dark Ages begin.

Across the Dardanelles, the almighty Hittite civilisation is also crumbling. Hattusa has lost its pole political position, cuneiform writing stops and the site at Boğazköy with its gold-mine of archives is abandoned. By 1175 BC the Hittites have ceased to exist. Troy was destroyed by fire, perhaps the fire of the invading forces of Agamemnon, Odysseus, Menelaus and Achilles, but more likely the fire of native malcontents. Vandals burning down a city that had already been seriously weakened by natural disasters, chronic incursions and in-fighting.

One phrase archaeologists and historians use today to describe the end of these proto-empires is 'systems collapse'. If the Mycenaeans, the Hittites and the Egyptians were indeed intimately linked, if they consistently traded with one another, married each other's women and stole each other's men, then the fall of one would bring the fall of another. Once the nations of heroes, they were now giant skittles tumbling around an empty sea.

The Bronze Age was ending, and with the new Iron Age would come a time of insecurity and inactivity. Gone are the fine twists of Mycenaean painting, the microscopic perfections of delicate, ambitious metalwork. Grand palaces are no longer built, the art of writing is eclipsed, this is a time of retrenchment rather than expansion.

But in those quiet, long, isolated evenings that men and women spent together, clearly what lasted, with absolute vitality, was storytelling. Throughout the 'Dark Ages' the bard and his lyre maintain a presence in art – these men did not disappear, they did not stop transmitting their tales. Oral culture is a transparent space in the eyes of the historian or the archaeologist, but within its time it can be the most effective method of transmitting images, information and ideas about the world and the past. And one of the brightest stars in this imaginary firmament was Helen. The rich and headstrong queen of Sparta would not be forgotten, she would not die. Now liberated from the prison of her beautiful body, she was no longer to be worshipped only by a Greek hero or a Trojan prince. This immortal, legendary luminary could now be adored by everyone, man and woman, labourer and lord.

35

'FRAGRANT TREASURIES'

@@@@@@@@@@@@

are you a witch?
a vulture, a hieroglyph,
the sign or the name of a goddess?
what sort of goddess is this?

H.D., *Helen in Egypt*[1] (1961)

To find the shrines associated with Helen, I have had to make difficult, lonely journeys through the Aegean landscape. The travel writer of the Roman period, Pausanias, led me to one holy spot – the sanctuary of Bridal Aphrodite founded, he says, by Theseus when the hero 'married' Helen.[2] The site is about 18 km up into the mountains from the little harbour of Hermione on the eastern coast of the Peloponnese. To get to the sanctuary from Hermione, as ancient devotants would have done, I had to struggle up a somewhat perilous and neglected path.[3] Approaching through the mountains from the west there were no signs to guide me. Even locals have forgotten the stories of the place – ask for directions in the town of Hermione and you are led on a wild goose chase from florist to pharmacy, all enquiries being met with blank stares and shrugs of the shoulder.

But there are still two visible clues to the vicinity of the shrine: a mountain spring and a gargantuan stone known as 'Theseus' Rock'. It was under this rock that the ancients believed King Aegeus had hidden a sword and a pair of lattice-leather boots for his son Theseus. When the adolescent Theseus was strong enough to lift the rock with his bare hands, then and only then – resplendent in his new footwear and brandishing a glinting weapon – could he claim to have come of age.

Sitting there in the sun on Theseus' rock with one small tortoise for company, I tried to think back two-thousand-odd years. To picture the scene, when a farmer or fisherman or weaver from the region would have made the selfsame journey here in order to celebrate or assuage the sexual power of Bridal Aphrodite, a power made manifest by beautiful Helen. Although the position of the sanctuary is sylvan in the extreme – peaceful now as it was two thousand years ago (judging from the modest remains here, this was not a large religious complex) – the settlements it served along the coast were lively, populous developments.

In antiquity, Hermione was famous for its water-sports. It held a kind of mini-aqua-olympics, with boat racing and what may be translated either as diving or swimming competitions.[4] Boys were sent underwater to rescue objects from the bottom of the harbour; in the bays nearby they can still be found doing the same thing. These were popular events and attracted quite a crowd – one-man rowing boats jostling for position with the bigger sailing boats, rigging and linen sail-cloths fluttering as the craft lined up for the regatta.

There were musical contests at Hermione too, the fun and games all in honour of Dionysus of the Black Goat – the most debauched of all the Olympian deities. But in the maudlin hours after the drinking and carousing, one can imagine men's minds turning to their 'hero ancestors', those who had sailed and rowed from the harbour with a more serious purpose – to avenge Greek honour in the Trojan War. Homer lists in his Catalogue of Ships the contingent that left from Hermione.[5] Along with '*the men of Argos and Tiryns with her tremendous walls*', he talks of '[the men of] *Hermione and Asine commanding the deep wide gulf*'. In Hermione's folk memory the Trojan War was writ large. And as those locals recalled their long-dead ancestors, their thoughts, inevitably, must have turned to the cause of the war – white-armed, loose-robed Helen.

As I sat on that rock way above Hermione, the Bay of Hydra below, I tried to envisage how Aphrodite – and her earthly counterpart Helen – would have been commemorated at the nearby shrine. To help, I picked from Pausanias a selection of entries for ritual activity in the region.[6] These were rites actively practised in the 2nd century AD, many having their roots in classical Greek culture. To 21st-century sensibilities, few made comfortable reading.

One entry describes rites at the sanctuary of Demeter. Here (Pausanias writes), men, women and children – dressed in white, with wreaths of wild hyacinths woven into their hair – led a wild heifer 'still untamed and prancing', to Demeter's temple. Other cows lined up behind. Within the temple four old women waited with a scythe. The leading cow would be coaxed into the religious building and the doors shut. Then the slaughter would begin, first one cow and then another and another and another.

In nearby Methana, Pausanias recounts another ritual whereby each year, farmers tried to calm the fierce winds that threatened their newly shooting vines. A pair of farm-hands would take a white cockerel and tear it in half. The two men would then run around the vineyard in opposite directions – their hands wet with blood, the bird's torn feathers flying – before they buried the cockerel where they met. These were visceral times. We know that Helen too was honoured with animal sacrifice.[7] Helen's cult worshippers would typically have been men and women whose fingernails were black with grime and gore.

Pausanias paints a vivid picture of ritual activity in the 2nd century AD – but in most instances much of the finer detail of the mechanics of worship has been lost. The fixtures and fittings of religious sanctuaries and shrines rarely survive in the archaeological record. Religious paraphernalia were generally too flimsy, too transient to last or too precious to leave *in situ*. That which is left – the hefty, basic building blocks of ancient religious centres, bleached bones lying in the grass or still standing proud – give a rather reserved feel to temples and sanctuaries and shrines. But the impressions of an Ancient Greek visitor, of an acolyte of Helen, would have been very different.

In 2002 an excavation on the island of Kythnos in the Cyclades produced a rare and precious glimpse into the elusive world of Greek religious ritual.[8] Here, a shrine dating to the 7th century BC was destroyed in the 5th century BC by one of the region's traumatic earthquakes. This was not a shrine dedicated to Helen but it did house a female deity – almost certainly Hera or Aphrodite. The shrine was in use at the moment of disaster and, as a result, a moment in historical time has been frozen.

The goddess here commanded quite some respect. The most sacred part of the sanctuary, the *adyton* (literally 'no-go area') was preserved intact when it was covered in rubble by the earthquake. Protected by its very destruction, none of the *adyton*'s ephemera had been removed by locals, grave-robbers or amateur archaeologists. In the first stage of the excavations alone, a staggering 1,500 precious and significant artefacts – the majority of them left as votive offerings – have been discovered. This uniquely rich excavation offers us an unusually holistic sense of the ambient and rich experience of goddess-worship in the distant past.

It seems this *adyton*, a small sunken room, was partially obscured by a curtain of laced sea-shells. Niches in the walls held little clay figures. On one shelf, around the time that Homer's words were being written down, someone has dedicated jewellery from the Minoan-Mycenaean period – a grand heirloom given the greatest honour, becoming a gift for the gods. Scattered around the *adyton* were beads – carnelian and rock crystal: shiny objects appropriate for the magpie tastes of divinities. There are skeletal remains here too and little pots containing organic matter. On another surface are rows of coral – the offering of the 'common' crowd, harvested straight from the sea. For the poor 5th-century BC inhabitants of the Cyclades, coral was a gift that could be garnered without trade, without barter or cash.[9]

The 5th-century BC poet Pindar was right to call these inner sanctums 'fragrant treasuries'.[10] As well as burning oils and incense, there would have been animal sacrifices here; the olfactory hint of roast meat and the sharp smell of blood – and all heightened by an aural environment. Worshippers met their gods accompanied by the other-worldly tone of the aulos, the rattle of the sistra, and the clash of cymbals. And when the musicians stopped, there was another drone – the insistent and intrusive hum of swarms of flies, hiding in the cool shade of the inner sanctum or feeding off the sweat of transported ritual dancers.

It would have been in environments such as this that Helen would have been worshipped. And not just in the Peloponnese. Because she had come to be of particular significance to the Dorians – the *arriviste* inhabitants of Sparta – as they travelled, they took her cult westwards to Magna Graecia, east to Rhodes and across the Libyan Sea to Egypt, helping to keep the name, not just of Helen of Troy, but Helen of Sparta, alive.

In Egypt, where there had been Spartan–Arcadian incursions,[11] there was a tenacious Helen cult.[12] Herodotus tells us in his *Histories* of the statue of Helen, the daughter of Tyndareus, at Memphis where she was worshipped as 'the foreign Aphrodite'.[13] That particular identification may have been incorrect, but there were certainly cults of Helen in North Africa.[14] In the Cairo Museum there is a lovely gold dish, fairly beaten up, but with a series of minute letters – each only about a millimetre high – just legible around the edge:[15] a dedication, scratched into the surface, offering the gold object, used in the preparation of cosmetics, to 'Helen, sister of Aphrodite';[16] Helen the sister or rather the *equal* of Aphrodite in *beauty* is probably the implication.[17]

The Thorikos calendar – inscribed in stone at some point around 340 BC – records devotions to Helen in Attica too.[18] Here, in the month of Elaphebolion (the month of shooting stars: March/April), full-grown animals were sacrificed to her. This was indeed an honour. Other heroines are typically given only *trapezai* – wine and grain; blood is not shed for them. In the poem *Alexandra* written by Lycophron of Chalcis at the end of the 4th century BC, we hear that at Iapygia in southern Italy, Helen's fur-lined slippers were venerated in a shrine.[19] The story went that the footwear was dedicated by a dejected, lonely Menelaus as he searched for Helen after the fall of Troy – having discovered that all the Trojan city protected was an *eidolon*, a ghost.

Meanwhile back at Troy, in the 2nd century AD, we learn from a letter written to the Roman co-emperors, Marcus Aurelius and Commodus, that Helen was even invoked by the city which she had brought to its knees. In AD 176 a Christian called Athenagoras begged the emperors for tolerance, pointing out that across their empire all other kinds of eccentric cults were practised without persecution:

> The inhabitants of your empire, greatest of kings, follow many customs and laws, and none of them is prevented by law or fear of punishment from cherishing his ancestral ways, however ridiculous they may be. The Trojan calls Hector a god and worships Helen, regarding her as Adrasteia; the Lacedaemonian venerates Agamemnon as Zeus.[20]

Adrasteia is an alternative name for the vengeful spirit Nemesis. With the broken walls of Troy as their backdrop, locals clearly remembered Helen as a potent and malign force.

෨෧ඏ෧ඏ෧

As I write, an excavation of a Mycenaean complex in Pellana, 25 km north-west of Sparta, is reaching its final stages. Today Pellana is one of those sites that gives the impression of hunkering back down into the ground, quietly collapsing, contented and insignificant; dormant until archaeologists start to poke at it and encourage it to speak of the past. When I last visited the excavations out of hours, a tethered donkey in the adjacent farmyard, unused to visitors, brayed and hollered incessantly.[21] I asked the donkey's owners about the digs, as they tried to sell me their home-grown cabbages, they laughed at the idea that the ruin in their backyard might be the haunt of heroes.

Yet one of the chief excavators, Dr T.G. Spyropoulos, has made an extraordinary claim. Pellana, he says, was Lakedaimon, the capital of ancient Lakedaimonia, or Lakonia – and it was Helen's home. To date the digs have focused on two giant *tholos*-style tombs (cut into the rock these are in fact chamber tombs), 50 feet (15 m) deep, the graves of Mycenaean aristocrats. Rich artefacts have emerged. There are gorgeous piriform vases, one, for instance, decorated with a lush marine landscape, the surface wrapped with a seaweed motif and inlaid with ivory. The style of decoration is evidence of close contact with Minoan Crete. A monumental Mycenaean wall, snaking up from the foot of the acropolis, is an indication that a wealthy clan controlled this rich corner of the Peloponnese.

Along with the magnificence of the Late Bronze Age architecture here, the excavators' key evidence for this being the home of the famous King and Queen of Lacedaemon is a temple monument erected in the proto-geometric period *c.* 1050 BC and rebuilt *c.* 700 BC. Someone has left offerings for the spirit or deity honoured here. The votive gifts – a hoard of pottery and a collection of perforated clay discs (so far, thirty have been found) – are credible evidence of cult activity. The discs are all inscribed with an epsilon, a Greek 'E'. E, some claim, for Eleni.[22]

A number of *tholos*-style tombs have yet to be excavated. The new digs at Pellana are a chance to make more sense, if not of Helen's home then certainly her homeland. Spyropoulos' claims are significant not just because they witness the emergence of another Late Bronze Age centre from the ground, another cult of a female spirit, but also because they are a reminder that Helen is still a woman that men are drawn to, whom they choose to pursue.

36

THE DAUGHTER OF
THE OCEAN

◎◎◎◎◎◎◎◎◎◎◎◎◎

APOLLO (to Orestes): First as to Helen, whom you meant to kill,
and move/ Menelaus to rage – your purpose failed; for this is she,
whom you see here, enfolded in the sparkling sky;/ Not dead at
your hands, but preserved. I snatched her up/ At Zeus her father's
bidding, and saved her from your sword./ From Zeus immortal
born, immortal she must live,/ Reverenced as the goddess who saves
seamen's lives,/ enthroned beside her brothers in the folds of heaven.

So, Menelaus, choose for your home another wife;/ For Helen's
beauty was to the gods their instrument/ For setting Greeks and
Trojans face to face in war/ And multiplying deaths, to purge
the bloated earth/ Of its superfluous welter of mortality. So
much for Helen.

. . .

MENELAUS: Helen, daughter of Zeus, farewell! What happiness
For you, to find a home among the blessed gods!

EURIPIDES, *Orestes*[1]

AT SPARTA HELEN WAS WORSHIPPED both as a goddess and as a
heroine, in Egypt as a decorous, seemly wife, and across the Greek
mainland as a spirit of earth, air and sky. She is chameleon. But
just as in the epics she makes long physical journeys across the vast waterways of the Aegean, so her most common guise is that of a spirit associated
with water.

In the ancient world divinities and nymphs with pronounced sexual
power were typically thought to inhabit brooks, rivers and oceans.[2] Aphrodite
was herself conceived within the sea. One fragmentary poem attributed to
Hesiod claims that Helen's mother was not Leda but a 'daughter of the

Ocean'.³ And so the search for Helen's cultic shrines frequently leads to water-sources and shorelines.

A few miles south of Corinth and a stone's throw from the classical ruins of Kenchreai is the tiny village of Loutra Elenis – Helen's Baths – or, as it was marked on Greek maps and road-signs until a few years ago, Τὰ λουτρὰ τῆς ὡραίας Ἑλένης the baths of the beautiful Helen'. The therapeutic waters were first described as a ritual site by Pausanias.⁴ Now the springs are hard to find. Once you reach the shore, a good clue to the location is the sight of the charming Greek ladies (generally rather elderly and overweight) who use the place religiously.

The path to the mouth of the spring is hedged with laurels and scattered with the used baby wipes that appear as a constant companion to the lesser-known sites of antiquity. Balancing on the rocks, the silvery bubbles of gas produced by the spring are easy to trace, floating up through the clear water. I was cynical about how efficacious the 'holy waters' could possibly be – until I took the plunge myself. Swimming in the outflow of the spring I had the most curious sensation of passing through distinct layers of alternately warm and freezing cold water. Pausanias describes the warm sea as 'boiling' and you can just feel the underwater bubbles as they nudge their way up to the surface. This (naturally) is supposed to be a beautifying experience; it is certainly an invigorating one.

During my last visit I had an extraordinary conversation about Helen, while in the fizzing water of the spring, with an ex-merchant seaman, who was wearing only a pair of very small, black Speedos. The sailor had become a chef after he left the navy and because of standing up cooking day in, day out, suffered from dreadful circulation problems. One of his legs, he told me firmly, was once as black as his trunks, whereas now (and here he showed off a trim leg with a small patch of grey on the ankle) there was next to no problem. The mysterious cure, he assured me, had come with his visits to Loutra Elenis.

Helen's latter-day devotee then pointed out the epicentre of the spring – the point at which the fresh water, filtered through Mount Oneia, meets the sea. As the spring has been channelled, diverted and enclosed, it is now necessary for the visitor to half-swim, half-clamber, into a little niche where fresh water meets saline. Hanging onto the rocks there just above head height, fierce jets of water pummelled me from toes to chest. I could suddenly see why that faithful sailor had had such good results. Devotees are adamant that the place is efficacious both because Helen was worshipped here and because she herself used the spring.

On a hazy day, when atmospheric conditions blur and block out the shapes of modern buildings, the view here cannot have changed an iota down the millennia. To the east, clustering over the current archaeological dig at Kenchreai, there are fields of asphodel. With its lance-like leaves and pale-pink starry flowers the asphodel was a familiar sight in ancient Greece. In popular Greek thought, the meadow of asphodel in Hades received the fleshless corpses of the dead, and Homer describes fallen heroes eating the plant. The fields of asphodel at Kenchreai are a striking sight, each plant standing tall and straight like a man: it is easy to see why the ancients equated the spiny stems with the bones of their ancestors.

Throughout the classical period the outlines of boats on the horizon would also have been visible, making their way into the port of Corinth. Finds testify to visitors from across the region, from maritime centres such as Morocco, Cyprus and Chios. Many of these sailors would have followed up their visit to Helen's Baths by paying their respects to Aphrodite, her sister in beauty, making a bee-line to worship the goddess of love with *ta aphrodisia*, literally 'the things of Aphrodite' – sex.

A number of the remains at Kenchreai have been lost during road-construction – the present rubbing out the past. Those that are left seem most beloved by local fishermen who use them as platforms from which to cast off. We know that, from at least the Roman period onwards, Aphrodite had a temple and a large statue at Kenchreai itself,[5] but to reach the site of Aphrodite's grandest religious complex one has to pass through the old town of Corinth (a jumble of Roman ruins[6] obliterating most of the Greek stones, where tourist shops sell the image of Aphrodite on everything from aprons to doormats), and head for the unfeasibly dominant, sky-scraping, mottled grey rock that is Acrocorinth. Travellers making their way up to Acrocorinth (and it is a 4 km climb) any time from 500 BC onwards might well have seen gaggles of the prostitutes and temple servants descending to meet devout customers in the town.[7]

We hear from a fragment of Pindar's poetry that a doubly victorious Olympic champion called Xenophon, to commemorate his triumphs in 464 BC, dedicated one hundred girls to Aphrodite at Acrocorinth.[8] Strabo tells us that in his day there were a thousand of these women working for the goddess of love.[9] One has to imagine, since their clients were primarily the port-hopping sailors, that a number of these holy whores would have left the musky-sour stench of venereal disease on the air as they passed.

But the site of Aphrodite's temple on Acrocorinth, 1,880 feet (570 m) above sea level, runs against the squalid and clandestine stereotype of the brothel. Here the breeze is balmy and fresh. Where pillars and architraves once would have been there is a panoramic view out across the Gulf of

Corinth and over to the mountains of the Peloponnese. Just below the temple in the classical period a spring brought fresh water. The location feels exultant and secure. A female phi-type figurine found here, dating from the end of the Mycenaean period, testifies that in the Late Bronze Age Mycenaeans would also have stood on this spot to look and wonder.[10] We cannot know precisely why they came or to whom they prayed when they arrived, but the fact that they brought with them votive offerings does show that a visit here was an important spiritual experience.

Worried by the popularity of Aphrodite's cult in the classical period, the early Christians assiduously obliterated the pagan temple under one of their churches.[11] Now the most explicit reminders of the significance of the goddess of love, the armed protector of Corinth and its environs, are locked away in a restricted storeroom in Corinth museum.[12] A collection of offerings and artworks commemorating the power of erotic love is thought to be unsuitable for public consumption.

But Helen − the daughter, sister, incarnation of Aphrodite, and as always close to her in body and spirit − is still openly worshipped by modern-day believers. 'Magic!' shout the old Greek men and women as they swim in Helen's Baths, just down the hill from Acrocorinth: '*Ephcharisto ōrea Eleni*' − 'Thank you, beautiful Helen.'[13]

A Byzantine commentator writing in the second quarter of the 6th century AD, recorded that 200 km east of Loutra Elenis, close to the Turkish coastline on the island of Chios, Helen's cult revolved around a spring.[14] Pausanias described the spring, near Helen's Temple on the hill of Therapne in Sparta,[15] and another close to the shrine of Bridal Aphrodite founded on the occasion of Helen's union with Theseus.[16] And at Rome, in the south corner of the Forum Romanum, Helen's image − holding a large torch − could be found on the marble altar at the Lacus Juturnae, itself a spring-fed pool dedicated to the water-nymph Juturna.[17] The Lacus Juturnae altar was constructed at the time of Trajan,[18] and stood between the Temple of Castor and Pollux and the Atrium Vestae. Once again, as at Sparta and in Egypt, Helen finds her worship endorsed by the authorities.

Not that Helen needed state sponsorship to perpetuate her appeal. For the Roman people her influence was not just to be found in official religious sanctuaries and works of great literature − it seeped into the culture of the street. There is a plant whose Latin name is still *Inula helenium* − Helen's Flower. Pliny the Elder, in his *Natural History*, tells us the flower was thus named because it grew where Helen's tears fell. *Inula helenium* was enthusiastically used as a beauty aid by ageing Roman women and giddy girls alike who ground up the bitter plant to a beautifying paste. Another common practice was to burn its seeds or drink an infusion of *helenium* extract, all the while praying that by doing so the hopeful user would acquire just a fraction of Helen's dangerous beauty. Caesar Augustus' daughter, Julia, took a daily dose of 'Helen's Flower'. To overcome its bitterness, it was 'dried and pounded into flour and seasoned with some sweet juice' or else 'mixed with boiled-down grape-juice or flavoured with honey or raisins or juicy dates'.[19] Our source, Pliny, enthusiastically promoted its efficacy, describing the plant's reputation for keeping the face and body fresh and for increasing sex appeal. And if *helenium* did not work as a love-charm, it had handy secondary uses too – curing snake-bites and killing mice.

Because of its effective use as a tonic and a stimulant, 'Helen's Flower' has been a friend to doctors and pharmacists from antiquity through to the present day. Helenin (C_6H_8O) is a distillation from the root. Preparations from the plant can be prescribed by herbalists to regulate menstruation, or indeed encourage the onset of a girl's periods. The connection with Helen is a significant one. This herb brought pre-pubescent girls to sexual maturity and therefore to beauty. The ancients imagined the first ever Helen's Flower springing from the dark little pools where the tears of the most beautiful woman in the world fell on the ground. They imagined her weeping as she remembered the pain that came with erotic love, weeping as she guided young girls onto the sexual path she herself knew only too well.

It was on one of 'Helen's Islands',[20] *Helene*[21] now called Makronissos, that the plant *Inula helenium* was first said to have sprung from Helen's tears. Makronissos has a horrific and disturbing history. Today it is still and silent. No boats in the bay, no smudge of movement from a goat or a sheep, no clothes fluttering on a line. During the Greek Civil War,[22] this was the site of the 'white terror'. Over a hundred thousand political prisoners were rounded up and held on the island in a sealed, sadistic concentration camp. There were massacres and terrible tortures. The screams of the inmates could be heard from the mainland. The island has been left empty, a heavy monument to man's dreadful folly and blood-lust. Prophesying Makronissos' tragic history, it was said in antiquity that this was a sombre place, a place where Helen sighed.

☙❧☙❧☙❧

And on rough nights, those sailors who heard Helen sigh on the isle of *Helene* could have sensed her above them too, materialising from the ether, because along with her brothers, Castor and Pollux – the *soteres*, saviours riding their white horses across the oceans – a starry Helen was thought to keep watch over those in danger on the sea and to bring rather alarming illumination in the form of St Elmo's Fire. Anyone caught out at night on a stormy sea and blinded by the sudden arrival of St Elmo's Fire will be left in no doubt as to the real respect the ancients must have felt for Helen.[23] Called simply *Helene* in the ancient world, before the phenomenon was appropriated by a Christian saint, St Elmo's Fire is an electrifying event. In the highly charged atmosphere of a storm, gas can become ionised, causing an electro-luminescent discharge to leap in double or triple jets from sharp points on ships' rigging. Bluish-white streamers of flame seem to appear from thin air. The effect is breathtaking and disconcerting.

These corposants (literally 'holy bodies') typically appear singly or in pairs. The flames can provide a welcome source of light in a pitch black, storm-tossed night; they can also spark fires – a particular problem in antiquity when masts and rigging were made entirely of wood and hemp or papyrus. And so, whereas the twin brothers Castor and Pollux were thought to bring only relief, the single 'Helen flame' was often blamed for the devastation caused. A fragment of a work by one Hellenistic author called Sosibius[24] suggests that Helen's light was a bad omen, and another Roman author is loquacious on the matter: 'The ship is lost when the brothers of Therapne have deserted the sails doomed by the fire of their sister.'[25] Even out in the middle of the ocean, Helen was believed to crackle with a dangerous energy.

THE FACE
THAT LAUNCHED
A THOUSAND
SHIPS

37

HELEN IN ATHENS

@@@@@@@@@@@@

After they heard that Helen had returned to her home in
Mycenae, all Europe rushed in dense crowds, wondering
at Plisthenes' daughter-in-law, and were on fire to see the face
that overthrew Asia. Indeed, she was proud to have inflamed
leaders, to have torn apart the world in war, and to have gained
an infamous reputation for her shameful beauty.

JOSEPH OF EXETER, *Trojan War* (*c.* AD 1180)[1]

IF A BRONZE AGE Helen really did travel back to Sparta from Troy,
following her misadventures, as she looked out over the ragged, bucolic
coastlines of Turkey, Egypt and Greece, little could she have imagined
that the mediocre pre-historic ports and tiny settlements she and the other
survivors of the Trojan War passed would have become great classical cities:
Thebes, Corinth, Athens. And could she have ever guessed that in the future
she would live on in these cities, as one of their most significant and
contentious symbols of womanhood? That her story would be played out
again and again in the philosophers' academies and grand public theatres
to a drunk, demanding, intellectually greedy and polyglot crowd?

The memory of Helen would come to be particularly resonant not just
in her home town of Sparta, but in classical Athens. In the 5th century BC,
thanks to the new art of theatre, and then to the dialogues of philosophers and rhetoricians, Helen's story takes a significant turn. She was already
being worshipped in cultic shrines in the Peloponnese, her song sung in
grand mansions, her face etched into metal and applied to vases, but she
was about to become a political animal. Once the Spartan queen stepped
onto the Athenian stage, the *idea* of Helen became central to the Athenian
democratic experience, and therefore central to the blueprint for western
society.[2]

For an ambitious *polis* such as Athens, Helen's story embraces compelling
themes: death and duty, civic responsibility and individual ambition, the

relationship between stranger and kin; the purpose of war, the purpose of women; why humanity is flawed. And with Helen embodying a primal force – sexual power – there is the question of how the imperfect, the spontaneous, the animal, can become part of the social, political body.

Homer's Helen is always ambiguous, always intriguing. But it is on the Athenian stage that she becomes a paradox: a creature of pantomime polarity, either very, very good or very, very bad. It is here that the fervent debate about Helen really starts. What does Helen mean? How can she be dealt with? Even when she only has a walk-on part in Greek drama, she upstages the other characters and her presence bleeds beyond her scenes. The language the Greek playwrights used was designed to knock the breath out of their audience. And in the plays of Aeschylus, Sophocles and in particular Euripides, how they must have gasped at Helen.

In Athens, it is still possible to visit the Theatre of Dionysus (the structure still standing was built in the 4th century BC) where much Greek tragedy was premiered. The site is at the geographical heart of the ancient Athenian *polis*, a generous stone's throw from the acropolis, the agora and the assembly. The best time to visit is after the tourists have gone back to their hotels and the 21st-century Athenians are out on the streets, promenading up and down the marble walkways, chatting, chewing on figs and spitting out the husks of seeds and nuts much as Athenians would have done two and a half thousand years ago. Street vendors selling cheap religious icons are a reminder of the spiritual impact the location would once have had – the theatre was originally part of a religious sanctuary, the precinct of the louche, debauched god of wine and fertility, Dionysus. It was hemmed in with temples and shrines, littered with votive offerings.

Greek theatre was born out of religious ritual and was therefore by definition political, a part of the fabric of the *polis*. As one scholar puts it, 'the [theatre] festivals were . . . political because they were religious, since in ancient pre-Christian Greece the religious and the political were fabrics of thought and behaviour woven from the same threads'.[3] It was in the theatre, with a mass audience present, that the Greeks (who relished analysis) could ask themselves who they were, what they should think and how they should live. Helen was at the heart of that interrogation.

So it was to the sanctuary of Dionysus in the 5th century BC, that people would have come to watch Helen's story picked over – in particularly exposed form in the work of Euripides.[4] In his easy, colloquial, charismatic language, Euripides introduced Helen as a central figure to the tragic stage. And in his vacillating, complicated, portrayal of her, he summed up beautifully the way men have wanted Helen both to be perfect, and to be a perfect scapegoat. Euripides made it clear that the pre-historic Helen had become a Classical Greek everywoman, that there was a 'Helen' in every girl-child and virgin, wife and prostitute who inhabited the Greek world.

In the *Trojan Women* (first produced in 415 BC), Helen and her one-time mother-in-law Hecuba, widow of dead Priam, mother of dead Paris and Hector, fight a war of words. Menelaus is poised to kill his adulterous spouse but Helen insists she is not responsible for the death and destruction at Troy and does not deserve to die.[5] The Trojan queen counters, laying the blame four-square at Helen's door. The language lunges and thrusts across the stage. This is a rhetorical *agon* or competition. Cleverly, Hecuba emphasises Helen's 'Eastern', 'Barbaric' tastes and loyalties; she is reminding Menelaus that Helen has spent ten years in a Trojan's bed. The old woman argues desperately, convinced that, once again, Helen's beauty will floor the man in front of her. Knowing their Homer as they do, Euripides' audience senses the pathetic futility of the old woman's words. Hecuba is right: Menelaus cannot resist Helen, he will forgive her. He will let his eyes wander over her wonderful body and face, and decide to take his Queen back home. Paris' desire for Helen tramples over social codes and international etiquette. Menelaus relinquishes a cuckolded warrior's right to revenge.

Through the antiphonal dirges sung by the chorus, and the moaning accompaniment of *auloi* – the banshee-like oboe of the classical world – the central tenet of the play shouts out loud: Helen is dangerous, women are not be trusted, least of all those who are articulate, attractive, charismatic and crafty. These are the creatures who bring about the death of civilisations.

In Athens it was a civic duty to attend the theatre and tragic playwrights became society's unofficial educators. It has been estimated that in the 4th century BC, 50 per cent of the qualified citizenry would have gone to the theatre.[6] That is the greatest single collection of citizens (the Olympic Games and first-division battles excluded) that would ever gather in time or space in the Greek world, and all of them staring at a small stage; all – almost certainly at some point in their lives – watching Helen's story being played out in front of them.[7]

As part of a religious celebration, the experience of Athenian theatre was full-blooded. And one festival in particular had developed into a jamboree of epic proportions – the Great Dionysia. The atmosphere in Athens during the Great Dionysia, held in late March or early April, must have been electric. Men from across the Greek world, rich and poor alike,[8] flooded into the city. The festival opened with an exuberant and ostentatious parade.

Leading the procession was a fine bull, richly decorated, garlanded, sprin-kled with perfume and destined for a bloody sacrifice – like countless other animals in the city over the next three days. Behind the bull, a virgin carrying a golden basket. Dancing, singing and drinking carried on hard into the night.

Since these carnivalesque events offered many men a rare holiday, a chance to lay down hoes and sickles and ploughshares,[9] there must have been a number who watched Euripides' *Helen* and *The Trojan Women* with extremely sore heads. For some this was an annual event, for others a once-in-a-lifetime experience.[10] The plays performed at the Great Dionysia were rivals, all in competition with each other. Expectations and emotions ran high. The tragic Helen was paraded in front of a charged and voluble crowd.

Male members of the recognised tribes in Attica would have taken their theatre tickets,[11] either made out of lead or chipped from bone or ivory, and sat under the shadow of the Parthenon to listen and to learn. Inscrip-tions imply that blocks of seats were assigned depending on social standing. Members of the *boule* in one, war orphans in another, foreigners possibly in a separate section, *metics* and perhaps a tiny, token scattering of slaves elsewhere. The seats of the *theatron*, the watching place, in the Theatre of Dionysus were originally made of wood, but towards the end of the 4th century BC more money had been invested in the outfit and the audience perched on warm stone benches, enjoyed the refreshments that hawkers sold around the theatres and watched the action below them in the *orchestra* – the dancing place.[12]

The rock of the acropolis offered a geological cradle for the theatre. Here the gradient creates a natural auditorium with excellent acoustics.[13] Towering over the theatre on the Parthenon – Athens' symbol of power and piety – was an image of Helen, the beautiful problem immortalised in stone on the western end of the northern metopes. Menelaus fiercely confronts Paris while Helen shelters beneath a statue of Aphrodite.[14] It was under this masonry reminder of the Spartan queen's crimes, that the theatrical Helen would be judged.

Women, it seems, were absent from the theatres although some scholars argue that they would have been ranged in the worst, hottest seats in the auditorium.[15] The actors were all men.[16] Imagine the theatre on a warm April morning: the debris of the night before still fluttering in the streets, wine spilt in the Dionysiac debauches attracting the flies. And in the theatre itself, anywhere between fourteen and seventeen thousand men staring down at the masked male actor playing Helen, men trying to make some sense of their world, and of the women in it.

The man (or boy) who played Helen would have become the most beautiful woman in the world by reciting his lines through the rigid mask of tragic theatre. Made of linen or cork and wood with realistic hair, the masks would have been a pleasing neutral cover through which to transmit ideas about the power of beauty.[17] Used skilfully, this artificial second skin can magnify the thoughts and ideas and actions of the performer. At the end of the production, actors left their masks for the god in the temple in Dionysus' sanctuary. These were more than mere props, they were the triggers that allowed men to speak the words and thoughts of another, and to explore life's fundamental questions.

In the mystical, drunken atmosphere of the festival, audiences were sensitized to the drama before them. Plutarch, commentating in the 2nd century AD, tells the story of a 4th-century BC Thessalian tyrant called Alexander, famous for his hideous brutality. Alexander's show-stoppers included burying enemies alive or wrapping them in animal-hides before setting dogs on them. But at a production of *The Trojan Women* the despot rushed out of the theatre so that the cowed citizens should not see the tears that gushed, could not witness his weakness, his appreciation of Hecuba's and Helen's human tragedy.[18]

And because the *The Trojan Women* contains such stunning imagery, such muscular rhetorical speeches, such plangent exploration of the human condition, Euripides' play became a textbook through the Hellenistic, Roman, medieval and Renaissance periods. Alexander the Great, for instance, recited chunks of Euripides' *Andromeda* as one of his party tricks,[19] and two thousand years later Elizabeth I was taught to translate his plays.[20] Euripides promotes Helen as a bitch-whore, a gold-digger, a murderess; his plays are works of genius and they ensure that the West remembers her as a problem.

Other playwrights also damned Helen on stage. In Aeschylus' *Agamemnon* she is known simply as 'woman' – 'that filthy woman' is the implied tone. Begrudgingly, once she comes back to Menelaus, she is given a name, although the chorus makes much of the fact that '*Helenan*' has a sinister ring, because she is also *Helenas* (ship-destroyer), *Helandros* (man-destroyer) and *Heleptopolis* (city-destroyer).[21] Simon Goldhill has pointed out that a translation true to the original spirit of the words, would read something like this:

> *Whoever named you so, in absolute accuracy?*
> *Could it be someone unseen in foreknowledge*
> *Of what had to happen using his tongue to the mark,*
> *Who named you, spear-bride, fought-over*
> *Helen?*

Appropriately named, since hell for ships,
Hell for men, hell for cities . . .[22]

The Athenians of the 5th century BC hated Helen for her very activity, for the fact that she appeared to have catalysed a significant change in the status quo. Her story marked the end of the Age of Heroes and the end of the Mycenaean civilisation; she distracted men from their linear development. A man making love to a woman cannot lay a foundation stone, cannot write his own history, cannot fight.

೦಄೦಄೦

On Athenian vases of the archaic and classical periods, Helen is frequently in flight, running away after the fall of Troy, from a condemnatory and vengeful Menelaus.[23] The Athenians did not want to remember a proud, powerful queen. For many, with their own women penned and silenced at home, Helen encapsulated everything that a 'bad woman' could be. Self-sacrifice rather than self-fulfilment would be the act to earn an Athenian woman a good reputation.

For a 5th-century BC Greek audience, Helen could tot up an impressive list of depravities. She abandons her child, she sleeps with barbarians, she submits to carnal pleasure and she proves that, even once shackled by marriage, women still have the capacity to give men a run for their money. Euripides puts into the mouth of Clytemnestra a typical classical, male Greek judgement of Helen. Clytemnestra articulates why she murdered her husband Agamemnon, who had sacrificed their daughter Iphigeneia to please the gods and then returned ten years later with his concubine:

If he had killed her to avert the capture of our city or to benefit our house and save the other children, one for the sake of many, it would have been forgivable. But as things were, because Helen was a slut and her husband did not know how to control a treacherous wife, for those reasons he killed my girl.[24]

But in a sense Helen's greatest crime is simply her notoriety. Just over fifteen years before Euripides wrote *The Trojan Women*, Athenians would have heard their golden boy Pericles driving home a singularly repressive message. In his famous Funeral Speech of 431 BC he declares that the greatest *kleos* (fame or reputation) would be won by women who remained invisible: '*Perhaps I should say a word or two on the duties of women to those among you who are now widowed. I can say all I have to say in a short word of advice . . . the greatest glory of a woman is to be least talked about by men, whether they are praising you or criticising you.*[25] Xenophon adds his exhortations in his volume *Household Management*: '*So it is seemly for a woman to remain at home and not be out of doors; but for a man to stay inside, instead of devoting himself to outdoor pursuits, is disgraceful.*'[26] The ideal 5th-century BC Athenian woman was not seen, not heard, not heard of. Given these prerequisites, Helen was not just loose, she was a travesty of womanhood, an enemy to civilised man.

Helen's resilience is therefore particularly remarkable given her crimes. Within three years of staging *The Trojan Women*, Euripides produces another play, *Helen*, and this time the central character is an innocent, the Helen described by Stesichorus who spends the duration of the Trojan War living blamelessly in Egypt. Whether it is because he is seduced by the idea of the woman or himself fears the wrath of Helen the immortal, or whether he is writing a comedy elaborating on a grand joke (what could be funnier than the idea that Helen is not to blame), it seems Euripides too is a victim of Helen's charms.[27]

On occasion she is, literally, satirised, turning up as the subject of satyr plays, the rowdy, bawdy, comic works that rounded off a day of tragedies at one of the great theatre festivals. The complete texts of almost all the satyr plays are now lost (with the exception of Euripides' *Cyclops*); they would probably have been played alongside tragedies such as *Hecuba*. Just imagine the crowd roaring along to these lines, thumping their seats, as a satyr quizzes Odysseus on his way home from Troy.

> *When you took that woman, did you all take turns*
> *and bang her? She liked variety in men*
> *the fickle bitch! Why, the sight of a man*
> *with embroidered pants and a golden chain*
> *so fluttered her, she left Menelaus,*
> *a fine little man. I wish there were*
> *no women in the world — except [some] for me.*[28]

We also know of the name of one satyr play which seems to have revolved entirely around Helen. Called the Ὁ Ἑλένης Γαμὸς Σατυρικός 'The Satyric Marriage of Helen', it offered chortles and titillation aplenty, dealing with the timelessly romantic moment when Helen and Paris consummate their love affair on the island of Kranai.[29] Scrappy fragments of four other comedies about Helen exist, written by the 4th-century BC playwright Alexis.[30] Helen made the audiences of Athens laugh as well as cry.[31]

In Athens, just a year after the opening of Euripides' play *Helen*, in 412 BC, (probably at the Theatre of Dionysus), we come across Helen's other extant theatrical outing, in the premiere of Aristophanes' comedy, *Lysistrata*. Aristophanes' Helen is to be wondered at, not feared or damned. Here it is Helen's spirituality and her special relationship with young virgins that are being lauded and broadcast. Helen is simply mentioned (as Leda's daughter) right at the end of the play. Earlier on in the action, we have already been reminded what gorgeous creatures Spartan girls famously were. In one fabulous scene, a character called Lampito, whose breasts are being admired, describes how she goes to the gym to make her buttocks hard. The closing lines are playful, the atmosphere rapturous.

> SPARTAN [singing as the couples dance]:
>
> *Step it, hey!*
> *prance lightly, hey!*
> *that we may hymn Sparta,*
> *which delights in dances in honour of the gods*
> *and in the stamp of feet,*
> *and where beside the Eurotas*
> *the maidens prance*
> *like fillies, raising clouds*
> *of dust with their feet,*
> *and their hair bobs*
> *like the hair of bacchants who sport and ply the thyrsus;*
> *and they are led by Leda's daughter,*
> *the pure and comely chief of their chorus.*[32]

And so the play finishes as the spirit of Helen is invoked – leading those gorgeous young Spartan girls 'like fillies' off the stage and on into men's imaginations.

38

HELEN LOST AND
HELEN FOUND

nisi Taenario placuisset Troica cunno
Mentula, quod caneret, non habuisset opus.

If Trojan cock had not brought Spartan cunt such fun,
This Homer fellow's book could not have been begun

PRIAPEA: 'Poems for a Phallic God'[1]

EARLY IN THE 19TH CENTURY AD a rather over-enthusiastic librarian called Angelo Mai set to work on a rare, early manuscript of Homer. This precious document, created in the 5th century AD and known as the Ambrosian *Iliad* or the Milan Homer – kept in the Ambrosian library in Milan for two hundred years – had been butchered and botched. Pieces of paper were stuck to the back of the miniature illustrations. Mai realised there were lines of Homer underneath the paper-sheets, and was keen to get to them; perhaps here lay secrets, a version of the *Iliad* that had been lost for centuries.[2]

So Mai dissolved the glue that stuck the paper to the manuscript and used reagent chemicals to try to bring the words out of the vellum. One portion that he treated vigorously included, on the reverse side, a picture of Helen (dressed as though in purdah, with an aubergine-coloured apron and matching hem to her full skirts) and Paris, sitting, companionably, next to each other. There was a slight danger that the chemicals might soak through and the images be damaged in the process, but Mai went ahead.

A fine facsimile of this illustration is now housed in the Rare Books Room of the University of Cambridge Library. This is one of the most beautiful, vigorous representations of the Troy story from the Byzantine Empire. Resting on the salmon-pink cushions provided by the library, warriors race across petrol-green landscapes, hemmed in only by the tangerine frames of the manuscript around them, a colour scheme still vivid after 1,500 years.

But the chemicals that Mai used did indeed destroy as well as preserve; and it is the image of Helen that is particularly soiled. She still sits demurely, Paris by her side, but her name is barely legible. Her face, touched too often and for too long, has become an ugly, shady blur.

ᚖᚖᚖᚖᚖᚖ

Between 13 and 15 April 1204 AD, a sailor travelling up the Bosphorus, looking towards Constantinople, would have seen a sky red with fire. A joint force of Frankish and Venetian crusaders was running amok in the capital of the Byzantine Empire. Against the Pope's wishes, the forces of the Fourth Crusade had taken this rich Christian city. Hanging over the invaders was the threat of excommunication: but so too was the lure of silver and spoil.

In the centre of the city of Constantinople was the Hippodrome. Able to accommodate up to 100,000 spectators this was the sporting and social hub of the Byzantine Empire. Work on the Hippodrome may have begun as early as the 2nd century AD; it was certainly completed by the 4th century AD. By 1204 the race-track doubled up as a forum for grand celebrations, civic, political and religious. It hosts less lofty events now: the workers of Istanbul eat their sandwiches here at lunchtime, a rusting fun-fair sits unused under its tarpaulin covers, letter writers tap out missives for the illiterate of the city.

In its day the site boasted the finest collection of antiquities anywhere in the world. Here were the great and the good of Greece and Rome, cast in bronze and carved in stone: Heracles, Zeus, Romulus and Remus; Paris handing Aphrodite the Golden Apple; the Emperor Augustus. Here too was Helen. And for three apocalyptic days in 1204, it was here in the Hippodrome that the crusaders' fires burnt the fiercest.

There were cogent reasons for the desecration. The majority of the statues were pagan icons or personalities. Crusaders still thought these metal and stone shells contained spirits and demons. The Venetians and the Franks had already earned the disapproval of the Pope and his Church; they did not want to risk taking on the old gods as well. And of course all that molten bronze was very, very useful. The Hippodrome was a mine without the effort of digging. Tonnes of statuary and metal decoration were hacked down, smelted and then re-cast as coin. The only artworks to survive and be imported intact to Venice were four bronze horses – now world-famous

– that galloped across the emperor's box. Replicas of the horses still stand on the Basilica di San Marco today.[3]

But Helen was not so lucky: when the mob came to her, things got personal. An eyewitness (who clearly adored this metal vision, ranged as she was with her companions along the spine of the race-course), the Byzantine imperial secretary, Nicetas Choniates, described the scene:

> What of the white-armed Helen, beautiful-ankled, and long-necked Helen, who mustered the entire host of the Hellenes and overthrew Troy, whence she sailed to the Nile and, after a long absence, returned to the abodes of the Lakonians? Was she able to placate the implacable? Was she able to soften those men whose hearts were made of iron? On the contrary! She who had enslaved every onlooker with her beauty was wholly unable to achieve this, even though she was apparelled ornately; though fashioned of bronze, she appeared as fresh as the morning dew, anointed with the moistness of erotic love on her garment, veil, diadem and braid of hair. Her vesture was finer than spider webs, and the veil was cunningly wrought in its place; the diadem of gold and precious stones which bound the forehead was radiant, and the braid of hair that extended down to her knees, flowing down and blowing in the breeze, was bound tightly in the back with a hair-band. The lips were like flower cups, slightly parted as though she were about to speak; the graceful smile, at once greeting the spectator, filled him with delight; her flashing eyes, her arched eyebrows, and the shapeliness of the rest of her body were such that they cannot be described in words and depicted for future generations. O Helen, Tyndareus' daughter, the very essence of loveliness, offshoot of Erotes, ward of Aphrodite, nature's most perfect gift, contested prize of Trojans and Hellenes, where is your drug granted you by Thon's wife which banishes pain and sorrow and brings forgetfulness of every ill? Where are your irresistible love charms? Why did you not make use of these now as you did long ago? But I suspect that the Fates had foreordained that you should succumb to the flame's fervour so that your image should no longer enflame spectators with sexual passions.[4]

Although Nicetas himself thought the destruction of the statue was motivated purely by material gain – to appropriate more bronze – the rumours ran through Christendom that this Helen had been destroyed by the Venetians to avenge their Trojan ancestors. Just as Troy had been 'laid waste by the firebrand because of [Helen's] scandalous amours',⁵ so the Venetians had smashed and pulled Helen apart, fired up by vengeance and greed.

So today the Hippodrome is devoid of colossal statues. Only a couple of obelisks remain, stripped of their gilded bronze skins – stumps where once there were towering artworks. Helen used to be here; today she is a ghost.

And throughout history this is what Helen has become, a woman who has inspired such lust and such loathing she is forced into being a will-o'-the-wisp – always changing her form, here today, gone tomorrow. She is Protean and because of that she is perfect. She can become whatever the men around her want her to be; whether, like the ill-fated statue in the Hippodrome, a gleaming reminder of the glory of female sexuality, or, following the desecration of 1204, an amputated, broken memento of man's talent for acts of greed and execration.

☙☙☙☙☙

Helen's journey through history has been as tempestuous as her journey from Sparta to Troy and back again. She has been harried and destroyed in a multitude of ways. When she endures, she often does so by the skin of her teeth. The Queen of Sparta might have survived the historical battles of the Bronze Age, but there were new struggles to come. Great epics such as the *Cypria* – similar in size and scope to the *Iliad* and the *Odyssey* – telling of her early life and love affair with Paris were lost in the Medieval Dark Ages. Tragic and satirical plays that dealt with Helen, and Helen alone, were destroyed by the great fire in the library at Alexandria in Egypt. Painted vases illustrating lesser known episodes of her life were smashed or still lie buried underground. Cult offerings left to her at springs have been washed away by the waters. She leads us a merry dance. The path from the past to the present can be a rocky one. But during her tempestuous journey through time, Helen has had an important ally in the form of Homer: an artist whose work was itself so iconic that, thanks to its preservation and parody, an inky Helen has fluttered on fragments of papyrus and parchment out of antiquity and into the modern world.

39

HELEN, HOMER AND THE
CHANCES OF SURVIVAL

@@@@@@@@@@@@

Homer on parchment pages!
The Iliad and all the adventures
Of Ulysses, foe of Priam's kingdom!
All locked within a piece of skin
Folded into several little sheets!

MARTIAL, *Epigram* 14 (*c.* AD 40–103)[1]

I N AN UNASSUMING CASE in the British Museum there is a small piece
of plank designed to hang on a wall.[2] It dates from the Roman occupation of Egypt and was probably intended for display in a bar. With
its metal handle and schoolboy scrawl, it looks for all the world like a
swinging, Wild West saloon sign, or one of those Victorian homily boards:
'*There's no place like home*' or '*God bless this house*'. In fact the words written across
the uneven wooden surface are Homer's *Iliad* 1.468–73 in which the bard
celebrates the joys of drinking. The plank displaying Homer's lines is a
brave traveller from antiquity, now rather beaten up and splintered; nine
parts driftwood, one part treasure. This rough sign is testimony to the fact
that Homer pervaded antiquity, and that for the thousands of Roman citizens who walked, and drank, underneath it the poet's words were a familiar
rubric. Helen's biographer was a civilisation's popular prophet.

The physical passage of Homer's epics – and of most texts from classical
antiquity through to the modern world – was perilous. Helen was one of
the select host of characters who made this difficult journey. Many great
works of literature, many histories and many inhabitants of the classical
past were lost on the way. It was an expedition littered with obstacles, and
marked by character-changing experiences. Those who survived often did
so in idiosyncratic circumstances.

&&&&&&

On 21 February 1888, William Flinders Petrie, a British Egyptologist, was excavating at the cemetery of Hawara, in Fayum, Egypt. He found the mummy of a woman from the 2nd century AD. Attached to her skull there were still two thin plaits of her jet black hair, and underneath her head a scroll of papyrus. The outer layer of papyrus was already damaged but, carefully unfurling it, Petrie could make out some script firmly inked on the inside.[3]

As the layers got deeper the script became clearer – until it was apparent that here there were large gobbets of books 1 and 2 of the *Iliad*. Now the fragments of the papyrus scroll are stored between plates of glass within the Bodleian Library in Oxford.[4] A number of the pieces of papyrus have, through time, become raw and spidery. In the body of the manuscript itself and around the edges, fronds of the papyrus reed are clearly visible. Given the volatility of the organic writing surface, the Greek characters – formed in carbon-based ink – are unfeasibly neat. Across the tobacco-yellow papyrus Homer's words appear as a regular, confident stream.

It is perhaps significant that that nameless Egyptian woman from Hawara should have chosen Book 2 of the *Iliad* to cushion her journey into the afterlife. Helen first appears in Book 2 and on one, much damaged section of papyrus it is still possible to make out a sliver of her name – three little letters left at the end of '*ELENES*': . . . *NES*. The Hawara Homer is one of the earliest and most complete surviving copies of any of the books of the *Iliad*. With those three letters, Helen enters the written record.

Now the Hawara Homer is treated with absolute reverence. If you go to visit it in Oxford, your bags are locked away by security guards on the ground floor, and you bring your pencil and your notepaper in a clear plastic folder and then wait in the enveloping, 15th-century beauty of Duke Humfrey's Reading Room while the librarian takes different keys out of a series of boxes and drawers, each to unlock another container, the last key eventually unlocking the cupboards that contain the papyri sheets.

On other rare manuscripts in the Duke Humfrey's, Helen leads a medieval hunt, or, as a plump Germanic maiden, is plucked by Paris from a temple in the German countryside.[5] Before careful collectors and librarians were able to preserve these unique pieces, worms had done their best to destroy them. In one valuable volume, Helen sits, quietly, deep in the pages of vellum, but even hidden here, tenacious annelida (the original bookworms) have managed to bore their way through to the Spartan queen.

෧෧෧෧෧

For two thousand years the survival of Homer's Helen depended entirely on individuals, each hand-copying Homer's words. The *Iliad* itself was not printed until 1488, in Florence, when it was produced in a kind of facsimile version, one that strove to replicate handwriting. The *Iliad* was first translated into English (from French rather than Greek or Latin) by Arthur Hall in 1581. Of course by now the colossally influential technology of printing had arrived. Close on six thousand different printed texts were to follow. High-profile translators include Thomas Hobbes, Percy Bysshe Shelley, Gladstone and T.E. Lawrence. Pope's translation (1688–1704) has been published in more editions than any other. Over the years Homer has also been translated into an abundance of languages including Turkish (1887), Serbo-Croat (1915), Yiddish (1924), Farsi (1925), Esperanto (1930), Twi (1957), Basque (1985), Azerbaijani (1986) and Luxembourgish (1995).[6]

When Homer was first written down, 'books' – such as the Hawara Homer – took the form of a papyrus scroll.[7] Papyrus is the name of a particular kind of reed that grows profusely in the Nile Delta. If you pick up a piece of modern papyrus and hold it up to the light, you can clearly see how it is made – a criss-cross of fibrous strips, firmly pressed together.[8]

Throughout antiquity there were various recipes for ink (oak gall mixed with diluted egg-white is one, lamp-black in water is another). The pen was a reed sharpened to a point, the end split up the middle. The skill of the scribes who used these materials is admirable. Despite the unpredictable and uneven surface of a piece of papyrus, and the hideous propensity that reeds and quills have of splitting and spraying the text with blobs of ink as they do so, a number of the surviving scrolls from the ancient world show line after line of regular, perfect Greek or Latin script. The majority of the work was done in the great libraries of antiquity. Writing was just on one side, the papyrus was coiled up and then unwound, column by column, left to right, as it was read. Since each papyrus had to be rolled up again as the reader went through the text, in readiness for the next visitor, those libraries would have been filled with a rhythmic scratch and rustle of furling, recycled reeds.

We know that Helen was golden-haired, that she made men bristle with fear, or that she loved her child Hermione, thanks to those careful scribes and calligraphers, copying and transcribing and re-copying the works of Greek and Roman authors – in particular of Homer. Papyri fragments bear witness to Homer's fundamental influence. To date 1,550 Homeric fragments on papyrus have been found (and the figure rises as the years go on). No other author from antiquity comes close.

∽∽∽∽∽

The well-placed library at Alexandria did most of all to preserve Helen's name. The quayside here is still a vivacious place. Holding their own against the tankers, fishing and pleasure craft bob up and down, their hulls wildly decorated, their sails gaudy with streamers and flags. Animated visitors arrive from across the Eastern Mediterranean and beyond. From all accounts, the ancient city had an equal brilliance. Alexandria's famous lighthouse, which reflected the sun's rays by day and naked flame by night, beckoned in freights of both learning and the learned. Alexandria's founder – Alexander the Great – would have approved of Homer's cult status; for him the *Iliad* and the *Odyssey* were totemic handbooks. On crossing into Asia Minor in 334 BC, Alexander went on a pilgrimage to visit Troy and it was said that this monumentally ambitious, glittering, grabbing young man slept with a dagger and a copy of the *Iliad* under his pillow; one wonders which he found more inspirational.[9] During his imperialist and expansionist campaigns, Alexander promoted himself as a champion of the Greeks – he was fighting for them in retribution for the 5th-century BC Persian Wars, just as the Persian leader Xerxes claimed the Persian Wars had been a retribution for Troy.

Founded by Ptolemy I at the end of the 4th century BC, and then augmented by his son Ptolemy II, the library at Alexandria had a voracious appetite for ancient texts. The older the manuscripts, the higher the price they commanded. The logic was simple. The fewer copyists' hands a manuscript had passed through, it was argued, the more likely it was to be the 'authentic' version. Often manuscripts were seized from ships docking at Alexandria – the originals ended up in the libraries while duplicates were returned to their owners. The Library and the Museum at Alexandria ensured the survival of much literary material featuring the Spartan Queen through into the modern world.[10]

The papyri at Alexandria were stored alphabetically (for the first time in the world) on shelves in vast rolls – probably sitting in rooms behind the colonnades where scholars and readers would pore over selections of ancient works.[11] Many rolls were labelled with little tabs, giving the name and ethnic derivation of the author. If the librarians had not been so methodical, we could easily have lost track of the character of Helen.

There were a vast number of papyri rolls here, over 500,000 altogether in the city – some duplicates, many variant versions of the same text; parochial *Iliads* and *Odysseys* that originated from all the corners of the ancient world, from Babylon, Macedonia and Egypt. The scholars and literary enthusiasts who worked here had a mammoth task on hand – to generate standardised versions of the texts in the collection.

Our problem in the search for the primordial Helen is that the Homer we read today has been much tinkered with. Many scribes and copyists and librarians brought their own viewpoints to the ancient texts. Zenodotus, the first director of the library in the Museum in Alexandria in 284 BC, censored four lines from *Iliad* 3 in which the goddess Aphrodite fetched a stool for Helen,[12] because he thought it unseemly for a divinity to act in such a subservient way. In fact for us, this particular reference – in its original form – gives a clue to the intimacy of Helen's relationship with Aphrodite, and to Helen's elevated, privileged status in the eyes of the gods. Zenodotus was wrong to meddle.

Other authors were subject to similar excisions. In the British Museum there is a 15th-century manuscript of the *Aeneid*.[13] Scribbled into the margin are lines 567 to 588 of Book 2 – a vivid vignette featuring Helen. Aeneas has chased the Spartan queen through Troy and, as she cowers in the Temple of Vesta, he stands with his sword aloft – and stops just short of killing her. We know of this segment from a single source, quoted in a commentary on Virgil by Servius in the 4th century AD. Servius claims the lines were originally cut out by Virgil's editors, Varius and Tucca. The censors had chosen to act because '*turpe est viro forti contra feminam irasci*' – 'it is shameful for a brave man to rage against a woman'. If we did not have that little commentary entry, the lines would have been lost and the only Helen we would have known from the *Aeneid* would have been an evil murderess, her name choked out through the trailing flesh and sinew that passed for the mouth of the mutilated corpse of Deiphobus in Hades: '*These are reminders of Helen*.'[14]

❧❧❧❧❧

It was in the 2nd century AD that technology dictated the fate of much literature – deciding which classical texts should survive and which should fall by the wayside – to be lost for ever. Papyrus rolls started to go out of fashion, to be replaced by the codex – the forerunner of our book. Parchment or vellum (treated animal-skin) had been used sporadically in the ancient world, but now parchment leaves, bound together by a thong or a clasp, were recognised as being easier to read and easier to store.[15] Because there was a demand for texts in this compact, new-fangled format, a large number of works were transferred from papyrus to codex. During the transfer many papyri rolls were ditched; we shall never know what was written on them, never know what thoughts and poetry and histories, what Helens, have been lost.

Once Helen had survived the white-water ride through the classical period, there was also the bottleneck of the medieval Dark Ages to deal with, when the transmission of antiquity became the responsibility of a relatively tiny number of people. Much in classical writing was inimical to Christian thought, but fortunately for us some texts (Euripides, for example) were still considered an essential teaching aid for schools and universities – a select corpus was therefore preserved. It is thought that around nine or ten plays by Euripides were 'on the syllabus'. The play *Helen* does not appear to have been one of these. But thankfully a *single* manuscript with nine other plays of Euripides grouped alphabetically E to K, survived – and Eleni starting with an epsilon (our E) was one.[16] A Byzantine scholar Demetrius Triclinius came upon this unique, precious codex in the 14th century.

Many works were not so lucky. From the 6th century until the 10th century, in many countries the parchment that texts were written on came to be of more value than the texts themselves. Verse, philosophies, plays and political speeches were scraped or washed off parchment sheets to make way for other written documents thought to be more cogent or useful – a treatise on law, or a theological tract. In some cases we only know about a classical text thanks to a modern scholar's painstaking, forensic research – carefully tracing the ghost of a script left behind another. These are palimpsests, like Helen, eradicated and redrawn time after time.

40

VEYN FABLES

◎◎◎◎◎◎◎◎◎◎◎◎◎◎

veyn fables . . . hyde trouthe falsely under cloude,
And the sothe of malys for to schroude

LYDGATE, *Troye Book*, Prologue, 265–6

I N HIS *TROYE BOOK*, composed between 1412 and 1420, John Lydgate
denies that Homer can tell the truth of Troy.[1] Homer is Helen's greatest
advocate, but he does not have a monopoly on her. In the ancient
world, there were in fact a number of 'anti-Homer' versions of Troy, and
therefore different ways of understanding Helen. There were the variant
myths and misplaced epics that still circulated and which we find hinted
at on Greek vases or referred to by philosophers, politicians, poets and playwrights. Stesichorus tells us that Helen spent the duration of the Trojan
War in Egypt. Herodotus concurs – saying he has spoken to Egyptian
priests who confirmed that this was the 'real' story of Helen.[2] Thucydides
casts a more analytical eye and pumps Peloponnesians for their local knowledge, to back up his theory that it was economic ambition and bullying by
Agamemnon that sent the Greek ships scurrying across the water to Troy
– not love of Helen but rather '*in my opinion, fear played a greater part than loyalty*'
he says.[3]

Some alternatives are more extreme. Dio Chrysostom's *Trojan Discourse*,
written some time between AD 60 and 120 during his peripatetic life around
the Roman Empire, states that Troy was, in fact, never sacked. The rationale
seems audacious and unexpected until one takes into account that the
Romans claimed to be direct descendants of the Trojans, thanks to Aeneas
who started out in life as a Trojan shepherd (or prince depending on which
version of the story one favours) and then escaped from Troy – begetting
children whose descendants, Romulus and Remus, founded Rome. So, for
the Romans, the 'West' was created by their 'ancestors' the Trojans. In Roman
popular culture the beloved Trojans needed panegyrics, to be commemorated as triumphant military heroes.

Helen had been there at the birth of the Greek democratic ideal, and now she found herself at the centre of the Roman Empire's foundation myth. Because the Troy story gave the West its family tree, something rather interesting happens to Homer through the Fall of Rome and the medieval period. Many writers turn their backs on the great bard. While Virgil's version of Troy, the *Aeneid*, keeps its popularity, with the spread of Roman propaganda and then Christianity, the *Iliad* and the *Odyssey* lose their canonic status.

Homer, a mere poet, is viewed in a number of quarters as an inappropriate source for moral discourse and a dubious witness to politically relevant events. Suddenly he is not someone to be relied on; he is an 'artiste' who shrouds the truth in falsehoods.[4] Homer was merely inspired by the Muse; much more could be discovered about Troy via an 'autopsy', a scientific analysis of the facts, of hard evidence and of the statements of interviewees. This became a popular standpoint.[5] We even have a word for this anti-Homeric stance – 'Homerepanorthosis', the correction of Homer.[6]

And there are two unlikely characters, Dictys and Dares, who championed their own 'real' alternatives to Homer. They are a curious pair; the former wrote around the 2nd century AD, the latter in the 6th century AD, from the Greek and Trojan points of view respectively.[7] Throughout antiquity and the medieval period, there was never any doubt that the Trojan conflict took place. Remember that for Isidore of Seville, Helen's rape was a seminal moment in world history. Dictys and Dares set themselves up as that fabulously valuable resource, on-the-ground war-reporters at an epoch-making military engagement – and the medieval world loved them for it.

Of course, since they were writing at least one and a half thousand years after the event, these men could not have been there at the time, but they both boldly claimed that they were, and Dictys even goes so far as to create his own back-story to prove how 'real' he is, casting himself as a soldier in the retinue of the Cretan king, Idomeneus, whom Homer details in the *Iliad* as coming to Troy with eighty black ships.[8]

Dictys' Prologue, claiming to be God's truth, is a wonderful exercise in imagination. It describes Dictys as a contemporary of the great heroes, Achilles, Ajax and Hector, who ensures that the sole copy of his eyewitness account is buried with him in a grave near Knossos. After a massive earthquake in AD 66 the grave splits open and local shepherds, spotting the furled pieces of papyri, rescue the manuscript. Eventually the precious document ends up in the hands of the Emperor Nero himself, who insists that it is translated from ancient Phoenician into Greek. An impressive piece of self-promotion.

The account that follows is rather stodgy – as befits Dictys' purpose. After all, he was selling his story as a verbatim report rather than a poetic tale.[9] Helen is a quiet little thing here. Menelaus seems more affected by the desertion of his female relatives Aethra and Clymene (two of Helen's attendants) than he does by the loss of his wife. Paris (called Alexander in this version), a pernicious Eastern barbarian, is as covetous of Helen's treasure as he is of Helen, 'driven astray by greed for booty and lust'.[10] When the Trojans revolt and refuse to harbour Helen, Paris masterminds a wholesale slaughter of the Trojan population. The killing stops only when Antenor (a Trojan elder and counsellor of King Priam) intervenes.

Menelaus is not won back by the sight of Helen's breasts, as he is in the more licentious earlier Greek versions, but instead negotiates for her return through the intercession of Odysseus. Helen and Menelaus' journey home is emotionless, the prose reading as a terse and denuded guidebook. If Dictys' version were the sole surviving chronicle of Helen's life, it is more than likely that this uninspiring, incidental creature would have been long forgotten.

Dares, on the other hand, enjoys the opportunity to explore the love interest of the tale. Dares probably produced his Trojan version in the 6th century AD as a counter to Dictys' Hellenophile construction. In the Dares retelling of the story Helen and Paris catch a glimpse of each other for the first time while Helen is at the sea-port of Helaea worshipping in the temple of Diana and Apollo. The pair spent some time just staring, 'struck by each other's beauty'.[11] Helen leaves with Paris and, after a brief moment of hesitation on the island of Tenedos, enthusiastically takes up court in Troy.

Dares promotes his 'eyewitness' credentials by attempting to blind the reader with an impressive quotient of statistics. Here we hear that the war lasted for ten years, six months and twelve days. He tells us there were 866,000 Greek casualties and 676,000 Trojan dead. There is an incidental point of interest in Dares' account: Helen is seized tit for tat, as part of an ongoing series of affronts and insults traded between the House of Priam and the Greeks. Dares' version approximates to the truth of the Bronze Age where women would be used for barter and as diplomatic trading chips. There is a slim chance that Dares had in fact picked up on a bardic or oral memory that preserved Late Bronze Age accounts of the bride market of the Eastern Mediterranean in the 13th century BC.

What is significant is that Dares is sufficiently dismissive of Helen to adumbrate her fine features. This is not a Helen who has the face of a goddess – wonderful, terrible, unspeakable. This Helen is a mortal beauty, simply. Dares' Helen would not make anyone tingle with fear. She is said to be like her brothers, 'blond haired, large eyed, fair complexioned, and well built . . . She was beautiful, ingenuous, and charming. Her legs were the best; her mouth the cutest. There was a beauty-mark between her eyebrows.' [12]

The character of Helen might wax and wane through antiquity, but she never vanishes. *Anno Domini* she is as tenacious as ever. The Judaic tradition had already established Eve as the primordial transgressive female, so how would a faithless Queen of Sparta be dealt with in an increasingly Christianised world?

41

HELEN OF TROY AND THE BAD SAMARITAN

☙☙☙☙☙☙☙☙☙☙☙☙

Whose love is given over-well
Shall look on Helen's face in hell,
Whilst those whose love is thin and wise
May view John Knox in paradise.

DOROTHY PARKER[1] 1936

As THE WRITER DOROTHY PARKER pointed out with characteristic
wit, in mainstream Christian theology, Helen is clearly not the sort
of woman who should go to heaven. She belongs in hell.

But had you travelled on the stony road from Mount Carmel to
Jerusalem between Christ's crucifixion and the 4th century AD, you would
have encountered a Helen, in the heartlands of the Christian faith.

In the summers of 1931 and 1932, a team of Anglo-American excavators
working in Samaria-Sebaste discovered, in a patchwork of fields and fruit
orchards, a deserted sanctuary. Scattered around the perimeter of the sanctuary were the broken remains of a statue which had been smashed into a
number of pieces. The sorry sculpture had once been a lovely woman.
Draped in a chiton and a himation (a looped layer of clothing hung over
the left shoulder and under the right) she cut a distinguished figure. On
her head was a stephane (a wreathe or a crown) and a delicate veil. In her
left hand she carried a pomegranate and an ear of wheat or barley, in her
right a huge torch which blazed above her head and reached right down to
the ground. She was labelled simply *Kore* – 'girl'.

Traces of paint on the stonework demonstrated that the stone figure
had once been carefully decorated. On the wreath were hints of green. Red
tinges still visible on the flame of the torch and on the veil could well have
been the base for gilding. At some point, the girl's clothes too had been

richly coloured. The carved letters of the inscription she stood above had been freshly touched up.[2]

But someone had found this handsome creature deeply offensive. In fury or fear they had brutally violated her. The leader of the excavations, Professor J.W. Crowfoot, found her head and part of the torch in a cistern, hard up against the enclosure wall. The rest of the torch and her right hand were missing. The breaks in the stone were clean and violent. Scattered around the temple were fifty or so candlestick lamps – evidence of some kind of abandoned cultic activity.

Clearly this girl was thought to be potent – at least quasi-divine. Grain is a symbol of fertility, and pomegranates of death and sex. Although Helen's association with these powerful indices would not be surprising, any number of divinities could lay claim to the same attributes. The pomegranate and grain alone are insufficient diagnostics but the torch is a clue that this figure might have some connection with the Spartan queen. At this point in time, thanks partly to Virgil's striking description in the *Aeneid* where Helen stands on the towers of Troy, welcoming the Greeks into the city with an enormous lit firebrand, the torch had become one of Helen's hallmarks.[3] It was something else, however, which encouraged experts to re-label the *kore* '*Eleni*'. The discovery, elsewhere at the site, of sections of a relief made of hard, local limestone, showing two curiously shaped caps, make the identification of the statue with Helen almost certain.

Here, it seems, represented by their trademark headgear, were the Dioscuri, Helen's brothers, Castor and Pollux, the twins who, in Greek legend, had rescued Helen as a young girl from the clutches of Theseus. On their crowns were their characteristic emblems, 'omphalos-like cones wreathed with olive leaves and surmounted with six-pointed stars'.[4] There are stone carvings of similar design from Sparta, and Rome too, where Helen is also flanked by her brothers; a trio of heavenly beings.

What Professor Crowfoot and his team had found in Palestine was a religious precinct dating from, at the very latest, the 2nd century AD and vehemently destroyed around the middle of the 4th century: the epoch of some of the fiercest battles between Christians and pagans. A precinct devoted to mystical, possibly astrological worship. And there at the middle, standing well over a metre tall, was a gaudy, celestial Helen.

How do you explain a cult of Helen here in the Middle East? A cult vigorously worshipping a woman at the exact time the Christian Church was struggling to establish itself? To get closer to the answer we have to move from the archaeological evidence to written sources. Cue the curious tale of Helen, and a man who has been affectionately labelled the Bad Samaritan.[5]

᭛᭛᭛᭛᭛

The recorded story starts with Simon Magus, a charismatic, maverick figure who, we are told, lived in Samaria some time around AD 35. Famous for his sorcery and tricks (hence the name Magus, 'magician'), he seems to have enjoyed quite some influence in the busy, cosmopolitan town; he 'amazed the people of Samaria', say the Acts of the Apostles 8:9–12.[6] Although Samaria's inhabitants were considered impure by the Jews, this was an oasis for traders, and the perfect place for hucksters, opportunists and showmen to congregate. The Acts tell us that one day, fleeing persecution in Jerusalem, Philip, one of the original evangelists, began to perform miracles in one of the towns of the region, quickly attracting a crowd and a number of converts.

Simon Magus was curious; he needed to find out more about this rival magic-man. The local sorcerer went to watch Philip's miracles, and like many other Samaritans, he converted, although Simon's later attempt to buy the gift of the Holy Spirit from Peter and John (giving rise to the phrase an 'act of simony') suggests he was more interested in the intrinsic conjuring power of Christianity than in any central spiritual or theological message.[7]

Simon Magus' interpretation of the gospel was liberal. We are told that he embraced the idea that he had been physically imbued with the power of God. He declared he was in fact God in human form – the very incarnation of the 'Dunamis', the power of the godhead. Forming his own sect, based on these beliefs, Simon Magus would be branded the Christian Church's first heretic. Up until the 6th century AD, the Magus (and his followers the Simonians) is firmly inscribed in the heresiological lists – becoming one of history's most celebrated heretics. And bizarrely, Helen appears to have been at the centre of his idiosyncratic, libertine faith.

The bulk of Simon Magus' story was written down by the disapproving orthodox Christian authors, Justin Martyr and Irenaeus (a Bishop of Lyons) in the 2nd century AD and then – possibly – by Hippolytus of Rome, a disciple of Irenaeus in the 3rd century AD.[8] A guiding principle of these tracts was to identify and discredit heretics, so we have to take some of the highly coloured details they contain with a pinch of salt. Justin, for example, accuses the Simonians of eating 'meals of human flesh'.

It is in Justin that we first get an explicit reference to a woman called Helen or Helene[9] involved in the Magus' sect. The Simonian Helen is a hybrid creature – a flesh-and-blood woman with extraordinary sexual power, a woman who, it was claimed, was a reincarnation of the Greek Helen of Troy. Although she also has a metaphysical presence, this Helene is identified as a real woman – a prostitute who lived in Tyre. Hippolytus is particularly sceptical of Magus' motives in 'rescuing' Helene from Tyre and initiating her into his sect: 'the rogue having fallen in love with the hussy, the so-called Helene, and having bought her, enjoyed her [carnally] . . .'[10]

The Magus and Helene (if indeed she existed) seem to have been a couple of those magnetic characters to whom men and women gravitated, like travellers to an oasis. Some scholars argue that high-born women from the Greek 'courtesan' class were prominent members of the crowd that gathered in ever larger numbers around the pair.[11] The Simonian religious splinter group quickly established a footing in the region and then expanded throughout the Roman Empire. Come the 2nd century AD, the Magus and Helene were still actively being worshipped at Rome itself.[12]

Simon Magus' teachings appeared to have advocated sex as a path to salvation. According to Hippolytus' *Refutation of All Heresies*, Simon endorsed ideals of free love, and his followers had a proclivity to drug abuse and sexual excess. They used aphrodisiacs and love charms, they summoned up demons and they tampered with men's dreams. Although these accusations come from a hostile source, it is still credible that the incipient priority of the cult was simply Simon's sexual fulfilment and it is certain that this was a sect that both embraced women, and promoted the *idea* of the charismatic, potent female.

Simon's sect became part of a movement known as the Gnostics – so-called because its followers were thought to have privileged access to divine *gnosis*, 'knowledge', to understand fully the truth about God. We are told by the Christian Fathers that central to their belief was the idea that in the universe there existed an absolute wisdom, and that this wisdom had *female* form.[13] Because our main sources for Simon are post-dated, this radical interpretation of Christian belief could be little more than a slur on the part of the Christian Fathers, a sensational way of bringing the Simonians into disrepute. The evidence is certainly open to interpretation. But in 1945, fragments of Gnostic texts, written in Coptic, were found at Nag Hammadi in Egypt. The papyrus sheets had been bound in leather and packed into a red earthenware jar – discovered by chance by farmers at the foot of the Gebel el Tarif mountain. Once translated it was clear that these texts did indeed place a female life-force at the heart of the Gnostic doctrine:

> the image of the invisible, the virginal perfect spirit, the aeon of
> the glory, Barbelo, the glory who was perfected through the
> aeons of glory by the revelation of the glory of the virginal
> spirit . . . This is the first thought of his image. She became the
> mother of the All, for she existed before them all . . .'

There are echoes of these ideas in the thinking attributed to Simon Magus. He, too, seemed enamoured of this female life-force, the 'sacred feminine'. Perhaps there is indeed more to his story than the smears of the Christian Fathers. But whether his gyno-centric theology – with Helene commanding a pivotal role – was real or fashioned by his critics, is almost immaterial. The significant thing is that three centuries or so into the evolution of Christianity, the Magus and his prominent female companion called Helene were believable as manifestations of cultic power. A pagan Helen finds herself discussed in worried tones by the Christian Fathers. Helen of Troy was still sufficiently significant to be feared in her reincarnation as Helene of Samaria and whether or not her worship was promoted in concert with the Simonian sect, a Helen certainly ends up surveying her own shrine in Palestine.

⊗⊙⊗⊙⊗

If you pick and mix the writings of the Christian Fathers with contemporary Jewish and Samaritan accounts, it is possible to concoct an outline of the – rather complicated – Simonian credo and of Helen's place within it. It runs as follows. As a godhead himself, Simon descended to earth to rescue his *Ennoia* – his first concept, his first thought – a thought and primal life-force that was female. The female thought, the *Ennoia* (sometimes called the *Epinoia*), was a simple but ambitious one – the creation of the angelic host. But just as this *Ennoia* had finished her angelic opus, the angels themselves, jealous of this prism of pure female perfection, rebelled and imprisoned the *Ennoia* on earth in a sequence of female forms. The *Ennoia* was then reincarnated as (among others) Helen of Troy – a female spirit, the very cognition of God himself, trapped inside an exquisite female body. This female spirit in the form of Helen of Troy is taken and abused by many men, polluted by many lovers.

Over a thousand years later, the *Ennoia* reappears on earth as a woman called Helene, a Phoenician slave and prostitute from Tyre. This is the Helene who appears in the historical records as the Magus' lover.[14]

The Magus seems to have taken it upon himself to release the *Ennoia* from her centuries of captivity, and thus bring about the salvation of mankind. He effected this philanthropic design by recognising the *Ennoia* in Helene (of Tyre), where others just saw a base whore. We are told by some sources[15] that Simon Magus first caught sight of Helene as she held a torch one night on a rooftop in Tyre.[16] A rooftop is a euphemism for a brothel (the Greek word *tegos* can be used for both), and it may just be that in this account we are getting a mangle of literary and social references (with a sprinkling of fantasy) rather than historical fact. In Book 3 of the *Iliad*, Helen, the Spartan queen, too had stood on a high perimeter wall to identify the heroes of Greece. Another possibility is that the character of Helene was invented by Simon's followers in Rome as late as the 2nd century AD. But again, the question of whether Helene was real or not, is in one sense sophistic, subordinate to a broader question. What is significant to this enquiry is that the Magus' consort should be identified so closely and credibly with the figure of Helen, that her name still carried weight.

Those who wrote about the Magus and his followers were keen to highlight the connection with Helen and the Trojan Wars.[17] Authors such as Hippolytus vigorously took up the Trojan theme:

> she . . . ever dwelling in many women troubles the powers in the cosmos by her transcendent beauty. Wherefore also the Trojan War occurred on account of her. For Epinoia herself dwelt in Helen at that time, and all the authorities suing for her (favours), faction and war arose among the nations in which she appeared.[18]

It is significant that Helen's power, in these early years of the 1st millennium AD, is still thought to come from some kind of internal, divinely generated strength. She is no shallow lovely, but a blistering life-force. Helen's beauty might have 'confounded the powers' in the world, but it was her central core, her life-spirit, her intelligence that was recognised as an agent of change. In Simonian sanctuaries, the Magus was frequently represented as Zeus, and Helene/Helen as Athena/Minerva. Although the Helene described by Christian authors sounds more like a friend of Aphrodite, her equation with Athena/Minerva by her worshippers paid compliment to her perceived wisdom.[19]

The pagan Helen was given a series of impressive names: Sophia[20] (Greek for wisdom), Pallas Athena, Minerva, Sapientia, the Mother of All, the principle of knowledge, and, most significantly perhaps, Sophia Prouneikos. A Sophia Prouneikos is a wisdom that is catalysed, agitated, by the pursuit of pleasure, stimulated by beauty. Helen's flirtation with Christianity speaks of a time when the boundary between pagan and Christian, between the old gods and the new, was still blurred. Of a time when the world could imagine that a primordial wisdom, would, naturally, be female.[21]

❦❦❦❦❦

Early examples of Christian historical fiction — written between the 1st and 4th centuries AD, and extremely popular throughout the medieval period, such as the *Clementine Homilies* and *Recognitions*, cast Simon as a pantomime villain, with Helen (described as Luna or Selene) an embodiment of perfect divine power. In these Simon discusses his passion for the Helen figure, but says he wants to enjoy her 'honourably'. The frisson and cliffhangers (will he, won't he violate her?) go part of the way to explaining the huge popularity of these texts. In these influential morality tales, we hear again that the Trojan War was fought because both sides recognised Helen for what she was – not a spirit but THE SPIRIT . . .

> And he says that he has brought down this Helena from the highest heavens to the world; being queen, as the all-bearing being, and wisdom, for whose sake, says he, the Greeks and barbarians fought, having before their eyes but an image of truth; for she, who really is the truth, was then with the chiefest god.[22]

The Greeks might have thought of Helen as an instrument of the gods or as a demi-goddess: in her time as Christian heretic she becomes the godhead itself.[23]

Simon Magus was considered by some to be a sorcerer, by some a devil, and by all Christian authorities a distinct threat. But whereas the Magus could be damned as a heretic outright, Helen is treated more gingerly – with a begrudging respect. Early Christian writers[24] equated her (in her incarnations as Helene and as Helen of Troy, and as the *Ennoia* herself) not with the devil, but with the lost sheep of the Jesus parable.[25]

Helen might have strayed, but no one, not even the most critical of Christian Fathers, can deny her allure. Like that lost sheep she is cherished even more for her adventuring spirit. She is cast in the light of a woman wronged, lost and found again, rather than condemned as a slutty sexual commodity. The Gnostic Helen is an abused innocent. Helen had come down to earth and suffered great torment on behalf of man. Her rapes had been an act of sacrifice. By redeeming Helene (both the prostitute and the reincarnated Helen of Troy) Simon Magus was saving humankind. While the characters from the old world are kept in play, the echoes of orthodox Christianity come to the fore.

ᝍᝍᝍᝍᝍ

Think back to that broken pagan statue in Samaria-Sebaste. A clothed, rainbow-coloured mystical creature. A woman who bore more resemblance to strong, wise Athena than to naked, carnal Aphrodite. As was suggested by one of the first scholarly visitors to the newly excavated site, perhaps the cult of Helen had come first.[26] The Magus and his followers did not promote Helen as a novel addition to their sect; instead, she nurtured them. If a pagan Helen was being honoured here, as she was in other shrines across the Eastern Mediterranean, it is quite possible that Simon was indeed a magus, one of the 'magi' or astrologers who worshipped in her sanctuary. A votary to a charismatic life-force. A votary who had his own ambitions, and who took a substitute human Helen (the prostitute named Helene) along with him for the ride.[27]

Maybe the female divinity, this painted Helen, was a viable female alternative to the male-dominated sects and movements, including Christianity, which jostled for position from the 1st to the 4th centuries AD. No one is branded with heresy unless they threaten. The idea of a divine Helen – representing a form of spirituality pre-dating Christianity – would have put up quite a challenge to Jesus Christ's insecure 4th-century AD followers. Certainly someone was sufficiently fearful to try to eradicate her, to smash her statue in Samaria with intemperate passion.

ᘒᘒᘒᘒᘒ

From this time on, in the Christianised world, Helen wanders from the angelic to the diabolic. She is both the lost lamb and a wolf in sheep's clothing. Once the whore Helen had been worshipped in Samaria and lauded in Simonian theology as a female God, the Christian authorities would never be able to ignore her.[28] She was suppressed, but not annihilated. And for one extraordinary female leader of Christendom of the 12th century AD, the fact that Helen straddled the angel/whore divide, the fact that Christianity could neither destroy nor categorise her,[29] could not package her away neatly, offered a unique opportunity for political self-advancement.

42

'PERPULCHRA' – MORE THAN BEAUTIFUL

❦❦❦❦❦❦❦❦❦❦❦

'And were you pleased?' they asked of Helen in Hell.
'Pleased?' answered she, 'when all Troy's towers fell;
And dead were Priam's sons, and lost his throne?
And such a war was fought as none had known;
And even the gods took part; and all because
of me alone! Pleased?
I should say I was!'

LORD DUNSANY, 'An Interview' 1938

AT NUMBER 111 CANNON STREET near the City of London, embedded in the offices of the Oversea-Chinese Banking Corporation, is a grimy, chipped shape, about the size of a small television set. This unpromising object is half-hidden by an iron grille, but by crouching on your knees and peering, it just about becomes clear that this is a stone. In fact this is the remains of the London Stone, a pre-historic lump of the limestone known as oolite.

Originally part of a much larger block – possibly an altar – in popular imagination the London Stone had magical powers. Throughout the city's history this was where oaths were sworn and laws passed; Elizabeth I's sometime sorcerer, John Dee, was convinced the London Stone possessed supernatural properties; there are those today who delight in the notion that its miraculous survival during a German bombing raid in 1941 was not by chance alone – but thanks to the protection of the ley line over which it was laid. Although now it sits stubborn, dimpled and diminished, looking like a lump of sugar sucked by a giant's child, the stone has been, in its time, the subject of great veneration.

The London Stone fits into Helen's story because it was brought to London three thousand years ago, by a Trojan. Or at least that was the version of events that circulated (in a variety of forms) in Britain, throughout the Medieval period. After the Sack of Troy, the city's inhabitants and their descendants were scattered across the globe. The most famous refugee tale of course is that of Aeneas, the young man who left Troy carting his ancient father Anchises on his back, and then carried on to found Rome.[2] As we have seen following this adventure, the Romans claimed not Greek but Trojan ancestry and as the centuries went on, European dynasties and cities invested in the same foundation fantasy.

Britain was no exception. As early as the 9th century AD, we hear from the *Historia Brittonum*, attributed to a man called Nennius, that a certain Brutus (variously described as Aeneas' brother and as his great-grandson) came to an island (in later sources, called Albion) and 'filled it with his people and lived here'. And, so the story goes, from henceforth the island was known as the land of Britto (hence Britons, British, Britain) after its well-travelled first immigrant.

This, of course, is pure invention. However, archaeological evidence has revealed something rather curious. In the mud at the bottom of the Thames a black two-handled cup has been found. It is Late Bronze Age/Early Iron Age and originated in Anatolia – modern-day Turkey.[3] At the end of the tenth century BC, a trader, either European or Anatolian, brought exotica back from Paris' homeland. It might not have been at first hand, but those scattered groups who lived around the islands and inlets of the Thames may possibly have been visited by eastern traders, they may have heard Trojan tales, they certainly held Anatolian artefacts in their hands.

In the 12th century AD the Trojan foundation theme was picked up and amplified by Geoffrey of Monmouth in his best-selling *Historia Regum Britanniae*. Political successions were being challenged across Christendom – from Scotland to Syria. For rulers with imperial ambitions, lineage was suddenly vitally important, buttressing as it did individual claims to old territories and to new lands. After various Herculean struggles, Geoffrey tells us, Brutus founded Troia Nova, or Trinovantum, on the banks of the Thames (a sad slip; the real etymology in fact derives from the name of a tribe living in Essex, the Trinovantes). Now it was 'official', London, or the New Troy, and its rulers were the avatars of Priam, Paris, Hector, Hecuba and the rest. Helen, the limb-loosener and one-time Trojan princess, found herself, once again, entwined in international politics.

For the rulers of the day, all this was very convenient. The Trojan story was a useful one to manipulate. It spoke to a medieval population of military and heroic prowess, of a direct connection to the almighty Roman civilisation and, most importantly, of impeccable dynastic credentials. If

Aeneas was the *fons et origo* of the might that was Rome, and a ruler claimed descent from Aeneas, then he could argue he had an undisputed claim to European lands. If a dynasty could trace its territories and lineage back to the Kings of Troy, and from there back to God himself (Brutus is son of Silvius, is son of Ascanius, is son of Aeneas, is son of Priam, is son of Noah, is son of Adam),[4] it would command the political respect and spiritual confidence of the people.[5]

So, from the 11th century onwards, the Franks, the Normans and the English all vigorously perpetuated Trojan myth-histories. Chroniclers wrote 'factual' accounts of Trojan histories and genealogies that supported the Trojan spin. Poets composed new epic cycles based on the Troy story. These things were taken seriously; when Henry IV demanded fealty from the Scottish king he buttressed his legal claim by citing the genealogy of his family:[6] a genealogy that he could 'prove' stretched back to Brut the Trojan. Henry and his lawyers claimed that the genealogies in 'old chronicles' were as powerful as the law.[7] Henry VIII commands the first printed edition of *The Troye Book* in 1513 (when it becomes '*The hystorye sege and dystruccyon of Troye*'[8]) to help sway public opinion in his first French campaign. As late as 1714, a French scholar was jailed by the authorities because he dared to insist that the French people had German rather than Trojan ancestors.[9]

No coincidence then that after her accession to the throne as Henry II's Queen, the *Historia Regnum Britanniae* was turned into a French epic-poem, the *Roman de Brut* and was dedicated to that show-stopping medieval monarch, Eleanor of Aquitaine.

Eleanor 'Duchess of Aquitaine and by the Wrath of God Queen of England' was an extraordinary woman and a particularly wily magnate. The Trojan foundation stories were as useful to her as they were to any king. But Eleanor takes the Trojan connection one stage further. She had an almost impossible task ahead of her, to survive and rule in a man's world. In her journey from young heiress to dowager queen, she develops a striking and idiosyncratic relationship with Helen; a relationship that I am convinced was an important part of her quest for temporal power and iconic status.

The beating heart of the duchy of Aquitaine was the Ducal Hall in Poitiers. To get to it today one crosses a pleasingly typical French square, with ornate iron balconies and the smell of *pain au chocolat* in the air. The 12th-century hall was hidden in the 18th century by a neo-classical façade; the building still operates as the local Palais de Justice. In the past, to access the court, you would have taken your chances with Eleanor's henchmen, but now the greatest hazard is the plate-glass door that slides rather too quickly from one side of the entrance to the other. Lawyers of the Palais de Justice still pop in and out of the arches that line the walls, to take a mobile phone call or share a cigarette with the local gendarmes.

Even if the technology impedes a little, it is worth persevering, because inside, the hall is breathtaking. Straddling Romanesque and Gothic architecture with that peculiar hybrid, 'Angevin design', the Ducal Hall is a confident, clean, domineering place. The lines of the design are bold and simple, yet staring down at frequent intervals are the grotesque gargoyles and human heads so beloved of the medieval stone-mason. In its day the space would have been buzzing: subjects bringing petitions, advocates wrangling over the wording of charters, musicians strumming and courtiers jostling for favours. It was here that a new kind of Helen was delivered to the Angevin court, for here Eleanor and her husband Henry II would have sat to listen to Benoît de Sainte-Maure's 30,000-line epic, the *Roman de Troie*.

Written some time between 1165 and 1170, the *Roman* was a whirlwind of historical narrative, covert signals and overt emotion.

Because the *Roman* implicitly gave the Angevin court a family tree that stretched back a thousand years or so before the time of Christ, it became a work of fundamental importance. One 13th-century verse translation of the Bible incorporates the *Roman de Troie* in the Book of Exodus.[10] Benoît's epic was continually copied and translated – it spawned many imitations. This grand, romantic, sympathetic poem was one of the key devices that kept the profile of Helen and the Trojan War high among the literate and aristocratic classes through the medieval period and beyond.

What is unusual about the *Roman* is its surprisingly refined and respectful portrayal of Helen. This Helen is a fine lady, she is no whore. There is a good reason for the delicacy. The relationship between Helen and Paris could be read as mirroring that of Eleanor and Henry. Like Helen, Eleanor had left one husband (Louis VII) to marry his arch-rival (Henry II). Like Paris, Henry was 'enticed' to Eleanor, 'by the woman's high birth and especially by lust for the holdings she possessed, unable to endure love and any delay . . . within a brief time he attained his long desired union'.[11] Like Helen and Paris, the two medieval potentates seemed to share a mutual attraction that was played out in a rich courtly environment. Just as Henry and Eleanor rebuilt many of their fortress-palaces and kitted them out with new artworks, so, in the poem, Helen and Paris live in a land of busy builders and are given a *Chambre de Beautés* in which to consummate – and perpetuate – their love affair.[12]

Helen and Paris' illegitimate relationship as described by Benoît is, in fact, inspirational, decorous and decorative; it is the characters of Briseida (who started off life as Homer's Briseis) and her lover Troilus who are introduced to satisfy the need for a salacious sex scandal. Eleanor married Henry within eight weeks of leaving the King of France, Louis VII. The gossips were certain they had already embarked on an affair; an '*adulterino concubito*' says Gerald of Wales.[13] In the *Roman*, the adulterous affair between Helen and Paris is portrayed as a legitimate opportunity for private love. The consummation of their relationship is blatantly sexual but somehow not reprehensible:

> *Greatly did Paris comfort her*
> *And marvellously did he honour her.*
> *Greatly did he serve her well that night.*[14]

A comparison of Benoît's writing with the other accounts of Helen and Paris in circulation in the 12th century, and with which Eleanor had no connection, amplifies the poet's restraint.

ᏬᏯᏬᏯᏬ

Following Emperor Charlemagne's vision in the 780s of an intellectual and cultural revival of Gaul, whose focus was largely on expressive writing skills,[15] Helen's story had become a textbook for poetic expression. Writers used Helen as a vehicle for the development of their *artes poeticae*. On the face of it, a professional opportunity to elaborate ever more febrile epithets had presented itself, but, one suspects, so had the licence to publish private fantasies. Take one example: Matthew de Vendôme's 'educative' text called *The Art of Versification*.

Written in 1175 (at which point Eleanor, following a series of court intrigues, and, it was whispered, love affairs on Henry's part, was out of favour; she was to be kept under house arrest for fifteen years — her political power all but extinguished), *The Art of Versification*'s official purpose was to show how different tropes can be employed. There are standard metaphors: Helen has a face where 'rosy hue and snow-white skin contend in most delightful combat', and again, '*Her sparkling eyes rival the radiance of the stars, And with engaging frankness play ambassadors of Venus*'. But then some of the exemplary language gets very over-heated . . .

> *The glory of that countenance is her rosy lips*
> *Sighing for a lover's kiss, delicate lips*
> *That break into laughter as delicate as they . . .*

> . . . *Her smooth neck and shoulders whiter than*
> *Snow give way to firm but dainty breasts . . .*
>
> *Her chest and waist are narrow and compact, giving*
> *Way at last to the swell of her rounded abdomen.*
> *Next is the area celebrated as the storehouse*
> *Of modesty, the mistress of Nature, the delightful*
> *Dwelling of Venus. Of that sweetness which lies*
> *Hidden there, he that partakes can be the judge.*[16]

The Art of Versification prefigures the equally passionate language employed by another monk, Joseph of Exeter, to describe Paris' seduction, with Helen when she 'pressed him with her mouth and robbed him of his semen'.[17]

Unlike Benoît, Joseph of Exeter does not allow Helen any attributes other than the carnal. In a particularly intrusive and demeaning depiction of her, he shows he cares not a jot for who she is, but simply how she looks and how sexually arousing she can be:

Her ears are well-formed and not too large, her eyes ever
watchful, and her nose alive to every passing scent, each feature
in turn demanding admiration as they vie for praise. Her chin,
protruding slightly, gleams white, and her full lips swell a little
into a rosy pout, so that kisses may more gently be pressed deep
upon her mouth. Her neck seems to flow into her shoulders, her
modest chest all but conceals her breasts, both her arms and her
sides are short and dainty. When she walks, she glides with
playful step, her small feet kissing the earth as they fall, while
the graceful movement of her legs supports her limbs with easy
poise. A single blemish between her fine eyebrows dares to separate their delicate bows with a mole.[18]

Benoît's Helen is sexually powerful, but she is not the sex-object or the pin-up conjured by the pens of the poet's contemporaries.

∾∾∾∾

Illustrated versions of Benoît's *Roman* show Helen marrying Paris with a charming exchange of rings; she trips gracefully into Troy on the back of a white palfrey. Paris and then Priam hold the reins, a mark of great respect and an indication that these aristocrats, female and male, Greek and Trojan, have equal standing.[19] Mirroring the Spartan Queen, Eleanor was famously beautiful. 'By reason of her excessive beauty, she destroyed or injured nations', wrote Matthew Paris.[20] Another chronicler described the young heiress as 'perpulchra', 'utterly' or 'more than beautiful'.[21] The lines of the *Carmina Burana*, written in around 1204 with Eleanor in mind, could just as easily have been dedicated to Helen:[22] '*Were the world all mine, From the sea to the Rhine, I'd give it all, If so be the Queen of England, Lay in my arms.*'[23] Eleanor must have realised that those who listened to stories of Helen, in the resonating Ducal Hall, would have easily made the connection between a breath-taking but dangerous Spartan Queen, and the queen who sat, glinting with jewels and wrapped in furs, in front of them.

◌◌◌◌◌

Eleanor's grandfather, Duke William IX, was famously the first 'troubadour king' (although he was, in fact, only ever a duke). Troubadours sang of desire and longing, and among their influences they could count the clever, sensual poems of Ovid. Helen appears in a number of Ovid's works: the *Heroides, Metamorphoses, Amores, Ars Amatoria* and *Remedia Amoris*. Here she is often a minxy, duplicitous creature – a heart-breaker – but delightful enough to be well worth the trouble. The ladies in the troubadours' songs were always impossibly beautiful and always just out of reach. This '*civilisation de courteoisie*' was a highly eroticised environment; although cited in literary and musical terms, women's sexual power was being acknowledged and enshrined. These were the lessons of Eleanor's childhood.

Eleanor of Aquitaine's fabled courts of love were just that – a *fabula*. But even if there were no theatricalised legal judgments in the 12th-century palaces that dealt with the broken hearts and the ideals of lovers, there were still troubadours and there were still love poems. Although we have no piece of parchment that proves Eleanor commissioned the *Roman* from Benoît (nor do we for most comparable works of medieval literature) it is a distinct possibility that Eleanor, duchess and queen, knew exactly what she was doing when she encouraged the creation of this new Trojan epic, this new story of Paris and Helen. For Eleanor, Helen was an unusual but ideal icon. When Paris addresses Helen, his words are both tender and terrible:

> Now I have placed my heart so in you,
> And your love has so burned me,
> That I am completely enclined toward you.
> Loyal beloved, loyal spouse

295

> *You will henceforth be all my life:*
> *Of this fact you may be certain and confident.*
> *All will obey you*
> *And all will serve you.*[24]

Eleanor herself was exceptional, as the chronicler Richard of Devizes described her, a '*femina incomparabilis*'. She was unusually ambitious and unusually proactive in international and domestic affairs. To maintain her atypical standing and influence she needed actively to promote her own image as a powerful, desirable, threatening creature. She needed an irregular role-model. So when she heard those lines, drifting through the echoing acoustics of the Ducal Hall, speaking of Helen's ability to affect the world around her, I can imagine Eleanor thinking, this is really good, listen and tremble.

There is also another, more subtle, comparison to be made between the two women. Eleanor was deeply spiritual. In commemoration of their marriage, she and Henry had had their image built into the very fabric of the grand cathedral at Poitiers, Eleanor's home town. Eleanor still stares down from the glorious east window: dressed in blue and with a fine gold crown on her head, she is myriad fractured colours. The king and queen cradle a model of the cathedral between them like a newborn baby. This was not just vainglory. From her few letters, her many charters and her bequests to religious institutions it is clear that Eleanor was a true and pious believer. On her tomb at Fontevraud she lies peacefully reading a prayer book.

In his *Roman*, one of the details Benoît chooses to emphasise is that Helen was taken by Paris while she was offering up prayers in the Temple of Venus (Aphrodite) on the island of Kythera. This follows the 'real' version of events as laid out by Dares. In art galleries and private collections across Europe, paintings and manuscript illustrations (including those for the *Roman de Troie*) from the 12th to the 17th centuries frequently show Helen being plucked from her devotions to the Goddess of Love. Benoît's epic was the inspiration for many of these creations. In a number of the pictures the Spartan Queen is flanked by idols, and lit by candles: a Helen framed within religious architecture and iconography. Benoît's Helen (in tune with the feistier Helens that scatter the classical corpus) is not just an object but a subject.

By equating herself with a chivalric Helen, I think that Eleanor was sending out a coded message to Christendom. She was positioning herself as neither angel nor whore, but a potent combination of both. Like Helen, Eleanor was not content with watching from the sidelines. Through force of character and charisma, by using her intellect resourcefully, she sought to occupy a central position. She was a woman both lusty and sovereign. Like Helen, happy to exploit her God-given gifts.

Benoît's *Roman* did much for Helen's rehabilitation. Thanks, largely, to Eleanor's influence, Helen the hieratic potentate rather than the fantasy whore had a brief but significant reprieve. And so Helen is sung once again, and continues to be sung across the courts and mansions of medieval Europe. A Provençal poem called '*Flamenca*' from 1234 listed the fables that minstrels were expected to perform — Helen's story is one of them.[25] Helen is now a fixture in the world of the literate and the aristocratic. But her memory did not just hover in this rarefied atmosphere. Soon she was going to come hurtling back onto the street; this time as an agent of the devil himself.

43

DANCING WITH THE DEVIL

@@@@@@@@@@@@

> Was this the face that launched a thousand ships,
> And burnt the topless towers of Ilium?
> Sweet Helen, make me immortal with a kiss.
> Her lips suck forth my soul; see where it flies —
> Come, Helen, come give me my soul again.
> Here will I dwell, for Heaven be in these lips,
> And all is dross that is not Helena.

CHRISTOPHER MARLOWE,
The Tragical History of Dr Faustus c. 1549

WITHIN DAYS OF ITS PREMIERE IN LONDON, in the last decade of the 16th century, Kit Marlowe's perfect pentameter line, 'Was this the face that launched a thousand ships?' from Act V of his *Tragical History of Dr Faustus* was buzzing around the capital.[1] In the cut-throat commercial world of Elizabethan theatre, the play was an immediate success. The audience loved it, the money-men were happy. Its producer, Philip Henslowe,[2] kept meticulous production accounts in a journal. Henslowe's Diary is a valuable historical source, which records numerous performances of *Dr Faustus* at the Rose and at the other new playhouses in the capital. The show was still being performed regularly well into the 17th century. *Faustus* was a hit.

The Tragical History of Dr Faustus was one of eight-hundred-odd plays produced in London over a period of forty years from 1574 to 1616 (the year of Shakespeare's death).[3] The productivity of the playwrights in the Elizabethan capital was unprecedented. As well as the editions that have survived, there were scores of other plays lost to time, the manuscripts destroyed by dissatisfied authors or burnt in the less discriminating Great Fire of London of 1666. And yet in that maelstrom of theatrical creativity, one desperate, appalling, erotic line immediately gained currency in the popular imagination. Was this the face that launched a thousand ships?

The question is an expression both of utter bliss and of utter desolation.

At their inception, the words had simply been just part of another speech penned by Marlowe and then muttered over and over by a lone actor, as he paced up and down the South Bank, desperately trying to remember his lines. The dramas were in repertory, and there was a punishing turnover of scripts. Actors worked six days a week, forty-nine weeks of the year.[4] That is a lot of dramatic verse (some brilliant, some dreadful doggerel) to commit to memory.

Much of what was written was instantly forgettable. But 'the face that launched a thousand ships' was soon carried across the River Thames to the City of London on the tongues of thousands. It has been estimated that from three to four thousand men and women every afternoon would travel from the north bank of the river to the south bank and back again. They were pleasure-seekers using the services of the wherry-men who plied to and fro across the river carrying passengers to take in the entertainments on 'Bankside' – London's wild side, the suburbs of sin. Wherries wound their way across the Thames and along the London waterways that are now for ever clogged underground – lost rivers such as the River Fleet and the Oldbourne; Elizabeth I herself was rumoured to use these river taxis, in disguise, at night. In one of the largest cities in the West, a city that handled between two thirds and three quarters of the nation's trade,[5] in a newly burgeoning international axis, Helen's name was back on the great waterways and back on the streets.

One has to imagine the context in which Marlowe's line took hold of the capital. When *Faustus* was first staged, Elizabethan London was at its most fervent and fetid. Pox and plague stalked the streets. There were human heads on London Bridge and bears being ripped to shreds by mastiffs within sight of the theatres. Prostitutes picked up custom in the playhouses themselves, others sat a stone's-throw away in infamous brothels such as the Holland Leaguer.

Much of the South Bank has been sanitised now, but around one of the few remaining derelict areas, where plastic bags and tin-cans are heaped up on the ghosts of the past, prostitutes still street-walk. In Marlowe's day it was illegal to tout for custom. Calling out or throwing stones at passers-by was outlawed; so scores of 'trulls and flurts' stood waiting, some branded, some with their nipples painted, all desperate to earn a crust through the sale of their bodies. A punter could pick up a strumpette (a woman), an apple-squire (a rent-boy) or a young child whose maidenhead was restored every night. The impresarios of the theatre often had financial interests in the whore-houses.

Sexually transmitted diseases were endemic. A broadsheet of 1584, *A Mirror for Magistrates*, tells us 'forty shillings or better' would buy 'a pottle or two of wine, the embracement of a painted strumpet and the French Welcome'. Thefts of personal possessions are much talked about during a session at the 'stews' (the local brothels) with 'Winchester geese' or 'Flanders Mares'.[6] For the Elizabethan audiences, sex meant danger.

In one edition of the play, when Helen makes her entrance she is flanked by two cupids – an immediate signal to the audience that the incarnation of the sex goddess Venus/Aphrodite has arrived.[7] Marlowe also makes a clever, direct connection between his Helen of the 16th century and another sexually active Helen of the 1st century AD, Simon Magus' companion, Helene. Just before Helen and Faustus leave to have sex, Helen is exalted in fine poetic terms, reminiscent of the Song of Solomon, one of the texts referred to by Simonians and the Gnostics.

> *O, thou art fairer than the evening air*
> *Clad in the beauty of a thousand stars.*
> *Brighter art thou than flaming Jupiter,*
> *When he appeared to hapless Semele,*
> *More lovely than the monarch of the sky*
> *In wanton Arethusa's azured arms,*
> *And none but thou shalt be my paramour.*
>
> Exeunt

(V.i.102–8)

His paramour. Marlowe's Helen is daimonic, a diabolic spirit. The symbolism of the play goes so far as to suggest she is even the devil in female form, a succubus. If Faustus was leaving the stage to make love to this she-devil Helen, then many would have known that from this point on they were irrevocably condemned. Enjoying Helen was the ultimate delight that brought with it the ultimate, awful punishment: eternal damnation.[8]

◦◦◦◦◦◦

To catch the natural light at the Rose, or the other theatres on the South Bank, theatrical performances such as Marlowe's *Faustus* would normally be held around 2.00 p.m. There was no fixed roof over the new amphitheatres, which were an architectural hybrid of bear-pits and makeshift performance spaces in inn courtyards. Bankside was low-lying and marshy. Given that the Rose accommodated just over 1,600 people and that *Dr Faustus* was a commercial hit, in high summer, sitting or standing through the tragedy must have been a steamy and pungent experience. Added to the smell of immediate neighbours (for the unlucky, one of London's 'Stinkards' who reeked of garlic and urine) and those outside 'plucking the rose' (having a pee) was the distinctive stink of the South Bank: dyers, tanners and starchers all using the river as a free resource.[9]

The audience who met Helen in this rank environment at the Rose Theatre would have been mixed. The basic entry rate to London's new play-houses was one penny and although a few extra coins could buy a cushion or a better seat, theatre of this period was a democratic experience. Archae-ological investigation has shown the area close to the stage to be hard-worn and beaten – witness to crowds of Tudor playgoers 'moshing' – jostling around, flicking and grabbing the actors.[10] The highest percentage of the audience probably consisted of citizens and successful artisans, but along with these and well-to-do traders, there were also journeymen and students, dukes and duchesses, sitting across the way from pimps and prostitutes. It was for this catholic crowd that Helen danced with the devil.

To appreciate the physical setting in which the Elizabethan Helen made her mark, I visited the site of the Rose Theatre on London's South Bank during its excavation, and found a suitably Stygian setting.[11] The ghost of the stage is now 10 feet or so (3 m) beneath the current street level, submerged (for preservation) in 2 feet (0.6 m) of distilled water. Encased in a 1980s office building, the profile of the stage has been picked out by a scattering of grit and a snaking red light tube. The air is dank and musky – there are replicas of the earthenware pots at the entrance once used by the theatre's entrepreneurs to re-coup their investment, collecting pennies from lords and ladies, bishops, traders and spies. But the pots rattle no more – this is a site that has been silenced by concrete and by time.

So it was here on the South Bank, a stirring, sensuous, sordid location, that the most enduring Elizabethan Helen was born. The capital's trade-mark 'jangling' (gossip and chit-chat) gave the oxygen of publicity to its new resident. Tourists noticed that in the roughest inns and the finest dining houses, Londoners were always talking, talking, talking.[12] Courtiers were essential to the patronage of the players and play companies, and many of these sponsors and pundits met daily in locations such as the central aisle of St Paul's Cathedral (known as Paul's Walk or Duke Humfrey's Walk) to chat and exchange news. Two of the things they discussed were Marlowe's new play, and one of its most striking images, 'Sweet Helena'. Shakespeare and Jonson were among those who eagerly drew on and parodied Marlowe's line.[13] Word of mouth, like spoken poetry and oral history, covers its tracks. But what is certain is that, blasted by the bitter smell of gunpowder and the searing beauty of Marlowe's lines, the Elizabethan Londoners made Helen an icon in the popular imagination once again.

Marlowe's Helen arrived in the Elizabethan capital with a bang. Theatrical producers fed off the punters' taste for spook and spectacle. We know that in 1595 Philip Henslowe paid seven pounds two shillings for the tricks and trappings that made theatre so exciting to an Elizabethan audience. An early production of *Faustus* boasted a 'throne in the hevenes' and 'enterludes and music'. Later a dragon-machine was added. And in 1598, Henslowe appropriated from the Admiral's Men's properties store, a 'Hell's Mouth' into which Faustus could collapse.[14] In 1620, one audience member reported that 'shagge-hayr'd Devills runne roaring over the Stage with Squibs in their mouthes, while Drummers make Thunder in the Tyring-house and the twelve-penny Hirelings make artificiall Lightening in their Heavens'.[15] The special effects employed by the producers of the *Tragical History of Dr Faustus* were bumptious, brassy and wondrous to the Elizabethan audience. Their infernal nature was particularly appropriate for this play; because *Faustus* was a diabolic piece of work.

∽∽∽∽∽

Faustus had come into the consciousness of the Elizabethans via a volume published in Frankfurt and then translated into English, sometime around 1587, entitled, *The Historie of the Damnable Life, and Deserved Death, of Doctor John Faustus*. This was a 'true' story of dreadful temptation. Johann Faust did exist; he was a German scholar and conjuror who billed himself as a mid-16th-century disciple and double of Helen's old friend Simon Magus. As with Simon Magus, much of our evidence for Faust's life comes from hostile sources and so has to be read carefully. Lutheran reformers used Faust's story as a case-study of how *not* to engage with the spiritual world.

The details of Dr Faust's life are sketchy. But the *Historie* left its readers in no doubt that at some point the sorcerer's soul had indeed been sold to the devil in return for earthly pleasures, including the carnal knowledge of Helen:

> Now, in order that the miserable Faust could indulge in the
> desires of his flesh at midnight when he awoke, in the twenty-
> third year that had past, Helen of Greece entered into him . . .
> Now when Doctor Faust saw her, she so captured his heart that

he began to make love to her and kept her as his mistress: he became so fond of her that he could hardly be a moment without her. In the last year he made her pregnant and she bore him a son . . .'[16]

Helen as a captive mistress: it was a mortal delight that would lead Faust to eternal death. Temptation incarnate. We are told that students of the religious reformer Luther discovered evidence, at Faust's home, of a gruesome end: 'his brains cleaving to the wall: for the devil had beaten him from one wall against the other, on one corner lay his eyes, in another his teeth', and then moving outside they found 'lying on the horse dung, most monstrously torn and fearful to behold . . . his head and all his joints were dashed in pieces'.

Inspired by this ghastly story, Marlowe set to penning his work for the London stage.

In Marlowe's play Faustus is a man who cannot *not* sin – he is predestined for damnation. And one of the most significant staging posts on his journey into hell is his sexual relationship with the lascivious, luciferous spirit of Helen. Marlowe's Helen is not just an agent of destruction, she is an agent of the devil himself. Popular woodcuts of the time – the *Ars Moriendi* – show devils dragging a man's soul out from his mouth as he dies.[17] Just so, Helen's '*lips suck forth my soul; see where it flies –*' here Faustus is a necromancer and Helen a succubus, a spirit of the dead.

Helen has always been ambiguous, but there is something different going on here. Whereas classical authors imagined in her a brilliant source of light that permeated into the heavens itself, the light in her that balanced the dark, here Helen's glow is hemmed in with an oppressive gloom. Helen gleams in the pages of *Faustus* and on the stage of the Rose Theatre, but it is an aureole of light surrounded by impenetrable, stifling shadow.

The play met the tastes of the Tudor audience perfectly. Here on stage were the necromancers and occult illusions and witches that they knew to be real. In Europe, trafficking in spirits had recently been made a capital offence and the Lutherans were whipping up witch-hunt fever. In 1586 in Trier after a particularly late spring, 'a hundred and eighteen women and two men' had been burnt following their confession that 'the prolongation of the winter was the work of their incantations'.[18] In Britain on the other hand, an increasingly puritanical outlook went so far as to deny that such forces existed – but men and women wanted to believe in the supernatural. There were reports of great confusion and consternation among both the actors and the audience during one performance of Marlowe's *Faustus*, when some panicked, believing that there was one too many devils on stage.[19]

Just forty years before, all official public performances in England had taken the form of miracle plays and morality plays. These were unofficially sanctioned productions that peddled only ideas which met the approval of the Church. Much of Marlowe was blasphemous, and the impact for a live audience must have been thrilling. Here, for instance, was a man who was being made immortal thanks to the kiss of a whore-queen – not an idea to be found in the tenets of orthodox Christianity. But here too was a play of morals that seemed to reach beyond lessons of good and evil, asking questions about what it meant to be a woman, what it meant to be a man; about what it meant to be human. Two thousand years earlier, on the sun-baked slopes of the Athenian acropolis, the same questions had been asked, and now as then it was the spirit of Helen that was at the heart of the enquiry.[20]

Helen posed a problem – she was the perfect classical beauty that the Elizabethan Renaissance, with its love of antiquity, craved,[21] and yet her actions represented sin in its purest form as promulgated by the new, increasingly puritanical Church. The culture of the Renaissance keened for Beauty, but the prevailing Protestant mores upheld predestination and the unpardonable nature of sin.

And because playwrights such as Shakespeare, Marlowe, Dekker and Heywood had (although each to varying degrees) a broad knowledge of classical literature, their fertile minds were being exposed to the visceral, raw horrors of a classical world dominated by fickle and unforgiving gods. The result was a harrowing explosion of creativity. Elizabethan London was reeling under the impact of both a classical Renaissance and a Protestant clamp-down. This was an edgy world, when religious uncertainty kept the waters churning like a neap tide. And in the swell Helen slipped even further from the rank of heroic queen. Now losing yourself in Helen meant spinning into a vortex, where Aphrodite had no roses, only thorns.

Marlowe lived in stirring times. There are many parallels between 5th-century BC Athens and 16th-century AD London. The Elizabethan capital had the schizophrenic exuberance of an age in political, social and cultural transition. Londoners were beginning to experience foods, stimulants and stories from countries their grandfathers had never even dreamed existed. Live crocodiles were presented at court in 1605 and a camel was touted around the streets. Suddenly Londoners were tasting the unknown and the exotic and it was making the *fin-de-siècle* capital restless. In the fifty years since 1550, the London population had risen by nearly 70 per cent. The city was booming, it was humming with a cultural energy and Helen's name was quickly carried along the lines of current.

But also – as in 5th-century BC Athens – one of the spurs to this vivacity was the spectre of mass and premature death courtesy of the plague.

> *Beauty is but a flower,*
> *Which wrinkles will devour,*
> *Brightness falls from the air;*
> *Queens have died young and fair;*
> *Dust hath closed Helen's eye.*
> *I am sick, I must die*
> *Lord have mercy on us!*[22]

The poet and playwright Nashe describes the dreadful inevitability of death in an infected London. The Elizabethan Helen is indeed besmirched with dust: this is a time when even the immortal queen may succumb to death.[23] And although Marlowe's lyrical line 'the face that launched a thousand ships' has gathered to itself a wonderfully bright timbre, his inspiration may in fact have been the very dark work of the Greek satirist Lucian.[24] Lucian conjured up a vision of Helen's skull in Hades in one of his *Dialogues of the Dead*, written around AD 170. A new arrival to Hades, Menippus, is being given a guided tour by Hermes, and stands in front of a pile of bones and skulls:

HERMES: This skull is Helen.

MENIPPUS: And for this a thousand ships carried warriors from every part of Greece; Greeks and barbarians were slain, and cities made desolate.

HERMES: Ah, Menippus, you never saw the living Helen; or you would have said with Homer

> *Well might they suffer grievous years of toil*
> *Who strove for such a prize.*

We look at withered flowers, whose dye is gone from them, and what can we call them but unlovely things? Yet in the hour of their bloom these unlovely things were things of beauty.

MENIPPUS: Strange, that the Greeks could not realise what it was for which they laboured; how short-lived, how soon to fade.

HERMES: I have no time for moralising. Choose your spot, where you will, and lie down. I must go and fetch new dead.[25]

So, on the stage of the Rose, the face that launched a thousand ships was enjoying a true re-naissance, albeit in a shadow cast by classical antiquity. And whereas even the most hostile ancient sources allow Helen to escape death and ignominy as a star, a spirit in the oceans, or in Elysian fields making love to Achilles, for many Elizabethans Helen has become a symbol of endless death.[26]

Tottel asks of Helen in his *Songs and Sonettes* composed in 1557:

> Did not the worms consume
> Her carrion to the dust?
> Did dreadful death forbear its fume
> For beauty, pride or lust?

Thomas Proctor rewrites history by killing Helen off in Troy, in his poem 'Helen's Complaint' from the volume *The triumph of truth.*[27] And yet, still one feels Marlowe's Helen is attractive not repulsive; the playwright's saturated lines drip with a personal yearning. Marlowe had risen from a family of poor shoe-makers thanks to an education that introduced him to the characters who created and inhabited the classical texts he avidly read. Men like Homer and women like Helen, these were his heroes and his heroines, his path to enlightenment.

Marlowe's Helen was a Zeitgeist. She was dark, distinctive and transitory enough to become legendary once again. And the face that launched a thousand ships was particularly vivid for the very reason that she could get away without an actual appearance – Faust's Helen is a wraith, an appearance in spirit only. Rather than some callow boy dressed up as a woman trying to play the most beautiful woman in the world, the Elizabethan image of Sweet Helena could blossom in the minds of London's theatre-goers.

The stage directions of *Dr Faustus* distil, perfectly, one of the enduring and fundamental problems with Helen. Marlowe's Helen 'passeth over the stage' but never speaks. Is she real or is she a ghost? Is she an *eidolon* or an icon, a creation of the act of sex or of the sexual imagination? Is she Simon Magus' *Ennoia*, the sacred feminine, trapped in different bodies down the centuries, or one hapless woman with feet of clay, a real, tired matron who inspired many millennia of fantasies? How do you transmit the idea of Helen, how do you become her?

Theatre directors have dealt with the problem in a variety of ways. In 1950, Orson Welles put Eartha Kitt on stage as Helen, accompanied by the music of Duke Ellington. In 1966, as their offstage relationship crumbled, a plump Elizabeth Taylor was Helen to Burton's Faustus at the Oxford

Playhouse. The RSC production of 1968 had Helen naked, whereas in Manchester in 1981, Helen descended from the ceiling in a shower of gold-dust. In John Barton's 1974–5 staging (with Ian McKellen as Faustus), Sweet Helena was simply a marionette with a blonde wig, a mask and a chiffon nightie.[28] In the Young Vic's sell-out show of 2003 directed by David Lan, Helen was not there at all, it was only the movie-star beauty of Jude Law as Faustus that was allowed on stage.

Remember Zeuxis and his frustrating quest to find the perfect way to represent the ultimate beauty. Any physical Helen can only disappoint; but a poetic Helen has always the chance to embody absolute perfection. Marlowe's versification lifts Helen beyond the confines of a Faustian pact, out of the slavering, syphilitic fug of a theatre on Bankside. She is made immortal once again at the very moment she 'immortalises' Faustus with a kiss. For many she abides as 'the face that launched a thousand ships', a beautiful, formless poetic image, which first swirled around the heads of Elizabethan Londoners and which still hangs in the air.

44

HELEN'S NEMESIS

@@@@@@@@@@@@

Fame has indeed made great heralding of you, and there is
no land that knows not of your beauty; no other among
fair women has a name like yours – nowhere in Phrygia,
nor from the rising of the sun.

Paris comparing Helen's beauty to that of Venus in OVID, *Heroides*[1]
(1ST CENTURY AD)

WHEN ZEUS ADDRESSES APHRODITE in the *Iliad* he counsels:
'*Fighting is not for you, my child, the works of war. See to the works of
marriage, the slow fires of longing.*'[2] And the goddess of love obliges.
On an *amphoriskos* (a vessel used to contain cosmetics or perfumes) in the
Berlin Museum, painted in around 430 BC, Helen sits in Aphrodite's lap.[3]
Our heroine looks a slip of a thing, an ingénue, an innocent being drilled
in the facts of life. Aphrodite is giving the child-queen her instructions in
the ways of love. And just in case this young recruit buckles under the
strain, the goddess has brought along reinforcements. Eros is there, hovering,
naked at the corner, and tugging at the Trojan prince's arm, staring intently
up at him, is another, urgent young male figure, another son of Aphrodite
– *Himeros*, Desire.

> PARIS: That is just the thing that seems downright incredible to
> me, that she should be willing to abandon her husband and sail
> away with a foreigner and a stranger.
> APHRODITE: Be easy on that score; I have two beautiful pages,
> Desire and Love; these I shall give you to be your guides on the
> journey. Love will enter wholly into her heart and compel the
> woman to love you, while Desire will encompass you and make
> you what he is himself, desirable and charming. I myself shall be
> there too, and I shall ask the Graces to go with me; and in this
> way, by united effort, we shall prevail upon her.[4]

Helen was put on earth to catalyse desire. And for three millennia she has been hated for it: because in entertaining desire, we recognise our needs and our disappointments. Helen embodies mankind's drive to covet, yearn, raven for what it does not have.[5] Helen is both fantastical and terrible because however often she is enjoyed, she still promises more; no one stops wanting her. Theseus rapes her when she is a child but the heroes of Greece still queue up to win her hand. Paris takes her once again yet none the less thousands are prepared to die just to see her face. She has moved on to her second Trojan prince by the time Menelaus storms Troy, but still the Spartan king wants her back.

Helen's guises may change, but not her role. Like a drop of mercury that will always reunite however often it is split, she remains one thing: the incarnation of sexual promise. She is a woman blessed or cursed by that strange alchemical ability to fuse passion of the head and the heart and thus cause the world, despite its best intentions, to fall hopelessly, disastrously in love with her. She is a factotum for our fantasies. This is the secret of Helen's abiding celebrity, why she has won out over the many sensational women in Greek stories and histories: the other virgins who have been raped, the powerful queens, the seductive sorceresses. Here is a narrative not just of beauty, sex and death, but of eternal longing, a story born out of the first civilisation on the Greek mainland. Civilisation is restless, greedy – it always wants more, what it does not have. Longing propels us into uncharted territories, we go willingly and yet come to resent the journeys we have embarked on. *Eros, eris*; love and strife. Because we know we have to seek her, but because we know the consequences of the quest, Helen makes the world around her 'bristle with fear'. There is a frisson as she passes.

Down the ages, different cultures have interpreted Helen in a way that reflects their own preoccupations. We want to categorise her, but we cannot. She is an icon of beauty who flees from view.[6] Sometimes she is a victim of fate, sometimes a self-seeking force of evil. For some her beauty alone excuses her anything, for others it is proof that humankind is at its most frail when erotic passion impacts on human affairs. But without exception, all make it clear that once the person and image of Helen are distilled what is left is one irreducible element: a sex-appeal so powerful and so unknowable, that men will simply do anything – however cataclysmic – to possess it and therefore her.

And on that vase in Berlin we can read the punishment for being so desired. Helen is joined by another female figure who stands close by pointing an accusing finger at the thoughtful queen. She is Nemesis, the spirit of fate and revenge. She stares unwaveringly at Helen, inescapable. Some mythographers tell us that Nemesis — a sea-nymph — was Helen's mother; they make the connection between beauty and fate umbilical.[7] Mention Nemesis today and Greek men will swear and spit, to ward off her evil power. But Helen, the sometime child of Nemesis, has no heed of curses, and after two and a half thousand years of vilification, she is used to them.

⁓⊘⊙⊘⊙⁓

Helen whirls through history, often turning full circle as she does so. She is worshipped by the ancient Greeks as a sex-goddess, and becomes that again in the Gnostic tradition. Works of scholarship claim Helen's responsibility for a huge range of things from the Aryan ideal, fair-haired, blue-eyed superiority,[8] to Easter eggs (fertility symbols), from the Hollywood stereotype of blonde bombshell to fairies strung up on top of our Christmas trees — a much corrupted version of a tree-spirit.[9] Men seize her from the Spartan palace and entrap her in whichever sanctuary or castle or brothel or heaven or hell best befits their age. They are attempting, always unsuccessfully, to frame her beauty, both mentally and physically: creating ever more Helens as they do so.

> For since I crossed this threshold last, as duty bade,
> All unsuspecting, visiting Cythera's shrine,
> And there was ravished by an adventurer from Troy,
> Much has befallen: far and wide men tell the tale
> And take their pleasure in it. But no tale can please
> One round whose name legend spins its false report.[10]

⁓⊘⊙⊘⊙⁓

An aside. Just a week after September 11, 2001 I was taken to Heathrow Airport by my local mini-cab company. My destination was North America and, inevitably, we talked about the cause of the recent attacks. My mini-cab driver laid the responsibility for the entire tragedy at Monica Lewinsky's door. If it had not been for her, he said, the Bush administration would never have got in. In his opinion Bush was only in power (and therefore al Qu'eda was only so active) because a degenerate woman had made Bill Clinton 'weak around the trousers'. It is an opinion I am sure a number of classical male Greeks would have subscribed to.

The connection between Helen and Monica was made explicit by Jeffrey Toobin following the Clinton affair: 'As is demonstrated by the history of scandal from Helen of Troy to Monica of Beverly Hills, sex has a way of befogging the higher intellectual faculties.'[11] Like Helen, Monica Lewinsky was memorably described by Bill Clinton not by name but as 'that woman'.

Helen is an archetype. Men fall for her, have sex with her and then, when terrible things happen, it is she who gets the blame.[12]

We still – with woeful partiality – focus on the 'shame' rather than the triumph of Helen's life-story. For centuries we have chosen to adopt the post-Homeric, misogynist world-view, a view codified in cities such as Athens from the 5th century BC onwards, as a precedent for our own – but Helen springs from an earlier time. Since the birth of history her name has never been forgotten. Her very survival is proof of her significance. She is special because she is a consistent female presence, both sacred and profane, across three millennia. Worlds have changed, civilisations have come and gone, social, cultural and political sensibilities have shifted, poets have sung and been silenced, but Helen has outlasted them all.

And what of that elusive pre-historic Helen, the Bronze Age queen who sat on the limestone blocks of the Spartan palace? The aristocrat who controlled the men around her. The hieratic potentate who owned land. The woman who glistened as she passed, smelling of olive oil and roses, and who left the palace by night to officiate at heady cultic rituals. The queen who lived in a palace adorned with images, high priestesses, goddess-girls: who prepared narcotics, who walked hand in hand with the spirits of her land. A woman who had pole position – power, wealth and respect.

Evidence of this woman's life is embedded in the Peloponnesian and Anatolian landscape. She has left us many clues, but she has not left us a corpse. Although it seems from the conditions on the Spartan citadel that this is the one piece of Helen that has escaped for certain from the record, I will share my private fantasy of 'the world's desire': that one day her body will be found. Because it is only when Helen of Troy becomes a desiccated pile of bones, when men can look at a toothless jaw, a tarnished ring and hand that has become an incomplete claw, that she can, finally, be laid to rest. Only then that we will stop hounding her, stop blaming her for being the most beautiful woman in the world.

HELEN

All Greece hates
the still eyes in the white face,
the lustre as of olives
where she stands
and the white hands

All Greece reviles
the wan face when she smiles
hating it deeper still
when it grows wan and white
remembering past enchantments
and past ills

Greece sees, unmoved,
God's daughter, born of love,
the beauty of cool feet
and slenderest knees
could love indeed the maid
only if she were laid
white ash amid funeral cypresses.[13]

APPENDICES

@@@@@@@@@@@@@

THE MINOTAUR'S ISLAND

◎◎◎◎◎◎◎◎◎◎◎◎◎

There is a land called Crete . . .
ringed by the wine-dark sea with rolling whitecaps –
handsome country, fertile, thronged with people
well past counting . . .

HOMER, *Odyssey*[1]

To understand Helen's world more fully, we first have to go to the Peloponnesian coast and stare south, out in the direction of Africa, and search
for Bronze Age Crete just beyond the horizon. Crete, the Minotaur's island,
homeland of the legendary King Minos, the centre of Minoan culture, was
taken over by invading Mycenaean forces sometime around 1450 BC. The
urgent, vigorous Mycenaeans are vastly indebted to the Minoans. Minoan
civilisation had by 1450 BC already been established on its island home for
well over a millenium, dominant in the Aegean for close on five hundred
years.

Before Jason went in search of the Golden Fleece, before Paris stole
Helen and sparked the Trojan Wars, Crete was the jewel of the Aegean, a
pre-historic land of milk and honey. Naturally lush and fertile and protected
on all sides by miles of sea, the island was a secure, cultural hothouse.

Crete's axial position between three continents meant it became
unusually cosmopolitan, unusually early. Archaeologists have found evidence
of pre-historic ports and international trade on its north, south and east
coasts. It seems this was a favoured stopping-off point for traders from all
over the Eastern Mediterranean: from Egypt, from Syria, from the Greek
mainland and from Italy. In the east of the island at Vaï (where picture-
postcard palm trees shade an idyllic sandy beach) locals claim the first palm
grew when a pre-historic Egyptian sailor spat out the stone from one of
the dates he had brought with him from the banks of the Nile.

I last visited Crete to study new digs in the east of the island at
Palaikastro.[2] As the white sand at Vaï burnt the soles of my feet and the

46-degree midday sun blistered my shoulders, I understood why archaeologists prefer to describe the island as an outpost of the Middle East rather than to use its more traditional, Edwardian title, 'the birthplace of Europe'. After those cosmopolitan beginnings, Crete has never lost its eastern feel. During my stay I was lured into local bars by the siren song of Crete's native beat, a mixture of Rai, bouzouki and Afro-pop. Home-grown bananas line the streets like sunny chandeliers. Crete's micro-climate then and now yields exceptional crops. The island has a charmed feel about it; those who believe in their gods think it is blessed.

And in the Bronze Age, Crete, wealthy and highly cultured, was a prize worth claiming – Cretan palaces and ports offered rich pickings. Then the gods of the earth appeared to give another ambitious civilisation the opportunity they needed. The Minoans had already been weakened by the debilitating effects of a number of earlier earthquakes. The grand, terrible, spectacular eruption of the volcano at Thera set in train a series of religious and social dislocations. This was, perhaps, not 'apocalypse now', for the Minoans, but a slow lingering death.[3]

So when the ambitious Mycenaeans arrived in Crete, these would have been exciting times. In the centuries that preceded the takeover (a coup or a philanthropic rescue depending on your interpretation of the evidence), the Greek mainlanders perhaps felt they were living in the shadow of the big island to the south: Crete produced the finest of everything. The Cretans have been compared to the Japanese in the 1970s[4] – soaking up the best of global culture, adapting it and sending it out with a fresh, unique Minoan spin.

Name a technique or a material and as like as not the Minoans worked it up with audacious skill. Ultra-realistic stone-carving, exquisite jewellery, fresco paintings whose pastoral verve is both touching and uplifting: flying fish cover one wall, on another a cat stalks a richly plumed bird. There are jadeite axes made in the shape of black panthers and stone bulls with gilded horns, their rock-crystal eyes still contemplating the world around them.

Crete was also a breeding ground for vivid myths and stories. It was here that Europa was raped by Zeus in the form of a bull. Here the Minotaur, the monstrous half-man, half-bull hybrid, whose lair was at the heart of the palace of Knossos, and who lived off human flesh, was conceived when Queen Pasiphae satisfied her lust mounted by a great white bull. In Cretan skies, Icarus, the callow youth who tried to push human achievement just too far, headed for the sun and was sent plunging back down to earth, his home-made waxen wings bubbling, his flesh burnt.

But there is another myth from Crete, less well known. It tells of a giant metal robot made by that consummate inventor and craftsman,

Daedalus (father of ill-fated Icarus). This robot, Talos, had one task – to protect his birth-land, Crete, at all costs. The special island had to be shielded from unwanted intruders and invaders. Just as importantly, native Cretans must be prevented from leaving Crete's shores in search of pastures new. Talos made Crete a prison-fortress. In the Bronze Age imagination, Minoan talent was well worth guarding.

໑໑໑໑໑

In one sense such xenophobia was justified: there would have been plenty of chances for international exchange throughout the second millennium BC. The contact that Bronze Age Crete enjoyed with its neighbours is clearly demonstrated by a number of archaeological finds. In Heraklion Museum an elephant's tusk survives from Africa one of the storerooms at the palace at Zakro. Perhaps it had been displayed in the palace as an exotic novelty, or perhaps it was used for barter. Now the tusk is cinder-grey and sickeningly decayed, with a choppy perforated surface.

Time has been kinder to other artefacts. In the Sitia Museum there is an exquisitely carved *kouros*, a boy – probably a boy-god – dressed in hippopotamus ivory, a material prized for its delicate flesh-pink tone. The boy, found shattered in a sanctuary at Palaikastro on the east coast of Crete and then pieced back together again, with his gold and ivory decorations, earns the epithet a chryselephantine statuette.

The artists who made him carefully coloured the *kouros* with Egyptian blue and embedded rock crystal for his eyes. His hands are clenched and the veins and sinews in his flesh stick out. Each toenail and fingernail is perfectly carved – even though the latter dig into his palms and are therefore invisible to the human eye. The golden filaments that represented his hair would have been pressed around his beautifully proportioned face. Each time I stand and look at this powerful, poised creature I have to remind myself that this boy comes not from Michelangelo's studio, but from prehistory. It is no surprise that Minoan aesthetics were lauded and copied throughout the Aegean.

A number of communities around the Mediterranean, Thera included, appear to have been under the Minoan spell. When the Mycenaeans dress, it is Minoan fashions they ape; when they paint frescoes, they follow the example of the Minoan masters; when they make pots, they work to a Minoan pattern. A woman such as Helen apparently paraded in fashions dreamt up by her Cretan cousins, the sartorial innovators themselves having lain dead for centuries.

Giant pots with distinctive designs, octopuses and seaweed whorls – images previously thought to be exclusively Minoan – have recently been dug up near Sparta.[5] On the gold cups decorated with bulls and jumping figures from Vapheio, just south of Sparta, the Minoan influence (or craftsmanship) is striking. Sailing due north from Crete, the island of Kythera and the Lakonian port of Gythion would have been the Minoans' first ports of call. Carry on travelling due north, inland for half a day, and there is Sparta. While Minoan style has more élan, the Mycenaeans were masters of pottery production: their use of clays and slips is more discriminating, they understand better the technology of the furnace. Pots from the mainland are of finer quality. There would have been a consistent and comprehensive two-way traffic of goods and ideas between Lakedaimonia and the fervent Cretan islanders before and during Helen's lifetime. In the *Iliad*, Helen describes the close connection between Crete and the Peloponnese. Speaking of the Cretan king, Idomeneus, she says: '*How often Menelaus, my good soldier, would host him in our halls.*'[6] King Idomeneus sends eighty '*black ships*'[7] to the Trojan war effort. And of course Menelaus was burying his grandfather on Crete when Paris stayed at Sparta and took a fancy to the Spartans' queen, Helen.

Minoan hallmarks crop up throughout the Argolid and Lakonia. Around 1550 BC the Mycenaeans even start to bury their dead in round *tholos* tombs as their Minoan counterparts did in the south of Crete. But there is one marked difference: for the Minoans these were shared graves, where large numbers of the community would end up together, but in the settlements such as Mycenae the tombs are for kings, aristocrats and their families. It is a telling enthusiasm for an architecture that, even in death, gives individual warriors preferential treatment, raises them even further above the group. Minoan burial chambers were there for the community; Mycenaean tombs celebrate heroic achievement and encourage clan posturing.

One of the most significant Minoan attributes, gathered up by the Mycenaeans, and then used for their own purposes, seems to have been the gift of writing.

The Cretans invented the first-ever script in Old Europe, 'Cretan Hieroglyphic', around 2000 BC, closely followed by another, Linear A; to date, both remain undeciphered. Evidence of these two scripts was uncovered by Arthur Evans when he excavated Knossos on Crete in 1900. But Evans also discovered another script – Linear B – that would prove not quite so elusive. Twelve years after Evans' death, in 1953, Michael Ventris, an architect who had worked closely with the brilliant, chain-smoking American scholar Alice E. Kober (the 180,000 rectangles of graph paper that represented much of the leg-work necessary for cracking Linear B were filed in old Lucky and Fleetwood cigarette boxes),[8] deciphered Linear B and showed it to be an early form of Greek.

Inspired by the innovators to the south, it appears the Mycenaeans took the idea of writing from the Minoans, but used it to express the early form of Greek that they spoke.

At a stroke, thanks to Ventris' decipherment, the Greeks had been given approximately one thousand years more attributable history. The excitement of Ventris and his collaborator John Chadwick is endearing and contagious. When Chadwick took the first Linear B documents to Cambridge University Press he celebrated by writing a postcard to Ventris (who was then in Greece) in Linear B.[9]

.1   i-jo-a-na, mi-kae, ka-re-e
.2   sa-me-ro, pu-pi-ri-jo
.3   tu-po-ka-ra-pe-u-si
.4   a-ka-ta, tu-ka
.5   ka-mo-jo, ke-pu$_2$ ra$_3$,
       i-jo-u-ni-jo-jo
.6   me-no, A-ME-RA 7

.1   John to Michael, Greetings!
.2   Today I gave the book
.3   to the printers.
.4   Good luck!
.5   At the Bridge of Cam . . .
.6   . . . Month of June, Day 7

It is thanks to these code-breakers that we have a direct textual window onto Helen's world. The Linear B tablets, found predominantly at Knossos and Chania on Crete and at Pylos, Mycenae, Tiryns and Thebes on the mainland, turned out not to bear fine poems or diplomatic treatises – in a first flush of disappointment, scholars called them 'laundry lists'. But still, laundry lists can tell us what men and women wear, how much washing costs and who runs the launderettes. Although the language is abbreviated and riddled with baffling terms, the equivalent of the legalese we might struggle through in the small print of a mortgage application, these sludgy-coloured blocks yield vivid details – odd words that can carry the reader back into the Mycenaean world. Some, for instance, detail the number of sheep in one shepherd's herd, others the impressive amount of olive oil given as a gift to a high priestess, there are even the names of individual cattle: Blacky, Spotty, White-Nose and White-foot.[10]

Once they were writing, the Mycenaeans did not look back. Year by year more of the Cretans' turf became theirs, until the moment came when the Greek mainlanders themselves were in charge. The Mycenaeans, a great civilisation in their own right, were also great plagiarists, happy to appropriate the successes of another culture to serve their own ends. The Minoans were to the Mycenaeans what the ancient Greeks would be to Rome – an inspiration and a pervasive cultural resource. They became a civilisation whose ghosts appear in a world tightly controlled by Mycenaean bureaucrats.[11] A woman such as Helen would have benefited greatly from her Cretan inheritance.

For me it is at the hilltop burial site of Phourni, near the north coast of Crete, that the shift from Minoan to Mycenaean can be felt most poignantly. As the sun falls behind Mount Juktas – itself sheltering the sacred cave of Anemospilia – the haloes of buttery-yellow sunset-light around the graves are extinguished in a stroke. Suddenly all that is left are the hunched shapes of the reconstructed burial chambers of the Early Minoan period, modest stone igloos designed to shelter the bodies of men and women who lived in a changing world – at a time when infant societies were each jostling for pole position. And further down the hill, just visible, are the later Mycenaean tholos tombs. Now the Mycenaeans are burying their dead in separate clan groups, with swaggering pomp.

Investigating the graves, one has a strong sense of peoples and powers moving through time, leaving footprints as they pass. It is odd to think that up there on the hillside, many of the sounds can have changed not an iota over the millennia, regardless of which ruler was enjoying the upper hand in Crete: Minoan, Mycenaean, Turkish, German or Greek. There are ducks in the farm down below, bees buzzing from one wild sage to another and a dog's chipper bark, followed by a man's voice drifting up from the valley, shouting out a word that appears on the Linear B tablets, written three and a half thousand years ago, as ME-RI: 'MELI!' the man calls. 'Bring more honey!'

LA PARISIENNE

◎◎◎◎◎◎◎◎◎◎◎◎

> From what source, then, did the beauty of Helen
> whom men fought for shine out, or that of all women
> like Aphrodite in beauty?
>
> PLOTINUS, *On the Intelligible Beauty*[1] *c.* AD 260

What is desperately difficult to judge is how far the Minoans influenced the Mycenaean mind-set; particularly when it came to women and religion. And yet it is a compelling line of inquiry, particularly because, on Crete, the 'fairer sex' (in Minoan-Mycenaean art, women are painted white, men brown) appear prominent, dynamic and distinctive. When Arthur Evans began to dig at the site of Knossos in 1900, on Day 2 he found a figurine 'goddess' whom he immediately labelled Aphrodite. When frescoes were uncovered in the 'palace-complexes' women were found, clustering on the surface, often with symbols of divinity around them. Topless girls hurl themselves across golden signet rings, shaking trees, carrying armfuls of vegetation. Women collapse onto altars, they sit high on thrones.

I once had an ancient-history tutor with a taste for the sensational. One dismal, November afternoon my colleagues and I were gathered together for a slide show. It was pitch black, the air was fuggy, most of the class had their heads on their desks, ready for a snooze. Suddenly an extremely well-endowed, half-naked woman burst onto the projection screen. This was the famous (so-called) 'Snake Goddess' from Crete, a trenchant creature, with a wasp waist and furious, kohl-lined eyes, whose pneumatic breasts stood bare and proud above her tight bodice and flouncy, gaudily striped skirts. A giant snake coiled around her arms and neck. The image was bewitching. Billed as a goddess, this startling pin-up, three and a half thousand years old, seemed very much flesh and blood to me. Mortal or divine, she was clearly a symbol of female force and fecundity. I wanted to try to get to the bottom of her story.

My initial hunch about that goddess turned out to be right. The faience 'goddess' has four companions – two of whom exist only as small fragments.

All five of these figures were found at the palace of Knossos on Crete by Arthur Evans and his team in 1903. Dating from around 1600 BC, at some point each had been carefully broken, and buried deep in a stone-lined pit along with sea-shells and many other curious items under the floor of a storage room. The dislocated remains were contained in what seems to have been one of the most sacred parts of the grand palatial complex. Clearly these women, had been, in some way, demoted. But they were too powerful to treat without respect. The figurines were laid to rest with precision and care, as one colleague put it, as though their executors were dealing with radioactive waste.

Edwardian archaeologists deified these women, assuming that since they were so exquisitely made, and seemed so powerful, they must represent supernatural creatures. It is now thought more likely that the 'Snake Goddesses' were in fact living, breathing votaries – the high priestesses in some kind of Minoan nature-worship or fertility cult.

If one manages to arrive early enough or late enough to avoid the crowds at the Archaeological Museum of Heraklion (walking past concrete pillars painted the same blood-red as the columns at the palace of Knossos just up the road) it is possible to spend a few quiet minutes with these famous female images from the Bronze Age. Delicately fashioned out of faience, the fierce bare-breasted women glare from their glass-fronted prison. All three are dressed in the height of fashion. Waists are cinched in by a girdle. Beneath these girdles there are aprons and full, pleated skirts reminiscent of crinolines.

Now the 'Snake Goddess' is visible everywhere in Crete. Cheap, bootleg reproductions of her are on sale in back streets. In one of the nudist beaches on the south of the island a giant version has been painted on the outside walls of the concrete lavatories. Some scholars think that, in one sense, the Snake Goddess and her votaries would have been ubiquitous in Bronze Age Crete too. Whether she was divine or mortal, she speaks of a time when women were totemic. The Mycenaeans consolidated their interest in Minoans and took on board a huge amount of cultural baggage when they took over Crete around 1450 BC. And one of the cultural markers transposed to the Greek mainland was a delight in the representation of women.

If we look for the origins of Helen's potency, I think the trail starts in Crete. The iconography of the island brims with so many female images that a few bold scholars insist Minoan Crete was a matriarchy. This might be going too far, but there is certainly something unusual going on in Crete when it comes to women and the powers and privileges they enjoyed.

Our material evidence for religion in pre-history is localised, any generic description of worship has to be one part analysis, two parts speculation. But because Helen's world – both material and spiritual – was coloured and informed by that of its Minoan predecessors, and because the Mycenaeans seem to have been in charge there between around 1450 and 1200 BC, it is well worth looking at the evidence that Crete yields. Figurines, seal-stones, pottery tables and frescoes appear to give us clues to the beliefs and lives of the five hundred thousand or so people who lived and worked on the island.[2]

At a time when matters spiritual were so inalienable a part of the real, living, breathing world, it is no surprise that religious belief was manifest in gutsy, vivacious, mettlesome displays. Religion seems to have been high drama, circus, seance, rock concert and May Day rolled into one. And if the evidence for Crete is anything to go by, the highest class took an active and leading role in these heady religious practices. Some suggest that Bronze Age aristocracies may even have held power not by virtue of high birth but through earning their stripes as specialist mediators between the people and their deities.

Religious ritual was certainly central to a number of the palace-complexes, such as Knossos, Malia and the fine palace on the south of the island, Phaistos. To get to the palace of Phaistos one has to turn away from the Greek mainland, face south and travel down towards the Libyan Sea. Here the landscape is flatter, stranger: the road passes giant rocks marooned in the landscape – 'cheese-pies', locals call them (although you get the feeling these stones would have represented something less cosy to the early Cretans) – and then heads towards the coast, winding through the fertile Messara Plain to the palatial complex of Phaistos itself which, perched on a ridge and now surrounded by pine-trees, is reached by a steep climb. Hot dry winds whip around the site but the lively environment is balanced by a still, colossal presence to the West, the sacred bulk of Mount Ida with its trademark twin peaks.

I had come here to look for those early images of Minoan women that informed Helen's Mycenaean world.[3] A round pedestal table and clay bowl found in the palace at Phaistos, dating from around 1900 to 1700 BC, have both been lovingly designed and executed – so far, they are unique, suggesting they played a part in religious devotion. Perhaps they were brought out at certain times of the agricultural year to please the gods who filled the fields with wheat, brought olives to the trees and grapes to the vine. Both the bowl and the table are decorated with designs of women who seem to be dancing – their arms arc and sway, their skirts are full, some of the figures look as if they have beaks. One, centre stage, holds up a plant in bloom.

On seal-stones, carefully etched miniature scenes record processions and parades. Young women carry baskets full of orchard boughs and gather around trees that look as though they are in pots on a constructed plinth. The immediate impression is that these feisty, voluptuous girls are both honouring and marshalling nature: commanding animals and birds. Archaeologists have given them names such as 'Mistress of the Animals', 'Mistress of the Birds', 'Mistress of the Horses'.

In Minoan representations of nature, it is women who are ever-present, women who appear to be in charge. And, perhaps as a consequence, women elsewhere in Minoan iconography are given great respect.[5] One very damaged fresco from Knossos, the Procession Fresco also in the Heraklion museum,[6] shows a seated female figure – perhaps a goddess who has taken the human form of a high priestess – being escorted and worshipped by both men and women. The acolytes walk backwards in deference to this sublimely decorated being.

ᄋᄼᄋᄼᄋ

Female divinities seem to have been worshipped with the most frenzied devotion at extreme points in the landscape. The Bronze Age populations of Crete used their palaces and towns as religious centres, but they also travelled out to locations which, for them, had a predominantly religious function; the peaks of mountains, the banks of rivers or deep into the bowels of the earth. Shrines, sanctuaries and altars, some of which still survive, were built on these wild spots – but elsewhere nature's architecture was more than adequate to host Minoan devotions.

In these wildernesses the only clues we have to human activity are the small votive offerings left behind, items such as a tiny baked clay ox, or a woman who seems to be praying – standing with her arms pressed to her chest or her fist to her forehead in an act of adoration. Terracotta scarab beetles have been found, and, somewhat bizarrely, model weasels. One offering found by Arthur Evans in the Psychro Cave near Lasithi in Crete, is a plump, crawling baby, just under 2 inches long (5 cm) with a wonderfully pudgy bottom. The child's head is lifted enquiringly. Archaeologists also unearthed representations of disjointed legs or arms. In Catholic and Greek Orthodox churches today, remarkably similar metal versions are offered up when someone has a broken arm, a leg ulcer, breast cancer, and so on. *Tamata* the Greeks call them. It seems extremely likely that the pre-historic clay versions served the same propitiating purpose. Layers of ash on a number of the sites suggest that rituals there were accompanied by great fires.[7]

In Crete, museum curators tell a charming story of a young boy who drew their attention to one particular find – and site. Exploring in the Skotino Cave, just to the east of Heraklion and about an hour's walk inland, the child came across a tiny damaged bronze statuette of what seemed to be a man carrying a goat on his shoulders. The figure was three and a half thousand years old.

The Skotino Cave is 160 m deep. I have stumbled deep into the interior across the rugged cave floor, its rocks covered in a mixture of mud (the consistency of melted chocolate) and sage-green slime, in order to try to appreciate the extreme sites in which women worshipped and were revered. The further in one travels, the more the light itself colours – one is passing through air but quickly the sensation is of being underwater, of walking in a soft, green aqua haze.

There is a percussive soundtrack of trickles, splashes and drops; stalactites and stalagmites are still growing. Some minerals have formed monstrous globular masses in the cave's centre. Any visitor is dwarfed by these giants and the tortured bulk of the rocks inside, their surfaces thrown into relief every now and then by the odd clump of bright green moss and algae. Each patch of vegetation waits for its appointed moment of glory: once a day shafts of sunlight hit a line whose surfaces are not blocked by the Gormenghast forms of the cave's interior. For an hour or so points on the cave wall are bathed in light and the plant life that clings there has a brief, frenetic window to stay alive and produce its vital chlorophyll. It is in places such as this that we have to try to understand the spiritual landscape of pre-history.

☙☙☙☙☙

One persuasive interpretation of the female imagery on Bronze Age seal-stones and pots and figurines is that women were held responsible for nature's good health – for the germination of the seed and the ripening of the corn. A society that has moved from hunting and gathering to farming finds that nature, in its newly domesticated and artificial form, depends on the farmer as much as he does on it. So when nature becomes an agro-business, nature's CEOs, women, need to be kept on side. Grain supplies are stored in the palace-complexes of Knossos on Crete or Pylos on the Greek mainland and were perhaps guarded by priestesses, the *klawiphoroi*, the 'keepers of the keys'.

Knossos has been identified as the mother of all grain stores.[8] Many hundreds of *pithoi* were found lining its labyrinthine storerooms. Someone must have walked through those pregnant, malty chambers organising what went where, deciding how the wheat and barley and olives should be stored, saying what proportion was due to be offered back to the gods, marshalling the rations of a civilisation. The Grandstand and Temple frescoes from Knossos imply that women were present in the palace in huge numbers. This painted female host surely escapes its earlier identification as a chorus of dancing girls or a harem of silent, dutiful wives. The attractive woman from the Campstool Fresco, christened '*La Parisienne*' by Evans' team of excavators because she seemed the height of coiffeured urbanity, was almost certainly not there to be decorative. It is as likely that such women received the harvest, blessed it and then controlled its use and redistribution.

That would have been a powerful position to be in. Consider how fragile food production was in the Bronze Age. The panic caused by the prospect of seven years of famine in Egypt is well documented – but it has been calculated that it would take just two years of bad harvests to clear out the warren of food storage rooms in Knossos – the same or even less at the palaces of Pylos and Mycenae. The sex that controlled nature's larder would have been a phalanx to keep sweet and on side. Women were important, perhaps because they had some kind of privileged access to the mysteries of nature and the spirit world; they mattered. And a woman like Helen, if she stood out from the rest thanks to a god-given natural beauty, would have mattered a great deal indeed.

ᎧᎧᎧᎧᎧ

It is helpful to turn to the fuller, more eloquent data of the Hittites to get a feel for the tangible benefits high-powered religious women would have enjoyed in the Eastern Mediterranean. Contemporary Hittite sources describe temple-priestesses as a suitable match for a king. Some of the tablets give us an idea of just how much corporeal wealth women at the top of the religious (and, by default, temporal) pile, could accumulate.

As well as the SAL SANGA, the high priestess, in the temples there were also women of some influence called SAL.SUHUR.LAL. In about 1400 BC we hear of one particular woman of the temple called Kuvatalla – who had gifts positively showered on her by the king and queen of the time (Arnuvanda and Ašmunikal). One might imagine that this generosity was effected by the monarchs to win favour with the gods and plump up the resources of the temple itself – but no, these gifts were in perpetuity for Kuvatalla and to be inherited by Kuvatalla's children.

In the Istanbul Archaeological Museum the benefaction tablet that immortalised Kuvatalla's inheritance, just over 25 cm high and 17 cm across, now a rich, burnt ochre, inscribed with Hittite cuneiform, still survives. Although there are great cracks in the tablet and large chunks of text are missing, one can still make out much of the gift-list:

> . . . from Pulliya's house, 2 males (Pulliyani, Ašarta), 3 boys (Aparkammi, Iriyatti, Hapilu), 4 women (Tešmu, Zidandu, Ašakkummila, Huliyašuhani), 3 girls (Kapašanni, Kapurti, Paškuva), 2 old women (Arhuvaši, Tuttuvani) total 14 persons; 4 cattle, 2 donkeys, 2 cows, 1 calf, 1 plowing ox . . . from Hantapi's house in the Antarla, 7.5 (iku) vineyards, 13 houses, 30 men, 18 boys, 4 infant boys, 35 old women . . . total 110 [persons]. Among the servants, 2 artisans, 2 cooks, 1 cloth-maker, 1 Hurrian tailor, 1 shoemaker, 1 groom . . . 22 cattle, 158 sheep, 2 horses, 3 mules . . . The Great King Arnuvanda, the Great Queen Ašmunikal and the honourable Prince Tuthalia took [these things] and gave them to their servant, the priestess Kuvatalla, as a gift. In the future they will not demand anything back from her sons and grandsons. The promise of the Sovereign King, the Great King Arnuvanda and his wife Ašmunikal is of iron. It cannot be undone or broken. Anyone trying to change it shall lose his head.[9]

The high priestess Kuvatalla must have enjoyed quite a life-style.

WOMEN OF STONE AND CLAY AND BRONZE

⊙⊙⊙⊙⊙⊙⊙⊙⊙⊙⊙⊙⊙

The Mother of us all,
The oldest of all,
Hard,
Splendid as rock

Whatever there is that is of the land
it is she
who nourishes it,
it is the Earth
that I sing

Whoever you are,
howsoever you come
across her sacred ground
you of the sea
you that fly,
it is she
who nourishes you
she,
out of her treasures
Beautiful children
beautiful harvests
are achieved from you
The giving of life itself,
the taking of it back
to or from
any man
are yours . . .

Homeric Hymn to the Earth (Ge)[1]

One of the earliest pieces of figurative sculpture that we have from Sparta is of a woman. She is quite possibly some kind of a Mother Goddess, carved out of stone by a society that had barely discovered how to make pots, or how to work metal. The explicit social, political and cultural muscle of women in this distant past is almost impossible to gauge. But archaeological finds like this – sturdy, glowering, curvy life-givers – surely indicate how powerful early societies *thought* women to be.

Female figures and figurines turn up throughout the pre-historic levels of the Aegean. Many have been buried in domestic rubbish pits, others are found in graves, sometimes singly, sometimes a dozen or so clustered together. Some have been deliberately violated – often the neck has been neatly snapped and then the figure buried. An act of aggression and disrespect? Possibly not. Breaking a man-made object, particularly an anthropomorphic figure, in pre-history may well have been a recognition of its power, or a way of marking its journey on to another world: an act not of vandalism, but of devotion. Some of the female figurines have been taken to places of great religious significance – sanctuaries, the peaks of mountains, the bowels of caves – to be offered up as gifts to long-forgotten divinities.

There are thousands and thousands of these female figurines, of all shapes and sizes. Some are gloriously fat with elephantine thighs, some attenuated, angular and stringy. They start appearing around 29,000 BC (although some experts are more conservative, and put the date at 25,000 BC). They are most prolific in Greece and the Eastern Mediterranean from 8000 to 3500 BC. Whether curvaceous or cubist, whether designed to stand up or lie down, only a tiny fraction of the neolithic figures are distinctly male.[2] In the Cyclades, up until 2500 BC, huge numbers of female figurines continue to be produced.[3] Ultraviolet analysis of the stone surface shows that many of these were decorated with cinnabar and azurite – the red and blue tracing hair, jewellery, facial features, slashed or spotted tattoos, and in one startling instance single eyes pricked all over the effigy's face and thigh.[4]

Most of these little women who would watch with silent eyes the daily lives of their makers are (particularly those from the Cycladic islands) overtly sexualised. In a number the predominant incised decoration is a stark, pubic triangle and two simple breasts. These all-important marks of gender have simply been gouged out of the stone or terracotta. One woman is from Skoura in Lakonia, Helen's locale. She is about the size and shape of an average loaf of bread, a rather lumpen, amorphous clay creature, inanimate apart from the fingers of one hand which are spread wide, pointing directly down to her sex organs.[5]

For a number of years these female figurines, these 'mother-goddesses', were side-lined. Early collectors described them as 'barbaric' and 'repulsively ugly'. The simple, primitive forms could not compete with highly finished 'classical' Greek art and in the 19th century AD were typically thought suitable for academic rather than public interest. Today in the museums of Serbia, Croatia and Romania the odd lonely figurine can still be found on display in a back room with a ragbag of other pre-historic artefacts. No clue as to its provenance, no label hazarding a guess as to what it might be; here such figurines are still second-class citizens. Many more languish in storerooms, unstudied and half-forgotten.

It is little surprise though that in some quarters these elegant Henry Moore prototypes have become rather fashionable. When I go to Athens, I always make a bee-line for the Goulandris and Benaki Museums in a modish, up-market district, the Kolonaki. The Benaki in particular has an elegant mish-mash of artefacts spanning the period from pre-history to the Greek War of Independence. Emanuel Benakis made his money in the Nile cotton trade, appropriate credentials for a collection that itself would have started off life as a trade-commodity, travelling back and forth across the Eastern Mediterranean.

One comes into the museums out of the glare and urgency of the heart-stoppingly busy highway, the Vasilissis Sofias. The figurines are displayed in a respectful half-light. Children stop chattering; tourists stare long and hard at the stone women, trying to make some sense of them. Of course the purpose of these sexually blunt female figures has had scholars scratching their heads for decades. The problem is that where archaeological context is relatively sparse, the evidence can be manipulated to fit almost any theory. These charismatic effigies are no exception. Because the figures represent women – from a time when we cannot hear people's voices and rarely find their bones – they tempt one into an emotional reaction, into the hope that these mute creatures, tenderly shaped out of stone or clay or bone or ivory, offer us direct contact with a distant past.

But in fact there are as many different ways to interpret these figurines as they themselves have different body shapes. Although the mistake has been made in the past, it would be over-simplistic to assume that they have a constant, uniform meaning. There are thousands upon thousands of these viragos and one has to take into consideration the different contexts in which they were found and how they span the millennia. Talk to a roomful of archaeologists and the ideas come thick and fast; perhaps they were used for business as contractual tokens, as birth aids or educational tools, symbols of a rite of passage that mirrored the most extreme passage of all, birth.

Were they perhaps pre-historic portraits, images of longed-for babies, toys to satisfy the sexual and ludic appetites of the dead, or simply visual art representing a population that was apparently inhabited not just by men and women, but also by hermaphrodites and humans of no sex; were they, some even posit, treasured, pornographic playthings?[6]

Archaeologists rarely agree, but, over time, a consensus of sorts has emerged. Whatever their function, these forms have authority. They are fecund, uberous creations whose power rests primarily in their sex. The figurines represent, in its purest visual form, individual self-awareness. Each is trying to articulate something about the identity of the human race. With these human images comes, for the first time, hard evidence of how populations were using their creative imaginations to make sense of the world around them. And they seem to be making sense of that world primarily in female terms.[7] Whatever their precise purpose, these figurines tell us that Helen's direct and distant ancestors thought, for some reason, that women were the more noteworthy sex, and that it was essential to create images in their honour.

ELEMENTAL HELEN –
SHE-GODS AND
SHE-DEVILS

@@@@@@@@@@@@@@

Olympus let the other women die;
They shall be quiet when the day is done
And have no care to-morrow. Yet for me
There is no rest. The gods are not so kind
To her made half immortal like themselves.

SARAH TEASDALE,
Helen of Troy (1884–1933)

Partly inspired by the discovery of pre-historic female figurines, a traditional thesis of early human societies developed, in which God was a woman. This understanding of how pre-historic populations viewed and constructed their world is rather neat and goes on the following lines: a single supernatural mother – often thought to be Mother Earth or Mother Nature – was originally worshipped across the Eastern Mediterranean; some even argue, across the globe. This notion was passionately presented by archaeologists, historians and scientists of the late 19th and early 20th centuries. The Mother Earth theory was charismatic in its time, because it buttressed the idea that a society led (spiritually or politically) by women, was an 'early' form of humanity. A matriarchal, primitive world overseen by Mother Earth was the logical starting point for a race that was destined for greater, more progressive, and more manly things.

What people thought (and a number still think) was that at some point – perhaps with the discovery of bronze technology and the huge developmental leap which that discovery supported, perhaps with the invasion of nomads from the north – female authority gave way to male drive. The Stone Age came to its end, the Bronze Age started, and in the Aegean people set off on a spiritual path that led away from their omnipotent

Mothers and ended up with the creation of the Olympian pantheon, headed by a pushy, 'dark-browed'[1] Zeus.

It is not without irony that similar arguments, although with a very different rationale, have also been employed by 20th- and 21st-century feminists who see early pre-history as the domain of a She-God. From this viewpoint, the divine mother presided over a golden age of female superiority 'in the bedroom and the boardroom', in the streets and in sanctuaries. So (the arguments go) this was a world of theacracy, gynarchy and matriarchy, the world's natural state — women in control — realised and made manifest by its visionary and sensible early inhabitants. Men were not absent but they were acquiescent.

There are scholars who believe that Helen herself was one of these she-gods, perhaps *the* She-God. They argue that one all-embracing Mother Goddess, a goddess closely associated with the powers of nature, was worshipped up until the moment the invaders from the north came and disrupted the native inhabitants of mainland Greece. Many have pointed out that Helen's association with sex and rape and the natural world makes her the perfect candidate for a personification of this spirit. But I am not entirely convinced. When I look at the range of female figurines made and the variety of contexts in which they were found, I am struck not just by their similarities but by their differences. I do not see an omnipotent She-God, the pre-historic equivalent of Allah or Yahweh, without his manhood and his beard, the sole recipient of Stone Age and Early Bronze Age devotion. To my mind, it is a mistake to project our monotheistic world-view onto the distant past. What may well have been the case is that that gorgeous, piercing, flighty, invisible force — life — was thought of as female by the pre-historic and ancient worlds. And that this female spirit was recognised at every turn. As soon as literature arrives we hear tell of this life-spirit, Gaia — the female power that breathes life into humans and immortals.[2]

⊕⊕⊕⊕⊕

Much of the Bronze Age Eastern Mediterranean world was animist, believing that *animae*, 'life-forces', abounded, that they existed in spirit form. If it is accepted that the spirit of life itself was thought to be female then, in the Aegean Bronze Age, one has to imagine that the spirit in an ear of wheat, in the heavy olive bough laden with fruit, and in the ripening grape that darkens from electric green to blood-red, is female. On Bronze Age rings and seal-stones there are depictions of women gathering up branches and baskets of fruit and leaves while some kind of intense religious ceremony goes on – perhaps these were women tending to their agricultural sisters, in the earth, looking after their own.

The visual and oral evidence we have for the Bronze Age – figurines, storage jars, stories (including Helen's), seal-stones, frescoes, hymns – suggest that for most of pre-history, the majority of these spirits associated with the fundamentals of life, food, sun, wind, rain, and fire, were indeed female. They might have been 'virtual' women, but they were still feminine forces on whom life depended, beings who were wooed with a constant passion.

In the ancient world the language used to describe nature's larder was highly charged and overtly sexualised. Agriculture was thought to be the love-child of the *hieros gamos*, the sacred mating of heaven and earth. Desire for fertility and sexual desire were intimately linked. Much of the worship owed to Helen is appropriate for the worship of some kind of a nature divinity. The iconography of the Bronze Age suggests it was the job of the high priestess and her acolytes to summon all her resources to keep the earth fecund and responsive.

There is no doubt that Helen is consistently associated with natural abundance and the forces of nature. Standing up on Therapne in Sparta, surveying the town below in April or May, one might just have been able to catch a glimpse of an all-female procession, worshipping Helen in a pastoral ritual: the young girls of the town carrying boughs and branches and weaving wreaths out of the *hyakinthos* – almost certainly the *Orchis quadripunctata*[3] – a delicate, native plant that flowers in late spring. One festival is called the *Heleneia*, one the *Helenephoria* – in the latter 'holy things, beyond words' (perhaps Helen's flower *Helenium*) are carried in baskets.[4] It is unclear whether or not these two rituals were distinct but almost certain that they were designed to honour Helen and to celebrate the exuberance of the spring and of natural beauty.[5]

Helen's affiliation with the elements and natural features is further attested by a whole archipelago of islands that claim a connection with her. There is Pharos off the northern coast of Egypt near Memphis, also referred to as Helen's Island, where Helen was said to have planted seeds of her own flower to ward off an infestation of snakes.[6] At Cos, Plutarch tells us in his *Life of Solon*[7] that she threw a golden tripod into the sea which was then fished out and fought over by fishermen, until the Delphic Oracle (no less) stepped in to arbitrate. The Greek writer Pausanias offers other possibilities – Helen, he relates, married Achilles once they were both dead[8] (Achilles was known on Crete as *pemptos*, 'No. 5', because he was Helen's fifth husband) and lived with him for an eternity on the legendary 'White Island',[9] part of the Elysian Fields. For some this conjured up an image of a sublime union of the perfect hero and the perfect woman, but for others, Helen's time in the land of the blest was an excuse for a bawdy romp.

Lucian of Samosata, writing in the mid-2nd century AD, claims in his comic burlesque the *True Story* to have seen Helen making love to the finest specimens here until she is willingly abducted from the island by Cinyras, the son of Scintharus — '*a tall handsome lad, [who] had long been in love with Helen, and it was no great secret that she herself was madly enamoured of the boy*'. Menelaus, not wishing to be cuckolded yet again, raises a hue and cry. Helen's lover's ship is overtaken and secured with a 'hawser of roses'. Cinyras and his accomplices are bound together by their penises and then sent off '*to the place of the wicked*'.[10] Helen, crying and hanging her head in shame, gets away with a mild scolding.

Pausanias, who had ethnographic interests, writes of Helen's gruesome, vegetative connection with the island of Rhodes. This, he says, is what the Rhodian islanders told him of Helen. After Menelaus' death, Helen was exiled by Nikostratos and Megapenthes.[11] Rejected and homeless, the queen sought refuge with aristocratic allies on Rhodes. It was, as it transpired, a bleak choice. Polyxo, queen of the island, and an embittered Trojan war-widow, blamed Helen for her husband Tlepolemos' death. Determined to wreak her vengeance, Polyxo feigns friendship and hospitality. While Helen bathes in the sea the widow queen orders her servants to dress up as Furies. These imposters taunt and terrify the aged Helen and then hang her on a tree — watching and waiting until her body has stopped twitching, until the last breath has been squeezed out of a woman who mothered a generation of orphans. The most womanly of women murdered by her own kind.

But — ever irrepressible — Helen's story does not end there. Pausanias goes on to tell us that this gruesome murder is, paradoxically, why the Rhodian islanders (delighted by the fact that the Trojan Wars sapped the energy and resources of eastern raiders) honour Helen as Helen Dendritis, 'Helen of the Trees', with her own 'Sanctuary of the Trees'.

The fact that Helen was worshipped on Rhodes as Helen Dendritis could be proof that she was, after all, a vegetation goddess — a deity with no real connection to the lived, political events of the Late Bronze Age. Fertility symbols were hung in trees in Greece. Maybe *Eleni* was one of them. But the evidence from Rhodes has a twist. Built into the floor of a Christian church on the island was a long-overlooked stone inscription made in the 2nd century BC. This stone slab — now rescued and held by the Copenhagen National Museum[12] — is densely covered in close, careful script. Each line details the dedications at Lindos to the Temple of Athena. And here carved into the surface are the names of Helen and Menelaus. Menelaus bestows the helmet he tore off Paris on the plains of Troy, Helen offers up a pair of bracelets.[13] On Rhodes Helen is remembered both as a tree-spirit and as a distinguished visitor – a queen rich and devout enough to leave jewels for the gods of Mount Olympus.

It is on Rhodes that we meet the gloriously complicated Helen face to face. The Rhodians whom Pausanias met must have called their tree-spirit Helen Dendritis to distinguish her from Helen of Sparta – and yet Helen of Sparta was also said to have visited the island. So here on Rhodes we have two distinct Helens. Distinct but complementary. The life-cycle of each woman reflects the other. Both are forces of nature bringing life and death. Both are important, both are gravid and desirable. Both are beautiful, both demand homage. Perhaps men and women wanted to try to understand the power of the earth and the meaning of sex – and via stories of the colourful, globe-trotting inhabitants of pre-history they could explore these ideas. In the cast-list of the Age of Heroes – the Late Bronze Age elite – they found a human character big enough to take on some of these fundamental questions.

What links the divinity worshipped on Rhodes and the rich site of Therapne and the spirit that runs through bathers' fingers as they swim in Helen's Baths with the gleaming Spartan queen of the epics, is an unimpeached sense of the power of the female. This is a belief that seems to have been present throughout much of the Bronze Age. It was an idea firmly challenged by the establishment of the Olympian pantheon controlled by the entirely masculine Zeus. The tide had turned, as the poet Hesiod encapsulates so baldly in his revisionist mythological poem *Theogony* (describing how Zeus's creation of women punished man for Prometheus' theft of fire from the gods):

> *the deadly race and tribe of women who live amongst mortal men to their*
> *great trouble, no helpmeets in hateful poverty, but only in wealth . . .*
> *Zeus who thunders on high made women to be an evil to mortal men,*
> *with a nature to do evil.*[14]

❀❀❀❀❀

For some, a primordial Helen represents the greatest fire of them all – the sun. They argue that Helen and her twin brothers, the Dioscuri, could represent something rare in Greek mythology – pre-Hellenic Indo-European mythology. The worship of a sister and twin brothers, related to the all-powerful sun god, goes back to a time even before the Hellenes come to

Greece. Parallel myths surface in the Rig Veda and the folk-songs of Latvia[15] where a number of folk-traditions seem to have survived without being supplanted by the ideas and sentiments of the classical and Christian worlds.[16]

In this context, Helen's abduction by Paris was the equivalent of winter's abduction of summer – an event that also brought with it, each year, deaths and acute hardship. Some Greeks thought that during the winter, and when weather conditions were severe, the sun migrated to Africa.[17] The sun's – Helen's – departure is rarely forgiven.

☙❧☙❧☙❧

So a number of academics do argue (sometimes bullishly, often persuasively, always with great erudition) that Helen herself was either just one female spirit, or even the pre-eminent among such spirits, a queen among divinities who was 'trimmed down to size'[18] to became a fabulously feisty mortal to fit in with the Homeric template. Paris did not fall in love with a woman, but with a faded goddess.

The chronology of this thesis is rather odd. Why, one wonders, would Homer bother to mortalise Helen and immortalise her in verse at the same time? And why would subsequent populations decide to turn her back into a goddess again, as a kind of back-handed compliment to Homer and to his power of imagination? Surely it is more likely that the Homeric Helen represented one of those real flesh-and-blood people who simply seem extraordinary. That the memory of this vibrant, charismatic mortal was conflated with the memory of a vibrant, charismatic nature goddess. Although I do not think that Homer's Helen started out in life as a goddess, it is quite possible that a wildly attractive Lakonian queen was thought of as an appropriate candidate to graft onto an existing belief in sex-goddesses. Perhaps even, in this case, she was someone whose sexual power was indeed so marked that it was presumed by her peers (people who made little distinction between the physical and the spiritual) that she must be some kind of human incarnation of the spirit of fecundity.

Of course, those who argue that Helen was obviously an out-of-date goddess by-pass the possibility that a woman as sensational as Helen – a pivotal, clever, desirable creature – could have existed in the Bronze Age. And that, I think, is a mistake. We are so used to living in civilisations in which women traditionally have little recognition, it is easy to assume that when a spotlight is turned on the female sex the women represented must be extra-special, extra-terrestrial, even, ergo, goddesses. But maybe not. Imagine a world where the greatest and most powerful mystery of all –

the generation of life — clearly, visibly belongs in the domain of women, and then imagine that as a result, flesh-and-blood women are accorded huge, actual, day-by-day respect.

Hold in your mind the image of a world in which the stuff of life, agricultural produce, is thought to emanate from a female spirit. Imagine a landscape where that produce is marshalled and allocated not by men but by women and girls. Suddenly significant, commemorated women stop being unreal, liminal, supernatural oddities, but instead are seen as conscious powerhouses at the centre of society.

So Helen in her lifetime could well have walked the earth, light-footed. And after her death, memories and tales of this incandescent creature kept her spirit alive. Now that she is established as an immortal in the popular imagination, though, she becomes many things in the minds of men — a princess, a queen, a wife, a lover, a whore, a heroine, a star, a goddess of sex. And whatever her guises there is one constant — she is for ever Helen — '*Eleni*', the shining one.

ROYAL PURPLE –
THE COLOUR OF
CONGEALED BLOOD

⊚⊚⊚⊚⊚⊚⊚⊚⊚⊚⊚⊚

. . . wave after wave of purple, precious as silver . . .

AESCHYLUS, *Agamemnon* 959–60[1]

One of Helen's landfalls on her journey home from Troy was Matala.[2] For any boat travelling across the Eastern Mediterranean in the 13th century BC, Matala would have been a convenient, and possibly profitable, staging post. Tucked into its own westerly facing bay on Crete's south coast, perfectly placed to enjoy exquisite sunsets every night, Matala today is the home of a slightly alternative, international crowd – a new age community lived in the caves here until they were outlawed in the 1970s.[3]

Two and a half miles along the coast from Matala is the archaeological site of Kommos. I have retraced the boat journey that would have been made here from Troy. On arrival, first sailing and then rowing, the galley would have passed the extraordinary rock formation of this particular segment of the coastline – past bays that welcome like cupped hands, where layers of sandstone are reminiscent, from the water, of whipped meringue. Excavations only began at Kommos in 1976, but quickly it became clear that this was a sizeable Bronze Age port – perhaps servicing the palatial complex of Phaistos which lies 6 km inland.[4] The connection made between Helen and this stretch of the Cretan coast is fitting. Late Bronze Age traders and diplomats, aristocrats and the itinerant labourers of the sea would indeed have stopped off here.

And before they reached Kommos itself, its smell would have come out to meet them, because this was a centre of production for the colour purple – one of the most luxurious commodities of the ancient world. The manufacture of this colour of status is a messy business. It involves the harvest, dismemberment and then boiling – sometimes in urine – of a carnivorous sea-snail called the murex.

In Kommos many of these pre-historic sea-snails have been found with tiny, perfect holes bored into the shells – evidence that during factory farming they have turned cannibal, attacking their own kind to get food. Production here was on a substantial scale, providing dye for an international market.[5] A newcomer to Kommos would have been greeted by men and women with livid arms, dyed up to the shoulders with the murex's gift to humanity. Pliny described dye from the murex as being the colour of congealed blood.

While investigating the mechanics of Bronze Age trading systems, I have gone diving close to Kommos for these sea-snails. The trick is to lever oneself off the rocks 10 feet (3 m) or so below the surface and not to become a pin-cushion for sea-urchins in the process. Today sea-snails are fairly scarce, but local fishermen recount that forty years ago, when they were boys, the murex carpeted the sea-shore. With such a rich natural resource, Kommos would have been on the mental map of both traders and their clients – the great royal houses of the Eastern Mediterranean.[6] In the Late Bronze Age, in Hittite, Egyptian and Mycenaean societies, purple was the colour of royalty. Linear B tablets may provide one of our first records of the concept of Royal Purple, on a tablet which describes what seem to be textiles as *porphyreos*, 'of the colour purple', and *wanakteros*, 'royal, kingly'.[7] A concept which has not faded over three and half thousand years.

Even if our Bronze Age Helen never actually visited Kommos, she would, doubtless, have known of the place. Aristocratic women in both Mycenaean and Anatolian cultures would have been expected to weave, and the finest would have woven purple cloth. Homer relates that at Troy, Helen spent the bulk of her time in her apartments weaving a giant piece of cloth. Considering it would have taken 12,000 murex to produce enough dye to colour the hem of a single garment, Helen's ten-year oeuvre – her vast porphyry tapestry 'the colour of death' – would have kept the delivery boys from these centres of purple production very busy. So Helen sits and weaves. Murex shells used to create purple dye[8] have been found in some numbers around Troy, 10 kilos in one workshop.[10] Hittite tablets show that the city was famous for its textile production. There is no question that aristocratic women in this world would have sat and produced cloth. The intricate and delicate pieces they made might end up as gifts for visiting diplomats, might be worn in grand public ceremonies or might perhaps be offered to the gods, used to dress cult statues ceremonially. Hand-woven, pieces like this could take years to produce. Only the nobility devoted so many hours to so rarefied an activity. Homer envisages her:

> *weaving a growing web, a dark red folding robe,*
> *working into the weft the endless bloody struggles*
> *stallion-breaking Trojans and Argives armed in bronze*
> *had suffered all for her at the god of battle's hands.*[10]

Some see these lines as a metaphor for poetry — in which case Helen herself is the poet, pulling together the threads of men's lives, creating her own story, building an epic to be passed on to future generations. In a sense she (not Homer) is the bard, a woman fabricating the world around her.

It is significant that Helen's great tapestry is purple, a colour associated in the ancient world with power and death. Around her men are supporting unspeakable agonies and Helen sits and weaves the tales of their woe. Perhaps Homer is also trying to associate Helen with the great commodities of pre-literate society, a rich visual image and a story that lasts in popular memory. Pictures are articulate in the absence of literature. The most beautiful woman in the world is the child of, and breeds, both.

MYTH, HISTORY AND HISTORIA

@@@@@@@@@@@@@@

My name can be in many places: my person can only be in one.

EURIPIDES, *Helen*[1]

In the introduction to this book I made it clear that this was an *historia* – a mesh of inquiry, observation, analysis and myth. It has been, I hope, a valid approach: Helen herself is a conglomerate, an accretion of stories and histories. I have relied on four types of source: archaeological, topographical, historical and mythological. I have linked these with an attempt to understand Helen physically, by travelling through the landscape once inhabited by Bronze Age women and experiencing Helen in antiquity as the ancients would have done – exploring the worship of Helen, Helen on stage, Helen in art and politics.

The underpinning narrative has been provided by Homer, who in turn used myth-stories as inspiration.[2] Homer was not a contemporary of the Trojan War; in one sense, all he writes of Helen is imaginary. Helen would have died at least five hundred years before Homer lived – his stories were new versions of old memories, old mythologies.[3] Homer composed at a critical time. He lived on a fault-line in the development of European literature: growing up with the old techniques of oral poetry, growing into the new techniques of literacy.[4] My aim has been not simply to prove or disprove the historical accuracy of these epic sagas. Seeking to determine the historicity of myths word for word is a diverting but complicated exercise. Myths and stories are plastic creations – words and images from one world that can be moulded and used to colour another. The aim of the book has not been to set myth and reality up against each other – but to see why the two can be such happy bed-fellows, why some characters inhabit both worlds so confidently. They all laughed at Schliemann when he went in search of Homer's great war story, but then he found Troy, and ever since the world has had to think twice before it sneers.

It is worth looking in a little more detail at what 'myth' means. For the ancient Greeks, myths, '*muthoi*', were not a distinct, fantastical genre. We have chosen to view them as such, but much in Greek mythology emanated from the Mediterranean world's real beliefs, real history and actual life-experience. In a world before writing, '*muthoi*', oral traditions, meant 'things that were spoken – the transfer of information', and were a key way that knowledge was shared.[5]

At the same time, the purpose of the myth-merchant, the storyteller, was to hold his or her audience rapt and to transmit social and political messages, to explore man's place in the world, to dissect the human condition. Helen found in Homer the most brilliant of biographers. A man who dealt with the exigencies and triumphs of human nature – a man who tells us truths of all degrees. With such a recorded beginning, Helen's life was destined, down the centuries, to become as saleable as a modern-day icon's – a heady mix of headlines, strong visual images and bathos. She has been, and always will be, good box office. She might have died three and a half thousand years ago; she is unlikely to lose her relevance.

ABBREVIATIONS

⚬⚬⚬⚬⚬⚬⚬⚬⚬

The following abbreviations have been used in the text and endnotes:

BM British Museum

CMS *Corpus der Minoischen und Mykenischen Siegel*

CTH *Catalogue des textes hittites* (Paris: E. Laroche, 1971)

EA *The El-Amarna Letters*

EGF *Epicorum Graecorum Fragmenta* (Göttingen: M. Davies, 1988)

FrGrH *Fragmente Griechischen Historiker*, ed. F. Jacoby

I.G.M.E. Greek Institute of Geology and Mineral Exploration

KBo *Keilschrifttexte aus Boghazköi* (Leipzig and Berlin)

KUB *Keilschrifturkunden aus Boghazköi* (Berlin)

LBA Late Bronze Age

LCL Loeb Classical Library

LH Late Helladic

LIMC *Lexicon Iconographicum Mythologiae Classicae*

LM Late Minoan

MM Middle Minoan or Mycenae Archaeological Museum

NMA National Archaeological Museum, Athens

PMG *Poetae Melici Graeci* (Oxford: D. Page, 1962)

PMGF *Poetarum Melicorum Graecorum Fragmenta* (Oxford: M. Davies, 1991)

P.Oxy. *The Oxyrhynchus Papyri*

PRU IV *Le Palais Royal d'Ugarit IV (Mission de Ras Shamra Tome IX)* (Paris; J. Nougayrol, 1956)

RS Tablets from Ras Shamra

STC Short-Title Catalogue

NOTES

FOREWORD AND ACKNOWLEDGEMENTS

1 An epithet enthusiastically employed in the 19th century AD by writers such as H. Rider Haggard, Andrew Lang and Oscar Wilde.
2 An approach, I note, also embraced by Meagher (2002).
3 The Greeks were only thus called when populations from Italy encountered a tribe from the Balkan peninsula called the 'Graikoi'. The Italian aliens gave these people a collective name 'Graeci'. In the classical period the Greeks called themselves Hellenes.
4 See Latacz (2004), 133–4 for a useful summary.

INTRODUCTION

1 Labels noted during a site visit in 2002.
2 The stele can be read back to front, although in both readings it is Helen's face that melts Menelaus. Because the warrior appears taller and shaggier on one side, a sensible interpretation is that this is Menelaus after ten years on the Trojan plain: see Pomeroy (2002), 116–17.
3 Marlowe, *Tamburlaine*, Part 2, Act II, Scene 4, lines 87–8.
4 See Fragment 1 of the *Cypria*: '*Once upon a time the countless tribes [of mortals thronging about weighed down] the broad surface of the deep-bosomed earth. And Zeus, seeing this, took pity, and in his cunning mind he devised a plan to lighten the burden caused by mankind from the face of the all-nourishing earth, by fanning into flame the great strife that was the Trojan War, in order to alleviate the earth's burden by means of the death of men. So it was that the heroes were killed in battle at Troy and the will of Zeus was accomplished.*' Trans. M. Davies (1989), 33.
5 Hesiod, *Works and Days* 159–65. Trans. H.G. Evelyn-White.
6 Sappho, fragment 16 and Hesiod, *Catalogues of Women and Eoiae* 68.
7 West (1975), 2.
8 Southern Italy and Sicily.
9 The story is told in Cicero, *On Invention* 2.1–3 and Pliny the Elder, *Natural History* 35.64–6. Cicero sets the story in Croton, Pliny in Agrigentum.
10 François-André Vincent, *Zeuxis et les filles de Crotone*. Paris, Louvre INV.8543. The date of the painting is disputed: 1789–91. There are two versions by Vincent painted around the same time.
11 For comprehensive catalogues of Helen in ancient iconography, see Ghali-Kahil (1955) and the *Lexicon Iconographicum Mythologiae Classicae*, Vol. IV, nos. 1 and 2 (henceforth *LIMC*).
12 *Iliad* 6.357–8. This translation is taken from Austin (1994), 1. All subsequent extracts of Homer's *Iliad* and *Odyssey* are taken from the translations by Robert Fagles, with

his line references, unless otherwise stated. A Greek line reference from the Loeb Classical Library [LCL] editions of Homer will also be given. In this instance the LCL reference is [LCL 6.357–8].

13 A Semitic adaptation of the Phoenician script.

14 An *epos* (from which 'epic' derives) is a long narrative poem that tells the tales of heroes. The *epos* was originally composed for oral recital.

15 See Hesiod, *Works and Days* 159.

16 See, for example, Pausanias 3.22.9.

17 There were thought to be two generations of giants called Cyclopes. The first were loyal handymen to the gods on Mount Olympus, forging, for example, Zeus' thunderbolts. Odysseus meets the second in the form of Polyphemus during his long voyage home from Troy.

18 Descriptions of the relic indicate that the bone was probably the scapula of a mammoth. See Mayor (2000), in particular Chapter 3, and *passim*.

19 For example, see *Iliad* 5.336–43 [LCL 5.302–8].

20 Also those of Hesiod.

21 At the time of writing, the papyrology department at Oxford University, using infrared technology with the help of Brigham Young University, Provo, Utah, have announced the potential to trace 'lost' texts on pieces of Egyptian papyrus.

22 See Davies (1989), 32. Ancient tradition credited Homer or a man called Stasinus with authorship of the *Cypria*. Some even said that Homer had given the epic to his son-in-law Stasinus in lieu of a dowry for his daughter.

23 Cleopatra is the other. There are of course parallels between the appeal of both women. See, for example, Lucan's *Civil War* 10.59–62: 'Cleopatra, the shame of Egypt, the fatal Fury of Latium, whose unchastity cost Rome dear. As the dangerous beauty of the Spartan queen overthrew Argos and Troy town, in like measure Cleopatra fanned the frenzy of Italy.' Trans. J.D. Duff. Both Cleopatra and Helen are described as *Erinyes* – 'Furies' – Helen, for example, in Virgil, *Aeneid* 2.573.

24 Suetonius, *Nero* 38; Tacitus, *Annals* 15.39

25 See Foreville (1952), 198, 209.

26 Caxton *STC* [Short-Title Catalogue] 15375. '*The Recuyell*' roughly translates as a 'Collection of Trojan Histories'. It was begun by Caxton in March 1469, and actually printed for the first time in 1474 or 1475 at Bruges. It was a translation of a French work by Raoul Lefevre, the *Recueil des histoires de Troie*. A copy of Caxton's work, now in the Huntingdon Library in San Marino, California, was owned by Elizabeth Woodville, the wife of King Edward IV. For more details, see Blake (1976) and Painter (1976).

27 Euripides, *Helen* 22. Trans. R. Lattimore.

28 An opinion formed from the extant evidence. Fuller, more eloquent papyri may have been written in Late Bronze Age Greece and subsequently (although perhaps temporarily) lost.

29 Thanks to Silvan Kosak for advice on this matter, and for pointing out that as the pieces are often so fragmentary, this is a task that will by definition, be laborious and lengthy.

30 On medieval nuns and Ovid's *Heroides*, see M.W. Labarge (1986) *Women in Medieval Life* (Harmondsworth: Penguin), 220. For extant examples of homoerotic poetry from convents see J. Boswell (1980) *Christianity, Social Tolerance and Homosexuality: Gay People in*

Western Europe from the Beginning of the Christian Era to the Fourteenth Century (Chicago, IL: University of Chicago Press), 220–1.

31 See Maguire (forthcoming) *Shakespeare's Names.* Thank you to Dr Maguire for a preview.

32 See Jean-Luis Backé's essay in Brunel (1992), 522.

33 *La Belle Hélène* premiered on 17 December 1864, marking, so Saint-Saëns wrote, 'the collapse of good taste'.

34 J. W. von Goethe, *Maxims and Reflections.* Trans. E. Stopp (1998), 113–4 (London: Penguin). Goethe's personal correspondence indicates he spent many years struggling with the notion of Helen. In one letter of 1831 he writes that he carried Helen's story around with him as an 'inner fable'.

35 Thanks to Roman Roth for this example, from his forthcoming article on 'Myth and Female Identity in North Etruscan Burials of the Hellenistic Period: A Closer Look at the Urn of *velia cerinei* from Castiglioncello', in *Proceedings of the Sixth Conference of Italian Archaeology (Supplement to Bulletin Antieke Beschavingen).*

36 *Odyssey* 4.162 [LCL 4.145].

37 Euripides, *Andromache* 628.

38 Lycophron, *Alexandra* 850–1. Trans. G.W. Mair. This theme – Helen's degeneracy proven by her lack of male offspring – is picked up by a number of Elizabethan writers.

39 Shakespeare, *The Rape of Lucrece* 1471–7.

40 *Eidolon* gives us our word 'idol'.

41 As stated in the Foreword, Homer describes the Greek peoples as the Achaeans, the Danaans and the Argives.

42 For discussion of the possible dates for the end of Troy VI, see Mountjoy (1999).

CHAPTER ONE

A Dangerous Landscape

1 Homer, *Iliad* 13.20–4 [LCL 13.17–19].

2 The ancient Greeks described the island as '*kalliste*' (the most beautiful). The island's Greek name is Thira or Thera. It was renamed Santorini by conquering Venetians in the 13th century AD.

3 Dating of the eruption of Thera ranges from 1625 to 1550 BC depending on methodology. For a good summary of debates around the issue see Wiener (2003).

4 Forsyth (1997), 103. For another good overall summary of the data on the Theran eruption, see Manning (1999).

5 Forsyth (1997), 113ff.

6 See Minoura *et al.* (2000).

7 See Fitton (1995), 125ff.

8 Keftiu seems to be the name given to Bronze Age Cretans on the wall paintings of the tomb of Rekhmire in Egyptian Thebes.

9 For the impact of migration on disease in general see Arnott (2005a).

10 There are many ways of interpreting the interface between Minoans and Mycenaeans from the 16th to the 12th centuries BC. See Bibliography for a number of articles on the subject.

11 For 'Great King' epithets, see the Alakšandu treaty (*CTH* 76); the treaty between Hattusili III of Hatti and Rameses II of Egypt (*CTH* 91); the letter from Queen Naptera of Egypt to Queen Puduhepa of Hatti (*CTH* 167); the letter from Rameses II of Egypt to Queen Puduhepa of Hatti (*CTH* 158); the letter from Hattusili III of Hatti to Kadashman-Enlil II of Babylon (*CTH* 172); and the letter from Uhri-Teshshup (?) of Hatti to Adad-nirari I of Assyria (*CTH* 171). All examples, with translations, in Beckman (1996).

12 See Latacz (2004), 145.

13 Some of these earthquakes, it is estimated, must have measured up to 6.2 on the Richter scale. For 13th-century BC 'storms' see Nur (1998), 140. For comet impact, see Masse (1998), 53.

14 See Sampson (1996), 114.

15 In one potter's workshop at Gouves, close to the palatial complex of Knossos on Crete, a potter's tools have all been flung in the same direction, and the floor covered in sedimentary material. See Vallianou (1996).

16 Papadopoulos (1996).

CHAPTER TWO

A Rape, a Birth

1 The *Cypria*, fragment 8, has Nemesis as Helen's mother.

2 Euripides, *Helen* 212–18. Trans. R. Lattimore.

3 This mosaic can now be found in the Kuklia Museum in Paphos, from where it was stolen in 1980. It dates from the 2nd/3rd centuries AD. See *LIMC*, no. 42.

4 The stele in the Argos Museum is a Roman copy of a Greek original from the 6th or 5th century BC. This design was much copied; one version is on display in the British Museum: GR 2199.

5 Painted for Duke Alfonso d'Este of Ferrara and then sent to the French court – the original is now lost.

6 When the painting was given to the National Gallery by the Duke of Northumberland in 1838 the duke wrote a letter stating that it should not be displayed publicly. It is now on view: G1868.

7 Leonardo started a painting in 1505, but although many copies of it were made, the original is now lost.

8 *c.* 1598–1600.

9 Research trip 2003.

10 On the few Late Bronze Age frescoes that have survived, birds, particularly doves and swallows, flit across the painted surface alongside religious iconography.

11 On the 'egg' tradition of Helen's birth, see, for example, Euripides, *Helen* 257–9 and Pausanias 3.16.1; also Gantz (1993), 320–1. The First Vatican Mythographer (VM I 204) introduces a notion that two eggs were hatched, one containing Castor and Pollux, one with Helen and Clytemnestra.

12 Who, despite their mixed paternity, all came to be born in egg-shells.

13 Ancient sources come up with all possible permutations of paternity in relation to

Clytemnestra, Castor, Helen and Pollux. For a summary see Deacy and Pierce (1997), 85.

14 Apollodorus, *The Library* 3.117.

15 Thanks to Peter Warren for his help with LBA plant identification.

16 Lucian, *Judgement of the Goddesses* 14 (2nd century AD). Trans. A.M. Harmon.

17 Hera's typical epithet is 'white-armed': see, for example, Homer, *Iliad* 24.66 [LCL 24.55]. In the Louvre papyrus of Alcman's *Partheneion* (*PMGF* 1), Hagesichora's face is described as 'silver': on the use of this term to denote whiteness, see Hutchinson (2001), 89, n. 55.

18 See B.M. Thomas (2002) 'Constraints and Contradictions: Whiteness and Femininity in Ancient Greece', in L. Llewellyn-Jones, ed., *Women's Dress in the Ancient Greek World* (Duckworth and the Classical Press of Wales), 5, on the dried remains of white-lead carbonate found in women's graves. Xenophon and Aristophanes, writing in the 4th century BC, also mention the use of white lead, or *psimythion*, as make-up. See Aristophanes, *Ecclesiazusae* 878; Xenophon, *Household Management* 10.2.

19 German school, b. 1704, d. 1761.

20 J.G. Platzer, *The Rape of Helen*. The Wallace Collection: P634.

21 Joseph of Exeter, *Trojan War* 4.175–9. Translated by and reproduced with kind permission of Dr Neil Wright.

22 Pausanias lived and worked *c.* AD 120–180.

23 Pausanias 3.16.1. Trans. W.H.S. Jones and H.A. Ormerod.

24 J. Boardman (2002) *The Archaeology of Nostalgia* (Thames & Hudson).

25 Ten rolls of parchment or papyrus – a *volumen* is a roll in Latin.

26 Peter Brown as quoted in Freeman (1999), 148.

27 West (1975), 13, suggests that Helen's association with eggs may have a connection with our 'egg-honouring' at Easter time.

28 Aphrodite was said to have cursed the Tyndareid women with serial sexual encounters, 'twice-married and thrice-married and abandoners of their husbands', because King Tyndareus failed to honour the goddess with sacrifices. See Stesichorus 23 (*PMG*), and Gantz (1993), 321.

29 Ostrich eggs were in fact a feature of the Late Bronze Age; with their surprisingly durable shells, they were used as deluxe packaging for international trade. The most exquisite of goods would be tucked into the empty shells, and then the eggs sent off on long, dangerous voyages in flimsy boats to tempt other traders across the waters. They were also turned into *rhytons*, lavish vessels used in religious ritual. Thirteen ostrich-egg *rhytons* have been discovered in total (there is one on display in the Mycenae Museum, MM 1684). One particularly fine example from a shaft grave at Mycenae started off life in Nubia; it is richly decorated, with applied dolphins made of faience (an early form of glass): the dolphins' eyes and the curve of their bodies, arcing as they swim, are picked out in green and brown glaze. Faience decorations are also firmly stuck around the neck of the *rhyton*. Other eggs are beautified with silver or gilded bronze. In the 'Room of the Artists' at Mycenae, a tiny gobbet of yellowish material has been analysed and shown to be a mixture of resin and sulphur, which, when heated, becomes a browny-black glue. Creating these fragile works of art – sticking on the delicate, precious little details – would have been a stinking business.

All details from Sakellarakis (1990); also see Karo (1930–3), 238–9.

30 For further discussion see chapter 11.

31 The city's consortium of businesswomen call themselves the 'Daughters of Penelope' (Penelope in Homer's *Odyssey* being Odysseus' loyal and loving wife). These high achievers choose not to be Daughters of Helen.

32 See Wright (2004), 123, 160 and *passim*.

CHAPTER THREE

The Lost Citadel

1 Homer, *Odyssey* 4.79–85 [LCL 4.71–5].

2 New tablets were excavated at Thebes between 1993 and 1995 by Italian and French teams and published by Vassilis L. Aravantinos, Louis Godart and Anna Sacconi.

3 One new Linear B tablet from the Theban royal archive makes the first, tantalising Bronze Age reference to a 'son of Lakedaimon': Gp 227.2. See Aravantinos, Godart and Sacconi (2000) for the first publication of the tablets: reviewed by Palaima (2003).

4 See Catling (1977).

5 See Wright (2004), 123, 160 and *passim*.

6 Thompson (1908/9), 116.

7 The likely date of the foundation of the Menelaion is 700 BC: see Cartledge (1992), 55.

8 Herodotus 6.61.

9 Pausanias 13.9.9; Pindar's *Nemean Ode* 10.56 and *Pythian Ode* 11.62–3 report that the Dioscuri, Castor and Pollux, were buried at Therapne too; cf. Pomeroy (2002), 114.

10 The poet Alcman evokes the 'holy sanctuary of well-fortified Therapnai'. See Calame (1997), 201, n. 346, and Alcman, fragment 14(b).

11 Tryphiodorus, *The Taking of Troy* 520.

12 See Catling (1977), 37–8.

13 Or *kreagra*.

14 Isocrates, *Encomium of Helen* 10.63.

15 Catling (1976), 14.

16 All inscriptions are being re-studied by Professor Tony Spawforth of Newcastle University at the time of writing.

17 See Thompson (1908/9), 124.

18 Thanks to Richard Catling for this suggestion.

19 It is possible that virgins descended, ready, thanks to the perceived support of the spirit of Helen, to engage with Spartan men. See Chapter 11.

20 See *Odyssey* 4, *passim*, and Chapter 32, p. 234.

21 Figures from French (2002), 62 and Wardle and Wardle (1997), 17. As French points out, Knossos dwarfs all of the above, however, covering an area of *c.* 120,000 square feet [11,150 square m].

22 At the time of writing the excavation report for Therapne was still forthcoming. My thanks to Richard Catling and Dr Hector Catling for their help with this material.

23 Catling (1977), 33 and personal correspondence.

24 *ibid.*

25 *Odyssey* 4.80–1 [LCL 4.73–4].

CHAPTER FOUR

The Mycenaeans

1 *Odyssey* 3.344 [LCL 3.305]; *Iliad* 7.207 [LCL 7.180] and 11.52 [LCL 11.46].

2 Aeschylus, *Agamemnon* 909–11.

3 Thanks to Nicola Wardle. See *Inscriptiones Graecae* iv.4.9.7.

4 In fact Schliemann wrote a telegram to the Greek press saying: 'This corpse very much resembles the image which my imagination formed long ago of wide-ruling Agamemnon.'

5 The Bloomsbury group clump together, Sartre breaks convention by signing diagonally, Ginsberg leaves a short poem.

6 Current excavations at Thebes may show that this was in fact one of the most significant and powerful of the Mycenaean territories.

7 Mounts Agios Elias, Zara and Aëtovouno ('Eagle Mount').

8 There are other Mycenaean settlements across the Peloponnese at Argos, Sparta, Pylos, Tiryns, Asine, Kleonai, Midea, Pellana, Orchomenos and Ephyra (Corinth).

9 Tablet 714.1–2.

10 Military, religious and secular affairs alike were all controlled from the citadels. Food and supplies and luxury goods were brought into the palace-centres and then redistributed for subsistence or profit. Here records were kept, written in Linear B script onto soft clay tablets, recording people and possessions down to the last goat, the last jar of olives, the last cup of grain, the last fig. The native population and imported slaves would produce food for the palace and deliver it to the centralised storerooms. Those within the palatial economy would then be given their supplies in return. Villagers in the outlying settlements might be subjected to corvée labour – a hefty tax on human resources. The bean-counters, the scribes of Linear B – a literate elite that some argue were the rulers themselves – by insisting on extra deliveries of food or pressing farmers into military service could control whether or not a family had enough food to survive the winter.

11 See *Odyssey* 4, *passim*.

12 Those on display at Mycenae are replicas; the originals are in the National Archaeological Museum in Athens.

13 Found at the cult centre in Mycenae: MM 2084.

14 From shaft graves, finds dating between 1600 and 1300 BC.

15 Mycenae lady fresco fragment from the House of the High Priest, in the National Archaeological Museum in Athens (NMA 11670).

16 For a discussion of the historicity of Homer, see Latacz (2004), 216–49.

17 Hesiod, *Works and Days* 159.

18 Excavations by the German Archaeological Institute.

19 Iakovidis and French (2003), 22, n. 45.

20 Tablets Aa 701 and 515 from Pylos: see Chadwick (1988), 79. Chadwick also identifies groups of women from other parts of Asia Minor, including Milesians, Knidians, Chians and Lemnians (91).

21 We cannot tell for certain what kind of liberties, if any, the subject population enjoyed. Some from the bottom rung appear to have lived more like medieval bondsmen and women – free, with their own patches of land, but with fixed stringent duties owed to their overlords. In the Near East in the Late Bronze Age, women and children are recorded as serving a period of indentured service – working in bondage to pay back family debts, or to raise a dowry.

22 *Lawiaiai* at Pylos seem to be 'captives' or 'women taken as booty': Chadwick (1988), 83.

23 *c.* 1352 BC.

24 On this discovery, see A.B. Knapp (1992) 'Bronze Age Mediterranean Island Cultures and the Near East, Part 1', *Biblical Archaeologist* 55.2 (June 1992), 52–72, esp. 65–7.

25 A small temple was found at the site in 1955 when the airport was being built, three miles from Amman. Amongst other items, a quantity of Mycenaean pottery was discovered, and when the site was re-excavated in 1966, by the British School of Archaeology in Jerusalem, more Mycenaean artefacts were found. One example, recovered in 1955, is now in the museum in Amman (Amman 6261). It is a *krater*, restored from sherds, featuring a charioteer, and dated to LHIIIA2. Details from Hankey (1967), 128 and 131ff.

26 Details on the Mycenaean trade-horizon taken from Dickinson (1994); French (2002); Harding (1984); Wardle (2001).

27 The Mycenaeans happily appropriated Minoan cultural innovations – writing and inlaid pottery. See Appendix One.

28 Across Mycenaean Greece there were striking affinities. Rigidly efficient bureaucracies ran to the same systems. Administrative records from Pylos, Thebes, Mycenae and Tiryns, for instance, follow an identical pattern – there are the same systems of weights and measures, the same sealings used on casks of olive oil and jars of wine, the same language spoken, the same gods worshipped. Kings, queens and officials, priestesses and priests are distinguished in the same way. Those in power walk through corridors, archives, antechambers and storerooms whose architecture is strikingly isomorphic. Frescoes describing religious ritual and state occasions strongly resemble one another. There are corresponding shrines and sanctuaries, aristocrats across Greece are buried in the same way with the same funerary rituals. Commonalities such as these would have allowed for cultural and political liaison, and, when the time called for it, for consolidated military action.

29 Buried in Grave Circle B at Mycenae.

30 All 'war-wound' references in this paragraph from Arnott (1999), 500–1.

31 Goodison (1989), 106–7.

32 The Mycenaean Warrior Goddess perhaps evolves into Athena, the protecting goddess of Athens. For further discussion see Rehak (1999).

33 Linear B tablets provide close detail of the rigid social categories in Mycenaean society. The *wanax* is the king, or overlord – on occasions *wanax* appears to be used as a divine title: French (2002), 127. A *basileus* was only a chief of craft-groups. A more

important figure is the *lawagetas*. His title seems to mean 'leader of the host' although his exact function is unclear. The 'mayor' is the *koreter*, and the deputy mayor the *prokoreter*, followers are *hequetai* and then there is the *telestas* whose name could mean 'one who brings to fulfilment' in a religious context. Women are also given clear-cut designations, particularly in the religious sphere. There was a strict hierarchy, and it is worth remembering that the word comes from the ancient Greek *hieros*, 'sacred', and *arche*, 'rule'. Religious business is accounted for within palace archives – there is no distinction between 'church' and 'state'. Perhaps ruling in the citadel – particularly if you were a woman – was also thought to bring with it some kind of religious power. Thanks to Lisa Bendall for help with Linear B terminology in this paragraph.

CHAPTER FIVE
The Pre-historic Princess

1   The samples that produce these statistics are, by necessity, small. But for a good summary of latest figures see Arnott (2005a), 21–7.

2   Flowers were such an important harvest that one of the months in the Mycenaean calendar was called *wordewios* – 'the Month of Roses'.

3   *Murex trunculus* seems to have been the species most commonly used in Lakonia. Many thanks to Deborah Ruscillo for her help with *murex* queries.

4   Homeric examples of 'shining cloth' references: see *Iliad* 3.170 [LCL 3.141] and 3.487 [LCL 3.419]; for Linear B reference, see Pylos tablet Fr 1225: Ventris and Chadwick (1973), 482. Clader (1976), 58–9. See also Shelmerdine (1998), 109.

5   Divinities are also often described as shining or radiant. There are two possibilities here: the first is that Helen is being remembered as 'quasi-divine' because she was illustrious in life; the second that she was a mortal character being used as a foil for an idea about divinity. Time and again when we read about Helen, we are told that she glows with a white, bright luminosity. *'And Helen the radiance of women answered Priam'*, says Homer: *Iliad* 3.207 [LCL 3.171]. She wears cloaks that shimmer. It has been suggested that her name derives from an Indo-European root, *svaranā*, meaning 'the starry one' or 'the shining one', which gives us the Greek word *elene* that can mean a torch or light. See Skutsch (1987), 188–93. Homer often talks about Helen as 'Argive Helen'. The obvious interpretation is that she was a representative of the Greeks (also known as the Argives) or a woman whose influence resonated through the Argive plain, but there is also the possibility that the bard is playing on words. In the Greek language *arguros* first appears as a word in Homer's *Iliad*, where it means silver/silvery. For a further discussion of the 'shining' nature of Helen see Clader (1976), 56–64. Internal light was the mark of a goddess, but it was also the mark of one touched by divinity – of a mortal who has experienced or is experiencing an epiphany.

6   *Odyssey* 19.56–63 [LCL 19.53–8].

7   See tablet from Knossos, Sd 401 and Pylos tablet Ta 707. Ventris and Chadwick (1973), 366 and 342 respectively.

8   There is a fine example from the 14th century BC in the Heraklion Museum, Crete.

9   See Rehak (2005), 7.

10 Sakellarakis and Sapouna-Sakellaraki (1997), Vol. 2, 654 ff.

11 See also Chapter 14.

12 The Mycenaean palette was taken straight from the earth – pinks and rich yellows, greens, mauves and rusts ground down from natural clays and oxides. There was one notable exception: 'Egyptian blue'. This valuable tool in the artist's box acquired its evocative name because its production involved a chemical technique masterminded by Egyptians during the Old Kingdom (*c.* 2500–2100 BC). Blocks of this blue pigment were generated by heating frit, a glass-like element, with copper-bearing ore. Manufactured blues were probably a (rich) poor man's lapis lazuli, a trick to make the palace appear to boast, throughout, the precious lapis stone from Afghanistan or Iraq.

13 See Ventris and Chadwick (1973), 131.

14 Hypoplastic lines in dental enamel, see Arnott (2005a).

15 Todd Whitelaw has estimated the population of the Mycenaean settlement at Pylos at around 3,000 individuals, based on house sizes and densities at more extensively investigated Mycenaean sites, in Voutsaki and Killen (2001). Thanks to Todd Whitelaw for his help in discussing population figures for Aegean Late Bronze Age society.

16 The architecture of Mycenaean settlements at the end of the 13th century BC, too, is designed to deal with military engagement. The citadels grew more fortified – increasingly circled by those monstrous walls of huge, unworked limestone blocks. Across the Isthmus of Corinth a Cyclopean wall has been traced running a full kilometer west of the Saronic Gulf. And at Mycenae, and neighbouring Tiryns, gloomy, secret cisterns, Mycenae's over 18 m deep, have been hacked out of the bedrock to provide water in the event of a siege.

17 See Latacz (2004), 120–40, for analysis of these nominations. The term 'Mycenaean' is another 19th-century invention.

CHAPTER SIX

The Rape of 'Fair Hellen'

1 Hyginus, *Fables* 79.

2 Apollodorus, *Epitome* 1.23.

3 Diodorus of Sicily, 4.63.1–4.

4 Hellanikos *FrGrH* 4, 323a: F19 (168b). Hellanikos (*c.* 480–395 BC) was a noted mythographer and chronographer but only fragments of his work now survive. Later authors have certainly found this paedophiliac episode exciting. One Elizabethan writer – John Trussel in his *First Rape of Fair Hellen* (1595) – is insistent that Helen was only eight when she was raped. He describes the wheezing Theseus having to gasp for breath before he renews his advances. Another literary tradition claims that Theseus sodomised Helen to preserve her virginity: see Thornton (1997), 85 and n. 45.

5 Isocrates was an Athenian educationalist and a pamphleteer of a conservative persuasion, who lived from 436 to 338 BC.

6 Isocrates, *Encomium of Helen* 10.19. Trans. L. van Hook.

7 Site visit May 2001.

8 Trans. W. Barnstone (1962), quoted in Freeman (1999), 142.

9 The word 'rape' comes from the Latin *rapiere*, 'to seize'. In antiquity it does not necessarily mean a sexual violation but does carry the implication of an abduction by force.

10 Rose (1926), 401.

11 And probably earlier: see Cartledge (2002), 310.

12 Thompson (1908/9), 124 and 127.

13 Flogging to the death was almost certainly a Roman elaboration.

14 Plutarch, *Theseus* 26.

15 Variant myths say that Helen was pregnant by Theseus at the time and gave birth to a daughter – Iphigeneia, whom she then left with her sister Clytemnestra. Pausanias 2.22.6 summarises the literary tradition claiming that Iphigeneia was the child of Theseus and Helen: for example, Stesichorus (*PMGF* 191). Iphigeneia grows up to take her own place in legend, as a victim of human sacrifice. (See Chapter 27.) The young girl's fate was a tale at the heart of three of the most powerful of Greek tragedies: Euripides, *Iphigeneia at Aulis*; Euripides, *Iphigeneia among the Taurians*; and Aeschylus, *Agamemnon*.

16 Hellanikos *FrGrH* 4, 323a: F20 (134).

17 Plutarch, *Theseus* 32.3. Trans. B. Perrin. See also fragment 11 of the *Cypria* (scholiast on Homer, *Iliad* 3.242) that 'the Dioscuri, failing to find Theseus [in Aphidna], sacked Athens'. Trans. H.G. Evelyn-White.

18 Diodorus of Sicily gives one account of this story: 4.63.1–4. This is part of his multi-volume *Library*, a universal history of mythological times up to 60 BC, composed in Egypt and Rome 60–30 BC.

19 In 432 BC the Spartans had declared war on Athens. Their plan was to torch Athenian grainfields and force the Athenians to come out and meet them in fixed battle. For a city-state of professional soldiers the victory, the Spartans imagined, would be swift. But the Athenians were too canny to rise to the bait. Well connected to external food supplies via their port of Piraeus, the Athenians did not rush to meet the Spartans. Instead they waited to mount large-scale defensive military action on their own terms – Spartan success would not come easily. For the next twenty-seven years there would be victories and defeats as each power tested the strengths and weaknesses of the other. It was only when the Spartans took Persian gold and used their new-found wealth to become a sea- as well as a land-power that the pendulum started to swing in their direction. Athens' allies – with the exception of Samos – smelt defeat and the vulnerability of their overlord, and defected to the Spartan cause one by one. For an ideal overview of Spartan history, see Cartledge (2002).

20 Herodotus 9.73 and Thucydides 7.19.1.

21 Rape cases seem to have been more concerned with affronts to the honour of the city or *oikos* rather than issues of consensuality. Legendary rapes were often cited as historical and political catalysts; cf. the rape of Lucretia and the rape of the Sabine women. See R. Omitowju (1997) 'Regulating rape: Soap operas and self-interest in the Athenian courts', in S. Deacy and K.F. Pierce, eds (1997) *Rape in Antiquity* (London: Duckworth) and R. Omitowoju (2002) *Rape and the Politics of Consent in Classical Athens* (Cambridge: Cambridge University Press).

22 Helen's rape by Paris was cited by military leaders in the classical period. For example,

in his funeral oration of 322 BC, the orator Hyperides diagnoses the actions of the Greek general Leosthenes at the end of the first year of the Lamian War as a means of defending all Greek women from the affront of *hubris*. An affront suffered twice by Helen.

23 Deriving from Sparta's hinterland, Lakonia.

24 Rare mixed-blood offspring were labelled *mothakes*.

25 Given that all adult male citizens, 'Spartiates', were allowed only one profession – that of the soldier – the Spartans were a force to be reckoned with. Little surprise then that they should sustain a push-me-pull-you tussle with the other most prominent city-state of the period, Athens. Sometimes these two were close allies, and sometimes the bitterest of enemies. Conflict was inevitable as each became entrenched in its own social and political ideals – finally, after a long, bitter, bloody, dissatisfying war, in 404 BC Sparta triumphed, decisively, over Athens and Spartan warriors tore down the walls of the Athenian *polis*. Athens' flute-girls (prostitutes who lived outside the city walls) quickly changed sides and, dancing amid the flames, over the bodies of the Athenian dead, celebrated the end of an empire. See Xenophon, *Hellenica* 2.2.23. Sparta spent the next thirty-five years dominating much of the Greek world.

26 Thucydides 1.10.2.

27 Other than the acropolis, the theatre and the Menelaion almost all the digs in Sparta are now classified as 'rescue archaeology' – work can begin only when a building lot in the city is cleared for development or when someone's extension falls down, revealing, as it collapses, an ancient past in its foundations.

28 Hoplites formed the bulk of the Spartan army. Every male Spartan citizen who had been through the agoge system had to serve as a hoplite.

29 Pausanias 3.15.3.

30 Cartledge (2001), 150 and 161; see also L.H. Jeffery (1961) *The Local Scripts of Archaic Greece: A study of the origins of the Greek alphabet and its development from the eighth to the fifth centuries* BC (Oxford), 200, n. 24; M.N. Tod and A.J.B. Wace (1906) *A Catalogue of the Sparta Museum* (Oxford: Clarendon Press), 178, no. 447.

31 This ritual headdress is called a *polos*; it could perhaps have a connection with the *polos* worn in ritual circumstances by Mycenaean women.

32 For an astrological interpretation of this see Richer (1994).

33 Cults could have been established earlier but our first extant evidence is Hellenistic.

34 It is easy to understand why Helen and her brothers should be worshipped so full-bloodedly at Sparta – after all, Castor and Pollux were considered the protectors of the city, and Helen their emblem of perfect womanhood – but interesting that the popularity of the cult became widespread. Images of Helen and her brothers on coins from Asia Minor almost certainly bear witness to the cult spreading well beyond the Greek mainland. See Larson (1995), *passim*. And Chapter 36.

35 For fuller discussion see Spawforth (1992), *passim*.

36 Helen was also known as Argive Helen.

CHAPTER SEVEN
Sparte Kalligynaika

1 Peleus describes the problem of being married to Helen. Euripides, *Andromache* 595–600 (5th century BC). Trans. P. Vellacott.

2 *Odyssey* 4.341–2 [LCL 4.304–5].

3 A comprehensive overview of ancient sources shows Helen having a relationship with the following: Theseus, Menelaus, Paris, Enarsphoros the son of Hippocoon, Idas and Lynceus, Corythos, Deiphobus, Achilles and Theoclymenos. See Clader (1976), 71.

4 Excavated at Artemis Orthia and dating from the same century.

5 Carter (1988).

6 See Pomeroy (2002), 106, n. 2.

7 Later commentators even suggest the girls ate cakes in the shape of breasts. See Pomeroy (2002), 106, n. 3.

8 See Griffiths (1972), *passim*.

9 There is some, slightly questionable, evidence that Alcman started off life in Lydia.

10 *Partheneion* 3 (P.Oxy. 2387) is in the Papyrology Room at the Sackler Library in Oxford. *Partheneion* 1 is in the Louvre (P.Louvr. E3320). Many thanks to Nikolaos Gonis for his assistance.

11 Alcman, *Partheneion* 1 and 3. Trans. S.B. Pomeroy (2002), 6 and 7.

12 A reputation revived in the Roman period; see Plutarch, *Lycurgus* 18.4. Spartan girls were certainly well used to female company; given that all males from the age of seven to thirty lived on their own together in men-only army camps, the relationships between women must have been very strong.

13 See Larson (1995), 68, and 176, n. 53, citing C.M. Bowra, for a suggestion that Helen appears in Alcman as the dawn goddess Aotis.

14 This may also have been the case in the Late Bronze Age. Linear B tablets show the gods and goddesses of the Mycenaeans (not only their human representatives on earth) owning assets such as flocks of sheep and being listed as landholders. On the House of Potnia at Thebes, see Chadwick (1976), 93, 99; on landholding, see Chadwick (1976), 77, 114. A new Pylos join has revealed a 'Hearth of Dionysus'; see J.L. Melena (1996–7) '40 Joins and Quasi-Joins of Fragments in Linear B Tablets from Pylos' and '13 Joins and Quasi-Joins of Fragments in the Linear B Tablets from Pylos', in *Minos* 31–2: 159–70; on flocks of sheep, see Chadwick (1976), 93, 129.

15 *Odyssey* 13.469 [LCL 13.412].

16 The oracle at the religious site of Delphi in central Greece handed out judgments on current affairs, prophecies for the future and bon mots concerning state and personal histories. It was the Delphic Oracle that branded Spartan girls '*kallistai*' in the 7th century BC. Parke and Wormell (1956), Vol. 1, 82.

17 Athenaeus, *Deipnosophists* 13.566a–b.

18 Xenophon, *Constitution of the Lacedaemonians* 1.3. One very fragmentary vase found in Sparta shows men and women debauching together – there is no indication that these women are *hetairai* (prostitutes). It is currently held by the Sparta Museum. Pipili (1992) no. 196.

19 Plato, *Laws* 806A; cf. *Republic* 5.452A.

20 See Cavanagh and Laxton (1984), 34–6.

21 Athenaeus, *Deipnosophists* 13.600f–601a.

22 Clearchus of Soli, fragment 73.

23 See Xenophon, *Household Management* 7.10. Trans. S.B. Pomeroy (2002), 9.

24 Pollux 4.102.

25 See Pomeroy (2002), 112ff, for an account of Spartan girls' physical education, with sources.

26 See Bowra (1961), 53 on *poloi*; also Aristophanes, *Lysistrata* 1308–15.

27 Helen is herself compared to a '*Thessalian horse adorning its chariot*' in Theocritus, *Idylls* 18.31.

28 Sarah Pomeroy has pointed out that while Spartan girls have their long hair cut in preparation for marriage, Pliny in his *Natural History* links the cropping of a mare's mane with a reduction in libido. Pliny, *Natural History* 8.164.

29 The challenges of the sources available for Spartan studies, particularly the lives of women, are succinctly laid out by Pomeroy (2002), 139–70.

30 Augustus was said to have made this visit in 21 BC. See Cartledge and Spawforth (1989 reprinted 1991, 2002), 199, citing Cassius Dio 54.7.2.

31 Scholiast on Juvenal 4.53.

32 Ovid, *Heroides* 16.149–52.

33 Propertius lived from *c.* 50 BC to *c.* 2 BC.

34 Trans. A. Dalby; taken from Dalby (2000), 146.

35 Xenophon, *Constitution of the Lacedaemonians* 1.4 and see Pomeroy (2002), 25, for further discussion.

36 British Museum GR 1876.5–10.1.

37 For a further description of constructions on the Menelaion, see Tomlinson (1992).

38 Herodotus 6.61.

39 Pausanias 3.19.9.

40 Pausanias 3.7.7.

41 The fact that she was honoured with rituals that involved plants and flowers could suggest that her memory was being conflated with the primal vegetation goddess who gives her name (ἑλένη) to reeds or shoots and woven baskets in ancient Greece. Some would go so far as to say that she was nothing other than a nature goddess herself. See Clader (1976), 56–68. See also Appendix 4.

CHAPTER EIGHT

Tender-eyed Girls

1 *The Myth of Sisyphus and Other Essays* (2000). Trans. J. O'Brien.

2 See Hallager and McGeorge (1992), especially 43.

3 On girls' maturation rites, such as the *arkteia*, where young girls, who had not yet reached the age of menarche, served Artemis as 'bears' in her sanctuaries at Brauron and Mounichia, see C. Sourvinou-Inwood (1988) *Studies in Girls' Transitions: aspects of the arkteia and age representation in Attic iconography*. Athens: Kardamitsa.

4 See, for instance, NMA 3180.

5 See Rehak (2005) for a good summary and for a discussion of the Thera frescoes. I am very grateful to John Younger for allowing me to see an advance copy of this work.

6 The similarity of dress, adornment and ritual between Theran and Mycenaean society allows for close comparison of the two.

7 After investigations in the 1930s and tentative digging in the 1960s led by Spyridon Marinatos.

8 Because a monkey and a griffin are close by, this goddess could be a Mistress of the Animals, a *potnia theron*. A deity with particular responsibility for nature.

9 See Rehak (2005).

10 The 'Citadel House mould' from Mycenae shows that moon-shaped jewellery was also made at Mycenae.

11 For a good summary of all frescoes excavated, see Marinatos (1984).

12 Morgan (1988), 31.

13 For further discussion see Goodison and Morris (1998), 125.

14 Pliny, *Natural History* 21.17.31–2.

15 Ellen Davis has identified six different hairstyles at Thera, marking six stages of sexual development. See Davis (1986).

16 Here, too, above a doorway there is a religious symbol which can signify fecundity, the 'horns of consecration' – bull's horns which drip with blood. The image almost certainly represents both a sacrifice on an altar and a bleeding woman. Bulls had been symbols of fertility since the Palaeolithic era. A woman's womb is an organ that would have become clearly visible during excarnation or any sword-attack: see D.O. Cameron (1981) *Symbols of Birth and of Death in the Neolithic Era* (London: Kenyon-Deane), 4–5. A womb bears a marked resemblance to a bull's head – particularly to the head of the breed of bull common in pre-history, the auroch, a massive beast standing up to 2 m at the shoulder with long, slim horns measuring about 30 cm and a footprint the size of a man's head. The bleeding horns speak of female fecundity. The frescoes could well be a pictorial representation of activities which actually took place in the room – rites of passage such as initiation rites.

17 In the area of the 'lustral basin' situated below the saffron-gatherers' fresco.

18 On the ground floor of Xeste 3, Room 3. North Wall.

19 By the archaic and classical period one finds the hair of the statues of particular goddesses decorated with yellow or golden paint. The 6th-century BC towering 'Berlin Goddess', for example, in the Pergamon Museum, has her thick curls tinted yellow, and Praxiteles' famous sculpture of a naked Aphrodite was thought to have gilded locks. Both these goddesses were honoured for their pronounced eroticism. This could be the remnants of a pre-historic association of blondeness with 'special (sexual) powers'.

20 It is estimated that 250,000 crocus flowers are needed to produce 1 pound (0.45 kg) of saffron: see the *Cambridge World History of Food*, Vol. 2, eds. K.F. Kiple and K.C. Ornelas (Cambridge: Cambridge University Press, 2000), 1846. There are ideograms representing saffron on the Np series of Linear B tablets from Knossos on Crete: see Ventris and Chadwick (1973), 51.

21 Men are portrayed in other contexts at Thera. For an excellent survey see S. Sherratt (ed) (2000) *The Wall Paintings of Thera*. Proceedings of the First International Symposium.

Petros M. Nomikos Conference Centre, Thera, Hellas, 30 August – 4 September 1997. 2 Vols. Athens: Petros M. Nomikos and The Thera Foundation.

22 British Museum, E773.

23 See Chapter 14.

24 Visitors should check which representations of the frescoes are on display before visiting Thera.

CHAPTER NINE

A Trophy for Heroes

1 This episode in Helen's story has its counterpart in other sagas dealing with contests for the hand of a heroine: women such as Atalanta – who forced suitors to compete with her in foot-races; Jocasta – whose son Oedipus solved the riddle of the Sphinx and won the right to sleep with his mother and control the kingdom of Thebes; and Hippodamia, whose father took part in the chariot-races with her suitors and always won. But Hippodamia loved Pelops and wanted to share with him the kingdom of Elis, so when he took up the challenge she had wax pegs inserted into her father's chariot's wheels – the wax melted as the race went on and the chariot overturned, killing her father. The treachery eventually resulted in a curse being put on the House of Atreus. See Pindar, *Olympian Ode* 1.25–96 and Apollodorus, *Epitome* 2.3–10. All these women were competed for. Like Helen, they too had substantial estates to share with men who proved themselves worthy.

2 Hesiod, *Catalogues of Women and Eoiae* 68.

3 Apollodorus, *The Library* 3.10.8.

4 Euripides, *Trojan Women*, 987.

5 Hesiod, *Catalogues of Women and Eoiae* 68.

6 Excavation report: C. Tsountas (1889) 'Ereuna en te Lakonike kai ho taphos tou Vapheiou', in *Archaiologike Ephemeris* 129–72.

7 In the classical period, a statue of Apollo 9 m high would have towered above the site. Fragment 53 of Alcman's poetry describes the spread at one festival – moon-shaped buns with sesame-seeds, sweets of honey and flax seeds for the children. Although there is no specific reference to the worship of Helen at the Hyakinthia, similarities with the Heleneia are very strong – see Xenophon, *Agesilaus* 8.7 and Athenaeus, *Deipnosophists* 4.138e–139b.

8 Hesychius 1999. Hesychius of Alexandria compiled his Greek lexicon in the fifth century AD: it survives in a single manuscript from the fifteenth century.

9 Athenaeus, *Deipnosophists* 4.139ff; Xenophon, *Agesilaus* 8.7; Plutarch, *Agesilaus* 19.5–6.

10 Helen's rape by Theseus was commemorated on a throne at Amyklai along with other episodes from the Trojan War cycle. Pausanias, 3.18.10–16.

11 Hesiod, *Catalogues of Women and Eoiae* 68. Trans. H.G. Evelyn-White.

12 See Hesiod, fragments 204.78ff. and 197.4ff. in the Merkelbach and West edition (1967).

13 Hesiod, *Catalogues of Women and Eoiae* 68.102–5. Trans. H.G. Evelyn-White.

14 At every turn in Mycenaean society one's standing (or lack of it) was reinforced by

the bureaucrats – Linear B tablets show, for example, that only certain men were allowed the finest quality wool for their cloaks.

15 *Iliad* 2.56 [LCL 2.47].

16 *Iliad* 2.539–43 [LCL 2.455–8].

17 *Iliad* 10.306–10 [LCL 10.262–5].

18 Site visit Wildwood, UK, 2002.

19 See Chapter 17 for further details.

20 The Horse Book of Kikkuli of the Mitanni was already widely employed in the 14th century in Anatolia. Tablets inscribed with training methods can be seen in the Istanbul Archaeological Museum; for example, Bo 10407 (KBo III 5, IBoT II 136).

21 See Hood (1953).

22 See Konsolaki-Yannopoulou (1999) and (2000).

23 *Iliad* 2.26 [LCL 2.23].

24 Troy also earns this epithet [LCL 2.287].

25 Helen's brothers were also famous for their equestrian prowess. A *Homeric Hymn* describes them as 'riders on swift steeds'; the poet Alcman talks of them as 'masters of swift colts, skilled horsemen'; and Alcaeus as 'Castor and Polydeuces, who traverse the broad earth and oceans on swift-footed horses'.

26 And would our Bronze Age Helen have ridden out to meet them? There are images of women handling horses from the Late Bronze Age but they all appear in a religious context. There is one statuette from 13th-century BC Attica that represents a female figure riding side-saddle. From the Hélène Stathatos collection: see *Collection Hélène Stathatos* (1963) *Vol. III: Objets Antiques et Byzantins* (Strasbourg), 23–4 (no. 6) and Plate II, no. 6. Finely painted images from Mycenaean frescoes show women driving chariots. Their progress is stately, they wear elaborate hats – probably a religious procession. On the frescoes at Tiryns, females thunder across the walls in chariots, their boar's-tusk helmets an indication that these are perhaps the prototype warrior goddesses.

27 Hesiod, *Catalogues of Women and Eoiae* 68.1–6. Trans. H. G. Evelyn-White.

28 Hesiod, *Catalogues of Women and Eoiae* 68; Euripides, *Iphigeneia in Aulis* 49–71; Apollodorus, *The Library* 3.10.8; Hyginus, *Fables* 78.

29 Horses buried in the Bronze Age with their owners presumably were killed at the time of the owner's death (Marathon, Dendra). Pausanias 3.20.9 tells us there was a tomb called 'The Horse's Tomb' on the Sparta-Arcadia road which held the body of the very horse sacrificed by Tyndareus.

CHAPTER TEN

The Kingmaker

1 Euripides, *Iphigeneia in Aulis* 67–75. Trans. P. Vellacott.

2 It is clear from extant Hittite texts that athletic contests were mounted for the benefit of the gods at large social gatherings. Hoffner (2003) lists the events: boxing, wrestling, stone-throwing, foot-racing, archery and chariot-racing.

3 *Diethnes Politistiki Enosi Pammachon* – the International Cultural Pammachon Union. Many

thanks to Kostas Dervenis for co-ordination of this event.

4 See Dervenis and Lykiardopoulos (2005).

5 See Arnott (1999), 500.

6 Herodotus, 6.126ff.

7 For a fuller account of these issues, see Finkelberg (1991).

8 Pausanias 2.18.6.

9 *Odyssey* 4.12–14 [LCL 4.10–12].

10 Interesting that Megapenthes is not described as a bastard even though his mother was a slave, hinting perhaps at an accepted system of surrogate births. See Finley (1954).

11 Settlements along the Turkish coast show evidence of strong trading links – Mycenaean pottery has been found at Clazomenae, Panaztepe, Colophon and Ephesus. This was not unfamiliar territory.

12 See Neville (1977), 5 and n. 13.

13 The Gortyn law code from Crete – inscribed in the 5th century BC but it may well describe legislation rooted in the Late Bronze Age – also details the rights a woman has over property.

14 Linear B information in this paragraph derived from personal correspondence with Dr Michael Lane, May 2004–April 2005. See also Ventris and Chadwick (1973), 232ff.

15 At a place called *pakijana*. The scribes seem to recognise an unresolved dispute between Erita and 'allotment-holders' who can claim certain benefits to the land. Erita has a special plot of land described as *etonijo* which appears to be dedicated to some 'god' and also has given a woman named *uwamija a kera* a 'gift of honour' in the form of the benefit of a parcel of land. In the eyes of the scribes, Erita the priestess has clear rights to the possession and disposal of her property in land, which include passing claims on to another woman.

16 In another series, many landholders are subjected to religious 'taxes' – perhaps one tenth of the product of their land as suggested by another series of tablets from Pylos (Es series). These tablets imply that 'taxation' is proportionate to the 'benefit' a person holds.

17 Hyginus, *Fables* 78 – see note by the translator M. Grant, 74, who mentions a similar story told by Aristotle as quoted in Athenaeus' *Deipnosophists* 576, where the daughter of a Gallic king, Petta, chooses her husband. See also Euripides, *Iphigeneia in Aulis* 68–75.

18 The custom certainly fed through to some parts of western Europe and was still practised until recently in parts of rural Germany, where young girls were auctioned to become the 'May-wife'. These girls started the spring as passive, obedient 'spouses' but come the early summer they got to choose their own 'dancing partners'. If a girl wanted to stay with her mate, she announced the fact by pinning a bunch of flowers to his hat. See West (1975), 12.

19 *Iphigeneia in Aulis* 68–75. Trans. P. Vellacott.

20 Hesiod, *Catalogues of Women and Eoiae* 68.

21 Hesiod, *Catalogues of Women and Eoiae* 68, 98–100.

CHAPTER ELEVEN
A Royal Wedding

1 Also called *Idyll* 18. Trans. A. Verity.

2 *Epithalamia* were songs or poems traditionally performed on the eve of a wedding, literally '*epi*' outside the '*thalamos*', the bridal chamber.

3 The choral leader who wrote so expressively in the 7th century BC about rituals for young Spartan girls down on the banks of the Eurotas.

4 Theocritus may also have got some of his detail from another poem written about Helen in the 6th century BC by the Sicilian poet Stesichorus. Only the tiniest fragments of Stesichorus survive now, but it seems this poem covered Helen's early life in some detail. See notes in Hunter (2002), 109.

5 Theocritus, *Idyll* 18.

6 Theocritus, *Idyll* 18. 43.6 Trans. S. B. Pomeroy (2002), 115.

7 Eighteen was late to marry by Greek standards, a peculiarity of the Spartan city-state, apparently endorsed from the Late Archaic period onwards.

8 Plutarch, *Lycurgus* 15.4.

9 See Hagnon of Tarsus in Athenaeus, *Deipnosophists* 13.602d–e.

10 See discussion in David (1992), 1.

11 See Griffiths (1972), 27.

12 Theocritus, *Idyll* 18.8.

13 V 659 (from Mycenae) and Vn 851 (from Pylos) on pallets.

14 For detailed analysis of foodstuffs at various sites, see Tzedakis and Martlew (1999), *passim*.

15 A tradition also referred to by Homer: e.g. the wedding feast at Sparta for Hermione; a feast in honour of Poseidon at Pylos; and something marked by its absence in the unruly, improper behaviour of Penelope's suitors. It is worth noting that a feast in honour of Poseidon at Pylos is recorded in the Linear B. tablets. See Sherratt (2004), 315.

16 There is an interesting comparison here with Iron Age British tribal gatherings.

17 Tablet Cn 1287.

18 Un 138. See also Un 418, 718, 853 and Cn 418.

19 Another tablet records the delivery of 197 sheep for a feast. Uc 161, from Knossos.

20 Some animals travelled 'over water' and across distances of 50 km to get to the table. Palaima (2004), 226.

21 Un 2 from Pylos, in Ventris and Chadwick (1973), 221.

22 Pylos Ta 716.

23 See Isaakidou *et al.* (2002). The flesh has been cut off the mandibles – this could, perhaps, correlate to the sacrifice of tongues described by Homer in *Odyssey* 3.373 (LCL 3.332).

24 Agia Triada sarcophagus: see Fitton (2002), 192 and Immerwahr (1990), 100–2.

25 Some figures in this and the following paragraph are derived from a lecture given by Lisa Bendall on 6 May 2004, 'Mycenaean Feasting at Pylos', at the McDonald Institute, Cambridge. Also conversations with John Killen and reference to Ventris and Chadwick (1973).

26 Uc 161, from Knossos.

27 Analysis of the pottery at cult sites shows that wine played a significant part in the more intimate sacral rituals of the Late Bronze Age as well as in the grand feasts – where huge amounts would have been drunk. In another room (Room 9) of the palace of Pylos, there are a further 600 kylikes. The traces of organic materials found in the cult centre at Mycenae bear witness to resinated wine, both locally made and imported from producers along the Palestinian coasts at Ugarit and Ras Shamra in large Canaanite jars. A clay mug held a mix of wine and mead. Elsewhere there is alcohol steeped in rue and sage. We think of rue as a token of remembrance but it can act too as a sedative; today pharmacists warn against its use because the risk:benefit ratio is too unstable. So while the gods might have felt very close to the inhabitants of the Late Bronze Age it seems that men and women were happy to use drugs, as well as alcohol, to bring them closer still.

28 *Iliad* 4.401 [LCL 4.346]. Honeyed wine is referred to on a sealing nodule recording a wine delivery at Pylos. I tried this Bronze Age drink with archaeologist Holley Martlew in October 2004. It is delicious and extremely efficacious.

29 The 'Campstool Fresco' from Knossos.

30 See Bendall (2004), on Room 60 at Pylos.

31 Sufficiently significant to be buried with the aristocrats – for example, at Vapheio two bronze jugs, a bronze ladle and a silver ladle, and a brazier.

32 For a fuller discussion of the topic of feasting and social display, see Bendall (2004).

33 For an excellent collection of references see Sherratt (2004), 316, n. 46.

34 *Odyssey* 9.3–11 [LCL 9.3–11].

35 *Odyssey* 17.270–1. Trans. E.V. Rieu. [LCL 17.270–1].

36 On the battlefield too, when the heroes describe the real pleasures of life, music and dancing are nearly always mentioned. In the midst of a seething, passionate torrent of abuse that a vengeful Menelaus is hurling at the Trojans, we get an idea – certainly of Iron Age pleasures, and most probably of Bronze Age ones.

> One can achieve his fill of all good things,
> even sleep, even of making love . . .
> rapturous song and the beat and sway of dancing.
> A man will yearn for his fill of all these joys
> before his fill of war. But not these Trojans –
> No one can glut their lust for battle! Iliad 13.733–8 [LCL 13.636–9].

37 Although ethno-musicologists have a difficult time reconstructing the sounds of the very distant past because many musical instruments were made entirely of organic material, and have simply rotted away, a few examples do remain. There could be a wealth – particularly of percussion instruments – enjoyed by Bronze Age society, which we cannot imagine today because their remains have been swallowed by time. One survivor is a rattle (sometimes made of bronze, sometimes of terracotta) called a *sistrum*. The *sistrum* is prevalent in antiquity. A strange hybrid of a fork, a maraca and an abacus, the *sistrum* gives out a sound that is at once eerie and intrusive. Bronze finger cymbals, not unlike those used today by Hari

Krishna devotees, were probably an oriental import to Greece. Found on Crete and in the Uluburun shipwreck. See Bass (1987) and (1996). Another import was a large whistle carved out of the tooth of a hippopotamus, and unworked tortoise shells destined for use as resonating boxes. In 1981, H. Roberts reconstructed a tortoiseshell lyre for the British Museum. See Younger (1998), 17 and H. Roberts (1981), 'Reconstructing the Greek Tortoise-Shell Lyre', in *World Archaeology* 12: 303–12. In the Mycenaean sanctuary of Phylakopi, on Melos, Late Bronze Age tortoise-shells were excavated with holes carefully drilled into the sides to allow for the attachment of lyre arms. See Renfrew (1985), 325–6. The tortoise-shell fragments were recovered from the east and west shrines, during the excavations between 1974 and 1977 by the British School of Archaeology at Athens. Renfrew notes that tortoises can still be found in the countryside around Phylakopi. *A Homeric Hymn* describes the creation of these musical instruments (also called the chelys-lyre) by Hermes.

38 See Younger (1998), 37 and Plate 24.3 (CMS II. 3.7).

39 Agios Nikolaos, Archaeological Museum 11246.

40 This is from Malia, and was found in a building at the far north-east corner of the palace. It dates from LMi (16th–15th centuries BC). See C. Baurain and P. Darcque (1983), 'Un triton en pierre à Mallia', in *Bulletin de Correspondance Hellénique* 107:3–73. Thank you to Peter Warren for details.

41 *Iliad* 9.225 [LCL 9.189].

42 See Plutarch, for the *Life of Alexander* (15) and Aelian, *Historical Miscellany* 9.38.

43 The Judgement of Paris, Attic black-figure amphora, *c.* 575–550 BC. Paris, Louvre F13.

44 Paris, Louvre, Département des Peintures INV. 3696.

45 Women, it seems, would on occasion play. From Palaikastro in East Crete there is a crude terracotta group of a woman holding a lyre while three others hold hands and dance in a semi-circle in front of her.

46 There is a particularly fine example from Amyklai, just 8 cm tall.

47 Lang (1969).

48 *Odyssey* 17.287 [LCL 17.261].

49 Theocritus, *Idylls* 18.54–5. Trans. A. Verity.

50 See Pantelia (1995), 79 for further discussion. The author points out that Ptolemy's marriage to (his sister) Arsinoe would also have 'strengthened both his claim to the Egyptian throne and his position as a figure of cult in Egypt'. There are echoes here perhaps of Helen's story.

CHAPTER TWELVE

Hermione

1 Ovid, *The Art of Love* 2.690f Trans. R. Humphries.

2 Although most literary sources say that Helen had only one child, a comprehensive account of 'Helen' references yields quite a list of children – from her liaison with Theseus, Iphigeneia; with Paris, Corythos, Boumonos, Idaios and Aganos as well as the seemingly fatherless Aithiolas and Nicostratus (for latter see Apollodorus, *The*

Library 2ii, 2i). Pleisthenes is mentioned in fragment 12 of the *Cypria* as another child of Helen and Menelaus.

3 Hesiod, *Catalogues of Women and Eoiae* 204.94–5, in Merkelbach and West (1967).

4 Could he be talking about a system of surrogacy, where aristocrats use slaves to increase the number of their offspring? *Odyssey* 4.14–17 [LCL 4.12–14]. Hittite tablets of the time indicate that in Anatolia at least, surrogacy was acceptable; '*if within two years the wife does not produce children, she will purchase a slave woman for her husband; but as soon as the slave produces a [male] child, the wife can sell the slave as she wishes*': Darga (1993), 34.

5 Ventris and Chadwick (1973), 127 and 310.

6 Material from 2002 site visit.

7 In the 7th century many terracotta figurines of the goddess were left as votive offerings in the sanctuary of Artemis Orthia in Sparta. See Farrell (1908).

8 Gg 705.

9 *Odyssey* 19.213–17 [LCL 19.186–9].

10 The Eileithyia Cave in Crete still has a folkloric reputation for causing miraculous pregnancies. Chemical analysis of the pure water found in the cave indicates that drunk in large quantities it could work as a laxative. See Rutkowski (1986), 65.

11 Pausanias 2.21.8.

12 Fragment 13 of the work of the poet Stesichorus claims that after Helen's abduction by Theseus, the Spartan queen founded the shrine. Argos' pride and joy is a massive Greco-Roman theatre. Originally built in the 3rd century BC, it can still hold an audience of 20,000. Today children mooch around the capacious remains on school trips but when a play is staged here the place hums again as it would have done in the classical period. Many of the women in that ancient press of tourists would also have visited Eileithyia's shrine, to thank the goddess for the gift of a child or to beg her for more, and as they did so they would have remembered its young founder, 'the most beautiful woman in the world'. Today experts think they have detected the site of the altar of Eileithyia, hidden underneath one of the town's Christian churches.

13 Angel (1977), 88–105. This method has had its critics, but combined with evidence from dental analysis, it seems to show that girls were sexually mature aged twelve/thirteen. There is no reason to believe a gap was left before they started to produce children. From the 5th century BC onwards it was thought that the gap between menarche and marriage for the *gyne* (a word meaning a mature female, although it can also translate as wife) should be as narrow as possible. It is likely that the ideal for most Late Bronze Age families was that girls should fall pregnant very young.

14 See evidence from Tomb 11 as published by Hallager and McGeorge (1992). See also opening of Chapter 8.

15 See Arnott (2005a).

16 The Mycenaean record is silent on beliefs and rituals concerning pregnancy and childbirth but Hittite tablets are inscribed with detailed descriptions of the *Papanikri*, the 'Birth Ritual'. The ritual sounds, quite frankly, uncomfortable. Women had to give birth on a wooden stool in the presence of the priest. If for some reason one of the legs or the seat of the stool broke, the priest would be roused to a frenzy, frantic to cleanse the evil that had been made manifest by the breakage. The mother would have to make a libation to the gods. Sheep and birds would be sacrificed, a lamb would

be bound with red yarn and dressed in red material with a hat on its head and rings and anklets on its feet and legs. On the following day, the newborn child seems to have been beaten with a stick by the men responsible for sacrifice. Procreation was not a private affair – it was the business of the whole community. See Darga (1993), 105: A1 35 (Istanbul Archaeological Museum Bo. 2001).

17 See Robertson (1990), esp. 24 and Riddle (1992) on contraception in the ancient world.

18 To date, Mycenaean objects have been found at twenty Egyptian sites. See Bryce (2005).

19 The oldest prescription for contraception appears to be in the Petrie papyrus, discovered at Kahun in 1889 and written during the reign of Amenenhat III of the Twelfth Dynasty. A wealth of information is contained in a group of documents now called the Papyrus Ebers which were written down in *c.* 1500 BC. Papyrus Ebers 716.

20 A papyrus fragment from around 1400 BC describes the wild murmurings and mutterings that would sometimes have served as medical attention – an incantation from the Land of the Keftiu (Crete) written at the time the Greek Mycenaeans were in control: '. . . Exorcism of the Asian sickness in the keftiu language . . . This spell is uttered over ferment, gas, fluid and urine.'

21 See Latacz (2004), 131–2, citing W. Helck (1979) *Die Beziehungen Ägyptens und Vorderasiens zur Ägäis bis ins 7. Jarhrhundert v. Chr.*, 2nd edition (Darmstadt), 97; and P.W. Haider (1988), *Griechenland-Nordafrika: Ihre Beziehungen zwischen 1600 und 600 v. Chr.* (Darmstadt), 139, 14, n. 48.

22 Pliny, *Natural History* 24.38.59 – used in wickerwork and perfumery as well as for medical purposes; details from King (1998), 86f.

23 For fuller discussion of this subject, see King (1983).

24 Plutarch, *Lycurgus and Numa* 3, 4. Trans. B. Perrin.

25 The female poet who probably lived in the 7th/6th century BC. See 378, n.2 for questions about Sappho's life.

26 P. Oxy 1231, fragment 14. Trans. D. A. Campbell.

27 She was even on the radar of Adhelm, an Anglo-Saxon theologian who wrote in a letter to one of his pupils Wihtfrith sometime between AD 673 and 706: '*What, pray, I beseech you eagerly, is the benefit to the sanctity of the orthodox faith to expend energy by reading and studying the foul pollution of base Proserpina, which I shrink from mentioning in plain speech; or to revere, through celebration in study, Hermione, the wanton offspring of Menelaus and Helen, who, as the ancient texts report, was engaged for a while by right of dowry to Orestes, then, having changed her mind, married Neoptolemus.*' Letter III, 'To Wihtfrith', in *Aldhelm: The Prose Works*. Trans. M. Lapidge and M. Herren (1979). (Cambridge: D.S. Brewer; Totowa, NJ: Rowman & Littlefield).

28 Euripides, *Helen* 282–3.

29 Andromache in Euripides, *Andromache* 206.

30 Written around about 20 BC.

31 Ovid, *Heroides* 8.91. Trans. H. Isbell.

CHAPTER THIRTEEN

A Welcome Burden

1 Tomb 8C; see Hallager and McGeorge (1992), 32.
2 Gates (1992) gives an extremely interesting and useful survey of objects found in children's graves.
3 In Grave Xi, Grave Circle B.
4 See Mylonas (1966), 105.
5 At Prosymna – the name that the travel writer Pausanias gives to the area around the Temple of Hera, Argos, 3.17.1 – children's bodies have been found with miniature terracotta animals – maybe creatures that could provide succour in the form of milk on the child's journey through the afterlife. There are even a few models of horses and chariots (although some academics hotly debate this identification), which could have been left, again, to help comfort the children in their journey. Weapons are conspicuous by their absence; these children were clearly not styled little soldiers.
6 The wife of a Victorian archaeologist and sponge merchant, a woman named Mrs Brown, allegedly committed the heinous crime of losing valuable Mycenaean goods from a child's grave. A gold doll, found at a Late Bronze Age site on Aegina, was smuggled out to Mrs Brown so that she could sail out of Greece with her illicit booty. But she died during the journey, her body was thrown overboard and the gold doll vanished from the record. Higgins (1979), 46–51; amplified by Gates (1992).
7 NMA 28092 (EUM–331).
8 Excavations of the cemetery began in 1969.
9 All references from Tzedakis and Martlew (1999), 211–79.
10 NMA 2899.
11 For a full description of the figurine, see Wace (1939); see also *American Journal of Archaeology* 45, no. 1: 91; and *American Journal of Archaeology* 43: 697 and Fig. 1.
12 In August 1989.
13 *Iliad* 3.207–13 [LCL 3.171–5].
14 Men are sometimes involved too, but the rituals are predominantly single-sex.
15 The Linear B tablets from Knossos, Pylos, Thebes and Mycenae show that a number of women had particular skills and particular job-titles. There are *raptriai* ('sewing women') and *lewotrokhowoi* ('bath-pourers') among many other examples.
16 KN Ap 639.
17 MY V 659. Thank you to Lisa Bendall for help with this list.
18 Olsen (1998) has a very clear description of the three categories: 384ff.
19 No Linear B tablets yet discovered talk about midwives or wet-nurses – a gap which is almost certainly a chance of survival or recording practices rather than a comment on Mycenaean practice. It is therefore difficult to know whether aristocratic women such as Helen would have nursed their own infants. Myth stories seem to imply that the high-born handed over their children to be raised. Apollo, for instance, was farmed out to Themis rather than fed by his own mother Leto. And in the *Iliad*, as Hector rushes to meet his wife Andromache, we get what appears to be evidence both of paternal affection and of wet-nursing:

She [Andromache] joined him now, and following in her steps
a servant holding the boy against her breast,
in the first flush of life, only a baby,
Hector's son, the darling of his eyes
And radiant as a star . . .
   (*Iliad* 6.471–5 [LCL 6.399–401])

20 Meeting with Dr Elizabeth French, September 2004. Once again, many thanks to Dr French for her help with this project.

21 See Chapter 14. Five 'smiting god' metal figurines have been found and a small number of non-phallic male figures from Phylakopi.

CHAPTER FOURTEEN

Helen, High Priestess

1 Pylos tablet Ae 303. Ventris and Chadwick (1973), 166.

2 *Iliad* 7.551–4 (LCL 7.476–9].

3 Hesiod, *Theogony* 47–9. Trans. H.G. Evelyn-White.

4 There is too a female Zeus, *Diwia*, in Linear B tablets, e.g. Tn 316. Lisa Bendall has pointed out that Zeus does get fairly lavish gifts when he is honoured, such as a gold bowl and a man (Hera gets a gold bowl and a woman) at Pylos.

5 See Renfrew (1985), 302–10.

6 See Meagher (2002), 72.

7 Centuries later we hear that Agesilaus (360/59 BC), a king of Sparta who died in North Africa, was embalmed in honey to be brought back home for burial. And Alexander the Great's body was said to have been carried from Babylon to Greece in a honey-and-wax cocoon. See Diodorus of Sicily 18.26.3. Studies in the University of Illinois showed neat honey to be a better preservative of turkey-meat than the traditional preservatives butylated hydroxytoluene and tocopherol.

8 Meagher (2002), 56.

9 Ae 303.

10 The Priestess of the Winds at Knossos on Crete was honoured with a gift of 30 l of olive oil.

11 Others with hieratic power are the enigmatic *ki–ri–te–wi–ja*. John Killen has pointed out that more data are needed to draw certain conclusions about the role of women in a religious context.

12 See for comparison CMS II.6 no. 74 (Plate 276) and CMS 1 no. 46 (Plate 505) in Krzyszkowska (2005). My thanks to Olga Krzyszkowska for her help.

13 Site visit October 2004.

14 Mycenae Archaeological Museum, MM 294.

15 NMA 4575.

16 There are clues as to the kinds of rites that would have been carried out here in the cult centre in honour of that little goddess. A small clay bath-tub was once filled with water for purification, three hearths around the altar (itself only 60 cm high)

are ready to receive sacrificial offerings. Vessels were found here to carry wine and titbits to sustain the goddess. Gifts have been left to appease the spirits in the room: cooking pots, a stone bowl from Crete and the graceful ivory carvings that demonstrate the artistic genius of the Mycenaeans – a lion, the fine head of a young man.

17 Mycenae, Acropolis Treasure: NMA 942.

18 In another close association of women with nature, at Thebes, women process across a painted wall carrying lilies, papyrus and rock-roses. Warren (1988), 26.

19 For a recent survey of seal-stones, see Krzyszkowska (2005).

20 Thomas (1938–9), 65–87.

CHAPTER FIFTEEN
La Belle Hélène

1 *Iliad* 3.168–71 [LCL 3.139–42].

2 *Odyssey* 7.103–7. Trans. E.V. Rieu, revised D.C.H. Rieu [LCL 7.104–7].

3 *Iliad* 18.697 [LCL 18.596].

4 Pylos tablet Fr 1225.

5 See Shelmerdine (1985), *passim.*

6 Helen's 'gold curls' are referred to in Euripides, *Helen* 1224. Earlier, Sappho, in fragment 23, describes her as *xanthe* – 'golden', which may refer to her golden hair.

7 PY AN 656 and AN 218 may feature reference to braid-weavers.

8 Advice to visitors: double-check opening times of site of Pylos.

9 The most likely areas for production at the archaeological sites of Pylos are Courts 42 and 47.

10 Terebinth resin is the base of turpentine and is still harvested on an industrial scale on the island of Chios.

11 Thanks to Cynthia Shelmerdine for her help with this material and for pointing out that a lump of LBA terebinth resin she was given to handle had maintained its distinctive aroma.

12 Dayagi-Mendels (1998), 36.

13 For further details see Manniche (1999). The Papyrus Ebers (written *c.* 1500 BC, see 370, n.19) contained details of medical and cosmetic preparations. Recipes included those to fight wrinkles.

14 NMA 4575.

15 Thanks to Diana Wardle for allowing us to conduct a practical experiment based on the LBA findings.

16 Over a thousand years after these frescoes were painted, in Euripides' play *The Trojan Women*, Paris' mother accuses Helen of 'impudent flaunting' (*Trojan Women* 1028. Trans. J. Morwood), of making an extra special effort to attract Menelaus. But Euripides is giving Hecuba a classical rather than a Bronze Age voice. It is only around the 5th century BC that we have written evidence that make-up had come to be thought of as a means of deception – enhanced beauty enticing men into sexual activity – and as such had become the mark of a prostitute. The Bronze Age Helen would have

worn heavy, garish make-up that emphasised her physicality and her gender, but that would not have branded her a whore.

17 There are other styles of dress too. In a painting from Mycenae, a naturalistic female figurine is wrapped in a single robe. On an earlier ring made of electrum a woman wears either ankle bracelets or voluminous 'Ali-Baba' trousers under her skirt. On the frescoes, some women are shrouded in cloaks. The use of paint on frescoes at Mycenae and a tomb from Crete indicates that some women wore skirts made of wrapped animal hide.

18 See Rehak (2005) on ivory examples; for an example of a gold signet ring, see NMA 3180.

19 Euripides, *Trojan Women* 1042.

20 Hughes-Brock (1998), 260.

21 Propertius 3.14.17–20. Trans. A. Dalby (2000), 146.

22 *Heroides* 16, Paris' letter to Helen. Trans. H. Isbell.

23 Pliny, *Natural History* 33.23.81.

24 British Museum B376.

25 Trans. P. Forbes (1967) 363, from 'Le Sein d'Hélène', an essay of 1937; and congratulations to Vintage Direct for having such an intriguing website.

26 *Iliad* 3.273 [LCL 3.228].

27 Thanks to Peter Millett.

CHAPTER SIXTEEN

The Golden Apple

1 Isocrates, *Encomium of Helen* 54. Trans. L. van Hook.

2 The curved mirror-image was slightly distorted, the face reduced, the world behind clearly visible.

3 It was also quite common for classical artists and authors to pair Helen with a mirror. The imagery is potent; she is both an *eidolon* (a ghost, a reflection) and a woman whose image is deceptive. See Hawley (1998), 46–7 for a good further discussion. On Helen's appearance on mirrors, see 'Elina' in *LIMC*.

4 Fitzwilliam Museum GR.19.1904.

5 For example, *LIMC* nos. 83 and 86.

6 Euripides, *Trojan Women* 1107–8. Trans. J. Morwood.

7 Euripides, *Orestes* 1112. Trans. P. Vellacott.

8 For example, *Iliad* 3.146 [LCL 3.121].

9 Hesiod, *Catalogues of Women and Eoiae* 68.45 and *passim*.

10 Sappho, fragment 23; Euripides, *Helen* 1225. Down the centuries, heroes have been golden ever since. The Romans, masters of artifice that they were, even wore blond wigs – fashionable and a statement of their heroic credentials.

11 Quintus Smyrnaeus, *The Fall of Troy* 14.39–70. Trans. A.S. Way.

12 Ovid, *Metamorphoses* 3.138–252.

13 Byron, *Don Juan*, Canto the Fourteenth.

14 The Egyptians were obsessed with 'beauty': see Manniche (1999) on evidence for their expertise in cosmetics and other beauty-aids. There is also a love-poem, from the Papyrus Chester Beatty I, dated *c.* 1450–1500 BC, which lingers over the components of a woman's beauty: see trans. by M. Lichtheim (1976) *Ancient Egyptian Literature*, Vol. 2, 182–5. Thank you to Nicole Doueck for her help.

15 There is a hybrid word in Ancient Greek, '*kalokagathia*' which translates directly as 'beautiful goodness' or 'the joint nobility of appearance and conduct' – *kalos* means beautiful and *agathos*, good. It was thought by many that the two were inextricably linked. Men (the Greeks fought shy of applying the notion of *kalokagathia* to women) were good because they were beautiful – a perfect face was simply the patina of a perfect spirit. In the fairytale world of Snow White and Cinderella, too, absolute beauty indicates absolute virtue. *Kharis*, Helen's beauty, also demonstrates sexual maturity and sexual potency. Herodotus tells us of an Olympic victor called Philippus of Croton who was revered by the people of (non-Greek) Egesta as a hero purely because of his physical perfection. The town erected a hero's shrine on his tomb and his heroic cult continued for generations (Herodotus 5.47). In Plato's *Symposium*, Alcibiades – the lubricious renegade who for a time sided with Athens' arch-enemies, the Spartans – holds up Socrates (who was famously ugly) as a noted exception to the *kalokagathia* rule. And although the philosopher shifted his ideas during his life, in his earlier works, Plato seems to see beauty as an outward sign of virtue. Other thinkers doggedly kept alive the 'beauty equals goodness' theme. In AD 260, Plotinus, a man with a Latin name who seems to have been born in Egypt and who wrote in Greek, concluded in his best-known work, *On Beauty*, that *to agathon* was the ultimate form of *to kalon*. But Helen, 'the most beautiful woman in the world', worried him. In another treatise, *On Intelligible Beauty*, he asks: '*From what source, then, did the beauty of Helen whom men fought for shine out, or that of all women like Aphrodite in beauty?*' Plotinus, *On Beauty* (*Ennead* 1.6) and *On Intelligible Beauty* (*Ennead* 5.8). Trans. A.H. Armstrong.

16 In Neoplatonic thought, from the 5th century AD, Helen's beauty was interpreted as representing the beauty of the cosmos – a beauty that draws souls into a warring world. See Proclus, *Commentary on the Republic*.

17 Both Herodotus and Aristotle noted with interest that in a number of ancient cultures beauty or fineness of form justified political authority. Aristotle, *Politics* 1290b5. Trans. S. Everson: 'a government in which offices were given according to stature, as is said to be the case in Ethiopia, or according to beauty, would be an oligarchy; for the number of tall or good-looking men is small'. In Bion's *Ethiopian History*, we are told that the Ethiopians choose the most handsome men to be kings. Cf. Athenaeus, *Deipnosophists* 13.566c. See also Herodotus: 'These Ethiopians . . . are said to be the tallest and fairest of all men . . . they deem worthy to be their king that townsman whom they judge to be the tallest and to have strength proportioned to his stature.' Herodotus 3.20. Trans. A.D. Godley.

18 Gorgias was considered one of the finest speakers of his day and was said to have won plaudits in Olympia at the Olympic Games, where his audience would have been closer to 20,000 as well as in his homeland of Sicily. See Plato, *Gorgias* 458c for an indication of Gorgias' popularity in the ancient world.

19 I remember shivering outside the Institute of Contemporary Arts on the Mall in London, with a queue of other hopefuls, waiting to get returned tickets for the sell-out discussion, 'What is Beauty?' in 2004. We were a mixed bunch, artists and academics, tourists and lawyers, young men who looked as if they worked in advertising, young mothers who looked tired. In an age when beautiful things and beautiful people can be swiftly and easily manufactured, we still seem to want to believe that beauty itself has an abstract quality. The programme leaflet promised a lively exploration of the subject. Why does beauty have power? Can the essence of beauty ever be defined? What, indeed, is beauty? The question appears eternally fascinating.

20 Athenaeus, writing in the 2nd or 3rd century AD, reports such contests in his *Deipnosophists* at 13.565ff and 13.609ff, the latter a male beauty contest recorded by Theophrastus.

21 *Agones*: see p. 73.

22 Hawley (1998), 53, n. 7 lists a number of ancient sources on beauty contests held at Tenedos and Lesbos.

23 See Spivey (1996), 37, illustration no. 16: Staatliche Museen zu Berlin, no. F4221.

24 When describing the education of Athenian girls, Aristophanes articulates beauty as a defining quality of the *complete* young woman. See Calame (1997), 197, on Aristophanes, *Lysistrata* 641–7.

25 Scholiast on Theocritus' *Idylls* 18.22–5, 39–40.

26 This is of course a tradition that continues; in *Roman de la Rose* by Jean de Meun, a poem from the 13th century AD, Helen is also cited as the measure of all beauty.

27 Reference from M.E. Waithe (1992), *History of Women Philosophers*, Vol, 1: *Ancient Women Philosophers 600 BC–500 AD*: 198, citing Mozans, a pseudonym for J.A. Zahm (1913), *Woman in Science*, 197–9 (New York: Appleton).

28 Athenaeus, *Deipnosophists* 12.554c.

29 See Hawley (1998), 38; cf. Athenaeus, *Deipnosophists* 13.565.

30 See, for example, *Cypria*, fragment 1; *Iliad* 24.28–30 [LCL 24.29–30]; and Ovid, *Heroides* 16.51–88. See Gantz (1993), 567–71 for fuller literary and artistic sources.

31 Like Paris, Helen will be 'unmanned' by lust. Paris' mother Hecuba spits out at Helen in Euripides' play *Trojan Women*: *'My son was handsome beyond all other men. You looked at him and sense went Cyprian at the sight.'* Euripides, *Trojan Women* 991–2. Trans. M. Gumpert (2002), 79.

CHAPTER SEVENTEEN

Bearing Gifts

1 Diogenes Laertius, *Lives of Eminent Philosophers*, 5.18: 'Beauty he declared to be a greater recommendation than any letter of introduction.' Trans. R.D. Hicks.

2 A sculpture known as 'The Ephebe of Antikythera' – perhaps the work of Kleon of Sicyon or Euphranor.

3 Paris' preparations for combat take up several lines, compared to a terse two lines for Menelaus' own military toilette: 'magnificent Paris, fair-haired Helen's consort. *First he wrapped his legs with well-made greaves, / fastened behind the heels with silver ankle-clasps, / next*

he strapped a breastplate round his chest, his brother Lycaon's that fitted him so well./ Then over his shoulder Paris slung his sword,/ the fine bronze blade with its silver-studded hilt,/ and then the shield-strap and his sturdy, massive shield and over his powerful head he set a well-forged helmet,/the horsehair crest atop it tossing, bristling terror . . .'. Iliad 3.385–94 [LCL 3.239–37].

4   Those who knew of, or shared, the views of authors such as Herodotus, see Chapter 23.

5   See Hyginus, *Fables* 91; also Pindar, *Paean* 8a. The story was also the basis of the prologue to Sophocles' lost play, *Alexandros*.

6   *Iliad* 3.16–18 [LCL 3.15–17].

7   Dares, *The Fall of Troy: a History*, 12. Trans. R.M. Frazer, Jr.

8   *O Polemos tis Troados*: a Byzantine Iliad (*c.* 14th century AD). Trans. Myrto Hatzaki. Thanks to Dr Hatzaki for use of the translation.

9   Through a character called Nereus.

10 *Odes* 1.19–24, in T. Creech (1684) *The Odes, Satyrs, and Epistles of Horace: Done into English*. London.

11 Hittite gods are shown with their hair twisted into a ponytail and topped with a large conical cap.

12 See Hoffner (2003) and Macqueen (1975), 101.

13 We know from faunal remains that wolves, bears, leopards and panthers were hunted down by Bronze Age aristocrats in the forests of north-west Anatolia.

14 Latacz (2004), 28.

15 *Cypria*, fragment 1.

16 *Iliad* 3.44–5 [LCL 3.39].

17 Whose descendants Romulus and Remus would then go on to found Rome.

18 *Cypria*, fragment 10.

19 Knossos tablet Ld 573.

20 See, for example, Boccaccio, *Concerning Famous Women*, on 'Helen, wife of Menelaus'. Boccaccio continues to describe the story as love at first sight: 'There he fell in love with Helen as soon as he saw her resplendent in celestial beauty, wanton in royal elegance, and desirous of being admired.' See G.A. Guarino (1964), whose translation this is.

21 *Cypria*, fragment 1.

22 For a useful window onto the history of the relationship between the Hittites and Wilusa see the Alakšandu Treaty (*CTH* 76: there are numerous tablet fragments).

23 Genesis 23:3 and II Kings 7:6. See also Bryce (1998), 389–91.

24 For an overview of Hittite climate and geography, see Hoffner (2003).

25 Some from other centres of Hittite power: Tabigga in the Tokat province, Shapinuwa in the Corum province and Sarissa in the Sivas province.

26 M. Riemschneider (1954) *Die Welt der Hethiter* (Stuttgart: Kilpper), 93f.

27 Writing arrived, in the shape of cuneiform, in Anatolia in the early 2nd millennium BC.

28 See Bryce (2003).

29 *EA* 7:71–2 and *EA* 7:64–70: see Moran (1992). In this paragraph and the previous I have relied heavily on Bryce (2003). Once again, I owe him many thanks for being so helpful with this project.

30 *Cypria* fragment 1. Apollodorus in *Epitome* 3.3 reports that Menelaus entertained Paris for nine days, before leaving for his grandfather's funeral on the tenth day.

31 Hesiod, *Catalogues of Women and Eoiae* 67.7. Trans. H.G. Evelyn-White.

32 Herodotus 2.113–19.

33 Dio Chrysostom, the *Eleventh* or *Trojan Discourse*. Trans. J.W. Cohoon.

34 The whole story is told in Herodotus 2.112ff.

35 For example, *EA* 4:47–50 after Moran (1992).

36 In the reign of Tudhaliya (IV).

37 See Bryce (1998), 345 (RS 17.159 [PRU IV 126] 1–10).

38 See Bryce (1998), 344–7.

39 Trans. A.M. Miller (1996), 45.

CHAPTER EIGHTEEN

Alexander Helenam Rapuit

1 Duffy (2002). Reproduced by kind permission of the author.

2 Paris is also called Alexander by Homer and known by both names thereafter. Why did Homer do this? One possibility is that he is conflating historical reality with local Anatolian myth – and therefore gives his Trojan prince the names of heroes from both.

3 *Cypria*, fragment 1.

4 Apollodorus, *Epitome* 3. Trans. J.G. Frazer.

5 Ovid, *Heroides* 16 and 17. Trans. H. Isbell. In Dryden's 'Introductory Argument' to his translation of Helen's letter to Paris he opines: 'The whole Letter showing the extream artifice of Woman-kind'. Dryden, *Poetical Works*, 514 (Oxford Standard Authors), cited in R. Trickett, 'The *Heroides* and English Augustans', in Martindale (1988), 193.

6 Apollodorus, *Epitome* 3.3. Trans. J.G. Frazer.

7 Site visits 1985–2005.

8 Paris, Louvre OA 1839.

9 The artist is thought to be Gubbio: Paris, Louvre OA 1849.

10 Limoges, dated to the 16th century. Paris, Louvre OA 2044.

11 Paris, Louvre OA 7339.

12 See *Iliad* 24.33 [LCL 24.28] on the '*ate*' of Paris, and *Odyssey* 4.293 [LCL 4.261], where Helen refers to her own 'abandonment'. See also Lindsay (1974), 28.

13 Herodotus 2.120.

14 Croally (1994), 95.

15 *Iliad* 14.209–25 [LCL 14.170–83].

16 *Iliad* 3.62 [LCL 3.53].

17 *Iliad* 6.415 [LCL 6.350].

18 A term sometimes used to describe the consort of a goddess.

19 I was drawn to this idea by the work of Bella Vivante.

20 *Alexander Helenam Rapuit* is Isidore of Seville's entry explaining Helen's importance to his universal theory (compiled 7th century AD).

CHAPTER NINETEEN

The Female of the Species Is More Deadly Than the Male

1 This fragment was found in Egypt in 1906, and published in 1914 by Grenfell and Hunt. The translation used here is by Josephine Balmer, from (1984) *Sappho: Poems and Fragments* (London: Brilliance Books), reissued (1992) (Newcastle upon Tyne: Bloodaxe). Reproduced with permission. It appears in Margaret Reynolds (2003) *The Sappho History* (Palgrave: Macmillan), 6–7.

2 The 'Sappho debate' looks set to run and run. Some argue that she was a construct, invented to create a genre of 'female' poetry. For a taste of the arguments that she might be fictitious, see Prins (1999), 8.

3 Aelian, fragment 190. Trans. N.G. Wilson.

4 Plato, *Phaedrus* 235bc. Trans. M. Williamson (1995), 12.

5 *Palatine Anthology* 9.506; testimonia 60 in Sappho, trans. D.A. Campbell in *Greek Lyric*.

6 The papyri in question are the property of the Egypt Exploration Society and housed in the Sackler Library in Oxford, stored in paper folders or between glass sheets. They continue to be studied and more are published each year, but it will be several generations before the work of processing them is complete. Fragment 16 (known by its reference number of P.Oxy.1233) is kept in the Bodleian Library, Oxford.

7 Williamson (1995), 55.

8 See Pomeroy (2002), 46–8 on polyandry and ancient sources for its practice by Spartans.

9 Plutarch, *Lycurgus* 15.6–7.

10 Colluthus' work was written in the reign of the Emperor Anastasius I (AD 491–518).

11 Colluthus, *Rape of Helen* 314; 254; 393–4. Trans. A.W. Mair.

12 See Bate (1986), 19, for a more extensive list.

13 Illustration to Boethius' *Consolation of Philosophy*. Cambridge, Trinity Hall MS 12, folio 69r: see Baswell and Taylor (1988), 297. On the following page of the same manuscript, Agamemnon carries his daughter Iphigeneia's head on a plate.

14 See Peter Green's excellent 'Heroic Hype, New Style: Hollywood Pitted Against Homer', in *Arion* 12.1 (Spring/Summer 2004): 171–87.

CHAPTER TWENTY

Helen the Whore

1 Clement of Alexandria, *Paidogogos – The Instructor* 3.2: 'Against Embellishing the Body'. Trans. W. Wilson. Earlier, in a section entitled 'Against Excessive Fondness for Jewels and Gold Ornaments' (2.13), the author refers to women who richly adorn themselves without being truly beautiful, as 'Helens'. Clement was a Greek theologian, one of the founding fathers of Christian literature. He died *c*. AD 215.

2 The full title is *Ylias Daretis Phrygii*; for ease of reference, it will be referred to here as *Trojan War*.

3 *Trojan War* 4.189. Joseph based his account on Dares' *The Fall of Troy*. In chapter 12,

Dares also describes her *cruribus optimis*. Thanks to Neil Wright for his help with this and other passages.

4 Clement of Alexandria in the *Paidogogos* dealt in some detail with Helen's affair and disgrace: 'For the mind is carried away by pleasure; and the unsullied principle of reason, when not instructed by the Word, slides down into licentiousness, and gets a fall as the due reward of its transgression. An example of this are the angels, who renounced the beauty of God for a beauty which fades, and so fell from heaven to earth.' Chapter 2. Trans. W. Wilson.

5 And Joseph goes further, slicing Helen open to investigate her heart, lungs, spleen and 'lustful' liver: 'But the itch in her sensitive liver goads her on more lasciviously than it should, destroying the merits of her deserved fame and perverting the praise due to her inborn love. This liver is a monster that cannot be overcome by any voracious vulture, rolling stone, whirling wheel or receding water; when her lust, well slaked and cooling, seems dead and buried, then the old fires breathe afresh in its fertile tissues. So a single part totally sinks Helen, and rouses the very world to disaster as kingdoms clash in war.' *Trojan War* 4.193 ff. Trans. Neil Wright.

6 Joseph of Exeter, *Trojan War* 3.330–8. Trans A.K. Bate. The translation does depend on one's interpretation of *incumbens*, which supports either the notion of Helen being 'on top' or of her pressing into Paris' body.

7 De Lille was born at Lille *c.* AD 1120.

8 Alan de Lille, *The Plaint of Nature* 135 and 71. Trans. J.J. Sheridan. See also 217.

9 Payer (1984), 22.

10 Brundage (1993), 87.

11 See Baswell and Taylor (1988), 306.

12 From Thomas Proctor's *A Gorgeous Gallery of Gallant Inventions* (1578), in Rollins (1926), 81.

13 Ross, *Mystagogus Poeticus* 161.

14 Helen's beauty by definition was thought to make her unchaste. As Thomas Heywood would write in his *Troia Britannica* of 1609: 'Beauty and Chastity at variance are, / Tis hard to finde one Woman chast and faire . . .'

15 Ovid, *Art of Love* 359–72. Trans. J.H. Mozley.

CHAPTER TWENTY-ONE

The Pain of Aphrodite

1 Euripides, *Iphigeneia at Aulis* 544–51. Trans. R.E. Meagher (2002), 28. Euripides describes the white heat of engagement with Aphrodite, the goddess of love.

2 *Cypria*, fragment 4. Trans. M. Davies (1989).

3 Colluthus, *The Rape of Helen* 155–8. Trans. A.W. Mair.

4 *Iliad* 3.461–71 [LCL 3.400–7].

5 See the quotation that opens this chapter.

6 See B. Geoffroy-Schneiter (2003) *Greek Beauty* (New York: Assouline), 5.

7 Hesiod, *Theogony* 190–206.

8 Pausanias 7.23.1–3.

9 Ovid, *Heroides* 16.123–5. Trans. G. Showerman.

10 Ovid, *Heroides* 16. (excerpts) Trans. G. Showerman.

11 Propertius, *Elegies* 2.15.13–14. Trans. G.P. Goold.

12 For a full list of ancient sources that deal with this aspect of *eros* see Carson (1986), 148.

13 Eros was also thought to love beauty: '*For it is a universal truth that no one has escaped or will escape Eros as long as there be beauty and eyes to see it.*' Longus, *Pastorals of Daphnis and Chloe* (2nd–3rd century AD).

14 Xenophon, *Memorabilia* 1.3.12.

15 Hesiod, *Theogony* 121.911.

16 Vernant (1991), 101, translating a fragment of Alcman.

17 Aphrodite is often found in the natural landscape. In Aeschylus' play *Agamemnon* 741, Helen is a 'heart-eating flower of love'.

18 Marlowe, *The Tragical History of Dr Faustus*: see Chapter 43.

19 Gorgias, *Encomium of Helen* 4. Trans. D.M. MacDowell.

CHAPTER TWENTY-TWO

The Sea's Foaming Lanes

1 *Iliad* 3.54–7 [LCL 3.46–9].

2 Colluthus, *Rape of Helen* 328ff. Trans. A.W. Mair.

3 *Iliad* 3.516–28 [LCL 3.441–50].

4 Helen is shown on coins from Gythion as a tree between the Dioscuri: Lindsay (1974), 221, and n. 16, citing Chapouthier (1935), 149.

5 See Roscher (1884), 1950–1, on Helen.

6 Apollodorus, *Epitome* 3.3–4.

7 The nearby chamber tombs at Mavrovouni were used by the Germans as bunkers during the Second World War.

8 Paris, Louvre, Département des Arts graphiques INV. 20268.

9 Animal-skins would have played an integral part in currency since humans started to trade with each other, so it is little surprise that one precursor of metal coinage, talents, are ox-hide shaped blocks of bronze, some the size of small dogs.

10 Latacz (2004), 45.

11 A full list of destinations can be found in *Odyssey* 4.80ff.

12 A late scholiast was said to have given her star the name Ourania – see Lindsay (1974), 211, and the scholiast on Statius, *Thebaid* 7.92, for the notion of Helen as a star.

13 See, for example, R.A. Goldthwaite (1993) *Wealth and the Demand for Art 1300–1600* (Baltimore).

14 Dares, *The Fall of Troy* 10.

15 Cf. Helen on Etruscan tombs; see p. 11 (Introduction).

16 National Gallery, L667.

17 Site visit in 2003.

18 British Museum, ANE E29793 and E29785. For more information on the Amarna tablets, see Moran (1992).

19 Discovery close to the Mediterranean Turkish coast opposite the Greek island of Megisti.

20 An alternative dating system for the Aegean Bronze Age is summarised in Warren and Hankey (1989).

21 Cline (1994), xviii. Michael Wedde has pointed out to me that the fastest route to Egypt – hooking on to the north wind – might depart from Crete, head due south with a landfall at Libya and then on east to the Nile Delta. The return route could travel up the Syro-Palestinian coast utilising light winds blowing off the coast in the early evening light to travel northwards under sail. My thanks for his help with this passage.

22 Herodotus 2.117, citing *Cypria* fragment. Lloyd (1988) in his commentary on this passage, notes that other *testimonia* on the *Cypria* contradict Herodotus' report, claiming instead that Paris stopped off at Cyprus and Phoenicia on the way to Troy; cf. Apollodorus, *Epitome* 3, 1ff.

23 *Iliad* 6.341–6 [LCL 6.289–92].

24 On Linear B, see, for example, Ae 303: Ventris and Chadwick (1973), 166. See also Ventris and Chadwick (1973), 409–10 on the subject of foreign women captives and slaves. On Hittite sources, see Bryce (2002), 51–5, referencing, for example, KUB XIII 4, on appropriate punishments for slaves in the Hittite world.

25 Once again, only fragments of Stesichorus exist. His ideas and poetry resurface in the works of Plato and Euripides among others.

26 Isocrates, *Encomium of Helen* 64; Plato, *Phaedrus* 243a; Pausanias 3.19.11.

27 See West (1975); 7 and n. 10.

28 Herodotus, 2.112.

29 See Visser (1938) for further discussion of Helen's cult in Egypt.

30 A fragment of Hekataios also has Helen in Egypt: FrGrH1, F308, 309.

31 Herodotus 2.113–20. Trans. A. de Sélincourt.

32 Minoan-style frescoes have recently been identified in Egypt.

33 Minoan hegemony had allowed for close trade relations between Eastern Mediterranean countries but it is in the 13th century BC that we find strong, regular trade links across a comprehensive sweep of the Eastern Mediterranean.

CHAPTER TWENTY-THREE

East Is East and West Is West

1 Catullus 68.87ff. Trans. F.W. Cornish.

2 In the Roman period, a lump of stone was shaped to represent the *omphalos* and displayed at Delphi. It is still in the Delphi Museum.

3 Helen was present at Delphi on a frieze decorating the Siphnian treasury (carved perhaps in the 6th century BC). In Greek folklore Menelaus and Odysseus visited Delphi to ask if they should travel to Troy. The oracle advised that they first had to offer to Athena Pronaia a necklace which Aphrodite had once given to Helen. There does seem to have been Late Bronze Age cultic activity at Delphi – 175 Mycenaean

terracotta female figurines were found there at the sanctuary of Athena Pronaia.

4 Pausanias 10.12.2. Trans. W.H.S. Jones.

5 Thank you to Phiroze Vasunia for assistance on this point.

6 Hall (1996) in her introduction to her edition of Aeschylus' play *The Persians*, outlines how the performance of this play has been deployed for political ends on many other occasions.

7 P.Oxy.3965.

8 See Erskine (2001), 61–92, on the conflation of Persians and Trojans in fifth-century Athenian thought.

9 Herodotus 1.5 and 1.4. Trans. A.D. Godley.

10 Herodotus 6.32 and 6.31.

11 In the geographical area of Caria.

12 See McQueen (2000), vii.

13 Herodotus clearly had a showman's instinct. The historian is supposed to have given public recitations of his work – a good performance would merit a donation. He was one of the intellectual buskers of the ancient world. The story goes that Thucydides went to one of his recitals at Olympia and was moved to tears. But if there was a schoolboy crush, it did not last long, and the younger historian later denounced the elder (by implication) as a pedlar of tall tales.

14 The 5th-century BC Hippocratic treatise *Airs, Waters, Places* claims of the balmy conditions of Asia Minor that: '*Courage, endurance, industry and high spirit could not arise in such conditions either among the natives or among immigrants*' (12).

15 Euripides, *Trojan Women* 993–7. Trans. M. Hadas and J.H. McLean.

16 Euripides, *Helen* 926ff. Trans R. Lattimore.

17 See Hall (1996), 10, and for a slightly alternative view, Erskine (2001), 70–2 and 79–92 on Trojans and Persians in fifth-century iconography.

18 Isocrates, *Encomium of Helen* 67–9. Trans. L. van Hook.

19 Seneca, *Troade* 892–8. Trans. A.J. Boyle.

20 Describing the Carians (the historian Herodotus' geographical and perhaps genetic ancestors), Hellenistic and Byzantine commentators chose to see as 'typical' of the *Iliad* passages where Greek 'brain' wins over Trojan 'brawn' and so they proudly promoted Homer as a chauvinist in its original sense of the word, a fanatical supporter of (in this case, Greek) national interests.

21 The story of Troy was continually used for political ends, Byzantine writers promoted it as a demonstration of Greek supremacy and in 1580–1581 the romance poet Torquato Tasso published his *Gerusalemme liberata* ('Jerusalem Delivered'), which described Christian crusaders storming Jerusalem. The Scottish classical scholar Thomas Blackwell, in his work *An Inquiry Into the Life and Writings of Homer* (1735), describes the Greek invasion of Troy as '*a prodigious Rendezvous of the bravest Inhabitants, and Sons of the noblest Families of a free Country, wide and warlike; and engaged in a violent struggle of Passions and Arms, with another of more effeminate Manners*' (301): quoted in Williams (1993), 93ff.

22 KUB XIV 3 (*CTH* 181): see Bryce (1998): 321–4.

23 For full discussion of the designation Ahhiyawa, see Latacz (2004), 121–8.

24 Strabo, *Geography* 4.169.

25 Tablet KUB 26.91 (Bo 1485).

26 This text, discovered in 1924, has – so some claim – yielded new information; although the author was probably the Greek-speaking king of Ahhiyawa, it can be interpreted as being written in Hittite cuneiform. A king on the Greek mainland may have been sufficiently embroiled in Anatolian affairs to have to communicate in the same language. Material unpublished at time of writing.

27 The conflation of Helen's story with a natural disaster, the knock-on effect of dust-clouds from an asteroid, is one explanation offered for its drama. Some academics prefer more prosaic reasoning – there are well-researched arguments that the Trojan War was a conflict over fishing rights. But dendrochronological evidence from tree-rings buttresses the natural disaster theory. It is possible that a scandal involving Mycenaean and Trojan royalty was an inflammatory act in a period of increasing instability. Since recorded time, seismic climate changes and ecological disasters have been accompanied by human wars. Changes in food quantity and supply, the annihilation or creation of new paths of communication, and the destruction of settlements are all outcomes that frequently project human groups into states of conflict. There is little reason to think that this period in pre-history was any different. The ancients chose to pin the blame for the war, not onto storms and dust-clouds sent from the heavens, but on Helen. For discussion of cosmic activity in the period, see M. Baillie (2000) *Exodus to Arthur: Catastrophic Encounters with Comets*. London: Batsford.

28 Aristotle, *History of Animals* 551a (24).

29 *Iliad* 9.412.

CHAPTER TWENTY-FOUR

The Fair Troad

1 The poet Rupert Brooke writes one of his last letters home, to Violet Asquith, during the Great War of 1914–18. Keynes (1968), 662.

2 Site visit in 1988.

3 Margaret Adelaide Wilson, 'Gervais (Killed at the Dardanelles)', in Reilly (1981) 129.

4 Latacz (2004), 41.

5 Bryce (2005) points out that the three kingdoms of prime importance in western Anatolia were Mira, the Seha River Land and then Wilusa – what we now call Troy.

6 Textual evidence bears witness to curious imports such as a cult-image of a god sent from Ahhiyawa to one of the kings of the Hittites. KUB v. 6 (*CTH* 570) ii.57–64.

7 Bryce (2002), 5.

8 Greek words and names appear to have been absorbed into the Hittite language, and so were many from Luwian, the language possibly spoken in the Troad. Note, for instance, that the Luwian compound *priiamuua* means 'exceptionally courageous' – are we looking at the root of King Priam's name? A name thought suitable for great kings? See F. Starke (1997) 'Troia im Kontext des historisch-politischen und sprachlichen Umfeldes Kleinasiens im 2. Jahrtausend', in *Studia Troica* 7: 447–87, esp. 456–8.

9 In *Iliad* 6.138–282 [LCL 6.119–238] a story is told of the Trojan Glaucus and the Greek Diomedes who meet on the battlefield. Glaucus reveals that his ancestors originally came from Corinth on the Greek mainland, but were then exiled to Anatolia. The

reason for this humiliating expulsion from the homeland was the overblown sexual appetite and then rage of a lustful queen called Antea. Antea – originally from the region of Lycia – was infatuated with a beautiful prince of Corinth called Bellerophon, but her advances had been rejected: '*mad for Bellerophon, the lovely Antea lusted to couple with him, all in secret . . . she could never seduce the man's strong will, his seasoned, firm resolve.*' *Iliad* 6.188–90 [LCL 6.160–2]. Antea, addled with frustration, swore that Bellerophon had in fact tried to seduce her and her furious husband engineered Bellerophon's exile – packing into his luggage secret messages that demanded his execution. Homer's reference here to folded writing tablets – which have since been found preserved in the anaerobic conditions of the Uluburun shipwreck – is another indication that a number of the stories he tells come not from the illiterate 'Dark Ages' but from the Late Bronze Age. The Uluburun examples were made of wood, one still preserving scraps of wax and its ivory hinges. Exiled to Lycia in south-west Anatolia, Bellerophon in fact proves himself a true hero, killing, among other things, the monster the Chimaera and siring a new dynasty on Anatolian soil. *Iliad* 6.181–252 [LCL 6.154–211]. On 'dynasty', see *Iliad* 6.244–52 [LCL 6.206–11]. One of Bellerophon's descendants was the Lycian hero fighting for Glaucus. When the two warriors, Lycian and Greek, find their common roots they decide not to fight but to honour each other instead. They seal their newfound relationship in that way so beloved of the Bronze Age and Iron Age Greeks with an exchange of gifts: *xenia* in action. The two men are not brothers in arms, but find themselves to be brothers in blood. '*Both fighters sprang from their chariots, clasped each other's hands and traded pacts of friendship.*' *Iliad* 6.278–9 [LCL 6.232–3]. The little story of Glaucus and Diomedes is a useful one. It buttresses a stereotype of women as dangerous and untrustworthy. But it also commemorates the fact that the 'Heroic Age' was a time and a place of racial exchange – when peoples and individuals moved in both directions across the Dardanelles and the Bosphorus, a time when natural harbours such as Beşik Bay would have regularly hosted Mycenaean Greeks.

10 Some argue that Homer's epic derives partly from eastern sources as a result of this kind of interchange. Wandering minstrels in the Troad would have recited cycles, surprisingly similar to those that then turn up 500-odd years later in Homer. Homer's story itself could owe much to Hittite sources – or at least to Babylonian and Hurrian sources via the Hittite world. One literary work, *The Gilgamesh Epic* (originally Sumerian), has passages which, if you substituted Homeric for Gilgameshi names, would read like an echo of the other. There are female temptresses – pretty similar to Circe and the Sirens – and Ishtar, whom some equate with Aphrodite and even Helen herself. The Kumarbi Epic Cycle could be understood as having strong parallels with Hesiod.

11 102 were excavated, 35 contained skeletal remains representing 95 individuals. Thanks to Dr Hans Jansen for his help with this matter.

12 A decade after Mehmet the Conqueror sacked Constantinople in AD 1453, the sultan visited Troy. The trip was a piece of well-staged PR. Here the Ottoman ruler declared that by defeating the Greeks he had avenged his Trojan ancestors. See Rose (1998), 411.

13 Herodotus 7.43.

14 Cicero, *Pro Archia* 24. Trans. N.H. Watts.

15 In 48 BC, Julius Caesar toured the vicinity while in pursuit of his arch-rival Pompey,

declaring that: 'Pergamum [Troy] will rise Roman'. His visit was vividly immortalised by the Roman author Lucan: 'He walks around a memorable name – burnt-out Troy . . . now barren woods and trunks with rotting timber have submerged Assaracus' houses, and, with roots now weary, occupy the temples of the gods, and all of Pergamum is veiled by thickets: even the ruins suffered oblivion.' Lucan, *Civil War* 9.964–99. Trans. S.M. Braund.

16 The distance between the city gate and the fortress gate is only about 80 metres.

CHAPTER TWENTY-FIVE

The Topless Towers of Ilium

1 H.D., *Helen in Egypt* 2.6, in H. Gregory (1961), 242. Reproduced by kind permission of New Directions Publishing, New York. Note that this is Helen in Egypt, not Helen in Troy.

2 See Latacz (2004), 216, n. 4, citing M. Korfmann (1997), 'TROIA' – Ausgrabungen 1996, *Studia Troica*, 7; 1–71.

3 The Archaic Greeks called it *Ilion*; it then became known as *Ilium Novum*.

4 See Fitton (1995), 48. This graffito was recorded in the late 17th century.

5 Clarke's notion was published in London by William Gell in 1804 in a volume called *The Troad* or *The Topography of Troy*.

6 Fitton (1995), 59.

7 Schliemann's archaeological methods might have verged on the vandalistic, but he was in fact the last in a long line of improvident visitors to the site. Others had already, albeit inadvertently, done their best to destroy the Bronze Age remains buried in Hisarlik. Because Troy was such a strategic and (thanks to Homer and the epic cycle) culturally and emotionally significant site, it had been regularly levelled and then re-occupied down the centuries. Greek, Hellenistic, Roman and Byzantine settlers all cannibalised building materials and spliced through the surviving archaeology while they constructed their own lives.

8 Fitton (1995), 68.

9 Although Schliemann's conclusions (and excavation technique) were in part flawed, current excavations at the site support his basic assumption that the site of Troy on Hisarlik is both Homer's *Ilios* and the Late Bronze Age settlement of *Wilusa* – a wealthy town and a trading-post at the centre of a number of disputes in the 13th century BC. Developments in current excavations can be tracked on the Project Troia website or in the periodical *Studia Troica*.

10 Schliemann (1870) 'Les fouilles de Troie' in the *Levant Herald*, 3 June 1870; and see Allen (1999), 131.

11 For debate on the exact conditions of the discovery see Easton (1981) and Traill (1984).

12 For an account of the rediscovery of this hoard in the Pushkin Museum in Moscow, see M. Siebler (1994) 'Eine andere Odyssee: Vom Flak-Bunker zum Puschkin Museum', in *Troia-Geschichte-Grabungen-Kontroversen*. Mainz: Antike Welt. See also Easton (1994).

13 Moorehead (1994), 229.

14 Moorehead (1994), 92–5. Schliemann's diaries and letters are held by the Gennadius Library, Athens.

15 Moorehead (1994), 35.

16 H. Schmidt (1902) *Heinrich Schliemann's Sammlung Trojanischer Altertuemer* (Berlin), 232–3.

17 Hoards in Troy such as these do attest the continuous and exceptional wealth of the town – surely garnered through international trade.

18 Work started on the building in 1878.

19 *Iliou Melathron* itself is a menagerie of styles from across antiquity. Schliemann dug deep into his pockets to realise his domestic dreams and the project cost 439,650 drachmas. On the walls are copies of Pompeiian frescoes painted by a Slovenian artist, Yuri Subic. The mosaic floor incorporates motifs from Troy and Mycenae and the house is protected by solid gates and railings along which a series of stern sphinxes process. It is all a far cry from the mossy half-timbered cottage where Schliemann's life began. Now the *Iliou Melathron* is Greece's leading numismatic museum; how appropriate that the man who worshipped Mammon should inadvertently build the god one of his finest shrines.

20 Digs took place in 1932–8 under the supervision of Carl W. Blegen of the University of Cincinnati, and then were resumed in 1981 at Beşik Tepe by an international team under the supervision of Manfred Korfmann. The work continues to this day, and finds are stored in the Canakkale Museum. Details in *A Guide to Troia* (1999) by the Director and Staff of the Excavations (Istanbul: Ege Press).

21 Wilusa refers to the kingdom of Troy and would, almost certainly, also have been the name given to the city.

22 Detailed arguments around the issue of the identification of Wilusa as Troy, and of Hisarlik Hill with historical elements within Homer's epic can be found *passim* in Latacz (2004); for the designation Wilusa, see particularly 82–3.

23 Museum of Fine Arts, Boston, 13.186.

24 Madrid, Biblioteca Nacional no. 17805: Guido MS, fol. 46; (date *c.* 1350).

25 *Chronique Universelle, dite la Bouquechardière* (*Universal Chronicle*) of Jehan de Courcy. New York, Pierpont Morgan Library, M214, fol. 84.

26 Scherer (1963), 37, Fig. 37.

27 There is a wonderfully poised painting of Helen by the artist Guido Reni. The huge Reni canvas, painted in the 17th century, hangs in one of the long corridors of the Louvre. The Reni painting has its own, complicated symbolism (much of the composition seems to have been planned with European politics in mind) but it is a good example of an appreciation of Helen's narrative without the need for a rape at its heart. See Colantuono (1997).

28 Despite the fact that Homer, among others, tells us that chief among Helen's attendants was the matron Aethra (the aged mother of Theseus, herself abducted by Castor and Pollux when they rescued Helen as a girl from Aphidna).

29 A subject brilliantly discussed by Ruth Bernard Yeazell (2000) *Harems of the Mind: Passages of Western Art and Literature* (New Haven, CT: Yale University Press).

30 '. . . which Philaenis and Elephantine later imitated, who carried out further similar licentious acts'. Trans. H. Parker (1992), 92. Philaenis and Elephantine were two of

nine writers whose names we have as authors of sex manuals. Philaenis is thought to have lived c. 370 BC, and Elephantine c. 1st century BC: see Parker (1992), 94.

31 S.v. *Astyanassa*, 4. 261 in *Suidae Lexicon*, ed. A. Adler, Vol. 1, 393.

32 See Parker (1992) for further discussion of ancient sex manuals.

33 Aeschylus, *Agamemnon* 403–8.

34 *LIMC*, no. 191.

35 Manuscript details all from Baswell and Taylor (1988) with backup from Buchthal (1971).

36 *Iliad* 6.576 [LCL 6.483–5].

37 II Kings 7:6.

38 H.P. and M. Uerpmann (2001) *Leben in Troia — Pflanzen und Tierwelt*, in: Archiäologisches Landesmuseum Baden-Württemberg *et al* (eds), *Troia — Traum und Wirklichkeit* (Stuttgart: Theiss), 315, especially Fig. 325.

39 *CTH* 284.

40 For further information, see S. Penner (1998) *Schliemanns Schachtgräberund und der europäische Nordosten Studien zur Herkunft der frühmykenischen Streitwagenausstattung* [*Saarbrücker Beiträge zur Altertumskunde* 60] (Bonn).

41 For example, the stone grave stele from Shaft Grave V, Grave Circle A, Mycenae, now in the National Archaeological Museum in Athens, NMA 1428.

42 See, for example, Tiryns frescoes; deep bowl krater at Nauplion 14336; vase painting on amphoroid krater, London, BM C357.

43 Thanks to Mike Loades for researching, leading and co-ordinating the operation and to Robert Hurford, chariot builder and Jonathan Warterer, horse-trainer.

44 See Bryce (2005), chapter 4: 'The Aegean Neighbours'.

45 Sometimes four; a driver, an archer and two mobile infantry.

46 *Iliad* 8.76–7 [LCL 8.64–5].

47 *Iliad* 24.944 [LCL 24.804].

48 There were severe malaria epidemics across the Eastern Mediterranean in the Bronze Age.

CHAPTER TWENTY-SIX

The Golden Houses of the East

1 *Iliad* 2.912–14 [LCL 2.803–4].

2 The picture that emerges from the tablets of the Hittite civilisation is of a powerful entity, made up of a number of states or kingdoms — most of them with a ruling king and queen. Some were controlled directly from Hattusa, some had their own local rulers, others were 'buffer zones' — dividing, for example, the Hittite world and the Hurrian kingdom of Mitanni (which covered much of northern Mesopotamia, northern Syria and parts of Eastern Anatolia).

3 I have relied heavily here on Bryce (2002) — an essential starting point for an understanding of the Hittite world.

4 Discussed at length by A. Ünal (1994) 'The Textual Illustration of the "Jester Scene" on the Sculptures of Alaca Höyük', in *Anatolian Studies* 44: 207–18.

5 See A. Goetze (1957) *Kulturgeschichte Kleinasiens* (Munich: Beck), 94.

6 We also hear some royal women referred to as the SAL LUGAL.GAL (the Great Queen, legal queen).

7 *CTH* 76.

8 See Latacz (2004), 118.

9 At the very least it should not escape notice that Homer is using names for his characters which are perfectly appropriate to their time and place. On Linear B tablets, 58 names have been found which also appear in Homer, including an Achilles, whose name is inscribed on a tablet from Pylos in a rations list for workers at a festival (Fn 79), and a Hector, who is a 'slave of the god' in the Pylos land tenure tablets (for example, Eb 913 and En 74).

10 The 'Milawata Letter': *CTH* 182 (KUB 19.55 and KUB 48.90). The 'Milawata Letter' points to intrigue at the Trojan court, detailing a king of Troy (Walmu) who had been deposed and was then to be restored thanks to the agency of the Hittites.

11 Edict of Telipinu: *CTH* 19.

12 Apology of Hattusili III.9.3.3 (*CTH* 81).

13 Aphrodite does not appear on Linear B tablets – an absence that some scholars apply to the suggestion that Helen is a proto-Aphrodite figure.

14 Hurrian Hymn to Ishtar, KUB XXIV (*CTH* 717) i.38–40, adapted by G. Beckman (2000) in 'Goddess Worship – Ancient and Modern', in *A Wise and Discerning Mind: Essays in Honor of Burke O. Long*, ed. S.M. Olyan and R.C. Culley (Providence), 11, from a translation by H. Güterbock (1983) 'A Hurro-Hittite Hymn to Ishtar', *Journal of the American Oriental Society* 103: 156.

15 Stamps still survive: e.g. Stamp Seal of Hittite Queen Puduhepa, in the Corum Museum 1.973.90.

16 RS 17.133.

17 There are no recorded dates for this event – which possibly fell in Urhi-Teshub's reign *c.* 1272–1267 BC during the civil war with Hattusili.

18 The daughter of Puduhepa, in the autumn of 1246, was finally dispatched on a journey organised and monitored by her mother to Egypt to marry Rameses II. But here the story peters out: like so many women who formed part of the human traffic between aristocratic courts, Puduhepa's tardy daughter seems to become just another member of the harem at Fayum. See Bryce (2002), 125.

19 See Bryce (2002), chapter 2: 'The People and the Law'.

20 Clause 28a, 'The Laws'.

21 Clause 197, 'The Laws'.

22 'If he brings them to the palace gate [the royal court] and says: "My wife shall not die," he can spare his wife's life, but must also spare the lover. Then he may veil her [his wife]. But if he says, "Both of them shall die", and they "roll the wheel", the king may have them both killed or he may spare them.' (Clause 198, 'The Laws').

CHAPTER TWENTY-SEVEN
A Fleet Sets Sail

1　Aeschylus, *Agamemnon* 414–19. Trans. A. Carson.

2　See *Cypria*, fragment 1.

3　In Dictys' version of the story, Menelaus sends a diplomatic mission from Crete as soon as he hears the news of Helen's infidelity in Sparta.

4　*Iliad* 3.247–69 [LCL 3.205–24] and Apollodorus, *Epitome* 3.28–9. According to the *Cypria*, the Greeks send an embassy after an initial attempt at landing and a skirmish on the Trojan shore. According to Herodotus 2.118, envoys were sent after the Greek army landed at Troy, but were met with the intelligence that Helen and the treasure were actually in Egypt, not Troy.

5　*Iliad* 11.143–65 [LCL 11.122–42].

6　Trans. Beckman (1996), 91–2.

7　Extracted from KBo I 10 + KUB III 72 (*CTH* 172). Trans. A.L. Oppenheim (1967), *Letters from Mesopotamia* (Chicago and London), 139–40. Quotation taken from Bryce (1998), 293.

8　See paragraph 1 of the Alakšandu tablet.

9　See Beal (1995), 547.

10　See Gantz (1993), 576–82.

11　In some versions of the story, the fleet has already set sail, and the diplomatic embassy is sent once the Greeks have landed on Trojan soil. This might be the suggestion in the *Iliad*: see *Iliad* 3.247–69 [LCL 3.205–24].

12　*Iliad* 2.265 [LCL 2.227].

13　*Iliad* 8.331–2 [LCL 8.291–2].

14　Generally presumed to be Clytemnestra's daughter, although in variant myths she is Helen's child. In the imagination of some it was Helen's overpowering allure that brought Iphigeneia her life and that dragged her towards an early death. See also Gantz (1993), 582–8, for a summary of ancient sources for this story.

15　It is in Euripides' *Iphigeneia among the Taurians* and *Iphigeneia at Aulis* that we first find mention of the Achilles ploy. See Gantz (1993) for Euripidean variations.

16　Aeschylus, *Agamemnon* 259–78 [LCL 225–43]. Trans. A. Shapiro and P. Burian (2003).

17　Euripides, *Iphigeneia at Aulis* 1166–70. Trans. P. Vellacott. Production seen at The Gate. J.W. von Goethe, *Under the Curse*; a new version by Dan Farrelly.

18　Euripides, *Iphigeneia at Aulis* 1264–5. Trans. R.E. Meagher.

19　Although in Euripides, *Iphigeneia at Aulis*, Iphigeneia embraces her death as an honour.

20　*Iliad* 2.573ff [LCL 2.484ff].

21　See E. Visser (1997) *Homers Katalog der Schiffe* (Stuttgart and Leipzig: Teubner), 746.

22　Summary of discovery in Latacz (2004), 240ff.

23　Godart and Sacconi (2001), 542.

24　Latacz (2004), Fig. 24.

25　See Latacz (2004), 92–100, for fuller discussion.

26　Latacz (2004), 154ff. and 260ff.

27　Letter from the King of Ugarit to the King of Alashia (part of Cyprus): RS 20.238, lines 27–31, from the archive of Ugarit. Published in *Ugaritica* 5 as no. 24.

28 Thanks to Michael Wedde for his detailed help with this passage and for the intelligence that around 1200 BC Ugarit had a fleet of 150 ships.

29 For a fine, fuller picture, see Morgan (1988), chapters 9–10 and Colour Plate C.

30 Although, as I have pointed out, Troy is in fact very close to Sparta by sea, in the epic imagination this had become a vast distance, as Achilles says (*Iliad* 1.184–5 [LCL 1.156–7]), when observing he has no personal quarrel with the Trojans and that this is a pre-emptive strike. '*Look at the endless miles that lie between us . . . shadowy mountain ranges, seas that surge and thunder.*'

CHAPTER TWENTY-EIGHT

Helen – Destroyer of Cities

1 *Iliad* 2.420–3 [LCL 2.354–6].

2 στυγέω (to loathe, shrink from) and ὀκρυόεις (causing a chilling fear) are also used in association with Helen; see Clader (1976) for further discussion.

3 *Iliad* 2, *passim*.

4 *Iliad* 1.1–2 [LCL 1.1–2].

5 *Iliad* 1.33–6 [LCL 1.29–31].

6 *Iliad* 13.830 Trans. J.–P. Vernant (1991), 100.

7 *Iliad* 13. 959–60 [LCL 13.829–31].

8 For an excellent summary of the aggressive/sexual incarnations of the eastern goddess Ishtar (Aphrodite's equivalent) see Bryce (2002), 147.

9 And just as desire and death, sex and violence, were, in the minds of the Greeks, two sides to the same coin, two different ways of expressing the same primordial urge, so one could lead to the other. As Plato neatly summed up, 'there is no cause of battles and wars and civil strifes other than the lusts of the body'. Plato, *Phaedrus* 66c.

10 *Iliad* 2.183–90 [LCL 2.157–62].

11 *Iliad* 3.196ff. [LCL 3.162ff.].

12 *Iliad* 3.179ff. [LCL 3.149ff.].

13 *Iliad* 3.185–90 [LCL 3.145–8].

14 See R. Naumann (1971) *Architektur Kleinasiens von ihren Anfängen bis zum Ende der hethitischen Zeit* (Tübingen: Ernst Wasmuth), 252. Homer describes Troy as boasting '*eudmetos purgos*' (a well-built tower).

15 Marlowe, *Dr Faustus* (B-Text) V.i.95.

16 See Korfmann *et al.* (2004) 'Was There a Trojan War?' For detraction of Korfmann's claims, see D. Hertel and F. Kolb (2003) 'Troy in Clearer Perspective', in *Anatolian Studies* 53: 71–88 and F. Kolb (2004) 'Troy VI: a Trading Centre and a Commercial City?', in *American Journal of Archaeology* 108: 577–614.

17 Korfmann (1993), 27ff.

18 *Iliad* 16.816ff. [LCL 16.698ff.].

19 See Latacz (2004), 40 and n. 47, and Korfmann (1998).

20 Site visit in 1995.

21 Manchester Museum 1977.1048. In many versions of this popular vase design, the

men are so absorbed that Athena has to appear to remind them that a battle has started to rage around them.

22 The campaigning season was typically April to September.

23 Alakšandu Treaty, 20.

24 1997–8.

25 Latacz (2004), 83.

26 *Iliad* 22.183 [LCL 22.153].

27 For a useful overview, see Korfmann *et al.* (2004).

28 For alternative dates for Troy VI, see Mountjoy (1999).

29 The use of an earth 'cushion' above the bedrock when rebuilding Troy VII after Troy VI may suggest that the Trojans, having experienced severe earthquake damage, attempted to accommodate further seismic activity within their architecture. For further discussion see Mountjoy (1999), 254–6, and Rapp and Gifford (1982), chapter 2.

CHAPTER TWENTY-NINE

Death's Dark Cloud

1 *Iliad* 16.407–13 [LCL 16.344–50].

2 *Iliad* 3.516–28 [LCL 3.441–50].

3 *Iliad* 6.68–70 [LCL 3.58–60].

4 As is shown in Chapter 42, in the medieval period Homer's wild, muddy blood-bath becomes a tale of morality, prudence and statecraft.

5 *Iliad* 5.161–4 [LCL 5.145–7] and 5.321–5 [LCL 5.290–3].

6 See Korfmann (1996), 34.

7 *Iliad* 2.650 [LCL 2.560].

8 A skeleton found in Grave Gamma at Mycenae, indicates that another warrior also survived a cranial investigation.

9 All information from Arnott (1999). Many thanks to Robert Arnott for his help with this project.

10 See Mayor (2003), 41–62 for a discussion of biological warfare in the Heroic Age.

11 *Iliad* 1.60 [LCL 1.52].

12 Bryce (2005). Text from KBo IV 6 (*CTH* 380), obv. 10'–15'. Trans. O. Gurney.

CHAPTER THIRTY

A Beautiful Death – Kalos Thanatos

1 Sorley (1922), 82. In the same work are found the lines: '*The tales, after the port went round! The wondrous wiles of old Odysseus, old Agamemnon and his misuse of his command, and that young chit Paris – who didn't care a bit for Helen – only to annoy her he did it really . . .*'

2 Ideas discussed elegantly and comprehensively in Vernant (1991).

3 The Spartans were taught to welcome death on the battlefield.

4 In a world in which the life of the community was lived, almost exclusively, in a series of public spaces, public recognition was a *raison d'être*. As Vernant elucidates: 'the same

words – *agathos, esthlos, aretē* and *timē* – can denote high birth, wealth, success, martial courage, and fame. There is no clear distinction among the concepts.' Vernant (1991), 56.

5 For neolithic examples from Britain see R. Mercer and F. Healy, eds (forthcoming), *Hambledon Hill, Dorset, England: Excavation and Survey of a Neolithic Monument Complex and its Surrounding Landscape*. English Heritage Archaeological Reports.

6 Sorley (1922), 85.

7 Pelly (2002), 10.

8 Patrick Shaw-Stewart, 'Untitled', in B. Gardner, ed. (1986) *Up the Line to Death: The War Poets 1914–18* (London: Methuen), 59–60. Shaw-Stewart was killed in action in 1917. See also Chapter 37 n22.

9 *Iliad* 18.623–6 [LCL 18.535–8].

10 J.-K. Huysmans wrote of the painting, 'She stands out against a sinister horizon, drenched in blood, and clad in a dress encrusted with gems like a shrine. Her eyes are wide-open in a catatonic stare. At her feet lie a pile of corpses. She is like an evil goddess who poisons all that approach her.'

11 First site visit February 1995.

12 On all Moreau's canvases the Spartan queen is strong and sinewy. Preserved in swinging racks along the walls of his old home there are scores of pencil, pen-and-ink and conté sketches of life-models. One woman, long-legged and fit, is the prototype for Helen. Along with the Helens she modelled for, this woman is not like most of the other female figures in the room – limp, naked and available – she is hard-cored.

13 In one painting on the third floor, Helen's smooth empty oval face is echoed by the pale globe of the moon above her. Inv. No. 58.

CHAPTER THIRTY-ONE

The Fall of Troy

1 Euripides, *Helen* 256ff. Trans. D. Kovacs.

2 *Iliad* 6.407 [LCL 6.344].

3 See *Iliad* 3.218 [LCL 3.180]; 6.408 [LCL 6.344]; 6.421 [LCL 6.356]; and *Odyssey* 4.162.

4 *Iliad* 6.415–16 [LCL 6.351–2].

5 Here is another hero who has died for her, and yet, in his dying, achieves *kleos*. See Clader (1976) for further discussion.

6 *Iliad* 24.909–13 [LCL 24.773–5].

7 When Odysseus disguises himself as a beggar and steals into the city to assess the Trojan fortifications, Helen has the wits to recognise him but does not hand him over to her new allies. Instead she bathes the lord of Ithaca and anoints him with oil, swearing that she has had a change of heart and longs to go home. Years later this story is being told back in the Spartan palace, but is trumped by Helen's attempted betrayal of the Greeks in the Trojan horse.

8 Particularly in Virgil's version of the story in *Aeneid* 6.

9 Virgil, *Aeneid* 6.515–19.

10 This story is told in *Odyssey* 4.310–24 [LCL 4.277–89].

11 Lesches, via Apollodorus, apparently suggested it was 3,000, but the figure is

disputed by scholars: see Gantz (1993), 649 and n. 86.

12 *Little Iliad*, Fragment 20.

13 BM 1899.2–19.1.

14 From KUB XIII 4, see Bryce (2002), 52.

15 431–404 BC.

16 Thucydides, 3.67.

17 Thucydides, 5.116.

18 Paraphrase from Tyrone Guthrie's New York production. Thanks to Michael Wood for his help.

19 Thebes reference TH Gp 164: Godart and Sacconi (2001), 541.

20 Bryce (2002), 105.

21 Ovid, *Metamorphoses* 12.607–8, pictures Achilles' disgust at being felled by an arrow – wielded by Paris' 'feminine hand'.

22 Paris' character is reformed, though, by the European dynasties of the medieval and Renaissance periods who traced their ancestry back to the Trojans. Thus we find Proctor in his *Gallery of Gallant Inventions* remarking how 'If Hellen had not bin so light; Sir Paris had not died in fight'; see Rollins, ed. (1926).

23 Both Hittite and Judaic texts refer to the practice of a widow marrying her husband's brother; it is known in the Old Testament as levirate marriage.

24 Hyginus, *Fables* 240 has Helen killing Deiphobus herself.

25 Virgil, *Aeneid* 6.494–512. Trans. D. West.

26 Stesichorus, 201 *PMG*. See Gantz (1993), 651.

27 *Little Iliad*, fragment 19, *EGF*.

28 Euripides, *Orestes* 1286. Trans. M.L. West.

29 The double entendre was certainly not lost on the ancients; come the Roman period, a woman's genitals are given the name of a sword-sheath, '*vagina*'.

30 Mykonos Museum 2240 (*c.* 675 BC). *LIMC* no. 225; see E.C. Keuls (1985) *The Reign of the Phallus: sexual politics in ancient Athens* (Berkeley and London: University of California Press), 397–9.

31 For a fuller discussion of all examples, see Hedreen (1996).

32 Translation after Clement (1958), 49.

33 Euripides, *Andromache* 629–30. Trans J.F. Nims in Grene and Lattimore (1958).

34 British Museum, GR 1865.7–12.4.

35 See Pipili (1992), 179–84, esp. 183–4, on 6th-century bronze shield-bands from the Peloponnese seeming to show the recovery of Helen by Menelaus, or else perhaps her abduction by Paris.

36 See French (2002), 16.

37 *The Collected Poems of Rupert Brooke* (New York: John Lane, 1915).

CHAPTER THIRTY-TWO

Home to Sparta

1 Gladstone (1858), Vol. 2, 488.

2 *Odyssey* 4.631–41 [LCL 4.561–9].

3 So far, from the Mycenaean tombs analysed, this seems to be a population with terrible teeth from the early twenties onwards. A forty-year-old weaver (admittedly in dental terms a hazardous occupation), buried at the Armenoi cemetery on Crete some time between 1340 and 1190 BC, has lost twenty-three out of his thirty-two teeth.

4 Euripides, *Trojan Women* 1046—50. Trans. K. McLeish.

5 Euripides, *Trojan Women*. Trans. K. McLeish.

6 Agamemnon's murder is referred to from the 7th century BC onwards. The first certain attestation to its taking place in a bath is to be found in Aeschylus, *Oresteia*. It is Aeschylus who puts the knife in Clytemnestra's hand.

7 *Odyssey* 4.234 [LCL 4.210].

8 *Odyssey* 4.141 [LCL 4.127].

9 *Odyssey* 4.90—5 [LCL 4.81—5].

10 See also Euripides, *Helen, passim.*

11 Herodotus 2.119.3.

12 In 360 BC, Agesilaus, a famous Spartan king, died in Libya at a place called 'the Harbour of Menelaus'. Menelaus' harbour is mentioned in Strabo, *Geography* 17.3.22.

13 Aristodemus, *FrGrH* 22 F (1a).

14 See Hughes (1989) for a good general study. One Linear B tablet (Pylos tablet Tn 316) has been tentatively interpreted as listing the victims of a human sacrifice along with the gold that was also being offered to the gods. On the Greek mainland, tombs have been excavated that contain skeletons in atypical positions or configurations. At the modest site of Kazarma, where a tholos tomb was excavated in the 1960s; two kneeling skeletons were reported as being found just inside the entrance. These were clearly poor men; they had no grave goods with them, simply a necklace made out of olive and apricot stones. Could they have been slaves or favoured servants who had been killed on the pile of stones at the entrance of the tomb? Slaughtered so they could travel with their lord or lady to the afterlife? Drive for twenty minutes or so from Mycenae, and you will find the confident, hilltop site of Prosymna. Here, in Tomb VII, there is another curious figure from the Late Bronze Age, a skeleton stretched over a pile of stones with a large limestone slab pinning down the bones. In the lower city of Mycenae, in Tomb 15, six individuals who appear to have died or been killed at the same time have been laid one over the other. All data in this note from Hughes (1989).

15 Site visit in 2001.

16 See Sakellarakis and Sapouna-Sakellaraki (1997) for an introduction to the finds around Archanes.

17 We have such exceptional evidence for this dreadful scene only because at the very moment the ritual was being carried out, Crete was rocked by an earthquake. The walls of the sanctuary toppled, crushing those still left alive inside. Perhaps the Minoans believed Poseidon, the earth-shaker, had already sent warning tremors through the land. Perhaps the sacrificial victim, a man in his prime, was being offered up as a desperate attempt to appease the fickle, awful gods? Poseidon appears on the Linear B tablets: see Ventris and Chadwick (1973), 126, for examples attested at Knossos and Pylos, e.g. Un 718.

18 *Odyssey* 4.146—7 [LCL 4.130—2].

19 Barber (1994).

20 Paris was buried alongside his first wife Oenone according to Strabo, *Geography* 13.1.33, written some time under the reigns of Augustus and Tiberius. Estimated dating of the *Geography* ranges from *c.* 7 BC to *c.* AD 18.

21 An eagle flies by with a goose clutched in its talons as foretelling Odysseus' triumphal reclaim of his wife Penelope and his palace in Ithaca.

22 Euripides, *Orestes* 62–6. Trans. D. Kovacs.

23 See *Odyssey* 4 for a description of Helen and Menelaus' Spartan palace.

24 See Bergen (1981) for a discussion of Helen's use of drugs defining the duality of her character.

25 *Odyssey* 4.220–6 [LCL 4.220–6]. Trans. E.V. Rieu.

26 Thanks to Professor Bradley C. Lenz for information that, given Helen's and the Mycenaeans' Egyptian connections, this drug could also have been mandragora, which, when mixed with wine, produces a trance-like state.

27 Hughes-Brock (1998), 251. There were also beads in the shape of figure-of-eight shields.

28 A seal-stone from Ipsopata is inscribed with the image of a woman who seems to be rising up out of the earth, helped by a young man – an epiphany brought on by narcotic use? Thomas (1938–9).

29 Opium is referred to in a Theban papyrus of 1552 BC.

30 See Arnott (2005b).

31 Even *Papaver rhoeas L.*, the red poppy, which would have grown more commonly on the mainland (and Crete), acts as a mild sedative.

32 *Odyssey* 4.341–342.

CHAPTER THIRTY-THREE

The Death of a Queen

1 Euripides, *Orestes* 1130–1310. Trans. P. Vellacott. The Mycenae story was relocated to Argos by Athenian playwrights following Athens' alliance with Argos in the 5th century BC.

2 Euripides, *Orestes* 1639–43. Trans. P. Vellacott.

3 Euripides, *Orestes* 1683–90. Trans. P. Vellacott. The chorus has a three-line closing statement, but other than that, these are the last words of the play. Vellacott suggests in his introduction that perhaps Euripides, in 'his last personal address to his fellow-citizens' (1972: 68), before he leaves Athens for Macedon at the end of his career, is keen to set straight the ambiguity with which he has always imbued his representations of Helen, by depicting her here as a wholly sympathetic character – ultimately deified at the will of her father, Zeus.

4 Ovid, *Metamorphoses* 15.232. Trans. F.J. Miller.

5 Pausanias 3.19.9 on the story of Helen's hanging by a vengeful Polyxo.

6 For three hundred years or so before the Trojan Wars, the elite on the Greek mainland had been burying their dead with ever more ostentation. Many tholos tombs are first of all intricately furnished and then abandoned, while chamber tombs boast rich offerings. It was becoming de rigueur to give your kin or your rulers a fabulous send-off,

to make that transition between this world and the afterlife as showy as possible. By the end of the 14th century it seems that belts were tightened a little; goods were kept for the living rather than the dead. Thanks to Sofia Voutsaki for her help with this section.

7 Both so-called; we do not know the names of the kings and queens who were in fact buried here.

8 For example, the Turkish governor Veli Pasha sacked the Tomb of Clytemnestra, an action which made him an extremely wealthy man overnight. Wace (1964) points out that the tomb had probably been plundered before Veli got to it, but that Veli Pasha almost certainly destroyed the dome.

9 And although a wealth of skeletal material has been discovered, this has often been sexed incorrectly, or not sexed at all. It can be very difficult to tell which artefacts belong to whom.

10 See Persson (1931), 16, on the discovery of a carnelian seal-stone found by the left wrist of a queen.

11 Tholos D, Archanes, Crete, dated to LHIIIA2 (c. 1350 BC). See account by Sakellerakis and Sapouna-Sakellaraki (1997). For gold diadem reference: 186. There are *tholoi* at Phourni (see Appendix One).

12 As previous note.

13 Cavanagh and Mee (1998), 109.

14 Terracotta *larnakes* that show these scenes are held by the Thebes Museum: see also Cavanagh and Mee (1995), 45–61; and Immerwahr (1995), 109–21.

15 Children could be here for a number of reasons. Were these sons or daughters? Was the child apotropaic? Could the youngster somehow be gathering life-experience from the corpse before it was interred or burned? Were children symbols of continuity and renewal?

16 The tomb of Clytemnestra was excavated by Sophia Schliemann.

17 Wace (1921–3).

18 Tholos D at Archanes.

19 Sakellarakis and Sapouna-Sakellaraki (1997), 186.

20 Visit in May 2004.

21 Thanks to Dr Freisenbruch. Excavation report from Persson (1931), 13–14.

22 See Demakopoulou (1990), 122. Tomb dates LHIIB-LHIIIA1.

23 These were *kylikes*.

24 See the lyre-player on one long side of the Agia Triada Sarcophagus (also known as Ayia Triadha and Hagia Triada). Illustrations available in Immerwahr (1990), Plates 50–3.

25 In one tomb at Asine, a couple, both around forty years old, were curled around each other. The woman's skull lies partially over the man's: see Hughes (1989), 43. Could this be a ritual murder or suicide? A loyal wife (or even a loyal husband) following her or his partner to death?

CHAPTER THIRTY-FOUR

The Age of Heroes Ends

1 Barkan (2000), 106, translating Boccaccio, *Concerning Famous Women*.

2 See Forsdyke (1956) 62ff.: Herodotus estimated the date at *c.* 1250: omitting Douris' 'extravagant assumption' of 1334 BC, the average of ancient calculations of the date for the Trojan War was 1203 BC.

3 Thanks to Dr Spyros B. Pavlides for assistance with instrumental seismological data for the Aegean; see also Ambraseys (1996) on the seismicity of Greece between the 5th century BC and 18th century AD.

4 See Nur (1998), 144, on the effect of construction methods on fatalities in an earthquake: compare the earthquake in Armenia in 1993, with a magnitude of 6.8, which killed 10,000 people, with the Californian earthquake in 1989, measuring M.7.0, which resulted in the deaths of 50 people.

5 See Papadopoulos (1996).

6 Thanks to Tim Kirby.

7 Thanks to Ken Wardle, Diana Wardle and Elizabeth French.

8 The figurines of 'Smiting' gods and 'Storm-gods' have distinct eastern characteristics – and either individually or as an iconographic influence could have been imported from, for example, Syria. See Houston-Smith (1962); also D. Collon (1972), 'The Smiting God: A Study of a Bronze in the Pomerance Collection in New York', in *Levant* 4: 111–34; J.V. Canby (1969), 'Some Hittite Figurines in the Aegean', in *Hesperia* 38: 141–9.

9 *Iliad* 2.661 [LCL 2.570].

CHAPTER THIRTY-FIVE

'Fragrant Treasuries'

1 H.D., *Helen in Egypt*, 1.8 (Palinode), in Gregory (1961), 16: Achilles to Helen.

2 Pausanias 2.32.7–8.

3 Notes taken during a first site visit in 1988.

4 Pausanias 2.35.

5 *Iliad* 2.650 [LCL 2.650].

6 Pausanias 2.35.5–8 and 2.34.2.

7 Isocrates, *Encomium of Helen*, 10.63.

8 Notes made on 10 November 2003 at a lecture organised by the Greek Archaeological Committee (UK) and given by the excavator, Professor Alexander Mazarakis-Ainian, in the Great Hall, King's College London.

9 See *Archaeological Reports* 2002–3: 75–6 for current published evidence. A forthcoming publication will appear as 'Inside the Adyton of a Greek Temple: Excavations on Kythnos (Cyclades)', in *Architecture and Archaeology in the Cyclades: Colloquium in honour of J.J. Coulton, Oxford University, Lincoln College*. Thanks to Professor Mazarakis-Ainian for information on this point.

10 Pindar, *Olympian Ode* 7.32. Thanks to Simon Hornblower.

11 The Spartan–Arcadian incursions continued into the 4th century BC. See Wide (1893) and Cartledge (1987), 328–9 for Aegesilaus' campaign in Egypt in the 360s.

12 The Egyptian Helen counted the influential (Greek) Ptolemaic dynasty among her admirers.

13 Herodotus 2.212.

14 F.T. Griffiths (1979), 88, says that the cult of Helen, particularly the chaste Helen, was popular in Egypt, and cites Herodotus 2.112 as one reference, with his identification of the shrine of 'Foreign Aphrodite' as Helen's; but there is also Plutarch, *Moralia* 857b, who said that Helen and Menelaus were much revered among the Egyptians. In the *Pannychis* (fragment 227 Pf.) Callimachus (a Hellenistic poet who was the royal librarian in Alexandria in the 3rd century BC) celebrates her as a goddess together with her brothers the Dioscuri (*Diegesis* 10.7). See also Hunter (1996); Visser (1938), 19–20 and Wide (1893), 345.

15 The gold dish was bought by the museum in 1908. It has no clear provenance.

16 The inscription was made on 9 January in AD 58 (the fifth year of the reign of Nero) by a certain Ploutas. Perdrizet (1936), 5–10 and Plate 1.

17 Chapouthier (1935).

18 Rosivach (1994), 28.

19 Lycophron, *Alexandra* 852–5.

20 'A Plea for Christians': W.R. Schoedel, ed. and trans. (1972) *Athenagoras: Legatio and De Resurrectione* (Oxford: Clarendon Press).

21 October 2004.

22 This letter, when prefixed by the asper ᶜ (which denotes rough breathing) becomes in ancient Greek 'He'.

CHAPTER THIRTY-SIX

The Daughter of the Ocean

1 Euripides, *Orestes* 1629–43, 1673–4. Trans. P. Vellacott.

2 Anthropomorphic idols in fertility cults were regularly taken out of shrines and sanctuaries by temple-officials to be washed and refreshed in streams and springs; the water was believed to renew their purity and virginity.

3 Hesiod, Fragment 24 in Merkelbach and West (1967). Nemesis too – another maternal candidate – started her mythological life as a sea-nymph.

4 Pausanias 2.2.3.

5 Pausanias 2.2.3.

6 The Romans destroyed the town in 146 BC, only to build it up again in 44 BC.

7 See Williams (1986), 21, for the suggestion that sex did not take place in the temple sanctuary itself.

8 Pindar, fragment 107, 11.18ff.

9 Strabo, *Geography* 8.6.20.

10 See Williams (1986), 18.

11 The Christians were only too aware of the hold Aphrodite had over men's imaginations and actively engaged in a struggle to wrest the faithful's focus away from carnal

to spiritual love. Contrary to popular opinion, the Christians did not deny Eros' power; they recognised it, as Sophocles, Euripides and other dramatists did, as 'a killer'. In his *Letter to the Corinthians*, Paul, who had lived for two years in Corinth with the Temple of Aphrodite towering above him, was not talking about hell-fire when he declared: 'It is better to marry than to burn with vain desire' (I Corinthians 7.9). He was using Greek symbolism and imagery.

12 For an interesting discussion of the root of Helen's name as attested on two early 6th-century *kraters* see Skutsch (1987), 190; also R. Arena (1967), *Le inscrizione Corinzie su vasi. Accad. Dei Lincei*, series 8 xiii 2 (Rome): nos. 15 and 29.

13 Some modern Greeks still offer up imprecations to ἁγια 'Ελένη (and occasionally on Lesbos this is the name given to a rainbow), although there may be a conflation here with St Helena, Constantine's mother. See Skutsch (1987), 92.

14 Stephanus of Byzantium, *Ethnika* 265.5. A grammarian living in Constantinople at this time, Stephanus of Byzantium was probably a contemporary of the Roman emperor Justinian.

15 Called Messeis: Pausanias 3.19.9.

16 Pausanias 2.32.7.

17 Although Helen was honoured at a number of locations by both republican and imperial Romans, for them she was a vexed figure of womanhood. Unlike Lucretia who honourably committed suicide following her rape by Sextus Tarquinius, Helen post-Troy lived on, unrepentant and unpunished. She was certainly not the model of a good Roman girl. As with other female characters in the Roman canon – Medea and Cleopatra – Helen challenged the Roman concept of *virtus*.

18 Trajan was emperor of Rome from AD 98 to 117. For an illustration of the altar, see *LIMC* no. 19.

19 Pliny, *Natural History* 19.92. Trans. H. Rackham. Cf. Dalby (2003), 131.

20 Pliny, *Natural History* 21.59.4.

21 Strabo, *Geography* 9.1.22.

22 The Greek Civil War lasted from 1946–9.

23 Also known as St Erasmus' Fire.

24 We know very little about Sosibius, other than that he was from Sparta, probably writing in the 3rd century BC.

25 Statius, *Thebaid* 792–3. Trans. O. Skutsch (1987), 192. See also *Silvae* 3.2.8–12; and Sosibius *FrGrH* 595.

CHAPTER THIRTY-SEVEN

Helen in Athens

1 Joseph of Exeter, *Trojan War* 6. 953–8. Translated by Neil Wright and reproduced with his kind permission.

2 When the Dorians claimed Heraclid descent during their take-over of Sparta, it was important to emphasise their connection to local heroes and heroines – one of the reasons that Helen's cult was promoted. They needed to prove they were autochthonous. In this sense Helen had already enjoyed political influence.

3 Cartledge (1997), 6.

4 Euripides lived c. 485–406 BC.

5 The arguments are simple but clever: 'Well, you gave birth to Paris,' says Helen at one point. For a good general study of Euripides' *Trojan Women*, see Croally (1994).

6 Cartledge (1997), 17.

7 See Goldhill (1997), 57–8. An estimate of around 14,000 spectators in the theatre audience is given.

8 For a powerful account of the Great Dionysia, see S. Goldhill (1990), 'The Great Dionysia and Civic Ideology', in J.J. Winkler and F. Zeitlin, eds, *Nothing to Do with Dionysos? Athenian Drama in Social Context* (Princeton, NJ: Princeton University Press).

9 See Isager and Skydsgaard (1992), 44–66 on agricultural implements.

10 See Taylor (1999), 21–2, on the excitement of the festival atmosphere. The Theoric fund was established (probably at the time of Pericles) so that even the poorest citizens on the deme roll could claim the price of a ticket (c. 2 obols). Women did not qualify. See Goldhill (1997), 67.

11 A few still survive in the Athenian Agora Museum although there is fierce debate as to whether all these examples are tickets or gaming counters.

12 See Pickard-Cambridge (1988), 272 who describes how in the 'Rural Dionysia' dried fruit and nuts and confectionery could also be used as missiles if the acting became boring or bad. See also Demosthenes, *On the Crown* 262.

13 Visiting the site today, one realises that the acropolis would also have created its own stagey backdrop. Vast rocks of marble shot through with red veins loom above the visitor. The other-worldly stone mass was living proof, as far as many Greeks were concerned, that the gods too were capable of an earthy *coup de théâtre*.

14 Boardman (1985), 234: metopes 24 and 25.

15 Also likely in the Colosseum at Rome. On women at the theatre, see Cartledge (1997), 8 and Goldhill (1997), 62ff.

16 On women in Greek drama, see Foley (1981).

17 See Taylor (1999), 18, on masks and actors' properties.

18 Plutarch, *Life of Pelopidas* 29. 4–6.

19 Athenaeus, *Deipnosophists* 12.537d.

20 Roman tragedians such as Seneca and Ennius attempted their own versions of *The Trojan Women*. It was one of ten Euripidean tragedies chosen for study in schools of the ancient world in the first and second centuries AD. Despite the later popularity of Sophocles, when Erasmus translated Euripides' *Hecuba* into Latin in 1524, it became one of the most popular ancient plays of the Renaissance, and study of Euripides was revived. Under her tutor Roger Ascham, the future Elizabeth I translated Euripides as part of her education in ancient Greek. In the 20th century, *The Trojan Women* was performed more often than any other Euripides play, including at the foundation of the League of Nations in 1919 and 1920. All details from introduction to J. Morwood's translation (2000), except Elizabeth I's Greek, for which see Rice (1951), 47.

21 See Goldhill (1986), 20.

22 See Goldhill (1986), 19–20. The untitled poem, that Patrick Shaw-Stewart is believed to have written from Gallipoli in the First World War (see page 219), echoes Aeschylus'

play on Helen's name: 'O hell of ships and cities, / Hell of men like me, / Fatal second Helen, / why must I follow thee?'

23 The finest examples of Helen's abduction and her return can be found in L.B. Ghali-Kahil's splendid *Les Enlèvements et le retour d'Hélène dans les textes et les documents figurés* (1955).

24 Euripides, *Electra* 1018–34 (1997) *Euripides: Medea, Hippolytus, Electra, Helen*. Trans. J. Morwood. Intro. Edith Hall (Oxford: Clarendon Press).

25 Thucydides 2.46. Trans. Rex Warner.

26 Xenophon, *Household Management* 7.30.

27 For a good study of Euripides' *Helen*, see Foley (2001).

28 Euripides' *Cyclops* 179ff. Trans. W. Arrowsmith. The view has been put forward that the phrase *'peri meson ton aukhena'* would have been suggestive to a Greek audience, as the word for neck or middle is a double entendre for penis and the word for neck-lace can mean a prisoner's neck-shackle or dog-collar.

29 See Coles (1996), 123. Helen also made an appearance on the comic stage in the *Nemesis* (431 BC) and the *Dionysalexandros* of Kratinos (430 BC).

30 Fragments 70–6 in R. Kassel and C. Austin, eds (1983) *Poetae Comici Graeci*, Vol. 2 (Berlin: de Gruyter). Alexis lived *c.* 372–270 BC.

31 There is a Greek vase from Apulia in the museum at Bari, which shows Helen's birth and is probably the visual representation of a satyr play, mocking the harlot of Troy. Helen's step-father Tyndareus seems to be smashing open Leda's egg with an axe. The figures are leering caricatures. Bari, Museo Archaeologico 3899.

32 Aristophanes, *Lysistrata* 1302–16. Trans. A.H. Sommerstein.

CHAPTER THIRTY-EIGHT

Helen Lost and Helen Found

1 Trans. W.H. Parker (1988), 175 (No. 68).

2 For a description of the manuscript, see Bianchi Bandinelli (1955), 37–9.

3 Perhaps, too, the Lion of St Mark, now on the column of the Piazzetta: see Brown (1996), 17. The original horses can now be seen in the Museo Marciano.

4 Nicetas Choniates, *Historia* 10.652. Trans. H.J. Magoulias.

5 *ibid.*

CHAPTER THIRTY-NINE

Helen, Homer and the Chances of Survival

1 Trans. P.H. Young (2003), 59.

2 British Museum *GR* 1906. 10–20.2.

3 Petrie (1889), 24.

4 Oxford, Bodleian Library, MS. Gr.class. a. 1 (P)/1–10.

5 Thanks to Dr Bruce Barker-Benfield for locating these examples. The plump 'Germanic' Helen can be found on a battered fragment of a manuscript copy of Guido delle Colonne's *Historia Troiana*, made in southern Germany *c.* 1440: MS. Germ. D.1, fol. 5r.

Other examples from the Bodleian, featuring Helen, include a 1461 manuscript of *Histoire de Troye*, a French translation by Jacques Milet of Orléans: MS. Douce 336, fol. 167r; and a first volume of the *Miroir du Monde*, a universal history from the Creation to the birth of Christ, in French, dating probably from before 1463: MS. Douce 336, fol.32. The latter features a single miniature of Helen's abduction by ship.

6 All data in these two paragraphs gathered from P.H. Young's exhaustive work *The Printed Homer: A 3,000 Year Publishing and Translation History of the Iliad and the Odyssey* (2003).

7 The Homeric epics do not appear to have been written down until the 7th century BC. For the next fifteen hundred years, it would have been only the super-rich who had prized written copies of the poems, but more importantly Homer's words (and therefore the character of Helen) were also in the popular consciousness, kept alive for one generation after another by professional travelling bards. This was a tradition that continued right up until the 19th century; Schliemann claimed that when he was a child a drunk miller wandered into the little grocer's shop where the proto-archaeologist sold herrings and swept the floor, and started to recite the epics in return for a couple of glasses of whisky. See Schliemann (1880); see also Traill (1995), 17–18.

8 Pliny in his *Natural History*, 13.68–89 describes its production and lists the other uses of this wonder plant: '*The roots of the papyrus plant are used by local people for timber, not only to serve as firewood but also for making various utensils and containers. Indeed they plait papyrus to make boats and they weave sails and matting from the bark and also cloth, blankets and ropes. They chew it when raw and when boiled, but only swallow the juice.*' Trans. J.F. Healy.

9 Plutarch, *Life of Alexander* 8.2 and Strabo, *Geography* 13.594.

10 See Casson (2001), chapter 3, on the history of the library of Alexandria.

11 As I write, archaeologists are excavating at Alexandria, trying to get a clearer picture of exactly how the library and the museum worked together.

12 *Iliad* 3.492–7 [LCL 3.423–6].

13 Harley MS 2472f. 19b.

14 Virgil, *Aeneid* 6.494–512. Trans. D. West.

15 See Reynolds and Wilson (1991) for a comprehensive and authoritative study of the transmission of ancient texts.

16 The manuscript was known as 'L' and its copy as 'P': see edition and commentary by Dale (1967), xxix–xxxi for a brief account of the history of the text. We have no evidence for how the manuscript came into Demetrius Triclinius' possession, but it seems it must descend at least from a master edition made for the library of Alexandria in about 200 BC.

CHAPTER FORTY

Veyn Fables

1 John Lydgate, *Troye Book* (1412–20), Prologue, 265–6.

2 Herodotus, 2.113–20.

3 Thucydides, 1.9–11. Trans. Rex Warner.

4 '[*Homer*] *made lies / Feyning his poetries / And was to the Greeks favourable.*' Chaucer, *House of Fame* 3.386–8. See Myrick (1993), 8–9, n. 5, for further examples.

5 Take John Lydgate, for instance. Lydgate, a monk, was commissioned by Henry V while he was still Prince of Wales, to write *The Troye Book*. It was in the grand surroundings of the abbey at Bury St Edmunds, the broken skeleton of which still remains, that this new epic was penned. Lydgate's version is thought to be more 'cutting-edge', more 'true'. Along with other medieval authors and chroniclers, instead of using Homer as a source, Lydgate chooses men whom he considers to be eyewitnesses to the real Trojan War; men such as Dictys and Dares.

6 See Myrick (1993), 9 and n. 7.

7 Dating Dictys and Dares is a vexed issue: for a summary of the arguments, see Frazer (1966), Myrick (1993) and Merkle (1994). Frazer (1966), 7, points out that it was only at the turn of the 20th century that proof for a Greek original of the surviving Latin translation of Dictys was found – on a fragment of Greek papyrus, the back of income tax returns for the year AD 206.

8 *Iliad* 2.747 [LCL 2.652].

9 Merkle (1994) makes the interesting point that whereas the tale starts in a rather idyllic way, with the terrible news of Helen's rape begins a slow gradual descent of the great Greeks into moral degeneracy. Merkle suggest that Dictys might in fact be writing to reveal the disastrous effects of war on human character.

10 Dictys, 1.7. Trans. R.M. Frazer Jr.

11 Dares, 10 Trans. R.M. Frazer, Jr,

12 Dares, 12. Trans. R.M. Frazer Jr. Joseph of Exeter's *Trojan War*, Chaucer's retelling of the tale and the Irish story of Troy, *Togail Troi*, appear to be based on Dares.

CHAPTER FORTY-ONE

Helen of Troy and the Bad Samaritan

1 *The Collected Poems of Dorothy Parker* (1936), 94. (New York: The Modern Library). Heartfelt thanks to Rev. Peter Watkins for quotation.

2 All the descriptions are from Crowfoot *et al.* (1957).

3 Virgil, *Aeneid* 6.515–28.

4 See Vincent (1936), 221 and n. 1, citing J.W. Crowfoot.

5 A sobriquet derived from Edwards' article 'Simon Magus, the Bad Samaritan' (1997). Thanks to Mark Edwards for his help with this chapter.

6 Samaria had once been the capital of Israel, but after its invasion by the Assyrians in the 8th century BC, it was resettled by Babylonians, Aramaeans and a scattering of Israelites. The region was fertile, the town on a good defensive position overlooking the north/south route through Palestine.

7 Philip carried on towards Gaza (converting an Ethiopian eunuch on the way) and Simon was left in Samaria as a new acolyte of a fledgeling religion.

8 It is disputed whether a single author called Hippolytus was responsible for authorship of the Hippolytan corpus. See, for example, J.A. Cerrato (2002) *Hippolytus between East and West: The Commentaries and the Provenance of the Corpus* (Oxford: Oxford University Press) and A. Brent (1995) *Hippolytus and the Roman Church in the Third Century: Communities in Tension before the Emergence of a Monarch-Bishop* (Leiden: Brill).

9 Helene was a common spelling of the name at this time.

10 Hippolytus, *Refutation of All Heresies* 6.19. Trans. F. Legge.

11 See Hoffman (1995), 16, n. 30.

12 Justin Martyr, in his *First Apology* (*c.* AD 160) records the cult of Simon and Helen in Rome, and even refers to a statue being erected in Simon's honour, although it is generally thought he mistook the statue's identity.

13 Some argue that this female Wisdom, referred to as the Idea of the Godhead or the Mother of All, makes an appearance in the Book of Proverbs of the Old Testament; for example, Proverbs 9.1 and 8.19.

14 See the following note for the principal sources for Simon Magus and his consort Helene.

15 Hippolytus, *Refutation of All Heresies* 6.19; also Justin Martyr, *Apology* 1.26.3.

16 Tyre might be significant, as here and elsewhere in Phoenicia there was a conspicuous cult of the 'mother-goddess' Astarte/Selene. See Haar (2003), 264.

17 The Trojan Horse was used as an allegory for the ignorance of non-believers: '*as the Phrygians, in drawing it, unwittingly invited their own destruction, so the Gentiles – the persons outside the sphere of my knowledge – draw destruction on themselves through ignorance.*' Epiphanius, *Panarion* 21.3.3. Trans. F. Williams. And Helen's Trojan story does in fact lend itself rather well to being hijacked by this particular branch of heresy. For the Gnostics, Helen's suffering epitomises the 'tragic epic of womanhood . . . in which a female deity emerges as creative, good, but subject to loss, pain, humiliation and limits.' Mortley (1981), 55.

18 Hippolytus, *Refutation of All Heresies* 6.19. Trans. F. Legge.

19 The devotees of Simon and Helene had to remember to accord the cult-leaders the respect they deserved, calling their images Lord and Lady rather than Simon and Helene, otherwise 'he is cast out as being ignorant of their mysteries'. See Hippolytus, *Refutation of all Heresies* 6.20. Trans. F. Legge. Up until the 3rd century AD Simon's statue continued to be cast in the image of Zeus, and Helen, having left Aphrodite behind once and for all, embraced her mental acuity again, in the form of Athena. See Irenaeus, *Against Heresies* 1.23.4.

20 For the notion of 'Sophia' in Gnostic thought see S. Petrement (1990) *A Separate God: The Christian Origins of Gnosticism* (San Francisco: Harper) or E. Pagels (1978) *The Gnostic Gospels* (New York: Random House).

21 Epiphanius claimed that around a thousand years before, Homer too had recognised Helen not just as a wayward Greek, but as a manifestation of the one, true God. '*For this is Ennoia, she whom Homer calls Helen. And this is why Homer has to describe her as standing on a tower, signalling the Greeks her plot against the Phrygians with the lamp. But with its brightness, as I said, he indicated the display of the light from on high.*' Describing his prostitute companion, Simon Magus was supposed to have supported this argument himself: '*This woman was, then, she who by her unseen powers has made replicas of herself in Greek and Trojan times and immemorially, before the world and after. She is the one who is with me now, and for her sake I am come down.*' Epiphanius, *Panarion* 21.3.1. Trans. F. Williams.

22 *Clementine Homilies* 2.25. Trans. A. Roberts and J. Donaldson (1870). This work tells us that both Helene and Simon were disciples of John the Baptist.

23 Her story was used as a convenient model by the Gnostic movement. As one authority on the Gnostics has put it. '. . . the story of Helen and Simon symbolises the story of

the soul fallen into this world of darkness and ignorance, a whore, but ready to be converted and to receive her heavenly spouse, her liberator and Saviour. The charms of the eternal female and the magic arts of the male counterpart combine so cleverly as to produce a model and a legend destined to last for centuries.' Filoramo (1990), 149–50. Simon liberates Helene from sex-slavery in Tyre, just as Paris liberates Helen from slaving in the bed of an uninspiring husband. In this very carnal love affair was found an allegory of the journey of the soul. This is the Helen who – in a new heretical, but Christianised environment – suffers torment, but ends up redeemed, celestial.

24 Epiphanius, *Panarion* 21.3.5.

25 'How think ye? If a man have an hundred sheep, and one of them be gone astray, doth he not leave the ninety and nine, and goeth into the mountains, and seeketh that which is gone astray? And if so be that he find it, verily I say unto you, he rejoiceth more of that sheep, than of the ninety and nine which went not astray.' Matthew 18:12–13.)

26 See Crowfoot *et al.* (1957), 8.

27 Mark Edwards has pointed out to me that Simon Magus is sometimes considered to be a representative of an old Samarian tradition in which some 'Gnostic' assumptions (such as the contrast between the god who creates and the highest god) were already ensconced before the advent of Christian Gnosticism.

28 See Quispel (1975), 300. Also see *Reallexikon für Antike und Christentum* (1988), vol. 14: 343.

29 In the original Greek sense of the word, when a *kategoros* was an accuser in the assembly.

CHAPTER FORTY-TWO

'Perpulchra': More Than Beautiful

1 Lord Dunsany, 'An Interview' in *Mirage Water* (1938), 61 (London: Putnam).

2 Virgil's *Aeneid* is a tribute to this resourceful hero.

3 I.N. Hume (1956) *Treasure in the Thames*, 49–51 and Plate V. London: Frederick Muller.

4 This is the English royal lineage as described by Geoffrey of Monmouth; many different versions were produced by other authors and other nationalities.

5 For a fuller discussion of these themes, see Waswo (1995). For an excellent overview of the uses and abuses of the Troy story in medieval England, see Benson (1980).

6 Robert III, 1390–1406.

7 Nicholson (1974), 220.

8 *STC* 5579.

9 Simon (1961).

10 Jean Bonnard (1884) *Les Traductions de la Bible en vers français au moyen âge*.

11 Gervase of Canterbury, writing after 1160.

12 O'Callaghan (2003), 311–13.

13 Giraldus Cambrensis, *De Principis Instructione Liber* 8.300.

14 Benoît de Sainte-Maure, *Roman de Troie* 4769–71. Trans. T.F. O'Callaghan (2003), 307.

15 The degree of this cultural florescence is debated. It is sometimes known as the Carolingian Renaissance.

16 Matthew of Vendôme, *The Art of Versification* 56.23–57.8. Trans. A.E. Galyon (1980).

17 Joseph of Exeter, *Trojan War* 3.329ff. Trans. A. K. Wright.

18 *Trojan War* 4.180–92. Trans. N. Bate.

19 The subtleties of these arguments are discussed at length in O'Callaghan (2003).

20 Thanks to Alison Weir for sourcing this quote.

21 See A. Weir (1999) *Eleanor of Aquitaine* (London: Jonathan Cape).

22 Codex 4660, Bayerische Staatsbibliothek, Munich. Hecuba, Paris and perhaps Helen are also mentioned in the songs.

23 Ezra Pound conflates the two women – Helen and Eleanor – in Canto II. See also C.F. Terrell (1993) *A Companion to the Cantos of Ezra Pound* (Berkeley, Los Angeles and London: University of California Press), 5–6.

24 Benoît de Sainte-Maure, *Roman de Troie* 4741–8. Trans. T.F. O'Callaghan (2003), 306.

25 See Highet (1949), 580, 46.

CHAPTER FORTY-THREE

Dancing with the Devil

1 The first recorded performance of Marlowe's *Dr Faustus* was on 30 September 1594 at the Rose Theatre on Bankside, London. See Bevington and Rasmussen (1993), 48. There were possibly earlier productions at the Theatre in Shoreditch.

2 Henslowe was an entrepreneur if ever there was one, trading in goat-skins and coinage as well as in theatrical talent.

3 Hall (1998), 114.

4 In the 1594–5 'season' the Admiral's Men (who first staged Marlowe's *Dr Faustus*) put on thirty-eight plays, twenty-one of which were new.

5 Figures from Hall (1998), 114–59.

6 For a good summary, see Emerson (2002).

7 Marlowe's *Dr Faustus* was not published until after his death. There are two early versions of the play, the A text (1604) and the B text (1616), which differ significantly from each other. Helen's entrance between cupids occurs only in the B text, Act V, scene i.

8 The interpretation of this scene is much debated. Although the consensus is that Helen is indeed a succubus, and that as a result of sex with her, Faustus is eternally damned, there are alternative readings. See, for example, Ormerod and Wortam (1985), Allen (1968) and Greg (1946).

9 The boom in tanners and starchers is particularly to be found in the 17th century. For the context of Bankside and the Rose see Bowsher (1998), *passim*.

10 Bowsher (forthcoming).

11 Site visit, July 2003.

12 Shakespeare had King Lear bemoaning the propensity for tittle-tattle (known as 'jangling' since the medieval period), 'As if we were God's spies' with our talk of 'who's in, who's out'.

13 Thanks to Jonathan Bate for his help with this point. See Bate (1997), 113–15, on Shakespeare's adaptation of the line in *Richard II* (4.1.271–9).

14 See Bowsher (1998), 67.

15 See Sir John Melton, *Astrologaster; or the Figure-Caster*.

16 Quispel (1975), 301: *Faustus*, Chapter 55, English version: *The Damnable Life and Deserved Death of Dr John Faustus* (London: 1592). Trans. P.F. Gent. (New York, Da Capo Press; Amsterdam: Theatrum Orbis Terrarum, 1969) It was Gent's translation that Marlowe used as his basis for *Dr Faustus*.

17 See Hattaway (1982), 181.

18 Riggs (2004), 234.

19 For famous cases of this neurosis see Chambers (1923), Vol. 3, 423. Thanks to Julian Bowsher for his help with this passage.

20 Particularly in Euripidean and Aeschylean tragedy.

21 Elizabeth I herself was described as a 'beauteous second queen of Troy': see James (1997), 18.

22 Thomas Nashe, 'Summer's Last Will and Testament' (1590–6).

23 When Shakespeare writes of Helen, he typically couples her with death: '*For every false drop in her bawdy veins / A Grecian's life hath sunk; for every scruple / Of her contaminated carrion weight / A Troyan hath been slain*' (*Troilus and Cressida*, 4.1.70–73) and '*Show me the strumpet that began this stir, / That with my nails her beauty I may tear! / The heat of lust, fond Paris, did incur / This load of wrath that burning Troy doth bear; / Thy eye kindled the fire that burneth here, / And here in Troy, for trespass of thine eye, / The sire, the son, the dame and daughter die*' (*Rape of Lucrece* 1.471–7).

24 Shades of the line can also be found in Seneca, *Troades* 26–7: '*Plunderers seize the Dardan spoils; A thousand ships cannot contain the booty.*' Trans. A.J. Boyle; see also Tertullian, *De anima* 34. And a popular school textbook of the time was one written by Baptista Spagnuoli, also known as Baptista Mantuanus. It comprised 10 Latin Eclogues. Interestingly enough, in the Fourth Eclogue, line 154 reads: '*Tyndaris Aegeas onerauit nauibus vndas*', 'Tyndarian Helen burdened the Aegean sea with ships'. Did Marlowe also know this launching Helen? See Baldwin (1944).

25 Lucian, *Dialogues of the Dead* 18. Trans. F.G. and H.W. Fowler.

26 Helen does have some Elizabethan apologists. John Ogle in his *Lamentation of Troy*, for instance, written in 1594, blames the gods for the war, and goes so far as to sanctify her.

27 Possibly written around 1595.

28 See Bevington and Rasmussen (1993), in the introduction to their edition of *Doctor Faustus*: 53–6.

CHAPTER FORTY-FOUR

Helen's Nemesis

1 Ovid, *Heroides* 16.141–4. Trans. G. Showerman.

2 *Iliad* 5.492–3 [LCL5. 428–9].

3 Heimarmene Painter, Berlin, Staatliche Antikensammlungen 30036.

4 Lucian, *The Judgement of the Goddesses* 15. Trans. A.M. Harmon.

5 See Plato, *Symposium* (200e): 'Eros is forever the desire of something, and that something is that which is lacking'. See Caldwell (1987) for further discussion of these ideas. Caldwell makes the point (p. 89) that 'Tartaros must come before Eros'.

6 Unlike Aphrodite, Helen is rarely portrayed naked. While the goddess is wantonly

available, Helen, typically cloaked, appears to be saving herself for someone. She is opaque. Men's eyes search for her but fear what they might find. When Paris sees her, the world changes; the *Cypria* (fragment 1) tells us that Achilles would fight only once he had looked upon Helen; one glimpse of Helen turns Menelaus' hate back to love. The ancients found in Helen the perfect tool to explore the notion that the origins of desire are in the seen. Alcman describes 'the liquid beam of the human eye as the source of erotic desire'. M.S. Cyrino (1995) *In Pandora's Jar: Lovesickness in Early Greek Poetry* (Lanham, MD), 83, citing Alcman fragment 3.61, as quoted in Worman (1997), 167, n. 53.

7 *Cypria* fragment 8 [Athenaeus 8.334b].

8 But, interestingly, the Nazis preferred Penelope as a loyal (blond) *hausfrau*: see, for example, H. Bengl (1941) 'Die Antike und die Erziehung zum politischen Deutschen', in *Die Alten Sprachen* 6: 5. Thanks to Katie Fleming for her help on this point.

9 There is a suggestion that the worship of Helen Dendritis at Rhodes stems from the hanging of images of the female on trees as part of a ritual act. Helen is often shown with fillets dangling from her arms, as if she could be strung from a tree. See West (1975), 13.

10 Goethe, *Faust*, Vol. 2. Trans. D. Luke.

11 Doniger (1999), 42.

12 One can only hope that the highest-paid Helen of the early 21st century, the German supermodel of Wolfgang Peterson's Hollywood epic *Troy*, does not represent our *Zeitgeist*. Helen is there shown as a simpering shell of a creature, a woman with no personality or power, a blandly beautiful face, malleable, decorative, a flummery – the antithesis of what any real, living Helen could have or would have been. Her essence in one sense was better captured by the pulp-fiction and Cinemascope productions of the 1950s and 1960s: see John Erskine's novel *The Private Life of Helen of Troy*, originally published in 1925 but reprinted in 1952 with a controversial cover of a buxom Helen by Earle Bergey. 'Her Lust Caused the Trojan War', this Popular Library edition screamed, also boasting on its cover that it is COMPLETE AND UNABRIDGED.

13 H.D. (1957) *Selected Poems* (New York: Grove Press).

APPENDIX ONE

The Minotaur's Island

1 *Odyssey* 19.194–6 [LCL 19.172–3].

2 Site visit 2003.

3 We still cannot tell whether the move from Minoan to Mycenaean was a glide or a bloody wrench, whether there was absorption of natives, a mutual integration or an annihilation. What is clear is that the transition was irreversible. In places such as Egypt, Syria and Cyprus, by 1450–1400 BC, Mycenaean pottery simply replaces that of the Minoans.

4 Thanks to Tim Kirby for this imaginative observation.

5 See finds from Pellana, reported in Spyropoulos (1998).

6 *Iliad* 3.277–8 [LCL 3.232–3].

7 *Iliad* 2.747 [LCL 2.652].

8 Details from 'The Education of Michael Ventris', a paper given by Thomas G. Palaima at the Institute of Classical Studies, University of London, March 2004.

9 'The Decipherment of Linear B and the Ventris-Chadwick Correspondence': exhibition in the Fitzwilliam Museum, Cambridge, 2003. The Mycenaean Epigraphy Group and the Chadwick Fund, Faculty of Classics, Cambridge. Exhibition catalogue by Lisa Bendall: 39.

10 Tablets featuring names of oxen come from Knossos, and include, in the order of names given above, Ch 896 (*Kelainos*); Ch 896 (*Aiwolos*); Ch 897 (*Stomargos*), Ch 899, 1029 (*Podargos*). See J. Killen (1992–3) 'The oxen's names on the Knossos Ch tablets', in *Minos* 27–8: 101–7.

11 A good, general discussion of this topic can be found in K.A. and D. Wardle (1997).

APPENDIX TWO

La Parisienne

1 (*Enneads* 5.8). Trans. A.H. Armstrong.

2 Thanks to Lesley Fitton for her help with this passage.

3 Site visit 1989.

4 Interestingly, Minoan seal-stones have never lost their totemic power. Many turned up at the beginning of the 20th century in peasant houses, where they were called galopetres (milkstones) and were still being used by mothers, the cold little spheres tucked in next to the nursing mothers' breasts to ensure good milk supply. Fitton (1995), 123. Even through the 'disappearance' of the Minoan civilisation, the fault-lines of Ottoman rule and the German invasion over a period of three and a half thousand years, locals must have passed on from generation to generation the notion that when fertility and nourishment were important, these cold little lumps of art had real potency.

5 The Ring of Minos – a fabulous thing, itself the size of a Kalamata olive – has a surface dense with images of some kind of tree ritual. The ring has travelled from one owner to another and only recently came to rest in the hands of the Greek authorities. The officials must be weak with relief to have this vagrant treasure back under lock and key.

6 See Immerwahr (1990), 174–5, for further details.

7 See Fitton (2002), 58–9.

8 See Fitton (2002), 70–2, and 134 on storerooms at Knossos.

9 See Darga (1993), 103: A131 (Istanbul Archaeological Museum, Bo. 2004).

APPENDIX THREE

Women of Stone and Clay and Bronze

1 *Homeric Hymns* (1980), 1. Trans. C. Boer. Reproduced by kind permission of Spring Publications, Texas.

2 Some argue that the figures may be asexual or hermaphrodite.

3 From around 2500 BC a few copper, lead and bronze figurines are produced. From 6000 BC onwards, terracotta is the material most commonly used for figurine-production. Thanks to Professor Colin Renfrew for his help with this passage.

4 See Broodbank (2002), 63–4. The tattooing seems to be representative – copper and bone needles with the remnants of pigments have been found.

5 Goulandris Museum Inv. 828 *c.* 7000–3000 BC.

6 See *Cambridge Archaeological Journal* 6:2 (1996), 281–307 *passim*.

7 From the evidence we have currently, it seems that the Upper Paleolithic Period (*c.* 35,000–9000 BC) is the era when humans first make images and symbols designed to last.

APPENDIX FOUR

Elemental Helen – She-Gods and She-Devils

1 *Iliad* 1.633 [LCL 1.528].

2 Note the *Homeric Hymn to the Earth* (Ge) at the beginning of Appendix Three.

3 West (1975), n. 5, quoting Gow on 10.8.

4 Pollux 10.191.

5 Theocritus, *Idyll* 18. See Chapter 11.

6 Helen was trapped on the island to escape the attentions of King Thonis of Egypt. It was Thonis' wife Polydamna who sent Helen there 'lest this alien should prove more beautiful than she' – see Aelian, *On the Characteristics of Animals* 9.21. Trans. A.F. Scholfield.

7 Plutarch, *Life of Solon* 4.

8 Philostratus, *Heroicus* 20.32ff., says there was in fact a temple of Helen and Achilles.

9 Pausanias 3.19.11–13.

10 Lucian, *True Story* 2.25–7. Trans. A.M. Harmon.

11 Pausanias 2.18.6 says that these boys were Menelaus' sons by a slave woman. Hesiod, *Catalogues of Women*, 70, says they were Helen and Menelaus' sons.

12 Copenhagen National Museum 7125, discovered in excavations at the beginning of the 20th century: see note 13.

13 B. 11: see C. Blinkenberg (1941) *Lindos II: Fouilles de l'Acropole 1902–14*. Inscriptions, Vol. I, 148–99, esp. 166 (Berlin: de Gruyter; Copenhagen: G.E.C. Gad).

14 Hesiod, *Theogony* 591–602. Trans. H.G. Evelyn-White.

15 See West (1975) and Skutsch (1987).

16 See West (1975).

17 Hesiod, *Works and Days* 527ff. and Herodotus 2.24–6.

18 See Clader (1976) and Meagher (2002) *passim*. Discussed, for example, in Austin (1994) p. 86.

APPENDIX FIVE

Royal Purple – The Colour of Congealed Blood

1 Aeschylus, *Agamemnon* 959–60. Trans. A. Shapiro and P. Burian.
2 Dictys 6.4 reports Helen and Menelaus' stop-over in Crete: 'When the Cretans heard of Helen's arrival, many men and women from all over the island came together, desiring to see her for whose sake almost all of the world had gone to war.' Trans. R.M. Frazer.
3 'The last real hippie', still wandered through the town when I last visited in 2003, roll-up in hand, tea cosy on his head.
4 The excavation reports at Kommos can be found in the series of publications by the excavators J.W and M.C. Shaw, eds (1995–2000) *Kommos: an excavation on the south coast of Crete by the University of Toronto and the Royal Ontario Museum under the auspices of the American School of Classical Studies at Athens.*
5 Some of these international journeymen left clues behind them. In the Late Bronze Age while a Syro-Palestinian boat was waiting in the bay, the anchor sheered off its rope (probably made of hemp or flax) and then lay, undetected, for the next three thousand years on the sea-bed. It is a simple thing, shaped like a Swiss cheese with just three holes bored through the block. But it speaks of a port filled with the babble of international voices. Of a place of exchange and communication, of visitors, of the victims of hostile ocean winds, of burgeoning international trade.
6 Linear B tablets seem to refer to *po-pu-re-ja* – female purple dyers. See D. Ruscillo (forthcoming) *To Dye For: Murex dye production in the Aegean and its social and economic impact in the Greek Bronze Age.* Thanks to Deborah Ruscillo for her help in this matter, and for allowing me to see a pre-publication copy of her work. There would too have been local production of purple in the Peloponnese.
7 Thanks to Lisa Bendall on this point.
8 *Murex brandaris* is the most common species in the region. Thanks once again to Deborah Ruscillo.
9 See Latacz (2004), 43 and n. 52, citing P. Jablonka.
10 *Iliad* 3.151–4 [LCL 3.125–8].

Epilogue – Myth, History and Historia

1 Euripides, *Helen* 588.
2 The authorship of the *Iliad* and the *Odyssey* is a question that will exercise scholars far into the future – but the current consensus is that Homer was one man, who lived in the 8th–7th centuries BC on the islands of the eastern Aegean (e.g. Chios) or the coast of Asia Minor.
3 In Greek mythology – passed on from the mouth of one male bard to another – there were four periods of human creation. The first beings were the children of the earth goddess Ge or Gaia, the female spirit who breathed life into both the immortals and humans. These firstborn lived in a golden age of peace and prosperity, and were known as the golden race of mankind. Next came the silver race – a society

of extreme matriarchy ignorant of the Olympian pantheon – who lived in abject misery. This troublesome group were replaced by the bronze race, phase one, who believed in the gods but were war-like and piteous, and, phase two, the heroes who believed in the gods, who were noble in soul who fought the Trojan War and then (as long as they fulfilled the necessary requirements) went on to dwell for ever in the Elysian fields. Archaic and Classical Greece was inhabited by the iron race, unjust, cruel, and *troubled*. Helen is a link with both bronze and silver. Each phase was violently, abruptly terminated. Current scientific research – which looks at the attenuated growth of many trees through the Bronze Age – suggests that this was a period of excessive cosmic movement. Some scientists posit that a globally catastrophic comet hit the earth around 2807 BC – a comet whose impact has been estimated at between 10^5 and 10^6 megatons. The creation tales of rock-men and giant abysses, of floods and divine destruction were perhaps monstrous versions of the terrible climate changes of around 2350 BC when a number of Bronze Age civilisations disappeared. They could have been a hazy memory of the impact of a major dust event on Aegean communities of 1800 BC – the fallout of more volcanic activity. For comet impact, see Masse (1998), 53; on climate change and dust event, see Verschur (1998), 51. Homer appears to commemorate both seismic and cosmic activity – in this case the arrival of a meteorite – on the battlefields of Troy. '*A crash of thunder! Zeus let loose a terrific bolt / and blazing white at the hoofs of Diomedes' team / it split the earth, a blinding smoking flash – / molten sulphur exploding into the air / stallions shying, cringing against the car – and the shining reins flew free of Nestor's grip.*' Iliad 8.152–7 [LCL 8.133–7].

4 Latacz (2004), 151.

5 One group of aboriginal Australians has detailed distinct story-memories of a distant, real place that was flooded eight thousand years ago. Divers exploring the sea-bed of the Persian Gulf found features 1,000 feet (305 m) below the waves, which precisely and minutely matched the aboriginals' descriptions. See C. Tudge (1988) *Neanderthals, Bandits and Farmers: how agriculture really began* (London: Weidenfeld & Nicolson).

EDITIONS OF ANCIENT TEXTS AND TRANSLATIONS

༺ઌ৩ઌ৩ઌ৩ઌ৩ઌ৩ঌ

The list of editions that follows includes only those titles from which specific translations have been quoted. All Greek and Latin text references that are cited without translation are taken from the relevant Loeb Classical Library editions.

AELIAN, *Historical Miscellany*
> N.G. Wilson (1997) 3 vols. Loeb Classical Library. Cambridge, MA: Harvard University Press.

AELIAN, *On the Characteristics of Animals*
> A.F. Scholfield, trans. (1959) 3 vols. Loeb Classical Library. Cambridge, MA: Harvard University Press.

AESCHYLUS, *Agammenon*
> A. Shapiro and P. Burian, trans. (2003) in *The Oresteia*. Oxford: Oxford University Press.

ALCAEUS
> A.M. Miller, trans. (1996) in *Greek Lyric: an anthology in translation*. Indianapolis and Cambridge: Hackett Publishing.

APOLLODORUS, *Epitome; The Library*
> J.G. Frazer, trans. (1921) 2 vols. Loeb Classical Library. New York and London: Heinemann.

ARISTOPHANES, *Lysistrata*
> A.H. Sommerstein, trans. (1990) Warminster: Aris & Phillips.

ARISTOTLE, *Politics*
> S. Everson, trans. (1996) in *The Politics and the Constitution of Athens*. Cambridge: Cambridge University Press.

Carmina Priapea
> W.H. Parker, trans. (1988) in *Priapea: Poems for a Phallic God*. London and Sydney: Croom Helm.

CATULLUS
> F.W. Cornish, trans. (1988) Loeb Classical Library. London: Heinemann; Cambridge, MA: Harvard University Press.

CICERO, *Pro Archia*
  N.H. Watts, trans. (1923) Loeb Classical Library. London: Heinemann;
  Cambridge, MA: Harvard University Press.
CLEMENT OF ALEXANDRIA, *The Instructor*
  W. Wilson, trans. (1867–8) Ante-Nicene Christian Library 12. Edinburgh.
Clementine Homilies and Recognitions
  A. Roberts and J. Donaldson, trans. (1870) Ante-Nicene Christian
  Library 17. Edinburgh.
COLLUTHUS, *The Rape of Helen*
  A.W. Mair, trans. (1963) in *Oppian, Colluthus, Tryphiodorus*. Loeb Classical
  Library. London: Heinemann.
Cypria
1) M. Davies, trans. (1989) in *The Epic Cycle*. Bristol: Bristol Classical Press.
2) H.G. Evelyn-White, trans. (1974) in *Hesiod: The Homeric Hymns and
   Homerica*. Loeb Classical Library. London: Heinemann; Cambridge, MA:
   Harvard University Press.
DARES, see next entry
DICTYS and DARES
  R.M. Frazer, Jr, trans. (1966) in *The Trojan War: The Chronicles of Dictys of
  Crete and Dares the Phrygian*. Bloomington and London: Indiana University
  Press.
DIO CHRYSOSTOM, the *Eleventh* or *Trojan Discourse*
  J.W. Cohoon, trans. (1932) 5 vols. Loeb Classical Library. London:
  Heinemann; Cambridge, MA: Harvard University Press.
DIODORUS of SICILY
  C.H. Oldfather, trans. (1933) 12 vols. Loeb Classical Library. London:
  Heinemann; Cambridge, MA: Harvard University Press.
DIOGENES LAERTIUS, *Lives of Eminent Philosophers*
  R.D. Hicks, trans. (1925) 2 vols. Loeb Classical Library. London:
  Heinemann; Cambridge, MA: Harvard University Press.
EPIPHANIUS, *Panarion*
  F. Williams, trans. (1987) 2 vols. Leiden and New York: Brill.
EURIPIDES, *Andromache*
1) P. Vellacott, trans. (1972) in *Euripides' Orestes and other plays*.
   Harmondsworth: Penguin.
2) J.F. Nims, trans. (1953) in R. Lattimore and D. Grene (eds), *Euripides*,
   Vol. III, *The Complete Greek Tragedies*. Chicago and London: University of
   Chicago Press.
EURIPIDES, *Cyclops*
  W. Arrowsmith, trans. (1956) in R. Lattimore and D. Grene (eds),

Euripides, Vol. II, *The Complete Greek Tragedies*. Chicago and London: University of Chicago Press.

EURIPIDES, *Helen*

1) R. Lattimore trans. (1956) in R. Lattimore and D. Grene (eds), *Euripides*, Vol. II, *The Complete Greek Tragedies*. Chicago and London: University of Chicago Press.

2) D. Kovacs. trans. (2002) Loeb Classical Library. Cambridge, MA and London: Harvard University Press.

EURIPIDES, *Iphigeneia in Aulis*

P. Vellacott, trans. (1972) in *Euripides' Orestes and other plays*. Harmondsworth: Penguin.

EURIPIDES, *Orestes*

1) P. Vellacott, trans. (1972) in *Euripides' Orestes and other plays*. Harmondsworth: Penguin.

2) D. Kovacs, trans. (2002) Loeb Classical Library. Cambridge, MA and London: Harvard University Press.

3) M.L. West, ed. with trans. and commentary (1987). Warminster: Aris & Phillips.

EURIPIDES, *The Trojan Women*

1) J. Morwood, trans. (2000) in *The Trojan Women and other plays*. Oxford World's Classics. Oxford: Oxford University Press.

2) M. Hadas and J.H. McLean, trans. (1936) *The Plays of Euripides*. New York: Dial Press.

3) K. McLeish, trans. (1995) in *After the Trojan War*. Reading: Absolute Books.

GORGIAS, *Encomium of Helen*

D.M. MacDowell, trans. (1982) Bristol: Bristol Classical Press.

HERODOTUS, *Histories*

1) A.D. Godley, trans. (1982) 4 vols. Loeb Classical Library. London: Heinemann; Cambridge, MA: Harvard University Press.

2) A. de Sélincourt, trans. (1954) Harmondsworth: Penguin.

HESIOD, *Catalogues of Women and Eoiae; Theogony; Works and Days*

H.G. Evelyn-White, trans. (1974) in *Hesiod: The Homeric Hymns and Homerica*. Loeb Classical Library. London: Heinemann; Cambridge, MA: Harvard University Press.

HESIOD, *Fragments*

R. Merkelbach and M.L. West (eds) (1967) Oxford: Clarendon Press.

HIPPOLYTUS, *Refutation of All Heresies*

F. Legge, trans. (1921) 2 vols. London: Society for Promoting Christian Knowledge; New York: Macmillan.

HOMER, *The Iliad*

R. Fagles, trans. (1998) London: Penguin.

HOMER, *The Odyssey*
1) R. Fagles, trans. (1996) New York: Viking.
2) E.V. Rieu, trans. (1991) revised D.C.H. Rieu. London: Penguin.

Homeric Hymns
C. Boer, trans. (1980) revised edition. Irving, TX: Spring Publications.

HYGINUS, *Fables*
M. Grant, trans. (1960) in *The Myths of Hyginus*. Lawrence: University of Kansas Publications.

ISOCRATES, *Encomium of Helen*
L. van Hook, trans. (1928) Vol. 3. Loeb Classical Library. London: Heinemann.

LUCAN, *Civil War*
1) S.M. Braund, trans. (1992) Oxford: Clarendon Press.
2) J.D. Duff, trans. (1928) Loeb Classical Library. London: Heinemann.

LUCIAN, *Dialogues of the Dead*
F.G. and H.W. Fowler, trans. (1905) in *The Works of Lucian of Samosata*. Oxford: Clarendon Press.

LUCIAN, *The Judgement of the Goddesses*
A.M. Harmon, trans. (1913) 8 vols. Loeb Classical Library. London: Heinemann.

LYCOPHRON, *Alexandra*
A.W. Mair, trans. (1921) Loeb Classical Library. Cambridge, MA and London: Harvard University Press.

OVID, *The Art of Love*
1) R. Humphries, trans. (1958) London: John Calder.
2) J.H. Mozley, trans. (1979) revised G.P. Goold. Loeb Classical Library. London: Heinemann; Cambridge, MA: Harvard University Press.

OVID, *Heroides*
1) H. Isbell, trans. (1990) London: Penguin.
2) G. Showerman, trans. (1977) revised G.P. Goold. Loeb Classical Library. London: Heinemann; Cambridge, MA: Harvard University Press.

OVID, *Metamorphoses*
F.J. Miller, trans. (1977) 2 vols, revised G.P. Goold. Loeb Classical Library. London: Heinemann; Cambridge, MA: Harvard University Press.

PAUSANIAS, *Description of Greece*
W.H.S. Jones and H.A. Ormerod, trans. (1918 1–171) 5 vols. Loeb Classical Library. London: Heinemann.

PLINY, *Natural History*
1) J.F. Healy, trans. (1991) Harmondsworth: Penguin.
2) H. Rackham, trans. (1938) 10 vols. Loeb Classical Library. London: Heinemann; Cambridge, MA: Harvard University Press.
PLOTINUS, *On Beauty; On the Intelligible Beauty*
A.H. Armstrong, trans. (1966) in *Enneads*, Vols. 1 and 5. Loeb Classical Library. London: Heinemann; Cambridge, MA; Harvard University Press.
PLUTARCH, *Lives: Lycurgus and Numa; Theseus*
B. Perrin, trans. (1914) Vol. 1. Loeb Classical Library. London: Heinemann; Cambridge, MA: Harvard University Press.
PLUTARCH, *On Sparta*
R. Talbert, trans. (2005 revised edition). Harmondsworth: Penguin.
PROPERTIUS, *Elegies*
G.P. Goold, ed. and trans. (1990) Loeb Classical Library. London: Heinemann; Cambridge, MA: Harvard University Press.
QUINTUS SMYRNAEUS, *The Fall of Troy*
A.S. Way, trans. (1913) Loeb Classical Library. London: Heinemann.
SAPPHO
D.A. Campbell, trans. (1990) in *Greek Lyric*, Vol. 1. Loeb Classical Library. Cambridge, MA: Harvard University Press.
SENECA, *Trojan Women*
A.J. Boyle, trans. (1994) in *Troades*. Leeds: Francis Cairns.
THEOCRITUS, *Idylls*
A. Verity, trans. (2002) Oxford: Oxford University Press.
THUCYDIDES, *History of the Peloponnesian War*
R. Warner, trans. (1972) Harmondsworth: Penguin.
VIRGIL, *The Aeneid*
D. West, trans. (1990) London: Penguin.

OTHER WORKS

∽∾∽∾∽∾∽∾∽∾

A Guide to Troia: by the Director and Staff of the Excavations (1999) Translated K. Gay and D.F. Easton. Istanbul: University of Tübingen: Troia Project.

Adler, A. (ed.) (1928) *Suidae Lexicon*. Vol. 1. Leipzig: Teubner.

Allen, D.C. (1968) *Image and Meaning: Metaphoric traditions in Renaissance poetry*. Baltimore, MD: Johns Hopkins University Press.

Allen, S.H. (1999) *Finding the Walls of Troy: Frank Calvert and Heinrich Schliemann at Hisarlik*. London and Berkeley: University of California Press.

Ambraseys, N.N. (1996) 'Material for the Investigation of Seismicity of Central Greece', in S. Stiros and R.E. Jones (eds), *Archaeoseismology*. Athens: IGME and the British School at Athens.

Angel, J.L. (1977) 'Ecology and Population in the Eastern Mediterranean', in World Archaeology 4.1: 88–105.

Angel, J.L. and Bisel, S.C. (1985) 'Health and Nutrition in Mycenaean Greece', in N. C. Wilkie and W.D.E. Coulson (eds), *Contributions to Aegean Archaeology: Studies in honor of William A. McDonald*. Dubuque, IA: Kendall/Hunt.

Aravantinos, V.L., Godart, L., Sacconi, A. (eds) (2000) *Les Tablettes en linéaire B de la Odos Pelopidou. Édition et Commentaire* (Thèbes Fouilles de la Cadmée 1). Pisa: Istituti editoriali e poligrafici internazionali.

Arkins, B. (1990) *Builders of My Soul: Greek and Roman themes in Yeats*. Gerrards Cross, Bucks: Colin Smythe.

Arnott, R. (1999) 'War Wounds and their Treatment in the Aegean Bronze Age', in R. Laffineur (ed.), *POLEMOS: Le contexte guerrier en Égée à l'Âge du Bronze*. Vol. 2. Liège: Université de Liège; Austin: University of Texas.

Arnott, R. (2005a) 'Disease and the Prehistory of the Aegean', in H. King (ed.), *Health in Antiquity*. London: Routledge.

Arnott, R. (2005b) *Disease, Healing and Medicine in the Aegean Bronze Age*. Leiden: Brill.

Åström, P. and Demakopoulou, K. (1996) 'Signs of an Earthquake at Midea', in S. Stiros and R.E. Jones (eds), *Archaeoseismology*. Athens: IGME and the British School at Athens.

Austin, N. (1994) *Helen of Troy and her Shameless Phantom*. Ithaca, NY: Cornell University Press.

Austin, R.G. (1964) *Virgil: Aeneidos liber secundus*. Text and commentary. Oxford: Clarendon Press.

Baldwin, T. (1944) *William Shakespere's Small Latine and Lesse Greeke*. Urbana: University of Illinois Press.

Barber, E.W. (1994) *Women's Work: The First 20,000 Years*. New York and London: W.W. Norton.

Barber, R.L.N. (1992) 'The Origins of the Mycenaean Palace', in J.M. Sanders (ed.), *Philolakon: Lakonian studies in honour of Hector Catling*. London: British School at Athens.

Barkan, L. (2000) 'The Heritage of Zeuxis: Painting, rhetoric and history', in A. Payne, A. Kuttner and R. Smick (eds), *Antiquity and Its Interpreters*. Cambridge: Cambridge University Press.

Bass, G.F. (1987) 'Oldest Known Shipwreck Reveals Splendour of the Bronze Age', in *National Geographic Magazine* 172.6: 692–733.

Bass, G.F. (1996) *Shipwrecks in the Bodrum Museum of Underwater Archaeology*. Museum of Underwater Archaeology Publications.

Bassi, K. (1993) 'Helen and the Discourse of Denial in Stesichorus' Palinode', in *Arethusa* 26: 51–75.

Baswell, C. (1995) *Virgil in Medieval England: Figuring the Aeneid from the twelfth century to Chaucer*. Cambridge: Cambridge University Press.

Baswell, C. and Taylor, P.B. (1988) 'The Fair Queene Eleyne in Chaucer's *Troilus*', in *Speculum* 63: 293–311.

Bate, A.K. (1986) Joseph of Exeter: *Trojan War: I–III*. Edited with translation and notes. Warminster: Bolchazy-Carducci Publishers; Atlantic Highlands, NJ: Aris & Phillips.

Bate, J. (1994) *Shakespeare and Ovid*. Oxford: Clarendon Press.

Bate, J. (1997) *The Genius of Shakespeare*. London: Picador.

Beal, R.H. (1995) 'Hittite Military Organisation', in J.M. Sasson (ed.), *Civilisations of the Ancient Near East*. New York: Scribner; London: Simon & Schuster and Prentice Hall International.

Beckman, G. (1996) *Hittite Diplomatic Texts*. Ed. H.A. Hoffner. Atlanta, GA: Scholars Press.

Bendall, L. (2004) 'Fit for a King? Exclusion, hierarchy, aspiration and desire in the social structure of Mycenaean banqueting', in P. Halstead and J.C. Barrett (eds), *Food, Cuisine and Society in Pre-Historic Greece*. Proceedings of the 10th Aegean Round Table, University of Sheffield, 19–21 January 2001. *Sheffield Studies in Aegean Archaeology* 5. Oxford: Oxbow Books.

Benson, C.D. (1980) *The History of Troy in Middle English Literature: Guido delle Colonne's* Historia destructionis Troiae *in medieval England*. Woodbridge: D. S. Brewer; Totowa, NJ: Rowman & Littlefield.

Bergen, A.T. (1981) 'Helen's "Good Drug": Odyssey IV 1–305', in S. Kresic (ed.), *Contemporary Literary Hermeneutics and Interpretation of Classical Texts*. Ottawa: Ottawa University Press.

Bergen, H. (1906) *Lydgate's Troy Book: AD 1412–20. Edited from the best manuscripts, with introduction, notes and glossary*. London: published for the Early English Text Society by Kegan Paul, Trench, Trubner.

Bettini, M. and Brillante, C. (2002) *Il Mito di Elena: immagini e racconti dalla Grecia a oggi*. Torino: G. Einaudi.

Bevington, D. and Rasmussen, E. (eds) (1993) *Doctor Faustus, A- and B-texts (1604, 1616)*. The Revel Plays. Manchester: Manchester University Press.

Bianchi Bandinelli, R. (1955) *Hellenistic-Byzantine Miniatures of the Iliad* (Ilias Ambrosiana). Olten: U. Graf.

Billigmeier, J.-C. and Turner, J.A. (1981) 'The Socio-Economic Roles of Women in Mycenaean Greece: A brief survey from evidence of the Linear B tablets', in H.P. Foley (ed.), *Reflections of Women in Antiquity*. New York, London and Paris: Gordon & Breach Science.

Birns, N. (1993) 'The Trojan Myth: Postmodern reverberations', in *Exemplaria* 5.1 (Spring): 45–78.

Blake, N.F. (1976) *Caxton: England's first publisher*. London: Osprey.

Blegen, C.W. (1963) *Troy and the Trojans*. London: Thames & Hudson.

Boardman, J. (1985) *The Parthenon and its Sculptures*. London: Thames & Hudson.

Boedeker, D. (ed.) (1997) *The World of Troy: Homer, Schliemann and the Treasures of Priam*. Washington, DC: Society for the Preservation of the Greek Heritage.

Bowra, C.M. (1961) *Greek Lyric Poetry: from Alcman to Simonides*. Oxford: Clarendon Press.

Bowsher, J. (1998) *The Rose Theatre: An archaeological discovery*. London: Museum of London.

Bowsher, J.M.C. (forthcoming) 'Encounters between Actors, Audience and Archaeologists at the Rose Theatre, 1587–1989'. CHAT 2003: Encounters between Past and Present: Archaeology and Popular Culture. Museum of London Archaeological Service.

Branigan, K. (ed.) (1998) *Cemetery and Society in the Aegean Bronze Age*. Sheffield: Sheffield Academic Press.

Brewster, H. (1997) *The River Gods of Greece: Myths and mountain waters in the Hellenic world*. London: I.B. Tauris.

Bridges-Adams, W. (1961) *The Irresistible Theatre*. London: Secker & Warburg.

Broodbank, C. (2002) *An Island Archaeology of the Early Cyclades*. Cambridge: Cambridge University Press.

Brown, P.F. (1996) *Venice and Antiquity: The Venetian sense of the past*. New Haven, CT and London: Yale University Press.

Brumble, H.D. (1998) *Classical Myths and Legends in the Middle Ages and Renaissance: A dictionary of allegorical meanings*. London and Chicago, IL: Fitzroy Dearborn.

Brundage, J.A. (1993) '"Let Me Count the Ways": Canonists and theologians contemplate coital positions', in J.A. Brundage (ed.), *Sex, Law and Marriage in the Middle Ages*. Aldershot, Hants: Variorum.

Brunel, P. (ed.) (1992) *Companion to Literary Myths, Heroes and Archetypes*. Translated from the French by W. Allatson, J. Hayward, T. Selous. London: Routledge.

Bryce, T. (1998) *The Kingdom of the Hittites*. Oxford: Clarendon Press.

Bryce, T. (2002) *Life and Society in the Hittite World*. Oxford: Oxford University Press.

Bryce, T. (2003) *Letters of the Great Kings of the Ancient Near East: The royal correspondence of the Late Bronze Age*. London: Routledge.

Bryce, T. (2005) *The Trojans*. London: Routledge.

Buchthal, H. (1971) *Historia Troiana: Studies in the history of medieval secular illustration*. London: Warburg Institute, University of London.

Calame, C. (1997) *Choruses of Young Women in Ancient Greece: Their morphology, religious role and social function*. Trans. D. Collins and J. Orion. Originally published in French in 1977. Lanham, MD and Oxford: Rowman & Littlefield.

Caldwell, R.S. (1987) *Hesiod's Theogony*: translated with introduction, commentary, and interpretive essay. Focus Classical Library. Newburyport, MA: R. Pullins.

Calnan, K.A. (1992) 'The Health Status of Bronze Age Greek Women'. PhD dissertation (unpublished). University of Cincinnati.

Camus, A. (2000) 'L'exil d'Hélène', in *The Myth of Sisyphus*. Trans. Justin O'Brien. London: Penguin.

Canfora, L. (1989) *The Vanished Library*. Trans. M. Ryle. London: Hutchinson Radius.

Carson, A. (1986) *Eros the Bittersweet: An essay*. Princeton, NJ: Princeton University Press.

Carter, J.B. (1988) 'Masks and Poetry in Early Sparta', in R. Hägg, N. Marinatos and G. Nordquist (eds), *Early Greek Cult Practice*. Proceedings of the Fifth International Symposium of the Swedish Institute in Athens, 26–9 June 1986. Stockholm: Swedish Institute in Athens.

Cartledge, P. (1987) *Agesilaos and the Crisis of Sparta*. London: Duckworth.

Cartledge, P. (1992) 'Early Lakedaimon: The making of a conquest-state', in J.M. Sanders (ed.), *Philolakon: Lakonian studies in Honour of Hector Catling*. Oxford: British School at Athens.

Cartledge, P. (1993 2nd edn, 2002) *The Greeks: A portrait of self and others*. Oxford: Oxford University Press.

Cartledge, P. (1997) '"Deep Plays": Theatre in process in Greek civic life', in P.E. Easterling (ed.), *The Cambridge Companion to Greek Tragedy*. Cambridge: Cambridge University Press.

Cartledge, P. (2001) *Spartan Reflections*. London: Duckworth.

Cartledge, P. (2002a) *Sparta and Lakonia: A regional history 1300–362 BC*. Second edition. London: Routledge.

Cartledge, P. (2002 revised edn.) *The Spartans: An epic history*. London: Channel 4 Books.

Cartledge, P. and Spawforth, A. (1989) *Hellenistic and Roman Sparta: A tale of two cities*. London: Routledge.

Casson, L. (2001) *Libraries in the Ancient World*. New Haven, CT and London: Yale University Press.

Catling, H.W. (1975) 'Excavations of the British School at Athens at the Menelaion, Sparta 1973–5', in *Lakonikai Spoudai* 2: 258–69.

Catling, H.W. (1976) 'Archaeology of Greece', in *Archaeological Reports* 22: 3–33. Published by the Council of the Society for the Promotion of Hellenic Studies and the Managing Committee of the British School at Athens.

Catling, H.W. (1977) 'Excavations at the Menelaion, Sparta, 1973–6', in *Archaeological Reports* 23: 24–42. Published by the Council of the Society for the Promotion of Hellenic Studies and the Managing Committee of the British School at Athens.

Catling, H.W. and Cavanagh, H. (1976) 'Two Inscribed Bronzes from the Menelaion, Sparta', in *Kadmos* 15: 145–57.

Cavanagh, W.G. and Laxton, R.R. (1984) 'Lead Figurines from the Menelaion and Seriation', in *Annual of the British School at Athens* 79: 23–36.

Cavanagh, W.G. and Mee, C. (1995) 'Mourning before and after the Dark Age', in C. Morris (ed.), *Klados: Essays in honour of J.N. Coldstream*. London: Institute of Classical Studies.

Cavanagh, W.G. and Mee, C. (1998) *A Private Place: Death in pre-historic Greece*. Jonsered: Paul Åströms Förlag.

Chadwick, J. (1976) *The Mycenaean World*. Cambridge: Cambridge University Press.

Chadwick, J. (1988) 'The Women of Pylos', in J.P. Olivier and T.G. Palaima (eds), *Texts, Tablets and Scribes: Studies in Mycenaean epigraphy and economy offered to Emmett L. Bennett Jr. Minos Supplement* 10. Salamanca: University of Salamanca.

Chambers, E.K. (1923) *The Elizabethan Stage*, Vol. III. Oxford: Clarendon Press.

Chapouthier, F. (1935) *Les Dioscures au service d'une déesse: étude d'iconographie religieuse*. Paris: E. de Boccard.

Clader, L.L. (1976) *Helen: The evolution from divine to heroic in Greek epic tradition*. Leiden: Brill.

Clarke, H. (1981) *Homer's Readers: A historical introduction to the Iliad and the Odyssey*. Newark: University of Delaware Press.

Clement, P.A. (1958) 'The Recovery of Helen', in *Hesperia* 27: 47–73.

Cline, E.H. (1994) *Sailing the Wine-Dark Sea: International trade and the Late Bronze Age Aegean*. Oxford: Tempus Reparatum.

Colantuono, A. (1997) *Guido Reni's Abduction of Helen: The politics and rhetoric of painting in seventeenth-century Europe*. Cambridge: Cambridge University Press.

Coles, L.H. (1996) 'Thinking with Helen: A reading of Euripides' *Helen*'. PhD dissertation (unpublished). University of Cambridge.

Croally, N. T. (1994) *Euripidean Polemic: The Trojan Women and the function of tragedy*. Cambridge and New York: Cambridge University Press.

Crowfoot, J.W., Crowfoot, G.M., Kenyon, K.M. (1957) *The Objects from Samaria*. London: Palestine Exploration Fund.

Crowley, J.L. and Laffineur, R. (eds) (1992) *Eikon: Aegean Bronze Age Iconography: Shaping a methodology*. Proceedings of the 4th International Aegean Conference, University of Tasmania, Hobart, Australia, 6–9 April 1992. Liège: Université de Liège.

Currie, S. (1998) 'Poisonous Women in Roman Culture', in M. Wyke (ed.), *Parchments of Gender: Deciphering the body in antiquity*. Oxford: Clarendon Press.

Dakoronia, P. (1996) 'Earthquakes of the Late Helladic III Period (12th Century BC) at Kynos (Livanates, Central Greece)', in S. Stiros and R.E. Jones (eds), *Archaeoseismology*. Athens: IGME and the British School at Athens.

Dalby, A. (2000) *Empire of Pleasures: Luxury and indulgence in the Roman world*. London: Routledge.

Dalby, A. (2003) *Food in the Ancient World from A–Z*. London: Routledge.

Dale, A. M. (1967) *Euripides' Helen*. Edited with introduction and commentary. Oxford: Clarendon Press.

Darga, M. (1993) 'Women in the Historical Ages', in *Woman in Anatolia: 9000 years of the Anatolian Woman*. Turkish Republic Ministry of Culture: General Directorate of Monuments and Museums.

Dassmann, E. and Klauser, T. (eds) (1988) *Reallexikon für Antike und Christentum*. Volume 14. Stuttgart: Anton Hiersemann.

David, E. (1992) 'Sparta's Social Hair', in *Eranos* 90: 11–21.

Davies, M. (1989) *The Epic Cycle*. Bristol: Bristol Classical Press.

Davis, E.N. (1986) 'Youth and Age in the Thera Frescoes', in *American Journal of Archaeology* 90: 399–406.

Dayagi-Mendels, M. (1989) *Perfumes and Cosmetics in the Ancient World*. Jerusalem: Israel Museum.

Deacy, S. and Pierce, K.F. (eds) (1997) *Rape in Antiquity*. London: Duckworth and the Classical Press of Wales.

Demakopoulou, K. (ed.) (1988) *The Mycenaean World: Five centuries of early Greek culture 1600–1100 BC*. Athens: Ministry of Culture.

Demakopoulou, K. (1990) 'The Burial Ritual in the Tholos Tomb at Kokla, Argolis', in R. Hägg and G. C. Nordquist (eds), *Celebrations of Death and Divinity in the Bronze Age Argolid*. Proceedings of the Sixth International Symposium at the Swedish Institute in Athens, 11–13 June 1988. Stockholm: Swedish Institute in Athens.

Demakopoulou, K. (ed.) (1996) *The Aidonia Treasure: Seals and jewellery of the Aegean Late Bronze Age*. Athens: Ministry of Culture.

Dervenis, K. and Lykiardopoulos, N. (2005) *Martial Arts of Ancient Greece and the Mediterranean*. Esoptron, Athens.

Dickinson, O.T.P.K. (1994) *The Aegean Bronze Age*. Cambridge: Cambridge University Press.

Doniger, W. (1999) *Splitting the Difference: Gender and myth in ancient Greece and India*. Chicago, IL: University of Chicago Press.

duBois, P. (1984) 'Sappho and Helen', in J. Peradotto and J.P. Sullivan (eds), *Women in the Ancient World: The Arethusa papers*. Albany, NY: State University of New York.

Duby, G. and Perot, M. (1992) *Power and Beauty: Images of women in art*. London: Tauris Park.

Duffy, C.-A. (2002) *Feminine Gospels*. London: Picador.

Easton, D.F. (1981) 'Schliemann's Discovery of "Priam's Treasure": Two enigmas', in *Antiquity* 55: 179–83.

Easton, D.F. (1994) 'Priam's Gold: The Full Story', in *Anatolian Studies* 44: 221–43.

Edwards, M. (1997) 'Simon Magus, the Bad Samaritan', in S. Swain and M. Edwards (eds), *Portraits: Biographical representation in the Greek and Latin literature of the Roman Empire*. Oxford: Clarendon Press.

Ehrenberg, M. (1989) *Women in Prehistory*. London: British Museum Publications.

Ehrhart, M.J. (1987) *The Judgment of the Trojan Prince Paris in Medieval Literature*. Philadelphia: University of Pennsylvania Press.

El-Abbadi, M. (1990) *The Life and Fate of the Ancient Library of Alexandria*. Unesco.

Emerson, G. (2002) *Sin City: London in pursuit of pleasure*. London: Granada.

Engels, D. (1980) 'The Problem of Female Infanticide in the Greco-Roman World', in *Classical Philology* 75: 112–20.

Erickson, C. (1999) *The First Elizabeth*. London: Robson.

Erskine, A. (2001) *Troy Between Greece and Rome: Local tradition and imperial power*. Oxford: Oxford University Press.

Faris, A. (1980) *Jacques Offenbach*. London: Faber.

Farnell, L.R. (1921) *Greek Hero Cults and Ideas of Immortality*. Oxford: Clarendon Press.

Farrell, J. (1908) 'Excavations at Sparta, 1908: Archaic terracottas from the sanctuary of Orthia', in the *Annual of the British School at Athens* 14: 48–73.

Fields, N. (2004) *Troy c. 1700–1250 BC*. (Fortress 17) London: Osprey.

Filoramo, G. (1990) *A History of Gnosticism*. Trans. A. Alcock. Oxford: Blackwell.

Finkelberg, M. (1991) 'Royal Succession in Heroic Greece', in *Classical Quarterly* 41.ii: 303–16.

Finley, M.I. (1954) 'Marriage, Sale, and Gift in the Homeric World'. Reprinted from *Seminar*, an annual extraordinary number of the *Jurist* 12: 7–33. Washington, DC: School of Canon Law, the Catholic University of America.

Fitton, J.L. (1995) *The Discovery of the Greek Bronze Age*. London: British Museum Press.

Fitton, J.L. (2002) *Minoans*. Peoples of the Past series. London: British Museum Press.

Foley, H.P. (1981) 'The Conception of Women in Athenian Drama', in H. Foley (ed.), *Reflections of Women in Antiquity*. New York: Gordon & Breach.

Foley, H.P. (2001) '*Anodos* Dramas: Euripides' *Alcestis* and *Helen*', in H.P. Foley (ed.), *Female Acts in Greek Tragedy*. Princeton, NJ: Princeton University Press.

Forbes, P. (1967) *Champagne: The wine, the land and the people*. London: Victor Gollancz.

Foreville, R. (ed.) (1952) *Guillaume de Poitiers: Histoire de Guillaume le Conquérant*. Edited with translation. Paris: Les Belles Lettres.

Forsdyke, J. (1956) *Greece Before Homer: Ancient Chronology and Mythology*. London: Max Parrish.

Forsyth, P.Y. (1997) *Thera in the Bronze Age*. American University Studies series. New York: P. Lang.

Frazer, J.G. (1898) *Pausanias's Description of Greece*. Translated with a commentary. 6 vols. London.

Frazer, R.M., Jr (1966) *The Trojan War: The chronicles of Dictys of Crete and Dares the Phrygian.* Translated with introduction and notes. Bloomington and London: Indiana University Press.

Freeman, C. (1999) *The Greek Achievement: The foundation of the western world.* London: Allen Lane, Penguin Press.

French, E. (2002) *Mycenae: Agamemnon's Capital.* Stroud, Glos: Tempus.

French, E.B. (1981) 'Mycenaean Figures and Figurines: Their Typology and Function', in R. Hägg and N. Marinatos (eds), *Sanctuaries and Cults in the Aegean Bronze Age.* Proceedings of the First International Symposium of the Swedish Institute in Athens, 12–13 May 1980. Stockholm: Swedish Institute in Athens.

Galaty, M.L. and Parkinson, W.A. (eds) (1999) *Rethinking Mycenaean Palaces: New interpretations of an old idea.* Los Angeles: Institute of Archaeology, University of California.

Galyon, A.E. (1980) *The Art of Versification: Matthew of Vendôme.* Translated with introduction. Ames: Iowa State University Press.

Gammond, P. (1980) *Offenbach: His life and times.* Speldhurst: Midas.

Gantz, T. (1993) *Early Greek Myth: A guide to literary and artistic sources.* Baltimore, MD and London: Johns Hopkins University Press.

Gardner, B. (1964) *Up the Line to Death: The war poets 1914–18.* London: Methuen.

Gates, C. (1992) 'Art for Children in Mycenaean Greece', in J.L. Crowley and R. Laffineur (eds), *Eikon: Aegean Bronze Age iconography: Shaping a methodology.* Proceedings of the 4th International Aegean Conference, University of Tasmania, Hobart, Australia. Liège: Université de Liège.

Ghali-Kahil, L. (1955) *Les Enlèvements et le retour d'Hélène dans les textes et les documents figurés.* 2 vols. Paris: E. de Boccard.

Gimbutas, M. (1999) *The Living Goddesses.* Berkeley, CA and London: University of California Press.

Gladstone, W.E. (1858) *Studies on Homer and the Homeric Age.* Vol. 2. Oxford: Oxford University Press.

Glenn, J.R. (ed.) (1987) *A Critical Edition of Alexander Ross's 1647 Mystagogus Poeticus, or The Muses' Interpreter.* New York: Garland.

Godart, L. and Sacconi, A. (2001) 'La Géographie des États mycéniens'. *Académie des Inscriptions et Belles-Lettres. Comptes Rendus des Séances de l'Année,* April–June 1999, Paris.

Goldhill, S.D. (1986) *Reading Greek Tragedy.* Cambridge: Cambridge University Press.

Goldhill, S.D. (1997) 'The Audience of Athenian Tragedy', in P.E. Easterling (ed.), *The Cambridge Companion to Greek Tragedy.* Cambridge: Cambridge University Press.

Goldhill, S.D. (2003) *Who Needs Greek?: Contests in the cultural history of Hellenism.* Cambridge: Cambridge University Press.

Goodison, L. (1989) *Death, Women and the Sun: Symbolism of regeneration in early Aegean religion. Bulletin of the Institute of Classical Studies,* Supplement 53. London: Institute of Classical Studies.

Goodison, L. and Morris, C. (eds) (1998) *Ancient Goddesses: The myths and the evidence.* London: British Museum Press.

Goold, G.P. (1990) 'Servius and the Helen Episode', in S.J. Harrison (ed.), *Oxford Readings in Virgil's* Aeneid. Oxford: Clarendon Press.

Graziosi, B. (2002) *Inventing Homer: The early reception of epic.* Cambridge: Cambridge University Press.

Green, P. (2004) 'Heroic Hype, New Style: Hollywood pitted against Homer', in *Arion* 12.1 (Spring/Summer 2004): 171–87.

Greene, E. (ed.) (1996) *Reading Sappho: Contemporary approaches.* Berkeley: University of California Press.

Greene, E. (ed.) (1996) *Re-reading Sappho: Reception and transmission.* Berkeley: University of California Press.

Greg, W.G. (1946) 'The Damnation of Faustus', in *Modern Language Review* 41: 97–107.

Gregory, E. (1997) *H.D. and Hellenism: Classical lines.* Cambridge: Cambridge University Press.

Gregory, H. (ed.) (1961) Helen in Egypt, *by H.D.* New York: New Directions.

Griffin, J. (2001) 'East is East and West is West', in *The Spectator*, October 2001.

Griffiths, A. (1972) 'Alcman's Partheneion: The morning after the night before', in *Quaderni Urbinati Di Cultura Classica* 14: 7–30.

Griffiths, F.T. (1979) *Theocritus at Court.* Leiden: Brill.

Guarino, G.A. (1964) *Boccaccio:* Concerning Famous Women. Translated with introduction and notes. London: Allen & Unwin.

Güterbock, H.G. (1984) 'Troy in Hittite Texts? Wilusa, Ahhiyawa and Hittite History', in M.J. Mellink (ed.), *Troy and the Trojan War*. A symposium held at Bryn Mawr College, October 1984. Bryn Mawr, PA: Bryn Mawr College.

Gumpert, M. (2001) *Grafting Helen: The abduction of the classical past.* Madison: University of Wisconsin Press.

Gurney, O. (1975) *The Hittites.* London: Allen Lane.

Guterl, F. and Hastings, M. *et al.* (2003) 'The Global Makeover', in *Newsweek,* 10 November 2003: Atlantic edition.

H.D. (Hilda Doolittle) (1957) *Selected Poems.* New York: Grove Press.

Haar, S.C. (2003) *Simon Magus: The first Gnostic?* Berlin: Walter de Gruyter.

Hägg, R. and Marinatos, N. (eds) (1981) *Sanctuaries and Cults in the Aegean Bronze Age.* Proceedings of the First International Symposium of the Swedish Institute in Athens, 12–13 May 1980. Stockholm: Swedish Institute in Athens.

Hägg, R. and Nordquist, G.C. (1990) *Celebrations of Death and Divinity in the Bronze Age Argolid.* Proceedings of the Sixth International Symposium at the Swedish Institute in Athens, 11–13 June 1988. Stockholm: Swedish Institute in Athens.

Hall, E. (1989) *Inventing the Barbarian: Greek self-definition through tragedy.* Oxford: Clarendon Press.

Hall, E. (ed.) (1996) *Aeschylus:* Persians. Translated with introduction and commentary. Warminster: Aris & Phillips.

Hall, E. (2000) 'Introduction' to *Euripides: Selections.* Ed. and trans. J. Morwood for Oxford World Classics. Oxford: Clarendon Press.

Hall, P. (1998) *Cities in Civilisation: Culture, innovation and urban order.* London: Weidenfeld & Nicolson.

Hallager, B.P. and McGeorge, P.J.P. (1992) *Late Minoan III Burials at Khania: The tombs, finds and deceased in Odos Palama.* Göteborg: Paul Åströms Förlag.

Hamilton, N. (1996) 'The Personal is Political', in *Viewpoint – Can We Interpret Figurines?,* in *Cambridge Archaeological Journal* 6.2: 281–307.

Hankey, V. (1967) 'Mycenaean Pottery in the Middle East: Notes on finds since 1951', in *Annual of the British School at Athens* 62: 104–47.

Hanson, A.E. (1990) 'The Medical Writers' Woman', in D. Halperin, J. Winkler, F. Zeitlin (ed), *Before Sexuality: The construction of erotic experience in the ancient world.* Princeton, NJ: Princeton University Press.

Harding, A.F. (1984) *The Mycenaeans and Europe.* London: Academic.

Harding, J. (1980) *Jacques Offenbach: A biography.* London: Calder.

Hartog, F. (1988) *The Mirror of Herodotus: The representation of the other in the writing of history.* Translated from the French by J. Lloyd. Berkeley and London: University of California Press.

Hattaway, M. (1982) *Elizabethan Popular Theatre: Plays in performance.* London: Routledge & Kegan Paul.

Hawley, R. (1998) 'The Dynamics of Beauty in Classical Greece', in D. Montserrat (ed.), *Changing Bodies, Changing Meanings: Studies on the human body in antiquity.* London and New York: Routledge.

Hedreen, G. (1996) 'Image, Text, and Story in the Recovery of Helen', in *Classical Antiquity* 15.1: 152–84.

Hedreen, G. (2001) *Capturing Troy: The narrative functions of landscape in archaic and early Greek classical art.* Ann Arbor: University of Michigan Press.

Higgins, R.A. (1979) *Minoan and Mycenaean Art*. Revised edition. London: Thames & Hudson.

Highet, G. (1949) *The Classical Tradition: Greek and Roman influences on western literature*. Oxford: Clarendon Press.

Hoffman, D.L. (1995) *The Status of Women and Gnosticism in Irenaeus and Tertullian*. Lewiston and Lampeter: Edwin Mellen Press.

Hoffner, H.A. (2003) 'Daily Life Among the Hittites', in R.E. Averbeck, M.W. Chavalas, D.B. Weisberg (eds), *Life and Culture in the Ancient Near East*. Potomac, MD: CDL Press.

Hood, S. (1953) 'A Mycenaean Cavalryman', in *Annual of the British School at Athens* 48: 84–93.

Hood, S. (1978) *The Arts in Pre-historic Greece*. Harmondsworth: Penguin.

Hopkins, D.C. (2002) *Across the Anatolian Plateau: Readings in the archaeology of ancient Turkey*. Boston, MA: American Schools of Oriental Research.

Houston-Smith, D. (1962) 'Near Eastern Forerunners of the Striding Zeus', in *Archaeology* 15.2: 176–83.

Hughes, D.D. (1989) *Human Sacrifice in Ancient Greece*. London and New York: Routledge.

Hughes-Brock, H. (1998) 'Greek Beads of the Mycenaean Period (ca. 1650–1100 BC): The age of the heroines of mythology', in L.D. Sciama and J.B. Eicher (eds), *Beads and Bead-Makers: Gender, material culture and meaning*. Oxford: Berg.

Hunter, R. (1996) *Theocritus and the Archaeology of Hellenistic Poetry*. Cambridge: Cambridge University Press.

Hunter, R. (ed.) (2002) *Theocritus' Idylls*. With introduction and explanatory notes, and translated by A. Verity. Oxford: Oxford University Press.

Hutchinson, G. (2001) *Greek Lyric Poetry: A commentary on selected larger pieces (Alcman, Stesichorus, Sappho, Alcaeus, Ibycus, Anacreon, Simonides, Bacchylides, Pindar, Sophocles, Euripides)*. Oxford: Oxford University Press.

Iakovidis, S.E. and French, E.B. (2003) *Archaeological Atlas of Mycenae*. Athens: Archaeological Society at Athens.

Immerwahr, S.A. (1971) *The Athenian Agora: Results of Excavations Conducted by the American School of Classical Studies at Athens*. Vol. XIII: *The Neolithic and Bronze Ages*. The American School of Classical Studies at Athens: Princeton, NJ.

Immerwahr, S.A. (1990) *Aegean Painting in the Bronze Age*. University Park, PA and London: Pennsylvania State University Press.

Immerwahr, S.A. (1995) 'Death and the Tanagra larnakes', in J.B. Carter and S.P. Morris (eds), *The Ages of Homer: A tribute to Emily Townsend Vermeule*. Austin: University of Texas Press.

Ingram, A.J.C. (1978) 'Changing Attitudes to "Bad" Women in Elizabethan and Jacobean Drama'. PhD dissertation (unpublished). University of Cambridge.

Isaakidou, V., Halstead, P., Davis, J. and Stocker, S. (2002) 'Burnt Animal Sacrifice at the Mycenaean "Palace of Nestor", Pylos', in *Antiquity* 76: 86–92.

Isager, S. and Skydsgaard, J.E. (1992) *Ancient Greek Agriculture: An introduction.* London: Routledge.

James, H. (1997) *Shakespeare's Troy: Drama, politics and the translation of empire.* Cambridge: Cambridge University Press.

Jones, N. (1999) *Rupert Brooke: Life, death and myth.* London: Richard Cohen.

Jordan, R.H. (1999) *Virgil:* Aeneid *II.* Edited with introduction, notes, bibliography and vocabulary. Bristol: Bristol Classical Press.

Kallendorf, C. (1999) *Virgil and the Myth of Venice: Books and readers in the Italian Renaissance.* Oxford: Clarendon Press.

Kallet, L. (2000) 'The Fifth Century: Political and military narrative', in R. Osborne (ed.), *Classical Greece: 500–323 BC.* Oxford: Oxford University Press.

Karo, G.H. (1930–3) *Die Schachtgräber von Mykenai.* München: F. Bruckmann.

Kaster, R. (1990) *The Tradition of the Text of the* Aeneid *in the Ninth Century.* New York and London: Garland Publishing.

Kennedy, D. (ed.) (2002) *The Oxford Encyclopedia of Theatre and Performance.* Vol. 2 (M–Z). Oxford: Oxford University Press.

Keynes, G. (ed.) (1968) *The Letters of Rupert Brooke.* London: Faber.

Kilian, K. (1996) 'Earthquakes and Archaeological Context at 13th century BC Tiryns', in S. Stiros and R.E. Jones (eds), *Archaeoseismology.* Athens: IGME and the British School at Athens.

King, H. (1983, rev. edn 1993) 'Bound to Bleed: Artemis and Greek women', in A. Cameron and A. Kuhrt (eds), *Images of Women in Antiquity.* London and Canberra: Croom Helm.

King, H. (1998) *Hippocrates' Woman: Reading the female body in ancient Greece.* London and New York: Routledge.

Koloski-Ostrow, A.O. and Lyons, C.L. (1997) *Naked Truths: Women, sexuality and gender in classical art and archaeology.* London: Routledge.

Konsolaki-Yannopoulou, E. (1999) 'A Group of New Mycenaean Horsemen from Methana', in P. Betancourt, V. Karageorghis, R. Laffineur and W.-D. Niemeier (eds), *Meletemata II: Studies in Aegean archaeology presented to Malcolm H. Wiener as he enters his 65th year.* Liège: Université de Liège; Austin: University of Texas.

Konsolaki-Yannopoulou, E. (2002) 'A Mycenaean Sanctuary on Methana', in R. Hägg (ed.), *Peloponnesian Sanctuaries and Cults.* Proceedings of the Ninth

International Symposium at the Swedish Institute in Athens, 11–13 June 1994. Stockholm: Swedish Institute in Athens.

Korfmann, M. (1993) 'Troia – Ausgrabungen 1992', in *Studia Troica* 3: 1–37.

Korfmann, M. (1996) 'Troia – Ausgrabungen 1995', in *Studia Troica* 6: 1–63.

Korfmann, M. (1998) 'Troia: An ancient Anatolian palatial and trading center: Archaeological evidence for the period of Troia VI/VII', in *Classical World* 91: 369–85.

Korfmann, M., Hawkins, J.D., Latacz, J. (2004) 'Was There a Trojan War?', in *Archaeology* 57.3 (May/June): 36–41.

Kracauer, S. (2002) *Jacques Offenbach and the Paris of His Time*. Trans. G. David and E. Mosbacher. Foreword by G. Koch. New York: Zone; London: MIT Press.

Krzyszkowska, O. (2005) *Aegean Seals: An introduction*. Bulletin of the Institute of Classical Studies Supplement 85. London: Institute of Classical Studies.

Laffineur, R. and Niemeier, W.-D. (eds) (1995) *Politeia: Society and state in the Aegean Bronze Age*. Liège: Université de Liège.

Lang, M (1969) *The Palace of Nestor at Pylos in Western Messenia* Vol 2: *The Frescoes*. Princeton, NJ: Princeton University Press.

Larson, J. (1995) *Greek Heroine Cults*. Madison: University of Wisconsin Press.

Latacz, J. (2004) *Troy and Homer: Towards a solution of an old mystery*. Translated from the German by Kevin Windle and Ross Ireland. Oxford: Oxford University Press

Lewartowski, K. (2000) *Late Helladic Simple Graves: A study of Mycenaean burial customs*. BAR International Series 878. Oxford: Archaeopress.

Lexicon Iconographicum Mythologiae Classicae (1988) Vol. IV, nos. 1 and 2 (Eros-Herakles). Zurich and Munich: Artemis.

Licht, H. (1932) *Sexual Life in Ancient Greece*. Ed. L.H. Dawson and trans. J.H. Freese. London: Routledge.

Lichtheim, M. (1976) *Ancient Egyptian Literature*. Vol. 2. Berkeley: University of California Press.

Lindsay, J. (1974) *Helen of Troy: Woman and goddess*. London: Constable.

Lloyd, A.B. (1988) *Commentary on Herodotus Book II*. Vol. 3. Leiden and New York: Brill.

Luce, J.V. (1999) *Celebrating Homer's Landscapes: Troy and Ithaca Revisited*. New Haven, CT and London: Yale University Press.

Luke, D. (1994) *Goethe:* Faust Part Two. Translated with introduction and notes. Oxford: Oxford University Press.

Lyons, D. (1997) *Gender and Immortality: Heroines in ancient Greek myth and cult*. Princeton, NJ: Princeton University Press.

MacDonald, D.R. (1994) *Christianizing Homer: The* Odyssey, Plato *and the Acts of Andrew*. New York and Oxford: Oxford University Press.

MacLeod, R. (2001) *The Library of Alexandria: Centre of learning in the ancient world*. London: I.B. Tauris.

McQueen, E.I. (ed.) (2000) *Herodotus VI*. With introduction, commentary and bibliography. London: Bristol Classical Press.

Macqueen, J.G. (1975) *The Hittites and Their Contemporaries in Asia Minor*. London: Thames & Hudson.

Magoulias, H.J. (ed.) (1984) *O City of Byzantium: Annals of Nicetas Choniates*. Trans. H.J. Magoulias. Detroit: Wayne State University Press.

Mandel, C. (1980) 'Garbo/Helen: The self-projection of beauty by H.D.', in *Women's Studies* 7: 127–35.

Manniche, L. (1999) *Sacred Luxuries: Fragrance, aromatherapy and cosmetics in ancient Egypt*. London: Opus.

Manning, S.W. (1999) *A Test of Time: The volcano of Thera and the chronology and history of the Aegean and east Mediterranean in the mid second millennium BC*. Oxford: Oxbow.

Marchand, S.L. (1996) *Down from Olympus: Archaeology and philhellenism in Germany, 1750–1970*. Princeton, NJ: Princeton University Press.

Marinatos, N. (1984) *Art and Religion in Thera: reconstructing a Bronze Age society*. Athens: Mathioulakis.

Marinatos, N. (1993) *Minoan Religion: Ritual, image and symbol*. University of Columbia, SC: University of South Carolina Press.

Marinatos, N. (2000) *The Goddess and the Warrior: The naked goddess and mistress of animals in early Greek religion*. London and New York: Routledge.

Marrou, H. (1956) *A History of Education in Antiquity*. Trans. George Lamb. London: Sheed & Ward.

Marsh, J. (ed.) (1999) *Dante Gabriel Rossetti: Collected writings*. London: J.M. Dent.

Martindale, C. (ed.) (1988) *Ovid Renewed: Ovidian influences on literature and art from the Middle Ages to the twentieth century*. Cambridge: Cambridge University Press.

Martindale, C. and Martindale, M. (1990) *Shakespeare and the Uses of Antiquity: An introductory essay*. London: Routledge.

Masse, W.B. (1998) 'Earth, Air, Fire and Water: The archaeology of Bronze Age cosmic catastrophes', in B.J. Peiser, T. Palmer and M.E. Bailey (eds), *Natural Catastrophes During Bronze Age Civilisations: Archaeological, geological, astronomical and cultural perspectives*. BAR International Series 728. Oxford: Archaeopress.

Mayer, K. (1996) 'Helen and the Dios Boule', in the *American Journal of Philology* 117: 1–15.

Mayor, A. (2000) *The First Fossil Hunters. Palaeontology in Greek and Roman Times.* Princeton, NJ: Princeton University Press.

Mayor, A. (2003) *Greek Fire, Poison Arrows and Scorpion Bombs: Biological and chemical warfare in the ancient world.* London: Duckworth.

Meagher, R.E. (2002) *The Meaning of Helen: In search of an ancient icon.* Wauconda, IL: Bolchazy-Carducci.

Mee, C. (1998) 'Gender Bias in Mycenaean Mortuary Practices', in K. Branigan (ed.), *Cemetery and society in the Aegean Bronze Age.* Sheffield: Sheffield Academic Press.

Merkle, S. (1994) 'Telling the True Story of the Trojan War: The eyewitness account of Dictys of Crete', in J. Tatum (ed.), *The Search for the Ancient Novel.* Baltimore, MD: Johns Hopkins University Press.

Meskell, L. (1995) 'Goddesses, Gimbutas and "New Age" archaeology', in *Antiquity,* 69: 74–86.

Minoura, K., Imamura, F., Kuran, U., Nakamura, T., Papadopoulos, G.A., Takahashi, T., Yalciner, A.C. (2000) 'Discovery of Minoan Tsunami Deposits', in *Geology* 28.1: 59–62.

Moorehead, C. (1994) *The Lost Treasures of Troy.* London: Weidenfeld & Nicolson.

Moran, W.L. (1992) *The Armana Letters.* Edited with translation. Baltimore MD: Johns Hopkins University Press.

Morgan, L. (1988) *The Miniature Wall Paintings of Thera: A study in Aegean culture and iconography.* Cambridge: Cambridge University Press.

Mortley, R. (1981) *Womanhood: The feminine in ancient Hellenism, Gnosticism, Christianity and Islam.* Rozelle: Delacroix Press.

Mountjoy, P. (1999) 'The Destruction of Troy VIh', in *Studia Troica* 9: 253–93.

Murgia, C.E. and Rodgers, R.H. (1984) 'A Tale of Two Manuscripts', in *Classical Philology* 70: 145–53.

Mylonas, G.E. (1966) *Mycenae and the Mycenaean Age.* Princeton, NJ: Princeton University Press

Mylonas, G.E. (1983) *Mycenae Rich in Gold.* Athens: Ekdotike Athenon Publishers.

Myrick, L.D. (1993) *From the De Excidio Troiae Historia to the Togail Troí: Literary-cultural synthesis in a medieval Irish adaptation of Dares' Troy Tale.* Heidelberg: C. Winter.

Neville, J.W. (1977) 'Herodotus on the Trojan War', in *Greece and Rome* 24: 3–12.

Nicholson, R. (1974) *Scotland: The later Middle Ages.* Edinburgh: Oliver & Boyd.

Nikolaidou, M. and Kokkinidou, D. (1997) 'The Symbolism of Violence in

Late Bronze Age Palatial Societies of the Aegean: A gender approach', in J. Carman (ed.), *Material Harm: Archaeological studies of war and violence*. Glasgow: Cruithne Press.

Nilsson, M.P. (1932) *The Mycenaean Origin of Greek Mythology*. Cambridge: Cambridge University Press.

Nilsson, M.P. (1950) *The Minoan-Mycenaean Religion and Its Survival in Greek Religion*. Lund: C.W.K. Gleerup.

Nixon, L. (1981) 'Changing Views of Minoan Society', in O. Krzyszkowska and L. Nixon (eds), *Minoan Society*. Proceedings of the Cambridge Colloquium 1981. Bristol: Bristol Classical Press.

Nixon, L. (1994) 'Gender Bias in Archaeology', in L.J. Archer, S. Fischler and M. Wyke (eds), *Women in Ancient Societies: An illusion of the night*. Basingstoke, Hants: Macmillan.

Nixon, L. (1999) 'Women, Children and Weaving', in P. Betancourt, V. Karageorghis, R. Laffineur and W.-D. Niemeier (eds), *Meletemata II: Studies in Aegean archaeology presented to Malcolm H. Wiener as he enters his 65th year*. Liège: Université de Liège; Austin: University of Texas.

Norgaard, L. and Smith, O.L. (eds) (1975) *A Byzantine Iliad*. Copenhagen: Museum Tusculanum.

Nur, A. (1998) 'The End of the Bronze Age by Large Earthquakes?', in B.J. Peiser, T. Palmer and M.E. Bailey (eds), *Natural Catastrophes During Bronze Age Civilisations: Archaeological, geological, astronomical and cultural perspectives*. BAR International Series 728. Oxford: Archaeopress.

O'Callaghan, T.F. (2003) 'Tempering Scandal: Eleanor of Aquitaine and Benoît de Sainte-Maure's *Roman de Troie*' in B. Wheeler and J.C. Parsons (eds), *Eleanor of Aquitaine: Lord and Lady*. New York and Basingstoke, Hants: Palgrave Macmillan.

Olsen, B.A. (1998) 'Women, Children and the Family in Late Aegean Bronze Age: Differences in Minoan and Mycenaean constructions of gender', in *World Archaeology* 29.3: 380–92.

Ormerod, D. and Wortam, C. (eds) (1985) *Christopher Marlowe, Dr Faustus: The A-Text*. Nedlands: University of Western Australia Press.

Oswald, E. (1905) *The Legend of Fair Helen as told by Homer, Goethe and others: A study*. London: John Murray.

Painter, G.D. (1976) *William Caxton: A quincentenary biography of England's first printer*. London: Chatto & Windus.

Palaima, T.G. (2003) Review of V.L. Aravantinos, L. Godart and A. Sacconi (eds), *Les Tablettes en linéaire B de la Odos Pelopidou. Édition et Commentaire* (Thèbes Fouilles de la Cadmée 1), in *American Journal of Archaeology* 107.1: 113–15.

Palaima, T.G. (2004) 'Sacrificial Feasting in the Linear B Tablets', in J.C. Wright (ed.), *The Mycenaean Feast. Hesperia* 73.2: 217–46.

Pantelia, M.C. (1995) 'Theocritus at Sparta: Homeric allusions in Theocritus' Idyll 18', in *Hermes* 123: 76–81.

Papadopoulos, G. (1996) 'An Earthquake Engineering Approach to the Collapse of the Mycenaean Palace Civilisation of the Greek Mainland', in S. Stiros and R.E. Jones (eds), *Archaeoseismology*. Athens: IGME and the British School at Athens.

Parke, H.W. and Wormell, D.E.W. (eds) (1956) *The Delphic Oracle*. 2 vols. Oxford: Blackwell.

Parker, H.N. (1992) 'Love's Body Anatomized: The ancient erotic handbooks and the rhetoric of sexuality', in A. Richlin (ed.), *Pornography and Representation in Greece and Rome*. New York and Oxford: Oxford University Press.

Payer, P.J. (1984) *Sex and the Penitentials: The development of a sexual code 550–1150*. Toronto and London: University of Toronto Press.

Peiser, B.J., Palmer, T. and Bailey, M.E. (eds) (1998) *Natural Catastrophes During Bronze Age Civilisations: Archaeological, geological, astronomical and cultural perspectives*. BAR International Series 728. Oxford: Archaeopress.

Pelly, K. (2002) 'Trojan Themes and the Classical Ethos in British Poetry of the First World War'. MPhil thesis (unpublished). Faculty of Classics, University of Cambridge.

Perdrizet, P. (1936) 'Objects d'Or de la Période Impériale au Musée Égyptien du Caire: Hélène, soeur d'Aphrodite', in *Annales du Service des Antiquités de l'Égypte* 36: 5–10.

Persson, A.W. (1931) *The Royal Tombs at Dendra near Midea*. Lund: C.W.K. Gleerup.

Petrie, W.M.F. (1889) *Hawara, Biahmu and Arsinoe*. Ed. A.H. Sayce. London.

Pickard-Cambridge, A.W. (1968) *The Dramatic Festivals of Athens*. Second edition. Revised by J. Gould and D.M. Lewis. Oxford: Clarendon Press.

Pipili, M. (1992) 'A Lakonian Ivory Reconsidered', in J.M. Sanders (ed.), *Philolakon: Lakonian studies in honour of Hector Catling*. Oxford: British School at Athens.

Pomeroy, S.B. (2002) *Spartan Women*. New York and Oxford: Oxford University Press

Posluszny, P. (ed.) (1989) *Thomas Nashe, Summer's Last Will and Testament: a critical modern-spelling edition*. New York: Peter Lang.

Postle, M. and Vaughan, W. (1999) *The Artist's Model from Etty to Spencer*. London: Merrell Holberton.

Prag, J. and Neave, R. (1997) *Making Faces: Using forensic and archaeological evidence*. London: British Museum Press.

Price, T.H. (1978) *Kourotrophos: Cults and representations of the Greek nursing deities*. Leiden: Brill.

Prins, Y. (1999) *Victorian Sappho*. Princeton, NJ; Princeton University Press.

Quispel, G. (1975) 'Faust, Symbol of Western Man', in *Gnostic Studies* II (Istanbul): 288–307.

Raaflaub, K.A. (1998) 'Homer, the Trojan War and History', in *Classical World* 91.5: 405–13.

Rapp, G. and Gifford, J.A. (1982) *Troy: The archaeological geology*. Supplementary Monograph 4. University of Cincinnati for Princeton University Press.

Reckford, K.J. (1981) 'Helen in Aeneid 2 and 6', in *Arethusa* 14: 85–99.

Rehak, P. (1999) 'The Mycenaean Warrior Goddess Revisited', in R. Laffineur (ed.), *POLEMOS: Le contexte guerrier en Égée à l'Âge du Bronze*. Liège: Université de Liège; Austin: University of Texas.

Rehak, P. (2002) 'Imag(in)ing a Woman's World in Bronze Age Greece: The frescoes from Xeste 3 at Akrotiri, Thera', in N. Rabinowitz and L. Auanger (eds), *Among Women: From the homosocial to the homoerotic in the ancient world*. Austin: University of Texas Press.

Rehak, P. (2005) 'Children's Work: Girls as acolytes in Aegean ritual and cult' (ed. J.G. Younger), in J. Rutter and A. Cohen (eds), *Coming of Age: Constructions of childhood in the ancient world*. Princeton, NJ: American School of Classical Studies, Athens.

Rehm, R. (1992) *Greek Tragic Theatre*. London: Routledge.

Reilly, C. (ed.) (1981) *Scars Upon My Heart: Women's poetry and verse of the First World War*. London: Virago.

Renfrew, C. (1985) *The Archaeology of Cult: The sanctuary at Phylakopi*. London: British School of Archaeology at Athens. Thames & Hudson.

Reynolds, L.D. and Wilson, N.G. (1974, 3rd edn. 1991) *Scribes and Scholars: A guide to the transmission of Greek and Latin literature*. Second edition. Oxford: Clarendon Press.

Rice, G.P., Jr (1951) *The Public Speaking of Queen Elizabeth: Selections from her official addresses*. New York: Columbia University Press.

Richer, J. (1994) *Sacred Geography of the Ancient Greeks: Astrological symbolism in art, architecture and landscape*. Trans. C. Rhone. Albany: State University of New York Press.

Riddle, J.M. (1992) *Contraception and Abortion from the Ancient World to the Renaissance*. Cambridge, MA: London: Harvard University Press.

Riggs, D. (2004) *The World of Christopher Marlowe*. London: Faber.

Robertson, W.H. (1990) *An Illustrated History of Contraception*. Carnforth, Lancs: Parthenon.

Rollins, H.E. (ed.) (1926) *A Gorgeous Gallery of Gallant Inventions* (1578). Cambridge, MA: Harvard University Press.

Roscher, W.H. (1884) *Ausführliches Lexikon der griechischen und römischen Mythologie*. 6 vols. Leipzig: Teubner.

Rose, C.B. (1998) 'Troy and the Historical Imagination', in *Classical World* 91.5: 386–403.

Rose, H.J. (1929) 'The Cult of Artemis Orthia', in R.M. Dawkins (ed.), *The Sanctuary of Artemis Orthia at Sparta: excavated and described by members of the British School at Athens, 1906–1910*. London: Society for the Promotion of Hellenic Studies.

Rosivach, V. J. (1994) *The System of Public Sacrifice in Fourth-Century Athens*. Atlanta, GA: Scholars Press.

Rühfel, H. (1984) *Das Kind in der Griechischen Kunst: von der minoisch-mykenischen Zeit bis zum Hellenismus*. Kulturgeschichte der Antiken Welt 18. Mainz am Rhein: Verlag von Philipp von Zabern.

Rutkowski, B. (1986) *The Cult Places of the Aegean*. New Haven, CT: Yale University Press.

Rutter, J. (2003) 'Children in Aegean Prehistory', in J. Neils and J.H. Oakley (eds), *Coming of Age in Ancient Greece: Images of childhood from the classical past*. New Haven, CT and London: Yale University Press.

Said, E.W. (1978) *Orientalism*. London: Routledge & Kegan Paul.

Sakellarakis, J.A. (1990) 'The Fashioning of Ostrich-Egg Rhyta in the Creto-Mycenaean Aegean', in D.A. Hardy (ed.), *Thera and the Aegean World* III. Proceedings of the Third International Congress, Santorini, Greece, 3–9 September 1989. Vol. 1: *Archaeology*. London: Thera Foundation.

Sakellarakis, Y. and Sapouna-Sakellaraki, E. (1997) *Archanes: Minoan Crete in a new light*. 2 vols. Athens: Ammos Publications/Eleni Nakou Foundation.

Sampson, A. (1996) 'Cases of Earthquakes at Mycenaean and Pre-Mycenaean Thebes', in S. Stiros and R.E. Jones (eds), *Archaeoseismology*. Athens: IGME and the British School at Athens.

Saunders, C. (2001) *Rape and Ravishment in the Literature of Medieval England*. Cambridge: D.S. Brewer.

Schama, S. (1995) *Landscape and Memory*. London: HarperCollins.

Scherer, M. (1963) *The Legends of Troy in Art and Literature*. New York and London: Phaidon Press for the Metropolitan Museum of Art.

Schliemann, H. (1880) *Ilios: The city and country of the Trojans*. London: John Murray.

Schmitz, G. (1990) *The Fall of Women in Early English Narrative Verse*. Cambridge: Cambridge University Press.

Scranton, R., Shaw, J.W. and Ibrahim, L. (1978) *Kenchreai: Eastern port of*

Corinth. Vol. 1: *Topography and Architecture*. Leiden: Brill.

Sewter, E.R.A. (1953) *Fourteen Byzantine Rulers: The* Chronographia *of Michael Psellus*. Translated with introduction. London: Routledge & Kegan Paul.

Shapiro, H.A. (1999) 'Cult Warfare: The Dioskouroi between Sparta and Athens', in R. Hägg (ed.), *Ancient Greek Hero Cult*. Proceedings of the Fifth International Seminar on Ancient Greek Hero Cult, organised by the Department of Classical Archaeology and Ancient History, Göteborg University, 21–3 April 1995. Stockholm: Swedish Institute in Athens.

Shawcross, T. (2003) 'Reinventing the Homeland in the Historiography of Frankish Greece: The Fourth Crusade and the legend of the Trojan War', in *Byzantine and Modern Greek Studies* 27: 120–52.

Shelmerdine, C.W. (1985) *The Perfume Industry of Mycenaean Pylos*. Göteborg: Paul Åströms Forlag.

Shelmerdine, C.W. (1998) 'The perfumed oil industry' in J.L. Davis (ed.), *Sandy Pylos: An Archaelogical History from Nestor to Navarino*. Austin: University of Texas.

Shelmerdine, C.W. and Palaima, T.G. (eds) (1984) *Pylos Comes Alive: Industry & administration in a Mycenaean palace*. Papers of a symposium sponsored by the Archaeological Institute of America regional symposium fund. New York: Fordham University.

Sheridan, J.J. (ed.) (1980) *The Plaint of Nature: Alan of Lille*. Translation with commentary. Toronto: Pontifical Institute of Medieval Studies.

Sherratt, S. (2004) 'Feasting in Homeric Epic', in J.C. Wright (ed.), *The Mycenaean Feast. Hesperia* 73.2: 301–37.

Simon, R. (1961) *Nicolas Fréret, académicien, 1678–1749*. Geneva: Institut et Musée Voltaire.

Skutsch, O. (1987) 'Helen, Her Name and Nature', in *Journal of Hellenic Studies* 107: 188–93.

Snodgrass, A.M. (1967) *Arms and Armour of the Greeks*. London: Thames & Hudson; Ithaca, NY: Cornell University Press.

Sorley, C.H. (1922) *Marlborough: And other poems*. Cambridge: Cambridge University Press.

Sourvinou-Inwood, C. (1995) *'Reading' Greek Death: To the end of the classical period*. Oxford: Clarendon Press.

Spawforth, A.J.S. (1992) 'Spartan Cults under the Roman Empire' in J.M. Sanders (ed.), *Philolakon: Lakonian Studies in Honour of Hector Catling*. Oxford: British School at Athens.

Spencer, T. (1952) 'Turks and Trojans in the Renaissance', in *Modern Language Review* 47: 330–3.

Spivey, N.J. (1996) *Understanding Greek Sculpture: Ancient meanings, modern readings*. London: Thames & Hudson.

Spivey, N.J. (2004) *Ancient Olympics*. Oxford: Oxford University Press.

Spyropoulos, T.G. (1998) 'Pellana: The administrative centre of pre-historic Lakonia', in W.G. Cavanagh and S.E.C. Walker (eds), *Sparta in Lakonia*. Proceedings of the 19th British Museum Classical Colloquium held with the British School at Athens and King's and University Colleges, London, 6–8 December 1995. London: British School at Athens.

Stiros, S. and Jones, R.E. (1996) *Archaeoseismology*. Athens: IGME and the British School at Athens.

Suzuki, M. (1989) *Metamorphoses of Helen: Authority, difference and the epic*. Ithaca, NY and London: Cornell University Press.

Taplin, O. (1992) *Comic Angels: And other approaches to Greek drama through vase-paintings*. Oxford: Clarendon Press; New York: Oxford University Press.

Taylor, D. (1999) *The Greek and Roman Stage*. Bristol: Bristol Classical Press.

Taylour, Lord W. (1983) *The Mycenaeans*. Revised edition. London: Thames & Hudson.

Thomas, H. (1938–9) 'The Acropolis Treasure from Mycenae', in *Annual of the British School at Athens* 39: 65–87.

Thompson, D.P. (2003) *The Trojan War: Literature and legends from the Bronze Age to the present*. Jefferson, NC: McFarland.

Thompson, M.S. (1908–9) 'Terracotta Figurines: Lakonia I. – Excavations at Sparta 1909', in *Annual of the British School at Athens* 15: 116–26.

Thornton, B. (1997) *Eros: The Myth of Greek Sexuality*. Boulder, CO: Westview Press.

Tomlinson, R.A. (1992) 'The Menelaion and Spartan Architecture', in J.M. Sanders (ed.), *Philolakon: Lakonian studies in Honour of Hector Catling*. Oxford: British School at Athens.

Traill, D. (1995) *Schliemann of Troy: Treasure and deceit*. London: John Murray

Traill, D.A. (1984) 'Schliemann's "Discovery" of "Priam's Treasure": A re-examination of the evidence', in *Journal of Hellenic Studies* 104: 96–115.

Tringham, R. and Conkey, M. (1998) 'Rethinking Figurines: A critical view from the archaeology of Gimbutas', in L. Goodison and C. Morris (eds), *Ancient Goddesses: The myths and the evidence*. London: British Museum Press.

Tzedakis, Y. and Martlew, H. (eds) (1999) *Minoans and Mycenaeans: Flavours of their time*. National Archaeological Museum 12 July–27 November 1999. Athens: Kapon.

Vallianou, D. (1996) 'New Evidence of Earthquake Destructions in Late Minoan Crete', in S. Stiros and R.E. Jones (eds), *Archaeoseismology*.

Athens: IGME and the British School at Athens.

Vandiver, E. (1999) 'Millions of the Mouthless Dead': Charles Hamilton Sorley and Wilfred Owen in Homer's 'Hades', in *International Journal of the Classical Tradition* 5.3 (Winter): 432–55.

Ventris, M. and Chadwick, J. (1973) *Documents in Mycenaean Greek*. Second edition. Cambridge: Cambridge University Press.

Vernant, J.-P. (1991) *Mortals and Immortals: Collected Essays*. Ed. F.I. Zeitlin. Princeton, NJ: Princeton University Press.

Verschur, G.L. (1998) 'Our Place in Space', in B.J. Peiser, T. Palmer and M.E. Bailey (eds), *Natural Catastrophes During Bronze Age Civilisations: Archaeological, geological, astronomical and cultural perspectives*. BAR International Series 728. Oxford: Archaeopress.

Vincent, L.H. (1936) 'Le Culte d'Hélène à Samarie', in *Revue Biblique* 45: 221–32.

Visser, E. (1938) *Götter und Kulte im ptolemäischen Alexandrien*. Amsterdam: NV Noord-Hollandsche Uitgevers-Mij.

Voutsaki, S. (1992) 'Society and Culture in the Mycenaean World: An analysis of mortuary practices in the Argolid, Thessaly and the Dodecanese'. PhD dissertation (unpublished). University of Cambridge.

Voutsaki, S. (1998) 'Mortuary Evidence, Symbolic Meanings and Social Change: A comparison between Messenia and the Argolid in the Mycenaean period', in K. Branigan (ed.), *Cemetery and Society in the Aegean Bronze Age*. Sheffield: Sheffield Academic Press.

Voutsaki, S. and Killen, J. (eds) (2001) *Economy and Politics in the Mycenaean Palace States*. Proceedings of a conference held on 1–3 July 1999 in the Faculty of Classics, Cambridge. Cambridge Philological Society, Supplementary Volume 27.

Wace, A.J.B. (1921–3) 'Excavations at Mycenae: IX – the tholos tombs', in *Annual of the British School at Athens* 25: 283–402.

Wace, A.J.B. (1964) *Mycenae: An archaeological history and guide*. Reprinted edition. London: Hafner.

Wace, A.J.B. and Stubbings, F.H. (eds) (1962) *A Companion to Homer*. London: Macmillan.

Wace, H. (1939) 'The Ivory Trio: The ladies and boy from Mycenae'. Pamphlet.

Walton, J.M. (1987) *Living Greek Theatre: A handbook of classical peformance and modern production*. New York: Greenwood Press.

Wardle, D. (1988) 'Does Reconstruction Help? A Mycenaean dress and the Dendra suit of armour', in E.B. French and K.A. Wardle (eds), *Problems in Greek Prehistory*. Papers presented at the Centenary Conference of the

British School of Archaeology at Athens, Manchester, April 1986. Bristol: Bristol Classical Press.

Wardle, K.A. and Wardle, D. (1997) *Cities of Legend: The Mycenaean world.* London: Bristol Classical Press.

Wardle, K.A. (2001) 'The Palace Civilisations of Minoan Crete and Mycenaean Greece 2000–1200 BC', in *The Oxford Illustrated History of Prehistoric Europe.* Oxford: Oxford University Press.

Warren, P. (1988) *Minoan Religion as Ritual Action.* Göteborg: Gothenburg University.

Warren, P. and Hankey, V. (1989) *Aegean Bronze Age Chronology.* Bristol: Bristol Classical Press.

Waswo, R. (1995) 'Our Ancestors, the Trojans: Inventing cultural identity in the Middle Ages', in *Exemplaria* 7.22: 269–90.

Weir, A. (2000) *Eleanor of Aquitaine: By the wrath of God, Queen of England.* London: Pimlico.

West, M.L. (1975) *Immortal Helen.* Inaugural lecture at Bedford College, University of London.

Wide, S. (1893) *Lakonische Kulte.* Leipzig: B.G. Teubner.

Wiener, M. (2003) 'Time Out: The current impasse in Bronze Age archaeological dating', in K.P. Foster and R. Laffineur (eds), *METRON: Measuring the Aegean Bronze Age.* Proceedings of the 9th International Aegean Conference, Yale University, 18–21 April 2002. Liège: Université de Liège; Austin: University of Texas.

Williams, C.B. (1993) *Pope, Homer and Manliness: Some aspects of eighteenth-century classical learning.* London: Routledge.

Williams, C.K., II (1986) 'Corinth and the Cult of Aphrodite', in M.A. Del Chiaro and W.R. Biers (eds), *Corinthiaca: Studies in honour of Darrel A. Amyx.* Columbia: University of Missouri Press.

Williamson, M. (1995) *Sappho's Immortal Daughters.* Cambridge, MA: Harvard University Press.

Winkler, J.J. and Zeitlin, F. (eds) (1990) *Nothing to Do with Dionysos? Athenian drama in its social context.* Princeton, NJ: Princeton University Press.

Wood, M. (1985) *In Search of the Trojan War.* London: BBC Books.

Woodford, S. (1993) *The Trojan War in Ancient Art.* London: Duckworth.

Worman, N. (1997) 'The Body as Argument: Helen in four Greek texts', in *Classical Antiquity* 16.1: 151–203.

Wright, J.C. (ed.) (2004) *The Mycenaean Feast. Hesperia* 73.2. Princeton, NJ: American School of Classical Studies at Athens.

Wright, W.A. (ed.) (1904) *English Works of Roger Ascham.* Cambridge: Cambridge University Press.

Yates, F. (1975) *Astraea: The imperial theme in the sixteenth century.* London and Boston: Routledge & Kegan Paul.

Yener, K.A. and Hoffner, H.A. (eds) (2002) *Recent Developments in Hittite Archaeology and History: Papers in memory of Hans G. Güterbock.* Ed. with the assistance of S. Dhesi. Winona Lake, IN: Eisenbrauns.

Young, P.H. (2003) *The Printed Homer: a 3,000 Year Publishing and Translation History of the* Iliad *and the* Odyssey. Jefferson, NC and London: McFarland.

Younger, J.G. (1998) *Music in the Aegean Bronze Age.* Studies in Mediterranean Archaeology and Literature, Pocket-book 144. Jonsered: Paul Åströms Förlag.

Zeitlin, F. (1981) 'Travesties of Gender and Genre in Aristophanes' *Thesmophoriazousae*', in H.P. Foley (ed.), *Reflections of Women in Antiquity.* New York: Gordon & Breach.

Zeitlin, F. (1996) *Playing the Other: Gender and society in classical Greek civilisation.* Chicago, IL: Chicago University Press.

Zweig, B. (1993a) 'The Only Women Who Give Birth to Men: A Gynocentric, Cross-Cultural View of Women in Ancient Sparta.' In Mary DeForest, ed, *Woman's Power, Man's Game: Essays on Classical Antiquity in Honor of Joy King,* pp 32–53. Wanconda, IL: Bolchazy-Carducci.

Zweig, B. (1993b) 'The Primal Mind: Using Native-American models to study women in ancient Greece', in N.S. Rabinowitz and A. Richlin (eds), *Feminist Theory and the Classics.* New York and London: Routledge.

INDEX

Abbate, Niccolò dell': *Abduction of Helen* 155
Achaioí/Achaeans xxxvi, 44
Achilles 10, 73, 86, 199, 204, 208, 215, 232, 334–5
Acrocorinth 252–3
    Aphrodite's temple 253–4
Adhelm (Anglo-Saxon theologian) 369n27
Adrasteia 248
Adrastus 79
adyton 246
Aegesilaus, King of Sparta 371n7
Aegeus, King 244
Aeneas 6, 119, 122, 155, 277, 290–1, 293
Aeneid see Virgil
Aeschylus 5, 260
    Agamemnon 184, 191, 195(n16), 206, 224–5,
        227, 263, 339, 380n17
    Oresteia 35
    Persians 166–7
Aethra 51, 279
Agamemnon, King of Mycenae xxv, xxvii, 34,
    80
    at Helen's marriage contest 73, 81
    death 24, 195, 230
    kills Iphigeneia 194–6
    and Trojan War 7, 10, 78, 157, 193, 194, 204,
        211, 279
'Agamemnon's Mask' 35
'Age of Heroes' 5, 6, 33
Agia Triada, Crete: palace 241
Agia Triada Palaioboukounia, Elis: *krater* 238
Agios Nikolaos Museum, Crete: stone conch
    85–6
Agrigentum, Sicily: temple of Hera 3
Ahhiyawa, land of 169, 170
aiamenos (inlay) 42
Aigisthos 78, 195, 230
Ajax 39, 199, 204, 208, 222, 230
Akhenaten, pharaoh 127
Akkadian (language) 126
Akrotiri 63
    see Thera
Alaca Höyük, Turkey: golden spindle 232
Alakšandu Treaty 187, 207, 350n11
Alcaeus 130, 363n25
Alcibiades 374n15

Alcman 31, 53, 81, 152, 362n7, 363n25
    Partheneia 56–8, 351n17
Alexander the Great 86, 175, 263, 274, 371n7
Alexander, tyrant 263
Alexandria, Egypt 81, 261, 274
    Library 272, 274, 275
    Museum 274
Alexis: comedies about Helen 265
Amarna *see* Tel el Amarna
Ambrosian *Iliad* 267
Amenophis III, pharaoh 39, 93
Ammistamru II, King of Ugarit 129
Amurru 129
Amyklai 71–3, 242
Anatolia/Anatolians xxxvi, 8, 12, 80, 124–5
    rival potentates 187–9
Anchises 290
Anemospilia ('Cave of Winds'), Crete 231, 320
Angelico, Fra 7
animal sacrifices 31, 85, 247–8, 262
animism 334–5
Anticlus 220
Antikythera: statue of Paris 120
Antimachos 191
Aphidnia: hill-fortress 51
Aphrodite xxxii, xxxiii
    conception and birth 148–50, 250
    curse on Tyndareid women 354n28
    and Eros 151
    and Helen 10, 104, 132, 135, 146, 148, 151, 152,
        275, 308
    and 'Judgement of Paris' 121, 148–9
    and *kharis* 56
    lovers 204
    saves Paris 210–11
    shrines 157, 246–7
    temple on Acrocorinth 252–3
    temple at Kenchreai 252
    see also Bridal Aphrodite, sanctuary of
Aphrodite Kallipugos, temple of (Sicily) 118
Apollo xxv, 72, 118, 182, 207, 212, 236, 250,
    370n19
Apollodorus: *Epitome* 3 132
Ap(p)aliunas 207
Archaiai-Kleonai: archaeological site 242

Archanes, Crete: female skeletons 42, 115
Ares xxv, 204
Argeioí/Argives xxxvi, 44, 134, 165, 205
Argos 76, 245, 395*n*1
　　Greco-Roman theatre 368*n*12
　　shrine to Eileithyia 92
Argos Museum
　　terracotta figurine 98–9
　　tombstone 23
Ariston, King of Sparta 61
Aristophanes: Lysistrata 59, 224, 266
Aristotle 5, 117, 120
　　Politics 374*n*17
Armenoi cemetery, Crete
　　drinking and cooking vessels 239
　　skeletons 39, 97
Arnuvanda, King of the Hittites 326, 327
aromatics 108, 183
Artemis 194, 196
Artemis Orthia, sanctuary of 50–1, 54, 59
aryballos (perfume jar) 31
Asia Minor see Anatolia/Anatolians
Asine, Greece: skeletons 39, 396*n*25
Asmunikal, Queen of the Hittites 326, 327
asphodels 252
Assyrians 403*n*6
Astyanassa 182
Astyanax 221
Atalanta 362*n*1
Athena xxxii, 58, 104, 119, 205, 211
Athenaeus: Deipnosophists 375*n*20
Athenagoras: letter to Marcus Aurelius and
　　Commodus 248
Athens/Athenians 30, 52, 67, 222, 242, 259–60,
　　304, 305
　　Great Dionysia 261–2
　　museums 330, see also National
　　　Archaeological Museum
　　theatre 216, 260–2
　　Theatre of Dionysus 260, 262, 266
　　women 72
Athos, Mount 225
Atreus, House of xxxiii, 80, 81, 363*n*1
Attarssiya 184
Augustine, St 117
Augustus, Emperor 59
Aulis, Greece 194–6, 197
Avelli, Francesco Xanto: Abduction of Helen
　　platter 133

Babylon/Babylonians 126, 127, 192

Bankside, London 299, 300
'barbarians'/'barbarism' 125, 168, 169
Barton, John: Marlowe's Doctor Faustus 307
beauty 2, 25, 113–14, 117, 120
　　Helen's 2, 3, 25–6, 60–1, 117–18, 119, 173,
　　　241
beauty contests (kallisteia) 117
Benaki Museum, Athens 330
Benakis, Emanuel 330
Benteshina, King of Amurru 129
'Berlin Goddess' (6th century) 361*n*19
Berlin Museum: amphoriskos 308, 309
Berlioz, Hector 7
Besik Bay 173–5, 176, 198, 220
　　cemetery 175
Besik Tepe ('Mound of Achilles') 175–6
birth trays, Italian 157
boar's-tusk helmets 40, 74–5
boats/ships 12, 19, 64, 119, 156, 158, 159, 196,
　　200–1, 245
Boccaccio, Giovanni: Concerning Famous Women
　　240, 377*n*20
Bodleian Library, Oxford 137; Hawara Homer
　　272
Bodrum, Turkey 167
Boethius: Consolation of Philosophy 139(*n*13)
Boğazkale, Museum of 189
Boğazköy 242
　　rock-carvings 124
Boiotia, Greece 21, 196, 197, 238
Bosphorus, the 166, 225
Boston Museum of Fine Arts: Helen vase
　　180–2
Bridal Aphrodite, sanctuary of 244–5, 253
Briseida 292
Briseis 204, 292
Britain, 'founding of' 290
British Museum, London
　　Aeneid 275
　　Amarna tablets 158–9
　　breast-shaped cup 111
　　plank with lines from Homer 271
　　pyxis 66
　　vase 222
Britten, Benjamin 35
Brooke, Rupert 7, 172
　　'Menelaus and Helen' 225–6
Brut the Trojan 291
Brutus 290, 291
Burna-Buriyash, King of Babylon 127
Burton, Richard 306

Caesar, Julius 384*n*15
Cairo Museum: gold dish 247
Callimachus: *Pannychis* 398*n*14
Calvert, Frank 178
Camus, Albert 7
  'Helen's Exile' 62
Canons of Theodore 145
Capitoline Museums, Rome 23–4
Carchemish: rock-carvings 124
Carmina Burana 295
Cassandra xxxiii, 66, 184, 203, 221, 230
Castor and Pollux/the Dioscuri xxxi, 24, 26,
  51, 53–54, 80, 282, 336
  as stars 156, 254–5
Catullus 165
Caxton, William: *The Recuyell of the Historyes of*
  Troye 7
Chadwick, John 319
Chania, Crete
  Linear B tablets 319
  tombs 62, 96
Chaos xxvi, 150, 205
chariots/charioteers 183–5
Charlemagne 293
Chaucer, Geoffrey 7, 146
children 96, 97–99, 221–3
  burials 62, 97
Choniates, Nicetas 269–70
Christian writers/Christianity 144–6, 253, 255,
  268, 281–2, 304
  see also Gnostics; Magus, Simon; Orthodox
    Church, Greek
Christie, Agatha 35
Chryseis 204
Chryses 204
Cicero 6
  On Invention 347*n*9
Cinyras 335
Cithairon 225
Clarke, Edward 177
Cleisthenes, tyrant of Sicyon 78
Clement of Alexandria: *The Instructor* 144, 378*n*4
Clementine Homilies 287
Cleopatra 348*n*23
Clinton, Bill 310–11
Clymene 279
Clytemnestra xxxi, xxxiii, 24, 34, 66, 79, 194,
  195, 230, 235, 236, 264
coinage 75, 109, 156
Colluthus of Lycopolis: *The Rape of Helen* 139,
  149, 153

Colonne, Guido delle 182
Constantine, Emperor 177
Constantinople 177, 268, 384*n*12
  Hippodrome 268, 270
  see also Istanbul
contests
  beauty 117–9
  boxing and wrestling 73, 78
  marriage 71, 73–5, 76, 77, 78–9, 362*n*1
  musical 245
  Olympic Games 252, 261
  Pythian Games 165
  water-sports 245
contraceptives 93
Corinth 67, 252, 259
  Museum 253
Corpus Christi College, Cambridge: Parker
  Library manuscript collection 143
Cos, island of 334
cosmetics 25, 53, 108, 109, 159, 253, 308
Courcy, Jehan de: *Chronique Universelle, dite la*
  Bouquechardiere 181(*n*25)
Creech, Thomas: *The Odes . . . of Horace* 121
Crete 156, 161, 317
  axes 84
  'Cretan Hieroglyphic' 318
  goddess with seedhead diadem 233
  Gortyn law code 364*n*13
  Linear A 318
  Linear B tablets *see* Knossos
  Minoan 19, 315, 320, 321, 322; *see* Knossos
  under Mycenaeans 20, 39, 80–1, 315, 316, 322,
    323
  myths 316–17
  sarcophagus 85
  votive offerings 324–5
  see Agia Triada; Agios Nikolaos;
    Anemospilia; Archanes; Armenoi;
    Chania; Eileithyia Cave; Isopata;
    Knossos; Komnos; Palaikastro; Phoumi;
    Vaï
Crowfoot, Professor J.W. 282
Crusades/Crusaders 268
Cyclades, the 159
  figurines 257, 329
  see also Kythnos; Thera
Cyclopean masonry 5, 38, 170, 356*n*16
Cypria 6, 122, 132, 148–9, 159, 270, 347*n*4, 350*n*1,
  389*n*4, 408*n*6
Cyprus 22, 150, 156, 159
Cythera *see* Kythera

Daedalus 317
Danaoí/Danaans xxxvi, 44
Dante Alighieri 7
    Inferno 146
Dardanelles, the 172, 173, 242
Dares 121(*n*7), 278, 279–80, 298
Darius I, of Persia 166
'Dark Ages', Greek (1100–800 BC) 37, 193, 241, 242, 243, 278
Dark Ages, medieval 275–6, 290
David, Jacques-Louis: *Les Amours de Paris et d'Hélène* 86–7
death, glory of 214–7
death-masks, Bronze Age 3
Debussy, Claude 35
Dee, Dr John 289
Deiphobus xxxi, 223, 275
Dekeleia 51
Dekker, Thomas 304
Delphi 165–6
Delphic Oracle 58, 165, 166, 167, 231, 334
Demeter, sanctuary of 245
Dendra: tomb finds 74–5, 238–9
Dictys 278–9
Dio Chrysostom 128
    Trojan Discourse 277
Diogenes Laertius 120
Diomedes 80, 211
Dionysus, Theatre of (Athens) 260, 262, 266
Dionysus of the Black Goat 245
Dioscuri, the *see* Castor and Pollux
diseases 19, 41, 97
Dorians 50, 51–2, 167, 247
dress-styles
    Minoan 109, 317–18
    Mycenaean 98, 109–10, 111
dromos 238
Dryden, John 7, 377*n*5
Duffy, Carol Ann: 'Beautiful' 131
Dumas, Alexandre: *Les Mohicans de Paris* 1
Dunsany, Edward Plunkett, 18th Lord: 'An Interview' 289
Durrell, Lawrence: 'Troy' 41
dyes 41, 64, 109, 339–40

earthquakes 20–1, 240–1, 316
eggs: as symbols 26–7
Egypt/Egyptians 11, 39, 78, 81, 102, 126, 189, 233, 242, 326
    and beauty 376*m*14
    contraceptives 93

'Eternal Treaty' with Hittites 192
Helen in 128, 156, 160–1, 230–1, 232, 277
Helen's cult 247, 250
trade 158, 159
    see also Hawara; Oxyrhynchus
eidolon 11, 160, 219
Eileithyia xxxii, 91–2
    shrine 92
Eileithyia Cave, Crete 92
Elateia, Phokis: citadel 242
Eleanor of Aquitaine 291, 292, 293, 294, 295–7
    tomb 296
Electra 224, 232, 235
Eleon 197
Elephantine 182
Elis
    beauty contests 117, 118
    chariot races 363*m*
Elizabeth I 263, 289, 299
Ennius: *Trojan Women* 400*n*20
Ennoia 285, 287, 306
Epic Cycle 6, 205
    see also Cypria; Little Iliad
Epiphanius: *Panarion* 404*n*17, 404*n*21
Erasmus, Desiderius 400*n*20
Eris 119, 150, 204
Erita ('the Priestess') 80
Ermioni, Greece 158
Eros xxvi, 148, 151, 152, 180, 308, 309, 400*m*11
'Eternal Treaty' 192
Etruscans, the
    mirror 225
    urns 11
eunomia 52
Euripides 6, 117, 205, 230, 260, 276
    Andromache 11(*n*37), 55, 95, 224
    Andromeda 263
    Cyclops 265
    Electra 264
    Hecuba 265, 400*n*20
    Helen 8, 22, 95, 121, 168, 204, 220, 262, 265, 266, 276, 342
    Iphigeneia at Aulis 78, 81, 148, 149, 150, 195–6
    Orestes 116, 235, 236–7, 250
    Trojan Women 71, 106, 109–10, 116, 168, 222, 230, 260–1, 262, 263, 372–3*m*16, 375*n*31, 400*n*20
Europa, rape of 316
Eurotas, River 22, 30, 49, 50, 54, 55, 118, 156
Evans, Arthur 19, 318, 321, 322, 324, 326,
Excidium Troie 139

Erskine, John: *The Private Life of Helen of Troy* 408*n*12

Faust, Dr Johann 302–3; *see also* Marlowe, Christopher
festivals 72, 165, 261–2, 334
fibulae 31
figurines/figures
    female 72, 329–31
        bronze/metal (Spartan) 47, 53, 59
        Cycladic 257, 329
        'goddess' 103, 109, 329–30
        terracotta 30, 31, 53, 98–9, 101, 238
        see also 'Snake Goddesses'
    male 75, 99, 101
Firaktin relief, Capadocia 188
Fitzwilliam Museum, Cambridge: Helen mirror 115–16
Flamenca (Provençal poem) 297
flax-products 43, 109
food and drink 30, 31, 41, 58, 72, 82–4, 239, 353*n*10, 362*n*7
Franks, the 291
French, Dr Elizabeth 225
frescoes 101
    Minoan 85–6, 105, 316, 321, 324, 326
    Mycenaean 25, 30, 37, 42–3, 62, 98, 102, 107, 108, 109, 110, 354*n*28
    from Pylos 73, 87, 105, 109
    from Thera 63, 64–6, 71, 109, 111, 198
Fry, Roger 35

Gaia xxvi, 150, 333
Gallipoli 173, 216
Ganymede 121
Gassulawiya, Queen of the Hittites 213–14
Geoffrey of Monmouth: *Historia Regum Britanniae* 290
German Oriental Society 125
gift-exchanges 123, 126–7, 128, 129, 156
Gilgamesh Epic, The 384*n*10
Ginsberg, Allen 35
Gladstone, William 7, 229, 273
Gnostics 284–5, 287, 309, 404*n*23
'goddess' figures/figurines 103, 109, 329–31
'god-stones' 207–8
Goebbels, Joseph 35
Goering, Hermann 35
Goethe, Johann von 7, 10
    Faust 310(*n*10)
    Iphigenie auf Tauris 195

Goldhill, Simon: *Reading Greek Tragedy* 263–4
goldwork 36–7, 42, 62, 72, 104, 109
Gorgias: *Encomium* 117, 152(*n*19)
Great Dionysia 261–2
Greece/Greeks xxxv–xxxvi, 12, 20
    and 'barbarians' 125, 168, 169, 170
    Persian Wars 166–7
    see also Athens, Delphi *and other cities*; Mycenaeans; Sparta
Greek Civil War 254
Grenfell, Bernard Pyne 138
Guillaume de Poitiers 7
Gythion 154, 155, 172, 318

hair-styles
    female 64–5, 83, 107
    male 107, 122
Halicarnassus 167
Hall, Arthur: (trs.) *Iliad* 273
Hatti, Great Kings of 124, 125
Hattusa 124–5, 189, 242
    Hittite tablets and texts 125–6, 174, 190
Hattusili III, King of the Hittites 169, 189
Hawara, Fayum, Egypt: *Iliad* 272, 273
H.D.
    Helen 312
    Helen in Egypt 177, 244
Hector xxxi, 10, 120, 122, 171, 177–9, 183, 204, 220, 370*n*19
    death 215, 219, 220
    tomb 177
Hecuba xxxiii, 109, 151, 168, 261
Helen xxxi, 3–4
    and Aphrodite 146, 148–9, 151, 152, 157, 210–11, 247, 275, 308
    and Athenian theatre 259–60
    beauty 3, 25–6, 60–1, 115–16, 117–18, 172, 206, 240
    birth 24–5, 26
    breasts 109–11, 224
    Christian attitudes to 281–88
    conception 22–4
    cults/cult sites and shrines 9, 11, 27–8, 31, 32, 53, 55–6, 58, 59, 60, 156, 158, 246–48, 250–2, 254
    Dares' 279–80
    death 235–7, 240
    and Deiphobus 223–4
    and Delphic Oracle 166, 167
    dress 109–10, 111, 317–18
    in Egypt 128, 156, 160–1, 230–1, 232, 277

Helen (*cont.*)
Eleanor of Aquitaine and 291, 292, 293, 294–7
funeral speech for Hector 219
as goddess 11, 24, 333, 334, 335–8; *see also* cults
and Hermione 91, 94–5, 153, 232
Homer's 4–5, 6, 10–11, 55, 81, 91, 98, 102, 106, 111, 135, 145, 149, 203–5, 206, 220–1, 232–4, 270, 277, 340–1, 342, 343
and human sacrifice 231–2
and 'Judgement of Paris' 118–19, 148
in Marlowe's *Doctor Faustus* 298, 299, 300, 301–7
marriage contest for 71, 73–5, 76, 77, 78
and Menelaus 80–3, 85–6, 91, 106, 224–5, 229–31
on mirrors 115–16
names given to 286
and Nemesis 309–10
paintings/pictures of 2–3, 9, 10, 24–5, 132–3, 134, 155, 157–58, 218–19, 386n27, *see also* vase
palace of 29–30, 31–2
and Paris's rape/seduction and flight to Troy 7, 122–3, 127–30, 132–5, 136, 138–40, 144–7, 151, 153–58, 171, 190, 265–6, 279, 292–3
raped by Theseus 49, 50, 51, 62, 71, 92
rehabilitation of 292–3, 294–7
as St Elmo's Fire 255
'shining' appearance of 41, 106–7, 110
statues 133, 268, 269–70
on stelae 1–2, 53
and the Trojan Horse 11, 221
and the Trojan War 204–5, 206, 215, 218–20
in Troy 10, 128–9, 183, 190, 191, 194, 203, 206
vase portrayals 4, 6, 116, 180–1, 182, 264, 308, 309–10
as whore 11, 105, 143–6, 292
Helen Dendritis 335, 336, 408n9
Helen of Troy Ltd 2
Helene (in Magus sect) 283–6
Helene, island of *see* Makronissos
Heleneia (festival) 72, 334
helenin (C_6H_8O) 253
Helenium see Inula helenium
Helen's Baths *see* Loutra Eleni
'Helen's Temple', Therapne hill 30–1
Hellanikos 356n4
Henry II, of England 291, 292, 293, 294

Henry IV, of England 291
Henry VIII, of England 291
Henslowe, Philip 298, 302
Hepat of Arinna 188
Hephaestion 175
Hera xxv, 118, 119, 134, 205, 351n17
shrine on Kythnos 246–7
temple at Agrigentum 3
Heracles 5, 53, 198
temple at Kleonai 242
Heraklion Museum, Crete
bronze boat (remains) 157–58
elephant's tusk 317
Procession Fresco 324
'Snake Goddesses' 322
vase 101
Herculaneum: *Leda and the Swan* (wall-painting) 23
Hermes xxxii, 119, 204, 305
Hermione 79, 91, 94–5, 153, 232, 236
Hermione town, Peloponnese 244, 245
Herodotus 167–8
Histories 60–1, 78–9, 117, 128, 133, 159, 160–1, 167, 168, 230–1, 247, 277, 374n15, 374n17, 389n4
Hesiod 2, 37, 250–51
Catalogues of Women and Eoiae 2(n6), 71, 73, 76, 118(n9), 127
Theogony 102, 149–50, 152, 336
Works and Days 2(n5), 37(n17)
Heywood, Thomas 304
Hilareia 24, 26
Himmler, Heinrich 35
Hippokleides 77–8
Hippocratic Corpus 94
Hippodamia 78, 362n1
Hippolytus of Rome 283
Refutation of All Heresies 284, 286
Hisarlik Hill 34, 176, 177–8, 180, 185, 206
Historia Regium Britanniae 291
Historie of the Damnable Life, and Deserved Death of Doctor John Faustus, The 302
Hittites, the 8, 12, 78 123, 128, 129, 170–1, 187, 242
fashions 122
horses and chariots 183, 184, 185
laws 126, 190
marriage 190
priestesses 102, 326
'secondary wives' and concubines 187
tablets and texts 8–9, 126, 183, 186–7, 192–3, 197

Talagalawa letter 169
treaties 189, 192–3
and Troy 123–4
see also Gassulawiya, Queen; Hattusa;
  Mursili II; Puduhepa, Queen
Hobbes, Thomas: (trs.) *Iliad* 273
Homecomings 6
Homer 37, 79, 102, 112, 169, 177, 184, 197, 230,
  236, 267, 270, 278, 337, 341, 342, 343, 410*n*2
portrayal of Helen *see under* Helen
see also Iliad; *Odyssey*
Homeric Hymn to the Earth 328
Horace: *Odes* 121
Horse Book of Kikkuli (Hittite text) 183,
  363*n*20
horses/horsemanship 75–7, 183–5
human sacrifices 33, 194–6, 231–2
Hume, David 117
Hunt, Arthur 138
Hurrians 126, 127, 192
hymn to Ishtar 188
Huysmans, J.-K. 392*n*10
Hyakinthia (festival) 72
Hyakinthus 72

Icarus 316, 317
Ida, Mount 225, 323
Idaean Cave, Crete 157
Idomeneus, King of Crete 210, 278 318
Iliad (Homer) xxxv, 4–6, 44, 87, 174, 176
  'Ambrosian' (Milan Homer) 267–8
  Byzantine (*O Polemos tis Troados*) 121(*n*8)
  first printing 273
  fragments of 273
  survival of 271, 272–3
  translations of 273
  variant versions 274
  descriptions and quotations from:
    Ajax 39
    Andromache 183
    'Catalogue of Ships' 196–7, 198, 212, 245
    Glaucus and Diomedes 383*n*9
    Hector and Andromache 370*n*19
    Helen 4–5, 6, 80, 91, 98, 106, 111, 135,
      145, 146, 149, 153–4, 183, 203–5, 206,
      220–1, 234, 286, 340–1
    Hera 134
    Idomeneus 278, 318
    Menelaus 210–11
    Paris 86, 120, 121, 122, 135, 153, 154,
      159–60, 210–11, 220

Poseidon and the sea 17, 172
Trojan War 12, 21, 74, 184, 186, 194,
  197–8, 203–5, 207, 211, 213, 217
Zeus 100, 308
Iliou Melathron, Athens 179
Imbros 170
Innocent III, Pope 268
Inula helenium 253–4, 334
Iphigeneia xxxiii, 66, 194–6, 231, 264, 357*n*15
Irenaeus, Bishop of Lyons 283
iris, oil of 108
irrigation 38
Ishtar 188
Isidore of Seville 278
  Etymologies 7
Isocrates: *Encomium* on Helen 31, 49, 115,
  168–9
Isopata, Crete: gold ring 104
Istanbul
  Archaeological Museum tablet 326–7
  see also Constantinople
ivory/ivories 36, 41, 42, 53, 62, 97–98, 109, 156,
  158, 159

Jason and the Argonauts 119, 315
jewellery
  'Helen's Jewels' 163, 179
  Minoan 316
  Mycenaean 3, 36, 42, 43, 98, 104, 110, 333
Jocasta, Queen 78, 362*n*1
Jonson, Ben 301
Jordan: Amman Airport 39
Joseph of Exeter: *Trojan War* 25–6, 143–4, 259,
  294
'Judgement of Paris' 77, 118–19, 148–9
Juktas, Mount (Crete) 233, 322
Julia (daughter of Augustus) 254
Justin Martyr 283
  First Apology 404*n*12

Kadashman-Enlil II, King of Babylon 192
Kadesh, battle of 124, 183–4, 193
Kadesh, Treaty of ('Eternal Treaty') 192
Kadmeia, hill of: Mycenaean destruction layer
  21
Kallias, Peace of 167
kallisteia see beauty contests
kalyvia (shacks) 37–8
Kapatija ('the Keybearer') 80
Karabel: rock-carvings 124
Kastanas 233

Kazarma: *tholos* tomb 394*n*4
Kenchreai, ruins of 251, 252
Ker 150, 218
kharis 56, 61, 112, 229
Kitt, Eartha 306
Kleonai 242
kleos 112, 265
Knossos palace, Crete 20, 316, 321, 323
    frescoes 84–5, 105, 321, 324, 326
    Linear B tablets 91, 92, 96, 319
    'Snake Goddesses' 321–2
    storerooms 325–6
Kober, Alice E. 319
kohl, use of 108
Kokla, near Argos: *tholos* tomb finds 239
Komnos archaeological site, Crete 339–40
Korfmann, Professor Manfred 180, 206
Kranai, island of 154–5, 266
ktema 80
kudos 112
Kuvatalla (temple-priestess) 326–8
kylikes (drinking vessels) 83
Kythera (Cythera), island of 157, 159, 296, 318
Kythnos, island of: votive offerings 246–7

Lakedaimonia/Lacedaimon 29, 32, 248, 318
Lakonia, Greece 29, 248
    see Sparta
languages 20, 126, 169, 174
Law, Jude 307
Lawrence, D.H.: *Leda and the Swan* 23
Lawrence, T.E.: (trs.) *Iliad* 273
Leda xxv, 27, 250
    and the Swan 22–4, 25–6
Lefkandi, Euboia: citadel 242
Lelwani 213
Lemnos 170, 225
Leonardo da Vinci 7, 25
    Leda and the Swan 23
Lesbos: beauty contests 117
Leucippides, the (Hilareia and Phoebe) 24, 26
Lewinsky, Monica 310–11
Lille, Alan de: *The Plaint of Nature* 144–5
Linear A script 318
Linear B script/tablets 8, 38, 42, 43, 83, 98, 102, 109, 113, 318–20, 340
    from Knossos 91, 92, 96, 318
    from Pylos 36, 76, 80, 83, 107
    from Thebes 197, 198, 223, 319
    from Therapne 32
    from Tiryns 319

linen 109
Little Iliad 6, 223
London 290, 304–5
    Bankside 299, 300–1
    London Stone 289–90
    plague 305
    Rose Theatre 298, 300–1, 303, 305
Long, Edwin
    The Chosen Five 2–3
    The Search for Beauty 3
Louis VII, of France 292
Loutra Eleni (Helen's Baths) 251–2, 253, 336
Louvre Palace and Museum, Paris 57, 87, 132–4
Lucan: *Civil War* 348*n*23, 384–5*n*15
Lucian
    Dialogues of the Dead 305
    The Judgement of the Goddesses 25(*n*16), 308(*n*4)
    True Story 335
Lukka Lands 169, 170
Luther, Martin/Lutherans 302, 303
Lycia 170
Lycophron of Chalcis: *Alexandra* 11(*n*38), 247
Lycurgus ('the Law-Giver') 52
Lydgate, John: *The Troye Book* 277, 403*n*5
Lydia/Lydians 156, 167
Lygdamis 167
lyres 85, 87

McKellen, Ian 307
Magus, Simon 283–5, 286–8, 300, 302
Mai, Angelo 267–9
Makronissos, island of 254
Mallia (Crete), palace of 18, 109, 323
    stone conch from 85–7
Manchester Museum: *skyphos* 208
Marathon, battle of 51, 167
Marlowe, Christopher 7
    Tamburlaine 2(*n*3)
    The Tragical History of Dr Faustus 152(*n*18), 206, 298–9, 300, 301–2, 303–4, 305, 306–7
marriage contests 71, 73–5, 76, 77, 78–9, 362*n*1
Martial: *Epigram 14*, 271
'Master of the Judgement of Paris': birth tray 157
Matala, Crete 339
medicine 64, 93, 97, 212, 213, 233, 254
Megalostrata 59
Megapenthes 91, 335
Melos, battle of 222
Memphis, Egypt 160
    statue of Helen 247

Menelaion, the 30, 53, 61
Menelaus, King of Sparta xxv, 79, 80
  appearance 65
  children 80, 92
  contest for Helen and wedding 10, 73, 78,
    81, 83
  in Crete 127, 132, 147, 318
  fight with Paris 80, 210–1
  and Helen's death 235–6, 250
  and siege of Troy 191, 193, 194, 199
  sparing of Helen and return to Sparta 11,
    109–10, 156, 180–1, 229–31, 263, 279
  in Sparta with Helen 55, 233
Menippus 305
Methana, Peloponnese
  horseman figurines 75
  ritual 245
Michelangelo Buonarroti: *Leda* 23
Midea, near Argos 241
'Milan Homer' 267–69
'Milawata Letter' 188(n10)
Miletus 39, 80
Minoans 19, 20, 39, 93, 315, 316, 320, 321, 322–3
  burials 318
  dress-styles 109, 317–8
  frescoes 84–5, 105, 316, 321, 324, 326
  gold cups 318
  seal-stone 85
  writing 318–9
Minos, King 19
Minotaur 51, 317
Mirror for Magistrates, A 300
mirrors 53, 59, 115–6, 225, 238
Moreau, Gustave 218–9
  Helen at the Ramparts of Troy 218
  Helen at the Scaean Gate 219
mortality rates 31, 92–3, 97
Mother Earth/Goddess 329, 332–3
Mukana, Egypt 39
murex sea-snails 339–40, 341
Mursili II, King of the Hittites 223
music and musical instruments 59, 85–6, 87,
  100, 187, 261, 366–7n37
Muskebi 81
Mycenae 32, 33, 34–6, 44, 72, 242, 326
  cisterns 356n16
  cult centre 42, 93, 103–4
  figurines and idols 75, 99, 103, 241
  frescoes 42, 62, 102, 103, 108
  graves 39, 96–7, 212
  ivories 97, 98

  jewellery 69, 104
  Linear B tablets 319
  Lion Gate 35, 102–3
  Schliemann's excavations 34–5, 36, 39
  'Sphinx' head 103
  'Tomb of Clytemnestra' 237, 238
  'Treasury of Atreus' 237, 238
Mycenaeans, the xxxvi, 12, 19–20, 21, 79, 126,
  240–3
  chariots 183–4, 185
  citadels 225, *see also* Mycenae
  and Egyptians 95, 242
  expansionism 38, 78–9
  figurines and idols 30, 31, 72, 75, 98–9, 103,
    241, 253
  food and drink 84–6
  frescoes 25, 30, 37, 42–3, 98, 102, 107, 109,
    110, 111, 112, 354n28
  goldwork 36–7, 42, 62, 72, 109
  graves and burials 39, 42, 96–7, 212,
    237–9
  and Hittites 12, 170–2, 242
  ivories 36, 41, 42, 62, 97–8, 109
  jewellery 3, 36, 42, 43, 98, 104, 110, 333
  Minoan influences 317–8, 322–3
  pottery 30, 31, 32, 39, 41, 248–9, 318
  slaves 38
  tholos tombs 36, 42, 238, 248, 249, 318
  trade 12, 20, 39, 41, 43, 174
  and Trojans 128–30, 170–1
  weaponry 36, 39–40, 44
  writing 319, 320
  see also Mycenae; Pylos; Therapne; Tiryns
Mykonos, island of: *pithos* 223

Nafplion Museum 74
Nag Hammadi, Egypt 284
Nashe, Thomas
  Of Lenten Stuff 71
  'Summer's Last Will and Testament' 305
National Gallery, London: birth tray 157
Nefertiti, Queen: scarab 159
Nemesis 248, 309–10, 350n1
Nennius: *Historia Brittonum* 290
Nero, Emperor 7, 278
Nestor 203, 230
  palace *see* Pylos
New Scientist Magazine 2
Nikostratos 336
Normans, the 291
Nostoi, the 230

O Polemos tis Troados (Byzantine *Iliad*) 121(*n*8)
obsidian blades 108
Odysseus 10, 65, 78, 191, 193, 194, 199, 221, 230,
    265, 279, 348*n*17, 392*n*7
Odyssey (Homer) 4, 5, 34, 274
    descriptions and quotations from:
        Crete 315
        Eileithya caves 92
        Helen 6, 11(*n*36), 31, 55, 135, 146, 232
        Hermione 91
        marriage feasts 83–6
        Menelaus 229
        Odysseus 230, *see also* Odysseus
        on use of oil 106–7
        Sparta 58
        Spartan palace 29, 33, 36
        Telemachus 29, 31
        Trojan Horse 221
Oedipus, King of Thebes 78, 362*m*
Offenbach, Jacques: *La Belle Hélène* 10
oils, perfumed 107–8, 216–7
olive oil 41, 106–7, 241
Olympia, Greece 5, 58
Olympic Games 252, 261
Olympus, Mount 100, 119
Ombiaux, Maurice des: '*Sein d'Hélène*' 110–1
onata 80
Oneia, Mount 251
opium/opium poppies 233
Orestes 24, 79, 195, 235, 236
Orthia 50
ostrich eggs 27
Ouranus 150
Ovid 6
    Amores 295
    The Art of Love (*Ars Amatoria*) 91, 145, 146–7,
        295
    Heroides 9, 60, 95, 105, 110, 132, 151, 295, 308
    Metamorphoses 237, 295
    Remedia Amoris 295
Oxyrhynchus (Bahnasa), Egypt 137

Palaikastro, Crete 318
    kouros from 317
Palamidi-Pronoia cemetery: finds 212
Paphos, Cyprus: sanctuary of Aphrodite 22
papyrus rolls 273, 274–5
    Homeric fragments 273
Paris xxv, 8, 120–1
    alternative name of Alexander 187, 279
    appearance 120, 121–2

death 11, 223, 232
'Judgement' of 78, 118, 148–9
    and Menelaus 80, 154, 191, 193, 210–1
    as musician 86
    in Ovid's *Heroides* 308
    rape/seduction of Helen 7, 122–3, 127–9,
        132–5, 136, 138–40, 144–51, 157, 171, 279,
        292–3
    return to Troy with Helen 153–6, 159–60,
        180–2, 190, 265–6, 294–5
    scorned by Helen 211, 220
    statue (from Antikythera) 120, 122
Paris, Matthew 295
Parker, Dorothy 281
Parker, Matthew 143
Pasiphae, Queen 316
Patroclus 86, 175, 207, 230
Paul, St: letter to Corinthians 398–9*n*11
Pausanias 26
    Periegisis Hellados 26, 27, 61, 79, 92, 150,
        237(*n*5), 244, 245–6, 251, 253, 334, 335
Peitho 180
Peleus 118, 119
Pelion, Mount 86, 118, 119
Pellana: excavations 248–9
Peloponnese, the 20, 22, 77, 161, 172, 244–6,
    248–9
    earthquakes 20–1, 240
    opium poppies 233
    see also Mycenae; Sparta
Peloponnesian War 51, 222
Pelops, King of Elis 5, 79, 362*m*
Penelope 78, 230, 354*n*31, 408*n*8
perfumes 41, 107–8, 182–3
Peri Parthenion 94
Pericles: Funeral speech 264–5
Persephone 51
Persian Empire 120, 175
Persian Wars 166–7, 198, 274
Persson, Axel 238–9
Peter Damian, St 145
Petrie, William Flinders 272
Phaistos palace, Crete 323–4, 339
phi-type terracotta figurines 99–100, 253
Philaenis 182
Philip, St 283
Philippus 375*n*15
Philoctetes 73, 76
Phoebe 24, 26
Phourni, Crete: burial site 320
Pindar 50, 252

Olympian Ode 247
pithoi (storage jars) 41, 101, 226, 241, 325
plague 212–3, 231, 305
Plataea, battle of 167, 222
Platanistas: Helen cult site 53, 55–6, 58
Plato 6, 117, 137
 Symposium 374*n*15
Platzer, Johan Georg: *The Rape of Helen* 25
Pleisthenes, King of Mycenae 367–8*n*2
Pliny the Elder: *Natural Histories* 110, 253, 254,
 340, 347*n*9, 402*n*8
Plotinus
 On Beauty 374*n*15
 On the Intelligible Beauty 321, 374*n*15
Plutarch
 Life of Lycurgus 82, 94, 138, 139
 Life of Pelopidas 363
 Life of Solon 334
 Moralia 398*n*14
Poitiers, France: Ducal Hall 291, 292, 296
Polybius 138
polyandry, Spartan 138–9
Polyxo, Queen of Rhodes 335, 395*n*5
Pope, Alexander: (trs.) *Iliad* 273
Poseidon xxxii, 17
potnia 102
pottery *see* figurines; vases
Pound, Ezra 7
Praxiteles: *Aphrodite* 361*n*19
pregnancies 92–3
Priam, King xxxiii, 10, 119, 121, 128, 161, 187, 191,
 205, 294
 death 220
 palace 178
'Priam's Treasure' 179–80
Priapea: 'Poems for a Phallic God' 267
priestesses 102, 104–5, 325, 326–7
Proctor, Thomas
 Gallery of Gallant Inventions 393*n*22
 'Helen's Complaint' 306
 The Reward of Whoredome by the Fall of Helen 146
Propertius: *Elegies* 60, 110
Proteus, King of Egypt 128, 231
psi-type figurines 99
Psychro Cave, Crete: votive offerings 324
Ptolemy I 274
Ptolemy II 274
puberty rites 50–1
Puduhepa, Queen of the Hittites 188–90
 seal 189–90
purple dye 41, 339–41

Pylades 235, 236
Pylos 354*n*28, 356*n*15
 frescoes 62, 73, 86, 105, 109
 Linear B tablets 80, 83–4, 100, 107, 212, 223,
  319
 'Nestor's Palace' 31–2, 36, 43, 84, 107, 230,
  325, 326
 perfume manufacture 108
 slave women 38
Pythia 166
Pythian Games 165
pyxis (cosmetics box) 66

Quintus of Smyrna: *The Fall of Troy* 116

Rameses II ('the Great') 124, 183–4, 189, 193
Recognitions 287
Recuyell of the Historyes of Troye, The 7
Reni, Guido: *The Abduction of Helen* 386*n*27
rhapsodes 100, 220
Rhodes, island of 159, 335–6, 409*n*9
 goblet 110
Richard of Devizes 296
Rimbaud, Arthur: *Season in Hell* 49
rings, Bronze Age 3, 15, 42, 156, 333
Robinson, Richard: *The Reward of Wickedness* 146
Roman de la Rose (Jean de Meun) 375*n*26
Romanelli, Giovanni Francesco: wall-painting 9
Romans 7, 54, 271, 278
 see also Rome
Rome 7, 59
 Capitoline Museums 23–4
 Domus Aurea 7
 founding of 277, 290, 291
 Lacus Juturnae altar 227, 253
Rose Theatre, London 298, 300–1, 303, 305
Ross, Alexander: *Mystagogus Poeticus* 146
Rossetti, Dante Gabriel 7
 'Troy Town' 106
Rubens, Peter Paul
 Abduction of Helen 155
 Leda and the Swan 23
Russell-Cotes collection, Bournemouth 2

Sack of Ilium 6
Sackler Library, Oxford 57
saffron 41, 64, 66, 109
St Elmo's Fire 255
Sainte-Maure, Benoît de: *Roman de Troie* 292–3,
 294–7
Salamis, battle of 166

Samaria-Sebaste, Palestine 284
  female statue (broken) 281–2, 288
Samos, island of 167
Samothrace 170
Sapinuwa tablets 187
Sappho 2, 6, 94, 117, 136–7, 197
  Fragment 16 136, 137–8, 139
Saqqara, Egypt: papyri from 57
Sartre, Jean-Paul 35
'Satyric Marriage of Helen, The' (satyr play)
  265–6
Sayce, Reverend Archibald 124
Scamander River 177, 206, 209
Schiller, Friedrich 9
Schliemann, Heinrich 30, 34, 35, 36, 39, 178–80,
  186, 207, 342
Schliemann, Sophia (*née* Engastromenos) 179,
  396*n*16
scribes 273
sea-snails *see* murex
seal-stones 42, 101, 103, 104, 156, 189, 323,
  333–4
Seneca: *Troades* (*Trojan Women*) 169(*n*19), 400*n*20,
  407*n*24
Servius 275
Sesto, Cesare da: *Birth of Helen* 25
Shakespeare, William 7, 301, 304
  Lucrece 407*n*23
  Troilus and Cressida 292, 407*n*23
Shaw-Stewart, Patrick: untitled poem 217–8
Shelley, Percy Bysshe: (trs.) *Iliad* 273
ships *see* boats
Sicily 82, 160, 165
  temples 3, 118
Sicyon: House of 78
  marriage contest 79
Sidon 156
Simonians 283
Simonides 166
Sinon 221
Sitia Museum, Crete: *kouros* 317
Skotino Cave, Crete 325
Skoura, Laconia: figurine 329
slaves 38, 160, 222
'Snake Goddesses', Minoan 321–2
  votary of 317
Socrates 52, 118, 151–2, 160
Solon 136–7
Sophia Prouneikos 286
Sophocles 94, 260
  Helenes Apaitesis (lost play) 191

Sorley, Charles Hamilton
  'I Have Not Brought My *Odyssey*' 215
  'In Memoriam' 217
Sosibus 255
Souda (encyclopaedia) 182
Spagnuoli, Baptista (Baptista Mantuanus)
  407*n*24
Sparta/Spartans 27, 51–2
  acropolis 26
  climate 22
  codes of behaviour 53–4
  eunomia 52
  excavations and findings 27–8, 29, 47, 53,
    84, 87
  female rituals 55–8
  girls' training regime 58–60
  and Helen 3, 12, 27, 51, 52, 53–4, 55, 118
  'marriage by capture' 82
  marriage feasts 83–5
  Peloponnesian War 51, 222
  plague 231
  political and social systems 52
  polygyny 138–9
  and Sicily 81, 160
  xenelasia 52
  xenos/xenia 122–3
  see also Sparta Museum; Therapne
Sparta Museum 1, 31, 56, 91–2
  stele 1–2
Sparti 53
Spenser, Edmund 7
Spyropoulos, Dr T.G. 248, 249
Statius: *Thebaid* 255(*n*25)
Stephanus of Byzantium 253(*n*14)
Stesichorus 160, 224, 230, 265, 277, 365*n*4,
  368*n*12
stirrup jars 108
Strabo: *Geography* 170, 252
Strauss, Johann 7
Suessula cemetery, Italy: vase 180–1
Sumas de Historia Trojana 139
surgery, Bronze Age 141, 212
syssition 52, 82

Talagalawa letter 169
Talos 317
Tanagra, Boiotia: coffin paintings 238
Tartarus xxxii, 150
Taruwisa 197–8
tau-type figurines 99
Tauris 196

Tayegetus, Mount 24, 27, 60, 72
Taylor, Elizabeth 306
Teasdale, Sarah: *Helen of Troy* 332
Tel el Amarna 39
    tablets 124, 158–9
Telemachus 29, 31, 232
Telipinu, Edict of 188
Tenedos 2, 191, 221, 279
    beauty contests 117
terebinth resin 212
terracotta figurines *see* figurines
Thames, River: Anatolian artefacts 290
Thanatos xxxii, 150, 218
Thebes, Egypt 156
Thebes, Greece 21, 78, 105, 170, 197, 241, 259, 354n28
    fresco 110
    Linear B tablets 197, 198, 223, 319
Theocritus 81
    Epithalamium for Helen 81–3
    Idylls 87
Thera, island of 317
    eruption 17–19, 20, 63, 316
    excavations 63
    frescoes 63, 64–6, 71, 109, 111, 198
    saffron 64
Therapne hill, Sparta 1, 29–31, 32–3, 61, 253, 255, 334
Thermopylae, battle of 167
Theseus, King of Athens xxxi, 158
    rape of Helen 49, 50, 51, 62, 71, 92
'Theseus' Rock' 243
Thetis 118–9
Thisbe, Gulf of Corinth: ring 104
tholos tombs 36, 42, 238, 248, 249, 318
Thorikos calendar 247
Thucydides 53, 205, 277
Tippett, Michael 7
Tiryns palace complex 32, 37–8, 170, 233, 245, 354n28
    cisterns 356n16
    frescoes 62, 105
    gold ring from 15
    Linear B tablets 319
Titans 150
Tlepolemos 335
Toobin, Jeffrey 311
Tottel, Richard: *Songs and Sonettes* 306
trade/trade routes 12, 19, 20, 39, 41, 43, 52, 156, 158–60, 161, 165, 174, 230, 290, 316, 339, 340
trepanations 141, 212

Triclinius, Demetrius 276
Trinovantes, the 290
Trjumanna Saga 139
Troad, the 8
Troilus 292
Trojan Horse *see* Trojan War
Trojan War xxix, 7, 38, 166–7, 170–1, 245
    and communication between Greeks and Trojans 174
    dating of 3, 6, 188, 240
    destruction of Troy 170, 221–3, 240, 242, 290
    Greek negotiations before 191, 193–4
    Homer's descriptions 12, 21, 74, 184, 186, 194, 197–198, 203–6, 211, 217
    and launch of Greek ships 194, 196–7, 198–9, 203
    Siege of Troy 37, 208–9, 210, 211–12
    and Trojan Horse 11, 221
Trojanerkrieg 139
Trojanska Prica 139
troubadours 295
Troy 39, 170, 172, 174, 177, 182, 206, 207
    cloth production 341
    excavations and finds 12, 30, 34, 122, 178–80, 183, 186, 206–7, 208
    god-stones 207–8
    Helen in 10, 183, 190, 191, 194, 203, 206
    Hisarlik Hill as site of 34, 176, 177–8, 180, 185, 206
    and Hittites 8–9, 123–4, 183, 186
    Homer's names for 197–8
    horses 183
    myths about 7, 289–91
    prophecy of destruction 119, 121
    sacked by Heracles 198
    Scaean Gate 206, 207, 219
    siege of *see* Trojan War
    visited by Alexander the Great 274
    see Trojan War
Troy (film) 140, 408n12
Troy Book, The 291
Trussel, John: *First rape of fair Hellen* 356n4
Tryphiodorus: *The Taking of Troy* 31
Tsountas, Christos 72
Tucca 275
Tyndareus, King of Sparta xxxii, 22, 24, 128
    marriage contest 71, 75, 76, 77, 78

Ugarit 129
Uluburun shipwreck 159, 174, 212

Vaï, Crete 315–6
Vapheio, Peloponnese
    gold cups 318
    tomb 72
Varius 275
vases and vessels 39, 116
    amphoriskos 308, 309
    aryballos (perfume jar) 31
    Athenian 264
    depicting Trojan War (British Museum) 222
    drinking cup 117–8
    Italian 180–1, 182
    kylikes 85
    piriform (from Pellana) 248–9
    pithoi (storage jars) 41, 101, 224, 241, 325
    portraying Helen 4, 6, 116, 180–1, 182, 264,
        308, 309–10
    portraying Paris (Louvre) 86
    skyphos (from Attica) 208
    Warrior Vase 44–5
Vendôme, Matthew de: *The Art of Versification*
    293–4
Venice/Venetians 268, 270
    horses, St Mark's Cathedral 268–9
Ventris, Michael 318–9
Vimpos, Archbishop Theokletos 179
Vincent, François-André: *Zeuxis et les filles de
    Crotone* 3(n10)
Virgil 6
    Aeneid 221, 223, 233(n25), 275, 278, 282, *see
        also* Aeneas
Vitex agnus castus 93
votive offerings 30, 92, 157, 246–7, 249, 324

Walmu, King of Troy 188
Warrior Goddess 40
'Warrior Vase' 44–5
weaponry 39–40, 44, 70, 156, 201, 212, 215
Welles, Orson: Marlowe's *Doctor Faustus* 306
Wilhelm II, Kaiser 125
William I ('the Conqueror') 7
William IX, Duke 295
Wilson, Margaret Adelaide: 'Gervais (Killed at
    the Dardanelles)' 173
Wilton House, Wiltshire 25
Wilusa 123–4, 180, 187, 197–8, 207, 208
women

Athenian 265
    and beauty *see* beauty
    and contraceptives 93–4
    and cosmetics 108–9
    depictions in frescoes 27, 37, 62–3, 64–7,
        101–2, 111, 321, 324, 326
    dress 109, 111; *see also* jewellery
    and funerary rites 238
    Hittite 187, 326–7
    as kingmakers 78–9
    and menstruation 94, 254
    Minoan 322, 323–4, 325–6
    mortality 41, 92
    and pregnancy 92–3
    priestesses 102, 104–5, 325, 326–7
    puberty rites 50, 62
    slaves 38, 98, 160
    Spartan 53, 54, 55–60, 72, 81–2,
        138–9
    and theatre 262
    Trojan 204
    warrior 40
Woolf, Virginia 35
writing
    'Cretan Hieroglyphic' 318
    Hittite 126
    see also Linear A; Linear B

xenia, xenos, xenwia 122–3, 126, 127, 128
Xenophon (historian) 52
    Household Management 265
Xenophon (Olympic champion) 252
Xerxes I, of Persia 175, 275

Yeats, W.B. 7
    'Leda and the Swan' 22
    'Lullaby' 155

Zakro palace, Crete: elephant's tusk 317
Zenodotus 275
Zeus xxv, xxvi, 2, 58, 101–2, 119, 203, 242,
    308, 333, 338
    and Ganymede 121
    and Hera 134
    rape of Europa 316
    rape of Leda 22
Zeuxis 3, 307